Anonymous

Williams' Fort Wayne Directory, city guide and business mirror,

For 1864-1865

Anonymous

Williams' Fort Wayne Directory, city guide and business mirror,
For 1864-1865

ISBN/EAN: 9783337713157

Printed in Europe, USA, Canada, Australia, Japan

Cover: Foto ©ninafisch / pixelio.de

More available books at **www.hansebooks.com**

WILLIAMS'

FORT WAYNE DIRECTORY,

City Guide and Business Mirror,

FOR 1864-5.

TO WHICH IS APPENDED A

UNITED STATES POST OFFICE DIRECTORY.

THIRD ISSUE:

COMPILED BY WILLIAMS & CO.

FORT WAYNE:
N. P. STOCKBRIDGE,
No. 104 Columbia Street.

FRANKLIN Type & Stereotype Foundry,

168 VINE STREET, bet. 4th and 5th,

R. ALLISON, SUP'T. - **CINCINNATI.**

Manufacturers of and Dealers in

NEWS, BOOK & JOB TYPE, PRINTING PRESSES,

Cases, Galleys, &c., Inks and Printing Material,
OF EVERY DESCRIPTION.

STEREOTYPING of all KINDS, BOOKS, MUSIC,

Volumes of all sizes, in Modern and Ancient Languages, Cards, Labels, Stamps, in Type Metal or Copper.

WOOD ENGRAVING,
PATTERN LETTERS OF VARIOUS STYLES,
Electrotyping in all its Branches.

MANUFACTURER'S WAREHOUSE.

LOUIS SNIDER,

MANUFACTURER OF

FOURDRINIER

BOOK & NEWS PAPER,

No. 232 Walnut St.,   **CINCINNATI, O.**

☞ Highest Price Paid for Rags.

JOHN McCALL, Agent.

CLASSIFIED INDEX TO ADVERTISEMENTS.

AGRICULTURAL IMPLEMENTS,
  Ft. Wayne Agricultural Works.......... 70
  Comparet D. F........................ 52
ART GALLERY,
  Shoaff J. A.......................... 76
ATTORNEYS AT LAW,
  Chittenden E. L...................... 48
  Coombs Wm. H........................ 44
  Hartman Homer L..................... 48
  Hough John.......................... 44
  Randall F. P........................ 44
BANKS,
  First National Bank................. 76
BELTING,
  Oakley B. W......................... 50
BILLIARDS,
  O'Connell D......................... 50
BOOK BINDERS & BLANK BOOK MANUF.
  Siemon A. F. & Bro.................. 46
  Stockbridge N. P.................... 56
BOOKS, &c.,
  Siemon A. F. & Bro.................. 46
  Stockbridge N. P.................... 56
BOOKBINDERS' DIES, &c.,
  Lanphear W. K....................... 8
BOOTS AND SHOES,
  Prouty F. M......................... 72
BRASS FOUNDER,
  Hattersley Alfred................... 68
BUILDING STONE,
  Humphrey James...................... 44
  Underhill P. S...................... 64
CABINET WARE,
  Miller John M....................... 64
CASTINGS, (IRON AND BRASS),
  Bass & Hanna........................ 36
CIVIL ENGINEER,
  McArthur John W..................... 68
CLOTHING, &c.,
  Fleddermann John O. & Co............ 40
  Mossler Louis H..................... 40
  Stockbridge N. P.................... 56
COMMISSIONER OF DEEDS & MORTGAGES
  McArthur John W..................... 68
COMMISSION MERCHANT,
  Comparet D. F....................... 52
CONFECTIONERY, &c.,
  Huestis A. C........................ 52
COAL DEALERS,
  Ft. Wayne Gas Light Co.............. 38
COKE,
  Ft. Wayne Gas Light Co.............. 38
COLLECTING AGENT,
  Chittenden E. L..................... 48
  Hartman & Bossler................... 48
  Hough John.......................... 44
  Randall F. P........................ 44
DRUGGISTS,
  Meyer & Brother..................... 58
DRY GOODS,
  Abbott Wm. T........................ 2
  Mossler Louis H..................... 40
  Schwegman H. R...................... 54
EATING HOUSE,
  Rumsey Philo........................ 48
ENGRAVERS, (GENERAL),
  Evans Platt, Jr..................... 200
  Lanphear W. K....................... 8
FANCY GOODS,
  Mossler Louis H..................... 40
FILES, RASPS, MILL PICKS, &c.,
  Schmidt C. & Co..................... 42

FLOUR MILLS,
  Comparet D. F....................... 52
FURNITURE, CHAIRS, &c.,
  Miller John M....................... 64
GAS FITTER, &c.,
  Hattersley Alfred................... 68
GROCERIES,
  Abbott Wm. T........................ 2
  Brackenridge T. K................... 58
  Foellinger J. M..................... 68
  Huestis A. C........................ 52
  Schwegman H. R...................... 54
  Trentman B.......................... 38
HATS AND CAPS,
  Abbott Wm. T........................ 2
  Schwegman H. R...................... 54
HARDWARE, CUTLERY, &c.,
  Brandriff A. D. & Co................ 60
  Oakley B. W......................... 50
  Schmidt C. & Co..................... 42
HOTEL,
  Fletcher C. P. & J. F............... 52
INSURANCE,
  Aetna Insurance Company............. 1
  Hartman & Bossler................... 48
  Hough John.......................... 62
  Randall F. P........................ 44
  State Insurance Co., Geo. W. Babcock,
    General Agent................... 72
KNITTING MACHINES,
  Kirby James A....................... 70
LAW AND COLLECTION OFFICE,
  Hough John.......................... 44
LUMBER, SHINGLES, LATH, &c.,
  Hurd & Clark........................ 60
MACHINISTS,
  Bass & Hanna........................ 36
  Ft. Wayne Agricultural Works........ 70
MARBLE WORKS,
  Underhill P. S...................... 64
MATTRESSES,
  Miller John M....................... 64
MONUMENTS, TOMBSTONES, &c.,
  Underhill P. S...................... 64
MUSICAL INSTRUMENTS,
  Anderson & Irving................... 42
  Stockbridge N. P.................... 56
NEWSPAPERS,
  Dawson's Ft. Wayne Times............ 35
  Ft. Wayne Gazette................... 82
  Ft. Wayne Sentinel.................. 74
OILS, WINDOW GLASS, &c.,
  Meyer & Brother..................... 58
OMNIBUS LINE,
  O'Connell J......................... 50
PAINTS, DYE STUFFS, &c.,
  Meyer & Brother..................... 58
PAPER BOX MANUFACTURER,
  Jordan Chas. W...................... 20
PAPER DEALERS,
  Snider Louis........................ 6
PHOTOGRAPHERS,
  Shoaff J. A......................... 76
PIANOS, &c.,
  Anderson & Irving................... 42
PLANING MILLS,
  Baldwin F. S........................ 54
  Hurd & Clark........................ 60
PLOWS, THRESHING MACHINES, &c.,
  Ft. Wayne Agricultural Works........ 70
PLUMBER,
  Hattersley Alfred................... 68

CLASSIFIED INDEX TO ADVERTISEMENTS.

PRINTERS, (BOOK AND JOB.)
Dawson John W........................... 35
Jones & Jenkinson........................ 78
Siemon A. F. & Bro....................... 46
T. Tigar.................................. 74

PRINTING MATERIALS,
Franklin Type Foundry.................... 4

PRODUCE DEALERS,
Brackenridge T. K........................ 58
Comparet D. F............................ 52

PROVISIONS,
Brackenridge T. K........................ 58
Foellinger J. M.......................... 68

RAILROADS,
L. M. C. & N. & C. H. & D. & D. & M.,
[Inside back cover

REAL ESTATE AGENTS,
Hartman & Bossler........................ 48
Hough John............................... 66
Randall F. P............................. 44

RECTIFIER,
Trentman B............................... 38

RESTAURANT,
O'Connell D.............................. 50

SADDLERY & CARRIAGE TRIMMINGS,
Oakley B. W.............................. 50

SASH, BLINDS, DOORS, &c.,
Baldwin F. S............................. 54

SEAL PRESSES, SEALS, &c.,
Evans Platt, Jr.......................... 200

SEWING MACHINES,
Kirby James A............................ 70
Stockbridge N. F......................... 56
Wheeler & Wilson's....... Inside front cover

STEAM ENGINES, &c.,
Bass & Hanna............................. 36

STENCIL CUTTER,
Lanphear W. K............................ 8

STONE CUTTER,
Humphrey James........................... 41

STOVES,
Brandriff A. D. & Co..................... 60

SURVEYOR,
McArthur John W.......................... 68

TAILORS, (MERCHANT),
Fledderman John G. & Co.................. 40

TIN, COPPER AND SHEET IRON WARE,
Brandriff A. D. & Co..................... 60

TOBACCO, CIGARS, &c.,
Foellinger J. M.......................... 68

TYPE FOUNDRY,
Franklin Type Foundry.................... 4

WINDOW SASH, DOORS, &c.,
Schmidt C. & Co.......................... 42

WINES AND LIQUORS,
Trentman B............................... 38

PREFACE.

We have used all the means at our command and exercised the greatest care in the preparation of the present issue of the FORT WAYNE DIRECTORY, and confidently believe that our patrons will find the Work as accurate and complete as it is possible to make a book of the kind.

The Work embraces a General Directory—embracing a full list of the names and locations of the inhabitants of the City; a complete Business Directory—containing the name of each person and firm doing business in Fort Wayne; with a City Guide—containing the names of all the Streets, Alleys, Lanes and Avenues, giving their location and termini; also, the names of all Public Institutions, Banks, Churches, Societies, &c., in the City; together with a UNITED STATES POST OFFICE DIRECTORY—containing the name and location of every Post Office in the United States and Territories, arranged alphabetically, and corrected up to date. Also, a well-written "SKETCH OF THE CITY OF FORT WAYNE," prepared expressly for our Work by a prominent citizen of the place, to whom we return our thanks for the interesting matter thereby added to our volume.

Our General Directory will be found to contain about five thousand names of heads of families, adults, &c., whose localities could be fixed, and upon this basis, experience gained in other cities, would justify us in estimating the present population of the CITY OF FORT WAYNE at from sixteen to eighteen thousand—which fact not only indicates the rapid growth and importance of the City, but also the necessity for the ANNUAL publication of a City Directory.

The materials for this volume were mainly collected and arranged by our assistant compiler, H. THORNTON BENNETT, and to his experience and diligence the public are indebted for the completeness of the Work.

The Compilers return their thanks to the Press for the many flattering notices given during the canvass, and to the business men and citizens of the City for their patronage and very courteous treatment, and sincerely hope that their DIRECTORY for 1864-5 will meet with the approval of mercantile, professional and business men of the community, and be a fit representative of the public spirit and commercial importance of the CITY OF FORT WAYNE.

W. K. LANPHEAR,
134 West Fourth Street,
CINCINNATI, O.
GENERAL ENGRAVER,
DIE SINKER,

AND MANUFACTURER OF

Book Binders' Dies, Hand Tools and Rolls, Steel Stamps, Stencil Tools, and Stencil Plates for Marking Boxes, Barrels, &c.

ALSO,

COMMISSION MERCHANT BY SAMPLE,

For New York and Philadelphia Manufacturers and Importers,

Hunt's Celebrated Razor Straps, Pocket Books, Purses and Ladies' Chain Bags, Photograph Albums, Toy Books, A B C and Dissecting Blocks, Cabinet Photographs, Pocket Cutlery, Union Playing Cards, &c,

SOLE AGENT FOR

COLLIDAY'S SILK, LINEN AND OTHER STUFF BUTTONS,

Lyman's Dating and Canceling Machine, for Bankers and Business Men Generally. (No Ink required with this Press.) Price, $7 00.

GOODALE & SON'S
Celebrated Patent Stereoscopic Instruments,
For Parlor and Traveling Exhibitions.

POST OFFICE BOX 2566.

PRICES:

Steel Stamps, 20 cents per letter, and cost of forging and steel.
Seal Presses from $5.00 to $20.00.
Burning Brands, for Liquor Dealers, 25 cents per letter, and cost of casting and handle.
Stencil Tools from $15.50 to $100 per sett.
Brass Letters Engraved from 12 1-2 cents upward.

Coat-of-Arms, for seals, &c., vary in Price according to design.
Stencil Plates, 6 cents per letter and cost of Material.
Small Plates for Marking Clothing from 50 cents to $1.50.
Raised Work Plates, original or copies, in Copper, according to design and size of Plate.

☞ I employ none but first-class Workmen, and challenge competition from all sections.

SKETCH OF FORT WAYNE.

FORT WAYNE, situated on an elevated plain, at the junction of the St. Mary's and St. Joseph Rivers, has from an early period been a point of great interest. As early as 1700, the French visited it for the purpose of trade with the Indians, and prior to 1719 they established here a regular Trading Post, and it became one of their most important commercial centres. In the Miami dialect, the place was called Ke-ki-oug-gay, and Ke-ki-ouge in the Pottawattamie. Vandreuil, Governor of Louisiana, writing in 1751, located "Fort Miami" at this point. It was a small stockade fort, built by the French, situated near the St. Mary's, probably in the vicinity of the canal aqueduct. The dim outlines of this Fort were traced by General Wayne, in 1794, and by Colonel John Johnston, in 1800.

At different periods, four nations have held dominion here. The untutored Indian for centuries; and for half a century prior to the conquest of Canada, the tri-colored flag waved at the meeting of the St. Joseph and the St. Mary's; after that, in December, 1760, the British flag was run up in its stead, upon a fort erected upon the east bank of the St. Joseph, near its mouth. May 27, 1763, during Pontiac's war, a small garrison stationed there, was massacred through the treacherous influence of the French traders over the Indians. This was about the last exertion of French power on this continent, east of the Mississippi.

The Declaration of Independence, in 1776, was the commencement of an era that established the rule of the United States as the fourth power that reigned over this region, and still reigns, greater than all that preceded it. The sagacious mind of Washington, at an early period, fixed upon the junction of the rivers as of commanding importance for a strong military post; and the main purpose of the campaign of 1791, was for its occupation as a center of military operations for the North-West. His plans contemplated a garrison of one thousand or twelve hundred men, but the defeat of General St. Clair, within a day's march, defeated his well-matured plans, and at that time the American army failed to occupy this favorite rendezvous of the savage Indians—this "Federal city" of the tribes that formed the Miami confederation.

In 1794, the United States were more successful. After defeating the Indians at the Rapids of the Maumee, Gen. Wayne marched to this point, and selected here a commanding site for a fort; and in October of that year, "Fort Wayne" was completed. From that period, and bearing that name, for now sixty-nine years, this has been a center of American civilization and power. It continued to grow in importance until 1825, when the first plat of the town was made, and it was laid out and incorporated as the "Town of Fort Wayne." Since that time there has been a steady, uniform and healthy progress.

From time to time numerous additions have been made to the original plat—November, 1833, the County Addition; October, 1836, Ewing's, and May, 1837, Hanna's Addition, with many others since, that have extended the limits of the town something over two miles east and west, and nearly the same distance north and south; and the population has kept equal pace with its enlarged dimension.

In 1828, the population of the town and its immediate vicinity, was estimated at about 500; and in 1830 it was computed at about 800. In the winter of 1839 a Charter was granted by the Legislature for a City corporation, and on the 2d day of March, 1840, a vote of the citizens was taken upon the adoption or rejection of the Charter, which was adopted. The population was then about 1,200; in 1850, it reached 4,200; and in 1860 it was 10,300; at the present time, from the rapid growth of the past three years, the population must exceed 16,000.

The causes that produced this rapid growth, are apparent. The commanding situation of the town, in the center of a large and fertile scope of country that sought this point for trade, with no competing town, and the facilities for export and import, were important elements in its growth. The facilities for this commerce, resulted from the important internal improvements constructed so as to make this an important point in their routes.

The first of these was the Wabash and Erie Canal, completed from the west in 1838, and from the east in the fall of 1842, thus connecting Fort Wayne with Lake Erie, at Toledo. By affording the means of shipping direct to the Lake, the canal drew the trade of a large region of country, north and south, immediately to this point. The water power resulting from this improvement, furnished facilities for the erection of mills and manufactories that were of great importance in its progress; and from this period it took a new start, and this impetus continued till the era of Plank Roads, in 1848. These roads were constructed with much energy and rapidity to a great distance in every direction, attracting an increased trade from a large and fertile section of country. Lastly came the Railroads. The Ohio & Indiana R. R. was first located, in 1852, and completed in 1854. The Fort Wayne & Chicago R. R. commenced in 1854, and completed in 1857, which two roads being consolidated with the Ohio & Pennsylvania R. R., constitute the Pittsburgh, Fort Wayne & Chicago R. R. Company, making a line 467 miles in length, and inferior in importance to no road in the United States, and equal to any in its management and success.

Next followed the Toledo & Western Railroad, located in 1854 and completed in 1856, connecting Lake Erie with the Mississippi.

Aside from the travel and freight brought to Fort Wayne, thus adding largely to its commerce, it has the fortunate position of being a central point on these great lines, and hence was the best location for their extensive shops, for repair and the building of rolling machinery, for both the roads. They therefore erected shops so extensive that they should be visited and examined, to properly realize their magnitude and importance.

The T. & W. R. W. buildings consist of a round-house, 140 feet in diameter, with capacity for 24 engines; brick machine shop, 100 feet wide by 160 feet long; blacksmith shop, 40 feet wide and 160 feet long; wood shop, 30 feet wide and 200 feet long. These shops give constant employment for near 400 men, with a monthly pay-roll of $30,000.

The shops of the P., Ft. W. & C. R. W. exceed in size and importance in direct ratio with the increased length of the Road, and embrace a brick depot, two stories, 190 feet long by 70 feet wide ; freight house, 200 feet by 60 feet ; car shop, main building, two stories, 220 feet by 75 feet, with two wings, one story, 188 feet by 75 feet each; machine and blacksmith shop, 327 feet by 65 feet, two stories, with two wings for engine and boiler shops, each 100 feet by 50; round-house, 60 feet deep by 308 feet in diameter, with stalls for 40 engines. In the spring a new machine shop will be erected, two stories, 300 feet by 150. These shops cover six acres of ground, and furnish full employment for over 600 mechanics and laborers, with a pay-roll of over $40,000 per month. With the projected enlargement, the employees will not be less than 900, with a pay-roll of at least $75,000 per month. The car shop averages 50 new cars per month, requiring a constant supply of 700,000 feet of lumber, at a cost of $12,000 per month. The other shops require an outlay in proportion, for the materials used by them. Such immense expenditures by these two Roads do a large share to keep up the prosperity of the city, and are a permanent element in its growth.

Following the Railroad improvements, in March, 1855, the Fort Wayne Gas Company was incorporated and works at once erected so as to light the city in October. The amount of pipe now laid is over five miles, extending through the greater part of the city.

While thus contemplating the Public Works as the great cause of rapid growth, private enterprise must not be overlooked as an equally important element in the rapid increase and prosperity of the town.

The extensive water power of the canal and rivers has led to the erection of some seven extensive merchant mills, whose manufacture command the highest price in the Eastern market. Also, eight planing mills and sash and door factories, employing over 200 men, to whom they give constant employment, together with four large steam tanneries, with work for 150 men.

Prominent among private enterprises are the machine shops and foundries of the "Fort Wayne Machine Works" of Bowser & Story and of Murray & Bennigin, employing in all over 150 men, with an aggregate pay-roll of $20,000 per month. All these works are employed to their fullest capacity, and are unable to keep up with the demand for their work, which is of the most superior character and finish.

The large woolen factory of French, Hanna & Co., four stories in height, 105 feet in length by 55 feet in width, giving employment for forty workmen, with a demand for their manufacture that they can not supply, is another important enterprise. Also, the extensive hub, spoke and bending factory of Olds, Hanna & Co., with employment for 70 men, and unable to meet the increasing call for their work. Nor must the large cabinet works of J. M. Miller, employing from 40 to 50 men, be overlooked. These, with numerous other manufactories, which the limits of this sketch do not permit a full description, are all elements of growth and prosperity, and readily account for our rapid progress, which is sure to be permanent, as the exhaustless supply of timber, of the finest quality, is attracting attention, and as the result, two large establishments are in course of erection for the manufacture of reapers, mowers and separators, with other agricultural implements. The buildings are nearly completed and by spring will be in active operation, and when fully completed will employ some 300 men each, with a monthly outlay of over $50,000. One is located in the Lewis Addition, at the junction of the Railroads, the other in the North-Side Addition, on the Canal Feeder.

Turning from this view of the public works and private manufactures to the commerce of the city, equal prosperity is apparent, and it has an amount and variety of trade not excelled by any city of its population in the West. Dry goods stores number 25; hardware and stoves, 15; boots and shoes, 30; grocery and provision, over 70; drug, book and jewelry stores, 17; clothing and hat stores, 15, with various other stores doing miscellaneous trade. The business of some of the houses exceed $200,000 annually, and all are in a healthy and sound condition, and the credit of no merchants in the West stands higher than those of Fort Wayne.

In its banking and financial resources it is also behind none, and it is sufficient to name the Branch of the Bank of the State, the banking house of Allen, Hamilton & Co., and the First National Bank, as evidence of the sound basis of our finances.

The most important items in a notice of the advantages of any city are the intellectual and religious privileges, and in these particulars Fort Wayne stands high. Three daily papers with large circulation and well supported, together with five weeklies—two in the German language—in connection with her large and well constructed free school edifices, with the schools admirably conducted, and educating, in the most thorough manner, in all the branches of study, 1,068 scholars, together with denominational and private schools of a superior order: the "Concordia University" and the Fort Wayne Female College—all are evidences of the superior advantages it possesses for intellectual culture.

The fifteen churches, some of them of the largest dimensions and of a high order of architecture, well supported with large and attentive congregations—all speak in highest terms as to the religious privileges and character of her people.

In the general appearance of the city—in the character and extent of the buildings, embracing over two hundred three and four story brick stores, with elegant and costly brick dwellings in proportion; a magnificent Court-house, costing some $80,000; the Aveline House, and other structures—all tell for the enterprise and taste of the population, and are the best evidence of prosperity and growth. The extent of building for the past year of large and extensive shops, of fine stores and dwellings has been such as to attract the attention and admiration of strangers, and is not surpassed, if equaled, by any city in the State, and the contracts already made with the prospective building for the next year promise far to exceed the present.

With a growth and prosperity founded upon so substantial a basis, little is hazarded in stating that the population of sixteen thousand in 1863 will exceed thirty thousand at the next census, and that few towns present so strong inducements to the merchant, mechanic, and business men of every class, for a permanent residence.

FORT WAYNE CITY GUIDE.

STREET DIRECTORY.

Baker, west from Calhoun next south of Douglas Av.
Barr, south from Duck next east of Clinton.
Bass, from Fairfield Av. east to Hoagland next north of Colerick.
Berry, east from Rockhill to Canal next north of Wayne.
Bowser, west from Lima Pland Road, Bloomingdale.
Brandriff, west from Webster to Hoagland next south of Melita.
Broadway, from Canal to Bluffton Plank Road next West of Fulton.
Buchanan, Lasselle's addition.
Butler, from Fairfield Av. east to Hoagland next south of Williams.
Calhoun, south from River to Piqua Road, between Harrison and Clinton.
Canal, from Clay to Monroe, north of Berry.
Cass, south from River to Berry between Ewing and Maiden Lane.
Cass, north from High to Douglas, Bloomingdale.
Charles, east from Lafayette to Hanna next south of Wallace.
Clay, south from Canal to Lasselle, between Lafayette and Monroe.
Clinton, south from Duck next east of Calhoun.
Colerick, from Fairfield Av. east to Hoagland next south of Bass.
College, south from Washington next east of Nelson.
Columbia, No. 1, from Harrison east to Lafayette next north of Main.
Columbia, No. 2, from Fulton east north of Canal.
Court, from Main to Berry between Calhoun and Clinton.
Dawson, west from Piqua Road to Hoagland, next south of Highland and Brandriff.

Douglas, west from Lima Plank Road, Bloomingdale.
Douglas Avenue, west from Calhoun next south of Lewis.
Durrie, east from Fairfield Av. to Hoagland next south of Butler.
Duck, from Calhoun east to River next north of Water.
Edsall, from Berry to Main next west of Jackson.
Erie, north from St. Louis next west of Fairfield Av.
Ewing, from River south between Griffith and Cass.
Fairfield Avenue, continuation of Griffith.
Force, Jones & Bass' Foundry addition.
Francis, south from Canal to Lewis next east of Hanna.
Fulton, from River south between Griffith and Broadway.
Garden, from Washington south next west of Nelson.
Gay, south from P., Ft. W. & C. R. R. next east of John.
George, west from Fairfield Av. next south of Sturgis.
Grant, east from Gay next south of Jones.
Griffith, from River south between Ewing and Fulton.
Hamilton, east from Hanna to Francis, next south of Lewis.
Hanna, south from Canal to corporation line next east of Monroe.
Harmer, south from Canal to Lewis next east of Francis.
Harrison, from River south next west of Calhoun.
Henry, west from Fairfield Av. next south of Poplar.
Herndon, Jones & Bass' Foundry addition.
High, west from Lima Plank Road, Bloomingdale.
Highland, west from Piqua Road to Webster next south of T. & W. R. W.
Hoagland, south from T. & W. R. W. next east of Fairfield Av.
Holman, east from Calhoun to Lafayette next south of Montgomery.
Hood, from Pritchard south to R. R. next east of West.
Horace, east and west of Gay next south of Grant.
Hough, east from Lafayette to Hanna next south of Holman.
Jackson, from Canal to corporation line next west of Van Buren.
Jefferson, east from corporation line to Harmer next south of Washington.
John, Jones & Bass' Foundry addition.
Jones, Jones & Bass' Foundry addition.
Jones, east and west of College next south of Wilt.
Kansas, south from T. & W. R. W. next west of Webster.
Lafayette, south from River to corporation line next east of Barr.
Lasselle, east from Lafayette to Hanna next south of Charles.
Lavina, west from Fairfield Av. next south of George.
Lewis, from Ewing east next south of Madison and Jefferson.
Locust, west from Fairfield Av. next south of T. & W. R. W.
Locust, No. 2, from Harrison to Calhoun next north of Water.
McClellan, south from Lewis next west of Webster.

STREET DIRECTORY. 17

Madison, east from Barr to Harmer between Jefferson and Lewis.
Maiden Lane, south from Canal to Berry between Cass and Harrison.
Main, east from River to Canal next north of Berry.
Marion, north from High to Douglas, Bloomingdale.
Maumee, east from Calhoun to Barr next south of Holman.
Melita, west from Webster to Hoagland, next south of T. & W. R. W.
Monroe, from Canal south to Lasselle between Hanna and Clay.
Montgomery, east from Barr to Hanna next south of Lewis.
Nelson, south from Washington between Garden and College.
Nirdlinger, west from Bluffton Plank Road next south of Wall.
Oakley, south from Taylor next west from Fairfield Av.
Pearl, from Fulton east between Main and Canal.
Pine, south from T. & W. R. W. next west of Fairfield Av.
Plum, from Water to St. Mary's River between Harrison and Cass.
Poplar, west from Fairfield Av. next south of Walnut.
Pritchard, west from Broadway next north of P., Ft. W. & C. R. W.
Rockhill, from Washington to Main next west of Union.
St. Francis, Lasselle's addition.
St. Louis, along north side T. & W. R. W. west from Fairfield Av.
Samuel, east and west of John next south of Horace.
Sturges, west from Fulton to Broadway next south of Jefferson
Taylor, west from Fairfield Av. next south of Locust.
Toledo, east from Lafayette to Hanna next south of Hough.
Union, from corporation line to Berry next west of Jackson.
Van Buren, from Canal to corporation line next west of Broadway.
Virginia, east from Lafayette to Hanna next south of Toledo.
Wall, west from Bluffton Plank Road next south of P., Ft. W. & C. R. W.
Wallace, east from Lafayette to Hanna next south of Virginia.
Walnut, west from Fairfield Av. next south of Taylor.
Washington, east from corporation line to Harmer next north of Jefferson.
Water, from Ewing east to River next north of Columbia.
Wayne, east from Rockhill to Harmer next north of Washington.
Webster, from Berry south to corporation line between Ewing and Harrison.
West, from Pritchard south to R. R. next west of Hood.
Williams, from Fairfield Av. east to Hoagland next south of Colerick.
Wilt, from Nelson east next south of Jefferson.
Wines, from Fairfield Av. to Hoagland next south of Williams

Boundaries of Wards.

FIRST WARD—Comprises all that part of the city lying east of Lafayette street.
SECOND WARD—Comprises all that part of the city lying west of Lafayette and east of Calhoun street.
THIRD WARD—Comprises all that part of the city lying west of Calhoun and east of Ewing street.
FOURTH WARD—Comprises all that part of the city lying west of Ewing and east of Broadway.
FIFTH WARD—Comprises all that part of the city lying west of Broadway.

CITY GOVERNMENT.

Municipal Election held first Tuesday in May.
City Council meets second and fourth Tuesdays in each month.
Council Chambers, west side Clinton between Main and Columbia.

MAYOR.

F. P. Randall, Office west side Clinton between Main and Columbia. Term expires May, 1865.

CLERK.

E L. Chittenden, Office at Mayor's Office. Term expires May, 1865.

TREASURER.

John Conger, Office at Mayor's office. Term expires May, 1865.

MARSHAL.

Patrick McGee, Office at Mayor's office. Term expires May, 1865.

CITY ATTORNEY.

Jos. S. France, Office at Mayor's office. Term expires May 1864.

CIVIL ENGINEER.

John S. Mower, residence, 25 Douglas Avenue. Term expires May, 1865. John W. McArthur, deputy.

MARKET MASTERS.

W. D. Henderson, Eastern Market; —————, Western Market. Terms expire May, 1864.

ASSESSOR.

John B. Rekers, residence s e c Ewing and Washington. Term expires May, 1865.

STREET COMMISSIONER.

C W. Lindlay, residence 109 W. Washington. Term expires May, 1865.

SUPERVISORS.

John M. Reidmiller. John Burt.

SEALER OF WEIGHTS AND MEASURES.

Vacancy.

NIGHT WATCH.

Conrad Pens, Captain; John Murray; John Sullivan; John Phillabaum; Wm. Schopman.

CITY COUNCIL.

F. P. Randall, Mayor, President.
E. L. Chittenden, Clerk.

1st Ward,	Edward Slocum.	Term expires, May,	1865.
	H. Monning.	" "	1867.
2d "	B. H. Tower.	" "	1867.
	Morris Cody.	" "	1865.
3d "	H. Neirman.	" "	1867.
	C. D. Pipenbrink.	" "	1865.
4th "	John S. Harrington.	" "	1865.
	Dennis Downey.	" "	1867.
5th "	B. H. Kimball.	" "	1865.
	A. F. Schele.	" "	1867.

School Department.

BOARD OF TRUSTEES.—Samuel Edsall, President; Christian Orff, Secretary; Dr. C. E. Sturgis, Treasurer: O. Bird and A. Martin. Meet first and third Mondays of each month.

BOARD OF EXAMINERS.—Hon. F. P. Randall, Dr. B. S. Woodworth, Rev. R. D. Robinson, Judge Morris, W. B. Walters, Isaac Jenkinson, Rev. W. P. Ruthrauff, Dr. J. S. Irwin, Judge Worden, Rev. J. M. Lowrie, Thomas Tigar, Prof. E. S. Green.

SUPERINTENDENT.—Prof. E. S. Green.

SCHOOL BUILDINGS.

No. 1, Eastern District, north-west corner Washington and Clay. Divided as follows: Primary Department, three grades; Secondary Department, two grades; Intermediate Department, two grades; Grammar Department, two grades.

No. 2, Western District, south-west corner Jefferson and Griffith. Divided as follows: Primary Department, three grades; Secondary Department, two grades; Intermediate Department, two grades; Grammar Department, two grades; High School Department, four years.

County Examiner.—R. D. Robinson.

Catholic Schools.—St. Patrick's School (English.) Building, west side Clinton between Jefferson and Lewis. Bro. Philip, Teacher.

Sisters of Providence School (English).—South side Jefferson between Calhoun and Clinton. Sister Theodore, Superior.

German Catholic Public School.—South side Jefferson between Lafayette and Clay. John E. Ohnhouse and Charles Geiger, Teachers.

Sisters of Providence School (German).—East side Lafayette between Jefferson and Madison. Sister Catharine, Superior.

Fire Department.

L. T. Bourie, Chief Engineer.
John Schuckman, First Assistant.
Jacob J. Kamm, Second Assistant.

Independent Alert Hook and Ladder Company No. 1.—House, Court Street between Main and Berry. Meeting Hall, east side Calhoun between Main and Columbia. Richard Rosington, Foreman.

Vigilant Engine Company No. 1, (Steam).—North-east corner Court and Berry. John Harrington, Foreman.

Mechanics' Engine Company No. 2, (Steam).—North-east corner Court and Berry. Hiram Poyser, Foreman.

Torrent Engine Company No. 3.—West side Clinton between Berry and Main. Henry Fry, Foreman.

The above three Companies meet in Fireman's Hall, north-east corner Court and Berry.

Eagle Engine Company No. 4.—Broadway between Berry and Wayne. Fred. Gross, Foreman.

Protection Engine Company.—South of T. & W. Railway Shops. Samuel C. Fletter, Foreman.

Banks and Bankers.

Bank of the State of Indiana, Branch at Ft. Wayne.—Southwest corner Main and Clinton. Organized January 1st, 1857. Capital, $125,000. Pliney Hoagland, President; Chas. D. Bond, Cashier; Pliney Hoagland, Samuel Hanna, B. W. Oakley, Chas. McCulloch, John E. Hill, Asa Fairfield, Charles D. Bond, Directors.

First National Bank of Ft. Wayne.—South-west corner Calhoun and Berry. Organized July, 1863. Capital, $150,000. J. D. Nuttman, President; W. B. Fisher, Cashier; Joseph D. Nuttman, Samuel Hanna, C. F. G. Meyer, John Brown, A. D. Brandriff, A. S. Evans, John Orff, John M. Miller, Fred. Nirdlinger, Directors.

Allen Hamilton & Co.—West side Calhoun opposite the Court House.

United States Internal Revenue.

W. H. Withers, Collector Tenth Congressional District of Indiana. Office, west side Calhoun, third door south of Main, over A. Hamilton & Co.'s Bank.

James S. Frazer, Assessor Tenth Congressional District. Residence at Warsaw, Kosciusko County.

N. B. Freeman, Assistant Assessor for Allen County.
T. Y. Dickinson, Assistant Assessor for DeKalb County.
Henry Linder, Assistant Assessor for LaGrange County.
Z. C. Thomas, Assistant Assessor for Noble County.
George Copeland, Assistant Assessor for Elkhart County.
Walter Scott, Assistant Assessor for Kosciusko County.
Alexander Hall, Assistant Assessor for Whitley County.

Official List of Justices of the Peace for Allen County.

Name.	Township.	P.O. Address	Term Expires.	
Simeon W. Stouder,	Aboite,	Ft. Wayne,	April	20, 1867
Ad. H. Bittinger,	Cedar Cr'k,	Leo,	May	2, 1867
J. W. Hutsell,	Eel River,	Eel River,	April	20, 1867
O. E. Jamison,	Marion,	Root,	May	20, 1867
Luke Lavanaway,	St. Joseph,	Ft. Wayne,	"	20, 1867
Geo. Smitley,	Washingt'n	"	April	20, 1867
A. McCormick,	Lake,	Arcola,	November	3, 1866
Nicholas Ladig,	Jefferson,	New Haven	"	3, 1866
Samps'n Newbrough	Perry,	Ft. Wayne,	April	27, 1866
Owen Hatfield,	Lafayette,	Zanesville,	"	27, 1866
John Kryder,	Cedar Cr'k,	Leo,	"	19, 1866
David McLain,	Marion,	Root,	"	27, 1866
Calvin F. Maynard,	Springfield,	Harlan,	"	27, 1866
C. V. N. Milliman,	Wayne,	Ft. Wayne,	"	19, 1866
Benj. Saunders,	"	"	June	25, 1865
Wm. W. Steevens,	"	"	April	28, 1864
James D. Werden,	"	"		22, 1864
Amasa Shaffer,	Madison,	Massillon,	June	20, 1865
Platt Squiers,	Scipio,	Halls Cor.'s	May	30, 1865
Jacob W. Hare,	Pleasant,	Little River	"	5, 1865
D. B. Litchfield,	Lake,	Randall,	"	3, 1865
Paoli S. Tarr,	Jefferson,	New Haven	April	23, 1865
Lorenzo D. George,	Milan,	Chamberl'n	"	16, 1865
Socrates Bacon,	Adams,	New Haven	"	16, 1865
Alonzo A. Baker,	Monroe,	Monroeville	"	16, 1865
Peter Bouter,	"	"	October,	29, 1864
Wm. Cutts,	Springfield,	Harlan,	"	29, 1864
Abraham Fulton,	Pleasant,	Little River	November	4, 1864
George Bullard,	Aboite,	Ft. Wayne,	May	7, 1864
Arnold Smith,	Madison,	Massillon,	July	12, 1864
James O. Beardsley,	Perry,	Huntertown	April	27, 1864
D. L. Whitaker,	Jackson,	Monroeville	"	27, 1864
Daniel Frisby,	Milan,	Chamberl'n	"	2, 1864
Orrin Rogers,	Adams,	New Haven	"	27, 1864
Samuel Shryock,	Eel River,	Perry,	"	28, 1864
Jacob W. Glass,	Lafayette,	Zanesville,	January	21, 1864
Asabel H. Wells,	Washingt'n	Ft. Wayne,	"	21, 1864

Notaries Public in Allen County.

Name.	Term Expires.
O. W. Jefferds,	Sept. 29, 1867
Henry H. Bossler,	June 2, "
William Lytle,	July 18, "
John S. Irwin,	June 22, "
Wm. S. Robison,	" "
D. Ryan,	" "
Wm. R. Nelson,	June 12, "
John Shaffer,	April 29, "
John Hough,	March 27, "
James F. Watkins,	" "
Henry H. Robinson,	April 11, "
Walpole G. Colerick,	" 8, "
William S. Smith,	Dec. 30, 1866
James C. Becks,	May 28, "
W. H. Withers,	April 11, "
Aug. H. Carier,	March 11, "
Frederick Buech,	Jan'y 10, 1865
Ward B. Chittenden,	Nov. 19, "
Charles McCulloch,	Oct. 2, "
William H. Jones,	" 16, "
Sol. D. Bayless,	Feb'y 2, "
David P. Whedon,	July 12, "
Daniel W. Bowen,	Jan'y 29, "
Samuel H. Bloomhuff,	April 9, "
George W. Wood,	Jan'y 23, "
David Colerick,	Dec. 12, 1864
Chr. Piepenbrink,	April 13, 1865
William Hamilton,	Oct. 26, 1864
James H. Myers,	May 21, "
L. M. Bowser,	Aug. 20, "
S. B. Bond,	" 18, "
Robert S. Taylor,	" 3, "
H. C. Hartman,	Aug. 6, "
Lewis E. Grove,	June 11, "
William Griffiths,	Feb'y 15, "
A. H. Hamilton,	" "

Township Officers.

TRUSTEE.—Isaac W. Campbell, office n w c Main and Calhoun, in Times Office. Term expires April, 1864.

JUSTICES OF THE PEACE.—Benjamin Saunders, office, west side Calhoun between Main and Columbia. Term expires June, 1865.

Wm. W. Steevens. Term expires April, 1864.
James D. Werden. Term expires April, 1864.
C. V. N. Milliman. Term expires April, 1866.

CONSTABLES.—D. B. Black; J. S. Leach. Terms expire April, 1864.

ASSESSOR.—George Fischer. Term expires April, 1864.

County Officers.

Court House east side Calhoun between Main and Berry.

CIRCUIT COURT.

Edwin R. Wilson, Judge of 10th Judicial Circuit, res. Bluffton. Term expires November, 1864.

COMMON PLEAS.

Joseph Brackenridge, Judge of 20th Common Pleas District. Term expires October, 1864.

CLERK OF CIRCUIT COURT.

Wm. Fleming, office Court House. Term expires November, 1866.
Wm. R. Nelson, Deputy.

SHERIFF.

Wm. T. Pratt, office Court House. Term expires October, 1864.
John McCartney, Deputy.

AUDITOR.

Geo. F. Stinchcomb, office Court House. Term expires October, 1865.
W. B. Chittenden and L. R. Hartman, Deputies.

TREASURER.

Alexander Wiley, office Court House. Term expires September, 1865.
Francis L. Furste, Deputy.

RECORDER.

Platt J. Wise, office Court House. Term expires June, 1864.
Clem. A. Rekers, Deputy and Recorder elect.

SURVEYOR

John W. M'Arthur, office Court House. Term expires Nov., 1864.

CORONER.

John P. Waters. Term expires October, 1864.

COUNTY COMMISSIONERS.

OFFICE, COURT HOUSE—MEETS QUARTERLY.

B. D. Miner. Term expires October, 1864.
John Shaffer. Term expires October, 1865.
David H. Lipes. Term expires October, 1866.

COMMON PLEAS PROSECUTOR.

David Colerick, office w s Calhoun opposite Court House. Term expires November, 1864.

COUNTY ATTORNEY.

Wm. W. Carson, office n s Main opposite Court House. Term expires June, 1864.

SUPERINTENDENT POOR HOUSE.

James Reed. Term expires June, 1864.

SCHOOL EXAMINER.

Rev. R. D. Robinson. Term expires June, 1864.

COUNTY PHYSICIAN.

C. E. Sturgis. Term expires June, 1864.

COURT HOUSE JANITOR.

Frank B. Kincade. Term expires September, 1864.

Benevolent Associations.

MASONIC.

Fort Wayne Commandery, No. 4—Knights Templars; instituted December, 1854. Meets in Stewart's Hall on second Thursday evenings in each month. Sir Charles Case, G. C. Sir John H. Bass, Recorder. Sol. D. Bayless, R. E. G. C. for Indiana.

Fort Wayne Council, No. 4—Instituted May 5, 1855. Meets in Wayne Lodge Room n w c Calhoun and Berry, on second Saturday evening in each month. Compn. Joseph Johnson, T. I. G. M. Compn. Benj. Saunders, Recorder. Sol. D. Bayless, M. I. G. M. for Indiana.

Fort Wayne Chapter, R. A. M., No. 19—Instituted May, 1851. Meets on first Wednesday evening of each month at Hall, n w c Calhoun and Berry. Companion Joseph Johnson, H. P. Companion Benj. Saunders, Secretary.

Wayne Lodge, No. 25, F. & A. M.—Instituted May, 1823. Regular meetings, Tuesday evenings on or preceding each full moon; adjourned meetings, Tuesday evening of each week. Hall n w c Calhoun and Berry. Sol. D. Bayless, W. M.; Benj. Saunders, Sec'y.

Summit City Lodge, No. 170—Instituted May, 1855. Hall n w c Calhoun and Berry. Regular meetings, on Friday evening preceding full moon; adjourned meetings, Friday evenings of each week. Wm. H. Nueman, W. M.; H. C. Hahn, Sec'y.

INDEPENDENT ORDER OF ODD FELLOWS.

HALL EAST SIDE CALHOUN, BET. MAIN AND COLUMBIA.

Fort Wayne Lodge, No. 14—Instituted October, 1843; meets every Monday evening. Platt J. Wise, Per. Sec.; O. W. Jefferds, Treasurer; O. W. Jefferds, M. Drake, Jr., Wm. H. Brooks, Trustees.

Harmony Lodge, No. 19—Instituted January 31, 1845; meets every Thursday evening. C. A. Fletcher, Per. Sec.; W. Waddington, Treasurer; Corydon Green, J. J. Kamm, Robert Erskine, Trustees.

Concordia Lodge, No. 228—Instituted January 15, 1862; meets every Wednesday evening. E. L. Sandmeier, Per. Sec.; C. Tresselt, Treasurer; F. Rehorst, C. Tresselt, L. Hause, Trustees.

Summit City Encampment, No. 16—Instituted November, 1849; meets first and third Saturday evening in each month.

INDEPENDENT ORDER OF GOOD TEMPLARS.

HALL 125 COLUMBIA STREET—THIRD STORY.

Total Abstinence Lodge, No. 26—Organized Feb. 25, 1859; meets every Saturday evening.

CHURCH DIRECTORY.

BAPTIST.

Baptist Church, west side Clinton, between Berry and Wayne, Rev. G. L. Stevens, Pastor.

GERMAN REFORMED.

St. John's Church, south side Washington, between Harrison and Webster. Rev. J. H. Klein, Pastor.

JEWISH.

Achduth Veshalom Synagogue, west side Harrison, between Wayne and Washington. Rev. Edward Rubin, Rabbi.

LUTHERAN.

English Lutheran Church, south east corner Clinton and Wayne. Rev. W. P. Ruthrauff, Pastor.

St. Paul's (German) Church, west side Barr opposite Madison. Rev. Wm. Sihler, Pastor. Rev. W. Stubnatzy, 2d Pastor.

St. John's (German) Church, south east corner Van Buren and Washington. Rev. Casimer Bauman, Pastor.

METHODIST EPISCOPAL.

Rev. S. N. Campbell, Presiding Elder.

Berry Street (M. E.) Church, morth east corner Harrison and Berry. Rev. John Hill, Pastor.

Wayne Street (M. E.) Church, south west corner Wayne and Broadway. Rev. R. Tobey, Pastor.

German (M. E.) Church, north side Washington, between Griffith and Fulton. Rev. F. A. Hoff, Pastor.

PRESBYTERIAN.

First Presbyterian (O. S.) Church, south east corner Clinton and Berry. Rev. John M. Lowrie, D. D., Pastor.

Second Presbyterian (N. S.) Church, south side Berry opposite Cass. Rev. ——— ———, Pastor.

PROTESTANT EPISCOPAL.

Trinity Church, south east corner Berry and Harrison. Rev. Joseph S. Large, Rector.

ROMAN CATHOLIC.

Right Rev. John H. Luers, Bishop of Fort Wayne.

Immaculate Conception Cathedral, east side Calhoun between Jefferson and Lewis. Very Rev. Julian Benoit, Rev. Patrick Madden, D. D., Pastors.

Mother of God (German) Church, south east corner Lafayette nd Jefferson. Rev. Joseph Weutz, Pastor.

Insurance Companies and Agencies.

HOME COMPANIES.

Banner Insurance Company—Office, 5 E. Main—Organized October, 1862.

OFFICERS.—B. W. Oakley, President; W. S. Smith, Vice President; L. A. Angell, Secretary; R. Morgan French, Treasurer; G. T. Angell, General Agent.

DIRECTORS.—B. W. Oakley, C. F. G. Meyer, W. S. Smith, Wm. T. Allen, R. Morgan French, G. T. Angell, Ira C. McAllaster, L. A. Angell, G. C. McAllaster.

Fort Wayne Insurance Company—Office, 5 E. Main—Organized October, 1863.

OFFICERS.—L. A. Angell, President; G. C. McAllaster, Secretary; Ira C. McAllaster, General Agent.

DIRECTORS.—A. M. Orbison, G. T. Angell, Wm. W. Fisk, D. F. Comparet, Ira C. McAllaster, C. Tresselt, L. A. Angell, I. W. Campbell, G. C. McAllaster.

State Insurance Company—Office, west side Clinton between Main and Columbia, (Hamilton's Old Bank,)—Organized November, 1863.

OFFICERS.—James L. Worden, President; O. Bird, Vice President; Hugh B. Reed, Treasurer; S. Lumbard, Secretary; G. W. Babcock, General Agent.

DIRECTORS.—James L. Worden, Hugh B. Reed, S. Lumbard, O. Bird, Geo. W. Babcock.

AGENCIES.

Ætna Fire Insurance Co. of Hartford, Conn.
Home Fire Insurance Co. of New York City.
>JOHN HOUGH, Agent,
>Office, 50 Calhoun,

Security Fire Insurance Co. of New York City.
New England Fire Insurance Co. of Hartford, Conn.
Home Fire Insurance Co. of New Haven, Conn.
Peoria Marine and Fire Insurance Co. of Peoria, Ill.
>SOL. D. BAYLESS, Agent,
>South-west cor. Clinton and Wayne.

North American Fire Insurance Co. of New York City.
Hartford Fire Insurance Co. of Hartford, Conn.
Connecticut Mutual Life Insurance Co. of Hartford, Conn.
     F. P. RANDALL, Agent,
  West side Clinton bet. Main and Columbia.
Liverpool & London Fire and Life Insurance Co.
     JOHN S. IRWIN, Agent,
  Office at Allen Hamilton & Co.'s Bank.
Phœnix Insurance Co. of Hartford, Conn.
City Fire Insurance Co. of Hartford, Conn.
Manhattan Fire Insurance Co. of New York City.
Lorillard Fire Insurance Co. of New York City.
Home Life Insurance Co. of Brooklyn, N. Y.
    HARTMAN & BOSSLER, Agents,
  Over Allen Hamilton & Co.'s Bank.
Metropolitan Fire Insurance Co. of New York.
Connecticut Fire Insurance Co. of Hartford, Conn.
    GEORGE R. HARTMAN, Agent,
  South-west corner Barr and Washington.
Equitable Life Assurance Society of New York.
    HENRY T. DUNHAM, Agent,
  South-west corner Main and Clinton.

Railroads.

Pittsburgh, Fort Wayne & Chicago Railway Co.—Extending from Pittsburgh, Pa. to Chicago, Ills., 468 miles. Principal office at Pittsburgh. George W. Cass, President, Pittsburgh; Samuel Hanna, Vice President, Fort Wayne; W. H. Barnes, Secretary, Pittsburgh; J. P. Henderson, Treasurer, Pittsburgh; T. D. Messler, Controller, Pittsburgh; John B. Jervis, General Superintendent, Pittsburgh; Wm. P. Shinn, Supt. Eastern Division, Pittsburgh; H. A. Gardner, Supt. Western Division, Ft. Wayne; J. J. Houston, General Freight Agent, Pittsburgh; H. R. Payson, General Passenger Agent, Pittsburgh.

Toledo & Wabash Railway Co.—Extending from Toledo to State Line, Illinois, 243 miles. Principal office at Toledo. A. Boody, President; W. Colburn, Vice President; J. N. Drummond, Secretary and Treasurer; George H. Burrows, General Superintendent; J. C. Baker, Assistant Superintendent; Charles Knox, General Freight Agent; J. E. Carpenter, General Ticket Agent.

Public Buildings, Halls, &c.

Townley's Block, north east corner Columbia and Calhoun.
Union Block, north-west corner Main and Clinton.
Masonic Hall, north-west corner Calhoun and Berry.
Odd Fellows' Hall, east side Calhoun between Main and Columbia.
Fireman's Hall, east side Calhoun between Columbia and Main.
Phœnix Block, north-west corner Main and Calhoun.
Court House, on Public Square.
Colerick's Hall, north side Columbia between Clinton and Barr.
Post Office, west end Columbia.
Miller's Block and Hall, north-west corner Berry and Calhoun.
Pratt's Hall, north-west corner Main and Harrison.
Robinson's Block, west end Columbia.
Templars' Hall, north-west corner Calhoun and Berry.
Stewart's Hall, west side Calhoun between Main and Berry.
Fireman's Hall, north east corner Court and Berry.

Miscellaneous.

Allen County Bible Society.—Organized April, 1833. Depository, 73 Columbia. Meets last Tuesday in each month. Rev. R. D. Robinson, President; G. R. Hartman, Secretary; A. S. Evans, Treasurer.

Indiana Land Agency.—John Hough, Proprietor. Office, 50 Calhoun.

Fort Wayne College.—West end of Wayne Street. Incorporated 1846, under the patronage of the North and North-West Indiana Conferences. Faculty—Rev. R. D. Robinson, President; Mrs. Mary K. Robinson, Governess; Miss Mary E. Dibble, Adjunct Teacher of Mathematics and Drawing; Henry Orff, Professor of Music; John T. Beaber; Instructor of Preparatory Department; Byron W. McLain, Instructor of Penmanship; Miss Louie S. Bragdon, Teacher of Primary Class. Officers of the Board of Trustees—Hon. Wm. Rockhill, President; Isaac Jenkinson, Secretary; John M. Miller, Treasurer.

Orphan's Home and Fort Wayne Hospital.—North-west corner Wayne and Webster. Bernard Rekers, Proprietor.

MISCELLANEOUS.

Pendagger Club.—Organized June 11, 1848. Meets the first Saturday evening in each month. Rooms, Columbia Street between Calhoun and Clinton. W. J. Van Schuyver, President; E. L. Chittenden, Secretary.

Lindenwood Cemetery.—Situated on Huntington Road, one and a half miles from the city. I. D. G. Nelson, President; C. D. Bond, Secretary and Treasurer; I. D. G. Nelson, J. L. Williams, H. McCulloch, P. Hoagland, O. P. Morgan, Directors.

Fort Wayne Gas Light Co.—Organized August, 1855. Capital, $68,900. A. P. Edgerton, President; H. H. Edgerton, Secretary; R. E. Fleming, Treasurer and Superintendent; Alfred Hattersley, Inspector; A. P. Edgerton, R. E. Fleming, William Rockhill, Platt J. Wise, H. H. Edgerton, Directors.

German Catholic Carl Barromœus Society.—Organized August, 1860. Hall in Baker's Building. H. Branger, President; Henry Monning, Secretary; John Mohr, Treasurer.

St. George's Benevolent Association of Fort Wayne.—Organized April, 1862. Meets in St. George's Hall on the first Saturday evening of each month at 8 o'clock, from April to September, and 7½ o'clock from October to April. Officers—Thomas Tigar, President; T. Rich and J. Stratton, Vice Presidents; R. Sulley, Treasurer; C. M. Thomas, Recording Secretary; A. Hattersley, Financial Secretary; E. Butland, J. Fowles, A. Bennett, Relief Committee.

Caledonian Society.—Organized February, 1860. Meets at room in Court House Building first Thursday evening in each month. Election of Directors annually in February.

Working Men's Institute and Library.—Organized August, 1854. Rooms in Court House Building. Number of Volumes, 1,300. Open every Tuesday and Friday evenings. Regular meetings every Friday evening. Election of Directors, December, annually.

Township Library.—In Court House Building. Open every Wednesday evening and Saturday afternoon. Number of Volumes, 1,100. Bernard Rekers, Librarian.

Fort Wayne Agricultural Works.—Situate on Canal Feeder, north end of Calhoun Street. Organized September, 1863. Capital, $30,000. Hugh B. Reed, President; Wm. H. Jones, Secretary; C. D. Bond, Treasurer; Hugh B. Reed, A. P. Edgerton, William Fleming, O. Bird, C. D. Bond, Directors.

Concordia College.—Situate north side Van Wert Road, east of Corporation Line. Under the auspices of the German Evangelical Lutheran Synod of Missouri, Ohio and other States. Board of Trustees and Inspectors: Rev. H. C. Schwan, Cleveland, O.; Rev. F. W. Husmann, Euclid, O.; Ch. Piepenbrink, Ft. Wayne; Rev. Dr. Wm. Sibler, President; G. A. Saxer, Director; C. Bonnet, Treasurer.

Newspapers.

Dawson's Fort Wayne Daily and Weekly Times.—Office, north-west corner Main and Calhoun Streets. John W. Dawson, Proprietor; Henry Higgins, Editor.

Fort Wayne Daily and Weekly Sentinel.—Office, west side Calhoun between Main and Columbia. Thomas Tigar, Editor and Proprietor; G. D. Hinkle, Associate Editor.

Indiana Staats Zeitung, (Weekly, German).—Office, north-east corner Clinton and Columbia. J. Sarnighausen, Editor.

Fort Wayne Daily and Weekly Gazette.—Office, No. 125 Columbia Street. Jones & Jenkinson, Editors and Proprietors.

Indiana Tri-Weekly and Weekly Demokrat, (German).—Office, north-west corner Calhoun and Berry. C. G. Jahn, Editor.

DAWSON'S
DAILY AND WEEKLY
FORT WAYNE TIMES.

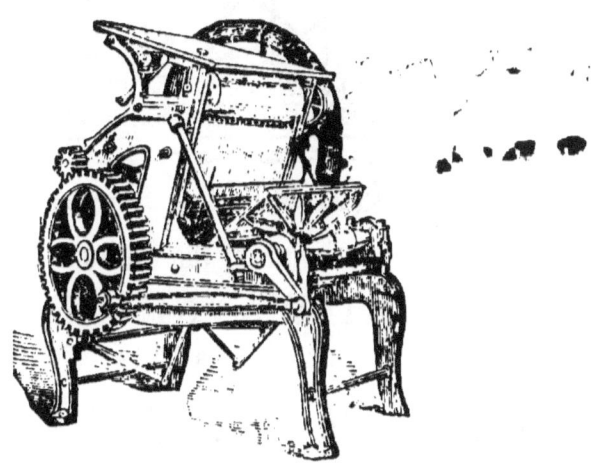

NEWS, BOOK, PLAIN,
— AND —
ORNAMENTAL JOB
PRINTING OFFICE,

North-West Corner of Main and Calhoun Sts.,

FORT WAYNE, IND.

JOHN W. DAWSON, Ed. and Proprietor.

TERMS:

Daily Times, per year, - - -	$6 00
Weekly " " - - -	2 00

FT. WAYNE MACHINE WORKS,

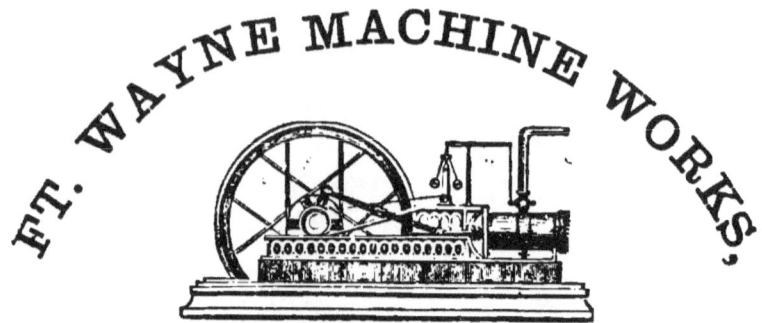

BASS & HANNA, Proprietors,

Hanna Street, South of the Railroad Crossing,

FORT WAYNE, IND.,

MANUFACTURERS OF

STEAM ENGINES,

BOILERS, MILL GEARING,

ASH LEACHES,
   TANKS,
      MULAY, SASH, AND
CIRCULAR SAW MILLS,
      RAILROAD CAR WHEELS,
BUILDING FRONTS,

And Every Description of

IRON AND BRASS CASTINGS.

REPAIRING ON

BOILERS, ENGINES AND MACHINERY,

Promptly Executed on Reasonable Terms.

WILLIAMS'
FT. WAYNE DIRECTORY,

FOR

1864.

ABBREVIATIONS.

al...........alley or allopathic.	cab. mkr.........cabinet maker.	mer...................merchant.
atty.......................attorney.	carp................carpenter.	mkr....................maker.
av........................avenue.	clk.....................clerk.	n........................north.
b......................between.	cof h..............coffee house.	not. pub........notary public.
bar k.................bar keeper.	com................commission.	nr.......................near.
bds......................boards.	confec...........confectioner.	opp....................opposite.
b. h..............boarding house.	e.......................east.	prov...................provision.
bk................book or brick.	ec.....................eclectic.	prop'r..............proprietor.
b. k.................book keeper.	eng....................engineer.	res....................residence.
bk layer..............brick layer.	ex....................exchange.	s................south or side.
bldr....................builder.	h.......................house.	srvt....................servant.
bldg..................building.	ho..................homoepathic.	w.......................west.
bo.....................botanic.	lab.....................laborer.	wh....................wholesale.
c........................corner.	manuf............manufacturer.	wks.....................works.

(A IN)

ABBOTT WM. T., Wholesale and Retail Dealer in Staple & Fancy Dry Goods, Carpets, Oil Cloths, Groceries, &c., 99 Columbia, h 213 W. Berry.

Achenbach Wm. teacher at Concordia College
Ackley Philip, res Mrs. Sarah Ackley's
Ackley Mrs. Sarah, widow h n s Wall w of Bluffton Plank Rd
Adair B. L. (A. & Hunter,) bds George R. Hartman's
Adair & Hunter, (B. L. A. & C. W. H.) fancy goods w s Clinton nr Main
Adams Elizabeth, h 138 E. Washington
Adams Israel, eng h 138 W. Wayne
Adams John, brakeman bds Mrs. Ann Graham's
Adkins Ormus W. conductor h n s Brandriff b Webster and Hoagland
Adler Francis, organist bds 181 Clinton

ÆTNA INSURANCE COMPANY of Hartford, Conn.; John Hough, Agent, 50 Calhoun, opp. Court House.

Agnew Edward, (Ash & A.) h 153 W. Berry
Agster Mrs. Anna M. h 156 Harrison
Ahlert Fred. watchman h s e c Jefferson and Nelson
Ainsworth Evans, bds Main Street Exchange

B. TRENTMAN,
WHOLESALE GROCER,
AND DEALER IN

Foreign and Domestic Liquors, Cigars, &c.

ALSO,

RECTIFIER OF EXTRA WHISKY,
86 Columbia St., Fort Wayne, Ind.

YOUGHIOGHENY COAL!

Of the best quality, and the price LOWER than elsewhere in this city. For sale at all times, in any quantity, at the Yard of the

FORT WAYNE
GAS LIGHT COMPANY,

On the Canal, corner of Barr and Water Streets,

FORT WAYNE, INDIANA.

Ainsworth J. H. clk n w c Columbia and Clinton, bds Main Street Exchange

ALBERT JULES, Market Bakery and Eating House, 88 Barr.

Albright S. blksmith wks P., Ft. W. & C. Railway blksmith shop

Aldenburg B. lab bds Steuben House

Aldrich E. hostler wks A. J. Read & Co.'s

Alexander C. G. blksmith h w s Fulton b Washington and Jefferson

Allbright Frank, blksmith h s e c Jones and John

Allemann John, mason h 88 Madison

ALLEN & CO., (W. T. A., Geo. H. Wilson & J. G. Schuckman,) Tin Roofers and Dealers in Stoves, House Furnishing Goods, and Manufacturers of Tin, Copper and Sheet Iron Ware, 77 Columbia.

ALLEN C. W., Carpenter, Builder and Lumber Dealer, Shop and Residence, s w c Wayne and Fulton.

Allen J. helper wks P., Ft. W. & C. Railway blksmith shop

Allen John, blksmith h 191 Lafayette

Allen W. T. (A. & Co.) h 20 E. Washington

Alliger D. (Neil McLachlan & Co.) h s s Water b Ewing and Griffith

Alter Jacob, painter h n w c Wilt and Van Buren

Alter Nicholas, plasterer h e s Force s of Jones

Altevogt Herman, h 10 W. Wayne

Alyo Delia, servt 139 W. Washington

Aman Charles, brakeman h 265 E. Washington

Aman Louis, plasterer h 265 E. Washington

Ame D. lab wks P., Ft. W. & C. Railway Co.'s Yard

Ame Frank, clk h 175 E. Wayne

AMEND ANDREW, Bakery and Eating House, 69 Columbia.

AMERICAN EXPRESS COMPANY, S. McElvain, Agent, n w c Calhoun and Berry.

AMERICAN HOUSE, B. H. Schnieders, Proprietor, s s Columbia b Calhoun and Harrison.

Amman M. W. foreman boiler mkrs P., Ft. W. & C. Railway Co.

Ammon Daniel, (A. & Henry,) h n s Wayne b Ewing and Griffith

AMMON & HENRY, (Daniel A. & H. H. H.) Butter and Egg Packers, and Flour and Feed Store, 51 Columbia.

Anderson A. M. mach wks P., Ft. W. & C. Railway machine shop

Anderson B. C. harness mkr bds T. W. Bayless'

Anderson Calvin, (A. & Evans,) h 117 W. Wayne

LOUIS H. MOSSLER,

FORMERLY THE

NEW YORK AUCTION STORE.

DEALER IN

STAPLE, FOREIGN AND DOMESTIC

DRY GOODS,

CLOTHING, FANCY GOODS, &C.,

AT THE OLD STAND,

No. 96 Columbia Street,

FORT WAYNE, IND.

JOHN G. FLEDDERMAN & CO.,

UNION CASH CLOTHING STORE,

COR. MAIN AND CLINTON STS.,

Fort Wayne, Ind.

All Kinds of Furnishing Goods.

CLOTHING

Of every Description made to Order in the most Fashionable Style.

Anderson David B. blksmith h n s Buchanan b Piqua Plank Rd and Clay
Anderson David H. clk Anderson & Evans', bds 174 W. Wayne
Anderson David L. brakeman bds n s Washington b Francis and Harmer

ANDERSON & EVANS, (Calvin A. & Edwin E.) Dealers in Family Groceries, Provisions, &c., n w c Calhoun and Main.

ANDERSON FELIX H., House, Sign and Ornamental Painter, 94 Columbia, up stairs; Resides Country.

Anderson Geo. fireman wks P., Ft. W. & C. Railway Co.
Anderson H. blksmith wks P., Ft. W. & C. Railway blksmith shop
Anderson Martin V. bds Summit City Hotel
Anderson Noah, barber bds 96 Madison
Anderson P. B. carriage painter bds Henry Montgomery's
Anderson Thos. P. (A. & Irving,) h n s Berry b Harrison and Maiden Lane
Andres John, carp h s e c Jones and John
Andrews & Conklin, (Dexter B. A. & Theodore C.) photographs west end of Columbia
Andrews David, boiler mkr h 231 Barr
Andrews Dexter B. (A. & Conklin)
Andrews E. C. clk P., Ft. W. & C. Railway Co. shops, bds Mayer House
Andrews John, carp wks T. & W. Railway shops
Andrews Marshall H. painter bds Jacob J. Kamm's
Andrews Wm. cooper wks C. S. Brackenridge & Co.'s
Angell Byron D. clk h 167 W. Wayne
Angell G. T. general agt Banner Ins. Co. 5 E. Main, bds 16 Madison

ANGELL L. A., Secretary Banner Insurance Co. Office 5 E. Main, h 16 Madison.

Angell Orange A. h 170 W. Berry
Ankanbruck Anthony, lab h n s Wayne b Hanna and Francis
Anthony Peter, gardener wks D. F. Comparet's
Anthony Wm. shoe mkr bds Union House
App Mathias, (Ketcher & A.) h 79 W. Washington
Appley J. lab wks P., Ft. W. & C. Railway lumber yard
Archibald Samuel, blksmith bds Old Fort House
Armbouster Ch. brakeman bds Wm. Beal's
Armstrong Mrs. Melinda, h s w c Berry and Union
Armstrong Nettie, h 240 E. Washington
Arney Susan, cook at Mayer House
Arnold John, carp h 125 W. Washington
Ash Mrs. Lucinda F. res 146 W. Berry
Ashley P. H. conductor bds 145 E. Jefferson

4

UNION FILE WORKS.

C. SCHMIDT & CO.,
MANUFACTURERS OF

Files, Rasps, Mill Picks,

STONE CUTTERS' TOOLS, &c.

Re-cutting Old Files, etc., done to order, and warranted equal to new. All kinds of Rasps and Files made to order.

ALSO,

Wholesale and Retail Dealers in Foreign and Domestic Hardware, Pine Sash and Doors, Nails, Glass, Paint, etc., at Factory Prices.

UNION BLOCK, OPP. STATE BANK,

FT. WAYNE, IND.

All Orders from the Country Promptly Attended to.

ANDERSON & IRVING,
DEALERS IN

Pianos, Melodeons, &c.,

No. 2, Aveline House Block, Calhoun Street,

FORT WAYNE, IND.

ANDERSON & IRVING, (Thos. P. A. & A. B. I.) Dealers in Piano Fortes, Melodeons, &c., No. 2 Aveline House, s e c Calhoun and Berry.

ASH & AGNEW, (Henry J. A. & Edward A.) Dealers in Stoves, Hardware, Cutlery, Nails, Sash, Glass, and Manufacturers of Tin, Copper and Sheet Iron Ware, 87 Columbia.

Ash Henry J. (A. & Agnew,) h 146 W. Berry
Atkins John, mach bds Mrs. Ann Graham's
Atkins Wm. mach wks T. & W. Railway shops
Auer Conrad, lab h 30 W. Wayne
Auer Daniel, h 215 E. Washington
Aufrecht Jacob, saloon w s Lafayette b Main and Columbia
Augustin Daniel, carp h s s Melitia b Webster and Hoagland
Augustine Wm. (Murray & Co.) h n s Pearl nr Fulton
Auman M. W. boiler mkr h s e c Douglas Av. and Webster
Autell V. blksmith wks P. Ft. W. & C. Railway blksmith shop

AVELINE F. S., Proprietor Aveline House, s e c Calhoun and Berry.

Aveline Frank H. res Aveline House

AVELINE HOUSE, F. S. Aveline, Proprietor, s e c Calhoun and Berry.

Aveline J. F. res at Aveline House
Axt Moses, carp h e s Francis b Lewis and Madison

AYRES H. P., Physician and Surgeon, Office n e c Main and Calhoun, h w s Clinton b Wayne and Washington.

Ayres Henry B. clk 140 Columbia, h 120 Clinton
Ayres Stephen C. phys h 120 Clinton

B

Baals George, carp h s e c Jones and Force
Babcock Cornelius, carp bds Kime House
Babcock G. carp wks P., Ft. W. & C. Railway carp shop

BABCOCK GEO. W., General Agent State Insurance Company, Office, w s Clinton b Main and Columbia, bds Aveline House.

Babcock W. C. carp wks P., Ft. W. & C. Railway carp shop
Bacon Franklin, blksmith h 40 Madison
Bacon M. F. blksmith h s w c Lewis and Lafayette
Bade Christ. h n s Douglas Av. b Webster and McClellan
Bade Ernst, carp h 198 Ewing
Bade H. lab wks P., Ft. W & C. Railway lumber yard
Bade Henry, h 193 Ewing
Bade Henry, lab h Bloomingdale
Bade Wm. warehouseman h 173 Harrison

JOHN HOUGH,
LAW AND COLLECTION OFFICE,
FORT WAYNE, IND.

WM. H. COOMBS.   JOHN HOUGH.

ATTORNEYS & COUNSELLORS AT LAW,

Practice in the Circuit Court of the United States, in the several State Courts, and make Collections throughout the State.

REFERENCES.

Allen Hamilton & Co., Ft. Wayne	Barcroft & Co., Philadelphia
A. T. Stewart & Co., New York	Levie, Ralsin & Co., "
Lathrop, Ludington & Co., "	Jay Cooke & Co., "
S. B. Chittenden & Co., "	Bullitt & Fairthorne, "
Spofford, Tileston & Co., "	Wm. Glenn & Sons, Cincinnati
Bliven & Mead, "	B. P. Baker & Co., "
Chase, McKinney & Co., Boston	Tweed & Andrews, "
Sidney, Shepard & Co., Buffalo	Hailman, Rahm & Co., Pittsburgh
Hon. H. McCulloch, Washington	Jones & Laughlin, "

F. P. RANDALL,
ATTORNEY AT LAW,
LAND AND INSURANCE AGENT,
OFFICE, WEST SIDE CLINTON, BET. COLUMBIA AND MAIN STREETS.
FORT WAYNE, IND.

JAMES HUMPHREY'S
STEAM SAND AND LIME-STONE WORKS,
CUT STONE FOR BUILDINGS,
Of all Kinds.
ORDERS FROM A DISTANCE PROMPTLY ATTENDED TO.
SHOP, CORNER FULTON AND MAIN STREETS,
FORT WAYNE, IND.

Bader Fred. lab wks T. & W. Railway shops
Bader Henry, watchman wks T. & W. Railway shops
Bagley Hugh, shoe mkr h 43 E. Water
Bahde Fred. lab h 182 W. Jefferson
Bahman A. carp wks P., Ft. W. & C. Railway carp shop
Bahman J. carp wks P., Ft. W. & C. Railway carp shop
Baier John, painter h n s Montgomery b Barr and Lafayette
Bailey E. fireman wks P., Ft. W. & C. Railway Co.
Bailey Geo. W. carp h 156 E. Jefferson
Bailey Jerome, fireman wks P., Ft. W. & C. Railway Co.
Bailey John, blksmith wks T. & W. Railway shops
Bailey Miss Libby, bds Christopher Wamsley's
Bailey Lucy, at Old Fort House
Bailey P. P. h n w c Clinton and Washington
Baistor Fred. carp bds 170 W. Wayne
Baker Aaron, lab res Philip Baker's
Baker C. teamster bds Union House
Baker C. lab wks P., F. W. & C. Railway lumber yard
Baker Charles, carp h 166 W. Washington
Baker Conrad, boots and shoes 19 Clinton, h 193 W. Berry
Baker Mrs. Elizabeth, widow h 151 Barr
Baker Geo. D. tailor h n s W. & E. Canal b Cass and Ewing
Baker Henry, (J., K. & H. B.) res Country

BAKER J., K. & H., (Jacob, Killian & Henry,) Saw Mill, s w c Water and Lafayette.

Baker Jacob, (J., K. & H. B.) h s s Main b Lafayette and Clay
Baker Jacob, teamster b ls Union House

BAKER JOHN, Blacksmith and Wagon Manufacturer, w s Lafayette b Main and Columbia, h e s Clinton b Washington and Jefferson.

Baker Killian, (J., K. & H. B.) h s s Main b Barr and Lafayette
Baker Mrs. Matilda, widow h e s Ewing b Wayne and Washington
Baker Philip, carp h n w s Bluffton Road s of Nirdlinger
Baker Wesley, carp wks F. S. Baldwin's
Baldock Alfred, carp h n s Main b Griffith and Fulton
Baldridge —— ——, conductor bds 225 W. Washington
Baldwin Albert B. asst checkman P., Ft. W. & C. Railway Freight Depot, bds Benjamin Morss'
Balwin C. S. clk 39 Columbia, res O. J. Baldwin's

BALDWIN F. S., Sash, Blind and Door Manufacturer, Scroll Sawing, &c., n s the Canal b Clinton and Barr, h 174 Griffith.

BALDWIN O. J., Veterinary Surgeon, Office, s s Berry b Calhoun and Harrison, h n s Main b Cass and Maiden Lane.

Baldwin S. contractor and builder, office, n s Canal b Clinton and Barr, h 174 Griffith

AUGUST F. SIEMON. RUDOLPH SIEMON.

A. F. SIEMON & BRO.,

WHOLESALE AND RETAIL DEALERS IN

BOOKS, STATIONERY,

Wall Papers, Pictures, etc.

PLAIN AND ORNAMENTAL

BOOK AND JOB PRINTERS,
BLANK BOOK MANUFACTURERS
—AND—

BOOK BINDERS.

PLAIN AND FANCY JOB PRINTING
OF EVERY DESCRIPTION

EXECUTED WITH NEATNESS AND DISPATCH.

BLANK BOOKS

Of any desired pattern, manufactured to order, at the shortest possible notice.

Books, Magazines, Newspapers, Pamphlets, &c.,
BOUND OR RE-BOUND IN THE MOST APPROVED STYLE.

Union Block, Clinton St., bet. Main and Columbia,
FORT WAYNE, INDIANA.

Ball J. W. conductor bds Mayer House
Ball Rudolph, lab h w s Piqua Plank Road b Virginia and Wallace
Balstz John L. lab h n e c Jefferson and College

BALTES M. & CO., (Michael B. & Wm. Wehrs,) Contractors and Dealers in Lime, Plaster, Cement, Stone, &c., e s Calhoun b Canal & Water.

Baltes Michael, (M. B. & Co.) h 14 E. Water
Balters Ernst, carp bds Wm. Muellerring's
Bamboo David, painter wks T. & W. Railway shops

BANNER INSURANCE COMPANY, Office, 5 E. Main, up stairs; B. W. Oakley, President; L. A. Angell, Secretary.

Banta Herman F. painter h s e c Washington and Union
Barbert Armand, cooper h 261 E. Washington
Barbier Peter F. saw repairer h s s Columbia b Barr and Lafayette
Barbour Lucius T. h 94 E. Washington
Barbour Myron F. lightning rods h 94 E. Washington
Barcorn F. helper wks P , Ft. W. & C. Railway boiler shops
Barcus Daniel, prop'r People's House w s Calhoun b Jefferson and Lewis
Barcus Hezekiah, candy mkr wks 83 Columbia
Barcus Isaac, marble cutter wks n e c Main and Cass
Barcus John L. painter bds People's House
Barcus Martin, carp h 154 E. Jefferson
Barcus Richard, candy mkr wks 83 Columbia
Bare John, engineer bds Mayer House
Barlow Isaac J. (B. & Kyle,) res Inwood

BARLOW & KYLE, (Isaac J. B. & Abram P. K.,) Pump Manufacturers, w s Harrison b Canal and Pearl.

Barnard C. carp wks P., Ft. W. & C. Railway carp shop
Barnard S. J. blksmith wks John Brown's
Barner Chas. carp h w s Francis b Hamilton and Railway
Barnes Joshua, mach wks T. & W. Railway shops
Barnett A. G. h on east branch Lima Plank Road n of St. Mary's River
Barnhard Christ, warehouseman P., Ft. W. & C. R. R. Freight Depot
Baron Mrs. Frances, widow h w s Hanna s of Lassello
Barr James S brakeman h 151 W. Washington
Barrand Frank, lab h w s Hanna b Montgomery and Holman
Barrand Joseph, lab h 165 E. Lewis
Barron John, h 123 Lafayette
Barrows H. P. lab bds 45 E. Main
Barry Thomas, core mkr h s s Montgomery b Barr and Lafayette

HOMER C. HARTMAN.   HENRY H. BOSSLER.

HARTMAN & BOSSLER,

Real Estate, Collecting

—AND—

INSURANCE AGENTS.

OFFICE:

NO. 4 West Side Calhoun St., over Allen Hamilton & Co.'s Bank,

FORT WAYNE, IND.

☞ Deeds, Mortgages and other Instruments drawn with care, and all kinds of NOTARIAL BUSINESS attended to.

PHILO RUMSEY,

PROPRIETOR

FT. WAYNE EATING HOUSE,

Junction Pittsburgh, Fort Wayne and Chicago and Toledo and Wabash Railroads,

FORT WAYNE, INDIANA.

Meals Served upon the Arrival of every Passenger Train.

E. L. CHITTENDEN,

CITY CLERK, ATTORNEY AT LAW

—AND—

GENERAL COLLECTING AGENT,

Office in Mayor's Office, up stairs.

Will promptly draft all Legal Instruments in Writing, collect Accounts and Notes by Suit, Foreclosures, etc. Particular attention paid to Divorces.

Bartels Ernst, cab mkr wks 50 E. Main
Bartholomew Hiram B. carp h w s Fairfield Av. b Locust and Taylor
Barton P. molder wks Ft. Wayne Machine Works
Base Ammon, butcher h 81 E. Wayne

BASH & EAKIN, (Solomon B. & Joseph S. E.,) Dealers in Wool, Furs, Hides, Pelts, Seeds, Butter, &c., 61 Columbia.

Bash Solomon, (B. & Eakin,) h 242 W. Berry
Bass Mrs. Eliza, widow h 139 W. Washington

BASS & HANNA, (John H. B. & Horace H. H.,) Proprietors Ft. Wayne Machine Works, e s Hanna s of Railroad Junction.

Bass John H. (B. & Hanna,) b ds Mayer House
Basse John, bklayer h w s Monroe b Madison and Lewis
Bateman W. helper wks P., Ft. W. & C. Railway blksmith shop
Batinfield John, eng wks John Brown's, bds Union House
Bauchinger Henry, sawyer wks J., K. & H. Baker's
Bauer Henry, harness mkr bds 98 E. Jefferson
Bauer Henry, porter American House
Baughman Jeremiah, carp h s s Douglas, Bloomingdale
Baughman Saml. miller h s s Lasselle e of Piqua Plank Road
Baughman Saml. C. clk Summit City Hotel
Baugier Joseph, res Xavier Baugier's
Baugier Xavier, h al b Clinton and Barr first n of Water
Bauman John, shoemkr h n w c Main and Harrison
Baumann Rev. C. h 199 W. Washington
Baumer Michael, h e s West b Pritchard and Railroad
Baumer Michael, miller wks Empire Flour Mill
Baxter John, conductor h 64 W. Wayne
Bayer Paul, shoemkr James H. Robinson's h 85 W. Jefferson

BAYLESS SOL. D., Insurance, Real Estate, Collecting and U. S. Pension Agent, Office and Residence, s w c Clinton and Wayne.

Bayless T. W. saddles, &c., 50 W. Main, h 53 Barr
Beaber A. J. h n w c Broadway and Wilt
Beaber Jacob, carp h 239 W. Wayne
Beaber John T. teacher at Fort Wayne College
Beach Byron, wks Olds, Hanna & Co.'s
Bealer Thos. fireman wks P., Ft. W. & C. Railway Co.
Beals Melvin M. bds Wm. Beal's
Beals Thomas C. fireman bds Wm. Beals'
Beals Wm. night watchman h w s Barr b Wayne and Washington
Beamer G. carp wks P., Ft. W. & C. Railway Carpenter Shop
Bear John, eng Vigilant Fire Co. bds Mayer House
Beard Thos. D. candy manuf 99 E. Berry
Bearrs Edward E. res Mrs. Esther Ewing's

D. O'CONNELL,
PROPRIETOR O'CONNELL'S BILLIARD

ROOM & RESTAURANT.

East side Calhoun St., bet. Mayer & Aveline Houses,

FORT WAYNE, IND.

J. O'CONNELL,
PROPRIETOR
FORT WAYNE OMNIBUS LINE,
OFFICE
At O'Connell's Billiard Room.

B. W. OAKLEY,
WHOLESALE AND RETAIL DEALER IN
FOREIGN AND DOMESTIC
HARDWARE,
SADDLERY AND CARRIAGE TRIMMINGS,
RUBBER AND LEATHER BELTING, Etc.,
79 COLUMBIA STREET,
FORT WAYNE, IND.

Beatty ——, mach bds Mrs. E. B. Grout's
Beatty Mrs. h n s Lewis b Francis and Hanna
Beattie Wm. blksmith wks T. & W. Railway Shop

BEAVER A. C., Contractor, Carpenter and Builder, 116 W. Main, h 170 W. Wayne.

BEAVER D. S., Miller, and Dealer in Flour, Feed and Grain, s w c Calhoun and Berry; residence, Glenwood Mills, on St. Mary's River, 2 1-2 miles from city.

Beaver George, blksmith h 182 E. Jefferson
Beaver John, b k D. S. Beaver's, res Glenwood Mills
Bechman Adam, carp res John Bechman's
Bechman John, carp h c s Hanna s of Jones
Becht Adam, h c s Calhoun b Washington and Jefferson
Becion W. fireman wks P., Ft. W. & C. Railway Co.

BECK FRANCIS J., Proprietor Bloomingdale Brewery, Bloomingdale.

Beck Henry, lab h e s West b Pritchard and Railroad

BECK JOHN, Dealer in Family Groceries, Produce, Provisions, &c., n w c Harrison and Main.

Beck Joseph, bklayer h 207 E. Washington
Beck M. melder wks Bowser & Story's
Beck Peter, lab h w s Nelson b Jefferson and Wilt
Beck Wm. lab h 189 Ewing
Beck Wm. L. warehouseman P., Ft. W. & C. Railway Freight Depot
Becker C. carp wks P., Ft. W. & C. Railway Carpenter Shop
Becker Christian, marble dealer n w c Main and Fulton, h 220 W. Berry
Becker Frederick, blksmith 9 and 11 E. Washington
Becker Geo. h e s Calhoun b Washington and Jefferson
Becker Henry, clk C. Schoerpf & Co.'s h 45 W. Washington
Becker Jacob, produce dealer h 140 W. Berry
Becker John J. mach bds Peter Becker's
Becker L. helper wks P., Ft. W. & C. Railway Boiler Shop
Becker Peter, lab h n w c Barr and Wayne
Beckett Mrs. Theresa widow h 200 E. Wayne
Beckette J. lab wks P., Ft. W. & C. Railway Lumber Yard
Becknece H. lab wks P., Ft. W. & C. Railway Lumber Yard
Beckus Jacob, lab h s e c Wilt and Nelson
Becquette John B. bklayer h 148 E. Main
Bedell Allen, conductor bds e s Piqua Plank Road b Virginia and Wallace
Bedell Amos, eng h e s Piqua Plank Road b Virginia and Wallace
Beebe James, bds 228 E. Jefferson
Beecher A. W. photographer h 95 W. Berry

A. C. HUESTIS,
WHOLESALE GROCER AND CONFECTIONER,

ALSO,

WHOLESALE DEALER

IN

Oranges, Lemons, Oysters, etc.

Nos. 83 & 85 Columbia St.,

FT. WAYNE, IND.

D. F. COMPARET.
MILLER AND COMMISSION MERCHANT,
FORT WAYNE, IND.

GENERAL DEALER IN ALL KINDS OF

Grain, Seeds, Salt, Fish, Produce,
AGRICULTURAL IMPLEMENTS, ETC.
BEST BRANDS OF FAMILY FLOUR.
☞ Liberal advances made on Produce in Store.

SUMMIT CITY HOTEL,
DIRECTLY OPPOSITE
Pittsburg, Ft. Wayne & Chicago & Toledo & Wabash Railroad Depots,

FORT WAYNE, IND.

C. P. & J. F. FLETCHER, - - Proprietors.

Beecher Mrs. Clorinda M. widow h 95 W. Berry
Beecher Martha S. teacher Western District School, h 95 W. Berry

BEEGAN M. P., Wholesale and Retail Dealer in Family Groceries, Provisions, Liquors, Salt, &c., 37 Columbia.

Beckman George W. clk Ft. Wayne Eating House
Beemer Philip, brakeman bds 151 Washington
Beer Benj. tinner bds 52 Columbia
Begue Edward, lab wks Murray & Bennigin's
Behner John, teamster h n s High, Bloomingdale
Beier Nicholas, carp res Valentine Beier's
Beier Paul, shoemkr h 85 W. Jefferson
Beier Valentine, carp h n s Douglas Av. b Harrison and Webster
Beirbaum Fred. h 203 E. Washington
Beirlein Geo. lab h n s W. & E. Canal b Broadway and Van Buren
Belcher Wm. T. clk 99 Columbia, bds 213 W. Berry
Belden Geo. A. carp h n s Brandriff b Webster and Hoagland
Bell Chas. teamster bds King House
Bell John M. carp h s s Washington b Rockhill and College
Bell Thos. boiler mkr h w s Ewing s of Jefferson
Bell Wm. blksmith bds Summit City Hotel
Bell Wm. J. engineer h n s Douglas av. b Calhoun and Harrison
Bellamy Albert F. painter h s s Main b Fulton and Broadway
Bellow J. helper wks P. Ft. W. & C. Railway Carpenter Shop
Benbow David, hatter bds 156 Harrison
Bender D. cooper wks Bloomingdale Browery
Bender Harrison, stone cutter bds David Gibford's
Bender Harvey, marble cutter wks n e c Main and Cass
Bender Henry, wagon mkr bds C. S. Pantlind's
Bender Henry, wagon mkr bds John Koch's
Bender Tenis, lab h s s Douglas, Bloomingdale
Benham B. H. photographs 106 Columbia, res Norwalk
Benham L. W. photographer 106 Columbia, bds Mayer House
Benham O. J. photographer bds Mayer House
Benner Conrad, painter h 135 E. Lewis
Benner John, lab wks P., Ft. W. & C. Railway Co. Yard
Bennett Abram, boiler mkr h 236 W. Washington
Bennett M. conductor bds 193 W. Washington
Bennett Robt. C. h s w c Water and Cass
Bennigin Henry, mach h 203 E. Lewis
Bennigin Hugh, (Murray & B.) h 203 E Lewis
Bennigin Hugh, jr. molder h 203 E. Lewis

BENOIT VERY REV. JULIAN, Pastor Immaculate Conception Catholic Cathedral, h n e c Calhoun and Lewis.

H. R. SCHWEGMAN,

Wholesale and Retail Dealer in

STAPLE AND FANCY DRY GOODS,

Millinery Goods,

HATS AND CAPS,

GROCERIES,

CROCKERY

Stone Ware, Wood and Willow Ware, &c.

NO. 101 COLUMBIA STREET,

Fort Wayne, Ind.

STEAM PLANING MILL.

F. S. BALDWIN,

MANUFACTURER OF

SASH, DOORS, BLINDS, MOULDINGS,

BRACKETS, &c.

Store Fronts, Circular Sash, Doors, &c., Made to Order at Short Notice.

CIRCULAR, PLANING AND SCROLL SAWING, OF ALL KINDS.

North Side of Canal, West of Gas Works,

FORT WAYNE, IND.

All Orders Neatly Executed and Promptly Filled.

Benskin A. marble cutter wks n e c Main & Cass
Bensman Rudolph, lab h 74 Madison
Bensman Rudolph, jr. h 74 Madison
Bensman Wm. boiler mkr h 74 Madison
Bent Wm. carp wks T. & W. Railway Shops.
Benton Alphonso, h w s Francis b Hamilton and Railway
Benz James, mach wks P., Ft. W. & C. Railway Machine Shop
Benz Joseph, mach bds James Maginnis'
Benz Philip, helper h 182 E. Jefferson
Benz W. helper wks P., Ft. W. & C. Railway Blacksmith Shop
Benziman Ralph, boiler mkr wks Ft. Wayne Machine Works
Benziman Wm. boiler mkr wks Ft. Wayne Machine Works
Bercot Francis, grocer 64 Columbia
Bergen Franklin H. carp h w s Fulton b Washington and Jefferson
Berger F. lab wks P., Ft. W. & C. Railway shops
Berger Jacob, house mover h 187 E. Washington
Berghorn Fred. lab h w s Lafayette b Montgomery and Holman
Bergman Peter, clk 101 Columbia
Bernar Mrs. Margaret, widow h e s Piqua Plank Road b Lasselle and Buchanan
Bernard Caroline, pastry cook Ft. Wayne Eating House
Bernard John, teamster 129 Columbia, h Bloomingdale
Bernard Josephine, waiter Ft. Wayne Eating House
Berning Conrad, h 206 Madison
Berr Geo. h n w c Bass and Hoagland
Berrickomm Benj. bds Jacob Aufrecht's
Berry Hiram, carp h s w c Jackson and Pritchard
Berry Mrs. Ruth, res B. W. Folsom's
Berry Theodore, fireman wks T. & W. Railway Co.
Bertalott Albert, clk 101 Columbia
Bessillia Peter, hostler wks Main Street Exchange
Beston C. P. (B. & McMaken,) h n e c Main and Lafayette
Beston Miss Kate, at Old Fort House
Beston & McMaken, (C. P. B. & C. S. McM.) carriages n s Main b Harrison and Maiden Lane
Bethel Mrs. Hannah, widow h 41 E. Water
Bethel Lorin, lab h 41 E. Water
Bethel Marion, miller h 41 E. Water
Betts A. fireman bds 145 E. Jefferson
Betz Fred. lab h west end Douglas, Bloomingdale
Betzinger F. boiler mkr wks P. Ft. W. & C. Railway boiler shop
Betzler Geo. cooper h s w c Bluffton Road and Nirdlinger
Beugnot Victor, printer bds Main Street Exchange
Beuret John, lab h e s Hanna s of Jones
Beuret Jules, tinner wks A. D. Brandriff & Co.'s, bds 52 Columbia

N. P. STOCKBRIDGE,

WHOLESALE AND RETAIL DEALER IN

SCHOOL AND MISCELLANEOUS
BOOKS,

STATIONERY, WALL AND WINDOW PAPER,

SHEET MUSIC, MUSICAL INSTRUMENTS,

Gold Pens, Toys, &c.

SEWING MACHINES, MELODEONS, &C.

BOOK BINDING DONE, AND BLANK BOOKS MADE TO ORDER.

Sign of the Book, No. 104 Columbia Street.

ALSO

WHOLESALE AND RETAIL DEALER IN

FASHIONABLE CLOTHING,

Gents' Furnishing Goods, Hats, Caps, Trunks, &c.,

No. 125 Columbia St., **FORT WAYNE IND.**

BEURET JUSTIN, Dealer in Watches, Clocks, Jewelry, Silver Ware, &c., 4 Union Block, n s Main b Calhoun and Clinton.
Bewley Cornelius, lab wks Summit City Hotel
Bewley Daniel, helper wks Bowser & Story's
Beyer Paul, shoe mkr h 85 W. Jefferson
Bezler Geo. lab h 198 W. Wayne
Bichner Casper, lab h s s Berry nr Harmer
Bicknehse Fred, helper bds Conrad Heitkamp's
Bicknese Henry, lab h 175 E. Lewis
Biddle Geo. helper wks P., Ft. W. & C. Railway carp shop
Bidwell J. W. candy mkr bds Main Street Exchange
Bidwell John, candy mkr wks 83 Columbia
Biemer George, wagon mkr h rear 88 Madison
Bierbaum Fred, boiler mkr wks Ft. Wayne Machine Works
Biettel George, lab h w s Francis b Hamilton and Railway
Bikeness J. helper wks P., Ft. W. & C. Railway b.ksmith shop
Billoo John, lab h n s High, Bloomingdale
Bilzer Mrs. Christina, widow h Bloomingdale
Binder Adam, lab h n w c Wines and Hoagland
Bird Ellen, servt Union House
Bird Lucy, teacher Eastern District School, bds 99 E. Wayne
Bird Oehmig, farmer h 23 E. Main
Birmingham John, wks Olds, Hanna & Co.'s
Birrell John, tailor h 171 Clinton
Bischof Mrs. Caroline, h w s Hanna b Madison and Jefferson
Bischoff William, cigar mkr bds John Koch's
Bischop Christian, lab h 123 E. Lewis
Bittikoffer John, watch mkr 88 Columbia
Bixler D. wks Olds, Hanna & Co.'s
Bixler William, lab h w s Cass, Bloomingdale
Black David H. constable h e s Barr b Lewis and Montgomery
Black Mrs. Sarah, h n s Washington b Harmer and Francis
Blair John, carp h s w c Calhoun and Berry
Blaisdell P. O. conductor h 21 E. Washington
Blakeley Mrs. Ruth, widow h w s Hanna s of Lasselle
Blanchard Priscilla, wks Main Street Exchange
Black Louis, lab bds Steuben House

BLASE LOUIS, Proprietor City Bakery, 62 Columbia.
Blee J. C. omnibus driver wks J. O'Connell's
Blee John, hostler wks A. J. Read & Co.'s
Bleke Deitrich, lab h 129 Madison
Bliler Lewis N. painter bds Union House
Blondiot Felix, candy dealer h s s Wayne b Monroe and Hanna
Bloomhuff Sidney C. broker h 146 W. Wayne

BLOOMINGDALE BREWERY, Francis J. Beck, Proprietor, Bloomingdale.

PHŒNIX GROCERY,

T. K. BRACKENRIDGE,
DEALER IN STAPLE AND FANCY
GROCERIES, PROVISIONS,
—AND—
COUNTRY PRODUCE, OF ALL KINDS.
West Side Calhoun Street, opposite Aveline House,
FORT WAYNE, INDIANA.

MEYER & BROTHER,
WHOLESALE DEALERS IN

Drugs, Medicines, Paints,
OILS, FRENCH & AMERICAN WINDOW GLASS,
Dye-Stuffs, Brushes, Spices,
&c., &c., &c., &c.

95 Columbia Street, . . . FORT WAYNE, IND.

Blumer Mrs. Louisa, widow h s s Sturgis w of Fulton
Blyler Benjamin F. mach h 185 W. Washington

BLYLER D., Dealer in Family Groceries, Provisions, &c., w s Broadway b Washington and Jefferson, h 185 W. Washington.

Blyler Louis M. painter h s w c Washington and Broadway
Boag Robert, mach wks T. & W. Railway shops
Boag William G. mach h n s George b Broadway and Fulton
Bockeloh Charles, (Peltier & B.) h 81 W. Washington
Boddie William, lab wks D. F. Comparet's
Bodenbeck Wm. lab h 65 Madison
Boerger Rudolph, cutter 93 Columbia, h n s Washington b Monroe and Clay
Boerger William, house mover h s c c Washington and Monroe
Bogan F. lab wks P., Ft. W. & C. Railway lumber yard
Bogart Adam, carp h w s Hood b Pritchard and Railroad
Bogasch Fred. shoe mkr h n e c Jefferson and Van Buren
Bohen Michael, lab h c s Calhoun b Wayne and Washington
Boling Lemuel, grocery s w c Barr and Wayne
Bollerman Henry, lab h n w c Jefferson and Rockhill
Bolley James, carriage maker h n s Baker b Webster and McClellan
Bollinger J. carp wks P. Ft. W. & C. Railway carp shop
Bolmahn Theodore H. carp wks Joseph L. Potter's
Boltz Conrad, dairyman h w s Lima Plank Road, Bloomingdale
Boltz Gustavus, clk W. Jacobs & Sons

BOND CHAS. D. Cashier Ft. Wayne Branch of the Bank of the of State Indiana s w c Main and Clinton, res Fairfield Ave.

Bond H. W. (Townleys, De Wald & B.) h 142 E. Main
Bond Harry, clk s w c Calhoun and Main, bds 122 W. Wayne
Bond S. B. (Allen, Hamilton & Co.) res country
Bond W. J. clk s w c Calhoun and Main, h 122 W. Wayne
Bonfield Mrs. Mary, widow h 34 Monroe
Bonnet Conrad, b k 101 Columbia, h 58 Madison
Bonnet Geo. clk 101 Columbia
Boon J. M. foreman machine shop P., Ft. W. & C. Railway, bds Mayer House
Borden James W. att at law, bds Aveline House
Boreland Thos. carp wks P., Ft. W. & C. Railway carp shop
Borgeons H. carp wks P., F. W. & C. Railway carp shop
Borgman Christian, lab h 208 Ewing
Borgman Wiliam, lab h 14 E. Water
Borman A. W. painter wks P., Ft. W. & C. Railway paint shop
Borneman Chas. tailor h 114 Harrison
Borr M. lab wks P., Ft. W & C. Railway lumber yard.
Bose Conrad, lab h n w c Harrison and Highland
Bose W. lab wks P., Ft. W. & C. Railway lumber yard

HURD & CLARK,
DEALERS IN
DRESSED AND UNDRESSED
LUMBER, SHINGLES, LATH, &C.,
FORT WAYNE, INDIANA.

A. D. BRANDRIFF & CO.,
WHOLESALE AND RETAIL DEALERS IN THE

VARIOUS KINDS OF STOVES.
Manufacturers and Dealers in
Tin Plate, Copper, Brass and Sheet Iron Ware.

ALSO,

Iron, Nails and Glass, English and American Hardware, Mechanics' Tools, Pine Doors, Sash, Blinds, Paints, Oils and Varnishes, Scythes, Grain Cradles, Forks, Shovels, Hoes. Leather and Rubber Belting, Mill Saws, Akron Stone Ware, &c., &c.

**NOS. 56, 58 AND 60 COLUMBIA STREET,
FORT WAYNE, IND.**

Boseker Chas, teamster h s s Jefferson b Rockhill and College
Boseker Christian, carp h 210 E. Jefferson
Boseker Henry, teamster h s s Jefferson b Rockhill and College
Boshenger Mrs. Susan, widow, h w s Lafayette b Lewis and Montgomery.
Boss Mrs. bds 136 W. Berry
Boss Wm. engineer bds 193 W. Washington
Bossler Henry H. (Hartman & B.) h s w c Lewis and Harrison
Bossman ———, painter, bds Albert H. Cook's
Bostick E. clothing 98 Columbia, h s s Wayne b Clay and Wayne
Bostwick Geo. R. molder h 171 Clinton
Both Theodore, clk 101 Columbus, h s s Jefferson b Barr and Lafayette
Bounce James, lab bds Thos. Dailey's
Bounds Clark, lab wks C. S. Brackenridge & Co.'s
Bounds James, lab wks C. S. Brackenridge & Co.'s
Bourie ———, bds King House
Bourie Louis T. h 22 E. Wayne
Bouse Lorenzo, brakeman h s s Bass b Prince and Fairfield Av
Bowen Dan'l C. molder wks Murray & Benningin's

BOWEN D. W., Attorney at Law and Notary Public, 1 Phœnix Block w s Calhoun b Main and Columbia, h w s Barr b Wayne and Washington.

BOWEN G. W., Homœopathic Physician and Surgon, office w s Calhoun opp Court House, h 91 Barr

Bowen Ira, carp bds 82 Barr
Bowen Wm. h e s Barr b Wayne and Washington
Bower J. F. clk Union House
Bower W. C. engineer wks P., Ft. W. & C. Railway Co.
Bowers Mrs. Laura, widow res Mrs. Electa Emerson's
Bowers Lewis L. (Moyer & B.) h w s Calhoun b Highland and Dawson
Bowers Mrs. Maria, h 262 W. Washington
Bowser Jacob C. (B. & Story) h 64 E. Berry
Bowser Lafayette M. atty h 64 E. Berry

BOWSER & STORY (Jacob C. B. and James S.) Iron Founders, Machinists, and Manufacturers of Steam Engines, Saw and Grist Mills, Plows, &c., s s Water b Calhoun and Harrison.

Boxberger Valentine, lab wks Bloomingdale Brewery
Boyce Wm. wks Olds, Hanna & Co.'s
Boyd B. F. fireman h n w c Lafayette and Montgomery
Boyer Wm. carder and spinner wks Summit City Woolen Mills
Boynds Clark, mach h s s Railroad b Harrison and Webster
Boynton D. T. traveling agent P. S. Underhill's, n e c Main and Cass
Boynton Edwin, collector wks n e c Main and Cass

ÆTNA INSURANCE COMPANY,

HARTFORD, CONN.

Cash Capital, - - - 1,500,000 00

Assets, July 1st, 1863, . . . $2,952,248 85
Liabilities, ... 142,735 95

T. A. ALEXANDER,　　　**H. Z. PRATT,**
President.　　　　　　　　Vice Pres.

L. G. HENDEE, Secretary.

J. B. BENNETT, - - - GENERAL AGENT, CINCINNATI, OHIO

Policies Issued and Losses Promptly Adjusted, by
JOHN HOUGH, AGT.,
NO. 50 CALHOUN STREET, - - - FORT WAYNE, IND.

HOME
INSURANCE COMPANY,
Office, Nos. 112 and 114 Broadway, New York.

CASH CAPITAL, ONE MILLION DOLLARS.

Assets, July 1st, 1863, - - $2,007,530 91
Liabilities, - - - - - 69,570 20

CHAS. J. MARTIN, PRES.　　A. F. WILMARTH, VICE PRES.

J. MILTON SMITH, SEC.

Policies Issued and Losses Promptly Adjusted by
JOHN HOUGH, AGENT,
NO. 50 CALHOUN STREET, - - - FORT WAYNE, IND.

Boyse Wm. II. carp bds Geo. W. Phillips
Bracht Joseph, fireman wks T. & W Railway Co.
Brackenridge C. S. (C. S. B. & Co.) h s w c Clinton and Wayne

BRACKENRIDGE C. S. & Co., Manufacturers of Cooperage and Cooper's Material, s s of the Railroad b Calhoun and Clinton.

Brackenridge Geo. W. farmer h n s Douglas Ave b Calhoun and Harrison

BRACKENRIDGE JOSEPH, Attorney at Law, Office w s Calhoun 3d door s of Main, up stairs, h w s Calhoun b Douglas Av and Baker.

Brackenridge Robert, atty office w s Calhoun 3d door s of Main up stairs, h s w c Clinton and Washington

BRACKENRIDGE T. K., Proprietor Phœnix Grocery, Dealer in Staple and Fine Groceries, Provisions, &c. w s Calhoun 3d door s of Berry, h w s Calhoun b Lewis and Douglas Av.

Bradford A. Clayton, brakeman bds 53 Barr
Bradford Mrs. M. A. (Mrs. M. A. B. & Co.) bds 53 Barr
Bradford Mrs. M. A. & Co. (Mrs. Margaret A. B. & Mrs. N. M. Dealing) millinery 2 Aveline House s e c Calhoun and Berry
Bradshaw Walter, mach wks Toledo & Wabash Railway shop
Bradtmueller Gottlieb, carpenter h s s Douglas Ave b Harrison and Webster
Bradway O. E. brass molder h 212 E. Lewis
Brady Henry, cooper bds Union House
Brady R. L. carp h s w c Washington and Van Buren
Brady Richard M. carp h s w c Van Buren and Washington
Brady Samuel A. h 47 W. Berry

BRADY W. H. & Co. (Wm. H. B. and Geo. Voorhis) Ladies' and Gents' Furnishing and Trimming Store, No. 3 Aveline House s e c Calhoun and Berry.

Brady Wm. H. (W. H. B. & Co.) bds 47 W. Berry
Bragdon Miss Louie S. teacher at Ft. Wayne College.
Brainard Mrs. Lydia, widow h 83 E. Main
Brandmeier Fred. molder h 174 Ewing

BRANDRIFF A. D. & Co., (Alfred D. B., A. J. Emerick, W. A Roberts, and W. S. Humphreys,) Dealers in Stoves, Hardware, Cutlery; and Manufacturers of Tin, Copper and Sheet Iron Ware, 56, 58 and 60 Columbia.

Brandriff Alfred D. (A. D. B. & Co.) bds Aveline House
Brandt Chas. lab h 93 W. Jefferson
Brandt Fred. (Krutop & Co.) h c Lewis and Harrison
Brandt Fred. G. carp h 178 Harrison
Brandt Henry, mach h 45 W. Jefferson

P. S. UNDERHILL,
FORT WAYNE STEAM MARBLE
—AND—
BUILDING STONE WORKS,

WEST MAIN STREET,   FORT WAYNE, IND,

MONUMENTS,

Head Stones, Tomb Tables, Mantle Pieces, Cabinet Slabs, &c., &c.,

—ALSO—

All kinds of Dressed and Sawed Building Stone, including Door Caps and Sills, Window Caps and Sills, Water Table and Coping, Stone Steps, Balustrades, &c., &c., &c.

ORDERS SOLICITED AND PROMPTLY ATTENDED TO.

JOHN M. MILLER,

MANUFACTURER AND DEALER IN

FINE FURNITURE AND CHAIRS,

HUSK AND HAIR MATTRESSES,

Looking-Glass Plates, &c.,

50 AND 52 MAIN STREET,

FORT WAYNE, IND.

Brandt John Fred. carp h 178 Harrison
Brandtmeyer Fred. molder wks Bowser & Story's
Brannan Mrs. Julia, h n c c Lewis and Monroe
Brannan M. blksmith wks P., Ft. W. & C. Railway
Branning Conrad, shoemkr h 49 W. Jefferson
Brase Fred, boatman b 75 W. Jefferson
Brawer Conrad, foreman James H. Robinson's, h 156 Ewing
Brayan Michael, lab h s s Bass b Prince & Hoagland
Bredemeier Wm., tailor 71 Columbia h 114 Harrison

BREEN & DUNN (James B. and James D.) Dealers in Family Groceries, Provisions, Liquors, &c., 53 Columbia.

Breen James (B. & Dunn) h 53 Columbia
Breene Michael, helper wks T. & W. Railway shop
Breidenstein Mathias, carp h 76 W. Washington
Breier Conrad, shoemkr James H. Robinson's h 156 Ewing
Bremerkamp Barney, wagon mkr wks Michael Fisher's
Bremers Henry, clk Conrad Heitkamp's
Brendel John, sawyer wks Herman Wilken's
Brennan Thos. M. clk T. B. Hedekin's, bds 82 E. Washington
Brennen Richard, clk Peter Pierr's bds Jacob Pierr's
Brennen David, h 15 W Wayne
Brenton Chas. F. clk 104 Columbia, h 210 W. Wayne
Brenton Mrs. Eliza, widow h 210 W. Wayne
Brenton Milton H. clk post office, h 210 W. Wayne
Bresancon Frank, lab h w s Hanna b Montgomery and Holman
Bressler Geo. carp bds n c c Broadway and Washington

BREWER GILBERT, Palace Hall Billiard Saloon w s Calhoun b Main and Berry.

Brewster Stephen, brakeman h w s Nelson opp Wilt
Briant W. H. bricklayer h 204 W. Wayne
Bridge Chas. F. carp h 90 W. Jefferson
Briggs G. E. peddlar h 56 E. Main
Brindle Samuel, daguerreotypist h 39 Clinton
Brick Jacob, cooper, h s c c Lewis and Harrison
Brink Joseph, cooper wks C. S. Brackenridge & Co.'s
Brinkruger Wm. shoemkr h Bloomingdale
Brinkman Ernst, clk Empire Flour Mills, h s c c Washington and Nelson
Brittingham W. B. phys h 154 W. Wayne
Broad Lewis, contractor bds Mayer House
Brockman Henry, tailor w s Calhoun b Berry and Wayne
Brodmiller Geo. carp wks T. & W. Railway shops
Bronnenkamt Deonis, shoemkr wks P. Kline's, h n s Nirdlinger w of Bluffton Road
Brooks Bryant, barber s c c Calhoun and Berry, h 96 Madison
Brooks Chas. carp bds D. J. Folsom's
Brooks Chas. C. barber, bds 58 W. Washington

INDIANA LAND AGENCY,

FORT WAYNE, IND.

The Subscriber, Proprietor of the above Agency, has for Sale a large amount of

CITY PROPERTY

In Fort Wayne, improved and unimproved, embracing over

TWO HUNDRED LOTS.

—ALSO—

20,000 Acres of Land in Allen County;
50,000 Acres in the Adjoining Counties;
10,000 Acres in North-Western Ohio;

With a large number of

IMPROVED FARMS.

Persons wishing to buy or sell Real Estate, would do well to call on him, as his long experience and great facilities enable him to act to advantage for all parties entrusting property in his hands.

JOHN HOUGH,
Office, No. 50 Calhoun Street.

Brooks Henderson, plasterer h 229 W. Washington
Brooks Henry, clk 85 Columbia
Brooks Lorenzo D. barber bds 96 Madison
Brooks Miss Minnie, bds s s Pearl b Harrison and Maiden Lane

BROOKS WM. H., Jr., Dealer in Books, Stationery, Musical Instruments, Wall Paper, &c., 2 Phœnix Block w s Calhoun b Main and Columbia, h 110 W. Main.

BROOKS WM. H., Sen., Physician and Surgeon, Office and Residence s w c Calhoun and Water.

Broom Ely, wagon manuf's s Main b Harrison and Maiden Lane
Broom John, wagon makr bds Ely Broom's
Brosserd Geo. blksmith n e c Main and Fulton, h Bloomingdale
Brosserd John, blksmith h Bloomingdale
Brown A. C. tinner wks 81 Columbia, bds Geo. R Hartman's
Brown Benj. H. blksmith bds s e c Clay and Wayne
Brown C. helper wks P., Ft. W. & C. Railway carp shop
Brown Mrs. Campbell, widow h 97 W. Washington
Brown Edward, h w s Calhoun b Jefferson and Lewis
Brown Eli, carp h n s Water b Cass and Ewing
Brown G. S. carp wks P., Ft. W. & C. Railway carp shop
Brown Geo. helper wks P., Ft. W. & C. Railway blksmith shop
Brown George W. res Alphonso Benton's
Brown H. P. road master T. & W. R. R. bds Summit City Hotel
Brown James, engineer h w s Calhoun b Railroad & Highland
Brown James, lab h s w c Montgomery and Lafayette
Brown James D. dentist at 32 E. Main
Brown Mrs. Jessie, widow h s s Lewis b Calhoun and Harrison

BROWN JOHN, Blacksmith, Plow and Wagon Manufacturer, s e c Clay and Main, h s e c Clay and Wayne.

Brown John, cook at D. O'Connell's Restaurant
Brown John, carp bds 166 E. Washington
Brown John, carp h e s West b Pritchard and Railroad
Brown John, engineer h n s Railroad w of McClellan

BROWN JOHN, Miller and Grain Dealer, n e c Pearl and Maiden Lane, h n e c Wayne & Broadway.

Brown John, jr, carp wks T. & W. Railway Shops
Brown John, jr., blksmith bds s e c Clay and Wayne
Brown Lewis, tailor h w s Broadway b Washington & Jefferson
Brown Mrs. Rewah, res Eli Brown's
Brown Wm. H. blksmith bds s e c Clay and Wayne
Brown Wm. W. engineer res James Brown's
Brucker Michael, cooper h w s Nelson b Wilt and Jefferson

BRUEBACH GEO. THEODORE, Physician and Surgeon, Office, n e c Calhoun and Main, h 45 W. Main.

FORT WAYNE ADVERTISEMENTS.

J. M. FOELLINGER,

DEALER IN

FAMILY GROCERIES,

PROVISIONS,

Fresh and Canned Fruits,

OYSTERS,

CIGARS,

TOBACCO, &c.

No. 5 PHŒNIX BLOCK,
Calhoun Street,
FT. WAYNE, IND.

ALFRED HATTERSLEY
GAS-FITTER AND PLUMBER, BRASS FOUNDER & FINISHER,
MAIN ST. FT. WAYNE, IND.
ON HAND
GAS FIXTURES, GAS STOVES, LIFT & FORCE PUMPS, AND ALL KINDS OF BRASS WORK.
ALE PUMPS MADE TO ORDER.

JOHN W. M'ARTHUR,

CITY ENGINEER, COUNTY SURVEYOR,

COMMISSIONER
—OF—
DEEDS AND MORTGAGES.

OFFICE, in Court House.

FORT WAYNE, ALLEN CO., IND.

Engineering, Drafting, and all Instruments of Writing Promptly attended to.

Brunett Mrs. Mary, h s s Douglas, Bloomingdale
Brunner John, shoe mkr h w s Hood b Pritchard & Railroad
Bruns Christian, carp h w s Harrison s of Dawson
Bruns Christian F. lab h 224 E. Jefferson
Bruntz Christ. carp. wks T. & W. Railway Shops
Brush H. C. fireman wks T. & W. Railway Co.
Bryant Geo. wks Olds, Hanna & Co.'s
Bryant J. wks Olds, Hanna & Co.'s
Bryant Mrs. Massie, h e s Hanna b Jefferson and Madison
Bryant Stephen, cooper h 245 E. Jefferson
Bryant Wm. H. engineer h e s Lafayette b Lewis and Montgemery
Bryson M. bds Main Street Exchange
Buchanan Henry J. carp wks Cochran, Humphrey & Co.'s
Buchfink Geo. lab h s s High, Bloomingdale
Buchfink John, (B. & Neff,) h 63 E Water
Buchfink & Neff, John B. & Jacob N.) meat store w s Calhoun b Wayne and Washington
Buchholz Christian, tailor h s s High, Bloomingdale
Buchholz Fred. tailor h w s Lima Plank Road, Bloomingdale
Buchwalter Louis, mach bds 156 Harrison
Buck Dietrich, tailor h n s Jefferson b Rockhill and College
Buck Fred. helper bds Conrad Heitkamp's
Buck Thomas W. mach bds 143 E. Lewis
Buckley H. blksmith wks P., Ft. W. & C. Railway blksmith shop
Buckley John, mach bds Mrs. S. M. French's
Buckmaster Geo. carp h s s Lasselle e of Piqua Plank Road
Buckwalter L, mach wks P., Ft. W. & C. Railway machine shop
Buckwalter Paul, mach h n s Holman b Lafayette and Clay
Buddemeyer H. carp wks P., Ft. W. & C. Railway carp shop
Bucak F. helper wks P., Ft. W. & C. Railway blksmith shop
Buech Frederick, (Morgan & B.) h 90 W. Main
Buech John, h n e c Fairfield Av. and Wines
Bueche Fred. miller res Geo. Bueche's, Bloomingdale
Bueche Geo. lab h Bloomingdale
Buegnot Victor, printer Dawson's Times Office, bds Main Street Exchange
Buehnemann John, cigars 100 Columbia
Buerker Henry, h 150 Barr
Bufink Geo, servt 33 W. Main
Buhart A. carp wks P., Ft. W. & C. Railway carp shop
Buhr Nicholas, painter h 79 W. Washington
Bulger John H. (McComb & Co.) h New York
Bulger Peter, carp bds John S. Harrington's
Bulu Daniel, blksmith h 151 E. Lewis
Bur Nicholas, painter h e s Piqua Plank Road b Wallace and Charles

FORT WAYNE AGRICULTURAL WORKS

SITUATED ON THE CANAL FEEDER AT NORTH END OF CALHOUN STREET,

FT. WAYNE, IND.,

MANUFACTURE

THRESHING MACHINES, REAPERS,

Mowers, Seed Drills,

PLOWS,

Besides the usual variety of

Foundry and Machine Shop Work.

Repairing in Wood or Iron Work Promptly done.

JAMES A. KIRBY,

Agent for the Singer Manufacturing Company

Sewing Machines

GREAT REDUCTION IN PRICES.

The best and Cheapest Family Machine in the World.

No. 2 Aveline House, Street,
FT. WAYNE, IND.

Also Agent for Aiken's Celebrated Knitting Machines.

Burg Nicholas, paper hanger bds Steuben House
Burger Henry, boiler mkr wks Fort Wayne Machine Works
Burger Louis, lab wks P., Ft. W. & C. Railway Co.'s yard
Burger Ludwig, lab h n s Jefferson b Van Buren and Jackson
Burger Theresa, servt Hedekin House
Burgess Mrs. Eliza, barber shop 78 Columbia
Burgess Francis, mach h w s Fulton b Jefferson and Sturges
Burhan Edward, meat store s s Main b Calhoun and Harrison
Burk Mrs Elizabeth, h 185 E. Jefferson
Burkas John A. clk 77 Columbia, h n w c Wayne and Barr
Burke Edward, lab h n s Buchanan e of Clay
Burke John, fireman wks P., Ft. W. & C. Railway Co.
Burke Thomas, lab h n s Bass b Hoagland and Prince
Burke Thomas, warehouseman P., Ft. W. & C. Railway Freight Depot
Burkhardt Thomas, lab h s w c Jackson and Pritchard
Burlager Geo. clk Kanne & Co.'s, h 141 E. Washington
Burlager Gerhard, dray h 157 E. Jefferson
Burlager John, dray h 155 E. Washington
Burnett Mrs. Sarah A. widow h 57 W. Berry
Burns Joseph, waiter at Mayer House
Burns Patrick, lab h n s Bass b Hoagland and Prince
Burns Patrick, mach wks T. & W. Railway shops
Burns S. L. h s e c Lewis and Clay
Burns Wm. lab h s w c Lewis and Monroe
Burr Mrs. E. L. artist bds Hamilton House
Bursley G. E. b k 79 Columbia, h 60 W. Berry
Burt Charles, bk mkr h s s Jefferson b Hanna and Francis
Burt John, lab wks Herman Wilken's
Burt John, bk layer h 205 E. Wayne
Burt John C. bk layer h 205 E Wayne
Burt Sallie, servt Hedekin House
Burt Wm. wks Olds, Hanna & Co.'s
Busch Fred. Albert, clk 79 Columbia, bds 79 W. Berry
Busche Henry, carp h w s Harrison b Highland & Dawson
Buschman C. P. blksmith bds Union House
Buschman Wm. M. mach bds Thomas Meegan's
Buschmann F. W. wagon manuf s s Water b Calhoun and Clinton, h n w c Clay and Holman
Buschmann Fred. Wm. boiler mkr h n w c Clay and Holman
Basse Wm. (Yergens & Co.) h w s Ewing s of Jefferson
Basser Wm. H. carriagesmith bds Henry Montgomery's
Bassey E. J. cab mkr b n s Wayne b Broadway & Van Buren
Buste Henry, carp wks T. & W. Railway shops
Buster Henry, mason h n s Jefferson b Broadway and Van Buren
But'and Edward L. carp h 24 W. Jefferson
Butler F. cooper wks C. S. Brackenridge & Co.'s

F. M. PROUTY,

WHOLESALE AND RETAIL DEALER IN
LADIES', GENTS' AND CHILDRENS'

BOOTS AND SHOES,

No. 7 East Main St., Opposite Court House,

FORT WAYNE, INDIANA.

STATE INSURANCE COMPANY,

Office, in Hamilton's Old Bank, Clinton Street,

FORT WAYNE, IND.

CAPITAL, - - - - $100,000

Insured and Authorized by State Authority.

OFFICERS:

JAMES L. WORDEN, President.   HUGH B. REED, Treasurer.
O. BIRD, Vice President.   S. LUMBARD, Secretary.

GEO. W. BABCOCK, GENERAL AGENT.

DIRECTORS.—James L. Worden, Hugh B. Reed, S. Lumbard, O. Bird, Geo. W. Babcock.

Insures Dwellings, Household Furniture, Barns, Hay and Grain and Live Stock therein, against Loss or Damage by Fire for the Term of Five Years.

Butler George, conductor bds 193 W. Washington
Butler Nathan, deputy county surveyor bds Phillips House
Butt Frank, lab h 208 E. Wing
Butt Fred. lab wks C. S Brackenridge & Co.'s
Butt Wm. carder wks Summit City Woolen Mills
Buttenbinder Henry, clk J. M. Foellinger's, h 175 Clinton

C

Cable J. G. carp wks Bowser & Story's
Cade Miss Charlotte E. milliner res Mrs. Elizabeth Sulley's
Caeurdevay Adelaide, housekeeper n e c Calhoun and Lewis
Caffrey J. helper wks P., Ft. W. & C. Railway blksmith shop
Cain George E. engineer bds 107 W. Wayne
Cairns James, mach h n w c Hood and Railroad
Caldwell Charles, bar k Palace Hall Billiard Saloon
Caldwell Miss Lottie, dress mkr bds 167 E. Lewis
Callahan Cornelius, clk Joseph Clark's, b ls Mayer House
Callahan Timothy, lab h n s Bass b Hoagland and Prince
Calley Joseph, carp h 103 Madison
Calligan Patrick lab h 237 E. Washington
Callison Absalom, butcher h 89 W. Washington
Calvert John W. brakeman h 89 E. Lewis
Calvin B. Y. miller h e s Maiden Lane b Main and Berry
CAMPBELL ISAAC W., Associate Editor Dawson's Fort Wayne Times, h n e c Barr & Berry.
Campbell J. C. carp wks P., Ft. W. & C. Railway carp shop
Campbell John, lab h 63 Madison
Campbell John, bar k Summit City Hotel
Campbell John G. carp b ls 174 E. Berry
Campbell Mrs. Mary F. widow h n s Jefferson b Nelson and Garden
Campbell Mrs. Mary S. widow h 266 W. Washington
Campbell Rev. S. N. h 151 W. Wayne
Candee Elisha, engineer bds 193 W. Washington
Cannan John K. mach h s s Washington b Fulton & Broadway
Cannon Johnson, fireman bds 151 W. Washington
Cantlen Mary, servt Fort Wayne Eating House
Carey Edward F. clk 90 Columbia, h c Monroe and Wayne
Carey H. S. conductor h 49 E. Jefferson
Carey Joseph, blksmith wks P., Ft. W. & C. Railway blksmith shop
CARIER A. H., General Land Agent and Notary Public, 95 Columbia, h s w c Berry and Monroe.
Carll George S cab mkr wks 50 E Main, h 134 E. Berry
Carll H. D. printer Dawson's Times Office
Carman C. mach wks P., Ft. W. & C. Railway machine shop

FORT WAYNE

DAILY AND WEEKLY SENTINEL.

TERMS:

Daily, - - - - $6 00 per annum.
Weekly, - - - - 2 00   "

Advertisements conspicuously inserted, at reasonable rates.

This is the oldest paper in Northern Indiana, having been established by the present proprietor in 1833. It affords unrivalled advantages to advertisers.

T. TIGAR, - - - - - - - Editor and Proprietor.

JOB PRINTING,

OF EVERY DESCRIPTION,

PLAIN AND ORNAMENTAL,

Promptly Executed at the Lowest Rates.

Having Power Presses of the latest and best construction, we are prepared to do all kinds of work, in superior style, and at short notice, and as cheap as any other establishment in the State.

Office, corner Calhoun and Pearl Sts., 3d story,
FORT WAYNE, IND.

Carns James, mach wks P., Ft. W. & C. Railway machine shop
Carpenter E. A. weaver and carder wks Summit City Woolen Mills
Carpenter Fred. h s s Berry b Griffith and Fulton
Carpenter G. Washington, fireman h n w c College and Jones
Carroll ———, printer bds Mrs. Hannah Whaley's
Carroll Charles, teamster bds 205 E. Wayne
Carroll Dinnandy, carp h n e c Prince and Colerick
Carroll John, bklayer h 222 E. Washington
Carroll John, molder wks Fort Wayne Machine Works
Carroll Patrick, lab h n s Water b Cass and Ewing
Carroll Peter, mach h 171 Barr
Carroll Thomas, lab h n e c Prince and Colerick
Carry Joseph, blksmith h 23 Monroe
Carry Mrs. Sarah, h 23 Monroe
Carson W. W. atty n s Main b Calhoun and Clinton, h n s Berry b Lafayette and Clay
Carter Isaac, pattern mkr h 57 E. Berry
Carter Wm. tinner h 123 W. Water
Cartwright John, blksmith wks T. & W. Railway shops
Cary James D. (C. & Knight,) h s s Douglas Av. b Webster and McClellan

CARY & KNIGHT, (James D. C. & J. H. K.,) Saloon and Billiard Room, n s Railroad Street b Calhoun and Clinton.
Case A. stock dealer bds Main Street Exchange
Case C. engineer h n s Douglas Av. b Harrison and Webster
Case Charles, (Withers, Morris & C.) h 203 W. Wayne
Case E. T. carder h n e c Wayne and Hanna
Case Samuel J. res E. T. Case's
Case Willis W. h 203 W. Wayne
Casey John, shoe mkr bds Main Street Exchange
Cassidy John J. clk h 53 Harrison
Cattez J. carp wks P., Ft. W. & C. Railway carp shop
Caul L. bds Phillip's House

CENTLIVRE L. & L. C., French Brewery, on W. & E. Canal Feeder, Lima Plank Road, n of St. Mary's River.
Centlivre L. (L. & L. C. C.) h on W. & E. Canal Feeder, Lima Plank Road n of St. Mary's River
Centlivre L. C. (L. & L. C. C.) h on W. & E. Canal Feeder, Lima Plank Road n of St. Mary's River
Cerdoe John, lab bds n e c Monroe and Lewis
Chadwick Joseph J. cook Summit City Hotel
Challenger J. W. mach h 227 E. Lewis
Chamberlain Henry, h 40 E. Jefferson
Chamberlain James C. h 126 W. Washington
Chamberlain Porter, mach h n s Lewis b Harrison and Webster

J. A. SHOAFF'S

ART GALLERY,

Nort-west corner Calhoun and Main streets, Times Building,

FORT WAYNE, IND.

PARTICULAR ATTENTION PAID TO CARTES DE VISITE

FIRST NATIONAL BANK,
—OF—
FORT WAYNE, IND.
CALHOUN STREET, OPPOSITE AVELINE HOUSE.

CAPITAL, - - - - - - $150,000.

J. D. NUTTMAN, President.   W. B. FISHER, Cashier.

DIRECTORS:

J. D. Nuttman,	John Brown,	C. F. G. Meyer,
Samuel Hanna,	Fred. Nirdlinger,	John Orff,
J. M. Miller,	A. S. Evans,	A. D. Brandriff.

Chamberlain Mrs. Sarah, widow h 126 W. Washington
Chamberlain Wm. H. asst engineer h 40 E. Jefferson
Chapin L. O. mach h n s Main b Calhoun and Harrison
CHAPIN MRS. M. E., Millinery, Cloak and Dress Making Rooms, n s Main b Calhoun and Harrison.
Chappell John, mach h e s Broadway b Jefferson and George
Chericorn X. mach wks P., Ft. W. & C. Railway machine shop
Cheritie Anton, h w s Piqua Plank Road b Virginia and Wallace
Cheviron Xavier, finisher bds 52 Columbia
CHITTENDEN E. L., City Clerk, Attorney at Law, and Notary Public, office at Mayor's Office, h 168 W. Berry.
Chittenden Mrs. Harriet, h 168 W. Berry
Chittenden Miss Hattie, 168 W. Berry
Chittenden W. B. notary public and deputy county auditor, bds 168 W. Berry
Chorpening Henry, roofer h s w c Pearl and Griffith
Chovey Chas. blksmith res John B. Chovey's
Chovey Frank, blksmith res John B. Chovey's
Chovey John B. blksmith n s Water b Calhoun and Clinton, h e s Piqua Plank Road b Lasclle and Buchanan
Christen John, clk 9 Calhoun bds James M. Kane's
Christensen Lars, lab at Concordia College
Christy Mrs. Angeline, widow res Geo. W. Jones'
Christy James H. omnibus driver wks John O'Connell's
Church Sylvanus, grain dealer n s s Pearl b Maiden Lane and Cass
Chuton Michael, helper wks T. & W. Railway shops
City Attorney's Office, w s Clinton b Columbia and Main
City Clerk's Office, w s Clinton b Columbia and Main, E. L. Chittenden, Clerk
CITY FLOUR MILLS, P. Hoagland & Co., Propr's, n w c Canal and Clinton.
City Marshal's Office, w s Clinton b Columbia and Main, Patrick McGee, Marshal
CITY READING ROOM, w s Calhoun b Main and Columbia, Lamley & Rosenthal, Proprietors.
City Treasurer's Office, w s Clinton b Columbia and Main, John Conger, Treasurer
Clare Michael, warehouseman P., Ft. W. & C. Railway freight depot
Clarence R. A. marble cutter wks n e c Main and Cass
Clark Mrs. Bridget, widow h Bloomingdale
Clark Edward, brakeman bds s e c Lewis and Lafayette
Clark H. C. engineer wks P., Ft. W. & C. Railway Co
Clark Irvin, teamster res B. H. Tower's
Clark J. H. (Hurd & C.) h 150 W. Wayne

NEW STEAM PRINTING HOUSE.

JONES & JENKINSON,

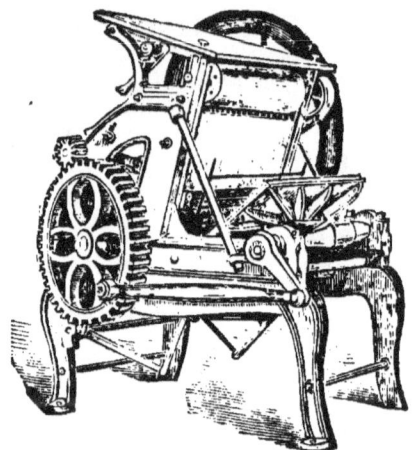

FT. WAYNE GAZETTE.

Daily and Weekly.

LARGEST CIRCULATION IN THE CITY.

TERMS—Daily Gazette, per annum, $6 00
Weekly Gazette, " 2 00

JONES & JENKINSON, Editors and Publishers.

No. 125 Columbia street.

ALSO
GENERAL JOB PRINTERS.

Being supplied with the most approved styles of Presses, Type, Borders, &c., are prepared to execute PLAIN and ORNAMENTAL Job Printing in a superior manner, and at the lowest prices, for Cash.

A good stock of Cards, Paper, Colored Inks, &c., on hand.

The only Steam Printing Establishment in Fort Wayne.

Clark James H. baggage master n s s Railroad b Webster and Kansas
Clark Joseph, tailor bds Geo. R. Hartman's
Clark Joseph, grocer w s Calhoun b Main and Berry, h 30 E. Wayne
Clark Joseph, mer tailor 4 Aveline House, h s w c Jefferson and Barr
Clark Lewis W. engineer h n e c Douglas Av and McClelland
Clark S. W. conductor h n s Montgomery b Lafayette and Clay
Clark Samuel, mach h s s Melita b Webster and Hoagland
Clark Samuel, engineer wks D. F. Comparet's
Clark Thomas R. teamster h 110 W. Water
Claus John, shoemkr bds 48 W. Washington
Clausz Christoph, shoemkr h n w c Broadway and Pritchard
Clawson I. vet surgeon bds 45 E. Main
Clawson Isaac, bds Phillips House
Clear Michael, lab h e s Prince b Bass and Colerick
Clerk Circuit Court Office, in Court House, Wm. Fleming, Clerk
Clist W. carp wks P., Ft. W. & C. Railway shop
Clist Wm. h 190 W. Washington
Clulow Geo. mach h w s Fairfield Av b Locust and Taylor

COCHRAN, HUMPHREY & CO., (John C., Geo. H., and Wm. McFee,) Carpenters, Builders, and Manufacturers of Sash, Doors, Blinds, &c., n e c Pearl and Fulton.

Cochran John (C., Humphrey & Co) h n w c Fulton and Sturgis
Cockell Richard, fireman bds 102 W. Water
Cody M. & Co. (Morris C. and P. McLain) ice dealers 53 Columbia
Cody Morris, flour mills office 53 Columbia, h n w c Water and Barr
Cody Patrick, tailor h n s Wayne b Hanna and Francis
Cogan Samuel, carp h 240 E. Washington
Coldridge Mary, dress mkr bds Thos. Rich's
Cole C. shoemkr bds American House
Cole Calvin, carp bds Phillips House
Cole Edward, lab h n s Railroad w of McClellan
Cole S. D. carp h e s Garden b Washington and Jefferson
Coleman Conrad, cupalo tender h w s Jackson b Pritchard and Railroad
Coleman H. lab wks P., Ft. Wayne & C. Railway shops
Coleman John, lab bds 156 Harrison

COLERICK D. H., Attorney at Law, Office w s Calhoun opp Court House, h 92 E. Berry.

Colerick David, district prosecuting atty office w s Calhoun opp Court House, res D. H. Colerick's

COLERICK E. F., h Junction Bluffton Road and T. & W. Railway.

COLERICK'S HALL, n s Columbia b Clinton and Barr, E. F. Colerick, Proprietor.
Colerick Henry, res John A. Colerick's
COLERICK JOHN A., Family Grocery and Confectionery, 5 Clinton b Main and Columbia.
Colerick Walpole G. atty and notary w s Calhoun opp Court House, res D. H. Colerick's
Colgan P., lab wks P., Ft. W. & C. Railway Co. yard
Collar D. W. saloon n e c Columbia and Clinton, h 156 Madison
Collar Geo. carp h s s Madison b Hanna and Francis
Collins Chas. boiler mkr h 227 Barr
Collins Chas. file cutter h 240 E. Washington
Collins Wm. mach bds Mrs. Ann Graham's
Colston Albert, engineer bds Luther Wright's
Colton Wm. C. h 224 E. Jefferson
COMPARET D. F., Miller, Commission Merchant and Dealer in Grain, Produce, Agricultural Implements, &c., East end of Columbia and Lafayette, h north end of Harmer.
COMPARET & HASKELL, (D. F. C. and Wash. H.) Proprietors Woodlawn Flax and Flour Mills, Office east end Columbia and Lafayette.
Comparet Joseph J. with D. F. Comparet h north end of Harmer
Concordia College, n s Van Wert Road e of city limits
Congdon John, tree dealer bds Old Fort House
CONGER JOHN, City Treasurer, Office at Mayor's Office, h 20 Madison.
Conklin Mrs. John J. h e s Ewing b Wayne and Washington
Conklin Wm. H. engineer h s w c Washington and Jackson
Conklin Theodore, (Andrews & C.) h 155 W. Washington
Conley Maggie, waiter at Mayer House
Connelley Pat. brakeman bds 193 W. Washington
Conner Mrs. Catharine, servt n w c Wayne and Webster
Conner J. mach wks P., Ft. W. & C. Railway machine shop
Conner Michael, teamster bds Main Street Exchange
Conners Cornelius, lab h 128 Madison
Conners Jerry, lab h s w c Madison and Francis
Connors J. helper wks P., Ft. W. & C. Railway blksmith shop
Connors P. helper wks P., Ft. W. & C. Railway blksmith shop
Conrad Daniel, cigar maker wks L. Dessauer's
Converse Wm. H. mach wks Toledo & Wabash Railway shops
Cook Albert H. h e s Piqua Plank Road b Virginia and Wallace
Cook E. D. engineer h s e c Barr and Lewis
Cook Edwin P. mach wks P., Ft. W. & C. Railway machine shop
Cook H. C. fireman h 125 E. Lewis
Cook Nathaniel, lab res Wm Cook's
Cook W. S. clk Ft. Wayne Eating House
Cook Wm. lab h e s Francis b Lewis and Madison

Cook Christ. carp wks T. & W. Railway shops
Cooke Robt. A. telegraph operator T. & W. Railway, bds Hamilton House
Coombes Mrs. Eliza, widow h w s Broadway b Wilt and Pritchard
Coombs Chas. H. clk res Wm. H. Coombs'

COOMBS & DRAKE, (J. M. C. and F. G. D.) Wholesale and Retail Dealers in Hardware, Cutlery, Iron, Nails, Steel, Belting, &c., 115 Columbia.

Coombs John M. (C. & Drake) h 99 W. Wayne
Coombs Wm. H. atty at law 50 Calhoun h n s Main b Cass and Ewing
Cooney Patrick, lab bds 70 Madison
Coons Andrew, fireman bds Fred Miller's
Cooper Cornelius, dray h Junction Bluffton Road and P., Ft. W. & C. Railway
Cooper E. O. conductor h s s Washington b Calhoun and Clinton
Cooper Mrs. Eleanor, widow, braid and embroidery stamping h 176 W. Washington
Cooper Wm. P. plasterer h 152 W. Wayne
Corcoran John, lab h Bloomingdale
Corcoran Michael, cooper bds Union House

CORCORAN PATRICK, Dealer in Family Groceries and Provisions, w s Calhoun b Main and Berry, h 199 E. Jefferson.

Core Mary, servt wks Main Street Exchange

CORNEILLE JOHN B., Clerk 99 Columbia, h 47 n s Water b Clinton and Barr.

Cornelle Jane, servt Hedekin House
Cortrey John, blksmith h 165 W. Washington
Cory Michael, brakeman bds 225 W. Washington
Cothrell Mrs. Ann, widow h 72 E. Main

COTHRELL JARED, Proprietor Mad Anthony Dining Room, 65 Columbia, h 169 E. Washington.

Cotter H. C. mach wks P., Ft. W. & C. Railway machine shop
Coulston A. engineer wks P., Ft. W. & C. Railway Co
Coulter C. M. marble cutter wks n e c Main and Cass

COUNTY AUDITOR'S OFFICE, in Court House, Geo. F. Stinchcomb, Auditor.

County Commissioner's Office, in Court House Building
County Jail, w s Calhoun n of Water

COUNTY RECORDER'S OFFICE, in Court House, Platt J. Wise, Recorder.

COUNTY TREASURER'S OFFICE, in Court House, A. Wiley, Treasurer.

Court House, Calhoun b Main and Berry
Courtney L. F. driller h w s Calhoun b Washington and Jefferson

Courtney Lawrence, mach wks Toledo & Wabash Railway shops
Cowan Miss M. J. bds 248 W. Wayne
Cowie Isaac, molder bds People's House
Cox John, lab h e s Hanna b Hamilton and Railway
Coyle Michael, lab bds Mrs. Catharine Mahan's
Coyle Peter, teamster Hedekin House
Cramer B. engineer wks P , Ft. W. & C. Railway Co
Cramer Eli, fireman h 85 E. Lewis
Cramer W. helper wks P., Ft. W. & C. Railway carp shop
Cran Chas. tailor h w s Union b Washington and Jefferson
Cran Charles, tailor h s e c Barr and Jefferson
Cran Chas. Jr. molder res Cnas. Cran's
Cran Robert, molder res Chas. Cran's
Cran W. H. clk T. & W. Railway freight office, bds s e c Barr and Jefferson
Crane Calvin D. inventor res Wm. M. Crane's
Crane & Smith (Wm. M. C. and Wm. S. S.) attys n w c Calhoun and Berry
Crane Wm. M. (C. & Smith) h n s Sturgis w of Fulton
Crary Charles N. boatman h w s Maiden Lane b Main and Pearl
Craw Edward L. clk post office bds 91 W. Wayne
Crawford Mrs. ——, widow h n s Jefferson b Nelson and Garden
Crawford Henry, mach bds Old Fort House
Crawford Joseph, brakeman h s w c Piqua Plank Road and Virginia
Crawford Richardville, butcher h e s Garden b Jefferson and Railroad
Crawford W. B. asst checkman P., Ft. W. & C. Railway Freight Depot, bds Benj. Morss'
Creditor Chas. teamster wks D. F. Comparet
Creighton Wm. mach h e s Broadway b Jefferson and George
Crimer C. lab wks P., Ft. W. & C. Railway shops
Crimmel C. carp wks P., Ft. W. & C. Railway carp shop
Crimmins Mrs. Margaret, widow h Common n of Baker and w of McClellan
Crist Joseph, clk h n s Wayne b Hanna and Francis
Croak Thomas, stone mason h 54 Barr
Cronan Francis, clk bds 199 E. Jefferson
Cropsey Chas. conductor bds Mayer House
Crosby Geo. T. mach h s s Jefferson b Rockhill and College
Crosby Nathan G. blksmith h s s Jefferson b Rockhill and College
Crout E. L. foreman h w s Lafayette b Lewis and Montgomery
Crow James, carp wks T. & W. Railway shops
Croxton P W. millwright h 200 W. Washington
Crumley Mrs. Elizabeth, bds F. P. Higgins'
Cudoo J. helper wks P., Ft. W. & C. Railway blksmith shop

Culbertson James, conductor h 25 W. Jefferson
Cull Conrad, lab wks T. & W. Railway shops
Cull Cornelius, lab h n s Railroad w of McClellan
Cull Edward, lab wks T. & W. Railway shops
Cullem W. J. mach wks P., Ft. W. & C. Railway machine shop
Cummings E. fireman bds 151 W. Washington
Cummings Wilson, engineer bds Wm. H. Bryant's
Cunningham Abraham, lab h n e c Jefferson and College
Cunningham John, carp h s w c Wilt and College
Currant S. S. carp wks P., Ft. W. & C. Railway carp shop
Currant Sylvanus, carp h s s Locust w of Pine
Curry Francis, lab h s s Railroad b Harrison and Webster
Curtin S. helper wks P., Ft. W. & C Railway blksmith shop
Curtis Frank, harness mkr h 245 E. Lewis
Curtis G. blksmith wks P., Ft. W. & C. Railway blksmith shop
Cushion J. helper wks P., Ft. W. & C. Railway machine shop
Cushion J. C. helper wks P. Ft, W. & C. Railway repair shops
Cushing Michael, lab h n s Wilt b Rockhill and College
Cutler Chas. conductor bds Mrs. Ann Graham's
Cyrenius Mrs. Elizabeth, res James H. Harcourt's

D

Dachsteiner J. W. & Co. (John W. D. and Wm. Frey) upholsterers e s Calhoun b Berry and Wayne
Dachsteiner John W. (J. W. D. & Co.) h n s High, Bloomingdale
Dahman Wm. potash manuf n s Canal b Lafayette and Clay
DAILY & ERWIN, (James W. D. & A. J. E.) Surgeons and Physicians, Office, e s Calhoun b Main and Columbia, up stairs.
Dailey John, lab wks Fort Wayne Gas Co.'s
Daily Isaac, mach wks T. & W. Railway shops
Daily James W. phys (D. & Erwin,) h 22 W. Berry
Daily Thomas, hostler h s s Lewis b Lafayette and Clay
Daily Thomas, lab h 28 E. Berry
Dale Joshua, mach wks T. & W. Railway shops
Dalman Mrs. widow h 153 W. Washington
Dalman James, h 60 W. Washington
Dalton Edmund, carp h s w c Jefferson and Union
Dalton Timothy, helper h s s Colerick b Hoagland and Prince
Damise H. blksmith wks P., Ft. W. & C. Railway blksmith shop
Dammeier Henry, blksmith h 209 Ewing
Dammeier Wm. boiler mkr bds Henry Dammeier's
Danel Peter, asst general agent State Insurance Co., bds Aveline House
Darker Wm. fireman h 136 W. Jefferson

Daum Jacob, grocer n e c Broadway and Washington
Davidson G. F. insurance agent h n e c Clay and Berry
Davis A. A. carp wks P., Ft. W. & C. Railway carp shop
Davis Alfred, carp h w s Hanna b Madison and Jefferson
Davis Benjamin, clk 75 Columbia, bds Aveline House
Davis Charles E. bkbinder wks A. F. Siemon & Bro.'s, bds Hedekin House
Davis Fred. marble cutter wks n e c Main and Cass
Davis Henry, bkbinder bds Hedekin House

DAVIS J. C., Freight and Ticket Agent P., Ft. W. & C. Railway Co.; Office, Railroad e of Calhoun, h e s Hanna b Madison and Lewis.

Davis John, fireman wks T. & W. Railway Co.
Davis Joseph, tinner wks A. D. Brandriff & Co.'s, bds American House
Davis Samuel F. mach h 23 Madison
Davis U. B. carp wks P., Ft. W. & C. Railway carp shop
Davis Wm. bds Aveline House
Davis Wm. H. bkbinder wks A. F. Siemon & Bro's, bds Hedekin House

DAWSON JOHN W., Proprietor and Publisher of Dawson's Daily and Weekly Fort Wayne Times, n w c Calhoun and Main, h s w c Clay & Berry.

Day Christian A. painter h 99 E. Washington
Day Henry, painter, shop e s Clinton b Main and Columbia, h 131 W. Water
Dealing Mrs. N. M. (Mrs. M. A. Bradford & Co.) bds 203 W. Wayne
De Armett Potter, mach wks P., Ft. W. & C. Railway machine shop
De Armett Vinton, helper wks P., Ft. W. & C. Railway blksmith shop
Decker John, h s s Wayne b Francis and Harmer
Decker Mrs. Mary, widow h s s Wayne b Francis and Harmer
DeFoy Alex. fireman h n s Holman b Barr and Lafayette
Degan Patrick, helper h s e c Prince and Colerick
Degitz Charles, cigar mkr h s s Colerick b Hoagland and Prince
Dehart Abraham, lab h w s Calhoun b Baker and Railroad
Dehart Mary, servt Summit City Hotel
Dehart Robert, bar k F. X. Goodman's
Dehaven James, brakeman h n w s Bluffton Road b Nirdlinger and Wall
Dehaven Jonathan, carp h w s Bluffton Road nr T. & W. R. R.
DeHaven John, fireman bds 112 E Berry
DeHaven Mrs. Maria, h s s Jefferson b Nelson and Garden
Dehner Wm. carp h 142 Madison
Deininger Joseph, confec bds W. Wiemann's
Deininger Joseph, tailor h over 92 E. Main

Deininger Ulrich, confec bds W. Wiemann's
Deirman Henry, carp bds 51 W Washington
Delavan Barney, lab h n w c Webster and Douglas Av
Delavan Bernard, contractor h 214 E. Wayne
Delmont Julius, miller bds Robert Gavin's
Delzell Martin, carp h n s Montgomery b Clay and Monroe
Dement R. mach wks P., Ft. W. & C. Railway machine shop
Dennis Anthony, hostler Union House
Dennis P. W. carp wks P., Ft. W. & C. Railway carp shop
Dennis Philip H. brakeman bds 175 E. Jefferson
Dent T. J. teacher Francisco's Com. College, bds George R. Hartman's
Depler G. W. conductor h w s Jackson b Pritchard and Railroad
Derome Solomon, carp h 252 E. Washington
Derry Mrs. Margaret, h 79 W. Main
Desopher ———, brakeman bds 107 W. Wayne
Dessauer David, clk 96 Columbia, bds s s Water w of Harrison

DESSAUER L., Manufacturer and Dealer in Cigars, Tobacco, Snuff, Pipes, &c., e s Calhoun b Main and Columbia, under Odd Fellows' Hall, bds Main Street Exchange.

Deuter John M. tailor h 89 W. Water
Devine Neil, helper wks T. & W. Railway shops
DeWald Anton, clk 107 Columbia, bds George DeWald's
DeWald Frank, clk 107 Columbia, bds Mayer House
DeWald George, lab h w s Fairfield Av b Locust and Taylor
DeWald George, (Townley's, DeW. & Bond,) h s s Berry b Clinton and Barr
DeWald Henry, tinner wks E. Weber's, h w s Fairfield Av b Locust and Taylor
DeWald L. shoe mkr h 186 W. Main
DeWald Nicholas, cooper res George DeWald's
Dibble Miss Mary E. teacher at Fort Wayne College
Dick Daniel, engineer h w s Ewing s of Jefferson
Dick John, packer wks Fort Wayne Flour Mills
Dickerson Chilion D. harness mkr bds T. W. Bayless'
Dickerson Joshua, butcher bds 149 W. Berry
Dickey Mrs. Rebecca, widow h 199 E. Jefferson
Dickey Robert, foreman boiler mkrs. wks T. & W. Railway shops
Dickey Samuel, h w s Broadway b Washington and Jefferson
Dickey William, wks Olds, Hanna & Co.'s
Dickey William, boiler mkr wks T. & W. Railway shops
Dieck John H. packer h 93 Clay
Diefler George, cab mkr h n e c Piqua Plank Road and St. Francis
Dierstein Anton, wagon mkr h s s Wall w of Bluffton Road
Dierstein Christian, carp h s s Wall w of Bluffton Road
Dierstein Curist, wagon mkr e s Court b Berry and Main

Dierstein Conrad, clk 81 Columbia, bds Paul Siemon's
Dierstein S. lab wks P., Ft. W. & C. Railway shops
Diether Charles, lab h w s Griffith b Washington and Jefferson
Diffindarfer Samuel, (J. W. McNamara & Co.) res country
Dill Mortimer, carp h w s Clay b Jefferson and Madison
Dillon James C. carp h 176 Griffith

DILLS HENRY, h 91 E. Main.

Dingman Daniel, engineer h w s Clinton b Water and Duck
Dinklage Henry, lab b n e c Washington and Francis
Dinklage Herman, dray h e s Calhoun b Berry and Wayne
Dinklague Herman, dray h s s Water b Cass and Ewing
Dinkler Barney, lab h n s Washington b Hanna and Francis
Dirkes August, lab h n s Jefferson b Lafayette and Clay
Dirkes Fred, lab h Bloomingdale

DOANE N. E., Inventor and Patentee of Doane's Weighing Wagon, shop n s Main b Harrison and Maiden Lane, h 189 W. Washington.

Dodez G. C. clk 90 Columbia, h n s Wayne b Ewing & Griffith
Dodge Arthur, bds Mayer House
Dodge I. T. engineer bds 193 W. Washington

DOELKER JACOB, Meat Store, w s Calhoun b Berry and Wayne, h 81 E. Berry.

Dofler George, cab mkr wks B. H. Tower's
Doll Ferdinand, h n s Jones e of John
Doll Fred, lab wks Fort Wayne Machine Works
Donaldson Leavens H. h 228 E. Jefferson
Donaldson Moses, h 228 E. Jefferson
Donaldson Wesley, foreman at Ft. Wayne Agricultural Works
Donehue John, h s s Jefferson b Van Buren and Jackson
Donohue John, fireman bds 107 W. Wayne
Donoughoo Joseph, h 90 E. Lewis

DONOVAN M. Canal Boat Captain, res. 141 E. Main.

DONOVAN TIMOTHY, Canal Boat Captain, res. 141 E. Main.

Dooley Mrs. Mary A. widow h w s Kansas s of Railroad
Doolin B. tinner wks A. D. Brandriff & Co.'s
Doolittle W. boiler mkr wks T. and W- Railway shops
Doran Patrick, lab b n s Colerick b Prince and Hoagland
Doran Wm. teamster bds 53 E. Main
Doremus Kate E. bds 20 Madison
Doster Henry, bar k n w c Lafayette and Holman
Douglas Wm. B. train dispatcher h e s Barr b Washington and Jefferson
Dow David, lab b n s Wall w of Bluffton Road
Downey Dennis, sawyer h 162 W. Jefferson
Downey Dennis, lab wks T. & W. Railway shops

Doyle Timothy, lab bds 70 Madison
Drain Oscar, cooper wks C. S. Brackenridge & Co.'s
Drake F. G. (Coombs & D.) bds Aveline House
DRAKE MOSES, Jr., Post Master, Office w s Harrison opp. Columbia, h 91 W. Wayne.
Drake W. R. lightning rod dealer h s s Jefferson b Calhoun and Harrison
Dreibelbiss Conrad, sr. h w s Fulton b Washington and Jefferson
Dreibelbiss, J. P. clk C. Schmidt & Co.'s h n e c Harrison and Jefferson
Drew John W. bar k, h s s Lasselle e of Piqua Plank Road
Driftmeier Ernst, carp h n s Madison b Hanna and Francis
Dripps Isaac, master machinist Western Division P. Ft. Wayne & C. Railway Co., office s e c Holman and Barr h 46 E Jefferson
Driscoll Edward, mach bds Thos. Meegan's
Droecher Henry, h 66 W. Washington,
Droegemeier J. A. clk s e c Calhoun and Columbia, h 70 W. Washington
Druecker Henry, h 66 Washington
Drury Maurice, lab bds 70 Madison
DuBois John B. atty h 209 E. Lewis
Duell Frank, engineer h w s Fairfield Av. b T. & W. R. R. and Locust
Duffy Edwin, cloth finisher wks Summit City Woolen Mills
Duffy Frank, clk 11 Calhoun, bds 94 W- Main
Dugan Patrick, blksmith wks T. & W. Railway shops
Dull Jacob, blksmith bds Joseph Harter's
Dulo C. mach wks Bowser & Story's
Dunbar C. helper wks P., Ft. W. & C. Railway blksmith shop
DUNCKLEBURG WM., Photograph and Ambrotype Gallery, 3 Phœnix Block w s Calhoun b Main and Columbia, bds Mayer House.
Dunham Henry T. b k Ft. Wayne Branch Bank, h 134 W. Wayne
Dunham J. L. peddlar h n w c Ewing and Jefferson
Dunn James, (Breen & D.) bds 53 Columbia
Dunn James, fireman bds 151 W. Washington
Dunn Wm. mach h e s Webster b Washington and Jefferson
Duplain Geo. harness mkr wks Good & Co.'s
Durkee Mrs. A. H. widow h 176 E. Wayne
Dwane Michael, cartman h s s Baker b McClellan and Ewing
Dwelly Chas. W. mach h 183 E Jefferson
Dyer Thos. engineer h 165 W. Washington

E

Eagle J. H. carp h 55 W. Water
Eakin John, tree dealer bds Old Fort House
Eakin Joseph S. (Bash & E.) h 149 W. Wayne
Earl Geo fireman bds Hedekin House
Earl Mrs. Sirenia, widow h 190 W. Washington
Earl W. H. clk 39 Columbia bds Hedekin House
Earl Wm. engineer wks P., Ft. W. & C. Railway Co.
Early Mrs. Bridget, widow h n s al b Clinton and Calhoun and Water and Duck
Eastern District School, n w c Clay and Washington

EATON & CO., (J. A. E., John Eaton, Jr., & F. Eaton) Dealers in Staple and Fancy Dry Goods, 49 Columbia.

Eaton J. A. (E. & Co.) bds Hamilton House
Eberhadrt Wm. stone mason h s s Wilt b College and Nelson
Ebner Lorenz, carp h 95 E. Washington

ECKHART FREDERICK, Meat Store n e c Barr and Wayne.

Eckhart Wolfgang, h 84 E. Wayne
Eckels James M. carp h 211 W. Washington
Eckert Tobias lab h Bloomingdale

EDGERTON ALFRED P., President Ft. Wayne Gas Light Co., President and General Superintendent W. & E. Canal Co., Office n w c Columbia and Clinton, res 154 W. Berry and Land Office at Hicksville, Ohio.

Edgerton Henry H. Sec. Ft. Wayne Gas Light Co., res 154 W. Berry

EDGERTON J. H., Attorney at Law, Office and res. 85 W. Wayne.

Edington Isaac, fireman h n s Wall w of Bluffton Road
Eller Francis, organist bds 181 Clinton
Edmonds J. helper wks P., Ft. W. & C. Railway blksmith shop
Edmonds T. M. conductor h on T. & W. Railway s of Taylor
Edsall E. P. res Samuel Edsall's.
Edsall Samuel, h s w c Main and Edsall

EDSALL WM. S., Pork Packer, Commission Merchant and Dealer in all kinds of Grain, Seeds, &c., s s Canal b Calhoun and Harrison, bds Aveline House.

Elsold Wm. h w s Griffith s of Jefferson
Edwards Daniel, carp h 184 W. Washington
Edwards Mrs. Maria, widow h 22 Madison

Edwards Wm. R. coppersmith h 22 Madison
Edzold Frank, lab wks T. & W. Railway shops
Edzold Henry, shoemkr b s Wilt b Rockhill and College
Egerte Geo. cab mkr h n s Washington b Barr and Lafayette
Ehinger Chas. lab h 200 Madison
Ehinger John, lab wks T. & W. Railway shops
Ehinger Rohman, tailor wks 105 Columbia h 168 E. Washington
Ehle August, cigar mkr h e s West b Pritchard and Railroad
Ehle Michael, lab bds August Ehle's
Ehlert Fred. watchman h s e c Jefferson and Nelson
Ehrman Andrew, lab h e s West b Pritchard and Railroad
Ehrman Chas. Fred. harness mkr wks S. H. Shoaff's
Ehrman Mathias, lab h s s Jefferson b Nelson and Garden
Eicher John, carp h 138 E. Washington
Eichhorn Christian, baker wks 67 Columbia
Eickhoff Francis, cab mkr h 134 E Wayne
Eickhoff Frank M. clk h 134 E. Wayne
Eickhoff John, cab mkr h 132 E. Wayne
Eilgenfritz Mary M. h 241 W. Washington
Eiten John, carp h n s Buchanan b Piqua Plank Road and Clay
Eiter Peter, h s w c Jones and John
Eix August, well digger h 60 W. Washington
Elbert H. clk bds Main Street Exchange
Elbert Henry, clk 90 Columbia
Eldridge Mrs. Clara, widow h 200 W. Main
Elker ———, lab h 167 W. Washington
Ellert Fred. watchman wks T. & W. Railway shops
Elligsen Henry, tailor h Bloomingdale
Elliott A. A. fireman wks T. & W. Railway Co.
Elliott C. E. clk 75 Columbia, h 213 W. Wayne
Elliott E. helper wks P., Ft. W. & C. Railway carp shop
Elliott Edward carpenter b ds Peoples House
Elliott Geo. W. printer h 50 Monroe
Elliott Willis barber 80 Columbia h 152 W. Jefferson
Ellis G. molder h 7 Water
Ellis Joseph S. engineer res James Brown's

ELM PARK NURSERY, De Graff, Nelson & Co., n s New Haven Road, 4 miles e of City.
Elward Amanda, waiter Avenue House
Ely Geo. W. bds 117 W. Wayne
Ely John, lab bds John Enright's
Embry James, huckster h n w c Fairfield Av. and Taylor
Eme C. F. clk 111 Columbia, h n s Wayne b Clay and Monroe
Emerich Henry, carp h 181 Madison
Emerson Almeron boatman res Mrs Electa Emerson's
Emerson Mrs. Electa, widow h s s Columbia b Barr and Lafayette
Emery H. carp wks P., Ft. W. & C. Railway carp shop

Emmert Leonhard, teamster h n s Bowser, Bloomingdale
Emons O. W. mach wks P., Ft. W. & C Railway shop
Emons Mrs. Susan, widow res Chas. G. Smalley's
Emons W, lab wks P., Ft. & C. Railway shops
Emory H. W. clk bds Mayer House.

EMPIRE FLOUR MILLS, John Orff, Proprietor, w end of Main.

Emrick A. J. (A. D. Brandriff & Co.) h n s Water b Calhoun and Harrison

ENGELKING FRED., Dealer in Family Groceries, Provisions, Liquors, &c., n s Main b Clinton and Barr.

Engelking Henry, shoemkr h s s High, Bloomingdale
Engeln Mrs. Catharine, widow h w s Calhoun b Jefferson and Lewis
Englair Geo. helper wks P., Ft. W. & C. Railway Machine Shop
Engle Joseph, cooper wks C. S. Brackenridge & Co's
Engler Julius, foreman Indiana Demokrat office bds Steuben House
Englert Frank, cooper wks Haswell & Pierce's
Enos Richard, bds 108 W. Main
Enright John, lab h n w c Calhoun and Lewis
Enright Michael, helper h w s Calhoun b Jefferson and Lewis
Ensign Richard, gun smith h n e c Water and Clinton
Eple John, lab h w s Hood b Railroad and Pritchard
Epslein Albert, clk bds Main Street Exchange
Erhardt Mrs. Lena, widow h 174 E. Jefferson
Erlenbach Adam, harness mkr wks L. Troub & Co.'s
Ernsteing Chas. lab h Bloomingdale
Erny Mrs. Ann, h n s Nirdlinger w of Bluffton Road
Errell Chas. mach wks P., Ft. W. & C. Railway Machine shop
Erskine R. B. foreman painter h e s Lafayette b Montgomery and Holman
Ervin Latimer, mason bds Geo. Harter's
Erwin A. J. phys (Daily & E.) bds Mayer House.
Erwin Mrs. M. J. B. milliner res Mrs. M. E Chapin's
Ettinger Jerry, printer Dawson's Times office h 19 W. Wayne
Etzel Christoph, cooper wks Bloomingdale Brewery
Eure Wm. blksmith bds Phillips House
Evans A. mach wks P., Ft. W. & C. Railway machine shop
Evans A. S. (E. & Co.) h 121 E. Wayne

EVANS & CO. (A. S. E. and B. W. Goode,) Wholesale Dealers in Dry Goods, Notions, Carpets, Boots and Shoes, &c., n w c Columbia and Clinton.

Evans Edwin (Anderson & E.) h 174 W. Wayne
Evans Mrs. Elizabeth, widow h 58 W. Berry

Evans John P. clk n w c Columbia and Clinton, h 121 E. Wayne
Evans Joseph A. mach h n c c Lafayette and Jefferson
Evans Miss Lizzie, res 58 W. Berry
Evers F. O. clk bds Hedekin House
Ewell John Charles, clk 101 Columbia, h 89 W. Water
Ewing Mrs. Esther, widow h 114 W. Berry

EWING GEO. W., Surviving Partner of W. G. and G. W. Ewing, Office 91 W. Main, res Chicago.

Ewing G. W. jr. 91 W. Main, bds Aveline House
Ewing Wm G. jr, h 114 W. Berry

EXCELSIOR AGRICULTURAL WORKS, w s Hanna s of the Railroad Junction, Reitzell, Shunk & Co., Proprietors.

Eyder Peter, lab wks Fort Wayne Machine Works

F

Facineau J. mach P., Ft. W. & C. Railway machine shop
Fahlsing Chas. W. clk 107 Columbia
Failing Patrick, lab h s s Bass b Prince and Hoagland
Fairfield Asa h s c s Bluffton Road near T. & W. Railway
Fairfield John, blksmith 106 E. Main, h 102 E. Main
Fairfield John jr, boatman h 102 E. Main
Fairfield Oliver, h 121 E. Wayne
Falconer John, blksmith h n s Sturgis w of Fulton
Falk L. liquors, &c., c s Calhoun b Columbia and Main, h 69 W. Berry
Falkner J. blksmith wks P., Ft. W. & C. Railway blksmith shop
Fallahey Patrick, lab h c s Prince b Colerick and Williams
Falls D. M. mach h n w c Fulton and George
Farber John Fred. lab h o s Hanna b Hamilton and Railway
Farmer Sylvester, mach h 77 W. Jefferson
Farmnal J. helper wks P., Ft. W. & C. Railway blksmith shop
Farnan John, blksmith res Owen Farnan's

FARNAN OWEN, Blacksmith, Shoeing Shop, and Dealer in Coal, s s Columbia b Barr and Lafayette.

Farrell J. D. fireman P., Ft. W. & C. Railway
Farrer W. B. at C. S. Brackenridge & Co.'s
Faulkner John, blksmith wks T. & W. Railway shops
Fay Miss Clara A. music teacher res T. P. Anderson's

FAY JAMES A., Attorney at Law, Office n w c Calhoun and Berry, up stairs, h 226 W. Berry.

Fayman Wm. H. (Keifer, Yergens & F.) bds 144 E. Berry
Fee T. W. chair mkr h 67 Clinton
Fehlinger Fred. fireman h 93 W. Water
Fenimore Benj. H. carriage smith h 220 W. Wayne

Fentman Ulrich, lab wks T. & W. Railway shops
Ferrah James, baker bds 92 E. Main
Ferrell J. D. currier h 43 Clinton
Ferris L. A. carp bds s w c Wayne and Fulton
Ferry Mrs. Caroline, widow h 191 W. Main
Ferry Geo. helper wks P., Ft. W. & C. Railway blksmith shop
Fetters Eliza, at Old Fort House
Feuhrer Fred. baker h 69 W. Washington
Fick John, bds Jacob Aufrecht's
Fiegel Wm. driver wks Bloomingdale Brewery
Fieler Wm. pattern mkr wks Fort Wayne Machine Works
Fieler Wm. Rudolph, carp h 194 E. Jefferson
Filley Samuel, carp wks n e c Main and Cass
Filson R. C. furs, &c., w s Calhoun 3d door n of Columbia, h 204 W. Berry
Fink Charles, grocer s s Columbia b Calhoun and Harrison, h 55 W. Main
Fink Francis, molder wks Fort Wayne Machine Works
Fink Mrs. Mary, widow h 174 E. Jefferson
Finley Bridget, waiter Aveline House
Finn John, tinner bds Luther Wright's
Finnegan Barney, lab bds 70 Madison
Firemen's Hall, e s Calhoun b Columbia and Main

FIRST NATIONAL BANK OF FT. WAYNE, s w c Calhoun and Berry, J. D. Nuttman, President, W. B. Fisher Cashier.

FISCHER A., Proprietor Union Saloon, 54 E. Main b Clinton and Barr.

Fischer Adolph, clk 95 Columbia, h 148 Harrison
Fischer Frank, mach 265 E. Washington
Fischer Geo. W. carp h w s Griffith s of Jefferson
Fischer Henry, clk 95 Columbia, bds Adolph Fischer's
Fischer Isaac, meat store h n w c Wayne and Ewing
Fischer Joseph, plasterer h 265 E. Washington
Fischer Mrs. Mena, res Chas. Granneman's
Fischer Michael, wagon mkr n s Water b Calhoun and Clinton, h 85 E Berry
Fischer Michael, stone cutter wks James Humphreys'
Fish Geo. F. engineer h e s Lafayette b Madison and Lewis
Fish H. L. engineer h s s Lewis b Lafayette and Clay
Fish John R. foreman machinists P., Ft. W. & C. Railway Co., h n s Railroad w of McClellan
Fisher E. brakeman bds s e c Harrison and Railroad
Fisher E. H. clk 107 Columbia, bds Aveline House
Fisher Francis, mach wks F. Wayne Machine Works
Fisher Geo. W. plasterer h 246 E. Washington
Fisher Henry D. clk 107 Columbia, bds Mrs. Mena Fischer's
Fisher J. H. mach wks P., Ft. W. & C. Railway machine shop

Fisher J. K. engineer wks P., Ft. W. & C. Railway Co.
Fisher Robert J. clk Reed & Wall's, bds Mayer House
Fisher S. H. conductor bds Mayer House
FISHER W. B., Cashier First National Bank of Ft. Wayne, bds Aveline House.
Fisk Josephus I. brakeman h e s Ewing b Wayne and Washington
Fisk Wm. W. ins agt h n e c Washington and Ewing
Fitzgerald J. helper wks P., Ft. W. & C. Railway blksmith shop
Fitzgerald M. lab wks P., Ft. W. & C. Railway carp shop
Fitzgerald Michael, lab bds 92 E. Main
Fitzgibbon J. carp wks P., Ft. W. & C. Railway carp shop
Fitzgibbon Mrs. Margaret, widow h Common n of Baker and w of McClellan
Fitzpatrick Bart. lab h w s Prince b Bass and Colerick
Fitzpatrick John, lab h n e c Fairfield Av and Bass
Fitzpatrick Michael, lab h n s Lewis b Calhoun and Harrison
Flaharty Patrick, lab h s s Jefferson b Fulton and Broadway
Flaherty Patrick, lab wks T. & W. Railway shops
Fledderman John G. (John G. F. & Co.) h n w c Main and Clinton
FLEDDERMAN JOHN G. & CO., Proprietors Union Cash Clothing Store, n w c Main and Clinton.
Fleischmann Henry, lab h w s Lima Plank Road Bloomingdale
Fleitner Jacob, butcher res John Weller's
Fleming J. C. eng h e s Lafayette b Lewis and Montgomery
FLEMING R. E., Treasurer and Superintendent Ft. Wayne Gas Co., s e c Barr and Water, h 162 W. Berry.
Fleming Mrs. Sarah, widow h 134 Ewing
FLEMING WM., Clerk Circuit Court Allen County, Office Court House, h 69 W. Wayne.
FLETCHER C. P. & J. F., (Chas. P. and J. Frank.) Proprietors Summit City Hotel, w s Calhoun opp P., Ft. W. & C., and T. & W. Railroad.
Fletcher & Co. (C. P. F., O. J. Baldwin, and J. F. Fletcher) livery stable e s Calhoun b Holman and P., Ft. W. & C. Railway
Fletcher Chas. A. carp h 221 W. Washington
Fletcher Chas. P. (C. P. and J. F. F.) res Summit City Hotel
Fletcher J. Frank. (C. P. and J. F. F.) h 191 Ewing
Fletcher Lucy B. teacher Eastern District School, bds Wm. H. Coombs
Fletter Henry A. watchman h s s Taylor w of T. & W. Railway
Fletter Samuel C. carp h n w c Bass and Prince
Flinn Alex. sculptor n e c Cass and Main
Flinn Geo. N. dray h w s Clinton b Water and Duck
Flood Ann, pastry cook Aveline House

Flood Michael, h e s West b Pritchard and Railroad
Flowers Samuel, painter wks T. & W. Railway shops
Foellinger Fred. clk Jacob Foellinger, h 144 Harrison

FOELLINGER J. M., Dealer in Family Groceries, Provisions, Fruits, Cigars, Tobacco, &c., 5 w s Calhoun b Main and Columbia, h 110 W. Wayne.

Foellinger Jacob, boots and shoes w s Calhoun b Main and Columbia, h 144 Harrison
Foellinger Jacob, jr. shoemkr h 144 Harrison
Fogle Mrs. Rebecca, res Samuel Gish's
Foley Cornelius, tinner bds Luther Wright's
Folsing Wm. clk 85 Columbia
Folsom B. W. carp h n s Wilt b Van Buren and Jackson
Folsom D. J. carp h e s Lafayette b Montgomery and Lewis
Forbing & Houser, (John F. and Michael H.) restaurant n s Main b Calhoun and Harrison
Forbing John, (F. & Houser) h St. Charles Restaurant
Forbing Peter, carriage smith bds n e c Main and Lafayette
Ford Mrs. Mary, widow h 191 E. Wayne
Fordney Geo. M. molder wks Fort Wayne Machine Works
Fordney Michael, molder h 51 Madison
Forsyth Mrs. Eliza, res E. F. Colerick's

FORT FLOUR MILLS, east end of Columbia and Lafayette, D. F. Comparet, Proprietor.

FORT WAYNE AGRICULTURAL WORKS, Manufacturers of the Sieberling (or Doylestown) Reaper and Mower, Factory on Canal Feeder n end of Calhoun.

FORT WAYNE BRANCH OF THE BANK OF THE STATE OF INDIANA, s w c Main and Clinton, Pliney Hoagland, President; Chas. D. Bond, Cashier.

FORT WAYNE COLLEGE, Rev. R. D. Robinson, President, w end of Wayne Street.

FORT WAYNE DAILY AND WEEKLY GAZETTE, Jones & Jenkinson, Editors and Proprietors, 125 Columbia.

FORT WAYNE DAILY AND WEEKLY SENTINEL, Thos. Tigar, Editor and Proprietor, Office s w c Calhoun and Pearl.

FORT WAYNE DAILY AND WEEKLY TIMES, John W. Dawson, Proprietor and Publisher, n w c Calhoun and Main.

FORT WAYNE EATING HOUSE, Philo Rumsey, Proprietor, Junction Pittsburg, Fort Wayne & Chicago, and Toledo & Wabash Railroads.

FORT WAYNE GAS COMPANY, s e c Barr and Water, A. P. Edgerton, President; R. E. Fleming, Treasurer and Superintendent.

Fort Wayne Insurance Co. office 5 E. Main, L. Angell, President, G C. McAllaster, Secretary

FORT WAYNE MACHINE WORKS, Bass & Hanna, Proprietors, Manufacturers of Steam Engines, Boilers, Mill Gearing, Machinery, &c., e s Hanna s of Railroad Junction.

FORT WAYNE PLANING MILL, Hurd & Clark, Proprietors, n s of the Canal b Clinton and Barr.

FORT WAYNE STEAM MARBLE AND BUILDING STONE WORKS, n e c Cass and Main, P. S. Underhill, Proprietor.

Fort Wayne Western Museum, w end of Columbia. P. O. Building

Foss Ernst, plasterer h 195 E. Jefferson
Foster Wm. B. mach h 136 Lafayette
Foster W. J. blksmith wks P., Ft. W. & C. Railway blksmith shop
Foster Wm. T. blksmith h 90 Madison
Fountain Eugene F. eng h e s Barr b Lewis and Montgomery
Fowles John, cutter 94 Columbia, h n s Water c Barr
Fox Bernard, carp h s s Walnut b Fairfield Av and Oakley
Fox Mrs. F. grocery 161 E. Jefferson
Fox Frank, blksmith h w s Lafayette b Wayne and Washington

FOX GEO., Gardener, h s s Taylor w of Oakley.

Fox Geo. lab h 161 E. Jefferson

FOX H. C., Proprietor Mayer House, s e c Calhoun and Wayne.

Fox J. lab wks P., Ft. W. & C. Railway lumber yard
Fox James, lab h 93 W. Washington
Fox John C. brass finisher wks 48 E. Main
Fox John R. gas fitter h e s Calhoun b Washington and Jefferson
Fox Mrs. P. at Mayer House
Fox Miss Sallie, at Mayer House
Fox Valentine, gardener res Geo. Fox's
Fraley C. lab wks P., Ft. W. & C. Railway Co. yard
Frame Margaret, h n s Montgomery b Clay and Monroe
France Joseph S. city atty office at Mayor's office, h w s Broadway b Washington and Jefferson
Francis Thos. P. mach wks T. & W. Railway Shops
Francisco Miss E. E. teacher of painting and drawing w end of Columbia, bds 108 W. Main

FRANCISCO M. J., Proprietor Francisco's Commercial College, w end of Columbia, bds 108 W. Main.

Franc P. lab wks Fort Wayne Machine Works
Frank Chas. clk J. M. Foellinger's, h s s Jefferson b Nelson and College
Frank Mrs. Ellen, widow h 140 E. Wayne
Frank Fred. tailor h e s Jackson b Pritchard and Railroad
Frank Henry, boatman h 140 E. Wayne
Frank Jacob, blksmith bds Steuben House
Franke Barney, night watchman P., Ft. W.& C.Railroad Freight Depot
Franke John, carp h s s Pritchard b Bluffton Road and Jackson
Franke Mrs Julia, widow h e s Clinton b Main and Berry
Franklin Horace B. h s s Berry b Griffith and Fulton
Fraser Thos. lab wks Toledo & Wabash Railway Freight Depot
Frederick D. M. eng wks P., Ft. W. & C. Railway Co.
Frederick Jacob, mach b n s St. Francis e of Piqua Plank Road
Frederick Peter, blksmith res Jacob Frederick's
Fredericks G. lab wks P., Ft. W.& C. Railway Shops
Fredericks Justus, painter h s s Washington b Nelson and Garden
Freeman Lieut. A. H. bds Aveline House
Freeman D. H. clk Banner Ins. Co. office 5 E. Main
Freeman J. clothing s e c Columbia and Calhoun, bds Main Street Exchange
Freeman Josephine, at 65 Columbia
Freeman M. D. (Griffith & Co.) h 180 W. Wayne
Freeman N. B. asst assessor U. S. Revenue office at Collector's office, res Washington Township
Freeman Rosetta, at 65 Columbia
Freeman Sophia, cook 65 Columbia

FRENCH CHAS. G., Contractor, Carpenter and Builder, Shop 85 E. Wayne, h 92 E. Wayne.
FRENCH, HANNA & CO., (R. Morgan F., Sam'l H., and Willis W. Hanna,) Proprietors Summit CITY WOOLLEN MILLS, s s Water b Barr and Lafayette.

French R. Morgan, (F., Hanna & Co) h 144 E. Washington
French Mrs. S. M. widow b h n s Montgomery b Barr and Lafayette
Frenking Barney, lab h 136 Madison
Frese Mrs. Sophia, widow h 169 W. Washington
Frey Mrs. ———, widow h Bloomingdale
Frey Wm. (J. W. Dachsteiner & Co) h 10 E. Washington
Friberger Simon, produce dealer rear 51 Columbia, h 34 W. Wayne
Fricke Henry, h 183 Lafayette

Fricke C. H. W. clk 107 Columbia, bds 66 W. Jefferson
Friday Henry, dray h n w c Webster and Brandriff
Friday Henry, sen. res Chas. Degitz's
Frimuth Mrs. ———, widow h w s Broadway b Jefferson and Wilt
Froelich Chas. lab h n w c Bluffton Road and Railroad
Frohmuth John, painter wks T. & W. Railway Shops
Fronefield Reuben, (F. & Todd) h 30 W. Water
Fronefield & Todd (Reuben F. and Robt. T.) sash and blinds al b Calhoun and Clinton 1st n of Water
Frost A. G. telegraph operator P., Ft. W. & C. Railway office at Depot, bds Geo. R. Hartman's

FRY J. B. & CO., (Joseph B. F., & J. M. Wilder,) Manufacturers and Wholesale and Retail Dealers in Boots and Shoes, 123 Columbia.

Fry Jacob, h 61 Lafayette
Fry Jacob, tanner and dealer in leather findings, &c., wareroom 123 Columbia, tannery and res w end of Aqueduct
Fry Joseph B. (J. B. F. & Co.) h 84 W. Water
Fry Orrin, carp bds Union House
Fry Mrs. Sarah J. widow h s s Water b Ewing and Griffith
Fuchs Joseph, lab h e s Force b Jones and Hernden
Fuherer Fred. bakery 25 W. Main
Fuller Frank C. clk bds 141 E. Washington
Fuller Henry, lab 141 E. Washington
Furlong A. b'ksmith wks P., Ft. W. & C. Railway Blksmith Shop
Furste Francis L. clk County Treasurer's office, h 22 W. Wayne
Futter Martin, chair painter h n e c Nelson and Wilt

G

Gable Christian, b h 40 Madison
Gable Mrs. Christina, widow h 29 W. Water
Gable Miss Hadnah (G. & Shordon) h w s Clinton b Main and Columbia
Gable Miss Mary, dress mkr h n w c Harrison and Wayne
Gable Peter, mach wks Fort Wayne Machine Shops

GABLE & SHORDON, (Miss Hannah G., & Miss Catharine S.,) Millinery and Dress Making Rooms, w s Clinton b Main and Columbia.

Gabler Geo. lab h s s High, Bloomingdale
Gaensslen Chas. A. clk 63 Columbia
Gaer Wm. carp h s s Lewis b Barr and Lafayette

GAFFENEY & McDONNELL, (Wm. G., & Patrick McD.,) Saloon and Dealers in Family Groceries, Provisions, &c., w s Calhoun near the P., Ft. W. & C. Railroad.

Gaffency Wm. (G. & McDonnell) res Columbia City
Gaffney Edward, helper h s s Bass b Prince and Fairfield Av
Gage Sarah, servt Summit City Hotel
Gailor Louis, carp wks T. & W. Railway Shops
Gaines Geo. L. tinner bds Phillips House
Gale Anthony, h s e c Lewis and Lafayette

GALE GEO. A., Dealer in Family Groceries, Provisions, &c., s e c Lewis and Lafayette.

Gales Mrs. Mary L. widow h n s Jefferson b Nelson and Garden
Gallagher A. helper wks P., Ft. W. & C. Railway blksmith shop
Gallagher M. helper wks P., Ft. W. & C. Railway blksmith shop
Gallnor Henry, carp wks T. & W. Railway Shops
Galmeier Fred. lab wks Hugh McCulloch's
Galvin James H. telegraph operator T. & W. Railway, bds Summit City Hotel
Gamble Mrs. Catharine, h 93 W. Washington
Gans Louis, lab h e s West b Pritchard and Railroad
Gansor Abram, fireman T. & W. Railway Co.
Ganzer John, porter Fort Wayne Eating House
Gardanier Mrs. Rebecca V. bds n w c Lafayette and Jefferson
Gardner Mrs. Charity D. widow h 46 W. Berry

GARDNER H. A., Superintendent Western Division P., Ft. W. & C. Railway, Office, at Depot.

Garney E. A. teamster wks Olds, Hanna & Co.'s
Garr Henry H. fireman bds Lewis C. Wheeler's
Garrett Samuel, miller wks City Flour Mills
Garretty Mary, waiter Mayer House
Garrison Albert, lab h s Colerick b Prince and Hoagland
Gartie Theodore, cab mkr bds American House
Gartie Simon, turner bds B H. Tower's
Gasper Fred. carp h 51 W. Washington
Gasper Rudolph, carp 51 W. Washington
Gauche J. blksmith wks P., Ft. W. & C. Railway blksmith shop
Gaucher John B. lab h s s Lasselle e of Piqua Plank Road
Gavin Robert, farmer h n end of Harmer
Gawky Bernard, helper wks T. & W. Railway shops
Gawze Louis, lab wks P., Ft. W. & C. Railway Co. yard
Gear W. carp wks P., Ft. W. & C. Railway carp shop
Gebel Fritz, shoemkr h s w c Jefferson and Rockhill
Gebhard Wm. mason h 209 Madison
Gebhardt Geo. bklayer h s s High, Bloomingdale
Geerken Geo. clk 17 E. Main h 80 Madison
Gehring Andrew, watchman h Bloomingdale
Geiger Mrs Catharine, widow h 62 Columbia
Geiger Chas. teacher h n s Jefferson b Lafayette and Clay
Geiler F. lab wks P., Ft. W. & C. Railway shops
Geiso Jacob carp h e s Piqua Plank Road b Wallace and Charles
Geisler Wm. lab h s s Jefferson b Van Buren and Jackson

Geisman Jacob, lab h n s Locust w of Pine
Geissinger Mrs. Lucinda bds n w c Main and Griffith
Geller George, lab h s w c Pritchard and Hood
Geller H. blksmith wks P., Ft. W. & C. Railway blksmith shop
Gellor Louis, lab h e s Francis b Lewis and Madison
Gerardine Anthony, carp wks T. & W. Railway carp shop
Gerardine H. carp wks P., Ft. W. & C. Railway shop
Gerhardt John, molder wks Ft. Wayne Machine Works
Gerke Henry, lab h Bloomingdale
German Reformed School, e s Webster b Washington and Jefferson
Geronx Mrs. Mary, widow h n s Railroad b Webster and McClellan
Gerrad John, carp bds 128 E. Washington
Gerry Catharine, teacher Eastern District School, bds 4 E. Wayne
Gers Philip, lab h w s West b Pritchard and Railroad
Gessler Fred. butcher h 65 E. Wayne
Gettel Martin H. clk 89 Columbia h n s Main b Griffith and Fulton
Geyer G. Henry, shoemkr h 140 Harrison
Gibford A. clk n w c Columbia and Clinton h 55 W. Wayne
Gibford David, farmer h w s Rockhill b Wilt and Pritchard
Gibson Frank, carp h n e c Wilt and Jackson
Gibson Mary, h 168 E. Jefferson
Gibson Wm. molder h 83 E. Main
Gidley Wm. h e s Pine b Locust and Railroad
Gilby John, lab h e s Hood b Pritchard and Railroad
Gilchrist Christopher, carp h s s Berry b Fulton and Griffith
Gilday Michael, lab h rear 161 E. Jefferson
Gilkison Wm. S. atty office at Mayor's Office, h 79 W. Main
Gillam David, eng bds Lewis C Wheeler's
Gillan James lab h n s Montgomery b Barr and Lafayette
Gillan Michael, lab h n e c Bass and Prince
Gilligan James, lab h e s Pine b Locust and T. & W. R. R.
Gillilan James, asst dispatcher P., Ft. W. & C. Railway
Gilliland James, lab h n s Montgomery b Barr and Lafayette
Gimbal Henry, lab h n e c Broadway and George
Girh W. helper wks P., Ft. W. & C. Railway carp shop
Gish Samuel, grocer w s Lafayette b Holman and Montgomery
Gitty C. lab wks P., Ft. W. & C. Railway Co.
Glecion T. fireman, wks P. Ft. W & C. Railway Co.
Glenn Martin, lab wks P., Ft. W. & C. Railway lumber yard
Glover Geo. N. Prin. High School Western District, bds W. S. Griffith s of Jefferson
Glutting Jacob, saloon 76 Columbia h s s Washington b Calhoun and Harrison
Glynn John, bar k 65 Columbia

GLYNN MATHIAS, Livery and Sale Stable 53 E. Main.

Gocke Anthony, clk 86 Columbia h 43 W. Wayne
Godfrey Wright eng h s w c Jefferson and Fulton.
Goebel Fred, shoemkr bds Geo. A. Hermsdorfer's
Goette Christopher lab h n s Buchanan e of Clay.
Golden T. helper wks P., Ft. W. & C. Railway blksmith shop
Golding Pat. laborer wks P., Ft. W. & C Railway Co. yard
Goler Fred. blksmith h w s Lafayette b Montgomery and Holman
Goll H. A. mach wks P., Ft. W. & C. Railway machine shop
Golsh Louis, lab bds Steuben House
Gonser Abraham, fireman bds 225 W. Washington
Goode B. F. (Evans & Co) bds 84 W. Berry
Goode & Co. (Geo. G. & Louis Traub,) saddles s s Columbia b Calhoun and Clinton.
Goode Geo. (G. & Co. and L. Traub & Co.) h 98 E. Jefferson.
Goodlip R. lab wks P., Ft. W. & C Railway Co. yard
Goodman Francis X. saloon w s Calhoun b Columbia and Canal h c Washington and Harrison
Goodman Jacob, lab wks Geo. W. Woods
Goodner J. carp wks P., Ft. W. & C. Railway carp shop
Goodrich John, clk 107 Columbia, bds Henry S. Dunham's
Goodspeed John, brakeman bds Mrs. Hannah Whaley's
Gordon H. bds Aveline House
Gordon Patrick, lab h s e c Colerick and Hoagland
Gosh Henry, saloon n s Railroad street near P., Ft. W. & C. Railway
Gosch Joseph, baker bds 92 E. Main
Gotsch Benj. teacher h w s Barr opp Madison
Gould Geo. upholsterer h s s Lewis b Barr and Lafayette
Gould Harvey H. eng h s s Lewis b Harrison and Webster
Gould Wm. F. fireman wks T. & W Railway Co.
Gouty T. A. planer wks Hurd & Clark's
Gowan Henry, carp h 182 W. Jefferson
Gowty Alex. h n s Railroad b Webster and McClellan
Grabner P. M. eng wks P., Ft. W. & C Railway Co.
Grady James, blksmith h 90 E. Lewis
Grady Michael, lab h n s Colerick b Prince and Hoagland
Graeffe Fred. (G. & Muehler) h w s Calhoun b Washington and Jefferson
Graeffe & Muehler, (Fred. G. & Chas. M.M.) saloon e s Calhoun b Columbia and Main
Graf Frank, shoemkr res John Graf's
Graf John, lab h n s Buchanan b Piqua Plank Road and Clay
Graff J. helper wks P., Ft. W. & C. Railway machine shop
Graff Lafayette, clk res Marx Graff's 84 Harrison
Graff Myer, clk res Marx Graff's 84 Harrison

GRAFF MARX, Importer and Wholesale Dealer in Brandies, Wines, Gin, Cigars, &c., w s Calhoun, one door n of Berry, h 84 Harrison.
GRAFFE H. C. Dealer in Watches, Clocks, Jewelry, Silver-ware, &c., 102 Columbia, h 88 Columbia.
Grage Fred. carp wks T. & W. Railway shops
Grage Fritz, lab h 177 W. Jefferson
Grage Wm. teamster h s s Sturgis w of Fulton
Graham Mrs. Ann, widow b h n s Holman b Clay and Monroe
Graham Catharine, wks Main Street Exchange
Graham James, eng h n w c Clinton and Wayne
Graham S. R. eng wks P., Ft. Wayne & C. Railway Co.
Graham Thos. eng h e s Barr b Lewis and Montgomery
Graham Wm. fireman res Mrs. Ann Graham's
Graham Wm. F. cooper bds Union House
Granneman Chas. lab h e s Harrison b Highland and Dawson
Granneman Henry G. carp h w s Harrison b Highland and Dawson
Grant David, mach wks P., Ft. W. & C. Railway machine shop
Grappy Samuel, porter 87 Columbia
Gratner John, eng wks P., Ft. W. & C. Railway Co.
Graumann Henry bk binder h 60 W. Jefferson
Gravener Peter, eng bds 40 Madison
Gray Thos. carp h w s Calhoun s of Dawson
Gray Wm. blksmith h n s Wilt b College and Nelson
Greathouse Henry, carp h 196 E. Wayne
Green C. produce dealer h 215 W. Wayne
Green Mrs. E. A. teacher Western District bds 145 W. Wayne
GREEN PROF. E. S., Superintendent of Public Schools, bds 145 W. Wayne.
Green Miss Esther, res Mrs. Esther Ewing's
Greene Wm. h 86 E. Wayne
Greensfelder Gustav, grocery n w s Bluffton Road b Pritchard and Railroad
Greenwood Henry blksmith h w s Calhoun b Jefferson and Lewis
Greer Rev. James, bds Mrs. Grout's
Grenaullet Jacque, lab h 100 Madison
Grenneman Chas. carp wks T. & W. Railway shops
Grenneman Henry, carp wks T. & W. Railway shop
Grey C. A. dry goods 84 Columbia
Gridley Mrs J. A. millinery and dress making 125 Columbia
Greib John, tailor h s s Lewis b Monroe and Clay
Griebel Adolphus L cab mkr h 58 E. Jefferson
Griebel Jno. Wm. cab mkr h 58 E. Jefferson
Griebel Ludwig, teamster h n s Bowser, Bloomingdale
Grier James, mach wks T. & W. Railway shops

GRIEBEL LOUIS, Cabinet Ware Manufacturer and Dealer, e s Clinton b Main and Columbia, h 85 E. Jefferson.

GRIFFITH & CO., (G. V. G. & M. D. Freeman) Potash Manufacturers n e c Ewing and W. & E. Canal

Griffith G. V. (G. & Co.) h c Jackson and Wayne
Griffith Geo. B. h 209 W. Wayne
Griffith Wm. clk 81 Columbia h w s Ewing b Washington and Wayne
Griffiths Wm. atty and notary h w s Ewing b Wayne and Washington
Grimes James molder h 140 E. Wayne
Grimple H. lab wks P. Ft. W. & C. Railway lumber yard
Griner C. watchman wks Olds, Hanna & Co.s
Groat Alfred T. fireman bds Wm T. Jackson's
Grob Louis, teamster h s s Pritchard b Bluffton Road and Jackson
Groezinger Christ. h w s Lima Plank Road, Bloomingdale
Grogeaun August, lab h n e c Lewis and Francis
Gronauer Anna res 160 E. Wayne
Gronauer Wm. G. h w s Ewing b Wayne and Washington
Gross Adam, lab h 114 Madison
Gross Mrs. Dorethea, widow h w s Calhoun b Washington and Jefferson
Gross Fred. lab. h o s Van Buren b Wilt and Pritchard
Grote H. A. cigars, &c. 30 W. Main
Grothel Wm. L. file cutter bds 156 Harrison
Grout Mrs. E. B. widow h w s Griffith s of Jefferson
Grout Wm. local train dispatcher P,, Ft. W. & C. Railway, office at depot, h w s Calhoun s of Railroad
Grove Maxwell J. boiler mkr h 134 Lafayette
Grover H. carp wks P., Ft. W. & C. Railway carp shop
Gruber Catharine, Matron Orphan's Home and Ft. Wayne Hospital n w c Wayne and Webster
Gruber Michael, tailor h n e c Wilt and Van Buren
Gruber Valentine, tailor h s s Taylor w of Oakley
Grund Fred. mason h s s Melita b Webster and Hoagland
Grund Fred. shoemkr wks E. Vordermark & Co.s
Gucot J. wagon mkr h s s Lasselle c of Piqua Plank Road
Guffey ———, carp bds 91 E. Washington
Guilday Michael, carp wks T. & W. Railway shop
Guin Russell B. stone cutter h 257 W. Berry
Guire J. carp wks P., Ft. W. & C. Railway carp shop
Gundy Geo. bklayer bds Wm Beals'
Gurney E. A. teamster h s e c Lewis and Harrison
Gushing John lab wks P., Ft. W. & C. Railway shops
Gust Dora L. servt wks Main street Exchange

Gutermuth Caspar, turner h s s Douglas Av. b Harrison and Webster.
Guthermuth Jno. Geo. h s. s. High, Bloomingdale
Guthman F. X. saloon h 39 W. Washington
Guywood C. H. lab wks Neil McLachlan & Co.'s

H

Haag John bklayer h s s Washington b Nelson and Garden
Habecker Elias, carp h 161 W. Washington
Habel Andrew, shoemkr h s w c College and Jones
Haberkorn Emil mach bds 164 E. Wayne
Haberkorn F. mach wks P., Ft. W. & C. Railway machine shop
Haberkorn Henry, mach h c s Lafayette b Madison and Lewis
Hachen P. S. clk bds Mayer House
Hachmeier Ernst lab h 208 Ewing
Hackeuse A. helper wks P., Ft. W. & C. Railway repair shops
Hackman John, tailor h 166 East Washington
Haddsnock J. lab wks P., Ft. W. & C. Railway Co. yard
Hadler C. carp wks P., Ft. W. & C. Railway carp shop
Hadley Wm. B. carp h s s Jones and Nelson and Garden
Hafleigh R. clk 50 E. Main h n s Wayne b Ewing and Griffith
Haffner M. blksmith wks P., Ft. W. & C. Railway blksmith shop
Hafner John, cab mkr bds 51 E. Jefferson
Hagan Wm. lab h rear 47 E. Water
Hagemann Wm. h s w c Pritchard and Bluffton Road
Hagerty Mrs. Deborah, h s c Harrrison and Railroad
Haggerty Hugh, boatman h n end of Harmer
Hagman J. helper wks P., Ft. W. & C. Railway blksmith shop
Hahmeyer Ernst lab, wks T. & W. Railway shops
Hahn Herman C. 1st Lieut. 128th Regiment Indiana Volunteers bds Aveline House
Haines Geo. carp bds Union House
Haines John L. eng h s w c Maiden Lane and Pearl
Hake Herman, dray h 159 E. Washington
Hall Geo. conductor bds Luther Wright's
Hall Goodwin, teamster h n s Railroad b Calhoun and Harrison
Hall Thos. blksmith h s w c Broadway and Wilt
Halstein Mrs. Louisa, widow h 20 E. Berry

HAMBROCK FRED., Saloon and Dealer in Family Groceries, Provisions, &c., n w c Calhoun and Washington h n s Lewis b Harrison and Calhoun.
Hamilton A. H. atty n s Main b Calhoun and Clinton, h s s Lewis b Calhoun and Clinton
Hamilton Allen, (Allen H. & Co.,) h s s Lewis opp Clinton

HAMILTON ALLEN & CO., (Allen H., Hugh McCulloch, Jesse L. Williams, S. B. Bond, and Chas. McCulloch,) Bankers and Exchange Dealers, w s Calhoun b Main and Berry.
Hamilton Mrs. Ann, at Hamilton House
Hamilton Mrs. Elizabeth, widow h e s Calhoun s of the Railroad
Hamilton Fred. proprietor Hamilton House 49 and 51 W. Berry
Hamilton James, blk-mith h 95 E. Jefferson
Hamilton John, grain dealer h 145 W. Wayne
Hamilton Miss Letitia, at Hamilton House
Hamilton Miss Mary, at Hamilton House
Hamilton Matilda J. servt wks Main Street Exchange
Hamilton R. H. eng T. & W. Railway, bds Summit City Hotel
Hamilton S. D. clk 107 Columbia, bds Geo. R. Hartman's
Hamilton Thos. jr. h s s Pearl b Maiden Lane and Cass
Hammond A. helper wks P., Ft. W. & C. Railway blksmith shop
Handrohen Wm. lab bds 70 Madison
Haney Edward, peddlar h e s Calhoun b Wayne and Washington
Hanks Miss Mary, seamstress res John Cochran's
Hanna Chas. h 62 Barr
Hanna Henry C. (Olds, H. & Co) res country
Hanna Horace H. (Bass & H.) h 215 E. Lewis
Hanna Hugh T. res Samuel Hanna's
HANNA SAMUEL, Vice-President P., Ft. W. & C. Railway Co., Office n w c Barr and Berry, h s s Lewis e of Hanna.
Hanna Samuel T. clk Samuel Hanna's, bds Aveline House
Hanna Willis W. (French, H. & Co.) bds Mayer House
HANNUM D. & CO., (Daniel H. & Chauncey Stauring,) The Lodge Saloon w s Calhoun b Berry and Wayne.
Hannum Daniel, (D. H. & Co.) h e s Calhoun b Washington and Jefferson
Hansher Henry, porter wks R. W. Taylor's
Harber Heter, mach bds Hedekin House
Harbard Isaac, mach wks Bowser & Story's
Harcourt James H. miller h e s Clay b Washington and Jefferson
Harcourt W. H. miller wks Fort Flour Mills
Harden Wm. molder wks Fort Wayne Machine Works
Hardendorf John, carp h 238 W. Wayne
Harder Mrs. Maria L. widow h 86 Madison
Hardich Ed. bds Aveline House
Hardike Edward, music teacher 54 Calhoun, bds G. Orff's
Hardindorff I. J. molder wks Bowser & Story's

Hardy Miss Emma, res Geo. L. Little's
Harmeier Wm. lab h s s High, Bloomingdale
Harmsdoerfer Adam, shoemkr h s w c Jefferson and Rockhill
Harries John, clk C. Schmidt & Co.'s, h s e c Jefferson and Ewing
Harrington Elias, carp h 101 W. Jefferson
Harrington James, carp bds Newcomb Ketchum's
Harrington John S. carp h s c c Hoagland and Melita
Harris Geo. W. eng h 154 E. Washington
Harris Mrs. H. M. e 176 E. Wayne
Harris Miss Melinda, bds 151 Barr
Harrison Milton, cab mkr h s s Lewis b Calhoun and Harrison
Harrison T. S. spring mkr h e s Ewing s of Jefferson
Harsh Jacob, harness mkr bds Hedekin House
Hart J. R. hackman h n s al b Calhoun and Clinton and Water and Duck
Hart John, lab bds American House
Harter Geo. b h w s Griffith s of Jefferson
Harter Joseph, blksmith n s Main b Fulton and Broadway, h n s Main e Broadway
Harter Philip, clk 90 Columbia, h 124 W. Washington
Hartman Adam, carp h w s Ewing s of Jefferson
Hartman Amos, cooper h 60 W. Washington
Hartman August, dray h 123 Lafayette

HARTMAN & BOSSLER, (Homer C. H. & Henry H. B.,) Real Estate, Collecting and Insurance Agents, w s Calhoun opposite Court House over Allen Hamilton & Co.'s Bank.

Hartman Geo. watchman h w s Nelson opp Wilt
Hartman Geo. R. b h s w c Barr and Washington
Hartman Gottfried, tailor h 205 E. Jefferson
Hartman Herman, brewery 128 E. Washington
Hartman Homer C. (H. & Bossler) h 173 W. Wayne
Hartman Isaac, cooper wks C. S. Brackenridge & Co.'s
Hartman L. R. deputy County Auditor, bds 149 W. Wayne
Hartmyer Fred. confectioner h 47 W. Main
Hartnett Richard, lab h n s Baker b Webster and McClellan
Hartnett Wm. cooper wks C. S. Brackenridge & Co.'s
Hartwell Wm. saloon 82 Barr
Harvey E. L. carp wks P., Ft. W. & C. Railway shop
Harvey L. D. carp bds Old Fort House
Haselhorst Henry, shoemkr h 252 E. Washington

HASKELL WASHINGTON, Commission and Produce Merchant, 39 Columbia, bds Main Street Exchange.

Haskins H. carp wks P., Ft. W. & C Railway carp shop
Hassett Barnard, painter wks T. & W. Railway shops.
Haswell S. P. (H. & Pierce) h n w c Main and Griffith

HASWELL & PIERCE, (S. P. H. & J. S. P.) Coopers and Stave Dealers, s w c Pearl and Griffith and n s Water b Calhoun and Clinton.
Hate Christ. clk C. Schoerpf & Co.'s, bds Jacob Hate's
Hate Jacob, eng h w s Lafayette b Lewis and Montgomery
Hate Jacob, mach wks P., Ft. W. & C. Railway Machine Shop
Hatfield Geo. W. res Philip Baker's
Hattendorf Wm. lab h s s High, Bloomingdale
HATTERSLEY ALFRED, Gas Fitter, Plumber, Brass Founder and Finisher, 48 E. Main.
Hausbach Jacob, lab h n s Wines b Fairfield Av and Hoagland
Hausper Jacob, mach wks Toledo & Wabash Railway Shops
Hausper Joseph, helper wks T. & W. Railway Shops
Hauss David, carp h 237 W. Washington
Haverley Anthony, blksmith h 168 Madison
Haws Isaac, cooper wks C. S. Brackenridge & Co.'s
Hay John, conductor h w s McClellan opp Douglas Av
Hayden John W. h 164 W. Wayne
Hayes Dennis, lab h s s Colerick b Prince and Fairfield Av
Hayes Thos. lab h s w c Colerick and Prince
Haynes ———, carp h w s Fairfield Av b T. & W. Railway and Locust
Haynes Frank, eng h s s Melita b Webster and Hoagland
Haynes Gilman, carp h s s Jefferson b Calhoun and Harrison
Hays Mrs. Ann, h 166 W. Jefferson
Hays Dennis, bklayer h 166 W. Jefferson
Hays John, carp h 166 W. Jefferson
Hays Miss Mary, h s s Pearl b Harrison and Maiden Lane
Hays Thos. molder b 166 W. Jefferson
Hays Thos. cooper wks C. S. Brackenridge & Co.'s
Haywood Byron, fireman bds 107 W. Wayne
Hazard Henry, painter wks T. & W. Railway Shops
Hazzard Henry, painter bds Mrs. E. B. Grout's
Hebert Oliver, fireman bds Hedekin House
Hebler Geo. W. miller h 102 W. Water
Hebsacker August, lab bds American House
Heckel David, carp bds 117 Madison
Heckens Andrew, lab h on 1st street s of Douglas Av b Webster and McClellan
HEDEKIN HOUSE, Eli Kearns, Proprietor, e s Barr b Main and Columbia.
Hedekin M. h 97 E. Main
HEDEKIN T. B., Wholesale and Retail Dealer in Groceries, Provisions, &c., s e c Columbia and Barr, h 82 E. Washington.
Hedges A. T. produce dealer h 39 Monroe
Hedges Edward, bar k St. Charles Exchange
Hedges Thos. J. carp h 122 W. Washington

Heet Alex. butcher h 84 E. Wayne
Heffer John, baker bds Henry Brockman's
Heffern Michael, lab bds 70 Madison
Heffner John, cab mkr wks 50 E. Main
Heffner Michael, blksmith n e s Hanna s of Jones
Heheringer Henry, lab bds Mathias Zattner's
Heidenreich Joseph, blksmith s s Water b Clinton and Calhoun, h Bloomingdale
Heider Alex. butcher wks 65 W. Main
Heier Fred. lab wks A. D. Reid's
Heil Fred. blksmith h Bloomingdale
Heilbroner S. vinegar mkr s w c Calhoun and Canal, h 30 W. Washington
Heilbroner Sigmund, res S. Heilbroner's
Heilbronner Abram, h w s Calhoun b Wayne and Washington
Heimbert John, lab h w s Hood b Pritchard and Railroad
Heine Fred. carp h s s Madison b Clay and Monroe
Heinlen Wm. helper h w s Harrison b Highland and Dawson
Heintzelman J. mach wks P., Ft. W. & C. Railway Machine Shop
Heit Amos, blksmith res Bloomingdale
Heit Anton, shoemkr h w s Griffith s of Jefferson
Heitenrech Armand, lab h n s Wines b Fairfield Av. and Hoagland

HEITKAMP CONRAD, Dealer in Family Groceries, Provisions, Liquors, &c., e s Lafayette b Lewis and Montgomery.

Heldt G. A. barber h w s Calhoun b Berry and Wayne
Heldt John M. (H & Shidel) h w s Calhoun b Berry and Wayne
Heldt & Shidel, (John M. H. & Chas. S.) barbers w s Calhoun b Berry and Wayne
Helker Fred. lab h n e c Jefferson and Van Buren
Hella Fred. eng wks Bowser & Story's
Helm Edwin, molder wks Fort Wayne Machine Works
Helm Mrs. Theodore, h 123 Lafayette
Helmkamp Henry, carp h n s Pritchard b Broadway and Van Buren
Hench Samuel M. carp bds Joseph Singmaster's
Henck D. carp wks T. & W. Railway Shops
Henderson A. R. sup't Summit City Woolen Mills, h s s Berry b Clay and Monroe
Henderson David, res A. R. Henderson's
Henderson John, brakeman bds Albert H. Cook's
Henderson Samuel C. mach h 79 E. Main
Henderson Wm. plasterer h 100 Madison
Henderson Wm. D. h 79 E. Main
Hendricks Christian, wagon mkr bds Julius Schaller's
Henkenius Frank, dray 86 Columbia, h Bloomingdale

Henning Chas. carder res Fred. Henning's
Henning Fred. lab h 51 E. Water
Henry Geo. C. clk res Hiram H. Henry's
Henry Hiram H. (Ammon & H.) h s e c Main and Van Buren
Henry Wm. hardware agent h w s McClellan b Lewis and Douglas Av.
Henry Wm. H. fireman res Hiram H. Henry's
Henschen Henry, teamster h 170 Ewing
Henschen Wm. h w s Francis b Hamilton and the Railroad
Hepler Louis, lab wks T. & W. Railway Shops
Hergenreter Max, mason h w s Piqua Pland Road b Virginia and Wallace
Hergenroether Joseph, bklayer h 237 W. Washington
Hermayer Wm. planer wks Hurd & Clark's
Hermsdoerfer Geo. Adam, shoemkr h c Jefferson and Rockhill
Hernigen Henry, lab wks Ft. Wayne Machine Works
Herrin Margaret, servt n w c Wayne and Webster
Herring Geo. teamster h 142 Madison
Herring Peter, mason h e s West b Pritchard and Railroad
Herrington H. J. carp wks P., Ft. W. & C. Railway carp shop
Herrington Miss Jennie, res Geo. T. Crosby's
Herrold Israel W. lab h s s Water b Cass and Ewing
Heseneier Wm. carp bds 86 W. Jefferson
Hess Ferdinand, clk 84 Columbia
Hess Franz, clk C. Schoerpf & Co.'s
Hess Jacob, lab h w s Broadway b Jefferson and Wilts
Hess N. W. plow stocker h n s Main b Griffith and Fulton
Hessenmauer John, lab h s w c Lima Plank Road and Douglas Av., Bloomingdale
Heton Joseph, lab h e s Clay b Washington and Jefferson
Hett Jacob, eng h w s Lafayette b Lewis and Montgomery
Hettler Christoph, carp b 246 E. Lewis
Heuer Herman, shoemkr h 59 W. Wayne
Hexter L. cigar mkr wks L. Dessauer's
Hezart Barnhart, lab h n s Main b Fulton and Broadway
Hiber Fred. blksmith b s s Holman b Clay and Monroe
Hibler Geo. W. miller h 102 W. Water
Hickman Daniel, clk b s w c Jefferson and Francis
Hickman Elijah, grocer n w c Berry and Barr, res country
Hickman Wm. res Daniel Hickman's
Higgins F. P. fireman h w s Lafayette b Wayne and Washington

HIGGINS HENRY, Editor Dawson's Fort Wayne Times, n w c Main and Calhoun, h s s Berry b Lafayette and Clay.

Higgins James, lab bds Union House
Hight Eugene, mach h e s Clay b Holman and Hough
Hildebrand Wm. (Walker & H.) h 226 W. Washington

Hilbrecht Henry, blksmith h n s Jefferson b Van Buren and Jackson
Hilgeman Ernst, spinner wks Summit City Woolen Mills, h 194 Ewing
Hilgeman Henry, carp h 194 Ewing
Hilgeman Wm. carp h w s Ewing s of Jefferson
Hilgemann Ernst, carp h 210 E. Washington
Hilgemann Henry, eng h 89 W. Jefferson
Hilgemann Wm. carp h 212 E. Washington
Hilker Chas. carp wks T. & W. Railway Shops
Hilker Chas. lab h e s Francis b Lewis and Madison
Hilker Fred. carp wks T. & W. Railway Shops
Hilker Henry, lab h w s Fairfield Av. b Locust and Taylor
Hilker M. lab wks P., Ft. W. & C. Railway Shops

HILL C. L., Dealer in Pianos, Musical Instruments, Sheet Music, Sewing Machines, &c., w s Calhoun opp. Court House, res. 34 W. Water.

Hill Daniel, boatman, h Bloomingdale
Hill J. A. (H. & Lemmon) h 46 W. Jefferson
Hill Rev. John, h 26 W. Berry
Hill John E. (H. & Orbison) h 84 W. Berry
Hill Mrs. John H. dry goods, millinery goods, &c., h w s Calhoun b Berry and Wayne
Hill John H. w s Calhoun b Berry and Wayne
Hill & Lemmon (J. A. H. & A. R. L.) carp n e c Main and Griffith
Hill O. G. clk 117 Columbia, h n s Jefferson b Griffith and Ewing
Hill & Orbison, (John E. H. & A. M. O.) com mers 129 Columbia
Hill Valentine, lab h n s Main b Fulton and Broadway
Hill Wm. R. res John H. Hill's
Hilt David, clk s w c Calhoun and Main
Hilt Fred. harness mkr bds T. W. Bayless'
Himbert John, carp wks T. & W. Railway Shops
Himbert Michael, dray h n s Railroad w of McClellan
Hine Wm. porter 177 Columbia
Hinke Dietrich, carp bds 206 Madison

HINKLE G. D., Assistant Editor Daily Sentinel, bds Aveline House.

Hinkle O. N. conductor h s w c Cass and Pearl
Hinlion Wm. mach wks T. & W. Railway Shops
Hinman H. F. carp h e s Union b Wayne and Washington
Hinton Samuel, h s s Melita b Webster and Hoagland
Hislop Mrs. Catharine, widow h s s Lewis b Monroe and Hanna
Hitchfield Fred. clk 121 Columbia, h 90 W. Water
Hitchman Henry, cooper wks C. S. Brackenridge & Co.'s
Hitzeman Fred. mason h 100 W. Jefferson
Hitzeman Gottleib, tailor 71 Columbia, h 100 W. Jefferson

Hitzerman Christ. wks 145 W. Water
Hitzfeld Mrs. Dorothea, h 90 W. Water
Hitzfeld Fred. h 90 W. Water
Hitzfeld John harness mkr h 90 W. Water

HOAGLAND P. & CO., (Pliney H. & Jesse L. Williams,) Proprietors City Flour Mills, n w c Clinton and Canal.

Hoagland Pliney, (P. H. & Co.) h n e c Ewing and Berry

HOBROCK WM., Bakery and Eating House, e s Calhoun b Holman and P., Ft. W. & C. Railroad, h w s Fairfield Av. b Locust and T. & W. Railroad.

Hochmeier Fred. lab wks T. & W. Railway Shops
Hockenburger John H. lab h s w c Jefferson and Van Buren
Hockstetter Wm. h n s Wall w of Bluffton Road
Hoff Rev. Fred. A. h s s Douglas Av. b Harrison and Webster
Hoffman Adam, carp h e s Force s of Jones
Hoffman Geo. carp h n s Wilt b Van Buren and Jackson
Hoffman Jacob, carp h 237 W. Washington
Hoffman Michael, carder h n w s Bluffton Road b Pritchard and Railroad
Hoffman P. helper wks P., Ft. W. & C. Railway Carp Shop
Hoffman Peter, carp h 179 Clinton
Hoffman Susan C. teacher Western District School, h s e c Fulton and Berry
Hoffmeister Henry, cooper n w c Lima Plank Road and Bowser, h Bloomingdale
Hogan John, lab bds 70 Madison
Hogan Michael, lab h e s Fairfield Av. b Colerick and Williams
Hogan Patrick, clk [s e c Calhoun and Railroad, bds Timothy Hogan's
Hogan Timothy, lab h n s Railroad w of McClellan
Hogan Timothy, saloon and grocery s e c Calhoun and Railroad
Hogan Wm. upholsterer wks 56 Columbia
Hogarth Thomas, stone cutter h 173 W. Berry
Hohing J. fireman h s s Durrie b Hoagland and Fairfield Av.
Hohnhaus Peter, carp h s w c Jefferson and Van Buren
Hoit David, asst foreman carp shop P., Ft. W. & C. Railway Co. h s e c Clay and Montgomery
Hoit L. H. atty bds Mayer House

HOKE JACOB, Dealer in Family Groceries, Provisions, &c., w s Calhoun one door n of Jefferson.

Hokemeier Chas. lab h s s Washington b College and Nelson
Holcher Chas. carp wks T. & W. Railway shops
Holker Fred. carp wks T. & W. Railway shops

HOLLEY H. H., Proprietor Union House, 49 E. Main.

Holley Mary, at Union House
Holmes Joshua cattle broker on Huntington Road 4 miles w of city
Holmes Wm. cattle broker on Huntington Road, 4 miles w of city
Holser Fred. saddler bds American House
Holswart A. helper wks P. Ft. W. & C. Railway blksmith shop
Holsworth Addison, clk 98 Columbia bds E. Bostick's
Holtz John C. molder bds Steuben House
Holzer Chas. lab h n w s Bluffton Road b Pritchard and Railroad
Holzer Fred. harness mkr bds American House
Holzworth Edward (Torbeck & H.) h n w c Bluffton Road and Railroad
Holzworth Geo. helper h s e s Bluffton Road b Pritchard and Railroad

HOME INSURANCE CO., of New York, John Hough, Agent, 50 Calhoun, opp. Court House.

Homeier Carl, lab h s s High, Bloomingdale
Homeier Wm. clk h s s Lewis b Harrison and Webster
Hondheim John J. lab n w s McClellan b Lewis and Douglas Av.
Honeck Henry, carp bds Wm. Muellerring's
Hontine Jacob, lab wks T. & W. Railway shops
Hood D. B. with W. E. Hood, bds Hamilton House
Hood Thompson N. ins agt bds Wm. Bowen's

HOOD W. E. Wholesale and Retail Grocer and Commission Merchant 88 w s Calhoun b Berry and Wayne, bds Hamilton House.

Hoolahen John lab h n s Railroad w of McClellan
Hooper Isaac Z. blksmith h n s Holman b Lafayette and Clay
Hooper J. blksmith wks P., Ft. W. & C. Railway blksmith shop
Horn Michael lab h al b Clinton and Barr, 1st n of Water

HORNUNG JOHN GEO., Proprietor Summit City Brewery e s Harrison b Berry and Wayne.

Horstmeier Henry carp bds Wm. Horstmeier's
Horstmeier Wm. carp h 205 Ewing
Horstmeyer Henry, carp h 242 E. Lewis
Horstmeyer Louis carp bds 242 E. Lewis
Hoskins Harry, carp bds D. J. Folsom's
Hosman C. painter h 82 W. Jefferson
Hosman Christian, lab h 86 W. Jefferson
Hosman Christian, gardener wks Hugh McCulloch's

HOUGH JOHN, Attorney at Law; Land and Insurance Agent, Office 50 Calhoun, opp. Court House, h 121 W. Wayne.

Hough Miss Martha, h 121 W. Wayne
Houghteling Peter G. bar k D. O'Connell's billiard rooms
Houghton Luther S. h n s Jefferson b Ewing and Griffith
Houser Geo. (H. & Kalbacher) res St. Nicholas Saloon

HOUSER & KALBACHER (Geo. H. & Andy K.) Proprietors St. Nicholas Saloon and Restaurant, w s Calhoun b Berry and Wayne.
Houser Michael, (H. & Forbing,) res St. Charles Saloon
Houston Christ. painter wks T. & W. Railway shops
Houston Wm. lab wks T. & W. Railway shops
Hovey Isaac, eng wks P., Ft. W. & C. Railway Co.
Howard Mrs. Alfred, bds n w c Lafayette and Jefferson
Howard C. carp wks P., Ft. W. & C. Railway carp shop
Howe James, clk Empire Flour Mills h 250 W. Berry
Howe James, lab bds 70 Madison
Howell David, carp h n s Berry nr Harmer
Howey Isaac, eng h 75 E. Jefferson
Howley B. blksmith wks P., Ft. W. & C. Railway blksmith shop
Howley & Patten, (Thos. H. & Charles P.) horse shoers s s Main b Harrison and Maiden Lane
Howley Thos. (H. & Patten) h n w c Pearl and Ewing
Huber Geo. eng bds Mrs. E. B. Grouts
Huber Geo. pro Andy's Express h 30 W. Wayne
Huber Tobias, bds 12 E. Berry
Hudrey Nicholas, carp h s s Montgomery b Monroe and Hanna
HUESTIS A. C. Wholesale Grocer and Confectioner; also, Wholesale Dealer in Oranges, Lemons, Oysters, &c., 83 and 85 Columbia, h 203 s e c Berry and Van Buren.
Huffet John, baker h w s Calhoun b Berry and Wayne
Huffman J. carp wks P., Ft. W. & C. Railway carp shop
Hughes James, lab h n s Bass b Prince and Fairfield Av.
Hugnean August, shoemkr wks 55 Columbia
Humbert Mr. Sarah, widow h 57 Barr
Humes Harvey, brakeman bds 107 W. Wayne
Humes John, fireman bds Sylvanus Currant's
Humphrey Geo. (Cochran, H. & Co.) h 175 W. Berry
Humphrey James conductor bds Mayer House
HUMPHREY JAMES, Steam, Sand and Limestone Works, n w c Main and Fulton, h 173 W. Berry.
Humphrey Joseph, carp h 106 Washington
HUMPHREY NOAH, Wholesale Boot and Shoe Manufacturer, 123 Columbia, up stairs, h 216 W. Wayne.
Humphrey Thos. stone cutter h 173 W. Berry
Humphreys W. S. (A. D. Brandriff & Co.) h 108 W. Main
Humphries Miss Emma L. milliner res Mrs. Elizabeth Sulley's
Hundertmark Louis. cab mkr wks John J. Kluehn's
Hunt C. D. fireman wks P., Ft. W. & C. Railway Co.
Hunt Mrs. Ellen, widow h 95 E. Berry.
Hunter C. W. (Adair & H.) bds Geo. R. Hartman's

Huntheim Jacob, carp h e s Pine b Taylor and Locust
Hunting W. H. switchman h 160 W. Washington

HURD & CLARK, (O. D. H. & J. H. C.) Proprietors Ft. Wayne Planing and Flooring Mill, n s the Canal b Clinton and Barr.
Hurd O. D. (H. & Clark) h 142 W. Jefferson
Hursh David, bds Mayer House
Hurst Joseph, hostler Hedekin House
Hurt B. carp wks P., Ft. W. & C. Railway carp shop
Hurtzell V. carp wks T. & W. Railway shops
Husner Wm. carp wks Cochran, Humphrey & Co.'s
Hutchinson Thos. J. n w s Bluffton Road b Pritchard and Railroad
Hutton Geo. lab h 123 E. Lewis
Hutzel John, teamster wks Ft. Wayne Machine Works
Hutzel John, h n s Washington b Broadway & Van Buren
Huxford M. W. h on East Branch Lima Plank Road n of St. Mary's river
Hyames L. L. Indian Doctor h 62 Columbia
Hyde John, wks Olds, Hanna & Co.'s
Hyne Christ. carp wks T. & W. Railway shops
Hyne Fred. carp wks T. & W. Railway shops

I

Iba W. boatman h e s Fairfield Av. b Colerick and Williams
Immel Henry, baker bds 20 E. Berry
INDIANA DEMOKRAT, Tri-Weekly and Weekly, German, Office n w c Calhoun and Berry, C. G. Jahn, Editor.
INDIANA LAND AGENCY, John Hough, Proprietor, 50 Calhoun, opp. Court House.
INDIANA STAATS, ZEITUNG (German Weekly) John D. Sarnighausen, Editor and Proprietor, n e c Columbia and Clinton.
Inglert Francis, cooper h n s Nirdlinger w of Bluffton Road
Inglert Geo. lab h s s Taylor w of Oakley
Iobst Alex. helper wks Bowser & Story's
Irey Miss Sarah, h w s Griffith s of Jefferson
Irving A. B. (Anderson & I.) h 15 Madison
Irwin John S. b k Allen Hamilton & Co.'s h 238 W. Berry
Irwin Thos. meat store w s Calhoun b Main and Berry h 103 Lafayette
Isabey Louis, boiler mkr wks T. & W. Railway shops
Isabey Louis C. helper h w s Cass, Bloomingdale
Ismer Chas. clk City Flour Mills, h n w c Wayne and Barr

Ismer Gottleib, eng h s e c Barr and Wayne
Ivars Geo. painter h n w c Wayne and Webster
Ives Miss Caroline, res E. O. Cooper's

J

Jackmeier H. helper wks P., Ft. W. & C. Railway blksmith shop
Jackson A. conductor bds 193 W. Washington
Jackson Anthony, eng bds n w c Ewing and Jefferson
Jackson Chas. brakeman bds 89 E. Lewis
Jackson John J. eng h n s Washington b Ewing and Griffith
Jackson Kirby, eng wks P., Ft. W. & C. Railway Co.
Jackson Thos E. mach h 161 W. Washington
Jackson Wm. T. eng h s w c McClellan and Lewis
Jacob Fred. painter h 68 W. Washington
Jacob Peter, lab h 114 Madison
Jacobs John H. (W. Jacobs & Son,) h 68 W. Berry
Jacobs W. & Son, (Wm. and John H.) boots and shoes s w c Calhoun and Columbia
Jacobs Wm. (W. J. & Son,) h 68 W. Berry

JACOBSON ELKAN, Dealer in Clothing, Gents' Furnishing Goods, Hats, Caps, Trunks, &c., 106 Columbia, h 73 W. Main.

Jacobson Vigdor, clothing e s Calhoun b Main and Columbia, h 54 W. Main
Jacoby Geo. pattern mkr h s w c Piqua Plank Road and Virginia

JAHN CARL G., Attorney at Law and Notary Public; Office, n w c Calhoun and Berry, up stairs, bds Main Street Exchange.

Jahn Nicholas, carp h e s Hood b Pritchard and Railroad
Jahn Nicholas, tailor, h s s Pritchard opp Van Buren
James Gilbert, harness mkr 122 Columbia, res country
Janks C. helper wks P., Ft. W. & C. Railway blksmith shop
Janks J. helper wks P., Ft. W. & C. Railway blksmith shop
Jautz Chas. helper h s s High, Bloomingdale
Jefferds O. W. notary public h 133 E. Wayne
Jefferds Thos. L. clk P., Ft. W. & C. R. R. freight office, h 133 E. Wayne
Jeneman J. lab wks P., Ft. W. & C. Railway shops

JENKINSON ISAAC, Attorney at Law, (Jones & J.) Office, n w c Calhoun and Berry, h 130 W. Jefferson.

JENKINSON MOSES, Attorney at Law, e s Calhoun b Columbia and Main, bds 105 W. Berry.

Jennert August, lab h rear 93 W. Water

Jennings J. W. grain dealer bds Main Street Exchange
Jennings Miss Rebecca J. res 109 Lafayette
Jerman A. S dyer h 57 W. Water
Jessup Danl. J. clk A. D. Brandriff & Co.'s, bds Geo. R. Hartman's
Jewish Synagogue, w s Harrison b Wayne and Washington
Jobson Mrs. Mattie, widow res Mrs. Mary Roope's
Jobst Alex. lab h n s Montgomery b Barr and Lafayette
Jockemeier Henry, lab h s s Jefferson b Harrison and Webster
Jocquel J. helper wks P., Ft. W. & C. Railway machine shop

JOCQUEL J. J., Dealer in Stoves and Manufacturer of Tin, Copper and Sheet Iron Ware, w s Calhoun b Main and Columbia, h 23 W. Jefferson.

Jocquel Mathias, mason h n s Wines b Fairfield Av. and Hoagland
John Andreas, lab h w s Francis b Madison and Lewis
John David P. eng h 50 E. Washington
Johnson Henry, lab wks T. & W. Railway shops
Johnson Henry B. sawyer h 75 W. Washington
Johnson Mrs Huldah, widow h 91 E Main
Johnson Joseph, carp h w s Griffith s of Jefferson
Johnson Martha, servt Union House
Johnson Samuel G. teamster bds Jacob Young's
Johnson Wm. blksmith wks T. & W. Railway shops
Johnston Wm. carp h e s Broadway b Jefferson and George
Johnston Wm. jr. b k 90 Columbia, bds Hamilton House

JONES C. K., Manager W. U. Telegraph Office, n w c Columbia and Clinton; h e s Jackson b Berry and Wayne.

Jones Chas. fireman wks P., Ft. W. & C. Railway Co.
Jones D. W. (Jones & Jenkinson,) h w end of Jefferson
Jones E. molder wks Ft. Wayne Machine Works
Jones Edward S. carp h 57 E. Berrry
Jones Geo. W. clk T. & W. Railway freight office, h s o c Jones and Nelson
Jones Harvey P. printer Ft. Wayne Gazette Office, res D. W. Jones'
Jones Harriet, servt wks Main Street Exchange
Jones Henry, eng wks P., Ft. W. & C. Railway Co.
Jones Irvin L. clk Main Street Exchange

JONES & JENKINSON, (David W. J. & Isaac J.) Editors and Proprietors Fort Wayne Daily and Weekly Gazette; Office, 125 Columbia.

Jones Joseph, h 110 W. Water
Jones Mrs. Mary, widow h 55 W. Water
Jones Myron B. fireman h 125 E. Lewis
Jones O. fireman wks P. Ft. W. & C. Railway Co.

Jones Resin V. h 202 W. Wayne
Jones Thos. L. carp bds 45 E. Main
Jones Wm. F. eng h c s Lafayette b Montgomery and Holman
Jones Wm. H. harness mkr bds Union House

JONES WM. H., Secretary Fort Wayne Agricultural Works, on Canal Feeder, n end of Calhoun, bds Hamilton House.

JORDAN JOHN P., Physician and Surgeon; Office, s w c Calhoun and Berry, bds Aveline House.

Jordan Miss Matilda L. res Mrs. Mary L. Shoaff's
Josse John M. phys h 96 W. Berry
Jung Mrs. Elizabeth, h w s Hood b Pritchard and Railroad

K

Kaag Jacob, clk 121 Columbia, bds 233 W. Berry
Kabisch Fred. saloon w s Calhoun b Berry and Wayne
Kabisch Julius, saloon n s Main b Calhoun and Harrison
Kabisch Rudolph, lab h w s Webster b Washington and Jefferson
Kable Geo. lab h 137 E. Lewis
Kaeliger Jacob, lab h 144 E. Jefferson
Kagle Leah, chambermaid at Mayer House
Kaiser Fred. tailor bds at Henry Thele's
Kaiser Henry, shoemkr wks Christian Pipenbrink's
Kalbacher A. (Houser & K.) res St. Nicholas Saloon
Kalbacher M. h 30 W. Wayne
Kalker J. helper wks P., Ft. W. & C. Railway blksmith shop
Kaly Andrew, bds Summit City Hotel
Kamm Adolphus, brewer wks Bloomingdale Brewery
Kamm Jacob J. (K. & Sweney,) h 77 E. Berry

KAMM & SWENEY, (Jacob J. K. and James L. S.,) House and Sign Painting, Graining and Paper Hanging, Post Office Building, West end of Columbia.

Kane James M. (James M. K. & Bro.) h n w c Calhoun and Water

KANE JAMES M. & BRO., (James M. K. and Patrick H. K.,) Wholesale and Retail Dealers in Yankee Notions, Cutlery, Jewelry, Fancy Goods, Toys, &c., e s Calhoun b Main and Columbia.

Kane Patrick H. (James M. Kane & Bro.) bds n w c Calhoun and Water
Kanne Fred Wm. (K. & Co.) h 33 Madison

KANNE & CO., (Fred. Wm. K., Wm. Muellering and Chas. Muellering,) Contractors and Dealers in Lime and Stone; Office, n s Columbia b Barr and Lafayette.

Kanning Louis, lab h 97 Madison
Kaplinger Jacob, eng h 51 Madison
Kappel J. helper wks P., Ft. W. & C. Railway boiler shop
Kappels Herman, lab h 180 E. Washington
Kappels Henry, h 180 E. Washington
Kappels John, h 180 E. Washington
Kariger Geo. tinner wks A. D. Brandriff & Co.'s bds People's House
Karll A. tinner wks P., Ft. W. & C. Railway repair shops
Kart F. lab wks P., Ft. W. & Railway carp shop
Kartholl Anthony, tinner h 149 E. Jefferson
Kartholl Mrs. Caroline, widow h 149 E. Jefferson
Kauffman Geoorge A. (K. & Thompson,) bds Main Street Exchange

KAUFFMAN & THOMPSON, (Geo. A. K. & Byron S. T.) Dealers in Watches, Clocks, Jewelry, Silver Ware, &c., n w c Calhoun and Main

Kauffman Tobias, trader h w s Lafayette b Washington and Jefferson
Kavanaugh James, polisher wks n e c Main and Cass
Kay Benj. brass finisher h n w s Bluffton Road b Wall and Nirdlinger
Kay Wm. saloon w s Clinton b Columbia and Main
Keafharbon G. helper wks P., Ft. W. & C. Railway carp shop
Kearns James, mach h n w c Hood and Railroad
Kearney Mrs. Mary, h 123 Lafayette

KEARNS ELI, Proprietor Hedekin House, e s Barr b Columbia and Main.

Kearns John, res at Hedekin House
Keder J. helper wks P., Ft. W. & C. Railway machine shop
Keech John, brakeman bds Mrs. Hannah Whaley's
Keefe Mrs. Catharine, widow h n s Holman b Barr & Lafayette
Keefer Christian, porter 81 Columbia, bds Martin Keefer's
Keefer M. carp wks P., Ft. W. & C. Railway carp shop
Keefer Samuel, (K., Yergens & Fayman,) h 144 E. Berry
Keefer Smith, carp wks F. S. Baldwin's
Keefer Wm. carp bds D. J. Folsom's

KEEFER, YERGENS & FAYMAN, (Samuel K., Christian F. W. Y. & Wm. H. F.,) Wholesale and Retail Dealers in Staple and Fancy Dry Goods, Carpetings, Oil Cloths, &c., 75 Columbia.

Keegal P. H. engineer h n s Wayne b Barr and Lafayette
Keelty Thomas, baker h n s Water b Clinton and Barr
Keever Nancy, servt 148 E. Berry

Keffer Mrs. Anna Maria, h 128 Madison
Kehn Wm. shoe mkr wks C. W. Sander's
Kehoe Thomas, teamster bds James W. Ryan's
Keifauver George, lab h w s Hood b Pritchard and Railroad
Keifer Mrs. Mary, widow h s w c Calhoun and Jefferson
Keil Herman, carp h n s Hamilton b Hanna and Francis
Keiser Fred. tailor bds Henry Thele's
Keistler James, mach wks P., Ft. W. & C. Railway machine shop
Keliker Peter. lab h c s Francis b Lewis and Madison
Kelker Anthony, engineer h w s Griffith s of Jefferson
Kelker George, mach h n s Washington b Clay and Monroe
Kelker H. engineer wks P., Ft. W. & C. Railway Co
Kelker John, engineer h 145 E. Lewis
Keller Caleb, clk 49 Columbia
Keller Charles, file cutter h Bloomingdale
Keller Sebastian, mason h s w c Jefferson and Union
Kellermeyer Henry, lab bds 60 W. Washington
Kelly E. W. conductor h 43 W. Berry
Kelly James, lab wks P., Ft. W. & C. Railway Co. yard
Kelly James J. mach h n s Montgomery b Barr and Lafayette
Kelly John, res James J. Kelly's
Kelly John, helper h w s Calhoun b Highland and Dawson
Kelly Patrick, lab h n s Bass b Prince and Fairfield Av
Kelly Timothy, lab h n s Baker b Webster and Harrison
Kelsey James T. butcher h 149 W. Berry
Kemp Edgar, clk 90 Columbia, h n s Main b Griffith and Fulton
Kemp W. P. blksmith wks P., Ft. W. & C. Railway blksmith shop
Kendall Jacob, carp wks P., Ft. W. & C. Railway carp shop
Kene William, shoe mkr bds 217 E. Jefferson
Kenlen Michael, watchman h 175 W. Jefferson
Kennedy Gust. plasterer h 229 E. Jefferson
Kennedy Joseph, peddler h e s Calhoun b Wayne and Washington
Kenning Fred. clk 86 Barr

KENNING WM., Family Grocery, Provisions and Saloon, 86 Barr.

Kennison Alex. carp bds Union House
Kent Wm. P. blksmith h 139 Clay
Kenton M. messenger wks P., Ft. W. & C. Railway Co
Keoble George, lab h 137 E. Lewis
Keough John, clk Anderson & Evans', bds 117 W. Wayne
Keplinger Jacob, engineer h 51 Madison
Keppler Mrs. Sabina, h 140 W. Main
Kept Gust. mason bds John Koch's
Kercheval Mrs. B. B. widow h 44 W. Wayne
Kerdoe John, lab bds n e c Monroe and Lewis

Kerkhoff Fred. shoe mkr h e s Broadway b Jefferson & George
Kerr James S. carp bds 90 W. Jefferson
Kers Peter, lab wks P., Ft. W. & C. Railway shops
Kersting Christoph, res John Wm. Dachsteiner's, Bloomingdale
Kertler Miss Dorothea, bds 10 W. Water
Kessler James, mach bds Mrs. Ann Graham's

KETCHER & APP, (Paul K. & Mathias A.,) Manufacturers and Dealers in Boots and Shoes, w s Calhoun b Berry and Wayne.

Ketcher Paul, (K. & App,) h 79 W. Washington
Ketchum Newcomb S. mach h n w c Bluffton Road and Nirdlinger
Kettler Mrs. Eliza, h 203 E. Jefferson
Keyser Anton, tailor 71 Columbia, h 125 Madison
Kief David, lab wks P., Ft. W. & C. Railway Co. yard
Kiefer Henry, elk 89 Columbia, h w s Broadway s of Jefferson
Kiefer Martin, carp h 166 E. Washington
Kieser Christ. h 125 Madison
Kieser Henry, shoe mkr h 125 Madison
Kilander Samuel, carp bds Union House
Killay Thomas, lab h s s Colerick b Prince and Fairfield Av
Killen & Morgan, (Miss Nan K. & Miss Sarah M.) dress and cloak mkrs n w c Clinton and Main
Killen Miss Nan, (K. & Morgan,) h n w c Main and Clinton
Killermeyer H. lab wks P., Ft. W. & C. Railway lumber yard
Kilpatrick James, carp h s s Canal b Broadway and Van Buren

KIMBALL BENJAMIN H., Carpenter and Builder, Shop, w s Fulton b Berry and Wayne, h n e c West and Railroad.

Kimball Laura A. teacher Western District School, h n e c West and Railroad
Kimball S. W. carp h e s Broadway b Jefferson and George
Kimball V. M. contractor h 244 W. Berry
Kimball W. P. carp res Benjamin H Kimball's

KIME HOUSE, J. W. Kime, Proprietor, n w c Wayne and Clay.

KIME J. W., Proprietor Kime House, 147 n w c Wayne and Clay.

Kimmel Michael, lab h e s Hanna b Hernden and Jones
Kindle Jacob, carp h s w c Lewis and Monroe
King David, fireman wks P., Ft. W. & C. Railway Co
King Enoch J. res George E. King's
King George, mach wks T. & W. Railway shops
King George E. engineer h n s Lewis b Harrison and Webster
King Jacob, jr., carriage manuf 106 W. Main, h w s Clinton b Main and Berry
Kingman J. blksmith wks P., Ft. W. & C. Railway blksmith shop
Kingsley Henry, conductor h s w c Railroad and Harrison

Kinkead F. B. janitor of Court House, h 142 W. Wayne
Kinlum Adam, lab wks Ed. Burhan's
Kintz A. blksmith wks P., Ft. W. & C. Railway blksmith shop
Kintz John, blksmith res Mrs. Sophia Kintz's
Kintz Louis, b k bds 22 W. Wayne
Kintz Mrs. Sophia, h e s Piqua Plank Road b Virginia and Wallace
Kintz V. helper wks P. F. W. & C. R. R. blksmith shop

KIRBY JAMES A., Agent Singer's Sewing Machines and Aiken's Knitting Machines, No. 2 Aveline House, s e c Calhoun and Berry, h 60 W. Berry.

Kirkham Mrs. Edward, b 137 Madison
Kirkhoff Fred. h s e c Washington and Nelson
Kiser Ambrose, clk h w s Ewing b Wayne and Washington
Kiser Charles, clk Peter Kiser's h 70 W. Wayne
Kiser David, brakeman bds Mrs S. M. French's
Kiser Dietrich, boatman h w s Broadway b Jefferson and Wilt

KISER PETER, Dealer in Dry Goods, Groceries, Hardware, Crockery, &c., e s Calhoun b Columbia and Main, h 70 W. Wayne.

Kiser Peter Jr., clk Co. Auditor's Office bds 70 W. Wayne
Kissan Daniel, lab h n s Bass b Hoagland and Prince

KLAEHN JOHN J., Cabinet-ware Manufacturer, e s Harrison b Main and Columbia, h s s Pearl b Harrison and Maiden Lane.

Klatt Jacob, expressman h Rockhill House
Klaus John, shoemaker bds 48 W. Washington
Klee John, painter bds Peter Ohneck's
Klein Rev. J. H. h s s Washington b Harrison and Webster
Kleinmiller Jno. Henry, teamster h 55 Madison
Kleinsorge Herman, res John H. Wefel's, Bloomingdale
Kley Fred. cooper n s Main b Jackson and Eksall
Klieber Christ, mason res Jones and Bass' Foundry Addition
Kline F. clk W. Jacobs & Son's, h n s Washington b Fulton and Griffith
Kline J. grocer 78 Columbia, h 126 E. Berry
Kline John, clk 78 Columbia, bds J. Kline's

KLINE PETER, Manufacturer of Boots and Shoes, and Dealer in Leather, e s Calhoun b Main and Columbia, h 13 E. Washington.

Kline P. W. saloon n w c Lafayette and Holman
Kline Samuel, carp h 118 E. Wayne
Kling John J. h s s Pearl b Harrison and Maiden Lane
Klinger H. meats w s Calhoun b Main and Berry, h 84 E. Main
Klingmann John, helper h e s Piqua Plank Road b Lasselle and Buchanan
Klist Wm. h 190 W. Washington

Klug Martin, carp wks Fronefield & Todd's
Klusman Henry, clk Peter Pierr's

KNAPP I., Surgeon Dentist, Office and Residence, 32 E. Main near Clinton.

Knave Wm. brakeman bds Mrs. Harriet Toland's
Knecht Dominick, shingles n s W. & E. Canal b Ewing and Griffith, h 24 W. Jefferson
Knecht Frank X. lab h s s High, Bloomingdale
Knight Charles, h n w s Bluffton Road b Wall and Nirdlinger
Knight Charles H. mach wks T. & W. Railway shops
Knight J. H. (Cary & K.) bds James D. Cary's
Knoesz Mrs. Caroline, h 198 W. Wayne
Knost John, lab wks C. S. Brackenridge & Co.'s
Knott Charles, mach wks P., Ft. W. & C. Railway machine shop
Knott Charles, clk 103 Columbia
Knotte Julius, (Krutop & Co.) h 51 E. Jefferson
Knowlton George W. (McDougal & Co.) res New York
Knust J. lab wks P., Ft. W. & C. Railway carp shop
Koegel Christian, carp h e s West b Pritchard and Railroad
Koenig Fred. blksmith h 64 Clinton
Koenig Jacob, blksmith e s Court b Main and Berry, h 64 Clinton
Koenig Jacob J. blksmith h 64 Clinton
Koester Christian, lime dealer h e s Harrison b Jefferson and Lewis
Koch Anton, dray h n s Lewis b Harrison and Webster
Koch Antony, lab wks T. & W. Railway shops
Koch Christian, h 45 W. Jefferson
Koch Christ, carp wks T. & W. Railway shops
Koch Christian F. grain dealer h 45 W. Jefferson
Koch F. lab wks P., Ft. W. & C. Railway carp shop
Koch Frank, carp h w s Calhoun b Washington and Jefferson
Koch John M. teacher h e s Calhoun b Berry and Wayne
Koch Wm. tailor h 123 Lafayette
Kochel Richard, engineer wks John Brown's, res country
Kochmeier Barney, carp wks T. & W. Railway shops
Kock Frank, lab h s s High, Bloomingdale
Kock John Wm. tailor h 123 E. Washington
Kockmeier Barney, carp h 268 E. Washington
Kohlbach A. wks Olds, Hanna & Co.'s
Kohlbecker A. lab wks P., Ft. W. & C. Railway shops
Kohler Daniel, eng h 61 Lafayette
Koko Louie, chambermaid Aveline House
Kolbacher Adam. lab bds 82 E. Jefferson
Komp Daniel, carp h w s Piqua Plank Road b Virginia and Wallace
Koons And. fireman wks P., Ft. W. & C. Railway Co.
Koontz Margaret, reeler res L. Ebner's

9

Kopp John, lab h w s Lima Plank Road, Bloomingdale
Kopple Henry, boiler mkr wks T. & W. Railway shops
Kopt Michael, lab wks Ft. Wayne Machine Works
Koster Christian, (Paul & K.) h s e c Jefferson and Harrison
Koster John, tanner n w c Jefferson and Webster
Kosters J. H. grocery w s Calhoun b Jefferson and Lewis
Kosters John G. boots and shoes w s Calhoun b Jefferson and Lewis
Kouder Benj. driver wks J. O'Connell's
Krah Christian, bklayer h n s Wall w of Bluffton Road
Kramer B. clk n w c Main and Clinton, bds Main Street Exchange
Kramer C. A. clk 103 Columbia h 128 Madison
Kramer Martin, blksmith bds 11 E. Washington
Kramer Wm. lab h 147 Madison
Krannichfeld John, carp h 124 Madison

KRATZSCH HERMAN, Dealer in Family Groceries, Provisions, Notions, &c., w s Calhoun b Berry and Wayne.

Krause Leopold, clk David Sachs', bds Main Street Exchange
Kreamer Wm. molder wks Murray & Bennigin's
Kreeger John, sawyer wks n e c Main and Cass
Kreite Deitrich, carp bds Wm. Horstmeier's
Kress Michael, lab h e s Pine b Taylor and Locust
Kretner Joseph, turner h s w c Wilt and Broadway
Kribel Ludwig, h n s Bowser, Bloomingdale
Krimmel Christian, carp h s s Jefferson b College and Nelson
Krimmel Traugott, tailor w s Calhoun b Wayne and Washington, bds Steuben House
Krone Henry, tinner h s s Douglas, Bloomingdale
Krohn Henry, tinner wks 81 Columbia, h Bloomingdale
Kronemiller Geo. lab h e s Calhoun b Wayne and Washington
Kronmeier John, lab h s s Douglas, Bloomingdale
Kronmiller Geo. lab h s w c Oakley and Taylor
Krueger John, sawyer h 139 Harrison
Kruse E. carp wks T. & W. Railway shops
Kruse Ernst H. lab h 211 Madison
Kruse Henry, lab h n s Montgomery b Clay and Monroe
Kruse John, lab h n s Lewis b Francis and Harmer
Krutop & Co. (John B. K., Fred. Brandt, Julius Knotte & Louis Schrader,) saw mill w s Cass b the Canal and Water
Krutop John B., (K. & Co.,) h 27 W. Jefferson
Kuhlman Conrad, h w s Jackson b Pritchard and Railroad
Kuhlman Sarah, servt Hamilton House
Kull H. lab wks P., Ft. W. & C. Railway shops
Kunz Andrew, fireman bds Fred. Miller's
Kunz G. J. teacher h w s Barr opp Madison
Kunz Jacob, mach h w s Hood b Pritchard and Railroad

Kunz Peter, lab wks Samuel Edsall's
Kunzs John, lab bds 128 E. Washington
Kupp Michael, lab h 236 E. Jefferson
Kuppel P. lab wks P., Ft. W. & C. Railway lumber yard
Kurz Jacob, blksmith h 190 W. Main
Kurz John H. printer Indiana Staats Zeitung office, bds 33 Madison
Kuttner Joseph, carp h 233 E. Jefferson
Kyle Abram P. (Barlow & K.) h 238 W. Wayne
Kyle Wm. B. pump mkr bds 238 W. Wayne

L

Lacey Mrs. Margaret, widow h s e c Main and Edsall
Lacey Patrick, carriage smith bds n e c Main and Lafayette
Laepple Christ. carp wks Murray & Bennigin's
Lafarnes Henry, polisher wks n e c Main and Cass
La France Henry, h n s Jefferson b Rockhill and College
Lagg Wm. carp h w s Broadway b Wilt and Pritchard
Lahmeier Henry, sawyer wks Hurd & Clark's
Lahmeyer Danl. carp h 205 Ewing
Lahmeyer John, cab mkr h n s Wall w of Bluffton Road
Laible Christ. lab h n s Wines b Fairfield Av. and Hoagland
Lamb Chas. bds 123 E. Washington
Lamb Robt. blksmith bds Mrs. Mary A. Saurs'
Lamb Thos. wks W. S. Edsall's
Lamley Moses, (L. & Rosenthal,) h 102 W. Berry

LAMLEY & ROSENTHAL, (Moses L. & Max R.,) Proprietors City Reading Room, and Manufacturers and Dealers in Cigars, Tobacco, &c.; also, Fruit Dealers, w s Calhoun b Main and Columbia.

Lampke Henry, boatman h 19 W. Washington
Lampman Seth, carp bds Union House
Lanagan Patrick, lab h s s Bass b Prince and Hoagland
Lancaster John, mach h rear 122 E. Wayne
Landeman F. helper wks P., Ft. W. & C. Railway repair shops
Landis Jacob A. carp h e s Clinton b Main and Berry
Landsman Fred. lab bds Chas. Prize's
Lane Mrs. Eleanor L. widow res Mrs. Laura McLaughlin's
Lanerky Fred. lab wks T. & W. Railway shops
Laney John, eng bds Albert H. Cook's
Lang Augustus J. b k 63 Columbia
Lang Geo. barber e s Calhoun b Columbia and Main, h o s Clay b Washington and Jefferson
Langan Michael, lab h al b Clinton and Barr 1st n of Water

Lange Rudolph, teacher at Concordia College
Langhan Martin, teamster wks J. K. & H. Baker's
Langohr John Wm. teamster h w s Lima Plank Road, Bloomingdale
Lankenau Francis, carp h 80 W. Jefferson
Lannan Mrs. Ann, h 97 W. Washington
Lape John F. blksmith h s e c Lewis and Webster
Lapp H. lab wks P., Ft. W. & C. Railway carp shop
Large Rev. J. S. h 210 W. Washington
Larue Mrs. Victoria, widow h 200 E. Wayne

LASSELLE FRANCIS D., Farmer, res. Pleasant View, e s Piqua Plank Road, s of the Railroad.

Lasselle Francis J. farmer res Francis D. Lasselle's
Latta Wm. bds Kime House
Lau Miss Susan, (Miss Shilling & Co.) h s w c Calhoun and Washington
Lau Thos. carp h s w c Calhoun and Washington
Laude Joseph, cab mkr bds Hypolite Mannier's
Lauer Conrad, lab h s s Van Wert Road e of corp line
Lauer John, lab wks T. & W. Railway shops
Lauer Paul, bklayer h n s Montgomery b Barr and Lafayette
Lauer Peter, cooper h w s Lima Plank Road, Bloomingdale

LAUFERTY ISAAC, Wholesale and Retail Dealer in Dry Goods, Clothing. Hats, Caps, Carpets, &c., 91 Columbia. h 75 W. Berry.

Lauferty M. J. with Isaac Lauferty 91 Columbia, h 25 W. Wayne
Lavelle Kate waiter at Mayer House
Law Miss Ellen, h 14 W. Washington
Lawler Jane, servt Summit City Hotel
Lawrence Edward E. conductor h 186 E. Washington
Leach Edward, carp h 64 Madison
Leach John S. carp h 160 W. Washington
Leach Reuben, eng bds 225 W. Washington
Lear Julia, waiter Ft. Wayne Eating House
Leaver Frank, cutter 94 Columbia, bds Mayer House
Le Barron Saml. T. conductor bds Mayer House
Lebbekass Joen, lab h n e c Main and Van Buren
Ledford Thomas, painter h s c c Lewis and Webster
Lee Mrs. Ann Maria, laundress Aveline House
Lee David, blksmith wks T. & W. Railway shops
Lee Israel, foreman h 135 Madison
Lee Sarah, laundress Aveline House
Lee Thos. bklayer bds 65 Columbia
Leecaff N. lab wks P., Ft. W. & C. Railway shops
Leeson John, mach bds 123 E. Washington
Leeson Thos. fireman wks P., Ft. W. & C. Railway Co.
Lefley Wm. fireman h w s Hanna b Hough and Holman

Legmeyer Fred. carp wks Cochran, Humphrey & Co.'s
Legras Joseph, eng res John Mangeot's
Lebarrar F. lab wks P., Ft. W. & C. Railway lumber yard

LEHMAN CHAS., Dealer in Lumber, Lath, Shingles, &c., s e c Berry and Clay, h 129 E. Washington.

Lebman John C. painter h 216 E. Washington
Lehncke Fred. helper h 157 Madison
Lehr Justis, plasterer h e s Calhoun b Washington and Jefferson
Lohr Tilghman, bkmkr bds Justis Lehr's
Leieb Henry, plasterer h 77 Madison
Leibold Christoph, cab mkr h w s Webster b Washington and Jefferson
Leifels J. J. b h e s Barr b Montgomery and Holman
Leikhauf Nicholas, lab h e s Hood b Pritchard and Railroad
Leimkuehle Rudolph, h w s Jackson b Pritchard and Railroad
Leinemeier Dietrich, boatman h s s Wilt b Rockhill and College
Leinker Henry, lab h Bloomingdale
Leiple Geo. helper wks P., Ft. W. & C. Railway carp shop
Leithner Mrs. Elizabeth, res Fred. Raab's
Lemkuhl F. foreman lumber yard P., Ft. W. & C. Railway Co.
Lemmon A. R. (Hill & L.) h n s Buchanan b Piqua Plank Road and Clay
Lendmeier Henry, carp wks T. & W. Railway shops
Lenker Henry, cab mkr wks 50 E. Main
Lenney John, eng wks P., Ft. W. & C. Railway Co.
Lennon Chas. clk h w s Barr n of Water
Leonard Lewis, brakeman bds Mrs. Harriet Toland's

LEONARD P. M., Physician and Surgeon; Office, 6 Phœnix Block, w s Calhoun b Main and Columbia, h 154. W. Wayne.

LEONARD WM., Gun Manufacturer, 66 Columbia, h s e c Lewis and Webster.

Leonhard Fred. lab bds 43 W. Water
Leonhard Henry, lab h e s Jackson b Pritchard and Railroad
Leppelo Christian, carp h s w c Railroad and Webster
Lepper Henry, carp h 240 E. Jefferson

LESMAN JACOB, Proprietor Main Street Exchange, n s Main b Calhoun and Harrison.

Lester Miss Sarah, milliner wks Flora Sexton's
Leterle Anton, cooper wks H. S. Brackenridge & Co.'s
Levor Frank, clk bds Mayer House
Lew John, lab h w s Piqua Plank Road s of Buchanan
Lewis Bayless A. dyer bds 57 W. Water
Lewis Clark A. printer Ft. Wayne Gazette office, h 57 W. Water
Lewis H. helper wks P., Ft. W. & C. Railway blksmith shop

Lewis J. J. carp bds Geo. Harter's
Lewis Miss Margaret, bds 245 E. Lewis
Lewis Saml. bds 47 W. Main
Lewis Saml. res Wm. D. McElfatrick's
Lewis Saml. candy mkr wks 83 Columbia
Liebald Christoph, cab mkr wks 50 E. Main
Lieber F. phys h 109 Lafayette
Liggett Robt. plow mkr wks A. D. Reid's, bds Union House
Lillie James, carp h 84 W. Water
Lindeman J. Henry, lab h n s Wilt b Rockhill and College
Lindeman Louis, shoemkr bds 101 W. Washington
Lindeman Louis, res J. Henry Lindeman's
Lindlag C. W. street commissioner h 109 W. Washington
Lindsay ———, tailor bds Geo. Harter's
Linck Thos. blksmith bds w s Lafayette b Main and Columbia
Link Geo. carp h s s Jefferson b Hanna and Francis
Linn C. B. watchmkr 102 Columbia, bds A. J. Emerick's
Liple Gottlieb, lab h s s Durrie b Hoagland and Fairfield Av
Lipler C. helper wks P., Ft. W. & C. Railway machine shop
Lischeid John, carp h n s Douglas Av. b Harrison and Webster
Lisher Jonathan, eng bds Wm. Bealls'

LITTLE GEO. L., Produce, Forwarding and Commission Merchant, w end of Columbia, h 145 W. Water.

Little Wm. brakeman bds s e c Harrison and Railroad
Littler J. C. switchman bds Wm Beals'
Litz Miss Mary E. res Casper Schoerpf's
Livingston Wm. mach wks T. & W Railway shops
Locklin S. W. millwright h s s Holman b Calhoun and Clinton
Loeffler Henry, h 66 W. Jefferson
Logan David A. tel operator T. & W. Railway, bds Mayer House
Lohmeier Henry, lab h s e c Monroe and Montgomery
Lomas Chas. molder h 251 E. Jefferson
Loment Mrs. Margaret, h e s Cass, Bloomingdale
Long John, butcher h 56 W. Wayne
Long John L. clk Wm. H. Brooks, jr. bds 110 W. Main
Longer Ann, cook Aveline House
Longhenry Andreas, h s s Sturgis w of Fulton
Longhenry Mrs. Mena, widow h s s Sturgis w of Fulton
Loomis Chas. molder wks Bowser & Story's
Loos Henry, helper, h e s Piqua Plank Road b Lasselle and Buchanan
Lose L. H. carp h s s Douglas Av. b Harrison and Webster
Lovet C, carp bds Phillips House
Lowe John, lab h w s Piqua Plank Road s of Buchanan
Lower Benedict, (Schille & L.) h n s Wayne b Calhoun and Clinton

Lowrie Gibson, h 106 W. Wayne
LOWRIE REV. JOHN M., D. D., Pastor First Presbyterian O. S. Church; residence, 106 W. Wayne.
Lowrie Matthew B. h 106 W. Wayne
Ludford Thos. painter wks T. & W. Railway Shops
Ludwick Benj. D. lab h n s Washington b Francis and Harmer
Lue John, helper wks P., Ft. W. & C. Railway carp shop
Luehrmann Christ. dray h 257 E. Jefferson
Luers Rt. Rev. John H., Bishop of Fort Wayne, h n e c Calhoun and Lewis
Lulay Frank, core mkr h s e c Jones and Hanna
Lulay Jacob, carp h n c c Hanna and Jones
Lulay Philip, molder h s s Lewis b Clay and Monroe
LUMBARD S., Secretary State Insurance Company, w s Clinton b Main and Columbia.
Lunday John, helper wks P., Ft. W. & C. Railway blksmith shop
Lundy Hugh, dray bds 21 W. Wayne
Lust John, lab wks P., Ft. W. & C. Railway carp shop
Luther Francis M. fireman h s e c Fairfield Av. and Bass
Luxenberger Philip, watchman h n w c Pine and Taylor
Lye L. N. confec h 193 Lafayette
Lynch J. lab wks P., Ft. W. & C. Railway Co. yard
Lynch James, blksmith h s s Railroad b Harrison and Webster
Lynch John, helper bds Thos. Lynch's
Lynch John, teamster res James McKnight's
Lynch Matt. lab h s s Bass b Prince and Hoagland
Lynch Thos. b h w s Kansas s of the Railroad
Lynn Lewis, clk 89 Columbia, h 197 W. Washington
Lytle Wm. b k 91 W. Main h 99 E. Main
Lytler Joseph, switchman P., Ft. W. & C. Railway
Lyward Robt. M. carp h 40 Madison

Mc

McAllaster G. C. Sec Fort Wayne Ins. Co. 5 E. Main, bds 16 Madison
McAllaster Ira C. general agent Fort Wayne Ins. Co. 5 E. Main, bds 16 Madison
McArdle A. J. foreman J. H. McArdle's, h 45 E. Washington
McArdle J. H. gun stock manuf n w c Water and Clinton, res Fremont, Ohio
McARTHUR JOHN W., City Engineer and County Surveyor, Office Court House, bds Mayer House.
McCabe John F. mach bds Thos. Meegan's

McCain Mrs. Margaret, h 62 Barr
McCall ———, bds E. D. Cook's
McCampbell James, wood yard n s Columbia b Barr and Lafayette, h 45 Madison
McCann James, blksmith h 171 E. Lewis
McCardel D. S. carp h 47 Madison
McCardel D. S. carp wks P., Ft. W. & C. Railway Shop
McCarter W. H. bklayer bds Kime House
McCarthy John, blksmith b w s Calhoun b the Railroad and Highland
McCartney John, deputy Sheriff bds Mayer House
McCartney P. coppersmith wks P., Ft. W. & C. Railway coppersmith shop
McCartney Patrick F. tinner h n s Jefferson b Nelson and Garden
McCarty Patrick, lab h s e c Colerick and Hoagland
McCary R. F. blksmith wks P., Ft. W. & C. Railway blksmith shop
McCaul John McG. clk P., Ft. W. & C. Railway Co. Shops, bds c Barr and Jefferson
McClain Wm. carp h e s Barr b Washington and Wayne
McClanahan Geo. cooper wks Haswell & Pierce's
McClaren Mrs. Nancy, widow h n s Main b Maiden Lane and Cass
McClelland A. C. eng wks P., Ft. W. & C. Railway Co.
McColgate James, carp h w s Kansas s of the Railroad
McColgin James, carp wks Cochran, Humphrey & Co.'s
McComb Judson, (McC. & Co.) h 148 W. Berry

M**cCOMB & CO.**, (Judson McC. & John H. Bulger,) **Wholesale Grocers and Vinegar Manufacturers, 117 Columbia.**

McConnell John J. saddler h e s Ewing s of Jefferson
McCormick Adam, teamster h s s Water b Cass and Ewing
McCormick John, brakeman bds Morgan Rose's
McCracken Miss Emily, teacher Eastern District School
McCracken J. K. ticket clerk P., Ft. W. & C. Railway Freight Office, bds Mayer House
McCreary B. F. blksmith h 196 Lafayette
McCulloch Chas. (Allen Hamilton & Co.) res w end of Water
McCulloch Hugh, comptroller of the currency b w end of Water

M**cCULLOUGH T. P., Physician and Surgeon, Office s w c Calhoun and Pearl, Phœnix Block, h n w c Harrison and Douglas Av.**

McCurdy A. R. painter bds Jacob J. Kamm's
McDember Edward, hostler wks Fletcher & Co.'s
McDermott J. brass molder wks P., Ft. W. & C. Railway Repair Shops
McDole John, mach h n e c Clay and Montgomery

McDonald J. carp wks P., Ft. W. & C, Railway carp shop
McDonald J. B. bklayer h n s Holman b Clay and Monroe
McDonnell Patrick, (Gaffeney & McD.) h w s Calhoun near P., Ft. W. & C. Railroad

McDOUGAL & CO., (John McD., E. C. Rurode, and Geo. W. Knowlton,) Proprietors New York Dry Goods Store, 90 Columbia.

McDougal John, (McD. & Co.) h 86 W. Wayne
McDowney John, blksmith bds 143 E. Lewis
McEldowney J. blksmith wks P., Ft. W. & C. Railway blksmith shop
McElfatrick Edward, carp h 152 E. Washington
McElfatrick J. helper wks P., Ft. W. & C. Railway carp shop

McELFATRICK J. B., Architect, Carpenter and Builder, res. 152 E. Washington.

McElfatrick Josiah H. carp h n s Washington b Barr and Lafayette
McElfatrick Samuel, lumber dealer s w c Main and Ewing
McElfatrick Wm. D. planing mill h s w c Clay and Montgomery
McElmeyer John, lightning rod dealer h n s Railroad b Calhoun and Harrison

McELVAIN S., Agent United States and American Express Companies, Office n w c Calhoun and Berry, h 27 W. Berry.

McElwee James, clk 87 Columbia, bds Geo. R. Hartman's
McFee Wm. (Cochran, Humphrey & Co.) h n w c Jefferson and Nelson
McFerson Wm. bklayer bds Wm. Beal's
McGee Owen, lab h s s Bass b Prince and Hoagland
McGee Patrick, Marshal, office at Mayor's office, h s c c Main and Harrison
McGowen Chas. conductor bds Hedekin House
McGovern Alice, servt wks Main Street Exchange
McGraw Thos. lab h n s Bass b Hoagland and Prince
McInnerney Thos. lab h w s Calhoun b Douglas Av. and Baker
McIntosh James, mach wks T. & W. Railway shops
McKanon Bernard, teamster h c s Lima Plank Road, Bloomingdale
McKean Wm. T. foreman at Fort Wayne Machine Works, h 189 E. Jefferson
McKeivey James A. brakeman h s s Webster b Washington and Jefferson
McKenzie Geo. mach h n s Sturgis w of Fulton
McKenzie Miss Mary, res Geo. McKenzie's
McKinley Wm. carp h s w c Fulton and Sturgis
McKnight James, blksmith h s s Lasselle c of Piqua Plank Road
McLachlan Neil (Neil McL. & Co.) h c s Calhoun s of city limits

McLachlan Neil & Co. (Neil McL., Alex. Muirhead, and D. Alliger) saw mill n s W. & E. Canal b Fulton and Griffith
McLain Byron W. teacher at Fort Wayne College
McLain Miss Clara, bds Rev. E. Snider's
McLain Mrs. Susan, bds Rev. E. Snider's
McLane Patrick, ice dealer h 228 E. Jefferson
McLaughlin Christ. molder bds n e c Monroe and Lewis
McLauglin Mrs. Isabella, weaver res Jacob Walter's
McLaughlin Jacob, bklayer bds 82 Barr
McLaughlin Mrs. Laura, widow h s s Jefferson b College and Nelson
McLaughlin Wm. h 231 Barr
McMahan Mrs. Ellen, h w end of Jefferson
McMahan John, h 141 Ewing
McMahan Wm. lab bds 70 Madison
McMaigle S. carp wks P., Ft. W. & C. Railway carp shop
McMaingal Josiah, conductor h 12 W. Washington
McMaken C. S. (Beston & McM.) h n e c Main and Lafayette
McMillan James, boiler mkr h w s Calhoun s of corp. line
McMillan R. P. conductor bds Hedekin House
McMullen Mrs. R. b h 91 E. Washington
McMullen Wm. H. clk 57 Columbia, h 91 E. Washington
McNally Thos. teamster h s s Montgomery b Barr and Lafayette

McNAMARA J. W. & CO., (John W. McN. & Samuel Diffindarfer,) Dealers in Copper and Iron Lightning Conductors, also Manufacturers and Dealers in the Queen of the West Washing Machines, and Ball's Hay, Straw and Fodder Cutter, Office at Orff & Co.'s, 103 Columbia.

McNamara John W. (J. W. McN. & Co.) h 33 W. Lewis
McNamara Thos. lab h 63 Madison
McNulty Geo. W. carp bds 91 E. Washington
McNulty Joseph, carp bds 91 E. Washington
McNulty P. J. carp wks P., Ft. W. & C. Railway carp shop
McNulty Thos. lab h s w c Bass and Hoagland
McNulty W. G. carp shop wks P., Ft. W. & C. Railway carp shop
McPhail Wm. mach h 202 Ewing
McPherson E. L. conductor bds Mayer House
McQuinston Wm. H. teacher Eastern District School

M

Macarthy Wm. printer Sentinel office, bds Kime House
Mack Mary, waiter at Mayer House
Mack Thos. lab h w s Calhoun b Douglas Av. and Baker

MAD ANTHONY DINING ROOM, Jared Cothrell, Proprietor, 65 Columbia.
Madden Rev. Patrick, D. D. h n e c Calhoun and Lowis
Maddux John, carp h s s Washington c Van Buren
Maddux John, carp h e s Griffith b Washington and Jefferson
Madison W. mach wks P., Ft. W. & C. Railway Machine Shop
Maers W. lab wks P., Ft. Wayne & C. Railway carp shop
Maginnis James, boiler mkr h w s Hanna b Hough and Holman
Magnus Chas. wagon mkr h n s Montgomery b Clay and Monroe
Magnus Mrs Louise, h 65 Madison
Magnus Wm F. harness mkr bds American House
Maguire Owen, telegraph repairer P., Ft. W. & C. Railway
Mahan Anthony, lab h n s Baker b Webster and McClellan
Mahan Mrs. Bridget, h n s Jefferson b Fulton and Broadway
Mahan Mrs. Bridget, widow h 103 W. Jefferson
Mahan Mrs. Catharine, widow, h al. b Clinton and Barr 1st n of Water
Mahan James, blksmith bds C. S. Pantlind's
Mahoney D. boiler mkr wks P., Ft. W. & C. Railway boiler shop
Mahoney E. helper wks P., Ft. W. & C. Railway blksmith shop
Mahurin Isaac, teacher h 219 W. Main
Mahurin Miss Matilda L. res Ft. Wayne College
Maier John A. clk 80 Columbia, h 78 Lafayette
Maier John G. grocer 80 Columbia, h 78 Lafayette
Maier Willis D. clk h 78 Lafayette
Maigland Fred. h 230 W. Washington
Mailand Fred. h 230 W. Washington

MAIN STREET EXCHANGE, Jacob Lesman, Proprietor, n s Main b Calhoun and Harrison.
Major John, carp h s s Berry b Calhoun and Clinton
Maley Patrick, helper wks T. & W. Railway Shops
Malline A. A. (Reitzell, Shunk & Co.)
Malone Mrs. Catharine, res John Beck's
Malone Mrs. Elizabeth, widow h o s Hood b Pritchard and Railroad
Malone Patrick, lab bds 70 Madison
Maloney Edward, lab h n s Buchanan b Piqua Plank Road and Clay
Maloney John, carp h 189 Ewing
Maloy Patrick, lab bds John Kelly's
Manaruy John C. carp h n w c Holman and Monroe
Manausch F. carp wks P., Ft. W. & C. Railway carp shop
Mangen John, wks Olds, Hanna & Co.'s
Mangeot John, grocery w s Lafayette b Main and Columbia
Manghin A. lab wks P., Ft. W. & C. Railway lumber yard
Mangun John, lab bds Matt. Lynch's
Manier Frank, carp h s s Lasselle e of Clay

MANIER HYPOLITE, Boarding House and Dealer in Family Groceries, Liquors, &c., 52 Columbia.
Manier J. helper wks P., Ft. W. & C. Railway Machine Shop
Manier L. helper wks P., Ft. W. & C. Railway Machine Shop
Manion Mrs. Bridget, h s w c Walnut and Fairfield Av.
Mannix Geo. blksmith h s w c Lafayette and Montgomery
MANNIX THOS., Boot and Shoe Manufacturer and Dealer, 55 Columbia, h s s Holman b Calhoun and Clinton.
Manocke J. J. blksmith wks P., Ft. W. & C. Railway blksmith shop
MANOK, NESTLE & CO., (Simon N., Philip N. & John Schellhorn,) Proprietors Union Tannery, n s W. & E. Canal b Harrison and Cass.
Manok Simon, (M., Nestle & Co.) h 137 s w c Wayne and Griffith
Mansdoerfer Jacob, weaver bds 156 Harrison
Manze F. lab wks P., Ft. W. & C. Railway lumber yard
Marchal Pierre, lab h s s Lasselle e of Clay
Marhenke Fred. shoemkr h s s High, Bloomingdale
Marhenke H. lab wks P., Ft. W. & C. Railway lumber yard
Marks A. clk 91 Columbia, bds 75 W. Berry
Marks S. lab h n s Holman b Barr and Lafayette
Marsh J. carp wks P., Ft. W. & C. Railway carp shop
Marshall P. lab wks P., Ft. W. & C. Railway shops
Marshall Thos. R. bds Mrs. Carrie Woodward's
Martin Albert, carp h 185 E. Jefferson
Martin Francis H. clk h e s Harrison b Berry and Wayne
Martin Gottlieb, shoemkr h s w c Washington and Nelson
Martin J. blksmith wks P., Ft. W. & C. blksmith shop
Martin J. helper wks P., Ft. W. & C. Railway carp shop
Martin John, lab 222 W. Washington
Martin Lambert, carp h 200 W. Washington
Martin N. carp wks P., Ft. W. & C. Railway carp shop
Martin Terrence, blksmith h 191 E. Jefferson
Martin W. watchman at P., Ft. W. & C. Railway Shops
Martins Wm. watchman h e s Monroe b Lewis and Madison
Marton A. painter wks P., Ft. W. & C. Railway paint shop
Martz ———, carp bds Jacob Aufrecht's
Mason Geo. blksmith h n s Holman b Clay and Lafayette
Mason John C. barber bds 96 Madison
Mason Ralph, lab h n s Colerick b Prince and Hoagland
Mason W. blksmith wks P., Ft. W. & C. Railway blksmith shop
Masters F. P. saddler h 54 W. Wayne
Matthews Samuel, clk bds 58 Madison
Matsch Christoph, carp h 33 W. Jefferson
Matsch Christoph, jr. clk bds 33 W. Jefferson

Matsch J. C. clk T. K. Brackenridge's, bds 33 W. Jefferson
Matsch Wm. carp h s s Lewis b Harrison and Webster
Maxfield Joel, eng h s s High, Bloomingdale
Maxfield Joseph, eng bds Phillips House
Maxfield Orange, miller s s High, Bloomingdale
Maxfield Mrs. Sarah, widow h s s High, Bloomingdale
May E. helper wks P., Ft. W. & C. Railway blksmith shop

MAYER CHAS., Physician and Surgeon, Office and Residence 111 Barr.

MAYER HOUSE, H. C. Fox, Proprietor, s e c Calhoun and Wayne.

MAYERS A., Dealer in Watches, Clocks, Jewelry, Silver Ware, &c., 88 Columbia, h s w c Wayne and Harrison.

MAYOR'S OFFICE, w s Clinton b Columbia and Main, F. P. Randall, Mayor.

Meegan Thomas, chief clk P., Ft. W. & C. Railway shops, h o s Clinton b Jefferson and Lewis
Meenzer Sebastian, tailor h 144 E. Jefferson
Megrady John, plasterer h rear 100 Madison
Mehing Henry, lab h s s Washington b College and Nelson
Mehre Louis, shoemkr h 197 E. Washington
Meichaelis Herman, cigar mkr bds 30 W. Main
Meiland Conrad, helper bds Fred. Berghorn's
Meily Lydia, res Mrs. S. M. French's
Meinhard Chas. A. mach h e s Lafayette b Montgomery and Holman
Meisner Chas. lab h 241 W. Washington
Melching Mrs. Charlotte, h s s High, Bloomingdale
Melia J. wks Olds, Hanna & Co.'s
Melliman C. fireman wks P., Ft. W. & C. Railway Co.
Meloy Bridget, waiter at Mayer House
Menze Fred. lab h 206 Madison
Merde L. mach wks P., Ft. W. & C Railway Machine Shop
Meredith I. P. brakeman h e s Ewing b Wayne and Washington
Meredith John, brakeman h w s Griffith b Washington and Jefferson
Meredith M. V. B. conductor h 136 W. Wayne
Merenke Christ. lab h 108 Madison

MERGEL REINHARD, Dealer in Family Groceries, Provisions, Yankee Notions, Toys, &c., 13 Calhoun, h 94 W. Main.

Merhenke Christ. lab wks Fort Wayne Machine Works
Merriam J. F. dentist 98 Columbia, bds 91 E. Washington
Merriman Orvis H. omnibus driver wks Jno. O'Connell's
Merz Joseph, carp h e s Pine b Taylor and Locust
Merz Peter, carp h 154 E Jefferson
Mesing Chas. blksmith h 75 W. Washington

Mesing Fred. clk Coombs & Drake's
Messersmith Geo. bds Mayer House
Metheany A. M. train dispatcher F., Ft. W. & C. Railway, bds Mayer House
Metheany Andrew, carp h n w c Jefferson and Van Buren
Metheany J. M. tel op P., Ft. W. & C. Railroad, office at depot, bds Mayer House
Mettler & Co., (Mathias M. & Adam Weik,) blinds n s Canal c Lafayette
Mettler Mathias, (M. & Co.) res Washington Tp
Metz George, cab mkr wks Nelson Wheeler's
Metzinger Mrs. h 175 Clinton
Metzinger John, mach h 175 Clinton
Mewroth A. coppersmith wks P., Ft. W. & C. Railway Coppersmith shop
Meyer ———, lab bds 128 E. Washington
Meyer B. molder bds s w c Barr and Jefferson

MEYER & BROTHER, (Christian F. G. & John F. W.,) Wholesale and Retail Dealers in Drugs, Medicines, Paints, Oils, Glass, Dye Stuffs, &c., 95 Columbia.

Meyer Charles F. W. clk C. L. Hill's, h 139 Harrison
Meyer Christian, carp h 45 W. Washington
Meyer Chistian F. G. (M. & Bro.) res Glendale Garden
Meyer Ernst, shoe mkr h 137 E. Lewis
Meyer F. C. clk post office, h 45 W. Washington
Meyer Fred. h 139 Harrison
Meyer Fred. carp h 175 E. Lewis
Meyer Fred. helper bds s w c Barr and Jefferson
Meyer Fred. molder h n s Lewis b Harrison and Webster
Meyer Fred. tailor h s s Wilt b Rockhill and College
Meyer Fred. teamster h n w c Douglas Av. and Webster

MEYER GEORGE, Bakery, w s Lima Plank Road, Bloomingdale.

Meyer Henry, blksmith shop s s Water b Calhoun and Clinton, h 150 W. Jefferson
Meyer Henry, clk 99 Columbia, bds Wm. Snyder's
Meyer Henry, clk bds 46 W. Washington
Meyer John, carp wks T. & W. Railway shops
Meyer John, rope mkr h s s Wall w of Bluffton Road
Meyer John F. W. (M. & Brother,) h 22 W. Washington
Meyer John H. clk 95 Columbia, h 118 Harrison
Meyer John M. lab h e s Hanna b Hernden and Jones
Meyer Lorenz, driver H & M. Niermann's, h 47 E. Jefferson
Meyer Louis, tailor h s s Montgomery b Barr and Lafayette
Meyer Nicholas, plasterer h 183 E. Jefferson
Meyer Sophia, serv't Hamilton House
Meyers Andrew, jeweler h 29 W. Wayne

Meyer Thomas C. engineer Western Division P., Ft. W. & C
Railway, office at depot
Meyers Charles F. clk post office, h 45 W. Washington
Meyers Fred. clk Charles Fink's, bds 55 W. Main
Meyers Fred. tailor wks 98 Columbia
Meyers Fred. lab wks 23 E. Main
Meyers Fred. lab wks Ft. Wayne Machine Works
Meyers George C. carp h 39 W. Jefferson
Meyers Henry, helper h n s Lewis b Clay and Monroe
Meyers John, clk bds Main Street Exchange
Meyers Mena, chambermaid Aveline House
Meyers Wm. H. phys h 186 E. Washington
Miener Michael, tanner h w s Lima Plank Road, Bloomingdale
Miles Charles, engineer wks P., Ft. W. & C. Railway Co.
Miles David, mach h e s Barr b Lewis and Montgomery
Millard Wm. carp h n s Butler b Hoagland and Fairfield Av.
Miller Andrew, carp h s s Washington b College and Nelson
Miller C. W. carp wks P., Ft. W. & C. Railway carp shop
Miller Chas. coppersmith h n s Taylor w of Pine
Miller Chas. lab wks T. & W. Railway shops
Miller Chas. tinner wks 87 Main
Miller Chas. T. tinner h w s Webster b Washington and Jefferson
Miller Christopher, clk bds 55 W. Main
Miller Clem. painter wks T. & W. Railway shops
Miller Clemens, bkmason h s s Locust w of Pine
Miller Mrs. Elizabeth, widow h 62 Columbia
Miller Mrs. Elizabeth, widow h n s Buchanan e of Piqua Plank
Road
Miller F. fireman wks P., Ft. W. & C. Railway Co.
Miller Fred. eng h s s Hough b Clay and Monroe
Miller Fred. lab h s w c Force and Hernden
Miller Geo. h 10 W. Berry
Miller Geo. fireman bds 225 W. Washington
Miller George, cooper bds Fred. Kley's
Miller H. mach wks P., Ft. W. & C. Railway Machine Shops
Miller Henry, bds Steuben House
Miller Henry, bklayer h 20 W. Jefferson
Miller J. J. h 81 E. Washington
Miller Jacob, clk 103 Columbia, h 200 E. Washington
Miller Jacob, chair mkr wks 50 E. Main
Miller John, wks James McCampell's*
Miller Jessamiah, carp bds Wm. Johnston's
Miller Jesse, carp wks Cochran, Humphrey & Co.'s
Miller John, lab h w s Griffith s of Jefferson
Miller John Henry, mach h e s Cass, Bloomingdale
Miller John, teamster h s s Washington b College and Nelson
Miller Louis, paint shop n s Main b Clinton and Barr
Miller Martin, b k h 10 W. Berry

MILLER JOHN M., Manufacturer and Dealer in Fine Furniture, Chairs, Husk and Hair Mattresses, Looking Glass Plates, &c., 50 and 52 E. Main, h 52 E. Jeff rson.
Miller Michael, carp h 218 W. Washington
Miller P. boiler mkr wks P., Ft. W. & C. Railway boiler shop
Miller Peter, b h n s Douglas Av. b Webster and McClellan
Miller Peter, carp bds Union House
Miller Sylvester, carp bds Mrs. Hannah Whaley's
Miller Valentine, blksmith bds Union House
Miller W. lab wks P., Ft. W. & C. Railway carp shop
Miller Wm. clk 63 Columbia h 200 E. Washington
Miller Wm. clk 129 Columbia, h 190 W. Main
Miller Xavier, watchman res Jones & Bass' Foundry Addition
Millering Chas. bklayer h 214 W. Washington
Miller's Hall, n w c Calhoun and Berry
Milliman C. V. N. justice of the peace, h s s Lewis b Lafayette and Monroe
Milliman R. L. clk T. K. Brackenridge's, h s s Lewis b Lafayette and Clay
Mills A. J. H. h s w c Wayne and Jackson
Mills Andrew, painter wks T. & W. Railway shops
Miner B. D. office 91 W. Main res country
Miner Wanton, lab h n s Pearl b Ewing and Griffith
Minnewisch Fred. carp h 200 Barr
Minnie Hattie, h n s Water b Clinton and Barr
Minton T. D. carp h w s Rockill b Wilt and Pritchard
Mischo Michael, stone cutter h w s Broadway b Wilt and Pritchard
Mitchell A. V. carp bds 112 E. Berry
Mitchell Alex. blksmith h 162 Ewing
Mitten James B. carp bds Union House
Moak Harrison, switchman wks T. & W. Railway shops
Moak Harry, eng bds Luther Wright's
Moehring M. E. h 69 W. Berry
Mohlmeister Henry, boots and shoes, w s Calhoun b Washington and Jefferson, h 129 W. Wayne
Mohr John, boots and shoes, 46 Columbia
Mohr Louis, shoemkr h 46 Columbia
Mohring Henry, lab wks Fort Wayne Machine Works
Mollring H., mach wks P., Ft. Wayne & C. Railway Machine Shop
Momer John, lab h s s Lewis b Clay and Monroe
Momer Louis, lab res John Momer's
Mommer Joseph, clk B. Phillips', h 133 W. Main
MONNING HENRY, Dealer in Groceries, Liquors, Wines, Cider, Vinegar, &c., 13 and 15 E. Main, h 69 Lafayette.

Monning John, h rear 7 W. Water
Montgomery David, helper wks T. & W. railway shops
Montgomery Henry, clk John Beck's, h e s Harrison b Main and Pearl
Moon Eugene W. printer Fort Wayne Sentinel office, bds 163 E. Berry
Mooney Wm. lab h o s Calhoun n of Water
Moore John, blksmith wks Bowser & Story's
Moore John, stone cutter bds American House
Moore John, lab bds John Kelly's
Moore John C. fireman h n s Jefferson b Broadway and Van Buren
Moore Miss Nancy, teacher bds 144 E. Main
Moore Thos. L. shoemkr h n e c Washington and Griffith
Moran P. fireman bds Luther Wright's
Moran Peter, ice dealer h 201 E. Wayne
Morehouse Mrs. Mary, h 18 E. Wayne
Morell Christian, lab h 16 W. Wayne
Morey Elwin, conductor bds 107 W. Wayne

MORGAN & BUECH, (Oliver P. M. & Frederick B.) Dealers in Stoves, Hardware, Cutlery, Iron, Nails, and Manufacturers of Tin, Copper and Sheet Iron Ware, 81 Columbia.

Morgan Geo. C. resident eng P., Ft. W. & C. Railway, bds Aveline House
Morgan John B. mach h w s Jackson b Berry and Wayne
Morgan Oliver P. (M. & Buech,) h 54 E. Washington
Morgan Miss Sarah, (Killen & M.) h n w c Main and Clinton
Morrell John, molder h s w c Force and Herndon
Morris Mrs. Ann, 16 W. Washington
Morris Mrs. Dora, widow h 191 W. Main
Morris Miss Ellen, h 16 W. Washington
Morris John, (Withers M. & Case) h 126 W. Jefferson
Morris John R. hostler bds Philips House
Morris Wm. h 16 W. Washington
Morrison A. M. carp bds 91 E. Washington
Morrison Patrick, tailor h. n s Water opp Ewing
Morrow Mrs E. M. widow h n s Wall w of Bluffton Road
Morse A. A. clk 107 Columbia, bds Hamilton House

MORSE CHAS. E., Master Transportation Western Division P., Ft. W. & C. Railway, Office at Depot, h 27 Douglas Av.

Morss Augustus B. messenger P., Ft. W. & C. R. R. Freight Depot, bds Benj Morrss
Morse Benj. checkman P., Ft. W. & C. R. R. Freight Depot, h n s Madison b Barr Lafayette
Morss Mrs. S. S. widow h n s Douglas Av. b Harrison and Webster

Morton James h 151 Barr
Morton J. boiler mkr wks P., Ft. W. & C. Railway boiler shop
Morton J. helper wks P., Ft. W. & C. Railway machine shop
Moseley E. clk bds Main Street Exchange
Moser Mathias, lab h w s Lima Plank Road, Bloomingdale
Mosshamer Mathias, boiler mkr h 56 E. Main
Mossler A. 96 Columbia h s s Water w of Harrison
Mossler H. clk 96 Columbia, bds s s Water w of Harrison

MOSSLER LOUIS H., Dealer in Staple, Foreign and Domestic Dry Goods, Clothing, &c., (formerly the New York Auction Store) 96 Columbia, bds s s Water w of Harrison.

Mower J. S. clk Superintendent's Office P., Ft. W. C. Railway h 25 Douglas Av.
Moyer, Albert L. messenger W. U. Telegraph, h 189 W. Washington
Moyer & Bowers (Lewis M. & Lewis L. B.) boots and shoes, n e c Calhoun and Railroad
Moyer Harman L. printer Ft. Wayne Gazette office, h 189 W. Washington
Moyer Lewis, (M. & Bowers) h 189 W. Washington
Mudge S. R. eng h s s Jefferson b Broadway and Van Buren
Muchlmeister Henry, shoemkr h 129 W. Wayne
Muehring Henry, lab h e s Monroe b Montgomery and Holman
Muellenbourgh Herman, cigar mkr bds Steuben House
Mueller Chas. Wm. baker bds 92 E. Main
Mueller Gustav, printer, Indiana Demokrat office, bds Steuben House
Mueller Henry, lab wks T. & W. Railway shops
Muellerring Chas. (Kanne & Co.)
Muellerring Wm. (Kanne & Co.) h s s Montgomery b Lafayette and Clay
Muellring Henry, mach h 55 E. Lewis
Muenzer Sebastian, tailor h 144 E. Jefferson
Muhl Geo. wagon mkr h 51 E. Water

MUHLENBRUCH D. & BRO., (Didrich & Gottreich) Wagon Manufacturers, s s Water b Calhoun and Clinton.

Muhlenbruch Didrich, (D. M. & Bro) h 213 E. Jefferson
Muhlenbruch Gottreich, (D. Muhlenbruch & Bro.) bds 213 E. Jefferson
Muhlenbruch Wm. wagon mkr h 148 W. Jefferson
Muhler Chas F. tinner h 29 W. Berry
Muhler Chas. M. (Graffe & M.) h 29 W. Berry.
Muirhead Alex. (Neil McLachlan & Co.) h n s Lewis b Harrison and Webster
Muirhead Alex. Jr. mach res Alex. Muirhead's
Mungovern Thos. C. blksmith wks T. & W. Railway shops

Munson Chas A. clk Geo L. Little's, h 176 W. Washington
Murchy Daniel, lab h n e c Jackson and Railroad
Murchy David, carp wks T. & W. Railway shops
Murchy David II. mach bds 156 Harrison
Murnay John, stoker h 81 E. Water
Murphy Dennis, watchman h 123 Lafayette
Murphy Edward, helper wks T & W. Railway shops
Murphy Geo. lab h s s Colerick b Hoagland and Prince.
Murphy Joseph, mach wks P., Ft. W. & C. Railway machine shops
Murphy Michael, lab h n s Madison b Hanna and Francis
Murphy Pat. helper wks P., Ft. W. & C. Railway blksmith shop
Murphy Patrick, spinner h n s alley b Clinton and Calhoun and Water and Duck

MURRAY & BENNIGIN (Kerr M. & Hug'i B.) Iron Foundry and Machine Shop e s Calhoun s of the Railroad.

MURRAY & Co. (G. W. M. & Wm. Augustine) Produce Dealers s s Columbia b Clinton and Barr.

Murray G. W. (M. & Co.) bds Aveline House
Murray John, carp wks P., Ft. W. & C. Railway carp shop
Murray John, mach wks P., Ft. W. C Railway machine shop
Murray John, stone cutter wks n e c Main and Cass
Murray Kerr, foreman machine shop T. & W. Railway, h 201 Ewing
Myers Bryan, molder wks Ft. Wayne machine works
Myers Deitrich, saloon n e c Main and Harrison
Myers Felix, hostler wks 45 Columbia
Myers G. carp wks P., Ft W. & C. Railway carp shop
Myers J. blksmith wks P., Ft. W. & C. Railway blksmith shop
Myers John, carp bds 177 Harrison
Myers Jerry, carp h w s Lafayette b Lewis and Montgomery
Myers W. H. lightning rod agt h w s Fairfield Av. b T. & W. R. R. and Locust
Myers Wm. blksmith bds Summit City Hotel

MYERS WM. H., Physician and Surgeon, s w c Calhoun and Main, h s w c Monroe and Washington.

Myerson David P. clk 106 Columbia bds Philip Myerson's
Myerson Philip, clk 105 Columbia, h 136 W. Berry
Myerson Raphael, res Marx Graff's
Myland C. helper wks P., Ft. W. & C. Railway shop
Myland F. carp wks Pt. Ft. W. & C. R. R. carp shop

N

Naab Geo. h e s Jackson b Pritchard and Railroad
Nabe C. lab wks P. Ft. W. & C. Railway lumber yard
Nachtrieb J. F. hats and caps 82 Columbia
Nagel Fred. lab h 93 W. Jefferson
Nagle Fred. porter Toledo & Wabash Railway office
Nagle John, harness mkr wks L. Troub & Co.'s
Napierski John, lab h e s Calhoun n of Water
Nash S. C. clk 125 Columbia, h 81 W. Main

NATER JOHN H., Saloon and Dealer in Family Groceries, Provisions, &c., w s Calhoun b Washington and Jefferson.

National Hotel, e s Barr b Montgomery and Holman
Nave Wm. brakeman bds Mrs. Harriet Toland's
Nay D. DeWitt, clk 107 Columbia, bds Hamilton House
Neary James, fireman bds 107 W. Wayne
Neeb Caspar, lab h w. end Bowser, Bloomingdale
Neerman J. blksmith wks P., Ft. W. & C. Railway blksmith shop
Neff John Jacob, (Buchfink & N.) h 63 E. Water
Neher Joseph, shoemkr h 111 W. Water
Neidhefer Wm. lab h n s Jefferson b Lafayette and Clay
Neireiter Caspar, harness mkr 122 Columbia, h 49 W. Wayne
Neireiter Christian, shoemkr h n e c Calhoun and Jefferson
Neireiter Conrad, h n e c Calhoun and Jefferson

NEIREITER CONRAD, Dealer in all kinds of Saddlery Hardware and Manufacturer and Dealer in Saddles, Harness, Collars, Trunks, &c. 122 Columbia h c Wayne and Griffith.

Neireiter J. lab wks P., Ft. W. & C. Railway carp shop
Neireiter John, hostler American House
Neill Lewis, mason h 18 E. Wayne
Nelson De Groff, (DeGroff N & Co.) h n s New Haven Road, 4 miles e of city

NELSON De GROFF & CO., (De Groff N. & Isaac D. G. Nelson) Elm Park Nursery, n s New Haven Road 4 miles e of city.

Nelson Elizabeth at Old Fort House
Nelson Elmore, hatter h 64 W. Wayne
Nelson Isaac D. G. (De Groff Nelson & Co.) h n e s New Haven Road, 4 miles e of city
Nelson Wm. R. deputy clk Circuit Court, bds Hamilton House
Nestel Daniel, b'ksmith h s w c Jefferson and Broadway
Nestle Philip, (Manok, N. & Co.) h n e c Lewis and Lafayette

Neumann Alex. tailor h 93 E. Jefferson
Neuroth Anton, coppersmith h s s Taylor b Fairfield Av. and Oakley
Neuthopper W. laborer wks P.. Ft. W. & C. Railway lumber yard
Newell Chas D. eng h 152 W. Washington
Newell Wm. brakeman bds Mrs. Harriet Toland's
Newhart Edward, clk James H. Robinson's, h 45 Barr
Newkirk Frank, bar k h s e Pearl and Maiden Lane
Newman John, mach bds Thos Meagan's
Newman W. H. agt T. & W. Railway Co., office Railroad w of Calhoun, h 128 E. Wayne
Ney Edward, striker h n w c Colerick and Hoagland
Niar Chas. carriage mkr bds s e c Calhoun and Washington
Nicholas John, carp wks T. & W. Railroad shops
Nichols Geo. M. lab h 103 W. Jefferson
Nichols Mrs. Harriet, widow h 60 Clinton
Nichols John L. h s s Holman b Clay and Monroe
Nichols John L. blksmith h 40 Madison
Nichols Lucinda, servt Helekin House
Nichter Joseph, watchman wks T. & W. Railway shops
Nickum Wm. teamster bks Patrick Mc Lane's
Niemann Gotlieb, clk n w c Calhoun and Washington
Niemeyer Henry, teamster h 157 Madison
Nier Chas. wagon mkr wks Thos. Stevens'

NIERMANN H. & M., (Hermann & Martin,) Proprietors Stone Brewery, s w c Water and Harrison.

Niermann Hermann, (H. & M. N.) h 46 W. Water
Niermann Martin, (H. & M. N.) h 43 W. Water
Nies Chas. tailor 71 Columbia, h 241 E. Washington
Nies Mrs. Helena, widow h 241 E. Washington
Nieser Barney, tinner wks 77 Columbia
Niesser Louis, mach h 20 W. Jefferson

NILL C., Boot and Shoe Manufacturer, 80 w s Calhoun b Berry and Wayne, up stairs; h n e c Washington and Harrison.

Nill Conrad, c'k George Nill's res Bloomingdale
Nill Geo. boots and shoes w s Calhoun b Columbia and Main, res Bloomingdale
Nill John, shoemkr h n w s Bluffton Road b Pritchard and Railroad
Ninde Lindley M. (N. & Taylor,) h Fairfield Av.

NINDE & TAYLOR, (Lindley M. N. & R. Stewart T.,) Attorneys at Law; Office, n s Main b Calhoun and Harrison, up stairs.

Nirdlinger Fred. (N. & Oppenheimer,) h 33 W. Main

NIRDLINGER & OPPENHEIMER, (Fred. N. & Abraham O.,) Merchant Tailors, Clothiers and Dealers in Gents' Furnishing Goods, 105 Columbia.

Nitsche Chas. saloon w s Lima Plank Road, Bloomingdale
Nix Valentine, shoemkr h 80 E. Jefferson
Noel F. A. carp wks P., Ft. W. & C. Railway carp shop
Noel Frank, bds 49 E. Lewis
Noel Mrs. S. C. widow bds Hamilton House
Noel Wm. brakeman bds Peoples House
Nohe Joseph, shoemkr h n e c Broadway and George
Nohe Wm. shoemkr h 173 E. Washington
Nolan Mrs. Catharine, widow h 66 Madison
Nolan James, brakeman bds 66 Madison
Nolan John, lab h n s Washington b Monroe and Hanna
Nolan Michael, lab b 128 Madison
Nolen Cyrus, carp h s s Wayne b Francis and Harmer
Noll Adam A. tinner res Geo. Noll's
Noll Alfred, tinner h 246 E. Lewis
Noll Benedict, clk 7 Clinton, h 115 Barr
Noll Chas. (N. & Ofenloh,) h 22 E. Berry
Noll Geo. lab h n s Lewis b Hanna and Francis
Noll John, cashier 103 Columbia, h 215 E. Lewis
Noll John F. clk 7 Clinton, h 115 Barr

NOLL MARTIN, Manufacturer of and Dealer in Boots and Shoes, 7 Clinton, h 115 Barr.

Noll Martin, res Peter Noll's
Noll Martin A. clk W. E. Hood's, bds Jacob Fry's
Noll & Ofenloh, (Chas. N. & Peter O.) saloon 22 E. Berry
Noll Peter, painter h n s Jefferson b Lafayette and Clay
Nongasser Louis C. turner h w s Hood b Pritchard and Railroad
Noonan James, blksmith bds n e c Monroe and Lewis
Norman Henry, cigar mkr bds St. Charles Restaurant
Nortman Henry, cigar mkr bds St. Charles
Norwall Wm. carp bds 51 W. Washington
Nugent Miss Ellen, milliner wks Flora Sexton's

NUTTMAN J. D., President First National Bank of Fort Wayne, h n e c Berry and Griffith.

Nye Lyman O. shoemkr b 132 W. Washington

O

Oahrle Geo. cab mkr wks 50 E. Main

OAKLEY B. W., Wholesale and Retail Dealer in Hardware, Cutlery, Saddlery and Carriage Trimmings, Belting, &c., 79 Columbia, h 79 W. Berry.

Oakley C. B. with B. W. Oakley 79 Columbia, h 79 W. Berry
O'Brian James, res Thos. O'Brian's
O'Brian Maria, waiter Aveline House
O'Brian Thos. helper h e s Webster b Highland and Dawson

O'CALLAHAN JOHN, Wholesale Dealer in Groceries, Provisions, Pure Liquors, Wine, &c., 120 Columbia, bds Mayer House.

O'CONNELL D., Billiard Room and Restaurant, e s Calhoun b Mayer and Aveline Houses, h 9 E. Wayne.

O'CONNELL JOHN, Ft. Wayne Omnibus Line; Office, at D. O'Connell's Billiard Room, h 9 E. Wayne

O.'Connors B. mach wks P., Ft. W. & C. Railway machine shop
O'Conner Bernard, h 213 W. Washington
O'Conner Cornelius, lab h 128 Madison
O'Conner James, h 213 W. Washington
O'Conner James, mach wks T. & W. Railway shops
O'Conner John, bds 49 E. Lewis
Odd Fellows Hall, e s Calhoun b Columbia and Main
Odery N. carp wks P., Ft. W. & C. Railway carp shop
Oehler Geo. carp bds John Koch's
Oelker ———, lab h 167 W. Washington
Oetzel Frank, lab h s s Jefferson b Fulton and Broadway
Ofenloh Michael, painter h w s Francis b Madison and Lewis
Ofenloh Peter, (Noll & O.) h 22 E. Berry
Ofenloh Peter, h w s Francis b Madison and Lewis
Ofenloh V. painter wks P., Ft. W. & C. Railway paint shop
O'Gorman Mrs. Bridget, b h n s Railroad b Calhoun and Harrison
O'Grady Danl. lab h n s Lewis b Francis and Harmer
O'Herron James, helper h e s Prince b Colerick and Williams
Ohneck Peter, painter n s Pearl b Calhoun and Harrison, h n s Jefferson b Barr and Lafayette
Ohnhouse John E. teacher h 140 E. Jefferson
Old Fort House, n e c Main and Lafayette

OLDS, HANNA & CO., (N. G. O., Samuel H., H. C. Hanna & Henry G. Olds,) Proprietors Fort Wayne Spoke, Hub and Bending Factory, s s of the Railroad e of Lafayette.

Olds Henry G. (O., Hanna & Co.) h 27 Madison
Olds John D. mach h 27 Madison
Olds N. G. (O., Hanna & Co.) h 27 Madison
Olds S. N. hatter 97 Columbia, h e s of Calhoun n of Water
O'Neil Andrew, servt Hamilton House
O'Neil Kitty, servt Hamilton House
Oppelt Joseph, lab h n w c Main and Fulton
Oppenheimer Abraham, (Nirdlinger & O.) h 43 W. Berry
Oppenheimer Jacob, clk Vigdor Jacobson's
Orbison Alex. M. (Hill & O.) h 88 W. Berry
Orff Christian, (O. & Co.) h 4 W. Water c Calhoun

ORFF & CO., (Christian O. & John Orff,) Dealers in Staple and Fancy Dry Goods, Millinery Goods, 103 Columbia.

Orff Gottleib, carp h 150 Clinton
Orff Henry, music teacher h 230 E. Washington

ORFF JOHN, Proprietor Empire Flour Mills, w end of Main, res Country.

Ornan C. lab wks P., Ft. W. & C. Railway carp shop
O'Rourke P. S. conductor h w s McClellan opp Douglas Av.

ORPHANS' HOME AND FORT WAYNE HOSPITAL, n w c Wayne and Webster, Bernard Rekers, Proprietor.

Orr John Wm. fireman h e s Lafayette b Lewis and Montgomery
Orr Robt. M. fireman bds John Wm. Orr's
Ortstadt John, cutter 71 Columbia, h 140 Harrison
Osgood Moses R. fireman wks T. & W. Railway Co.
O'Shaunnessey Bridget, waiter Aveline House
O'Shaunnessey Martin, lab h n s Bass b Hoagland and Prince
Osterman Henry, cooper bds Lambert Osterman's
Osterman Lambert, dray h n s Washington b Hanna and Francis
O'Sullivan J. blksmith wks P., Ft. W. & C. Railway blksmith shop
Otto Herman, lab h 124 Madison
Overley Martin, lab h w s Hanna s of Lasselle
Overley Thos. boatman h s s Canal b Broadway and Van Buren

P

Paals Geo. carp wks P., Ft. W. & C. Railway carp shop
Page E. B. fireman bds Summit City Hotel
Pageler John Henry, blksmith bds s w c Barr and Jefferson
Paielthorp Henry, lab h w s Oakley b Walnut and Poplar

PALACE HALL BILLIARD SALOON, Gilbert Brewer, Proprietor, n s Calhoun b Main and Berry.
PANTLIND C. S., Wagon and Blacksmith Shop, 28 Harrison, h n s Main b Griffith and Fulton.
Pantlind Henry D. h 60 Clinton
Pape Carl, teamster h s s High, Bloomingdale
Pape Wm. boatman h s s High, Bloomingdale
Parent H. bds Mayer House
Parent Hiram J. stable e s Calhoun b Wayne and Washington, h 206 W. Washington
Parent Mrs. Rachel, widow dress mkr h n o c Calhoun and Wayne
Parisoe Louis, h 89 Madison
Parisoe Louis, eng h 118 Clay
Parker J. R. helper h s w c Piqua Plank Road and Virginia
Parker R. R. (Spencer & P.) res Indianapolis
Parks Jonathan, h 170 W. Wayne
Parks Mrs. Mary, widow res Wm. Millard's
Parks Volney, bds Francis M. Luther's
Parnin August, clk 89 Columbia, h 206 E. Wayne
Parragy Peter, lab h 103 Madison
Parrott John P. wagon mkr h 167 W. Washington
Pasonoe Joseph, mach h 77 Madison
Patten Chas. (Howly & P.) h n s Water b Clinton and Barr
Patterson Miss Melinda, res Tobias Kauffman's
Patterson Harvey, cab mkr bds Hedekin House
Patton Chas V. brakeman h 156 Madison
Patton Geo. D. conductor h s s Madison b Hanna and Francis
Patton Jesse T. brakeman h 156 Madison
Paul Ben. carp wks Cochran, Humphrey & Co.'s
Paul Chas. boatman h s s High, Bloomingdale
Paul Ferdinand, blksmith h 63 W. Jefferson
Paul Fred. helper h s w c Harrison and Highland
Paul Henry, cab mkr wks 50 E. Main
Paul J. lab wks P., Ft. W. & C. Railway carp shop
PAUL & KOSTER, (William P. & Christian K.,) Cement, Lime and Stone Dealers, n e c Pearl and Cass.
Paul Wm. (P. & Koster.) h 16 W. Jefferson
Paulhamus J. H. eng wks P., Ft. W. & C. Railway Co.
Payne Wm. lab wks Fronefield & Todd's
Payne Wm. C. bds 26 W. Water
Pease ———, brakeman bds 225 W. Washington
Peirce Jacob, clk e s Calhoun b Washington and Jefferson
PELTIER & BOCKELOH, (Louis P. & Chas. B.,) Undertakers, 24 E. Berry.
Peltier Louis, (P. & Bockeloh,) h 49 E. Lewis

Pens C. E. h 196 W. Washington
Peoples House, w s Calhoun b Jefferson and Lewis
Pepler Jacob, clk n e c Calhoun and Main
Pepple Geo. W. carp h 233 E. Jefferson
Pequagnot Frank, carp h n s Buchanan e of Piqua Plank Road
Pequenot Felix, clk 79 Columbia, bds 79 W. Berry
Perot August, lab h n s Lasselle e of Piqua Plank Road
Perrey John Joseph. wagon mkr wks Michael Fischer's
Perry ———, cooper wks C. S. Brackenridge & Co.'s
Perry Jerome, wks Olds, Hanna & Co.'s
Perry John, eng h n s Washington b Clay and Monroe
Perry Melissa, clk 83 Columbia
Peters Wm. carp wks T. & W. Railway shops
Peterson David, conductor h w s Hanna b Madison and Jefferson
Peterson James, cooper bds Sylvanus Currant's
Petgen Nicholas, servt at Saml. Hanna's
Petrie ———, blksmith h s s Lewis b Monroe and Hanna
Petrie Frank C. mach h 96 E. Jefferson
Pettit Amelia, teacher Western District, bds 117 W. Wayne
Pettit Miss Sarah, school s s Berry b Griffith and Ewing, bds John E. Hill's
Pettyjohn Aug. clk W. E. Hood's
Pettys Nathan, mach h s e c Barr and Jefferson
Petzinger Fred. h w s Lima Plank Road, Bloomingdale
Pfeiffer Chris. cattle broker h e s Lima Plank Road n W. and E. Canal Feeder
Phelps Abbie, teacher Eastern District school, h 107 W. Wayne
Phelps C. N. 107 W. Wayne
Phelps Geo. brakeman h 107 W. Wayne
Phelps Willard, tinner bds 57 Barr
Philip Brother, teacher h n e c Calhoun and Lewis
Philley S. R. carp h 40 Monroe
Phillibam John, broom mkr h s s Railroad b Harrison and Webster
Phillips B. grocer e s Calhoun b Main and Columbia, h 121 W. Main
Phillips B. B. lab wks Neil, McLachlan & Co.'s
PHILLIPS GEO., Proprietor Phillips House, n w c Columbia and Lafayette.
Phillips Geo. W. carp h w s Calhoun b Highland and Dawson
PHILLIPS HOUSE, George Phillips, Proprietor, n w c Columbia and Lafayette.
Phillips Michael, lab h n s Colerick b Prince and Hoagland
Phillips Stephen W. blksmith h 131 E. Washington
Phœnix Block, n w c Main and Calhoun
PHŒNIX GROCERY, T. K. Brackenridge, Proprietor, w s Calhoun, 3d door s of Berry.

FORT WAYNE (POS) DIRECTORY. 147

Pickard Thos. foreman Fort Wayne Machine Works, h 78 Madison
Piepenbrink Adam, basket mkr wks 48 Columbia
PIEPENBRINK CHRISTIAN, Boot and Shoe Manufacturer, Notary Public, Foreign Express and Emigrant Agent, n w c Calhoun and Jefferson.
Piepenbrink Ernst, clk Adolph Spercisen's
Piepenbrink Ernst, shoemkr bds 43 W. Washington
Pierce Allen W. teacher bds Geo. Harter's
Pierce J. S. (Haswell & P.) h 257 W. Wayne
Pierr Jacob, clk Peter Pierr's, h e s Calhoun b Washington and Jefferson
Pierr Nathaniel, lab wks Ft. Wayne Machine Works
Pierr Nicholas, lab h 139 E. Washington
PIERR PETER, Dealer in Dry Goods, Groceries, Provisions, Dried Fruits, &c., s w c Calhoun and Pearl, h 39 W. Washington.
PIPENBRINK CONRAD D., Boot and Shoe Manufacturer and Dealer, 54 W. Washington, h 48 W. Washington.
Piper Fred. mach h 69 W. Jefferson
PITTSBURGH FT. WAYNE & CHICAGO RAILWAY CO.; Office and Depot, s end of Calhoun Street.
PITTSBURGH, FT. WAYNE & CHICAGO Railway Freight Depot and Office, Railroad e of Calhoun, J. C. Davis, Freight Agent.
PITTSBUGH, FT. WAYNE & CHICAGO Railway Machine, Blacksmith, Carpenter, Boiler, Paint, Car, Coppersmith, Tin and Brass Shops, s e c Holman and Barr.
Plock Herman, fireman h n s Jefferson b Broadway and Van Buren
Plohr Mrs. Lenore, widow h w s Calhoun b Jefferson and Lewis
Plugge Louis, lab h n s High, Bloomingdale
Plunkett Chas. peddler h s s Pearl b Maiden Lane and Cass
Pohle Christinia, cook Aveline House
Pohle Mrs. Julia, widow h 77 Madison
Point D. L. foreman bds Summit City Hotel
Point David, cooper wks C. S. Brackenridge & Co.'s
Polhamus Albert H. eng h 200 Lafayette
Polland James, lab wks Toledo & W. Railway freight depot
Poole E. H. carp bds E. O. Poole's
Poole E. O. eng h n s Jefferson b Ewing and Griffith
POST OFFICE, w end of Columbia, Moses Drake, Jr., Postmaster.
Poston Elisha W. carp h n s Jones b College and Nelson

Potter J. mach h 45 E. Washington
POTTER JOSEPH L., Carpenter and Builder, Shop n w c Main and Griffith, h n s Wayne b Union and Rockhill.
Powers Emmett, fireman wks Hurd & Clark's
Powers John Allen, h 158 E. Wayne
Powers Miss Nellie, res Geo. W. Wood's
Powers Thos. stone cutter wks n e c Main ann Cass
Poyser Hiram, carp h n s Jefferson b Fulton and Broadway
Pranger John H. carp h 204 E. Washington
Pratt Benj. D. bklayer res Geo. H. Pratt's
Pratt Geo. H. bklayer b s s Montgomery b Barr and Lafayette
PRATT WM. T., Sheriff Allen County; Office, Court House, w s Calhoun n of Water, at County Jail.
Preese Christ. carp wks T. & W. Railway shops
Prentiss Chas. mach h 47 W. Water
Prentiss Joseph R. clk Bowser & Story's, h 47 W. Water
Price Joseph, bds Main Street Exchange
Price L. H. carp wks Fronefield & Todd's
Printiss Joseph R. mach h n s Main b Van Buren and Jackson
Prize Chas. carp h s s Holman b Clay and Monroe
Probasco A. C. collector W. & E. Canal n w c Columbia and Clinton, h 112 E. Main
Probasco M. fireman wks P., Ft. W. & C. Railway Co.
Probst B. butcher h s s Nirdlinger w of Bluffton Road
PROUTY F. M., Wholesale and Retail Dealer in Boots and Shoes, 7 E. Main, bds Hamilton House.
Puhowgnik John, carp h s s Hough b Clay and Monroe
Pulch Danl. blksmith h 151 E. Lewis
Punk Ezra, cooper wks C. S. Brackenridge & Co.'s
Puregay F. helper wks P., Ft. W. & C. Railway blksmith shop
Putnam H. N. clk 79 Columbia, h 250 E. Wayne

Quicksell Peter, fireman bds 112 E. Berry
Quidore Nathan K. eng bds 146 W. Wayne
Quinn James, lab h 101 W. Jefferson
Quinn James, mach h w s Lafayette b Lewis and Montgomery
Quinn James E. helper wks T. & W. Railway shops
Quinn Wm. lab h w s Clinton b Water and Duck

R

Raab Fred. clk 92 Columbia, h 173 E. Washington
Raab John, grocer 92 Columbia, h n e c Jefferson and Ewing
Rabus John, tailor 71 Columbia, h Bloomingdale
Rabus Mathias, weaver h n s Bowser, Bloomingdale
Rabus Tobias, tailor wks 91 Columbia, h Bloomingdale
Racht Joseph, lab h s s Wilt b College and Nelson

RACINE AIME, Wholesale Horse Collar Manufacturer, west end of Columbia, bds Union House.

Racine Fred. collar mkr wks Aime Racine's
Rackgeber Joseph, cab mkr h 191 E. Washington
Radey Wm. lab h n s T. & W. Railway w of Fairfield Av
Ragland W. helper wks P., Ft. W. & C. Railway machine shop
Rahe Henry, cab mkr wks Chas Fink's; h Bloomingdale
Rahe Henry, carp h e s Broadway b Jefferson and George
Rakestraw Miss Emma, bds Christopher Wamsley's
Ralston A. mach wks P., Ft. W. & C. Railway machine shop
Rambo B W. watch mkr w s Calhoun b Main and Columbia, h 120 W. Washington
Ramsey Peter, mach h s s Jefferson b Van Buren and Jackson
Randall E. S. conductor h 122 E. Berry

RANDALL F. P., Attorney at Law, Land and Insurance Agent, Office w s Clinton b Columbia and Main, h n e c Lafayette and Berry.

RANDALL F. P., Mayor, Office w s Clinton b Columbia and Main.

Ranke Fred. mach wks Bowser & Story's

RANKE WM., Proprietor Eagle Bakery, 20 E. Berry b Calhoun and Clinton.

Ransman Barney, cooper wks C. S. Brackenridge & Co.'s
Ransman J. helper wks P., Ft. W. & C. Railway blksmith shop
Ranz Adam, lab h 180 E. Washington
Rapp Jacob, wagon mkr h s s Main b Fulton and Broadway

RASTETTER LOUIS, Machine Shop, and Town Clock Manufacturer, 42 W. Jefferson, h 156 Harrison.

Rau Casper, lab h w s Lima Plank Road, Bloomingdale
Rau G. lab wks P., Ft. W. & C. Railway shops
Rau Gustav, plasterer h w s Lima Plank Road, Bloomingdale
Rauner Joseph, painter h n s Wilt b College and Nelson
Rauth John, lab at Aveline House
Ray A. D. mach h s s Lewis b Monroe and Hanna
Ray Henry, carp wks T. & W. Railway shop
Rayhonser Gedeliah, printer n s Bowser, Bloomingdale

RAY WM. F., Master Mechanic Toledo & Wabash Railway Co., h 156 W. Jefferson.

READ A. J. & CO., (Asahel J. R. & Alex. Wiley,) Livery and Sale Stable, e s Court b Main and Berry.

Read Asahel J. (A. J. R. & Co.) h e s Clinton b Main and Berry

READ HENRY A., Veterinary Surgeon, e s Court b Main and Berry, h 89 W. Berry.

Redelsheimer David S. clk 93 Columbia, h 72 Griffith

REDELSHEIMER H., Optician and Dealer in Family Groceries, Fancy Goods, Toys, &c., e s Calhoun b Columbia and Main, h s e c Washington and Harrison.

REDELSHEIMER S., Wholesale Dealer in Groceries, Liquors, Wines, Cigars, Tobacco, &c., 93 Columbia, h 48 W. Wayne.

Reed Daniel M. conductor h n s Wayne b Ewing and Griffith
Reed Hugh B. (R. & Wall,) s w c Main and Van Buren
Reed Joseph, fireman bds Mrs. Sarah Toland's
Reed Joseph, mach bds Mrs. S. M. French's
Reed Mrs. Joseph, res Mrs. Laura McLaughlin's

REED & WALL, (Hugh B. R. & Watson W.) Wholesale Dealers in Drugs and Medicines, Chemicals, Paints, Oils, &c., 109, 111 and 113 Columbia.

Reffelt Henry, res Henry G. Granneman's
Reffelt W. R. carp wks P., Ft. W. & C. Railway carp shop
Regitz Ludwig, painter h Bloomingdale
Rehling C. blksmith wks P., Ft. W. & C. Railway blksmith shop
Rehling F. blksmith wks P., Ft. W. & C. Railway blksmith shop
Rehling W. carp wks P., Ft. W. & C. Railway carp shop
Rehm Christian, lab h rear 241 W. Washington
Rehm Samuel, carp h e s West b Pritchard and Railroad
Rehner Ulrich, mason h 58 W. Wayne
Rehorst Fred. carp h 218 E. Jefferson
Reichardt Henry, carp h n s Bowser, Bloomingdale
Reichert David, lab h w s Calhoun s of corp. line
Reid A. D. plow manuf 57 W. Main, h 59 W. Main
Reihling Ernst, boiler mkr bds 155 E. Lewis
Reihling Henry, boiler mkr h 155 E. Lewis
Reihling Philip Jacob, teamster h 220 Madison

RIELING AUGUST, Lock Manufacturer and Repairing Shop, n s Pearl b Ewing and Griffith.

Reiling Conrad, h n s Lewis b Clay and Monroe
Reiling Conrad, tailor bds Rudolph Boerger's
Reiling Henry, boiler mkr wks Fort Wayne Machine Works
Reiling Wm. carp h s s Sturgis w of Fulton
Reineke Christian, upholsterer h 105 Barr
Reiner John H. lab wks Geo. Meyer's

Reinewald Wm. lab h s w c Harrison and Dawson
Reinhardt John, cooper h n s Washington b Hanna and Francis
Reinhardt Mathias, shoe mkr h 239 E. Jefferson
Reinke Fred. W. steward at Concordia College
Reinking Fred. h 183 Ewing
Reiter Mrs. Christina, widow h 16 W. Jefferson
Reiter Edward, wheat buyer wks D. F. Comparet's
Reith Joseph, mason h 224 E. Jefferson
Reitze Tobias, carp h n s Pritchard b Broadway and Van Buren
Reitzell Peter N. (R., Shunk & Co.) h c s Lafayette b Montgomery and Holman

REITZELL, SHUNK & CO., (Peter N. R., Allen S., & A. A. Malline,) Proprietors Excelsior Agricultural Works, w s Hanna s of the Railroad Junction.

Rekers B. J. carp h s w c Washington and Ewing

REKERS BERNARD, Proprietor Orphan's Home, and Fort Wayne Hospital, n w c Wayne and Webster.

REKERS C. A., Recorder Elect Allen County, Office Court House, h 21 W. Wayne.

Rekers Gerhard, clk 15 E. Main, h n w c Wayne and Webster
Remerman Henry, blksmith h c s Broadway b Jefferson and George
Remment John, carp wks Murray and Bennigin's
Remmer John, carp bds 128 E. Washington
Remmert Herman, cooper b Bloomingdale
Remmort H. J. carp wks P., Ft. W. & C. Railway carp shop
Renean Miss Catharine, h 200 E. Wayne
Renner Leopold, lab at n c c Jefferson and Griffith
Renney Robt. currier wks Union Tannery
Rensman Henry, baker wks Wm. Hobrock's
Rentz Adam, clk Peter Pierr's, h 180 E. Washington
Repps Carl, carp h s s Jones e of John
Resing Mrs. Magdelana, widow h s s High, Bloomingdale
Resteusch Ludwig, brewer wks Bloomingdale Brewery
Revels Wilis, barber h 152 W. Jefferson
Reynolds C. L. printer h 53 Barr
Rheinerman Henry, blksmith wks T. & W. Railway shops
Rheinking Fred. clk 101 Columbia, h e s Ewing near Jefferson
Rheinwall Wm. lab wks T. & W. Railway shops
Rhinesmith Mrs. Elizabeth, widow h 218 W. Wayne
Rhinesmith John, express messenger h 218 W. Wayne
Rhoadamier Geo. eng wks T. & W. Railway Co.
Rhoadarmel J. K. brakesman bds People's House
Riale Sampson, barber w s Calhoun b Main and Berry, h 53 W. Washington
Rico Edwin A. fireman wks T. & W. Railway Co.

Rich Thos. carp h e s Lafayette b Wayne and Washington
Richards David, lab wks Murray & Bennigin's
Richards Emma, chambermaid Fort Wayne Eating House
Richey Amos, clk 81 Columbia, bds Mayer House
Richey James, h 57 W. Perry
Richmond A. L. carp bds Mrs. Ann Graham's
Richmond D. W. C. conductor h n s Montgomery b Lafayette and Clay
Ried J. mach wks P., Ft. W. & C. Railway Machine Shop

RIEDMILLER JOHN M., Dealer in Family Groceries, Provisions, &c., w s Broadway b Wilt and Pritchard.

Rieter Fred. dray h n e c Douglas Av. and Webster
Rieter Henry, mach h s s Washington b Fulton and Broadway
Riethmiller Geo. lab h s e c Wilt and College
Riuling Conrad, tail r wks J. Freeman's
Rihm Peter, lab h w end Bowser, Bloomingdale
Riley Barney, brakeman bds s e c Harrison and Railroad
Ring Eley A. waiter Fort Wayne Eating House
Ring Mrs. Hannah, h al. b Clinton and Barr 1st n of Water
Ring Lizzie, waiter Fort Wayne Eating House
Ring Margaret, servt Summit City Hotel
Rippe Wm. cab mkr wks 50 E. Main
Risor P. helper wks P., Ft. W. & C Railway boiler shop
Rissing August, shoemkr h Bloomingdale
Ritchey Mrs. Elizabeth, h 14 E. Water
Ritchey Joseph, b h 45 E. Main
Ritter Andreas, stone mason h w s Lima Plank Road, Bloomingdale
Ritter Henry, lab bds Steuben House
Ritter Philip Jacob, tailor h n s Bowser, Bloomingdale

RIVERS W. F., House, Sign, Carriage and Ornamental Painter, Shop s s Pearl b Calhoun and Harrison; h 53 W. Main.

Rizer Philip, bds Mrs. S. M. French's
Roberts W. A. (A. D. Brandriff & Co) bds Mayer House
Robertson Samuel B. carp h s s Washington b Nelson and Garden
Robbins Chas. G. carp h rear 161 E. Jefferson
Robinson Chas. H. eng h s w c Berry and Clay
Robinson Francis, bds Ambrose Kiser's
Robinson H. H. atty and notary with Sol. D. Bayless, bds Hamilton House
Robinson Henry A. foreman carp T. & W. Railway, h o s Harrison b Highland and Dawson

ROBINSON JAMES H., Boot and Shoe Manufacturer and Dealer in Shoe Findings, &c., w end of Columbia, bds Hamilton House.

Robinson Marvin S. teller Fort Wayne Branch Bank, bds Aveline House
Robinson Mrs. Mary K. governess Fort Wayne College, res at the College

ROBINSON REV. R. D., President Fort Wayne College, w end of Wayne

Rock Frank, hostler wks Jackson Swain's
Rockhill House, s w c Main and Broadway

ROCKHILL HON. WM., h s e c Berry and Rockhill.

Rodabaugh T. J. painter h e s Van Buren b Wilt and Pritchard
Rodener Geo. eng bds 151 W. Washington
Rodenbeck Fred. boiler mkr h 204 E. Jefferson
Rodenberg J. lab wks P., Ft. W. & C. Railway shops
Rodgers W. boiler mkr wks P., Ft. W. & C. Railway boiler shop
Roebel Gustave, shoemkr h s s Wall w of Bluffton Road
Roelle Frank, carp h w s Calhoun b Jefferson and Lewis
Roelle Jacob, carp h w s Calhoun b Jefferson and Lewis
Roelle Peter, h w s Calhoun b Jefferson and Lewis
Roelle Mrs. Susan, widow h w s Calhoun b Jefferson and Lewis
Roesler Henry, mach h c Poplar and Fairfield Av.
Rogers C. H. printer Ft. Wayne Gazette office, h n w c Calhoun and Wayne
Rogers John, h s e c Clay and Wayne
Rogers Wm. H. boiler mkr h 61 E. Jefferson
Rogge Wm. carp h 194 Ewing
Rohdenbeck C. helper bds Conrad Heitkamp's
Robley F. carp wks P., Ft. W. & C. Railway carp shop
Rohlmer W. painter wks P., Ft. W. & C. Railway paint shop
Rohlman Wm. lab h 181 Ewing
Rohs Henry, clk 84 Columbia
Rolage John, lab h 141 E. Washington
Rolf Fritz, mason h s s Pritchard opp Van Buren
Rolfing W. dray h 200 E Jefferson
Rolston James, mach h e s Clay b Holman and Hough
Romary Joseph, clk 87 Columbia
Roney John, eng wks P., Ft. W. & C. Railway Co.
Ronk John, lab h s s Water b Barr and Lafayette
Roope Mrs. Mary, widow h s s Lewis b Harrison and Webster
Rope Fred. cab mkr bds 81 W. Washington
Rope Wm. boatman h s e c Jefferson and Broadway
Rose B. B. carp wks P., Ft. W. & C. Railway carp shop
Rose D. B. carp bds James M. Wolfe's
Rose Geo. fireman wks T. & W. Railway Co.
Rose Henry, helper wks Bowser and Story's
Rose Katie, bds Morgan Rose's
Rose Morgan, lab h s e c Railroad and Harrison

11

Rosenthal Isaac, phys h 100 W. Berry
Rosenthal Max (Lamley & R.) h 102 W. Berry
Ross Geo. B. eng h s s Jefferson b Lafayette and Clay
Ross James L. clk Supt's office P., Ft. W. & C. Railway, bds Ft. Wayne Eating House
Rossbacher Chas. shoemkr h 80 E Jefferson
Rossington Richard, carp h 112 E. Berry
Rossington Wm. brakeman h 112 E. Berry
Rossman Wm. W. carp h rear 261 E. Washington
Rost Edward, mason h s w c Calhoun and Jefferson
Rotell Chas. carp wks Cochran, Humphrey & Co.'s
Rotermann Wm. cigar mkr h 200 Barr
Roth Bernhard, lab n w c Force and Jones
Rothaus H. carp wks P. Ft. W. & C Railway carp shop
Rothenbeck Fred. boiler mkr wks Ft. Wayne Machine Works
Rothenbeck J. helper wks P., Ft. W. & C. Railway blksmith shop
Rothenbeck Wm. boiler mkr wks T. & W. Railway shops
Rothenberger Geo. lab h n s Wines b Fairfield Av. and Hoagland
Rothert H. lab wks P., Ft. W. & C. Railway lumber yard
Rotter J. lab wks P., Ft. W. & C. Railway Co. yard
Rowan Mrs. Barbara A. widow h 74 E. Washington
Rowan Miss Jane, h 120 Clinton
Roy F. E. C. clk bds Mayer House
Roy J. N. clk bds Mayer House
Roy Louis clk 107 Columbia, bds Mayer House
Rubin Rev. Edward, h n s Main b Cass and Ewing
Ruby Arthur M. fireman h s s Railroad b Webster and Kansas
Ruby Geo. A. fireman h s e c Madison and Lafayette
Ruderdt Geo. butcher h 72 Ewing
Rudisill Mrs. E. h on East Branch Lima Plank Road n of St. Mary's Road
Rudolph Frank, harness mkr h s s Water b Cass and Ewing
Rudolph Frank, harness mkr h 156 Ewing
Rudolph John, carp h w s Lima Plank Road, Bloomingdale
Rue Nicholas T. teacher h n w c Webster and Wayne
Ruech John, storekeeper wks P.. Ft. W. & C. Railway Co.
Ruffington A. D. fireman wks P. Ft. W. & C. Railway Co.
Ruger Wm. carp wks T. & W. Railway shops
Ruh Dom, bar k Chas. Stein's
Ruhl Jesse F. carp bds n e c Jefferson and Jackson
Rumbold Gotlieb, lab h w s Hood b Pritchard and Railroad

RUMSEY JAMES B., Clerk Ft. Wayne Eating House.

RUMSEY PHILO, Proprietor Fort Wayne Eating House, Junction Pittsburg Ft. Wayne & Chicago and Toledo & Wabash Railroads.

FORT WAYNE (SAL) DIRECTORY. 155

Runck John, fireman wks J. K. & H. Baker's
Rundel Chas. conductor h 175 E. Jefferson
Rundell Miss Sarah J. bds 236 W. Washington
Runnell Nicholas, lab res Martin Overley's
Ruppel John, bk layer h n s Montgomery b Barr and Lafayette
Ruppel John, boatman h s w c Wayne and Francis
Ruppel Paul, lab h 258 E. Wayne
Rupert Ira, h 123 E. Washington
Rurode E. C. (McDougal & Co) bds Aveline House
Rushton Sam'l, blksmith h n s Lewis b Harrison and Webster
Russell John C. mach bds Benj Kay's
Russell Peter, bds Jacob Aufricht's
Russell Wm. painter h s e s Bluffton Road below the Railroad
Ruthrauff Chas. clk 75 Columbia, h 146 Clinton
Ruthrauff Rev. Wm. P. h s s Wayne b Clinton and Barr
Ryan Andrew, helper wks T. & W. Railway shops

RYAN D., Attorney at Law and Notary Public, Office with C. V. N. Milliman.

Ryan Dennis, lab h w s Fairfield Av. b T. & W. R. R. and Locust
Ryan Ellen, servt Mrs. M. E Chapin's
Ryan J. carp wks P., Ft. W. & C. Railway carp shop

RYAN JAMES W., Teamster and Contractor, h s w c Washington and Griffith.

Ryan John, dray h s s Pritchard b Bluffton Road and Jackson
Ryan John, lab h s s Pritchard b Bluffton Road and Jackson
Ryan Mary, housekeeper n e c Calhoun and Lewis
Ryan Michael, lab res Mrs. Rose Ann Ryan's
Ryan Michael B. boiler mkr h s s Jefferson b College and Nelson
Ryan Patrick, saloon w s Barr b Berry and Wayne
Ryan Mrs. Rose Ann, widow h e s Pine b Locust and T. & W. Railway
Ryan Wm. lab res Mrs. Rose Ann Ryan's

Sachs David, dry goods w s Calhoun b Main and Columbia, h 21 W. Berry
Sadler C. T. clk 7 E. Main
Saffen Thos. W. R. mach h n w c Montgomery and Monroe
St. Charles Exchange, n s Main b Calhoun and Harrison
St. Mary's German Catholic School, (males,) s w c Lafayette and Jefferson
St. Mary's German Catholic Female School, e s Lafayette b Madison and Jefferson
Salander Miss Mary E. res B. Y. Calvin's
Salgo Ferdinand, mason h 123 Madison

ST. NICHOLAS SALOON AND RESTAURANT, Houser & Kalbacher, Proprietors, w s Calhoun b Berry and Wayne.
Salisbury Phenias, fireman bds Sylvanus Currant's
Sallear Frank, carp h 101 Madison
Sallear John, carp h 101 Madison
Sallot J. F. carp h n e c Piqua Plank Road and Buchanan
Simpson Joseph, barber at Summit City Hotel
SANDER C. W., Wholesale and Retail Dealer in Boots, Shoes, Leather, Findings, &c., s w c Columbia and Clinton, h 101 W. Washington.
Sander Ernst, lab h 97 W. Jefferson
Sanders Chas. carp h o s Broadway b Jefferson and George
Sanders John, collar mkr wks 41 Columbia
Sanders Wm. h 86 W. Washington
Sandler Chas. cigar mkr wks L. Dessauer's
SANDMEYER A. L., Dealer in Drugs, Medicines, Chemicals, Homoeopathic Medicines, &c., w s Calhoun b Wayne and Washington, h c Harrison and Jefferson.
Sandoz Phillip, polisher h 229 E. Jefferson
Sands John, bds s o c Harrison and Railroad
Saners Peter, lab h n s Montgomery b Barr and Lafayette
Sanford Henry C. eng wks T. & W. Railway Co.
SARNIGHAUSEN JOHN D., Editor and Proprietor Indiana Staats Zeitung, (German Weekly,) Office, n e c Columbia and Clinton.
Sarns John, carp h 10 W. Wayne
Sauers John, lab h 60 Clinton
SAUNDERS BENJAMIN, Justice of the Peace, Office, 2 Phœnix Block, w s Calhoun b Main and Columbia, up stairs, h 101 E. Berry.
Saurs Henry S. lab res Mrs. Mary A. Saurs'
Saurs James T. fireman res Mrs. Mary A. Saurs'
Saurs Mrs. Mary A. widow h w s Fairfield Av. b T. & W. R. R. and Locust
Sauwen Chas. lab h Bloomingdale
Sauwen Mrs. Marian, widow h Bloomingdale
Sauwen Philip, lab h Bloomingdale
Savage ———, blksmith bds 140 E. Wayne
Savage Mrs. Hannah, widow h 225 W. Washington
Savage James, 20 W. Jefferson
Savage John H. fireman h 225 W. Washington
Sawin Wm. blksmith wks T. & W. Railway shops
Sawin Wm. P. switchman h s e c Bass and Prince
Saxer G. A. director Concordia College, res at College
Scarlett Chester, clk bds s w c Wayne and Jackson
Schabruck M. lab wks P., Ft. W. & C. Railway carp shop

Schacher Christian, lab h e s Jackson b Pritchard and Railroad
Schacher Leonard, shoemkr h w s Hood b Pritchard and Railroad
Schack Fred. Wm. shoemkr h n w c Pearl and Ewing
Schade John J. printer Indiana Staats Zeitung office, h n w c Jefferson and Harrison
Schaefer Geo. h 18 E. Wayne
Schaefer Michael, lab h s s Nirdlinger w of Bluffton Road
Schaefer Rienhard, h 122 E. Wayne
Schaeffer August, clk n e c Main and Calhoun
Schanck Louis, baskets, etc., 48 Columbia
Schaper Fred. clk h 71 Lafayette
Scharardy Hypolite, carp h n s Jefferson b Lafayette and Clay
Scheafer Wm. carp h n s Wilt b Van Buren and Jackson
Scheele Henry W. blksmith h n s Holman b Monroe and Hanna
Scheiman Ferdinand, mach wks Bowser & Story's
Scheimann Fred. tailor b 86 E. Jefferson
Schele A. F. (S. & Lower) h s e c Jackson and Pritchard
Schele August, mason h 56 W. Wayne
Schele John, bklayer h e s Jackson b Pritchard and Railroad
Schele & Lower, (August S. & Benedict L.) grocers 5 E. Main
Schellhorn John, (Manok, Nestle & Co.) h 107 W. Water
Schenerman P. carp wks P., Ft. W. & C. Railway carp shop
Schepf Andrew, mach res John Schepf's
Schepf John, mach h n s Taylor w of Pine
Scherer Andrew, lab h 51 Monroe
Scherer Fred. lab h e s Hanna b Hamilton and Railway
Scherer Fred. cab mkr b 95 E. Washington
Scherer John, h 51 Monroe
Scheuerman Peter, carp h w s Broadway b Wilt and Pritchard
Scheurman Christ. carp wks T. & W. Railway shops
Scheurman Fred. carp h s s Melita b Webster and Hoagland
Scheumerr Christ. carp bds 118 Harrison
Scheumerr Ferdinand, bds 118 Harrison
Schick Geo. teacher at Concordia College
Schiefer Christian, (E. Vordermark & Co.) h 124 E. Wayne
Schieferstein Philip, saloon n s Main b Clinton and Barr
Schildmeier Christian, h 172 W. Jefferson
Schilling Chas. lab h s w c Jefferson and Union
Schilling Frank, mason h s w c Jefferson and Union
Schilling Valentine, saloon e s Calhoun b Berry and Wayne
Schlaefer Gottfreid, cigar mkr bds John Koch's
Schlafer Fred. cigar mkr wks L. Dessauer's
Schmall Gottlieb, lab h e s West b Pritchard and Railroad
Schmalz Chas. J. tailor h e s Calhoun b Washington and Jefferson
Schmanner Henry, marble cutter wks n e c Main and Cass
Schmeker T. wks Olds, Hanna & Co.'s

Schmeller Henry, stone cutter h 242 W. Washington
Schmetzer Louis, clk A. F. Siemon & Bro.'s, h 33 W. Jefferson
Schmetzer M. Fred. c.k 71 Columbia, h s e c Jefferson and Harrison
Schmides Geo. carp h n w c Jefferson and College
Schmidt Adam, shoemkr h s s Wilt b College and Nelson
Schmidt Andrew, lab h n w s Bluffton Road b Pritchard and Railroad

SCHMIDT C. & CO., (Conrad S., Jr. & Conrad Schmidt, Sen.,) File Manufacturers and Dealers in Hardware, Cutlery, Tools, Sash, &c., Union Block, n s Main b Calhoun and Clinton.

Schmidt Conrad, jr. (C. S. & Co.) h 193 W. Wayne
Schmidt Conrad, sr., (C. Schmidt & Co.) h 193 W. Wayne
Schmidt Ernst, lab wks Bloomingdale Brewery
Schmidt G. A. taxidermist h 164 E. Wayne
Schmidt Geo. mason res Jones & Bass' Foundry Addition
Schmidt Gustav, clk C. Schoerpf & Co.'s
Schmidt Jacob, lab h w s Hood b Pritchard and Railroad
Schmidt Mrs. Jacob, res H. F. Banta's
Schmidt Peter C. carp h s e c Jefferson and Van Buren
Scmidt Wm. file mkr h c Griffith and Berry
Schmidtley Casper, helper Bowser & Story's
Schmidtley Mary, servt Hamilton House
Schmitt Gustav, h s w c Monroe and Madison
Schmitz Charles, phys office w s Calhoun b Wayne and Washington, h n w c College and Wilt
Schmocker T. B. lab h n s Baker b Calhoun and Harrison
Schmoe Louis, shoemkr h 171 Ewing
Schmucker Sebastian, clk 81 Columbia, res country
Schmuckle Fred. saloon 98 Columbia
Schneerline Geo. carriage smith bds Christian Reinecke's
Schneider Gottlieb, tailor bds 118 Harrison
Schneider John, lab h 12 E. Jefferson
Schneider K. mer bds Steuben House
Schneider Valentine, lab h c s Force b Jones and Hernden
Schneider Wm. shoemkr h 46 W. Washington
Schnelker Barney, mason h 170 E. Washington
Schnelker Henry, mason h n s Wayne b Hanna and Francis

SCHNIEDERS B. H., Proprietor American House, s s Columbia b Calhoun and Harrison.

Schoemaker Wm. janitor h 44 E. Lewis

SCHOENBEIN ALBERT F., Machinist, and Mechanical and Architectural Drawing School, h n w c West Main and Cass.

Schoenell Wm. shoemkr wks P. Kline's
Schoepf Andrew, mach wks T. & W. Railway shops
Schoerpf Casper, (C. S. & Co.) h 96 Columbia

SCHOERPF C. & CO., (Casper S. & Meyer & Bro.,) Dealers in Drugs, Medicines, Paints, Oils, Chemicals, &c., e s Calhoun b Columbia and Main.

Schoerpf Miss Sophia, res Casper Schoerpf's
Schone Barney, cooper wks C. S. Brackenridge & Co.'s
Schone Henry, grocer n w c Washington and Hanna, h 221 E. Washington
Schopman Wm. lab h n s Lewis b Francis and Harmer
Schopman Wm. cab mkr bds 49 E. Lewis
Schott Geo. J. clk s w c Calhoun and Main, bds Main Street Exchange
Schrack Joseph, carp bds 30 W. Water
Schrader Henry, h 55 Madison
Schrader Louis, (Krutop & Co.) h 179 W. Washington
Schrage Christ. tailor h 212 Madison
Schramm Frank, lab h s w c Jones and Force
Schrier Willard, mach wks T. & W. Railway shops
Schrimpf Frank, lab bds Adam Webel's
Schrimpf Henry, shoemkr bds 63 E. Water
Schroder Gottfried, tailor h 168 E. Jefferson
Schroder Gustavus, clk 11 Calhoun, bds 94 W. Main
Schroeder Fred. shoemkr h 123 Madison
Schroeder Henry, lab h e s Francis b Lewis and Madison
Schroeder Henry, teamster h n s High, Bloomingdale
Schroeder Louis, saw mill h s s Washington b Fulton and Broadway
Schroge Christ. tailor h 212 Madison
Schrouder Fred. lab wks C. S. Brackenridge & Co.'s
Schroup Mrs. Catharine, res Chas. Jautz's
Schrum John, h e s Piqua Plank Road b Wallace and Charles
Schrump ———, lab bds 63 E. Water
Schuber Fred. marble cutter wks n e c Cass and Main
Schuckman John G. (Allen & Co.) h n e c Calhoun and Wayne
Schuckman Henry N. tinner h 221 E. Washington
Schuler H. lab wks P., Ft. W. & C. Railway lumber yard
Schuler Mathias, lab h w Monroe b Madison and Lewis
Schuller John, lab h 214 E. Jefferson
Schulthes Benj. Carl, cutter 71 Columbia, h w s Griffith s of Jefferson
Schultz Mrs. Elizabeth, widow h w s Barr b Berry and Wayne
Schultz J. lab wks P., Ft. W. & C. Railway lumber yard
Schultz John, cooper h 124 E. Washington
Schultz Christ. h 25 W. Wayne

SCHULZ PETER, Manufacturer of Dealer in Boots and Shoes, 47 E. Main b Clinton and Barr, h n s Jefferson b Clay and Lafayette.

Schulz Wm. boots and shoes, 25 W. Wayne
Schumacker Barney, carp bds 52 Columbia

Schumacker Joseph, lab bds 52 Columbia
Schumacker Wm. janitor b 189 E Lewis
Schust Andrew, carp b 234 W. Washington
Schust Michael, carp h w c Wilt and Rockhill
Schwalm Herman, corp h c s Hanna b Hamilton and Railway
Schwart Meinhart, carp h n w c Bluffton Road and Railroad
Schwartz Chas. harness mkr wks L. Troub & Co.'s
Schwartz Fred. lab wks Griffith & Co.'s
Schwartz Geo. watchman at P., Ft. W. & C. Railway shops
Schwartz Geo. lab h w s Hood b Pritchard and Railroad
Schwarz Adam, teamster h w s Calhoun s of corp. line
Schwarz Fred. res Adam Schwarz's
Schwarz Rudolph, h s s Pearl b Griffith and Fulton

SCHWEGEL JACOB, Manufacturer and Wholesale Dealer in Horse Collars, 41 Columbia.

SCHWEGMANN H. R., Wholesale and Retail Dealer in Staple and Fancy Dry Goods, Millinery Goods, Hats, Caps, Crockery, Wood and Willow Ware, &c., 101 Columbia; h n w c Clinton and Jefferson.

Schweier Wm. boiler mkr wks Fort Wayne Machine Works
Schwier Wm. boiler mkr h 188 E. Jefferson

SCHWIETERS HERMAN, Old Fort Wayne Bakery, 67 Columbia.

Scott Geo. finisher h n s Jefferson b Rockhill and College
Scott Geo. O. carriage mkr bds n e c Main and Lafayette
Scott Howard, bds Geo. R. Hartman's
Scott James, h 19 W. Washington
Scott James, h 97 W. Washington
Scott James, carp wks T. & W. Railway shops
Scott W. H. clk T. & W. Railway freight office, bds Geo. R. Hartman's
Scott Wm. miller wks Empire Flour Mills, h 211 W. Wayne
Seacord H. blksmith wks P., Ft. W. & C. Railway blksmith shop
Seamon P. helper wks P., Ft. W. & C. Railway boiler shop
Sedgwick John, miller City Flour Mills, h w s Barr b Main and Berry
Sedgwick Joseph, res John Sedgwick's
Seek Mrs. Elizabeth, h n w c Harrison and Wayne
Seely A. J. cab mkr wks 50 E. Main
Seemeier Gottlieb, tailor h rear 16 W. Jefferson
Seibold Chas. F. painter wks T. & W. Railway shops
Seibold David, clk h s w c Lima Plank Road and Douglas, Bloomingdale
Seibold Gottlieb, lab h w s Pine b Taylor and Locust
Seibring Henry, shoemkr wks Noah Humphrey's
Selle Augustus, clk 95 Columbia

SEIDEL EDWARD, Wine and Lager Beer Saloon, and Ice Dealer, w s Calhoun b Main and Berry.
Selle Gustave, clk bds Main Street Exchange
Selover N. H. dentist with D. L. & A. P. Talbot, bds Hedekin House
Sells Gustavus, clk 90 Columbia, bds Mayer House
Sensency Mrs. Mary E. widow h 16 W. Washington
Sovencik Frank, h 123 Lafayette
SEXTON FLORA, Millinery Rooms and Dealer in Fancy Goods, &c., n s Main b Calhoun and Clinton, Union Block.
Seybold Chas. F. painter h 86 W. Jefferson
SEYBOLD FRED., Proprietor Steuben House, s e c Calhoun and Washington.
Shaddock B. bds Main Street Exchange
Shafer A. W. blksmith wks P., Ft. W. & C. Railway blksmith shop
Shafer Wm. L. hostler h 58 W. Main
Shaffer Chas. carp h w s Francis b Lewis and Hamilton
Shaffer Geo. P. eng h s s Berry b Griffith and Fulton
Shalloup Mrs. Catharine, widow h 17 W. Jefferson
Shanahan W. helper wks P., Ft. W. & C. Railway blksmith shop
Sharp Carrie B. teacher Western District, b n e c Water and Calhoun
SHARP H., Dealer in Hats, Caps, Furs, &c., 97 Columbia, h n e c Water and Calhoun.
Sharp John, clk h n e c Water and Calhoun
Shaw Benj. brakeman bds Wm. Beals'
Shaw James, b k 75 Columbia, bds Aveline House
Shaw John L. resident eng P., Ft. W. & C. Railway, bds Fort Wayne Eating House
Sheafer Wm. E. carp wks Cochran, Humphrey & Co.'s
SHEAFER WM. G., Carpenter and Builder, Shop and Residence 181 W. Wayne.
Shea Bart lab h s s Walnut b Fairfield Av. and Oakley
Shea Dennis, mach wks Bowser & Story's
Shea John, mach bds Mrs. Ann Graham's
Shea Mrs. Mary, widow h 191 Ewing
Shebley Edward, molder wks Fort Wayne Machine Works
Sheehan James, mason bds Patrick Ryan's
Sheehy Mrs. Ellen, widow h Junction Bluffton Road and T. & W. Railway
Sheering John, painter bds Jacob J. Kamm's
Shele John, helper bds 251 E. Jefferson
Shele Julius helper 251 E. Jefferson
Sheley John, helper wks P., Ft. W. & C. Railway blksmith shop
Sheridan Mrs. Sophia, widow h s w c Jefferson and Van Buren

Shepard A. fruits, etc., w s Harrison b Pearl and Canal, h s s
    Water b Cass and Ewing
Sheridan W. carp wks P., Ft. W. & C. Railway carp shop
Sheridan Wm. B. lab h s e c Barr and Montgomery
Sheriff's Office in Court House, Wm. T. Pratt, Sheriff
Sherwood Dorr, h 95 W. Berry
Sherwood Mrs. Eliza, widow h 169 W. Washington
Sherwood Wm. fireman wks T. & W. Railway Co.
Shidel Chas. (Heldt & S.) h w s Calhoun b Berry and Wayne
Shilling Miss & Co. (Miss Mary S. & Miss Susan Lau,) millinery
    w s Calhoun b Main and Columbia
Shilling Andrew, carp bds St. Charles Restaurant
Shilling Frank, stone cutter wks James Humphrey's
Shilling Miss Mary, (Miss S. & Co.) h s w c Calhoun and Washington
Shiman F. carp wks P., Ft. W. & C. Railway carp shop
Shipman R. M. conductor bds Mayer House

SHOAFF J. A., Photograph and Ambrotype Gallery, n w c Main and Calhoun; bds Hamilton House.
Shoaff Mrs. Mary L. widow h 88 W. Main
Shoaff Miles E. carp h 39 W. Jefferson
Shoaff Peter, saddler h 179 W. Washington
Shoaff S. H. saddles, etc., 119 Columbia, h 86 E. Berry
Shoaff Thos. B. with S. H. Shoaff, h 86 E. Berry
Sheaff W. C. h 76 W. Berry
Shordon Miss Catharine, (Gable & S.) h w s Clinton b Main and
    Columbia
Shoulter John, cooper wks C. S. Brackenridge & Co.'s
Shrigley Samuel H. fireman h 40 Madison
Shriner John, carp h 234 W. Wayne
Shunk Allen, (Reitzell, S. & Co.) h s s Montgomery b Clay and
    Monroe
Sibray Nathan, carp h 224 W. Wayne
Siebald Christian, grocery n w s Bluffton Road b Pritchard and
    Railroad
Siebold David, clk 80 Columbia, h Bloomingdale
Siebold John, teamster h s w c Jefferson and Van Buren
Siedrchlag Alex. clk 107 Columbia
Siemon August, F. (A. F. S. & Bro.) h n s Jefferson b Lafayette
    and Clay

SIEMON A. F. & BRO., (August F. & Rudolph,) Dealers in Books, Stationery, Wall Paper, and Pictures; also Book and Job Printers, Book Binders and Blank Book Manufacturers, Union Block, w s Clinton, b Main and Columbia.
Siemon Rudolph, (A. F. Siemon & Bro.)
Sihler Rev. W. h 176 Barr

Sillot V. carp wks P., Ft. W. & C. Railway carp shop
SILVER D. J., Contractor and Builder, Office 54 Calhoun Street, 3rd Story; h 64 E. Jefferson.
Silver J. M. bklayer h 248 W. Wayne
Silver Robert D. b k D. J. Silver's, n 64 E. Jefferson
Silver S. D. clk 99 Columbia, bds 18 E. Wayne
Simmons Wm. hatter bds Union House
Simon Paul, lab h 82 E. Jefferson
Simon S. lab wks P., Ft. W. & C. Railway shops
Simons Geo. eng wks P., Ft. W. & C. Railway Co.
Simpkins ———, brakeman bds 225 W. Washington
Sinclear Miss Frank, h s w c Main and Cass
Sinclear Miss Orlinda, h s w c Main and Cass
Singleton John, lab h 47 E. Water
Singleton Michael, stoker h w s Barr n of Water
Singmaster Joseph, lab h c s Jackson b Pritchard and Railroad
Sisters of Providence School, s e c Calhoun and Washington
Skillman ———, carp bds 112 E. Berry
Slagle Samuel, eng wks P., Ft. W. & C. Railway Co.
Slater Henry, fireman bds Lewis C. Wheeler's
Slater John, blksmith h s s Taylor b Fairfield Av. and Oakley
Slater Omer, eng h s s Holman b Clay and Monroe
Sleppy A. mach bds 91 E. Washington
Slocum E. foreman blksmith shop P., Ft. W. & C. railway Co, h 238 E. Lewis
Slocum John, firemrn bds 57 Barr
Small Geo. boiler mkr wks P., Ft. W. & C. Railway boiler shop
Smalley Chas. G. fireman h e s Lafayette b Montgomery and Holman
Smallhouse Fred. h e s Calhoun b Berry and Wayne
Smith ———, h s w c Berry and Griffith
Smith Alex. boiler mkr bds 143 E. Lewis
Smith A. T. eng wks P., Ft. W. & C. Railway Co.
Smith Alfred, eng h e s Lafayette b Montgomery and Holman
SMITH C. S., Physician and Surgeon, Office and Residence s s Lewis b Calhoun and Harrison.
Smith Charles, brakeman bds Francis M. Luther's
Smith Chas. carp wks T. & W. Railway shop
Smith Edward, bds 52 Columbia
Smith Eugene B. printer Dawson's Times office, bds 172 W. Washington
Smith Fred. lab h n s Lewis b Calhoun and Harrison
Smith Geo. boiler mkr wks P., Ft. W. & C. Railway boiler shop
Smith Geo. B. harness maker bds Hedekin House
Smith J. McNutt, tel opr h s s Douglas Av. b Harrison and Webster
Smith James H. fireman wks T. and W. Railway Co.
Smith James, mach h s s Jefferson b Van Buren and Jackson

Smith John, brakeman bds Mrs. Hannah Whaley's
Smith John, clk L. P. Stapleford's bds 85 Barr
Smith John, F. molder bds 65 Columbia
Smith John, painter h 37 Monroe
Smith John W. foreman painter T. & W. Railway Co.
Smith Joseph, wagon mkr bds John Baker's
SMITH LORIN, Post Office News Depot, w end of Columbia, Post Office Building, bds 47 W. Berry.
Smith Ohio, miller bds Mrs. Mary L. Gales'
Smith Orsin, eng wks P., Ft. W. & C. Railway Co.
Smith S. R. blksmith h e s Hood b Pritchard and Railroad
Smith Samuel, carp h e s Pine b Taylor and Locust
Smith Miss Sarah, bds s w c Fulton and Sturgis
Smith Miss Viola, res C. K. Jones'
Smith Wm. F. mach wks T. & W. Railway shops
Smith Wm. S. (Crane & S) h 172 W. Washington
Smithly Casper, lab h 122 E. Berry
Smyser Peter, clk 61 Columbia, bds 242 W. Berry
Snellbaker G. helper wks P., Ft. W. & C. Railway blksmith shop
Snellbaker Wm. blksmith bds 57 Barr
Snider Clark, eng h s s Washington b Griffith and Fulton
Snider Rev. E. h e s Garden b Jefferson and Railroad
Snively Henry J. carp h e s Lafayette b Lewis and Montgomery
Snively John M. carp h 153 W. Washington
Snow Wm. clk 129 Columbia, bds A. M. Orbison's
Snyder Adam, brakeman h s s Pritchard b Bluffton Road and Jackson
Snyder C. eng wks P., Ft. W. & C. Railway Co.
Snyder John, asst dispatcher P., Ft. W. & C. Railway
Snyder John, yard master h 72 W. Jefferson
Snyder Lorenzo, fireman bds C. Case's
Snyder Orelia, servt Hamilton House
Snyder P. lab wks F., Ft. W. & C. Railway lumber yard
Snyder R. fireman wks P., Ft. W. & C. Railway Co.
Snyder Wm. cooper wks C. S. Brackenridge & Co's
Solomon Miss Louie bds s s Pearl b Harrison and Maiden Lane
Somer John G. lab h w s Pine b Taylor and Locust
Somers Anthony, pattern mkr wks Bowser & Story's
Somers Chas. bkbinder h 30 E. Berry
Somers Henry, mach wks Bowser & Story's
Somers James, saloon w s Calhoun b Douglas Av. and Baker
Somers Joseph, millwright wks Bowser & Story's
Somers Morris, eng wks Ft. Wayne Machine Works
Somerville J. tinner bds Union House
Sommer Chas. photographer 106 Columbia, h s s Berry b Calhoun and Clinton
Sommer Fred. packer City Flour Mills, h Bloomingdale
Sommer Joseph, lab h 57 W. Jefferson

Soso John, carp wks T. & W. Railway shops
Souerwein Ernst, lab h Bloomingdale
Souct P. helper wks P., Ft. W. & C. Railway blksmith shop
Soule E. M. lab h s s Main b Van Buren and Jackson
Southern James, eng h 146 Barr
Southern Ralph, h 146 Barr
Southern Robt. brakeman h 146 Barr
Speidel Herman, lab h 200 E. Jefferson
Speiker Jacob, mach bds 156 Harrison
Spence Mrs. Mary J. widow h s s Jefferson b Van Buren and Jackson
Spencer Mrs. Ann M. h w s Calhoun b Lewis and Douglas Av.

SPENCER CHAS. E., bds Aveline House.

SPENCER MARTIN B., Attorney at Law and Notary, e s Calhoun b Columbia and Main, bds 105 W. Berry.

SPENCER & PARKER, (Stephen S. & R. R. P.) Dealers in Hats, Caps, Furs, and Gents' Furnishing Goods, 70 Calhoun opp. Aveline House.

Spencer Stephen, (S. & Parker) res Indianapolis

SPEREISEN ADOLPH, Lager Beer and Oyster Saloon, n s Main b Calhoun and Harrison.

Spereisen J. Alex. blksmith h n s Taylor w of Pine
Spereisen Mrs. Joseph, h n s Taylor w of Pine
Speigel August, tailor h n s Wall w of Bluffton Road
Speigel B. lab wks P., Ft. W. & C. Railway shops
Spiegel Ernst, clk 101 Columbia
Spiegel Gustav, shoemkr h s s Jefferson b College and Nelson
Spiker Philip, carp wks Cochran, Humphrey & Co.'s
Spittle H. lab wks P., Ft. W. & C Railway lumber yard
Sponsler C. B. blksmith wks P., Ft. W. & C. Railway blksmith shop
Spring Christ. h 51 Monroe
Spring John, h 51 Monroe
Springston Isaac, brakeman bds 107 W. Wayne
Sprinkel John J. saddler bds Heackin House
Sprinkle R K marble cutter wks n e c Cass and Main
Spyker Philip G. carp h 55 W. Berry
Stachlut Wm. h 167 Ewing
Stackhouse W. blksmith wks P., Ft. W. & C. Railway blksmith shop
Stagmeier Jacob, carp wks T. & W. Railway shop!

STANLEY C., Carriage Manufacturer 118 W. Main, h s w c Main and Jackson.

Stanley Thos. carriage trimmer 118 W. Main, bds E. Stanley's
Stanton James, marble cutter wks n e c Main and Cass
Stanton Wm. molder bds Francis M. Luther's

Stansbury Philip, brakeman h s w c Piqua Plank Road and Virginia
Stanbery Wm. brakeman b w s Calhoun b Washington and Jefferson
Stapleford Mrs. Edward, widow h 85 Barr

STAPLEFORD L. P., Auction and Commission Merchant and Real Estate Agent, 4 e s Calhoun b Columbia and Main, h 85 Barr

Stapleford Wm. H. printer bds 118 E. Berry
Stapleford Wm. R. auctioneer L. P. Stapleford's, h 102 E. Washington

STAR BAKERY, Xavier Valroff, Proprietor, 92 E. Main.

Starck Herman, shoemkr wks Henry Mohlmeister's
Starke Fred. h s s High, Bloomingdale
Starkey O. L. painter h 102 E. Main

STATE INSURANCE COMPANY, Office, w s Clinton b Main and Columbia, James L. Worden, President; S. Lumbard, Secretary; Geo. W. Babcock, General Agent.

Standacher Geo. h s s Wilt b Rockhill and College
Staunton James A. eng h 160 E. Wayne
Stauring Chaney, (D. Hannum & Co.) bds Mayer House
Steatton L. lab wks P., Ft. W. & C. Railway Co. yard
Steele James M. conductor T. & W. R. R., bds Summit City Hotel
Steer Henry, warehouseman P., Ft. W. & C. Railway Freight Depot
Steevens A. L. carp wks P., Ft. W. & C. Railway carp shop
Steevens Wm. W. atty h 89 W. Berry
Steger Rudolph, carp h w s Broadway b Jefferson and Wilt
Stegmeier Jacob, lab h s e Hood and Pritchard
Steiger Fred. lab bds 63 E. Water
Stein Charles, saloon n s Main b Calhoun and Harrison
Stein Fred. teacher h 219 W. Washington
Stein Gust. omnibus driver wks John O'Connell's
Stein Peter, shoemkr h s s Van Wert Road e of corp line
Stein Sebastian, cooper wks C. S. Brackenridge & Co.'s
Steinacher Fred. lab h s e corner Fairfield Av. and Locust
Steinman Adam, carriage mkr h w side Clinton b Main and Berry
Steinman Jacob, h n s Montgomery b Lafayette and Clay
Steinman Jacob, h 88 W. Main
Steinman Jacob, jr. h 88 W. Main
Steinman Wm. h 88 W. Main
Stelhorn Chas. F. H. shoemkr h 127 W. Water
Stellwagon Joseph, coppersmith bds Hedekin House
Stem W. P. carp bds Wm. Beals'

Stemler Philip, tailor h s s Lewis b Clay and Monroe
Stemelon Frank. collar mkr wks 41 Columbia
Stenner Fred W. clk 103 Columbia, bds 148 Harrison
Stephan Henry, lab h 107 Madison
Stephan Philip, carp bds John Koch's
Stephens Mrs. V. H. h n w c Lafayette and Jefferson
Sterder Ludwig, lab h s s Wilt b College and Nelson

STEUBEN HOUSE, Fred. Seybold, Proprietor, s e c Calhoun and Washington.

Steup Henry, wheat buyer h s e c Water and Ewing
Stevens Ephraim, carp bds Wm. Beals'
Stevens George, bds Rufus Stevens

STEVENS G. L., Oculist and Aurist; Office and Residence, 15 E. Jefferson.

Stevens Geo. E. ins agt bds 15 E. Jefferson
Stevens Mrs. Henry, res M. Hedekin's
Stevens R. L. harness mkr bds 15 E. Jefferson
Stevens Rufus, upholsterer h 131 E. Washington

STEVENS THOMAS, Carriage and Wagon Manufacturer; also, Carriage and Wagon Painting, e s Clay b Berry and Main, h 155 E. Berry

Stevens Samuel, wagon mkr h 17 Clay
Stevens Wm. carriage painter h 228 E. Lewis
Stewart Alex. mach h n s Railroad w of McClellan
Stewart Mrs. Alice, widow h 150 Barr
Stewart Chas. helper h s s Bass b Prince and Hoagland
Stewart Chas. A. clk Geo. L. Little's
Stewart Chas J. clk b w s Calhoun b Water and the Canal
Stewart John, res Chas. Stewarts'
Stewart Wm. h 54 W. Wayne
Stewart Wm. mach res Alex. Stewart's
Stiegerwald John A. lab h 209 E. Jefferson
Stier Henry, lab h 116 Lafayette
Stier Jacob, molder wks Murray & Bennigin's
Stier John, stone dealer h 129 E. Lewis
Stiese Wm. lab h 185 E. Jefferson
Stiles James A. conductor bds Eugene F. Fountain's
Stillhorn Henry, blksmith s w c Barr and Jefferson

STINCHCOMB GEO. F., Auditor Allen County; Office, Court House, bds Mayer House.

Stine Daniel, carp h w s Harrison b Highland and Dawson
Stockbridge Ira C. clk 104 Columbia, bds 219 W. Wayne

STOCKBRIDGE N. P., Dealer in Books, Stationery, Wall Paper, Musical Instruments and Sewing Machines, 104 Columbia; also, Clothing, Gents' Furnishing Goods, Trunks, Hats, Caps, &c., 125 Columbia, h 219 W. Wayne.

Stockbridge Joseph W. clk 104 Columbia, bds 219 W. Wayne

Stocking Henry, eng h 150 W. Washington
Stockman Chas. clk A. F. Siemon & Bro.'s
Stoddard John, eng h w s Fairfield Av. b T. & W Railway and Locust
Stokes John, lab h n s Baker b Webster and McClellan
Stokes T. fireman wks P., Ft. W. & C. Railway Co.
Stokes Thos. mach bds 154 E. Washington
Stoll Conrad, lab res Henry Stoll's, Bloomingdale
Stoll Henry, teamster h n s Bowser, Bloomingdale
Stone Wm. E. eng bds Luther Wright's
Stoner Harriet, servt Main Street Exchange
Stoner John M. millwright wks Bowser & Story's
Stonehouse James, cooper bds Union House
Stophlet Frank, tinner wks 87 Columbia, h 242 W. Wayne
Stoppenbach O. F. ins agt bds Luther Wright's
Story James, (Bowser & S.) h 16 W. Water
Story Wm. S. molder h 16 W. Water
Strahn N. W. clk John Brown's, bds Union House
Strater Melinda, 2d cook Ft. Wayne Eating House
Stratton Miss Anna, res 189 W. Wayne
Stratton John, bklayer bds 92 W. Washington
Stratton Joseph, bklayer h 92 W. Washington
Straughan J. R. h 91 E. Berry
Strausen Robt. mach wks T. & W. Railway shops
Straw Wm. F. tinner h 179 W. Washington
Streeper Clorinda, servt Dr. C. S. Smith's
Streiker Gottleib, carp h w s Lima Plank Road, Bloomingdale
Stricker A. lab wks P., Ft. W. & C. Railway lumber yard
Stricker G. carp wks P., Ft. W. & C. Railway carp shop
Strickland A. R. conductor bds 107 W. Wayne
Stroble Fred. cooper wks Bloomingdale Brewery
Strodel Geo. sausage mkr bds 12 E. Berry

STRODEL MATHIAS, Wine and Lager Saloon, and Bologna Sausage Manufacturer, 12 E. Berry.

Stroh Wm. F. coppersmith wks T. & W. Railway shops
Strole Andrew J. clk Reed & Wall's, bds American House
Strong E. R. clk Mayer House
Strong Henry, shoemkr h 62 Columbia
Strong Jared C. carp h s e c Barr and Lewis
Strong John H. carp bds John S. Harrington's
Strong M. B. conductor h s e c Jefferson and Jackson
Strope D. B. chief eng P., Ft. W. & C. Railway Co.
Strosser Robt. mach h s e c Jefferson and Ewing
Strout Mrs. Rebecca, widow h 143 E. Lewis
Strout Reuben W. mach h 143 E. Lewis
Strubey Chas. music teacher h 81 E. Jefferson
Stuuntz Christian, clk H. Redelsheimer's

Stubnatzy Rev. W. h 176 Barr
Stuck Christina, cook St. Charles Restaurant'
Studer Bernard, cab mkr h s s Douglas, Bloomingdale
Stumpf Christ. cab mkr bds Mrs. Hannah Whaley's
Stumpf Louis, lab h 64 Clinton

STURGIS CHAS. E., Physician and Surgeon, Office, s w c Calhoun and Main, h n e c Griffith and Jefferson.

Sturgis E. L. bds Aveline House
Sturgis W. G. E. clk s e c Calhoun and Berry, bds Aveline House
Sudbrink Mrs. Minnie, widow h 92 W. Jefferson
Sudbrink Wm. molder h 92 W. Jefferson

SULLEY MRS. ELIZABETH, Fashionable Millinery, Fancy Goods, Hosiery, &c., n w c Calhoun and Wayne.

Sulley Richard, h n w c Calhoun and Wayne
Sullivan Coney, lab bds 70 Madison
Sullivan Hannah, waiter Ft. Wayne Eating House
Sullivan John, helper wks P., Ft. W. & C. Railway blksmith shop
Sullivan Miss Mary, res Mrs. Ellen Hunt's
Sullivan Peter, helper wks T. & W. Railway shop
Sultzman John, brewery 18 Monroe

SUMMIT CITY BREWERY, John George Hornung, Proprietor, e s Harrison b Berry and Wayne.

SUMMIT CITY HOTEL, C. P. & J. F. Fletcher, Proprietors, w s Calhoun, opp P., Ft. W. & C. Railroad.

SUMMIT CITY WOOLEN MILLS, French, Hanna & Co., Proprietors, s s Water b Barr and Lafayette.

Suren John, carp wks T. & W. Railway shops
Suthern Henry, plasterer h n s Holman b Clay and Lafayette
Sutton John, mach wks T. & W. Railway shops
Sutton John, lab h w s McClellan b Lewis and Douglas Av.
Swager Peter, carp wks Cochran, Humphrey & Co.'s
Swain Conrad, lab wks T. & W. Railway shops
Swain Miss Elizabeth, res Mrs. Nancy McClaren's
Swain Geo. plasterer h n w c College and Jefferson
Swain Jackson, stable s s Berry b Calhoun and Harrison, h n s Main b Maiden Lane and Cass
Swan Mrs. Arabella, widow h 145 E. Lewis
Swart M. pattern mkr wks P., Ft. W. & C. Railway carp shop
Sweet Benj. cooper h w s Calhoun b Highland and Dawson
Sweet Wm. cooper res Benj. Sweet's
Sweetser Madison, h 113 W. Main

Sweney James L. (Kamm & S.) h s s W. Water b Cass and Ewing
Sweringen Hiram V. clk Reed & Wall's, bds Mayer House
Swimley Andrew, carp wks F. S. Baldwin's
Swinney T. W. h w end of Jefferson

T

Tagtmeyer David, (Yergens & Co.) h n s Wilt b Van Buren and Jackson
Tagtmeyer Fred. h n s Wilt b Van Buren and Jackson
Tagtmeyer Fred. W. shoemkr h w s McClellan b Lewis and Douglas Av.
Talbot Alfred P. (D. L. & A. P. T.) res David L. Talbot's
TALBOT D. L. & A. P., (David L. & Albert P.,) Surgeon Dentists; Office, 3 Phœnix Block, w s Calhoun b Main and Columbia, up stairs.
Talbot David L. (D. L. & A. P. T.) h s s Washington b Van Buren and Jackson
Tam Silas, jr. clk American Express Co. bds Mayer House
Tannehill Lewis, carp h e s Piqua Plank Road b Virginia and Wallace
Tapner Margaret, servt Main Street Exchange
Tate Saml. h 173 Barr
Tavlin Mrs. Mary, widow h n s Water b Barr and Lafayette
Taylor C. F. bds 34 W. Water
Taylor Henry G. clk 85 Columbia, bds A. J. Emrick's
Taylor Horace B. res John B. Dubois
Taylor L. P. mach P., Ft. W. & C. Railway machine shop
Taylor Lyman, clk P., Ft. W. & C. Railway freight depot, bds Geo. R. Hartman's
Taylor Maurice A. b k First National Bank of Ft. Wayne, h 77 W. Wayne
Taylor R. Stewart, (Ninde & T.) h Fairfield Av.
Taylor R. W. com mer n w c Pearl and Maiden Lane, h 77 W. Wayne
Teckenbrock Fred. lab h 176 E. Wayne
Tegtmeier Ernst, mach bds Wm. Muellering's
Tegtmeier Wm. mach h 94 W. Water
Tennery John E. phys w s Calhoun b Main and Columbia, bds Phillips House
Tennery R. F. conductor P., Ft. W. & C. Railway, h 145 E. Jefferson
Terry Geo. molder bds 45 Madison
Thaine John, mason h s e c Washington and Rockhill
Theins Geo. lab h e s Garden b Jefferson and Railroad

Thele D. lab wks P., Ft. W. & C. Railway lumber yard
Thele Henry, lab h n s Lewis b Calhoun and Harrison
Thieme Andrew, butcher h s e c Van Buren and Wilt
Thieme Gottfried, tailor h w s Griffith s of Jefferson
Thieme J. G. & Bro. (John G. & J. Fred.) tailors, 71 Columbia
Thieme John Fred, (J. G. Thieme & Bro.) h n s Lewis b Harrison and Webster
Thieme John G. (J. G. T. & Bro.) h 51 E. Wayne

THOMAS CHAS. M., Upholsterer, Carriage Trimmer, and Manufacturer and Wholesale and Retail Dealer in Mattresses, 56 Columbia, bds Hedekin House.

Thomas James, carp wks T. & W. Railway shops
Thomas John, helper 48 E. Main, bds F. Bercot's
Thomas L. painter h s e c Lewis and Webster
Thompson Mrs. Ann M. h junction Bluffton Road and T. & W. Railway
Thompson Byron S. (Kauffman & T.) res Bluffton Road, 1 mile from city
Thompson Mrs. Harriet E. widow h 186 E. Wayne
Thompson Jerry, teamster h rear 199 E. Jefferson
Thompson John, lab h s s Wayne b Hanna and Francis
Thompson Salathiel S. millwright bds 64 Columbia
Thompson Wm. currier bds American House.
Thompson Wm. jeweler bds Main Street Exchange
Thorp Miss Martha, h 257 W. Wayne
Thorp Miss Mary, h 257 W. Wayne
Thorp Wm. fireman, h 62 Madison
Threadgall John, janitor h w s Griffith s of Jefferson
Tibbles John H. chair mkr h 73 E. Berry
Tickenboo F. lab wks P., Ft. W. & C. Railway Co. Yard
Tiele Dietrich, h n s Jefferson b Fulton and Broadway
Tierney T helper wks P., Ft. W. & C. Railway carp shop
Tiernon Thos. lab h 75 Madison
Tigar John, printer Ft. Wayne Sentinel office, bds 163 E. Berry
Tigar P. helper wks P., Ft. W. & C. Railway machine shop
Tigar Philip, eng bds 40 Madison

TIGAR THOMAS, Editor and Proprietor Daily and Weekly Ft. Wayne Sentinel Office, w s Calhoun c Pearl, h 163 E. Berry.

Tilton James J. conductor bds 136 W. Wayne
Tinkham Milan H. fireman h s s Bass b Prince and Fairfield Av
Titus Theodore, fireman h 60 Madison
Tobe Ulrich, lab h 157 E. Lewis
Tobey Rev. R. pastor Wayne Street M. E. Church, h 189 W. Wayne
Tobin Louis, helper wks Bowser & Story's

Todd Robt. (Fronefeld & T.) h 26 W. Water
Toland Mrs. Hannah, widow h n s Holman b Clay and Monroe
Toledo & Wabash Railway Freight Office and Depot, Railroad w of Calhoun

TOLEDO & WABASH RAILWAY SHOPS, on Railroad w of Webster.

TOLERTON ALEXANDER, Physician and Surgeon; Office, 107 W. Wayne, h 105 W. Wayne.

Tonney Lucy, servt Union House
Tons Henry, ins solicitor 50 Calhoun, h 80 W. Washington
Toohey F. helper wks P., Ft. W. & C. Railway blksmith shop
Toohey Stephen, helper bds Thos. Lynch's
Toomy Ellen, servt Gerhard Rekers'
Torbeck & Holzworth, (John T. & Edward H.) blksmiths n s Main b Harrison and Maiden Lane
Torbeck John, (T. & Holzworth,) h W. Jefferson
Totten Miss Anna M. res Mrs. Julia A. Totten's
Totten Mrs. Julia A. h e s Ewing b Wayne and Washington
Tower B. H. cab manuf n w c Water and Clinton, wareroom 59 Columbia, h s w c Wayne and Lafayette
Tower B. H. jr. clk 59 Columbia, res B. H. Tower's
Townley J. W. (T., DeWald & Bond,) res New Jersey
Townley R. W. (T., DeWald & Bond,) res New Jersey

TOWNLEY, DeWALD & BOND, (J. W. T., R. W. T., Geo. DeW. & H. W. B.,) Wholesale and Retail Dealers in Dry Goods, Carpets, Oil Cloths, Notions, &c., n e c Columbia and Calhoun.

Township Library, in Court House Building, Bernard Rekers, Librarian
Towsley Wm. carp bds Francis M. Luther's
Trahim Fanny, servt Hedekin House
Trainer John, carriage mkr bds n e c Main and Lafayette
Traub Fred. lab h s s Douglas Av. b Harrison and Webster
Traub John, boiler mkr wks P., Ft. W. & C. Railway boiler shop
Trauebet S. wagon mkr h e s Piqua Plank Road b Lassello and Buchanan
Traud ———, lab h 176 E. Washington
Trauerman Isaac, cigar mkr h 92 W. Main
Trautman J. blksmith wks P., Ft. W. & C. Railway blksmith shop
Travelbee John, shoemkr h 90 W. Water
Trebea Wm. lab h 95 E. Berry
Tremmel C. tinner wks P., Ft. W. & C. Railway repair shops
Tremmel Conrad, lab h e s Hanna s of Jones
Tremmel John, helper res Conrad Tremmel's
Trenam Geo. carp h n s Main b Fulton and Broadway
Trenchett C. carp wks P., Ft. W. & C. Railway carp shop

TRENTMAN B., Wholesale Grocer and Dealer in Foreign and Domestic Liquors, Cigars, &c., 86 Columbia, h 10 W. Water.
Trentman B. H. chandler h 151 E. Wayne
Trentman Gust. chandler, h 151 E. Wayne
Trentman Gust. clk 86 Columbia, h 10 W. Water
Trentman Henry, clk 86 Columbia, h 10 W. Water
Trentman John, clk 86 Columbia, h 10 W. Water
TRENTMAN JOHN, Soap and Candle Manufacturer, 51 Clay; h 151 E. Wayne.
Tresselt Chas. cashier 101 Columbia, h s s Jefferson b Barr and Lafayette
TRESSELT CHRISTIAN, Clerk City Flour Mills, h 55 E. Jefferson.
Tresselt Herman, clk 101 Columbia
Trevallee Oscar, shoemkr wks Jacob Foellinger's, bds 137 W. Main
Triplet Miss Hattie, res 189 W. Wayne
Tritchler John, file cutter wks C. Schmidt & Co.'s
Troub Fred. harness mkr L. Troub & Co.'s
Troub L. & Co. (Louis T. & Geo. Goode) saddles w s Calhoun b Main and Columbia
Troub Louis, (L. T. & Co.) h w s McClellan b Douglas Av. and Lewis
Troutman John, blksmith bds s w c Barr and Jefferson
Tubbs Asa, miller h 190 E. Wayne
Tubbs Chas. miller h 190 E. Wayne
Tubbs James, miller 190 E. Wayne
Tuchtenhagen Chas. h s e c Jefferson and College
Tullis John F. harness mkr bds American House
Turberg Maurice, lab h n s Hough b Clay and Monroe
Turner Mrs. Ann, h e s Barr b Lewis and Montgomery
Turner John H. mach wks T. & W. Railroad shops
Turner Levi, h n s Jefferson b Broadway and Van Buren
Tuttle Irwin, teamster wks B. H. Tower's
Tuttle Mrs. Sallie A. h 39 E. Water
Tyler Daniel L. clk 107 Columbia, bds H. W. Bond's
Tyler Mrs. Mary, widow h w s Van Buren b Wayne and Washington
Tyner Wm. blksmith bds C. S. Pantlind's
Tyner Wm. saddler h s s Water near Ewing
Tyrrell John R. carp h 220 W. Wayne
Tyrrell Volney B. eng h 177 Harrison
Tyson Harvey, cooper bds Thos. Dailey's

U

Ubelber Fred. plasterer h 141 Ewing
Uber Geo. eng bds Mrs. E. B. Grout's
Uebelhoer Fred. plasterer h n s Lavina b Broadway and Fulton
Uebelhoer Philip, shoemkr h e s Barr b Berry and Wayne
Ueltschi Gottlieb, clk 87 Columbia
Uhlman Henry, clk 49 Columbia, bds Geo. R. Hartman's
Underfoldt H. carp wks T. & W. Railway shops
Underhill F. W. foreman P. S. Underhill's, h e s Ewing b Wayne and Washington

UNDERHILL P. S., Proprietor Fort Wayne Steam Marble and Building Stone Works, n e c Main and Cass.

Underwood James H. carp h 229 E. Jefferson
Unger Andreas, lab h n s Wilt b Rockhill and College
Unger Fred. coppersmith wks T. & W. Railway shops
Unger Geo. phys h n w c Jackson and Washington
Union Block, n w c Clinton and Main

UNION HOUSE, H. H. Holley, Proprietor, 49 W. Main.

UNION TANNERY, Manok, Nestle & Co., Proprietors, n s W. & E. Canal, b Harrison and Cass.

UNITED STATES EXPRESS CO., S. McElvain, Agent, n w c Calhoun and Berry.

UNITED STATES INTERNAL REVENUE OFFICE, w s Calhoun, 3rd Door s of Main, W. H. Withers, Collector.

Updegraff Mrs. H. widow h n w c Harrison and Douglas Av.
Updegraff W. W. bds n w c Harrison and Douglas Av.
Upligger Chas. dyer wks Summit City Woolen Mill, b Bloomingdale
Upp Wm. carp h n e c Jefferson and Jackson
Urban John, lab h s s Berry near Harmer
Ure Wm. E. carriage smith bds Phillips House

V

Vail James D. train dispatcher h e s Fulton b Washington and Jefferson

VALROFF XAVIER, Proprietor Star Bakery, 92 E. Main.

VAN ALSTINE WM., Livery and Sale Stable, 45 and 47 Columbia; res. Country.
Vanandie Mrs. Eliza, widow h n w c Lafayette and Jefferson
Vanandie J. W. carp bds Phillips House
Van Giesen M. carp h n w c Broadway and Jefferson
Van Horn Joel, eng wks T. & W. Railway Co.
Van Horn Joseph, eng bds Luther Wright's
Van Norman Jacob, brakeman bds 57 Barr
Varelmann August, lab bds 43 W. Water
Vaughn Henry, butcher h 186 W. Main
Vaught Joseph, fireman bds 193 W. Washington
Vazeli Peter, lab wks T. & W. Railway shops
Vasie Frank, fireman wks T. & W. Railway Co.
Veglin Peter, lab h s s Walnut w of Oakley
Veith Peter, boatman h 263 E. Wayne
Vemont Mrs. M. bds Mayer House
Vemont Miss Mary, bds Mayer House
Vizzard Anthony, blksmith h n e c Bass and Prince
Vizzard John, lab h n w c Wilt and Van Buren
Vizzard Mrs. Rose, widow h n e c Bass and Prince
Vizzard Thos. lab wks T. & W. Railway shops

VOGEL C. G., Merchant Tailor, Clothier, and Dealer in Gents' Furnishing Goods, e s Calhoun b Columbia and Main.

VOGEL MRS. E., Fashionable Millinery, e s Calhoun b Columbia and Main.
Vogel Frank B. clk res C G. Vogel's
Vogt Fred. teamster wks Herman Wilken's
Voiroll Frank, clk 81 Columbia, h 75 Lafayette
Vollamer Daniel, clk Reed & Wall's, h 27 W. Water
Volland Henry, miller h s s Washington b Rockhill and College
Volmer Barney, carp wks T. & W. Railway shops
Volmer Barnard, lab h s s Locust w of Pine
Von Wilman R. E. phys h e s Calhoun b Washington and Jefferson
Voorhis Geo. (W. H. Brady & Co.) bds Aveline House
Vorce John, cook Fort Wayne Eating House

VORDERMARK E. & CO., (Ernst V. & Christian Schiefer,) Boot and Shoe Manufacturers and Dealers in Leather, Findings, &c., 4 Phœnix Block, w s Calhoun b Main and Columbia.
Vordermark Ernst, (E. V. & Co.) h 16 E. Washington
Vordermark Henry P. clk E. Vordermark & Co's, h 16 E. Washington
Voss Ernst, plasterer h 195 E. Jefferson
Voss Louis, plasterer h 195 E. Jefferson

WABASH & ERIE CANAL COLLECTOR'S OFFICE, n w c Columbia and Clinton, A. C. Probasco, Collector.
Waddington Wm. foreman carp shop P., Ft. W. & C. Railway Co., h n s Holman b Clay and Monroe
Wade Chas. M. mach h n s Wall w of Bluffton Road
Wadge Richard C. clk P., Ft. W. C. Railway office, h 49 E. Lewis
Wadge Wm. carp h 49 E. Lewis

WAGNER H. G., Dealer in Drugs, Medicines, Paints, Oils, Chemicals, &c., n e c Calhoun and Main; h s s Main b Maiden Lane and Cass.
Wagner John, carp bds s w c Barr and Jefferson
Wagner Theodore, lab wks T. & W. Railway Freight Depot
Wahmhoff Wm. h n s High, Bloomingdale
Wahmhuff Wm. carp wks Cochran, Humphrey & Co's
Walda Chas. carp h 215 E. Jefferson
Walda Christ, carp h s w c Washington and Nelson
Walda Fred. tailor h 217 E. Jefferson
Walda Fred, res Christ. Walda's
Walda Henry, carp h s w c Hanna and Wayne
Walda Herman, tailor bds 217 E. Jefferson
Walda Wm. carp h s w c Wayne and Hanna
Waldemuth Henry, lab wks T. & W. Railway shops
Walker F. J. (W. & Hildebrand) res country

WALKER & HILDEBRAND, (F. J. W. & Wm. H.,) Dealers in Family Groceries, Provisions, Wines, Liquors, &c., w s Calhoun b Wayne and Washington.
Walker James, trader h 53 W. Wayne
Walker Wm. plasterer bds Union House
Walkinshaw A. J. conductor bds n w c Ewing and Jefferson
Wall Watson, (Reed & W.) h s c c Main and Lafayette
Wallace Wm. plumber 48 E. Main, bds Hedekin House
Wallace Wm. blksmith bds 40 Madison
Wallace Wm. J. blksmith wks T. & W. Railway shops
Walles Fred. carp h 140 Harrison
Walls Mrs. Sarah, b h s w c Railroad and Kansas
Walraven J. C. boiler mkr h w s Broadway b Jefferson and Wilt
Walsh Eugene, bds Main Street Exchange
Waltemuth Henry, lab h 95 Madison
Walter Daniel, blksmith bds Christian Brun's

Walter Frank, shoemkr h w s Pine b Locust and T. & W. Railway
Walter John J. sorter Summit City Woolen Mills
Waltermuth Chas. boatman bds Wm. Rope's
Walters August, clk 100 Columbia
Walters W. B. h on east Branch Lima Plank Road n of St. Mary's River
Waltke Wm. polisher wks n e c Main and Cass
Waltke Wm. h n w c Madison and Monroe
Walmsley C. clk American Express Co., bds Main Street Exchange
Walmsley Christopher, messenger h n w c Washington and Ewing

WARD H. N., Importer, Wholesale and Retail Dealer in China, Glass, Queensware, House Furnishing Goods, Wood and Willow Ware, &c., 121 Columbia; h 233 W. Berry.

Ward Samuel, whitewasher h 157 E. Wayne
Ward Wm. boatman h n end of Harmer
Waring A. manuf bds Mayer House
Warner D. S. mach wks P., Ft W. & C. Railway machine shop
Warner David S. fireman h n s Douglas Av. b Harrison and Webster

WARNER GUSTAVUS, Manufacturer and Dealer in Cigars, Tobacco, Snuff, Pipes, &c., w s Calhoun b Berry and Wayne.

Warren C. W. clk 90 Columbia, bds Hamilton House
Warren D. V. conductor T. & W. Railway, bds Summit City Hotel
Washburn A. molder wks Fort Wayne Machine Works
Washburn Ezra, molder bds Francis M. Luther's
Waters John P. h 193 W. Washington
Watkins James F. b k John Hough's, bds Aveline House
Watson Mrs. Ann M. h 128 Madison
Watson Miss Lucy A. bds 257 W. Wayne
Watters Miss Elizabeth, h 135 W. Water
Watters Miss Harriet, h 135 W. Water
Waugh James, fireman res L. H. Waugh's
Waugh L. H. eng h s e c Lewis and Clay
Weaver J. Jacob, h s Wilt b Rockhill and College
Weaver Martin, plasterer bds Union House
Weaver Martin V. plasterer bds Wm. McClain's
Webb A. B. carp h 234 W. Wayne
Webb J. helper wks P., Ft. W. & C. Railway blksmith shop
Webb Marion, clk bds 170 W. Wayne
Webb Wm. W. fireman bds 145 E. Lewis
Webel Adam, shoemkr h n s Montgomery b Barr and Lafayette
Weber Andrew, pattern mkr h 181 Clinton

Weber Benj millwright wks Fort Wayne machine works

WEBER E., Dealer in Stoves, and Manufacturer of Tin, Copper and Sheet Iron Ware, w s Clinton b Main and Columbia; h e s Clinton b Jefferson and Lewis.

Weber Fred. h n s Railroad b Webster and McClellan
Weber J. J. teacher h 55 W. Washington
Weber John, packer City Flour Mills h 268 E. Washington
Weber Peter, mason h u s Jefferson b College and Nelson
Webster N. D. baggage master P., Ft. W. & C. Railway, bds Summit City Hotel
Weed Frank, conductor bds Mayer House
Weehn Jacob, shoemkr h w s Calhoun b Jefferson and Lewis
Wefel Fred boat builder h s s High, Bloomingdale
Wefel John H. carp h n s High, Bloomingdale
Wefel Wm. carp h 19 E. Washington
Wefel Wm., jr. carp h 214 W. Washington
Wechman Henry, shoemkr wks 46 Columbia
Wehmer Mrs. H. widow h 93 Clinton
Wehmer Louis H. druggist h 93 Clinton
Wehmer Theodore G. clk 75 Columbia, bds n e c Clinton and Wayne
Wehmeyer Herman, dray h 124 Harrison
Wehrs Miss Emeline, res Fort Wayne College
Wehrbine Henry, porter Fort Wayne College
Wehrs Wm. shoemkr h 133 E. Lewis
Wehr Wm. (M. Baltes & Co.) res Huntington
Weibert Michael, cab mkr h Bloomingdale
Weibking Christ. carp h 96 W. Jefferson
Weick Adam, shoemkr h e s Jefferson b Van Buren and Jackson
Weidbrock Henry, teamster h n s Bowser, Bloomingdale
Weigman J. polisher wks n e c Main and Cass
Weik Adam, (Mettler & Co.) bds Mathias Mettler's
Weil Jacob, peddler h 41 E. Wayne
Weimeire F. helper wks P., Ft. W. & C. Railway blksmith shop
Wein Jacob, shoemkr h w s Calhoun b Jefferson and Lewis
Weis Adam, tailor h 19 Clinton
Weis Adam, tailor bds 93 W. Water
Weisenberger Ben. lab wks Sam'l Edsall's
Weisenberger Jacob, boatman h Bloomingdale
Weisenthall Moses, tailor e s Calhoun b Berry and Wayne
Weisman Jacob, b h 32 W. Main

WEISSER E. & CO., (Emanuel W., J. F. Schellkopf, Buffalo, & B. Schroeter, St. Louis,) Tanners and Dealers in Leather, Hides, Shoe Findings, Curriers' Tools, &c., 63 Columbia.

Weisser Emanuel, (E. W. & Co.) res Washington township
Weitzel Chas. R. fireman h s e c Barr and Lewis

Welbel Barney, lab bds 128 E. Washington
Welch Geo. W. eng h s s Milita b Webster and Hoagland
Welch John, lab h n w c Colerick and Hoagland
Welch Patrick, blksmith shop n e c Water and Barr
Welch Wm. tailor h 70 Madison
Wells A. dentist s w c Calhoun and Berry, h 128 W. Wayne
Weldon Francis R. fireman h 121 W. Washington
Weldon Mrs. Mary, widow h 121 W. Washington
Weleneg Henry, cab mkr h 63 W. Jefferson
Welklin John, lab h n s Taylor w of Pine
Weller Mrs. Barbara, widow h s e c Barr and Wayne
Weller John, meat store n s Main b Calhoun and Harrison
Wellman Fred. lab wks Hurd and Clark's
Wells Andrew, J., b k 89 Columbia bds A. J. Emerick's
Wells C. M. h 2 Madison
Wells Harvey, printer Ft. Wayne Sentinel office, h 128 W. Wayne
Wells Hiram A. clk 90 Columbia bds Mayer House
Wells Joseph, carp bds Philips House
Wels Henry, tailor 71 Columbia
Welsh John, tinner bds John J. Jocquel's
Wettling John, warehouseman P., Ft. W. & C. Railway Freight Depot
Welton Fred. helper 48 E. Main
Welton J. helper wks P., Ft. W. & C. Railway machine shop
Wendel Henry, cooper bds 128 E. Washington
Wendelen Henry, cooper wks C. S. Brackenridge & Co.'s
Wendt Wm. shoemkr h 133 Lewis
Wengler W. carp wks P., Ft. W. & C. Railway carp shop
WENTE WM., Dealer in Family Groceries, Provisions, Liquors, &c., 74 Barr.
Wercher P. watchman at P., Ft. W. & C. Railway shops
Werden James D. h 98 W. Berry
Werrell J. helper wks P., Ft. W. & C. Railway blksmith shop
Wers Wm. carp h 69 E. Jefferson
Werschen Samuel, whitewasher h Bloomingdale
Wescott D. L. vinegar manuf'h 117 E. Wayne
Wescott Robt. mach h 117 E. Wayne
Wessel John, lab h n s Montgomery b Barr and Lafayette
Westenfeld J. helper wks P., Ft. W. & C. Railway carp shop
Western District School, s w c Jefferson and Griffith
WESTERN UNION TELEGRAPH; Office, n w c Columbia and Clinton, up stairs, C. K. Jones, Manager.
Weutz Rev. Joseph, h 132 E. Jefferson
Whaley Mrs. Hannah, b h w s Barr b Wayne and Washington
Whallon Alfred, shoemkr wks Noah Humphrey's
Wheeler Lewis C. eng h s s Washington b Griffith and Fulton

WHEDON D. P., Attorney at Law and Notary Public; Office, n w c Main and Calhoun, bds Aveline House.

WHEELER NELSON, Manufacturer and Dealer in Cabinet Furniture, Chairs, &c.; Wareroom, 57 Columbia, h s e c Ewing and Main.

Whipke Richard, lab wks T. & W. Railway shops
White C. lab wks P., Ft. W. & C. Railway lumber yard
White J. B. tailor h 56 Barr
White Nellie, bds s e c Pearl and Maiden Lane
White Wm. h 56 Barr
Whitehead A. eng wks P., Ft. W. & C. Railway Co
Whitmore Daniel, carp h e s Calhoun s of the Railroad
Whitmore Elan F. harness mkr h 43 Clinton
Whitmore John, teamster bds 53 E. Main
Whittaker Mary, servt wks Main Street Exchange
Whoolahen John, lab h n s Railroad w of McClellan
Wibel Placidus, carp h n s Jefferson b Van Buren and Jackson
Wichant Sebastian, carp h e s Piqua Plank Road b Virginia and Wallace
Wichman Alfred C F. carp h 176 Lafayette
Wichman Christian, tailor h 241 E. Washington
Wichman Ferdinand, tailor h 93 W. Water
Wichman Henry, boiler mkr wks T. & W. Railway shops
Wichman Rev. Herman, h 241 E. Washington
Wiebke Deitrich, h 197 Ewing
Wiebke Henry, grocer 112 Columbia, bds American House
Wieble P. cab mkr wks 50 E. Main
Wiedbrauk Christ. butcher h 54 Lafayette
Wiedenman Ulrich, lab h w s Calhoun b Washington and Jefferson
Wiegmann Fred. lab h 206 E. Jefferson

WIEMANN W., Confectionery, Ice Cream and Oyster Saloon, Union Block, n s Main b Calhoun and Clinton.

Wiesenthal Moses, tailor and renovator e s Calhoun b Berry and Wayne, h s e c Main and Harrison
Wiesmer Nicholas, shoemkr h n s Buchanan e of Piqua Plank Road
Wiggins J. M. fireman wks P., Ft. W. & C. Railway Co.

WIGMAN HENRY, Dealer in Family Groceries, Provisions, &c., 17 E. Main.

Wigman Henry, h s s Sturgis w of Fulton
Wigman Henry, shoemkr h s s Berry near Harmer
Wigman Wm. blksmith h 97 W. Jefferson
Wike Adam, shoemkr h s s Jefferson b Van Buren and Jackson
Wilcox Mrs. Clark L. h 180 E. Wayne
Wilcox Lester, carp bds 212 E. Lewis

Wilde August, teacher h w s Barr opp Madison
Wilder E. fireman wks P., Ft. W. & C. Railway Co.
Wilder Henry J. h 107 W. Main
Wilder J. M. (J. B. Fry and Co.) h 107 W. Main
Wilder Joseph, shoemkr h 123 Columbia
Wilding James, plasterer h n s Wayne b Union and Rockhill

WILEY A., Treasurer Allen County; Office, Court House, h n w c Barr and Washington.

Wilke Joseph, watchmkr 88 Columbia

WILKEN HERMAN, Saw Mill and Lath Factory, e s Cass b W. & E. Canal and Water, h n w c Water and Cass.

Wilkening Gotleib, carp h 100 W. Jefferson
Wilkins Christ. butcher h n e c Water and Clinton
Wilkinson F. fireman wks P., Ft. W. & C. Railway Co.
Wilkinson Wm. helper bds 251 E Jefferson
Will Henry, helper bds 251 E. Jefferson
Willemburg Herman, cigar mkr 100 Columbia, bds Steuben House
Willett Wm. conductor h 158 W. Wayne
Willey Susan, chambermaid at Mayer House
Williams Henry, h 210 W. Berry
Williams Henry M. h 96 W. Wayne

WILLIAMS JESSE L., Civil Engineer; Office and Residence, 96 W. Main.

Williams John, lab h 172 W. Jefferson
Williams Ned, lab bds 64 Columbia
Willson Eliza J. teacher Western District School, h s w c Griffith and Berry
Willson O. J. clk Master Mechanic's office T. & W. Railway, bds n e c Barr and Lewis
Wilmington J. B. blksmith wks P., Ft. W. & C. Railway blksmith shop
Wilmot J. C. painter and paper hanger 66 E. Berry, h n s Berry b Clinton and Barr
Wilson Ael, carp bds John Sarns'
Wilson Geo. H. (Allen & Co.) h 132 W. Wayne
Wilson W. C. b k h s w c Berry and Griffith
Wilt John M. surveyor h w s Calhoun b Railroad and Highland
Winbaugh John, carp h s w c Lewis and Lafayette
Wineland J. blksmith wks P., Ft. W. & C. Railway blksmith shop
Wines Mrs. Elizabeth, h 155 W. Berry
Winkelmann Christian, lab h w s Griffith b Berry and Wayne
Winkler J. carp wks P., Ft. W. & C. Railway carp shop
Winn Jacob, shoemkr h w s Calhoun b Jefferson and Lewis

WINN LEVI, Clerk Aveline House.

Winte John D. helper h w s Calhoun b Highland and Dawson
Wirsche Peter, watchman h w s Jackson b Pritchard and Railroad

WISE PLATT J., Recorder Allen County; Office, Court House, h 230 W. Berry.
Wise R. fireman wks P., Ft. W. & C. Railway Co.

WITHERS, MORRIS & CASE, (W. H. W., John M. & Chas. C.,) Attorneys at Law; Office, w s Calhoun, 3d Door s of Main.
Withers W. H. (W., Morris & Case,) collector Internal Revenue, office w s Calhoun 3d door s of Wayne, res Washington township
Witte Christ. lab bds 75 Madison
Witte Mrs. Lizzetta, widow h 205 E. Jefferson
Wittenger Joseph, lab wks Ft. Wayne Machine Works
Wittie Wm. boiler mkr wks T. & W. Railway shops
Witzikreuter Max, clk 95 Columbia, bds John F. W. Meyer's
Woebking Christ. carp h 96 W. Jefferson
Wohnker Fred. h 203 E. Washington
Wolf Abraham, meat store 65 W. Main, b 67 W. Main
Wolf Adam, harness mkr bds Hedekin House
Wolf Chas. harness mkr bds Hedekin House
Wolf Mrs. Margaretta, widow h 117 Madison
Wolf Patrick, shoemkr b n e c Calhoun and Jefferson
Wolfe James M. carp h e s Hood b Pritchard and Railroad
Wolff J. M. carp wks P., Ft. W. & C. Railway carp shop
Wolke F. H. clk P., Ft. W. & C. Railway freight office, h s w c Calhoun and Wayne
Wolke Fred. A. carp h s w c Calhoun and Wayne
Wolke Fred. Louis, h s w c Calhoun and Wayne
Wolph John, blksmith bds n e c Main and Lafayette
Wood G. W. land agt n w c Barr and Perry, h 50 W. Water
Wood Marvin, fireman wks P., Ft. W. & C. Railway Co.
Wood Thos. L. helper wks T. & W. Railway shops
Wood Thos. foreman blksmiths T. & W. Railway Co. h w s Broadway b Jefferson and Wilt

WOODLAWN FLAX AND FLOUR MILLS; Office, east end of Columbia and Lafayette.
Woodley Louisa, servt Hedekin House
Woodward Mrs. Caroline, widow h 20 E. Berry
Woodward Mrs. Carrie, widow h n s Main b Lafayette and Clay
Woodward Miss Hattie, school n s Wayne b Clinton and Calhoun, b 144 E. Main
Woodward Jesse, brakeman bds n w c Lafayette and Montgomery
Woodward M. E. (W. & Young) h 144 E. Main
Woodward & Young, (M. E. W. & N. B. Y.) tailors, 94 Columbia

Woodward R. H. Indian phys 94 Columbia, h n s Berry b Van Buren and Jackson
Woodworth B. S. phys n w c Calhoun and Main, h 234 W. Berry c Jackson
WORDEN & COOK, (W. H. W. & E. D. C.) Dealers in Family Groceries, Provisions, &c., 19 Clinton.
Worden J. L. Judge Supreme Court, h 99 E. Jefferson
Worden W. H. (W. & Cook,) h 137 W. Main
Worden Willis, clk 103 Columbia, bds Christian Orff's
Working Men's Institute Rooms, in Court House Building
Wort J. M. wks 154 W. Berry
Wortman August, shoemkr bds 52 Columbia
Wright John, clk bds 85 Barr
Wright Luther, carp h w s Calhoun b the Railroad and Highland
Wynekend Rev. ———, h on east branch Lima Plank Road n of St. Mary's River
Wyrick Joseph, cooper wks C. S. Brackenridge & Co.'s

X

Xavier ———, lab bds 48 Columbia

Y

Yates Wm. umbrella mkr h n s Wayne b Hanna and Francis
Yergens Christian F. W. (Keefer, Y. & Fayman,) bds Mayer House
Yergens & Co. (Wm. Y., David Tegtmeier & Wm. Busse,) saw mill w s Ewing b the Canal and Water
Yergens Wm. (Y. & Co.) h 85 W. Washington
Yeoke Henry, carp wks Bowser & Story's
Yeoman Chas. tailor bds Kime House
Yingst Jacob, saw filer h 66 E. Berry
Yobst Alex. lab h n s Montgomery b Barr and Lafayette
Yobst Ammandt, lab h 151 E. Lewis
Yobt B. butcher h s s Nirdlinger w of Bluffton Road
Yobt Bruno, cooper wks C. S. Brackenridge & Co.'s
Young Chas. tanner wks Union Tannery
Young Mrs. Elizabeth, h w s Hood b Pritchard and Railroad
Young Fred. carp bds n c Jefferson and Jackson
Young Jacob, lab bds 63 E. Water
Young Jacob, stable al b Columbia and Main and Calhoun and Clinton, h 52 W. Main

Young Michael, clk bds 14 E. Water
Young N. B. (Woodward & Y.) bds Mayer House
Young Philip, lab h n s Lewis b Francis and Harmer
Youngblood R. fireman wks P. Ft. W. & C. Railway Co.
Youngblood Saml. eng h 167 E. Lewis

Zahn Wm. lab h 210 E. Jefferson
Zang Valentine, lab h 258 E. Wayne
Zauner Mathias, fireman h e s Force s of Jones
Zekind Mrs. Dorothea, widow h 140 W. Wayne
Zern Xavier, lab res Jones & Bass' Foundry Addition
Ziegler Adam, wagon mkr h s s Wilt b College and Nelson
Ziegler G. W. carp wks P., Ft. W. & C. Railway carp shop
Zimmerly John W. painter h 92 E. Jefferson
Zimmerman Anthony, driver, h 15 E. Wayne
Zimmerman Anton, shoemkr h n s Wall w of Bluffton Road
Zimmerman Anton, driver at 92 E. Main
Zimmerman David, shoemkr h w s Lima Plank Road, Bloomingdale
Zimmerman Francis E. clk 75 Columbia, bds Mayer House
Zimmerman Mathias, lab wks Murray & Bennigin's
Zimmerman Martin, helper bds 174 E. Jefferson
Zimmerman Stephen, boots and shoes 92 Columbia up stairs, h Bloomingdale
Zimmerman T. E. clk bds Mayer House
Zinck John, lab h s s Locust w of Pine
Zollinger Fritz, turner wks 50 E. Main
Zucker James, cooper wks C. S. Brackenridge & Co.'s
Zuger S. helper wks P., Ft. W. & C. Railway boiler shop

Fort Wayne Business Mirror.

For Residence and Business Location see Alphabetical List of Names in the body of the Work.

Agents, Collecting.

BAYLESS SOL. D.
CARIER A. H.
CHITTENDEN E. L.
HOUGH JOHN

Agricultural Implements.

COMPARET D. F.
COOMBS & DRAKE
FORT WAYNE AGRICULTURAL WORKS
OAKLEY B. W.
REITZELL, SHUNK & CO.

Architect.

McELFATRICK J. B.

Artist.

Burr Mrs. E. L.

Attorneys at Law.

BAYLESS SOL. D.
Borden James W.
BOWEN D. W.
BRACKENRIDGE JOSEPH
BRACKENRIDGE ROBERT
Car-on W. W.
CHITTENDEN E. L.
COLERICK D. H.
Colerick David
Colerick Walpole G.
Coombs Wm. H.
Crane & Smith
Dubois John
EDGERTON J. K.
FAY JAMES A.
Gilkison W. S.
Griffiths Wm.
Hamilton A. H.
HARTMAN H. C.
HOUGH JOHN
JAHN CARL G.
JENKINSON ISAAC
Jenkinson Moses
NINDE & TAYLOR
RANDALL F. P.
Robinson H. H.
RYAN D.
SPENCER MARTIN V. B.
Steevens Wm. W.
WHEDON D. P.
WITHERS, MORRIS & CEAS

Auction and Commission.

STAPLEFORD L. P.

Bakeries.

ALBERT JULES
AMEND ANDREW
BLASE LOUIS

Fuherer Fred.
HOBROCK WM.
MEYER GEO.
RANKE WM.
SCHWIETERS HERMAN
VALROFF XAVIER

Bankers.

FIRST NATIONAL BANK OF FORT WAYNE
FORT WAYNE BRANCH OF THE STATE BANK
HAMILTON ALLEN & CO.

Barbers.

Brooks Bryant
Burgess Mrs. Eliza
Elliott Willis
Heldt & Shidel
Lang Geo.
Riale Sampson

Basket Dealer.

Schanck Louis

Bath House.

Brooks Bryant

Belting.

COOMBS & DRAKE
OAKLEY B. W.

Bending Factory.

OLDS, HANNA & CO.

Billiard Rooms.

CARY & KNIGHT
HANNUM D. & CO.
O'CONNELL D.
PALACE HALL, (GILBERT BREWER)
Stein Charles

Blacksmiths.

BAKER JOHN
Becker Fred.
Brosserd Geo.
BROWN JOHN
Chovey John B.
Fairfield John
FARNAN OWEN
Harter Joseph
Heidinreich Joseph
Koenig Jacob
Meyer Henry
PANTLIND C. S.
Stillhorn Henry
Torbeck & Holzworth
Welch Patrick

Blank Books.

SIEMON A. F. & BRO.
STOCKBRIDGE N. P.

Boarding Houses.

Aufrecht Jacob
Beals Wm.
Bercot Francis
French Mrs. S. M.
Gable Christian
Graham Mrs. Ann
Hamilton House
Harter Geo.
Hartman Geo. R.
Leifels J. J.
Lynch Thos.
McMullen Mrs. R.
MANIER HYPOLITE
Miller Peter
O'Gorman Mrs. Bridget
Old Fort House
Phelps C. N.
Ritchey Joseph
Walls Mrs. Sarah
Weisman Jacob
Whaley Mrs. Hannah

Boiler Manufacturers.

FORT WAYNE MACHINE WORKS

Book Binders.

SIEMON A. F. & BRO.
STOCKBRIDGE N. P.

Books, Stationery, &c.

BROOKS WM. H., Jr.
SIEMON A. F. & BRO.
STOCKBRIDGE N. P.

Boots and Shoes.

Baker Conrad
EVANS & CO.
Foellinger Jacob
FRY J. B. & CO.
HUMPHREY NOAH
Jacobs W. & Son
KETCHER & APP
KLINE PETER
Kosters John G.
MANNIX THOMAS
Mohlmeister Henry
Mohr John
Moyer & Bowers
NILL C.
Nill George
NOLL MARTIN
PIPENBRINK CHRISTIAN
PIPENBRINK CONRAD D.
PROUTY F. M.
ROBINSON JAMES H.
Sachs David
SANDER C. W.
SCHULZ PETER
Schulz William
VORDERMARK E. & CO.
Zimmerman Stephen

Brass Founder.

HATTERSLEY ALFRED

Breweries.

BECK FRANCIS J.
CENTLIVRE L. & L. C.
Hartman Herman
HORNUNG JOHN GEORGE

NIERMANN H. & M.
Sultzman John

Building Stone Works.

HUMPHREY JAMES
UNDERHILL P. S.

Butter and Egg Packers.

AMMON & HENRY
MURRAY & CO.

Cabinet Ware.

GRIEBEL LOUIS
KLAEHN JOHN J.
MILLER JOHN M.
Tower B. H.
WHEELER NELSON

Canal Office.

WABASH & ERIE

Candle Manufacturer.

TRENTMAN JOHN

Candy Manufacturers.

Beard Thos. D.
HUESTIS A. C.

Carpenters and Builders.

ALLEN C. W.
Baldwin S,
BEAVER A. C.
Breidenstein Mathias
COCHRAN, HUMPHREY & CO.
FRENCH CHARLES G.
Harrington John S.
Hill & Lemmon
KIMBALL BENJ. H.
McELFATRICK J. B.
POTTER JOSEPH L.
Rekers B. J.
SHEAFER W. G.

Carpets, Oil Cloths, &c.

ABBOTT WM. T.
EVANS & CO.
KEEFER, YERGENS & FAYMAN
LAUFERTY ISAAC
TOWNLEYS, DE WALD & BOND

Carriage Manufacturers.

Beston & McMaken
King Jacob, jr.
STANLEY C.
STEVENS THOMAS

Chain Pump Manufacturer.

Mettler & Co.

Chair Manufacturers.

MILLER JOHN M.
WHEELER NELSON

Children's Cabs.

Schanck Louis

China, Glass, &c.

WARD H. N.

Cigars, Tobacco, &c.

Buchnemann John
DESSAUER L.
FOELLINGER J. M.
GRAFF MARX
Grote H. A.
LAMLEY & ROSENTHAL
REDELSHEIMER S.
TRENTMAN B.
WARNER GUSTAVUS

Civil Engineers and Surveyors.

McARTHUR JOHN W.
WILLIAMS JESSE L.

Clothiers.

Bostick E.
FLEDDERMAN JOHN G. & CO.
Freeman J.
JACOBSON ELKAN
Jacobson Vigdor
LAUFERTY ISAAC
MOSSLER LEWIS & CO.
NIRDLINGER & OPPENHEIMER
STOCKBRIDGE N. P.
VOGEL C. G.
Woodward & Young

Coal Dealers.

EDGERTON ALFRED P.
FARNAN OWEN

Collecting Agents.

BAYLESS SOL. D.
HARTMAN & BOSSLER
HOUGH JOHN

Colleges.

CONCORDIA COLLEGE
FT. WAYNE COLLEGE

Commercial College.

FRANCISCO M. J.

Commissioner of Deeds.

McARTHUR JOHN W.

Commission Merchants.

COMPARET D. F.
EDSALL WM. S.
HASKELL WASHINGTON
Hill & Orbison
HOOD W. E.
LITTLE GEO. L.
Taylor R. W.

Confectioners.

COLERICK JOHN A.
HUESTIS A. C.
WIEMAN W.

Contractors.

Baldwin S.
BALTES M. & CO.
BEAVER A C.
FRENCH CHARLES G.
KANNE & CO.
RYAN JAMES W.
SILVER D. J.

Cooperage & Coopers' Material.

BRACKENRIDGE C. S. & CO

Coopers.

HASWELL & PIERCE
Hoffmeister Henry
Kley Fred.
Reinhardt John

Cutlery.

KANE JAMES M. & BRO.

Dentists.

KNAPP I.
Merriam J. F.
TALBOT D. L. & A. P.
Wells A.

Drawing School.

SCHOENBEIN ALBERT F.

Dress Makers.

CHAPIN MRS. M. E.
Gable Miss Hannah
GABLE & SHORDON
Gridley Mrs. J. A.
Killen & Morgan
Parent Mrs. Rachel
SEXTON FLORA

Druggists.

MEYER & BROTHER
REED & WALL
SANDMEYER A. L.
SCHOERPF C. & CO.
WAGNER H. G.

Dry Goods.

ABBOTT WM. T.
EATON & CO.
EVANS & CO.
Grey C. A
Hill Mrs John H..
KEEFER, YERGENS & FAYMAN
KISER PETER
LAUFERTY ISAAC
McDOUGAL & CO.
MOSSLER LOUIS H.
ORFF & CO.
PIERR PETER
Sachs David
SCHWEGMANN H. R.
TOWNLEYS DE WALD & BOND

Dyer.

Jerman A. S.

Eating Houses.

ALBERT JULES
AMEND ANDREW
COTHRELL JARED
FT. WAYNE EATING HOUSE
HOBROCK WM.

Embroidery and Braid Stamping.

Cooper Mrs. Eleanor

Emigrant Agency.

PIEPENBRINK CHRIST.

Express Companies.

AMERICAN EXPRESS CO.
UNITED STATES EXPRESS CO.

Fancy Goods.

Adair & Hunter
KANE JAMES M.
MERGEL R.
REDELSHEIMER H.
SEXTON FLORA
SULLEY MRS. ELIZABETH

File Manufacturers.

SCHMIDT C. & CO.

Flax Mill.

COMPARET & HASKELL

Flooring Mills.

HURD & CLARK
Tower B. H.

Flour and Feed Stores.

AMMON & HENRY
BEAVER D. S.

Flour Mills.

BEAVER D. S.
BROWN JOHN
Cody Morris
COMPARET D. F.
COMPARET & HASKELL
HOAGLAND P. & CO.
ORFF JOHN

Foreign Express and Emigrant Agent.

PIEPENBRINK CHRISTIAN

Foreign Fruits

HUESTIS A. C.

Freight Office and Depot.

PITTSBURGH, FT. WAYNE & CHICAGO
Toledo & Wabash

Fruit Dealers.

FOELLINGER J. M.
LAMLEY & ROSENTHAL
PIERR PETER
SHEPARD A.

Fur Dealers

BASH & EAKIN
Filson R. C.

Gas Company.

FORT WAYNE GAS COMPANY

Gas Fitter

HATTERSLEY ALFRED

Gents' Furnishing Goods.

Bostick E.
BRADY W. H. & CO.
Clark Joseph
FLEDDERMAN JOHN G. & CO.
Freeman J.
JACOBSON ELKAN
NIRDLINGER & OPPENHEIMER
SPENCER & PARKER
VOGEL C. G.
Woodward & Young

Grain Dealers

BROWN JOHN
COMPARET D. F.
EDSALL WM. S.
Hill & Orbison
LITTLE GEO. L.
Taylor R. W.

Groceries.

ABBOTT WM. T.
ANDERSON & EVANS
BECK JOHN

BEEGAN M. P.
Bercot Francis
BLYLER D.
Boling Lemuel
BRACKENRIDGE T. K.
BREEN & DUNN
Clarke Joseph
COLERICK JOHN A.
CORCORAN PATRICK
Daum Jacob
ENGELKING FRED.
Fink Charles
FOELLINGER J. M.
Fox Mrs. F.
GAFFENEY & McDONNELL
GALE GEO. A.
Gisb Samuel
Greensfelder Gustavo
HAMBROCK FRED.
HFDEKIN T. B.
HEITKAMP CONRAD
Hickman Elijah
Hogan Timothy
HOKE JACOB
HOOD W. E.
KENNING WM.
KISER PETER
Kline J.
Kosters J. H.
KRATZSCH HERMAN
Maier John G.
Mangeot John
MANIER HYPOLITE
MERGEL REINHARD
MONNING HENRY
NATER JOHN H.
O'CALLAHAN JOHN
Phillips B.
PIERR PETER
Rabb John
REDELSHEIMER H.
REDELSHEIMER S.
RIEDMILLER JOHN M.
Schele & Lower
Schone Henry
SCHWEGMAN H. R.
Seibald Christian
WALKER & HILDEBRAND
WENTE WM.

Wiebke Henry
WIGMAN HENRY
WORDEN & COOK

(*Wholesale.*)

HEDEKIN T. B.
HUESTIS A. C.
McCOMB & CO.
TRENTMAN B.

Gunsmith.

LEONARD WM.

Gun Stock Manufacturer.

McArdle J. H.

Hardware, Cutlery, &c.

ASH & AGNEW
BRANDRIFF A. D. & CO.
COOMBS & DRAKE
KISER PETER
MORGAN & BUECH
OAKLEY B. W.
SCHMIDT C. & CO.

Hats and Caps.

JACOBSON ELKAN
Nachtrieb J. F.
SCHWEGMAN H. R.
SHARP H.
SPENCER & PARKER
STOCKBRIDGE N. P.

Hides, Pelts, &c.

BASH & EAKIN
Filson R. C.
Heilbroner S.
ROBINSON JAMES H.

Homœopathic Pharmacy.

SANDMEYER A. L.

Horse Collar Manufacturers.

NEIREITER CONRAD
RACINE AIME
SCHWEGEL JACOB

Horse Shoeing.

Becker Fred.
Fairfield John
FARNAN OWEN
Howly & Patten

Hosiery, &c.

Adair & Hunter

Hotels.

AMERICAN HOUSE
AVELINE HOUSE
HEDEKIN HOUSE
KIME HGUSE
MAIN STREET EXCHANGE
MAYER HOUSE
PHILLIPS HOUSE
STEUBEN HOUSE
SUMMIT CITY HOTEL
UNION HOUSE

House Furnishing Goods.

ALLEN & CO.
ASH & AGNEW
BRANDRIFF A. D. & CO.
WARD H. N.

Hub and Spoke Manufacturers.

OLDS, HANNA & CO.

Ice Cream and Oyster Saloons.

HUESTIS A. C.
WIEMANN W.

Ice Dealers.

Cody M. & Co.
SEIDEL EDWARD

Insurance Agents.

BAYLESS SOL. D.
Fisk Wm. W.
HARTMANN & BOSSLER
Hartman Geo. R.
HOUGH JOHN
RANDALL F. P.

Insurance Companies.

BANNER INSURANCE CO.
Fort Wayne Insurance Co.
STATE INSURANCE CO.

Iron Founders.

BASS & HANNA
BOWSER & STORY
FT. WAYNE AGRICULTU-
RAL WORKS
MURRAY & BENNIGIN

Iron, Nails, &c.

BRANDRIFF A. D. & CO.
COOMBS & DRAKE
MORGAN & BUECH
OAKLEY B. W.
SCHMIDT C. & CO.

Justices of the Peace.

Milliman C. V. N.
SAUNDERS BENJAMIN

Knitting Machines.

KIRBY JAMES A., Agent

Ladies' Furnishing Store.

BRADY W. H. & CO.

Lamps.

ASH & AGNEW
MEYER & BROTHER
REED HUGH B. & CO.
SCHOERPF C. & CO.

WAGNER H. G.
WARD H. N.

Land Dealers.

CARIER A. H.
EDGERTON ALFRED P.
HOUGH JOHN
RANDALL F. P.
WOOD G. W.

Lath Factories.

BAKER J. K. & H.
WILKEN HERMANN

Leather Dealers.

Jacobs W. & Son
KLINE PETER
Nill George
ROBINSON JAMES H.

Leather Findings, &c.

Fry Jacob
ROBINSON JAMES H.
SANDER C. W.
VORDERMARK E. & CO.
WEISSER E. & CO.

Lightning Rods.

Barbour M. F.
McNAMARA J. W. & CO.

Lime, Plaster and Cement.

BALTES M. & CO.
KANNE & CO.
PAUL & KOSTER

Liquors, Wines, &c.

BEEGAN M. P.
BREEN & DUNN
Clark Joseph
Falk L.
Graeffe & Muhler
GRAFF MARX

Kline J.
MEYER & BROTHER
MONNING HENRY
O'CALLAHAN JOHN
Phillips B.
Raab John
REDELSHEIMER S.
TRENTMAN B.
WALKER & HILDEBRAND

Livery and Sale Stable.

Fletcher & Co.
GLYNN MATHIAS
Parent Hiram J.
READ A. J. & CO.
Swain Jackson
VAN ALSTINE WM.
Young Jacob

Locksmith.

REIEING AUGUST

Looking Glass Plates.

MILLER JOHN M.

Lumber Dealers.

ALLEN C. W.
HURD & CLARK
LEHMAN CHAS.

Machinists.

BOWSER & STORY
FT. WAYNE AGRICULTU-
    RAL WORKS
FT. WAYNE MACHINE
    WORKS
MURRAY & BENNIGIN
RASTETTER LOUIS

Marble Dealers and Workers.

Becker Christian
UNDERHILL P. S.

Mattress Manufacturers.

Dachsteiner J. W. & Co.
MILLER JOHN M.
THOMAS CHAS. M.

Meat Stores.

Buchfink & Neff
Burhan Edward
DOELKER JACOB
ECKART FREDERICK
Fischer Isaac
Irwin Thos.
Klinger H.
Weller John
Wolf Abraham

Millinery.

Bradford Mrs. M. E. & Co.
CHAPIN MRS. M. E.
GABLE & SHORDON
Gridley Mrs. J. A.
Hill Mrs. John H.
ORFF & CO.
SCHWEGMAN H. R.
SEXTON FLORA
Shilling Miss & Co.
SULLEY MRS. ELIZABETH
VOGEL MRS. E.

Mill Gearing and Machinery.

BOWSER & STORY
FORT WAYNE MACHINE WORKS

Moulding Manufacturers.

BALDWIN F. S.
Mettler & Co.

Musical Instruments and Sheet Music.

BROOKS WM. H., Jr.
HILL C. L.
STOCKBRIDGE N. P.

Music Teachers.

Fay Miss Clara A.
Hardik Edward
Orff Henry
Strubey Chas.

Newspapers.

DAWSON'S FORT WAYNE TIMES
FORT WAYNE GAZETTE
FORT WAYNE SENTINEL
INDIANA DEMOKRAT
INDIANA STAATS ZEITUNG

News Stand.

SMITH LORIN

Notaries Public.

BOSSLER HENRY H.
BOWEN D. W.
CARIER A. H.
CHITTENDEN E. L.
Chittenden W. B.
Colerick Walpole G.
Griffiths Wm.
Hamilton A. H.
HARTMAN HOMER C.
JAHN CARL G.
PIEPENBRINK CHRISTIAN
Robinson H. H.
RYAN D.
Smith Wm. S.
SPENCER, MARTIN V. B.
TAYLOR R. STEWART
Watkins James F.
WHEDON D. P.

Notions.

Adair & Hunter
KANE JAMES M. & BRO.
KRATZSCH HERMAN
MERGEL REINHARD
TOWNLEYS, DE WALD & BOND

Nursery.

NELSON, DE GROFF & CO.

Oculist and Aurist.

STEVENS G. L.

Omnibus Lin

O'CONNELL JOHN

Optician.

REDELSHEIMER H

Oranges, Lemons

HUESTIS A. C.

Oysters.

FOELLINGER J. M.
HUESTIS A. C.

Painters.

Altor Jacob
ANDERSON FELIX H.
Day H.
KAMM & SWENEY
Miller Louis
Ohneck Peter
RIVERS F. W.
Wilmot J. C.

Paints, Oils, &c.

MEYER & BROTHER
REED & WALL
SCHOERPF C. & CO.
WAGNER H. G.

Paper Hanging.

ANDERSON F. H.
KAMM & SWENEY
Wilmot J. C.

Paper Hangings.

BROOKS WM. H., Jr.
SIEMON A. F. & BRO.
STOCKBRIDGE N. P.
WARD H. N.

Periodical Depot.

SMITH LORIN

Photographs.

Andrews & Conklin
Benham B. H.
Brindle Samuel
DUNCKLEBURG WM.
SHOAFF J. A.

Physicians and Surgeons.

AYRES H. P.
BOWEN G. W.
Brittingham W. B.
BROOKS WM. H., Sen.
BRUEBACH GEO. THEO-
    DORE
DAILY & ERWIN
JORDAN JOHN P.
Josse John M.
LEONARD P. M.
Lieber F.
McCULLOUGH T. P.
MEYER CHAS.
MYERS WM. H.
Rosenthal Isaac M.
Schmitz Charles
SMITH C. S.
STURGIS CHAS. E.
Tennery John E.
TOLERTON ALEXANDER
Unger Geo.
Von Wilman R. E.
Woodward R. H.
Woodworth B. S.

Pianos, &c.

ANDERSON & IRVING
HILL C. L.
STOCKBRIDGE N. P.

Planing Mills.

BALDWIN F. S.
Fronefield & Todd
HURD & CLARK

Plow Manufacturers.

BAKER JOHN
BOWSER & STORY
BROWN JOHN
Buschman F. W.
Reid A. D.

Plumber.

HATTERSLEY ALFRED

Pork Packer.

EDSALL WM. S.

Potash Manufacturers.

Dohman Wm.
GRIFFITH & CO.

Printers.

DAWSON JOHN W.
INDIANA DEMOKRAT
INDIANA STAATS ZEI-
  TUNG
JONES & JENKINSON
SIEMON A. F. & BRO.
TIGAR THOMAS

Produce Dealers.

COMPARET D. F.
Friberger Simon
HASKELL WASHINGTON
LITTLE GEO. L.
MURRAY & CO.

Pump Manufacturers.

BARLOW & KYLE

Railroad Offices.

PITTSBURGH, FT. WAYNE
  & CHICAGO
Toledo & Wabash

Real Estate Agents.

BAYLESS SOL. D.
HARTMAN & BOSSLER
HOUGH JOHN
RANDALL F. P.
STAPLEFORD L. P.

Reaping and Mowing Machines.

FORT WAYNE AGRICUL-
  TURAL WORKS
REITZELL, SHUNK & CO.

Renovator.

Wiesenthal Moses

Restaurants.

O'CONNELL D.
St. Charles
ST. NICHOLAS
SPEREISEN ADOLPH

Saddles, Harness, &c.

Bayless T. W.
Goode & Co.
NEIREITER CONRAD
Shoaff S. H.
Troub L. & Co.

Saddlery Hardware.

NEREITER CONRAD
OAKLEY B. W.

Saloons.

Aufrecht Jacob
CARY & KNIGHT
Collar D. W.
ENGELKING FRED.
FISCHER A.

FLETCHER C. P. & J. F.
GAFFENEY & McDONNELL
Gish Samuel
Glutting Jacob
Goodman F. X.
Gosch Henry
Graeffe & Muhler
HAMBROCK FRED.
Hartwell Wm.
HEITKAMP CONRAD
HOGAN TIMOTHY
HOUSER & KALBACHER
Katisch Fred.
Kabisch Julius
Kay Wm.
KENNING WM.
Kline P. W.
MANIER HYPOLITE
MONNING HENRY
Myers Deitrich
NATER JOHN H.
Nitsche Chas.
O'CONNELL D.
Ryan Patrick
St. Charles
ST. NICHOLAS
Schieferstein Philip
Schilling Valentine
Schmuckle Fred.
SEIDEL EDWARD
Somers Jame
SPEKEISEN ADOLPH
Stein Charles
STRODEL MATHIAS
WENTE WM.
WIGMAN HENRY

Sash, Doors, &c.

BALDWIN F. S.
COCHRAN, HUMPHREY & CO.
Fronefield & Todd

Sausage Manufacturer.

STRODEL MATHIAS

Saw Mills.

BAKER J. K. & H.
Krutop & Co.

McLachlan, Neil & Co.
WILKEN HERMAN
Yergens & Co.

Scales.

COOMBS & DRAKE
Hill & Orbison

Seeds, &c.

BASH & EAKIN

Select Schools.

Pettit Miss Sarah
Sisters of Providence
Woodward Miss Hattie

Sewing Machines.

HILL C. L.
KIRBY JAMES A.
STOCKBRIDGE N. P.

Shingle Manufacturer.

Knecht Dominick

Silver Ware.

BEURET JUSTIN
GRAFF H. C.
KAUFFMAN & THOMPSON
MAYERS A.

Soap and Candles.

TRENTMAN JOHN

Spoke, Hub and Bending Factory.

OLDS, HANNA & CO.

Stave Dealers.

HASWELL & PIERCE

Straw, Hay and Fodder Cutters.

McNAMARA J. W. & CO.

Steam Engines.

BOWSER & STORY

FORT WAYNE AGRICUL-
TURAL WORKS
FORT WAYNE MACHINE
WORKS

Stone Dealers.

BALTES M. & CO.
KANNE & CO.
PAUL & KOSTER

Stone Yards.

HUMPHREY JAMES
UNDERHILL P. S.

Stoves, Hollow Ware, &c.

ALLEN & CO.
ASH & AGNEW
BRANDRIFF A. D. & CO.
JOCQUEL J. J.
MORGAN & BEUCH
WEBER E

Tailors, Merchant.

Bostick E.
Clark Joseph
FLEDDERMAN JOHN G. &
CO.
Freeman J.
Krimmel Sraugott
LAUFERTY ISAAC
NIRDLINGER & OPPEN-
HEIMER
Schmalz Chas. J.
Thieme J. G. & Bro.
VOGEL C. G.
Wiesenthal Moses
Woodward & Young

Tanneries.

Fry Jacob
Koster John
MANOK, NESTLE & CO.
WEISSER E. & CO.

Telegraph Company.

WESTERN UNION

Threshing Machines.

FORT WAYNE AGRICULTU-
RAL WORKS
REITZELL, SHUNK & CO.

Tin, Copper and Sheet Iron Ware.

ALLEN & CO.
ASH & AGNEW
BRANDRIFF A. D. & CO.
JOCQUEL J. J.
MORGAN & BEUCH
WEBER E.

Tin Roofers.

ALLEN & CO.
ASH & AGNEW
BRANDRIFF A. D. & CO.
WEBER E.

Town Clock Manufacturer.

RASTETTER LOUIS

Trimming Store.

BRADY W. H. & CO.

Trunks.

NEREITER CONRAD
Shoaff S. H.
STOCKBRIDGE N. P.

Undertakers.

Fink Charles
PELTIER & BOCKELOH

United States Pension Agent.

BAYLESS SOL. D.

Upholsterers.

Dachsteiner J. W.
THOMAS CHAS. M. & CO.

Veterinary Surgeons.

BALDWIN O. J.
READ HENRY A.

Vinegar Manufacturers.

Heilbroner S.
McCOMB & CO.
MONNING HENRY

Wagon Makers.

BAKER JOHN
Beston & McMaken
Broom Ely
BROWN JOHN
Buschmann F. W.
Dierstein Christ.
Fischer Michael
King Jacob, jr.
MUHLENBRUCH D. & BRO.
PANTLIND C. S.
Rapp Jacob
STEVENS THOMAS
Torbeck & Holzworth

Washing Machines.

McNAMARA J. W. & CO.

Watches, Jewelry, &c.

BEURET JUSTIN
GRAFFE H. C.
KANE JAMES M. & BRO.
KAUFFMAN & THOMPSON
MAYERS A.

Weighing Wagon.

DOANE N. E.

Wood and Willow Ware, &c.

Schanck Louis
SCHWEGMAN H. R.
WARD H. N.

Window Blind Manufacturer.

Mettler & Co.

Wood Yard.

McCampbell James

Wool Dealer.

BASH & EAKIN

Woolen Mill.

FRENCH, HANNA & CO.

EVENS' VARIETY WORKS,

SOLE MANUFACTORY OF EVENS' PATENT

SEAL PRESSES,

For the use of Courts, Lodges, Societies, and Business Seals.

P. EVENS, JR.,

64 West Fourth St.,   CINCINNATI, O.

CHAS. W. JORDAN,

PLAIN AND FANCY

PAPER BOX MANUFACTURER,

Keeps constantly on hand a full and complete assortment of

DRY GOODS AND DRUGGISTS' BOXES,

NORTH-EAST CORNER FIFTH AND WALNUT,

CINCINNATI, O.

N. B.—Orders from a distance promptly attended to.

WILLIAMS' POST OFFICE DIRECTORY,

OF THE

UNITED STATES AND TERRITORIES.

Alabama.

Post Office.	County.
Abbeville	Henry
Aberfoil	Macon
Abernethy	Calhoun
Abeda	Marion
Adam's Store	Coosa
Addison	Tuscaloosa
Aflonee	Bibb
Air Mount	Clark
Albertville	Marshall
Alexandria	Calhoun
Allen's Factory	Marion
Allenton	Wilcox
Allsborough	Franklin
Almond	Randolph
Alpine	Talladega
Andalusia	Covington
Anderson's Creek	Lauderdale
Annawaika	De Kalb
Antioch	Pickens
Anvil	Sumter
Apple Grove	Morgan
Arbacoochee	Randolph
Arbor Vitæ	Pike
Argue	Montgomery
Arkadelphia	Walker
Armadillo	Butler
Asbury	Fayette
Ashville	St. Clair
Athens	Limestone
Auburn	Macon
Aurora	Marshall
Autaugaville	Autauga
Avoca	Lawrence
Bailey Spring	Lauderdale
Barnes' X Roads	Dale
Barryton	Choctaw
Barton	Franklin
Bartonville	Walker
Bashams' Gap	Morgan
Bashi	Clark
Bayou Labatre	Mobile
Bay Spring	Hargrove
Beaver Creek	Dale
Beaver Dale	Fayette
Beaverton	Marion
Beaver Valley	St. Clair
Beebe Springs	"
Bellefonte	Jackson
Belleville	Conecuh
Belleview	Dallas
Bell's Landing	Monroe
Belmont	Sumter
Bennettsville	St. Clair
Benson	Bibb
Benton	Lowndes
Berkley	Madison

Post Office.	County.
Bethol	Wilcox
Bethlehem	Chambers
Beulah	"
Bexar	Marion
Bibb	Pike
Big Creek	Dale
Big Coon	Jackson
Big Pond	Fayette
Big Spring	Marshall
Bigalow	Marion
Black Creek	Choctaw
Black Water	Walker
Bladon Springs	Choctaw
Blairsville	St. Clair
Blakely	Baldwin
Blake's Ferry	Randolph
Blocker's	Tuscaloosa
Blount Springs	Blount
Blountsville	"
Blue Lick	Franklin
Blue Mountain	Calhoun
Blue Pond	Cherokee
Blue Spring	Morgan
Bluff Port	Sumter
Bluff Spring	Talladega
Boligee	Greene
Bowdon	Talladega
Bradford	Coosa
Braggs	Lowndes
Branchville	St. Clair
Breckinridge	Conecuh
Brewersville	Sumter
Brickville	Lawrence
Bridgeport	Jackson
Bridgeton	Shelby
Bridgeville	Pickens
Broken Arrow	St. Clair
Brooklyn	Conecuh
Brooksville	Blount
Broomtown	Cherokee
Brownsville	Talladega
Bruceville	Pike
Brundidge	"
Brush Creek	Perry
Buchanan	Randolph
Buckhorn	Pike
Buena Vista	Monroe
Buford	Barbour
Bulger's Mills	Coosa
Bullock	Coffee
Burleson	Franklin
Burnsville	Dallas
Burnt Corn	Monroe
Bushville	Barbour
Butler	Choctaw
Butler Springs	Butler
Buyckville	Coosa
Buzbeeville	Coffee
Cababa	Dallas
Caiuland	Calhoun

Post Office.	County.
Calhoun	Lowndes
Cambridge	Dallas
Camden	Wilcox
Campbell's Home	Shelby
Campbell's Store	Blount
Camp Hill	Tallapoosa
Camp Spring	Lawrence
Carlowsville	Dallas
Carrollton	Pickens
Carthage	Tuscaloosa
Catoma	Montgomery
Cave Spring	Fayette
Cedar Bluff	Cherokee
Cedar Grove	Jefferson
Cedar Plains	Morgan
Cedar Springs	Cherokee
Central Institute	Coosa
Center	Cherokee
Center Hill	Limestone
Center Star	Lauderdale
Centerville	Bibb
Chalk Bluff	Marion
Chambers C. H.	Chambers
Chanahatchee	Tallapoosa
Chandler's Spring	Talladega
Chepultepeo	Blount
Cherokee	Franklin
Chestnut Creek	Autauga
Chestnut Hill	Perry
Chester	Jefferson
Chickasaw	Franklin
Childersburg	Talladega
China Grove	Pike
Chinnibee	Talladega
Choctaw Corner	Clark
Choctawhatchee	Barbour
Chulafinnee	Randolph
Chuneuuggee	Macon
Churubusco	Franklin
Citronelle	Mobile
Claiborne	Monroe
Clauselville	"
Clay	De Kalb
Clay Hill	Marengo
Claysville	Marshall
Clayton	Barbour
Clear Creek Falls	Winston
Clifton	Wilcox
Clinton	Greene
Clintonville	Coffee
Clio	Marengo
Clopton	Dale
Cochran's Mills	Pickens
Coffeeville	Clark
Cokerville	Monroe
Colbert	Russell
Coleta	Talladega
Collinsville	De Kalb
Coloma	Cherokee
Columbia	Henry

1

POST OFFICES—ALABAMA.

Post Office.	County.	Post Office.	County.	Post Office.	County.
Columbiana	Shelby	Flint River	Morgan	Huntington	Autauga
Commerce	Conecuh	Florence	Lauderdale	Huntsville	Madison
Conchardee	Talladega	Forkland	Greene	Hurricane Creek	Choctaw
Concord	Lawrence	Fort Browder	Barbour	Hurtville	Russell
Coosa Valley	St. Clair	Fort Deposit	Lowndes	Independence	Autauga
Cordova	Fayette	Forts	Dallas	Ingram	Randolph
Corn Grove	Calhoun	Fox Creek	Randolph	Intercourse	Sumter
Corn House	Randolph	Fosters	Tuscaloosa	Ironville	Perry
Cotton Valley	Macon	Frankfort	Franklin	Island Home	Tallapoosa
Cottonville	Marshall	Franklin	Henry	Isney	Choctaw
County Line	Randolph	Fredonia	Chambers	Ivy Bluff	Morgan
Court Hill	Talladega	Friendship	Bath	Jackson	Clark
Courtland	Lawrence	Gadsden	Cherokee	Jackson's Camp	Tallapoosa
Cove Creek	Calhoun	Gainestown	Clark	Jacksonville	Calhoun
Cowikee	Barbour	Gainesville	Sumter	Jamestown	Conecuh
Coxville	De Kalb	Gandy's Cove	Morgan	Jasper	Walker
Crawford	Russell	Gap	Walker	Jay Bird	Marshall
Creek Stand	Macon	Garland	Butler	Jefferson	Marengo
Cross Keys	"	Gaston	Sumter	Jena	Tuscaloosa
Cross Plains	Calhoun	Gaylesville	Cherokee	Jericho	Perry
Cropwell	St. Clair	Geneva	Coffee	Jernigan	Barbour
Cubahatchee	Macon	Georgiana	Butler	Jones' Bluff	Sumter
Cureton's Bridge	Henry	Gilbertsborough	Limestone	Jonesborough	Jefferson
Curry	Talladega	Girard	Russell	Kansas	Walker
Cushing	Tuscaloosa	Glenville	Barbour	Kelly's Creek	St. Clair
Cusseta	Chambers	Gnatsville	Cherokee	Kelly's Spring	Talladega
Dadeville	Tallapoosa	Gold Ridge	Randolph	Kemp's Creek	Calhoun
Daleville	Dale	Goldville	Tallapoosa	Kendall's ⋈ Roads	Chambers
Danncelley's Mills	Baldwin	Goline	Dale	Kennamer	Marshall
Danville	Morgan	Goodwater	Coosa	Kimulga	Talladega
Davidville	Butler	Gordo	Pickens	Kings	Barbour
Davis Creek	Fayette	Goshen	Cherokee	King's Hill	Cherokee
Davis ⋈ Roads	Cherokee	Grantley	Calhoun	Kingston	Autauga
Daviston	Tallapoosa	Gravelly Spring	Lauderdale	Kinlock	Lawrence
Dayton	Marengo	Green Bay	Coffee	Kirk's Grove	Cherokee
Dead Fall	Butler	Green Hill	Lauderdale	Kirkville	Butler
Dead Level	Clark	Greensport	St. Clair	Knoxville	Greene
Deer Park	Washington	Greensboro'	Greene	Kowaliga	Tallapoosa
Decatur	Morgan	Greenville C. H.	Butler	Lacey's Spring	Morgan
Delta	Randolph	Grove Hill	Clark	Ladiga	Calhoun
Democrat	Walker	Guerrytown	Macon	LaGrange	Franklin
Demopolis	Marengo	Guntersville	Marshall	Lamar	Randolph
De Soto	Tallapoosa	Hackneyville	Tallapoosa	Lamington	Russell
De Sotoville	Choctaw	Haden's	Madison	Landersville	Lawrence
Detroit	Marion	Haley's	Marion	Langston	Jackson
Dick's Creek	Macon	Hall's Mills	"	La Place	Macon
Dickson	Franklin	Hallsville	Pike	Larkin's Fork	Jackson
Dixon's Mills	Marengo	Hamburg	Perry	Larkinsville	"
Dodsonville	Jackson	Hamby's Mill	Walker	Lawrenceville	Henry
Dotham	Dale	Handy	Fayette	Lebanon	DeKalb
Dover	Russell	Hannegan	Cherokee	Leesburg	Cherokee
Dry Creek	Lawrence	Hanover	Coosa	Leighton	Lawrence
Dublin	Fayette	Hardaway	Macon	Leon	Covington
Duck Spring	De Kalb	Harpersville	Shelby	Letohatchee	Lowndes
Dudleyville	Tallapoosa	Hartwood	Autauga	Lewis Station	Conecuh
Eagle Hill	"	Hatchechubbee	Russell	Lexington	Lauderdale
Easta Boga	Talladega	Hatcher's	Talladega	Liberty Hill	Dallas
Eastville	Randolph	Havanna	Greene	Lilly's Store	Wilcox
East Georgia	Butler	Haw Ridge	Dale	Limeville	Shelby
Echo	Dale	Haye's Store	Madison	Lincoln	Talladega
Egypt	Henry	Hayneville	Lowndes	Linden	Marengo
Elba	Coffee	Haywood	Randolph	Line Creek	Montgomery
Elliottsville	Shelby	Head Spring	De Kalb	Little Oak	Pike
Eldridge	Walker	Hebron	Randolph	Little River	Cherokee
Elm Bluff	Dallas	Helicon	Lowndes	Littlesville	Winston
Elyton	Jefferson	Henderson	Pike	Little Warrior	Blount
Emuckfaw	Tallapoosa	Henrysville	Marshall	Livingston	Sumter
Enon	Macon	Hernando	Macon	Loachapoka	Macon
Equality	Coosa	Hester's	Fayette	Loango	Covington
Escatawpa	Washington	Hickory Flat	Chambers	Long Creek	Butler
Estill's Fork	Jackson	Hickory Grove	Montgomery	Long Island	Jackson
Eufaula	Black	High Bluff	Dale	Lost Creek	Randolph
Eutaw	Greene	High Falls	"	Louina	"
Evergreen	Conecuh	Highland	Shelby	Louisville	Barbour
Fairfield	Pickens	Hill	Fayette	Lower Peach Tree	Wilcox
Fairplay	Calhoun	Hillahee	Talladega	Lowndesborough	Lowndes
Fairview	Walker	Hillian's Store	Marshall	Lucky Hit	Limestone
Farland	Dale	Hilliardsville	Henry	Lyonville	Jackson
Farmersville	Lowndes	Hillsborough	Shelby	McCammac	DeKalb
Farriorville	Pike	Hine's Precinct	Russell	McCloskey's	Marshall
Fatama	Wilcox	Hinton's Grove	Pickens	McConnell's	Tuscaloosa
Fayette C. H.	Fayette	Hoke's Bluff	Cherokee	McKinley	Marengo
Fayetteville	Talladega	Hollow Square	Greene	McMath's	Tuscaloosa
Fernvale	Tuscaloosa	Holly Grove	Walker	Macon	Marengo
Fife	Talladega	Hopewell	Greene	Madison ⋈ Roads	Madison
Fish Pond	Tallapoosa	Hopkinsville	Perry	Madison Station	"
Five Mile	Perry	Honorville	Butler	Manack	Lowndes
Five Points	Coosa	Horse Shoe Bend	Tallapoosa	Manningham	Butler
Flag Pond	Henry	Houston	Winston	Mantua	Pickens
Flat Rock	Talladega	Howell's ⋈ Roads	Cherokee	Mapleville	Bibb

POST OFFICES—ALABAMA.

Post Office.	County.	Post Office.	County.	Post Office.	County.
Marble Valley	Coosa	North Port	Tuscaloosa	Randolph	Bibb
Mardisville	Talladega	North River	"	Rawlingsville	De Kalb
Marietta	Lawrence	Notasulga	Macon	Read Level	Covington
Marion	Perry	Oak Bowery	Chambers	Recltown	Tallapoosa
Mars	Bibb	Oakfusky	Randolph	Reavesville	Calhoun
Masonville	Lauderdale	Oak Grove	Montgomery	Red Creek	Choctaw
Maysville	Madison	Oakland	Lauderdale	Red Hill	Marshall
Mechanicsville	Russell	Oak Level	Calhoun	Reese's Mills	De Kalb
Mellon Valley	Randolph	Oakley	Montgomery	Reform	Pickens
Meltonsville	Marshall	Oakmulga	Perry	Rehoboth	Wilcox
Memphis	Pickens	Oakville	Lawrence	Reubenville	De Kalb
Morey Bay	Henry	Oaktuppa	Choctaw	Richmond	Dallas
Meridianville	Madison	Oaky Streak	Butler	Ringgold	Cherokee
Mexico	Jefferson	Oceola	Cherokee	Rio Grande	"
Middle Ridge	Talladega	Odenville	Talladega	River Ridge	Monroe
Middleton	Calhoun	Ogee	Blount	Roanoke	Randolph
Midway	Barbour	Old Texas	Monroe	Rock Creek	Franklin
Military Springs	Fayette	Old Town	Coffee	Rockford	Coosa
Mill Grove	Henry	Oleander	Marshall	Rock Mills	Randolph
Millport	Fayette	Olinda	Fayette	Rockville	Jefferson
Millry	Washington	Olney	Pickens	Rocky	Butler
Milltown	Chambers	Oluste Creek	Pike	Rocky Head	Dale
Millville	Butler	Opelika	Russell	Rocky Spring	Jackson
Milner	Randolph	Open Pond	Henry	Rogersville	Lauderdale
Milo	Pike	Oregon	Jefferson	Romulus	Tuscaloosa
Milton	Antauga	Oregonia	Tuscaloosa	Rose Hill	Covington
Mobile	Mobile	Orion	Pike	Rosserville	Sumter
Monroeville	Monroe	Orison	Conecuh	Round Hill	Tallapoosa
Monterey	Butler	Orrville	Dallas	Round Pond	St. Clair
Montevallo	Shelby	Osanippa	Chambers	Rural Hill	Conecuh
Montgomery	Montgomery	Otho	Henry	Rustic Bower	Jackson
Monticello	Pike	Owen's X Roads	Madison	Russellville	Franklin
Moore's Bridge	Tuscaloosa	Oxford	Calhoun	Saint Paul	Clark
Mooresville	Limestone	Ozark	Dale	Saint Stephen's	Washington
Morgan's Springs	Perry	Paint Rock	Jackson	Salem	Russell
Morrisville	Calhoun	Palestine	Calhoun	Sal Soda	Butler
Morvin	Clark	Palmetto	Pickens	Sand Fort	Russell
Moscow	Marion	Palo	Marion	Sand Mountain	De Kalb
Moseley's Grove	Dallas	Panola	Lowndes	Sand Rock	Cherokee
Moulton	Lawrence	Park's Store	Jackson	Sandy Ridge	Lowndes
Mountain Home	"	Peak's Hill	Calhoun	Santa	Jackson
Mountain	Talladega	Pelham	Choctaw	Sapp's X Roads	Blount
Mountain Spring	Franklin	Perdue	Coffee	Sardis	Dallas
Mount Alvis	Blount	Perote	Pike	Scottsborough	Jackson
Mount Andrew	Barbour	Perryville	Perry	Scottsville	Bibb
Mount Hebron	Greene	Persons	Macon	Seal's Precinct	Mobile
Mount High	Marshall	Pettusville	Limestone	Seale's Station	Russell
Mount Hilliard	Pike	Pickensville	Pickens	Sebastopol	Wilcox
Mount Hope	Lawrence	Pierceville	De Kalb	Selma	Dallas
Mount Ida	Pike	Pigeon Creek	Butler	Sepulga	Conecuh
Mount Jefferson	Chambers	Pikeville	Marion	Shady Grove	Lawrence
Mount Moigs	Montgomery	Pilgrims' Rest	Fayette	Sharpesville	Montgomery
Mount Niles	St. Clair	Pinckneyville	Tallapoosa	Sheffield	Fayette
Mount Olive	Coosa	Pine Apple	Wilcox	Shelby Springs	Shelby
Mount Pinson	Jefferson	Pine Flat	Talladega	Shiloh	Marengo
Mount Pleasant	Monroe	Pine Grove	Pike	Shoal Creek	Calhoun
Mount Polk	Calhoun	Pine Hill	Wilcox	Shoal Ford	Limestone
Mount Rozzell	Limestone	Pine Level	Montgomery	Shorterville	Henry
Mount Sterling	Choctaw	Pinetucky	Perry	Silver Run	Talladega
Mount Vernon	Mobile	Pineville	Marengo	Mipsey Turnpike	Tuscaloosa
Mount Willing	Lowndes	Pintlala	Montgomery	Six Mile	Bibb
Mud Creek	Fayette	Plantersville	Perry	Skipperville	Dale
Mulberry	Autauga	Pleasant Gap	Cherokee	State Hill	Randolph
Mullins	Shelby	Pleasant Grove	Pickens	Snow Hill	Wilcox
Murphree's Valley	Blount	Pleasant Hill	Dallas	Soccopatoy	Coosa
Nanafalia	Marengo	Pleasant Ridge	Greene	Society Hill	Macon
Narrow Valley	Calhoun	Pleasant Site	Franklin	Somerville	Morgan
Nathansville	Conecuh	Pleasant Valley	Washington	Souchahatchee	Tallapoosa
Nauvoo	Franklin	Plum	Tuscaloosa	South Butler	Butler
Nebo	Jefferson	Pond Town	Dale	South Florence	Franklin
Nelson	Shelby	Poplar Spring	Randolph	Sparta	Conecuh
Newbern	Greene	Porter	Marshall	Springfield	Greene
New Bethel	Calhoun	Porterville	DeKalb	Spring Garden	Cherokee
Newburg	Franklin	Portland	Dallas	Spring Hill	Marengo
New Harmony	Chambers	Post Oak Flat	Jefferson	Springville	St. Clair
New Hope	Madison	Prairie Bluff	Wilcox	Spruce Pine	Franklin
New Lexington	Tuscaloosa	Prairie Ridge	Choctaw	Starkville	Pike
New Market	Madison	Prattville	Autauga	Starlington	Butler
New Potosi	Macon	Princeburg	Jackson	Steep Creek	Lowndes
New Providence	Pike	Princeton	"	Sterling	Cherokee
New River	Fayette	Providence	Pickens	Sterritt	Shelby
New Site	Tallapoosa	Pushmataha	Choctaw	Stevenson	Jackson
Newton C. H.	Dale	Pascus	"	Stockton	Baldwin
Newtonville	Fayette	Rchhittown	Calhoun	Stow's Ferry	Tallapoosa
New Topia	Barbour	Redfordville	Perry	Straight Creek	Jackson
Newton Academy	Monroe	Rainorsville	Butler	Strata	Montgomery
New Wakefield	Washington	Raleigh	Pickens	Suggsville	Clark
Nicholson's Store	Choctaw	Ramer	Montgomery	Sulphur Springs	Calhoun
Nixburg	Coosa	Ranch	Autauga	Summerfield	Dallas
North Bend	DeKalb				

POST OFFICES—ARKANSAS.

Arkansas.

Post Office.	County.
Summer Hill	Dale
Summitt	Blount
Sumterville	Sumter
Suspension	Marion
Sweet Water	Marengo
Sydney	Marshall
Sylacauga	Talladega
Sydenham	Sumter
Sylvan Grove	Dale
Talladega	Talladega
Tallassee	Tallapoosa
Taylor's	Jefferson
Tehopeka	Tallapoosa
Ten Islands	Calhoun
Texasville	Barbour
Thacker's Creek	Blount
Thorn Hill	Walker
Tolnea	Butler
Tompkinsville	Sumter
Town Creek	Lawrence
Traveller's Rest	Coosa
Trenton	Jackson
Triana	Madison
Trion	Tuscaloosa
Trout Creek	St. Clair
Troy	Pike
Truss	Jefferson
Turkeytown	Cherokee
Tuscaloosa	Tuscaloosa
Tuscumbia	Franklin
Tuskegee	Macon
Uchee	Russell
Union	Greene
Union Springs	Macon
Uniontown	Perry
Uphaupee	Macon
Valhermose Springs	Morgan
Valley Head	De Kalb
Van Buren	
Vienna	Pickens
Village Springs	Blount
Vilula	Russell
Vinesville	Jefferson
Violy	Blount
Waccoochee	Russell
Waco	Franklin
Waldrop's Mills	Jefferson
Walnut Grove	Blount
Walnut Hill	Tallapoosa
Warrenton	Marshall
Warrior Stand	Macon
Water Cure	Cherokee
Warsaw	Sumter
Waterloo	Lauderdale
Waverly	Chambers
Weedowee	Randolph
Woewoeaville	Talladega
Weebadkee	Randolph
Wehoga	Calhoun
Wellborn C. H.	Coffee
Welton	Greene
Woogufka	Coosa
Wesobulga	Randolph
Westmorelandville	Lauderdale
Westover	Covington
Westville	Dale
Wetumpka	Coosa
Whistler	Mobile
White Plains	Calhoun
Whitesburg	Madison
White Water	Pike
Wilcox Springs	Wilcox
Williams' X Roads	Choctaw
Williams' Mill	Covington
Wilsonville	Shelby
Wills Valley	Cherokee
Wind Creek	Tallapoosa
Winston	Randolph
Winterborough	Talladega
Wolf Creek	St. Clair
Woodstock	Tuscaloosa
Woodville	Jackson
Worth	De Kalb
Yellow Creek	Fayette
Yongesborough	Russell
York	Walker
Yorkville	Pickens
Youngsville	Tallapoosa
Zachary	Marshall

Post Office.	County.
Aberdeen	Monroe
Ada	Washington
Adamsville	Bradley
Adrian	Sevier
Akin's Store	Saline
Alder Brook	Independence
Albany	Hempstead
Allensville	Sevier
Alpine	Clark
Amity	
Antioch	Hot Springs
Antoine	Pike
Anvil	Clark
Apple Orchard	Benton
Arkadelphia	Clark
Arkansas Post	Arkansas
Armstrong Academy	Choctaw
Ash Flat	Lawrence
Askew	Philips
Atlanta	Union
Auburn	Arkansas
Augusta	Jackson
Back Bone	Sebastian
Baptist Mission	Cherokee
Barfield	Mississippi
Barkada	Drew
Bartholomew	Chicot
Batesville	Independence
Bayou Metoe	Pulaski
Beech Bluff	Dallas
Beech Creek	Clark
Beech Grove	Philips
Belfast	Saline
Bellville	Sevier
Belmont	Crawford
Benbrook's Mills	Izard
Bennett's Bayou	Fulton
Bennett's River	
Benton	Saline
Bentonville	Benton
Berlin	Ashley
Berryville	Carroll
Bethel	Pulaski
Big Bend	Polk
Big Flat	Searcy
Big Fork	Montgomery
Big Pond	Marion
Big Spring	Izard
Birnum Wood	Lafayette
Billingsley	Washington
Black Jack	Scott
Black Oak	Independence
Black Ferry	Randolph
Bland's	Saline
Bledsoe's Shop	Bradley
Bledsoe's Landing	Crittenden
Bloomer	Sebastian
Bloomington	Benton
Blue Mountain	Izard
Bluffton	Yell
Boggy Depot	Choctaw
Boonsboro'	Washington
Boone's Grove	
Booneville	Scott
Borland	Newton
Boston	Washington
Branchville	Drew
Brawley	Scott
Brazil	Saline
Breckinridge	Sebastian
Bright Star	Lafayette
Brocton	Pike
Brooks	Jefferson
Brownstown	Sevier
Brownsville	Prairie
Brunner	Sebastian
Buchanan	Washita
Buck Horn	Incependence
Buena Vista	Washita
Buffalo	
Buffalo City	Marion
Burney Academy	Chickasaw
Burrowsville	Searcy
Butler	Desha
Byrd's Spring	Jefferson
Cachemasso	Dallas
Cadron	Conway

Post Office.	County.
Caddo Grove	Montgomery
Calhoun	Columbia
Calvert	St. Francis
Camanche	Lawrence
Camden	Washita
Campabello	Greene
Campbell	Desha
Cane Creek	Conway
Caney	Washita
Cannon	Pope
Canton	Lawrence
Carouse	Washita
Carrollton	Carroll
Casa	Perry
Caseyville	Poinsett
Cass	Franklin
Casscoe	Arkansas
Cat Island	Crittenden
Cave Creek	Newton
Cedar Creek	Scott
Center Hill	White
Centre Point	Sevier
Centerville	Montgomery
Chalk Bluff	Greene
Chambersville	Dallas
Champagnolle	Union
Chappell	Dallas
Charleston	Franklin
Cherokee Bay	Randolph
Cherry Grove	Saline
Cherryville	Prairie
Chester	Ashley
Chickalah	Yell
Chismville	Scott
Chocoville	Sebastian
Choctaw Agency	Choctaw
Churchville	Pulaski
Cincinnati	Washington
Clamanda	Lawrence
Clarendon	Monroe
Clark's Mills	Hempstead
Clarksville	Johnson
Clear Creek	Marion
Clear Lake	Prairie
Clear Point	Arkansas
Clear Spring	Clark
Clitty	Madison
Clinton	Van Buren
Cobbsville	Johnson
Cold Water	Poinsett
Cold Well	White
Colerain	Jackson
Collegeville	Saline
Columbia	Chicot
Columbus	Hempstead
Como	Dallas
Constitution	Franklin
Convenience	Independence
Coody's Bluff	Cherokee
Cornersville	Drew
Cotton Plant	St. Francis
Council Bend	Crittenden
Cove	Polk
Covington	Lafayette
Creek Agency	Creek Nation
Crockett's Bluff	Arkansas
Crooked Creek	Carroll
Crosson's Store	Randolph
Cross Plains	Fulton
Crowley	Greene
Crystal Hill	Montgomery
Comfort	Van Buren
Cummins	Arkansas
Curia	Independence
Cut-Off	Drew
Cypress	Monroe
Cypress Creek	Desha
Cypress Mills	Perry
Dallas	Polk
Damo	Dallas
Danielsville	Cherokee
Danville	Yell
Dardanelle	
Darysaw	Jefferson
Dayton	Polk
De Armond's Mills	Drew
De Gray	Clark
De Rochey	Hot Springs
De Rosey	Franklin
Des Arc	Prairie

POST OFFICES—ARKANSAS.

Post Office.	County.	Post Office.	County.	Post Office.	County.
De Witt	Arkansas	Hobron	Pope	Lone Grove	Washita
Doaksville	Choctaw	Helena	Philips	Long Point	Arkansas
Dorcheato	Columbia	Henderson	Hot Springs	Long Prairie	Sebastian
Double Spring	Benton	Henslee's Springs	Saline	Long View	Ashley
Dover	Pope	Hermannsburg	Washington	Luda	Washita
Dubuque	Marion	Hermitage	Bradley	Luk-fah-tah	Choctaw
Due West	Monroe	Herndon	Greene	Lynch's Prairie	Washington
Duncan	"	Hickman's Bend	Mississippi	McHenry's Creek	Pulaski
Dutche's Creek	Yell	Hickory	Benton	McNeely's Ridge	Clark
Duvall's Bluff	Prairie	Hickory Creek	Hempstead	Madison	St. Francis
Eagle	Fulton	Hickory Grove	Clark	Magnolia	Columbia
Eagle Creek	Bradley	Hickory Plain	Prairie	Magnire's Store	Washington
Eagletown	Choctaw	Hickory Valley	Independence	Marble	Madison
East Fork	Conway	Hickory Flat	Saline	Marianna	Philips
Edge Hill	Polk	Hicksville	Columbia	Marie Saline	Ashley
Edmondson	Crittenden	Hico	Benton	Marion	Crittenden
Edwardsburg	Philips	Highway	Clark	Marlbrook	Hempstead
El Dorado	Union	Hillsborough	Union	Marshal Prairie	Searcy
Elgin	Jackson	Hilochee	Washington	Mars Hill	Drew
Elm Springs	Washington	Hixe's Ferry	Randolph	Martin's Creek	Lawrence
Elm Wood	Carroll	Hodge's Prairie	Sebastian	Mary Green	Saline
Elon	Ashley	Hollywood	Clark	Marysville	Columbia
Eminence	Independence	Holly Springs	Dallas	Masona	Chicot
Equality	Benton	Holmes' Mills	Perry	Mayhew	Choctaw
Eubank's Mills	Johnson	Hot Springs	Hot Springs	Maumelle	Pulaski
Eudora	Chicot	Howell	Pope	Maysville	Benton
Evansville	Washington	Huddleston	Pike	Meeks	Union
Evening Shade	Lawrence	Hungary	Saline	Miceo	Creek Nation
Eunice	Chicot	Huntsville	Madison	Middletown	Van Buren
Eureka	St. Francis	Hurricane	Saline	Midway	Hot Springs
Fair Dale	Arkansas	Indian Bay	Monroe	Mill Creek	Izard
Fair Play	Hot Springs	Ion	Drew	Millwood	Sevier
Fair View	Dallas	Jackson	Lawrence	Milor	Sebastian
Falcon	Columbia	Jacksonport	Jackson	Molina del Ray	Arkansas
Farmington	Sevier	James' Fork	Sebastian	Monticello	Drew
Fayetteville	Washington	Jasper	Newton	Montonga	"
Fitzhugh's Mills	Hot Springs	Jeffersonville	Philips	Morelaud	Pope
Flat Bayou	Jefferson	Jennings' Ferry	Benton	Moro	Monroe
Flint	Cherokee	Jenny Lind	Sebastian	Moro Bay	Bradley
Florence	Desha	Johnsville	Bradley	Moscow	Hempstead
Forest Grove	Lafayette	Jonesborough	Craighead	Mound City	Crittenden
Fort Arbuckle	Choctaw	Jones' Hill	St. Francis	Mount Adams	Arkansas
Fort Gibson	Cherokee	Jupiter	Madison	Mountain Spring	Carroll
Fort Smith	Sebastian	Judson	White	Mount Clairimier	Cherokee
Fort Washita	Chickasaw	Justus' Mills	Hempstead	Mount Elba	Bradley
Fountain Hill	Ashley	Kentucky Valley	White	Mount Holly	Union
Fourche Dumas	Randolph	Kenyon	Jackson	Mount Ida	Montgomery
Franklin	Fulton	Kedion	Cherokee	Mount Moriah	Washita
Frazier's Point	Washita	Kinderhook	Van Buren	Mount Olive	Izard
Freco	"	King's River	Carroll	Mount Parthenon	Newton
Fulton	Hempstead	Kingston	Madison	Mount Pleasant	Carroll
Gage's Point	St. Francis	Laconia	Desha	Mount Silvan	Lawrence
Gainesville	Greene	Lacy	Drew	Muddy Bayou	White
Galley Creek	Pope	Lagle	Bradley	Murfreesboro'	Pike
Galloway	Independence	La Grange	Philips	Myatt	Lawrence
Game Hill	Franklin	La Grue	Prairie	Napoleon	Desha
Gap Springs	Polk	Lake Bluff	"	Nashville	Hempstead
Geesville	Pope	Lake Enterprise	Ashley	Natural Dam	Crawford
Genoa	Clark	Lake Village	Chicot	Nelta Boe	Sevier
Gillen's Landing	Philips	Lamartine	Washita	New Gascony	Jefferson
Glass Village	Pope	Lanark	Bradley	New London	Union
Goldsboro'	Poinsett	L'Anguelle	St. Francis	Norristown	Pope
Good Hope	Pulaski	Larissa	Prairie	North Creek	Philips
Gordon's Ferry	Fulton	Laura Town	Lawrence	North Fork	Izard
Graham	Independence	Latona	Ashley	North Point	Pulaski
Grand Glaize	Jackson	Lenton	Poinsett	Norwoodville	Sevier
Grand Lake	Chicot	Lead Hill	Marion	Oak Bluff	Green
Grand Saline	Cherokee	Leake's Store	Columbia	Oak Grove	Arkansas
Gravelly Hill	Yell	Lebow	"	Oak Hill	Lafayette
Gravel Ridge	Bradley	Lee's Creek	Crawford	Oakland Grove	Prairie
Grave's	Hempstead	Lehi	Jefferson	Oak Ridge	Craighead
Grayson	Crittenden	Lenark Falls	Cherokee	Oasis	Lawrence
Greenbrier	Conway	Lewisburg	Conway	Oil Trough	Independence
Greenbush	Izard	Lewisville	Lafayette	Okolona	Clark
Green Grove	Conway	Liberty	Washita	Oldham	Crittenden
Green Mount	Drew	Liberty Springs	Van Buren	Old Hickory	Conway
Greensborough	Greene	Liddesdale	Columbia	Oldtuwn	Philips
Grenville	Washington	Lima	Randolph	Olio	Scott
Greenwood	Sebastian	Linden	St. Francis	Olive Creek	Conway
Gun Log	Pope	Line Ferry	Lafayette	Olivia	"
Gum Spring	Lawrence	Linn Spring Mills	Benton	Onyx	Perry
Gum Wood	Prairie	Linwood	Lawrence	Orion	Ashley
Hamburg	Ashley	Lisbon	Union	Osage	Carroll
Hamilton	Prairie	Little Rock	Pulaski	Osage Mills	Benton
Hampton	Calhoun	Little Spring	Madison	Oceola	Mississippi
Harmony Springs	Benton	Little Verdegris	Cherokee	Ouachita	Washita
Harold	Montgomery	Lockben	Poinsett	Owensville	Saline
Harrisburg	Poinsett	Locust Cottage	Jefferson	Oznn	Hempstead
Harris' Mill	Choctaw	Locust Grove	Searcy	Ozark	Franklin
Hasle Grove	Lawrence	Ludi	Pulaski	Pacific Place	Crittenden

POST OFFICES—CALIFORNIA.

Post Office.	County.
Paint Rock	Franklin
Polarm	Pulaski
Palestine	Columbia
Puraclifta	Sevier
Parkersburg	Yell
Parks	Scott
Pastoria	Jefferson
Patterson's Bluff	
Pea Ridge	Benton
Pearson's Mill	Arkansas
Pocan Point	Mississippi
Pekin	Johnson
Pennington's Mills	Pulaski
Perryville	Perry
Petersburg	Washita
Petite Jean	Yell
Petra	Craighead
Pigeon Hill	Union
Pilot Hill	Fulton
Pine Bluff	Jefferson
Pine Grove	Monroe
Piney	Johnson
Pittsburg	
Planters	Philips
Pleasant Hill	Franklin
Pleasant Plains	Independence
Pleasant Valley	Yell
Plum Bayou	Jefferson
Pocahontas	Randolph
Point Cedar	Clark
Point Meers	Johnson
Point Peter	Searcy
Point Pleasant	Ashley
Poke Bayou	Independence
Polk	Carroll
Pontotoc	Chickasaw
Poplar Bluffs	Ashley
Portland	
Port Williams	Scott
Post Oak	Calhoun
Powhatan	Lawrence
Prairie Landing	Desha
Prattsville	Saline
Princeton	Dallas
Providence	Searcy
Purn	Van Buren
Qitman	
Quito	Polk
Randolph	Lafayette
Rapp's Barrens	Fulton
Red Bird	Dallas
Red Fork	Desha
Red Hill	Washita
Red Land	Pike
Reed's Creek	Lawrence
Relf's Bluff	Drew
Revilee	Scott
Richland	Jefferson
Richmond	Sevier
Riggsville	Izard
Rob Roy	Jefferson
Rock Creek	Yell
Rock Fish	Searcy
Rock Hill	Pope
Rock Point	Independence
Rock Port	Hot Springs
Rocky Bayou	Izard
Rocky Comfort	Sevier
Roller's Ridge	Benton
Rolling Prairie	Marion
Rome	Clark
Rondo	Lafayette
Rose Bud	White
Roseville	Franklin
Rover	Yell
Royal Colony	White
Royston	Pike
Russellville	Pope
Saint Charles	Arkansas
Saint Paul	Madison
Santa Fe	Craighead
Scotland	Union
Searcy	White
Selma	Desha
Seminary	Washita
Shakespeare	Greene
Sharon	Arkansas
Sharp's X Roads	Independence
Shawnee Village	Mississippi
Sheriff's Ridge	Hot Spring

Post Office.	County.
Shetucket	Polk
Shiloh	Ashley
Shoal Creek	Johnson
Short Mountain	Franklin
Sidney	Lawrence
Smithland	Columbia
Smithville	Lawrence
South Bend	Arkansas
Spavinaw	Benton
Spring Bank	Lafayette
Spring Creek	Randolph
Springfield	Conway
Spring Hill	Hempstead
Spring Mill	Washington
Springvale	Clark
Star of the West	Pike
Stephens	Union
Sterling	Philips
Stony Point	White
Stover	Dallas
Stranger's Home	Lawrence
Strawberry	
Sub Rosa	Franklin
Sugar Grove	Lawrence
Sugar Loaf	Sebastian
Sullivan Springs	Independence
Sulphur Rock	
Sulphur Springs	Columbia
Summerville	Bradley
Sumpter	
Surrounded Hills	Monroe
Swan Lake	Arkansas
Sylamore	Izard
Table Rock	
Tahlequah	Cherokee
Taney	Washington
Taylor's Creek	St. Francis
Terre Noir	Clark
Texas	Scott
The Narrows	Crawford
Thomas' Store	Calhoun
Three Creeks	Union
Tishemingo	Chickasaw
Tolbert's Ferry	Marion
Tuboxky	Choctaw
Tomahawk	Searcy
Tremont	Union
Trenton	Philips
Trott's Mill	Benton
Trouble Hill	Scott
Tulip	Dallas
Turtu	Sabine
Twin Springs	Benton
Two Mills	
Tyler's Bluff	Perry
Uberty	Pulaski
Ultima Thule	Sevier
Union	Fulton
Union Springs	Union
Vache Grass	Sebastian
Valley	
Vallonia	Randolph
Van Buren	Crawford
Velvet Ridge	White
Village Creek	Columbia
Viola	Fulton
Violet Hill	Izard
Waldron	Scott
Wallace Creek	Independence
Walnut Bend	Philips
Walnut Fork	Newton
Walnut Grove	Independence
Walnut Hill	Lafayette
Walnut Plains	Prairie
Walnut Tree	Yell
War Eagle	Madison
Warren	Bradley
Washington	Hempstead
Watensaw	Prairie
Watersekv	Jefferson
Watkinsville	Newton
Waverly	Pulaski
Webbers Falls	Cherokee
Wesley	Madison
West Fork	Washington
West Point	White
Wheelock	Choctaw
White Bluff	Jefferson
Whiteley's	Newton
White Oak	Jefferson

Post Office.	County.
White Oak Shoals	Sevier
White River	Desha
White's Hill	Newton
White Sulphur Springs	Jefferson
Whiteville	Marion
Whittington	Saline
Wild Haws	Izard
Wiley's Cove	Searcy
Wilmington	Union
Wilton	Pike
Wittsburg	St. Francis
Witt's Spring	Searcy
Wolcott	Greene
Wolf Bayou	Independence
Woodlawn	Washita
Yellville	Marion

California.

Post Office.	County.
Agua Frio	Mariposa
Alameda	Alameda
Alamo	Contra Costa
Albion	Mendocino
Alleghany	Sierra
Alpha	Nevada
Alvarado	Alameda
Alviso	Santa Clara
American Ranche	Shasta
Anderson	Mendocino
Angel's Camp	Calaveras
Antelope	Yolo
Antioch	Contra Costa
Arcata	Humboldt
Areata	Trinity
Auburn	Placer
Bangor	Butte
Bear Valley	Mariposa
Bellota	San Joaquin
Belmont	San Mateo
Benicia	Solano
Bidwell's Bar	Butte
Big Bar	Trinity
Big Oak Flat	Tuolumne
Big Valley	Napa
Bloomfield	Sonoma
Bodega	
Brooklyn	Alameda
Brush Creek	Butte
Buckeye	Yolo
Bucksport	Humboldt
Burnt Ranche	Trinity
Burwood	San Joaquin
Butte Mills	Butte
Butte Valley	
Cache Creek	Yolo
Calpella	Mendocino
Callahan's Ranche	Siskyon
Campo Seco	Calaveras
Camptonville	Yuba
Cedarville	El Dorado
Central Ho	Butteuse
Centerville	Alameda
Charleston	Yolo
Cherokee	Butte
Chico	
Chinese Camp	Tuolumne
Clairsville	Mendocino
Clarksville	El Dorado
Clay's Bar	Calaveras
Cloverdale	Sonoma
Cold Spring	El Dodado
Colloma	
Columbia	Tuolumne
Colusa	Colusa
Cosumne	Sacramento
Cottage Grove	Klamath
Cottonwood	Tehama
Crescent City	Del Norte
Damascus	Placer
Danville	Contra Costa
Denverton	Solano
Diamond Spring	El Dorado
Don Pedro Bar	Tuolumne
Dougherty's Station	Alameda

POST OFFICES—CALIFORNIA.

Post Office.	County.	Post Office.	County.	Post Office.	County.
Douglas City	Trinity	Liberty	San Joaquin	Redwood City	San Mateo
Downieville	Sierra	Linden	San Joaquin	Reynolds' Ferry	Calaveras
Dry Town	Amador	Lisbon	Placer	Rich Gulch	
Duroc	El Dorado	Little Lake	Mendocino	Richland	Sacramento
Dutch Flat	Placer	Little York	Nevada	Rio Seco	Butte
Eel River	Humboldt	Long Bar	Yuba	Rio Vista	Solano
Eight Mile Corner	San Joaquin	Los Angelos	Los Angelos	Rock Creek	Tehama
		Loving's Ferry	Stanislaus	Rockville	Solano
Elderton	Shasta	Lower Lake	Napa	Rough and Ready	Nevada
El Dorado	El Dorado	Lynn's Valley	Tulare	Sacramento City	Sacramento
Elk Camp	Klamath	McCartysville	Santa Clara	Saint Helena	Napa
Elk Grove	Sacramento	Marietta	San Joaquin	Saint Louis	Sierra
Empire Ranche	Yuba	Mariposa	Mariposa	Salinas	Monterey
Eureka	Humboldt	Martinez	Contra Costa	Salsbury	Sacramento
Eureka North	Sierra	Marysville	Yuba	Salmon Falls	El Dorado
Fair Play	El Dorado	Maxwell's Creek	Mariposa	San Andreas	Calaveras
Ferndale	Humboldt	Mayfield	Santa Clara	San Antonio	Monterey
Ferry Point	Del Norte	Meadow Valley	Plumas	San Bernardino	San Bernardino
Fiddletown	El Dorado	Mendocino	Mendocino	San Diego	San Diego
Firebaugh's Ferry	Fresno	Merced Falls	Merced	San Francisco	San Francisco
Folsom City	Sacramento	Meridan	Sutter	San Gabriel	Los Angelos
Forbestown	Butte	Musserville	Trinity	San Jose	Santa Clara
Forest City	Sierra	Michigan Bar	Sacramento	San Juan	Monterey
Forest Hill	Placer	Michigan Bluff	Placer	San Leandro	Alameda
Fork's House		Millerton	Fresno	San Lorenzo	Alameda
Forks of Salmon	Klamath	Mill Valley	Calaveras	San Luis Obispo	
Fort Goff	Siskyou	Millville	Shasta		San Luis Obispo
Fort Jones		Milpitas	Santa Clara	San Miguel	
Fort Tejon	Los Angelos	Mineraville	Trinity	San Pablo	Contra Costa
Foster's Bar	Yuba	Mission San Jose	Contra Costa	San Pedro	Los Angelos
Fourth Crossing	Calaveras	Mokelumne Hill	Calaveras	San Rafael	Marin
Fremont	Yolo	Monroeville	Colusi	Santa Barbara	Santa Barbara
French Camp	San Joaquin	Monte	Los Angelos	Santa Clara	Santa Clara
French Corral	Nevada	Monterey	Monterey	Santa Cruz	Santa Cruz
French Gulch	Shasta	Montezuma	Tuolumne	Santa Rosa	Sonoma
Fresno City	Fresno	Moon's Ranche	Colusi	Sanel	Mendocino
Garden Valley	El Dorado	Moore's Flat	Nevada	Sawyer's Bar	Klamath
Garrote	Tuolumne	Morman's Island	Sacramento	Scottsburg	Fresno
Georgetown	El Dorado	Mountain Ranche	Calaveras	Scott's River	Siskyou
Gibsonville	Sierra	Moanta n Springs	Placer	Searsville	San Mateo
Gilroys	Santa Clara	Mountain View	Santa Clara	Sebastopol	Napa
Goodyear's Bar	Sierra	Mountain Well	Nevada	Secret Ravine	Placer
Grafton	Yolo	Mount Ophir	Mariposa	Seiad's Valley	Siskyou
Grand Island	Colusi	Murphy's	Calaveras	Shasta	Shasta
Grass Valley	Nevada	Masquito		Shaw's Flat	Tuolumne
Green Spring	Tuolumne	Napa City	Napa	Sheldon	Sacramento
Green Wood	El Dorado	Natividad	Monterey	Smith's Ranche	Sonoma
Grizzly Bear House	Placer	Neilsburg	Placer	Snelling's Ranche	Merced
Grizzly Flat	El Dorado	Nevada City	Nevada	Sonoma	Sonoma
Grove City	Tehama	Newtown	El Dorado	Sonora	Tuolumne
Gwin	Merced	Nicolaus	Sutter	Soquel	Santa Cruz
Hamilton	Butte	North Bloomfield	Nevada	Spanish Flat	El Dorado
Hansonville		North Branch	Calaveras	Springfield	Tuolumne
Happy Camp	Del Norte	North Columbia	Nevada	Staple's Ranche	San Joaquin
Hay Fork	Trinity	North San Juan	Nevada	Star House	Sacramento
Haywood	Alameda	Oakland	Alameda	Stockton	San Joaquin
Healdsburg	Sonoma	Oloma	Marin	Stony Point	Sonoma
Henly	Siskyou	Omega	Nevada	Strawberry Valley	Yuba
Hermitage	Mendocino	Onion Valley	Plumas	Suisun City	Solano
Hicksville	Sacramento	Onisbo	Sacramento	Sutter's Creek	Amador
Honcut	Yuba	Ophirville	Placer	Sweetland	Nevada
Hornitas	Mariposa	Oregon House	Yuba	Table Rock	Sierra
Horsetown	Shasta	Orleans	Klamath	Tehama	Colusi
How's Branch	Tuolumne	Oro Fino	Siskyou	Temecula	San Diego
Humbug Creek	Siskyou	Oroville	Butte	Thompson's Flat	Butte
Illinoistown	Placer	Orr's Ranche	San Joaquin	Timber Cove	Sierra
Indian Diggins	El Dorado	Otittiewa	Siskyou	Timbuctoo	Yuba
Indian Gulch	Mariposa	Owsley's Bar	Yuba	Todd's Valley	Placer
Indian Spring	Nevada	Pacheco	Contra Costa	Tomalles	Marin
Ione City	Amador	Paterson	Nevada	Trinidad	Klamath
Iowa City	Placer	Pea Vine	Butte	Trinity	Trinity
Jacinto	Colusi	Pescadero	Santa Cruz	Trinity Center	
Jackson	Amador	Petaluma	Sonoma	Tule	Tulare
Jacksonville	Tuolumne	Petersburg	Tulare	Ukrah	Mendocino
Jamestown		Pilot Hill	El Dorado	Uncle Sam	Napa
Jay Hawk	El Dorado	Pine Grove	Amador	Unionville	El Dorado
Jenny Lind	Calaveras	Placerville	El Dorado	Upper Clear Lake	Napa
Johnson's Rancho	Sutter	Plumas	Yuba	Vacaville	Solano
Kayoto	Napa	Plum Valley	Sierra	Vallicita	Calaveras
Kelsey	El Dorado	Poland	San Joaquin	Vallejo	Solano
Keysville	Tulare	Poverty Bar	Calaveras	Virginia	Placer
Kingston	Fresno	Prairie	Yolo	Visalia	Tulare
Knight's Ferry	San Joaquin	Preston	Marin	Volcano	Amador
Knight's Valley	Napa	Princeton	Colusi	Walnut Grove	Sacramento
Lafayette	Contra Costa	Punta Arenas	Mendocino	Watsonville	Santa Cruz
La Grange	Stanislaus	Putah	Solano	Weaverville	Trinity
Lakeville	Sonoma	Quincy	Plumas	West Point	Calaveras
Lancha Plana	Amador	Rattlesnake Bar	Placer	West Butte	Butte
La Porte	Sierra	Red Bluff	Shasta	Whiskey Creek	Shasta
Lewiston	Trinity	Red Dog	Nevada	Windsor	Sonoma

POST OFFICES—CONNECTICUT.

Post Office.	County.
Wood's Ferry	San Joaquin
Woodside	San Francisco
Wyandotte	Butte
Wyatt's Store	Mariposa
Yankee Hill	Butte
Yankee Jim's	Placer
Yreka	Siskyon
Yolo	Yolo
Yuba City	Sutter

Connecticut.

Post Office.	County.	Post Office.	County.	Post Office.	County.
Abington	Windham	East Haddam	Middlesex	Middlefield	Middlesex
Andover	Tolland	East Hampton	Middlesex	Middle Haddam	Middlesex
Ansonia	New Haven	East Hartford	Hartford	Middletown	Middlesex
Ashford	Windham	East Haven	New Haven	Milford	New Haven
Avon	Hartford	East Kent	Litchfield	Mill Brook	Litchfield
Bakersville	Litchfield	East Killingly	Windham	Millington	Middlesex
Banksville	Fairfield	Easton	Fairfield	Mill Plain	Fairfield
Bantam Falls	Litchfield	East Windsor	Hartford	Milton	Litchfield
Barkhamstead	Litchfield	East Windsor Hill	Hartford	Monroe	Fairfield
Beacon Falls	New Haven	East Woodstock	Windham	Montville	New London
Berlin	Hartford	Ellington	Tolland	Moodus	Middlesex
Bethany	New Haven	Ellsworth	Litchfield	Moose Meadow	Tolland
Bethel	Fairfield	Enfield	Hartford	Moosup	Windham
Bethlehem	Litchfield	Essex	Middlesex	Morris	Litchfield
Black Rock	Fairfield	Fairfield	Fairfield	Mount Carmel	New Haven
Bloomfield	Hartford	Fair Haven	New Haven	Mount Hope	Tolland
Bolton	Tolland	Falls Village	Litchfield	Mystic	New London
Bozrah	New London	Farmers' Village	Hartford	Mystic Ridge	New London
Bozrahville	New London	Farmington	Hartford	Mystic River	New London
Brantord	New Haven	Fisherville	Windham	Naugatuck	New Haven
Bridgeport	Fairfield	Forestville	Hartford	New Boston	Windham
Bridgewater	Litchfield	Franklin	New London	New Britain	Hartford
Bristol	Hartford	Gales' Ferry	New London	New Canaan	Fairfield
Broad Brook	Hartford	Gardner's Lake	New London	New Fairfield	Fairfield
Brookfield	Fairfield	Georgetown	Fairfield	New Hartford	Litchfield
Brooklyn	Windham	Gilead	Tolland	New Hartford Center	Litchfield
Brook's Vale	New Haven	Glastenbury	Hartford	New Haven	New Haven
Buckland	Hartford	Glenville	Fairfield	Newington	Hartford
Burlington	Hartford	Goshen	Litchfield	New London	New London
Burrville	Litchfield	Granby	Hartford	New Milford	Litchfield
Campbell's Mills	Windham	Greenfield Hill	Fairfield	New Preston	Litchfield
Campville	Litchfield	Greenville	New London	Newtown	Fairfield
Canaan	Lite field	Greenwich	Fairfield	Niantic	New London
Canterbury	Windham	Griswold	New London	Noank	New London
Canton	Hartford	Groton	New London	Norfolk	Litchfield
Canton Center	Hartford	Guilford	New Haven	North Ashford	Windham
Central Village	Windham	Haddam	Middlesex	North Branford	New Haven
Center Brook	Middlesex	Haddam Neck	Middlesex	North Canton	Hartford
Center Groton	New London	Hadlyme	Middlesex	North Colebrook	Litchfield
Chapinville	Litchfield	Hamburg	New London	North Cornwall	Litchfield
Chaplin	Windham	Hamden	New Haven	Northfield	Litchfield
Cheshire	New Haven	Hampton	Windham	Northford	New Haven
Chester	Middlesex	Hartford	Hartford	North Granby	Hartford
Chesterfield	New London	Hartland	Hartford	North Greenwich	Fairfield
Clinton	Middlesex	Harwinton	Litchfield	North Guilford	New Haven
Cobalt	Middlesex	Hawleyville	Fairfield	North Haven	New Haven
Colchester	New London	Hazardville	Hartford	North Killingworth	Middlesex
Cold Spring	Fairfield	Hebron	Tolland	North Lyme	New London
Colebrook	Litchfield	Higganum	Middlesex	North Madison	New Haven
Colebrook River	Litchfield	High Ridge	Fairfield	North Norfolk	Litchfield
Cullumer	Windham	Hitchcockville	Litchfield	North Somers	Tolland
Collinsville	Hartford	Hockanum	Hartford	North Stamford	Fairfield
Columbia	Tolland	Hutchkissville	Litchfield	North Stonington	New London
Cornwall	Litchfield	Huntington	Fairfield	Northville	Litchfield
Cornwall Bridge	Litchfield	Huntsville	Litchfield	North Wilton	Fairfield
Cornwall Hollow	Litchfield	Jewett City	New London	North Windham	Windham
Coventry	Tolland	Joyceville	Litchfield	North Woodstock	Windham
Coventry Depot	Tolland	Kensington	Hartford	Norwalk	Fairfield
Cromwell	Middlesex	Kent	Litchfield	Norwich	New London
Curtisville	Hartford	Killingly	Windham	Norwichtown	New London
Danbury	Fairfield	Killingworth	Middlesex	Oakville	New Haven
Darien	Fairfield	Lakeville	Litchfield	Oneco	Windham
Darien Depot	Fairfield	Lanesville	Litchfield	Orange	New Haven
Deep River	Middlesex	Laurel Glen	New London	Ore Hill	Litchfield
Derby	New Haven	Lebanon	New London	Oxford	New Haven
Durham	Middlesex	Ledyard	New London	Pendleton Hill	New London
Durham Center	Middlesex	Leesville	Middlesex	Pequabuck	Litchfield
Eagleville	Tolland	Liberty Hill	New London	Phœnixville	Windham
East Berlin	Hartford	Lime Rock	Litchfield	Pine Meadow	Litchfield
East Canaan	Litchfield	Lime Stone	Fairfield	Plainfield	Windham
Eastford	Windham	Lisbon	New London	Plainville	Hartford
East Granby	Hartford	Litchfield	Litchfield	Plantsville	Hartford
		Long Ridge	Fairfield	Pleasant Valley	Litchfield
		Lord's Bridge	New London	Plymouth	Litchfield
		Lyme	New London	Plymouth Hollow	Litchfield
		Madison	New Haven	Pomfret	Windham
		Manchester	Hartford	Pomfret Landing	Windham
		Manchester Station	Hartford	Poquetanuck	New London
		Mansfield	Tolland	Poquonock	Hartford
		Mansfield Center	Tolland	Poquanoc Bridge	New London
		Mansfield Depot	Tolland	Portland	Middlesex
		Marble Dale	Litchfield	Preston	New London
		Marion	Hartford	Prospect	New Haven
		Marlborough	Hartford	Putnam	Windham
		Mashapang	Tolland	Quaryville	Tolland
		Meriden	New Haven	Rainbow	Hartford
		Merrow Station	Tolland	Redding	Fairfield
		Merwinsville	Litchfield	Redding Ridge	Fairfield
		Mianus	Fairfield	Ridgebury	Fairfield
		Middlebury	New Haven	Ridgefield	Fairfield

POST OFFICES—DELAWARE—DISTRICT OF COLUMBIA—FLORIDA. 9

Post Office.	County.	Post Office.	County.	Post Office.	County.
Robertsville	Litchfield	West Norfolk	Litchfield	Milford	Kent
Rockland	New Haven	West Norwalk	Fairfield	Millsborough	Sussex
Rockville	Tolland	Weston	Fairfield	Milton	"
Rocky Hill	Hartford	Westport	Fairfield	Newark	New Castle
Round Hill	Fairfield	West Redding	Fairfield	New Castle	"
Roxbury	Litchfield	West Stafford	Tolland	Newport	"
Salem	New London	West Suffield	Hartford	Odessa	New Castle
Salisbury	Litchfield	West Thompson	Windham	Pleasant Hill	"
Saugatuck	Fairfield	Westville	New Haven	Port Penn	"
Saybrook	Middlesex	West Willington	Tolland	Red Lion	"
Saybrook Ferry	Middlesex	West Winsted	Litchfield	Saint George's	"
Scitico	Hartford	West Woodstock	Windham	Saint Johnstown	Sussex
Scotland	Windham	Wethersfield	Hartford	Seaford	"
Seymour	New Haven	Whitneyville	New Haven	Selbyville	"
Sharon	Litchfield	Willimantic	Windham	Smyrna	Kent
Sherman	Fairfield	Willington	Tolland	Stanton	New Castle
Simsbury	Hartford	Wilton	Fairfield	Summit Bridge	"
Smith's Ridge	Fairfield	Winchester Center	Litchfield	Townsend's Station	"
Somers	Tolland	Windham	Windham	Tunnell's Store	Sussex
Somersville	Tolland	Windsor	Hartford	Vernon	Kent
South Britain	New Haven	Windsor Locks	Hartford	Whiteleysburg	"
Southbury	New Haven	Windsorville	Hartford	Williamsville	"
South Cannan	Litchfield	Winnipauk	Fairfield	Willow Grove	"
South Coventry	Tolland	Winstead	Litchfield	Wilmington	New Castle
Southford	New Haven	Winthrop	Middlesex		
South Glastenbury	Hartford	Wolcott	New Haven		
Southington	Hartford	Wolcottville	Litchfield	## Dist. Columbia.	
South Kent	Litchfield	Woodbury	Litchfield		
South Killingly	Windham	Woodstock	Windham	Post Office.	County.
South Lyme	New London	Woodstock Valley	Windham		
South Manchester	Hartford	Woodville	Litchfield	Georgetown	Washington
South Norfolk	Litchfield	Yautic	New London	Oak Grove	Washington
South Norwalk	Fairfield	Zoar Bridge	New Haven	Tennallytown	Washington
Southport	Fairfield			Washington City	Washington
Southville	Litchfield				
South Windham	Windham	## Delaware.		## Florida.	
South Windsor	Hartford				
Square Pond	Tolland	Post Office.	County.		
Stafford	Tolland			Post Office.	County.
Staffordville	Tolland	Angola	Sussex		
Stamford	Fairfield	Arthursville	Kent	Adamsville	Sumter
Stanwich	Fairfield	Black Bird	New Castle	Alatia	Hillsborough
Stafford Springs	Tolland	Black Water	Sussex	Almiraute	Walton
Stepney	Fairfield	Bridgeville	"	Ancilla	Jefferson
Stepney Depot	Fairfield	Bull's Mills	"	Apalachicola	Franklin
Sterling	Windham	Camden	Kent	Archer	Alachua
Sterling Hill	Windham	Cannon's Ferry	Sussex	Aspaluga	Gadsden
Stony Creek	New Haven	Canterbury	Kent	Atsena Otie	Levy
Stonington	New London	Cedar Creek	Sussex	Austinville	Santa Rosa
Stratford	Fairfield	Centerville	New Castle	Bailey's Mill	Leon
Suffield	Hartford	Chippewa	"	Baldwin	Duval
Tariffville	Hartford	Christiana	"	Bay Port	Hernando
Terryville	Litchfield	Claymont	"	Beaseley	Jefferson
Thompson	Windham	Clayton	Kent	Belleville	Hamilton
Thompsonville	Hartford	Concord	Sussex	Benhaden	Wakulla
Tolland	Tolland	Cooch's Bridge	New Castle	Benton	Columbia
Torringford	Litchfield	Cove Dale	Sussex	Black Dirt	Levy
Torrington	Litchfield	Dagsborough	Sussex	Blount's Ferry	Columbia
Trumbull	Fairfield	Delaware City	New Castle	Blue Creek	Liberty
Trumbull Long Hill	Fairfield	Dover	Kent	Bristol	"
Uncasville	New London	Farmington	Kent	Bronson	Levy
Union	Tolland	Felton Station	"	Bluff Spring	Escambia
Unionville	Hartford	Fieldsborough	New Castle	Callahans	Nassau
Vernon	Tolland	Frankford	Sussex	Campbellton	Jackson
Vernon Depot	Tolland	Frederica	Kent	Camp Yard	Marion
Voluntown	Windham	Georgetown	Sussex	Cane Brake	Holmes
Wallingford	New Haven	Glasgow	New Castle	Cedar Tree	Hernando
Warehouse Point	Hartford	Gumborough	Sussex	Centerville	Leon
Warren	Litchfield	Hall's Store	"	Cerro Gordo	Holmes
Washington	Litchfield	Harrington	Kent	Chattahoochee	Gadsden
Waterbury	New Haven	Hazletville	"	Cherry Lake	Madison
Waterford	New London	Henry Clay Factory	New Castle	China Hill	Gadsden
Watertown	Litchfield	Hollyville	Sussex	Clay Landing	Levy
Waterville	New Haven	Horsey's X Roads	"	Clear Water Harbor	Hillsboro'
Wauregan	Windham	Kenton	Kent	Columbus	Columbia
West Ashford	Windham	Laurel	Sussex	Concord	Gadsden
West Avon	Hartford	Leipsic	Kent	Coon Hill	Santa Rosa
Westbrook	Middlesex	Leipsic Station	"	Cork	Hillsborough
West Cheshire	New Haven	Lewis	Sussex	Cottage	Marion
West Chester	New London	Little Creek Landing	Kent	Crystal River	Hernando
West Cornwall	Litchfield	Loveville	New Castle	Douglassville	Walton
Westford	Windham	McClellandsville	"	Durham	Columbia
West Goshen	Litchfield	McDonough	New Castle	Econfina	Washington
West Granby	Hartford	Magnolia	Kent	Eight Mile	Walton
West Hartford	Hartford	Marshy Hope Bridge	"	Ellisville	Columbia
West Hartland	Hartford	Mermaid	New Castle		
West Haven	New Haven	Middleford	Sussex		
West Killingly	Windham	Middletown	New Castle		
West Meriden	New Haven				
Westminster	Windham				

POST OFFICES—GEORGIA.

Post Office.	County.
Enterprise	Volusia
Etoniah	Putnam
Fayetteville	Lafayette
Fernandina	Nassau
Finholloway	Madison
Flemington	Marion
Fort Dado	Hernando
Fort Gates	Putnam
Fort Hamilton	Madison
Fort Mead	Hillsborough
Fort Taylor	Hernando
Gainesville	Alachua
Greenwood	Jackson
Hamburg	Madison
Hawkinsville	Orange
Hibernia	Duval
Hodgson's Distillery	Leon
Houston	Suwannee
Huntsville	Columbia
Ichetucknee	Columbia
Indian River	Brevard
Iola	Marion
Jackson's Bluff	Leon
Jacksonville	Duval
Jamonia	Leon
Jasper	Hamilton
Jennings	"
Key West	Monroe
King's Ferry	Nassau
Knox Hill	Walton
Lake Butler Court House	New River
Lake City	Columbia
Lake George	Putnam
Lake Griffin	Marion
Lake Harris	Sumter
Lewisville	Nassau
Little River	Columbia
Long Pond	Levy
Long Swamp	Marion
McIntosh	Lafayette
McLellanville	Santa Rosa
McQueen	Lafayette
Madison	Madison
Magnolia Mills	Duval
Manatee	Hillsborough
Mandarin	Duval
Mariana	Jackson
Mayport Mills	Duval
Mellonville	Marion
Miami	Dade
Micanopy	Alachua
Miccosukee	Leon
Middleburg	Duval
Midway	Gadsden
Millwood	Jackson
Milton	Santa Rosa
Monticello	Jefferson
Morrison's Mills	Alachua
Mosely Hall	Madison
Mount Pleasant	Gadsden
New Boston	Suwannee
Newburg	Columbia
Newnansville	Alachua
Newport	Wakulla
New River	Columbia
New Smyrna	Orange
New Troy Court House	Lafayette
Oakland	Orange
Ocola	Marion
Ocean Pond	New River
Ochesee	Calhoun
Olustee	New River
Orange Hill	Washington
Orange Lake	Marion
Orange Mills	St Johns
Orange Spring	Orange
Palan	Clay
Palestine	Columbia
Palmyra	Sumter
Pawtuxett	Wakulla
Picolata	St Johns
Pierceville	Hernando
Pilatka	Putnam
Ponce De Leon	Holmes
Providence	Columbia
Quincy	Gadsden
Rickoe's Bluff	"
St. Andrew's Bay	Washington

Post Office.	County.
St. Austine	St. Johns
St. Helena	Columbia
St. Mark's	Wakulla
Sanderson Station	New River
Sandy Ford	Jefferson
Shell Point	Wakulla
Silver Spring	Marion
Sopchoppy	Wakulla
Spring Grove	Suwannee
Starke	New River
Sugar Grove	Alachua
Sumterville	Sumter
Suwannee Shoals	Columbia
Tallahassee	Leon
Tampa	Hillsborough
Tocoi	St. Johns
Trail Ridge	Clay
Tustenuggee	Columbia
Uchee Anna	Walton
Volusia	Volusia
Vernon	Washington
Wacahootie	Marion
Waldo	Alachua
Wardville	Walton
Warrington	Escambia
Waukeenah	Jefferson
Wekeira	Levy
Welaka	Putnam
White Springs	Hamilton
Yellow Bluff	Duval

Georgia.

Post Office.	County.
Abbeville C. H.	Wilcox
Acworth	Cobb
Adairsville	Cass
Adams	Irwin
Air Line	Hart
Albany	Baker
Alexander	Burke
Allendale	Habersham
Allatoona	Cass
Allen's	Richmond
Alpharetta	Milton
Alpine	Chatooga
Amandaville	Elbert
Americus	Sumpter
Ami	Forsyth
Amicalola	Lumpkin
Ammy's Creek	Habersham
Anderson	Whitfield
Andersonville	Sumter
Anthony Shoals	Elbert
Antioch	Troup
Appling	Columbia
Aquilla	Franklin
Arabia	Thomas
Argo	Hall
Arnuchee	Floyd
Asbury	Troup
Athens	Clark
Atlanta	De Kalb
Attapulgus	Decatur
Auburn	Gwinnett
Auburn Hill	Franklin
Augusta	Richmond
Auraria	Lumpkin
Ava	Lowndes
Bainbridge	Decatur
Bairdstown	Oglethorpe
Ball Ground	Cherokee
Barnesville	Pike
Barrettsville	Lumpkin
Barker's Store	Floyd
Bascobel	Jackson
Bascom	Scriven
Batesville	Habersham
Bear Creek	Henry
Beard's Creek	Liberty
Belair	Richmond
Belleview	Talbot
Belton	Franklin
Benevolence	Randolph
Bengal	Bullock
Berkshire	Gwinnett
Bersheba	Henry

Post Office.	County.
Berzelia	Columbia
Beslin	Banks
Bethel	Glynn
Bethlehem	Forsyth
Big Creek	
Big Shantee	Cobb
Bio	Hart
Black Creek	Scriven
Black Shear	Pierce
Black Spring	Baldwin
Bladen Creek	Stewart
Blairsville	Union
Blakely	Early
Bloomfield	Worth
Blountsville	Jones
Blowing Cave	Decatur
Blue Creek	Habersham
Blue Ridge	Gilmer
Bluff Spring	Talbot
Boggess	Campbell
Bold Spring	Franklin
Boltonville	Cobb
Bond's Mills	Baker
Boston	Thomas
Bottsford	Sumter
Bowdon	Carroll
Bowensville	"
Bowersville	Franklin
Box Spring	Talbot
Boxville	Montgomery
Brandon	Gwinnett
Brasstown	Union
Brick Store	Newton
Brooksville	Randolph
Broad River	Elbert
Brown's Bridge	Forsyth
Brownsville	Paulding
Brushy Branch	Berrien
Brunswick	Glynn
Buchanan	Haralson
Buck Creek	Scriven
Buck Eye	Laurens
Buck Head	Morgan
Buena Vista	Marion
Buffalo	Carroll
Buford	Randolph
Bull Creek	Tatnall
Bushyville	Houston
Butler	Taylor
Byrd's Mills	Coffee
Byromville	Dooly
Byron	Houston
Cains	Gwinnett
Cairo	Decatur
Calhoun	Gordon
Camilla	Mitchell
Campbellton Court House	Campbell
Cane Creek	Walker
Canoochee	Emanuel
Canton	Cherokee
Cardeville	Jones
Carnesville Court House	Franklin
Carrollton	Carroll
Cartersville	Cass
Carticay	Gilmer
Cassandra	Walker
Cassville	Cass
Cataula	Harris
Catoose	Lumpkin
Catoosa Spring	Catoosa
Cave Spring	Floyd
Cedar Branch	Campbell
Cedar Creek	Floyd
Cedar Grove	Walker
Cedar Spring	Early
Cedartown	Polk
Center	Talbot
Center Valley	Murray
Center Village	Camden
Chalybeate Springs	Meriwether
Chapel Hill	Campbell
Chanceville	Carroll
Chasoville	Murray
Chattoogaville	Chattooga
Chechero	Rabun
Cherokee Mills	Cherokee
Chenuba	Terrell
Cherry Grove	Gwinnett

POST OFFICES—GEORGIA.

Post Office.	County.	Post Office.	County.	Post Office.	County.
Chestnut Flat	Walker	Egypt	Effingham	Grooverville	Brooks
Chestnut Gap	Gilmer	Elberton	Elbert	Grove	Elbert
Chestnut Mountain	Hall	Eleno	Bibb	Gum Creek	Dooly
Chickasawhatchee	Lee	Ellaville	Schley	Gum Pond	Mitchell
Chiukapin Grove	Gwinnett	Ellersalie	Harris	Guyton	Effingham
Choestoe	Union	Ellejay	Gilmer	Hahira	Lowndes
Church Hill	Marion	Empire Mills	Campbell	Haleyondale	Scriven
Clarksville	Habersham	Enon Grove	Heard	Hall	Appling
Clay Hill	Lincoln	Erastus	Franklin	Halloca	Chattahoochee
Clayton	Rabun	Erin	Meriwether	Hamburg	Macon
Clayville	Telfair	Esom Hill	Polk	Hamilton	Harris
Clinton	Jones	Etna	Paulding	Hannahatchie	Stewart
Clyattsville	Lowndes	Etowa	Cass	Haralson	Coweta
Coal Mountain	Forsyth	Eubanks	Columbia	Harris' Mills	Dawson
Cohuttah Springs	Murray	Euharley	Cass	Hartwell	Hart
Colaparchee	Monroe	Everett's Spring	Floyd	Hassler's Mills	Murray
Cold Water	Elbert	Faceville	Decatur	Hawkinsville	Pulaski
Coleman's Depot	Randolph	Fairburn	Campbell	Haywood	Washington
Colquitt	Miller	Fairmount	Gordon	Haynoville	Houston
Columbus	Muscogee	Fair Play	Morgan	Head of Tennessee	Rabun
Columbia Mine	Columbia	Fairview	Franklin	Hearnville	Putnam
Concord	Fulton	Fall Creek	Clay	Hebron	Washington
Conyers	Newton	Fancy Hill	Murray	Henderson	Houston
Cool Spring	Wilkinson	Farmer's Academy	Macon	Herndon	Burke
Coosa	Floyd	Farmersville	Chattooga	Hiawassee	Towns
Coosawattee	Murray	Farmington	Clarke	Hickory Flat	Cherokee
Copeland	Telfair	Fayetteville	Fayette	Hickory Level	Carroll
Coriuth	Heard	Fenn's Bridge	Jefferson	High Point	Walker
Cork	Butts	Feronia	Coffee	High Shoals	Morgan
Cornucopia	Jones	Fillmore	Whitfield	High Tower	Forsyth
Cottage Mill	Chattahoochee	Fish Dam	Elbert	Hillsborough	Jasper
Cotton Hill	Clay	Flat Pond	Lee	Hinesville	Liberty
County Line	Campbell	Flat Rock	Henry	Hobbie	Dade
Covington	Newton	Flat Shoals	Meriwether	Hoganville	Troup
Cow Creek	Clinch	Flint River Factory	Upson	Hog Mountain	Hall
Craftsville	Elbert	Flintsville	Franklin	Holcombe	Burke
Crawford	Oglethorpe	Florence	Stewart	Hollingsworth	Habersham
Crawfordsville	Taliaferro	Floyd Springs	Floyd	Holly	Meriwether
Crashy	Habersham	Ford's Store	Franklin	Holly Creek	Murray
Cross Creek	Pulaski	Forsyth	Monroe	Homer	Banks
Cross Keys	De Kalb	Fort Buffington	Cherokee	Homersville	Clinch
Cross Hill	Lumpkin	Fort Gaines	Clay	Holmesville	Appling
Culloden	Monroe	Fort Lamar	Madison	Hopeful	Burke
Culverton	Hancock	Fort Valley	Houston	Hot House	Fannin
Cumming C. H.	Forsyth	Fragoletta	Marion	House Creek	Irwin
Currohee	Habersham	Franklin	Heard	Houston	Heard
Curry's Mills	Washington	Franklin Springs	Franklin	Houston Factory	Houston
Curtright	Greene	Frederica	Glynn	Howard	Taylor
Cussetta	Chattahoochee	Free Bridge	Gordon	Huntsville	Paulding
Cuthbert	Randolph	Freemansville	Milton	Ida	Greene
Cut Off	Walton	Friendship	Stewart	Indian Springs	Butts
Dahlonega	Lumpkin	Frick's Gap	Walker	Irwin's X Roads	Washington
Dallas	Paulding	Fryer's Pond	Burke	Irwinsville	Irwin
Dalton	Whitfield	Fulton	Cobb	Irwinton	Wilkinson
Damascus	Early	Furlow's	Calhoun	Isabella	Worth
Danburg	Wilkes	Gaddistown	Union	Island Creek	Hancock
Danielsville	Madison	Gainesville	Hall	Ivy Log	Union
Danville	Sumter	Gartroll	Campbell	Jackson	Butts
Darien	McIntosh	Gatesville	Early	Jacksonville	Telfair
Dark Corner	Campbell	Geneva	Talbot	Jamestown	Muscogee
Davisborough	Washington	Georgetown	Quitman	Jasper	Pickens
Davis Creek	Forsyth	Georgian	Franklin	Jateel	Meriwether
Dawson	Terrell	Ghentsville	Henry	Jefferson	Jackson
Dawsonville	Dawson	Gibson	Glasscock	Jeffersonton	Camden
Decatur	De Kalb	Gillians	Dougherty	Jeffersonville	Twiggs
Delhi	Wilkes	Gillaville	Hall	Johnson's Station	McIntosh
Dennis	Putnam	Girard	Burke	Johnstonville	Monroe
Deerland	Worth	Gladesville	Jasper	Jonesborough	Fayette
De Soto	Paulding	Glasgow	Thomas	Jones' Mills	Meriwether
Dirt Town	Chattooga	Glenalta	Marion	Juno	Lumpkin
Doctor Town	Wayne	Glenn Grove	Fayette	Kedron	Coweta
Double Branches	Lincoln	Glenmore	Ware	King	Chattahoochee
Double Bridges	Upson	Good Hope	Walton	Kingston	Cass
Douglass	Coffee	Goodman's X Roads	Harris	Kiokee	Columbia
Dover	Terrell	Goodson	Spalding	Knoxville	Crawford
Draketown	Paulding	Goodwill	Franklin	Lafayette	Walker
Drayton C. H.	Dooly	Gordon	Wilkinson	La Grange	Troup
Dry Forks	Oglethorpe	Goshen	Lincoln	Lanier	Macon
Dry Lake	Thomas	Grangersville	Macon	Laurel Hill	Carroll
Duane Street	Habersham	Grantville	Coweta	Lauren's Hill	Laurens
Dublin	Laurens	Graysville	Catoosa	Lawrenceville	Gwinnett
Duck Creek	Walker	Green Hill	Stewart	Lawson	Wilcox
Duncanville	Thomas	Greenbush	Walker	Leakesville	Jasper
Dykes' Store	Floyd	Green Cut	Burke	Leathersville	Lincoln
Eagle Grove	Elbert	Greenfield	Colquitt	Leo	White
East Point	Fulton	Greensborough	Greene	Lester's District	Burke
Eatonton	Putnam	Greenville	Meriwether	Lexington	Oglethorpe
Ebenezer	Morgan	Griffin's Mills	Lowndes	Liberty Hill	Pike
Eden	Effingham	Griffin	Spalding	Lincolnton	Lincoln
Edenfield	Irwin	Griswoldville	Jones	Linton	Hancock

POST OFFICES—GEORGIA.

Post Office.	County.	Post Office.	County.	Post Office.	County.
Little Prairie	Cass	Newborn	Newton	Richmond Factory	Richmond
Little River	Cherokee	New Bridge	Lumpkin	Riddlesville	Washington
Little York	Montgomery	New Manchester	Campbell	Ringgold	Catoosa
Locust Grove	Henry	New Market	Monroe	Rio	Coweta
Lodi	Coweta	Newnan	Coweta	Rising Fawn	Dade
Loganville	Walton	Newsville	Haralson	Rivertown	Campbell
Lombardy	Columbia	Newton	Baker	Rockalo	Heard
Long Branch	Tatnall	Newton Factory	Newton	Rockbridge	Gwinnett
Long Cane	Troup	Nochway	Randolph	Rock Spring	Walker
Long Street	Pulaski	Noonday	Cobb	Rocky Mount	Meriwether
Lookout Station	Dade	Oak Bower	Hart	Rocky Plains	Newton
Lost Mountain	Cobb	Oak Grove	Fulton	Rollin	Fannin
Loudsville	Habersham	Oak Hill	Newton	Rome	Floyd
Louisville	Jefferson	Oak Ridge	Meriwether	Rose Hill	Union
Lovejoy's Station	Clayton	Ocmulgeeville	Coffee	Rossville	Walker
Lumber City	Telfair	Oconee	Washington	Roswell	Cobb
Lumpkin	Stewart	Odchodkee	Randolph	Rotherwood	Carroll
Luthersville	Meriwether	Ogeechee	Scriven	Rough and Ready	Fayette
Lythonia	DeKalb	Oglethorpe	Macon	Ruckersville	Elbert
McBeen Depot	Richmond	Okapilco	Lowndes	Rural Vale	Whitfield
McDonough	Henry	O'Neal's Mills	Troup	Rushville	Appling
McElveensville	Baker	Ophir	Cherokee	Russellville	Monroe
McGuire's Store	Floyd	Orange		Rutledge	Morgan
McIntire	Wilkinson	Owen's Ferry	Camden	Saint Cloud	Heard
McIntosh	Liberty	Oxford	Newton	Saint Mary's	Camden
McItue's Store	Telfair	Pachitta	Calhoun	Saffold	Early
Macon	Bibb	Palmetto	Coweta	Salem	Clark
Madison	Morgan	Palo Alto	Jasper	Salt Spring	Campbell
Madison Springs	Madison	Palos	Gwinnett	Saluda	Coweta
Malloryville	Wilkes	Paoli	Madison	Salula Farm	Dade
Marble Works	Pickens	Pardues	Houston	Sandersville	Washington
Marcus	Jackson	Paris	Coweta	Sand Hill	Carroll
Marietta	Cobb	Parker's Store	Franklin	Sandy Ridge	Henry
Marion	Twiggs	Patterson	Pierce	Sardis	Burke
Marshallsville	Macon	Peaks	Henry	Satilla	Wayne
Matlock	Tatnall	Penfield	Greene	Santa Lucah	Gilmer
Maxey	Oglethorpe	Perry	Houston	Saunderstown	Pickens
Mayfield	Warren	Perry's Mills	Tatnall	Savannah	Chatham
Mechanicsville	Jasper	Phi Delta	Franklin	Saw Dust	Columbia
Molville	Chattooga	Philomath	Oglethorpe	Sawney's Mountain	Forsyth
Middle Ground	Scriven	Pierceville	Gilmer	Scarboro	Scriven
Middle Ridge	Newton	Pinckneyville	Gwinnett	Scienceville	Stewart
Middle River	Franklin	Pine Log	Cass	Screven	Appling
Midville	Burke	Pine Mountain	Rabun	Scull Shoals	Greene
Milford	Baker	Pineville	Marion	Seven Islands	Butts
Millard	Stewart	Piscola	Lowndes	Seward	Montgomery
Mill Creek	Union	Plains of Dura	Sumter	Shady Dale	Jasper
Milledgeville	Baldwin	Pleasant Hill	Talbot	Sharon	Taliaferro
Milkin	Burke	Pleasant Retreat	Lumpkin	Sharp Top	Cherokee
Mill Grove	Cobb	Poindexter	Schley	Sheffield	Newton
Mill Haven	Scriven	Point Peter	Oglethorpe	Sheltonville	Forsyth
Mill Ray	Bullock	Polksville	Hall	Shoal Creek	Hall
Mill Stone	Oglethorpe	Pomaria	Clay	Skitt's Mountain	
Mill Town	Berrien	Pond Fork	Jackson	Smithville	Lumpkin
Millwood	Dooly	Pond Spring	Walker	Snapping Shoals	Newton
Milner	Pike	Pond Town	Sumter	Sneed	Lee
Milton	Wilkinson	Popo Hill	Jefferson	Snow Hill	Catoosa
Mineral Bluff	Fannin	Poplar Springs	Hall	Social Circle	Walton
Minton	Irwin	Poverty Hill	Jones	Soda Town	Taylor
Missionary Station	Floyd	Powder Springs	Cobb	Sofkey	Decatur
Mobley Pond	Scriven	Powelton	Hancock	Sonora	Gordon
Moccasin	Rabun	Powers	Terrell	South Newport	McIntosh
Monroe	Walton	Powersville	Houston	Sparta	Hancock
Montevideo	Hart	Prattsburg	Talbot	Spier's Turnout	Jefferson
Montezuma	Macon	Preston	Webster	Spring	Henry
Morgan	Calhoun	Prince Edward	Gilmer	Spring Creek	Early
Morganton C. H.	Fannin	Proctor's Store	Monroe	Springfield	Effingham
Morris Station	Quitman	Providence	Sumter	Spring Place	Murray
Morven	Brooks	Pryor	Baker	Stanfordville	Putnam
Mosely's Store	Franklin	Pumpkin Pile	Polk	Stark	Butts
Moultrie	Colquitt	Pumpkin Vine	Paulding	Starkville	Lee
Mountain Hill	Harris	Quebec	Sumter	Starrsville	Newton
Mountain Scene	Towns	Quitman	Brooks	State Line	Heard
Mountain Town	Gilmer	Quito	Talbot	Statenville	Echols
Mount Carmel	Henry	Radford's Mills	Lowndes	Statesborough	Bulloch
Mount Eolia	Towns	Raysville	Columbia	Steam Factory	Muscogee
Mount Pleasant	Glynn	Raytown	Taliaferro	Steam Mill	Decatur
Mount Vernon	Montgomery	Red Bluff	Coffee	Stevens	Oglethorpe
Mountville	Troup	Red Bud	Gordon	Stephensville	Wilkinson
Mount Yonah	Habersham	Red Clay	Whitfield	Sterling	Montgomery
Mount Zion	Hancock	Red Oak	Fayette	Stilesborough	Cass
Mulberry	Jackson	Reedy Creek	Jefferson	Stockbridge	Henry
Mulberry Grove	Harris	Rehoboth	Wilkes	Stock Hill	Union
Nacoochee	Habersham	Reidsville	Tatnall	Stockton	Clinch
Nail's Creek	Franklin	Repose	Haralson	Stone Mountain	De Kalb
Nankin	Brooks	Republican	Warren	Stithville	Fayette
Naomi	Walker	Resaca	Gordon	Subligno	Chattooga
Nashville	Berrien	Reynolds	Taylor	Sugar Creek	Telfair
Naylor	Lowndes	Riceborough	Liberty	Sugar Hill	Hall
Nebraska	Columbia	Richland	Stewart	Sugar Valley	Gordon

POST OFFICES—ILLINOIS. 13

Post Office.	County.
Summervale	Elbert
Summerville	Chattooga
Suquee	Habersham
Suwanee	Gwinnett
Suwannoochee	Clinch
Swainsboro'	Emmanuel
Sweet Water	Gwinnett
Sylvania	Scriven
Tail's Creek	Gilmer
Talbotton	Talbot
Talking Rock	Pickens
Tallapoosa	Carroll
Tallokas	Lowndes
Tallulah	Habersham
Tally	Dawson
Talmage	Baldwin
Tanville	Warren
Traversville	Twiggs
Taylor's Creek	Liberty
Tazewell	Marion
Tebeauville	Ware
Tologa Springs	Chattooga
Temperance	Telfair
Tennille	Washington
The Rock	Upson
Thomaston	"
Thomasville	Thomas
Thompson	Columbia
Ti-Ti	Colquitt
Tiger	Rabun
Tifton	Whitfield
Tired Creek	Decatur
Toombsborough	Wilkinson
Town Creek	Gilmer
Trader's Hill	Charlton
Trenton	Dade
Trion Factory	Chattooga
Troup Factory	Troup
Troy	Cherokee
Tunnel Hill	Whitfield
Turin	Coweta
Twiggsville	Twiggs
Union Mills	Heard
Union Point	Greene
Unionville	Monroe
Upper King's Bridge	Whitfield
Upatoie	Muscogee
Utoy	De Kalb
Valdosta	Lowndes
Valley Store	Chattooga
Vanu's Valley	Floyd
Van Wert	Polk
Vanzandt's Store	Fanuin
Varnell's Station	Whitfield
Vernon	Troup
Vickery's Creek	Forsyth
Vienna	Dooly
Villanow	Walker
Villa Rica	Carroll
Walesca	Cherokee
Wallace	Jones
Walnut Grove	Walton
Walnut Hill	Franklin
Walthourville	Liberty
Walton's Ford	Habersham
Waresborough	Ware
War Hill	Hall
Warm Springs	Meriwether
Warnorville	"
Warrenton	Warren
Warsaw	Forsyth
Warthen's Store	Washington
Warwick	Worth
War Women	Rabun
Washington	Wilkes
Water Oak	Muscogee
Watkinsville	Clark
Waverly Hall	Harris
Waynesboro'	Burke
Waynesville	Wayne
Waynmanville	Upson
Way's Station	Bryan
Webster Place	Elbert
Wellborn's Mills	Houston
Well's Mills	Lowndes
Weston	Webster
West Point	Troup
Whaley's Mills	Terrell
White House	Henry
White Oak	Columbia

Post Office.	County.
White Path	Gilmer
White Plains	Greene
White Sulphur Springs	Meriwether
White Water	Fayette
Whitesville	Harris
Whitney	Calhoun
Willow Grove	Coweta
Wimberley	Carroll
Winchester	Macon
Windsor	Walton
Winfield	Columbia
Wisdom's Store	Harris
Woodbury	Meriwether
Woodlawn	Murray
Wood's Station	Catoosa
Woodstock	Cherokee
Woodville	Greene
Wooley's Ford	Hall
Worthville	Butts
Wrightsboro'	Columbia
Wrightsville C. H.	Johnson
Yarborough	Floyd
Yellow Creek	Lumpkin
Yellow River	Gwinnett
Yellow Stone	Polk
Young Cane	Union
Zebulon	Pike

Illinois.

Post Office.	County.
Abingdon	Knox
Accommodation	Effingham
Adams	Adams
Addison	Du Page
Adeline	Ogle
Ainsworth Station	Cook
Akin	Franklin
Albany	Whitesides
Albion	Edwards
Alden	McHenry
Aledo	Mercer
Alexander	Morgan
Algonquin	McHenry
Akron	Peoria
Alhambra	Madison
Allen's Springs	Pope
Alma	Marion
Alton	Madison
Alum Rock	La Salle
Amboy	Lee
Amity	Livingston
Ancona	"
Audalusia	Rock Island
Andover	Henry
Angola	Lake
Anna	Union
Annapolis	Crawford
Annawan	Henry
Antioch	Lake
Appanoose	Hancock
Apple Creek	Greene
Apple River	Jo Daviess
Arcadia	Morgan
Arcola	Coles
Areasville	Cass
Argo	Carroll
Argyle	McDonough
Arlington	Bureau
Armington	Tazewell
Armstrong	Wabash
Aroma	Kankakee
Asbury	La Salle
Ashby	Coles
Ash Grove	Iroquois
Ashkum	"
Ashland	Cass
Ashley	Washington
Ashmore	Coles
Ash Ridge	Massac
Assumption	Christian
Astoria	Fulton
Athens	Menard
Athensville	Greene

Post Office.	Parish.
Atkinson	Henry
Atlanta	Logan
Atlas	Pike
Attilla	Williamson
Auburn	Sangamon
Audubon	Montgomery
Augusta	Hancock
Aurora	Kane
Ava	Jackson
Avery	Jo Daviess
Aviston	Clinton
Avoca	Livingston
Avon	Fulton
Babcock's Grove	Du Page
Baileyville	Ogle
Bainbridge	Williamson
Baldwinville	Edgar
Bankston	Saline
Bardolph	McDonough
Barclay	Ogle
Barreville	McHenry
Barrington Station	Cook
Barr's Store	Macoupin
Barry	Pike
Basco	Hancock
Batavia	Kane
Bates	Sangamon
Bath	Mason
Beardstown	Cass
Bear Creek	Montgomery
Beaver Creek	Bond
Beaverton	Boone
Beaverville	Iroquois
Beck's Creek	Shelby
Bedford	Pike
Bedfordville	Henderson
Belden	McHenry
Bell Air	Crawford
Bell Plain	Marshall
Belle Prairie	Hamilton
Belleville	St. Clair
Bellview	Calhoun
Belvidere	Boone
Belwood	Iroquois
Bement	Piatt
Benton	Franklin
Berlin	Sangamon
Bernadotte	Fulton
Berryton	Cass
Berwick	Warren
Bethalto	Madison
Bethel	Morgan
Beulah	De Kalb
Beverly	Adams
Bible Grove	Clay
Biggsville	Henderson
Big Muddy	Franklin
Big Neck	Adams
Big Rock	Kane
Big Rush Creek	Jo Daviess
Big Spring	Shelby
Big Woods	Du Page
Birmingham	Schuyler
Bishop Hill	Henry
Blackberry	Kane
Blackberry Station	"
Black Oak	Wayne
Blair	Randolph
Blairsville	Williamson
Blandinsville	McDonough
Bliven's Mill	McHenry
Blood's Point	De Kalb
Bloomfield	Edgar
Bloomingdale	Du Page
Bloomington	McLean
Bloomville	Kankakee
Bloom	Cook
Blue Grass	Vermillion
Blue Island	Cook
Blue Point	Wayne
Blue Ridge	Jefferson
Blueville	Christian
Bluff Dale	Greene
Bluffville	Carroll
Bolton	Williamson
Bond's Point	Christian
Bon Pas	Richland
Bonus	Boone
Bonwell	Edgar
Book	Pope

14 POST OFFICES—ILLINOIS.

Post Office.	County.	Post Office.	County.	Post Office.	County.
Boone	Boone	Channahon	Will	Deer Plain	Calhoun
Boot	Richland	Charleston	Coles	DeKalb Center	DeKalb
Bourbon	Douglas	Chatham	Sangamon	Delavan	Tazewell
Bowling Green	Fayette	Chatsworth	Livingston	Delhi	Jersey
Boynton	Tazewell	Chebanse	Iroquois	Del Rey	Iroquois
Bradford	Stark	Chelsea	Will	Delta	McLean
Bradley	Jackson	Chemung	McHenry	Dement Station	Ogle
Breckinridge	Pope	Cheney's Grove	McLean	Denny	Warren
Breese	Greene	Chenoa	"	Derinda	Jo Daviess
Bremen	Randolph	Cherry Grove	Carroll	Detroit	Pike
Brickton	Cook	Cherry Valley	Winnebago	De Soto	Jackson
Bridgeport	Lawrence	Chester	Randolph	De Witt	De Witt
Brighton	Macoupin	Chesterfield	Macoupin	Diamond Lake	Lake
Brimfield	Peoria	Chicago	Cook	Dillon	Tazewell
Bristol	Kendall	Chili	Hancock	Dixon	Lee
Bristol Station	"	Chili Center	"	Doodsville	Schuyler
Broad Oaks	Pope	Chillicothe	Peoria	Dogtooth	Alexander
Broadwell	Logan	Chismansville	Gallatin	Dolson	Clark
Brooklyn	Schuyler	Circleville	Tazewell	Dongola	Union
Brookville	Ogle	Clark Center	Clark	Donovan	Iroquois
Browning	Schuyler	Clay	La Salle	Dorrance	Stark
Bruce	McDonough	Clay City	Clay	Dorchester	Macoupin
Brunswick	Peoria	Clayton	Adams	Dorset	DeKalb
Brush Creek	Wayne	Clear Creek Landing	Alexander	Douglas	Knox
Brushy Fork	Coles	Clermont	Richland	Dover	Bureau
Buck	Hamilton	Clifton	Iroquois	Downer's Grove	Du Page
Buck Hart	Christian	Clinton	De Witt	Downs	McLean
Buck Horn	Brown	Clintonville	Kane	Drury	Rock Island
Buda	Bureau	Clover	Henry	Dubois	Washington
Buenna Vista	Stephenson	Clyde	Whitesides	Duck Creek	Warren
Buffalo	Gallatin	Coal Valley	Rock Island	Dudley	Edgar
Buffalo Prairie	Rock Island	Coatsburg	Adams	Dudleyville	Bond
Bulkley	Iroquois	Cochranville	Stephenson	Duncan's Mills	Fulton
Bullbonas Grove	Kankakee	Cobb	Randolph	Dundas	Richland
Bunker Hill	Macoupin	Colchester	McDonough	Dundee	Kane
Bureau Junction	Bureau	Cold Spring	Shelby	Dunleith	Jo Daviess
Burkeville	Monroe	Collins' Station	Clinton	Dupage	Will
Burlington	Kane	Collinsville	Madison	Duquoin	Perry
Burns	Henry	Colmar	McDonough	Durand Station	Winnebago
Burnsville	McDonough	Colona Station	Henry	Durham	Hancock
Burnt Prairie	White	Columbia	Monroe	Dwight	Livingston
Burritt	Winnebago	Columbus	Adams	Eagle	La Salle
Burton	Adams	Como	Whitesides	Eagle Cliffs	Monroe
Bushnell	McDonough	Concord	Morgan	Eagle Point	Ogle
Butler	Montgomery	Conkey's Store	Vermillion	Earlville	La Salle
Byron	Ogle	Cooperstown	Brown	East Bend	Ford
Cairo	Alexander	Copperas Creek	Fulton	East Cambridge	Henry
Caledonia	Pulaski	Copper Creek	Rock Island	East Paw Paw	DeKalb
Caledonia Station	Boone	Coral	McHenry	East Wheatland	Will
Calhoun	Richland	Cordova	Rock Island	Eaton	Crawford
Camargo	Coles	Corinton	Cumberland	Edgington	Rock Island
Cambridge	Henry	Cornville	La Salle	Edwardsville	Madison
Camden	Schuyler	Cottage Hill	Du Page	Effingham	Effingham
Camden Mills	Rock Island	Cottonwood	Gallatin	Edgewood	"
Cameron	Warren	Cottonwood Grove	Bond	Egypt	Mason
Campbell	Coles	Coultersville	Randolph	Ela	Lake
Camp Grove	Stark	Council Hill	Jo Daviess	Elbridge	Edgar
Camp Point	Adams	Council Hill Station	"	El Dara	Pike
Canton	Fulton	Courtland Station	DeKalb	El Dorado	Saline
Carbon	Mercer	Courtright Mills	Iroquois	Eleroy	Stephenson
Carbon Cliff	Rock Island	Crab Orchard	Williamson	Elgin	Kane
Carbondale	Jackson	Crawford	Gallatin	Elida	Winnebago
Cary Station	McHenry	Crescent City	Iroquois	Eliza	Mercer
Carlinville	Macoupin	Crete	Will	Elizabeth	Jo Daviess
Carlyle	Clinton	Crittenden	Franklin	Elizabethtown	Hardin
Carment Prairie	Perry	Crotty	La Salle	Elk Grove	Cook
Carmi	White	Crow Meadows	Marshall	Elkhart City	Logan
Carpentersville	Kane	Cruger	Woodford	Elkhorn	Washington
Carrollton	Greene	Crystal Lake	McHenry	Elkhorn Grove	Carroll
Cartersville	Jasper	Cuba	Fulton	Elkton	Crawford
Carthage	Hancock	Cypress Creek	Johnson	Elliottstown	Effingham
Carter	Sangamon	Dakota	Stephenson	Ellis Grove	Randolph
Casey	Clark	Dallas City	Hancock	Ellison	Warren
Caseyville	St. Clair	Damascus	Stephenson	Ellisville	Fulton
Cass	Du Page	Danby	Du Page	Elm Grove	Adams
Catlin	Vermillion	Danforth	Tazewell	Elmore	Peoria
Cave	Franklin	Danville	Vermillion	Elmira	Stark
Cave in Rock	Hardin	Darion	Clark	Elm Point	Bond
Cayuga	Livingston	Davis	Stephenson	Elm Wood	Peoria
Cedar Bluff	Johnson	Darwin	Clark	El Paso	Woodford
Cedarville	Stephenson	Dawson	Sangamon	Elsah	Jersey
Centerville	Piatt	Daysville	Ogle	Elvaston	Hancock
Central City	Marion	Dayton	La Salle	Elwin	Macon
Centralia	"	Dearborn	McHenry	Elwood	Will
Center Point	Knox	Decatur	Macon	Eminence	Logan
Center Ridge	Mercer	Deep Cut	McHenry	Emma	White
Cerro Gordo	Piatt	Deer Creek	Tazewell	Empire	Whitesides
Chambersburg	Pike	Deerfield	Lake	Enfield	White
Champaign	Champaign	Deerfield Prairie	DeKalb	English Prairie	McHenry
Chandlerville	Cass	Deer Park	La Salle	Enon	Bureau

POST OFFICES—ILLINOIS.

Post Office.	Parish.	Post Office.	County.	Post Office.	County.
Enterprise	Wayne	Germantown	Clinton	Hickory Ridge	Hancock
Epler	Morgan	Gibson	Knox	Hicks' Mills	De Kalb
Equality	Gallatin	Gilead	Calhoun	Hidalgo	Jasper
Erie	Whitesides	Gilgal	Pike	Higginsville	Vermillion
Erin	McHenry	Gilespie	Macoupin	Highland	Madison
Erwin	Schuyler	Gilman	Iroquois	High Point	Mercer
Essex	Kankakee	Gilmer		High Prairie	La Salle
Etna	Coles	Girard	Macoupin	Hillsboro'	Montgomery
Eureka	Woodford	Glasgow	Scott	Hill's Grove	McDonough
Eugene	Knox	Glendale	Pope	Hodges	Greene
Evan's Mill	Morgan	Glencoe	Cook	Holland	Shelby
Evanston	Cook	Glenwood Mills	Livingston	Hollowayville	Bureau
Evansville	Randolph	Godfrey	Madison	Home	Wayne
Ewing	Franklin	Golconda	Pope	Homer	Champaign
Ewington	Effingham	Good Hope	McDonough	Hoover's Point	Macoupin
Exeter	Scott	Gooding's Grove	Will	Hope	Cook
Fairburg	Livingston	Goose Island	Alexander	Hopedale	Tazewell
Fairfield	Wayne	Grafton	Jersey	Hopewell	Macon
Fairhaven	Carroll	Grand Chain	Pulaski	Hopper's Mills	Henderson
Fairmont	Vermillion	Grand Cote Prairie	Perry	Hord	Clay
Fair Play	Jefferson	Grand Detour	Ogle	Hornsby	Macoupin
Fairview	Fulton	Grand View	Edgar	Houston	Adams
Fair Weather	Adams	Grand Tower	Jackson	Howard's Point	Fayette
Farina	Fayette	Grand Prairie	Kankakee	Howardsville	Stephenson
Farmington	Fulton	Granville	Putnam	Hoyleton	Washington
Farm Ridge	La Salle	Gray's Mills	Johnson	Hudson	McLean
Farmsville	Woodford	Grayville	White	Huntley Grove	McHenry
Farrowtown	Calhoun	Greenburg	Greene	Hnatsville	Schuyler
Fayette	Greene	Greenbush	Warren	Hurricane	Montgomery
Fayetteville	St. Clair	Green Dale	Marion	Hutsonville	Crawford
Ferdinand	Mercer	Greenfield	Greene	Hyde Park	Cook
Fiatt	Fulton	Green Garden	Will	Illiopolis Station	Sangamon
Fidelity	Jersey	Green River	Henry	Illinois City	Rock Island
Fieldon	"	Greenup	Cumberland	Illinoistown	St. Clair
Fillmore	Montgomery	Greenvale	Jo Daviess	Indianola	Vermillion
Fincastlo	Clark	Greenville	Bond	Industry	McDonough
Fish Hook	Pike	Greenwood	McHenry	Ingraham Prairie	Clay
Fitts Hill	Franklin	Greggville	Pike	Ionia	Warren
Fitz Henry	Ogle	Gridley	McLean	Ipava	Fulton
Flat Rock	Crawford	Griswold	Hamilton	Ira	Jo Daviess
Flora	Clay	Grouse	Kane	Iroquois	Iroquois
Floraville	St. Clair	Groveland	Tazewell	Irving	Montgomory
Florence	Pike	Guilford	Jo Daviess	Island Creek	Jasper
Florid	Putnam	Hadley	Will	Izoria	Rock Island
Forest Station	Livingston	Hadley's Station	Lawrence	Jacksonville	Morgan
Forksville	Lake	Hagley	Cass	Jamestown	Clinton
Foreston	Ogle	Hainesville	Lake	Jasper	Schuyler
Fort Hill	Lake	Haldane	Ogle	Jefferson	Cook
Fosterburg	Madison	Hale	"	Jefferson Corners	Whitesides
Fosters	Marion	Halgisaw	Boone	Jeffersonville	Wayne
Fountain Green	Hancock	Halt Day	Lake	Jericho	Kane
Four Mile Grove	Lee	Hall	Franklin	Jersey Prairie	Cass
Fowler's Station	Adams	Hallock	Peoria	Jerseyville	Jersey
Fox Lake	Lake	Hamburg	Calhoun	John's Creek	Sangamon
Frankfort	Franklin	Hamilton	Hancock	Johnson	McDonough
Franklin	Morgan	Hamlet	Mercer	Johnsontown	Cumberland
Franklin Grove	Lee	Hamshire	Kane	Johnsonville	Wayne
Franzonia	Richland	Hampton	Rock Island	Joliet	Will
Fredericksville	Schuyler	Hanover	Jo Daviess	Jonesboro'	Union
Fredonia	Williamson	Hardin	Calhoun	Jones' Creek	Randolph
Freeburg	St. Clair	Hardinsville	Crawford	Jordan	Vermillion
Freedom	La Salle	Harlem	Winnebago	Jordan's Grove	Randolph
Freeland	De Kalb	Harmony	McHenry	Kane	Greene
Freemanton	Effingham	Harrisburg	Saline	Kanoville	Kane
Fremont Center	Lake	Harris Grove	Jefferson	Kankakee Depot	Kankakee
Freeport	Stephenson	Harrison	Winnebago	Kansas	Edgar
French Village	St. Clair	Harrisonville	Monroe	Kappa	Woodford
Friend Grove	Wabash	Harristown	Macon	Kaskaskia	Randolph
Friendship	McDonough	Hartford	Saline	Kocno	Adams
Friendsville	Wabash	Hartland	McHenry	Keenville	Wayne
Fullersburg	Du Page	Harvard	"	Keithsburg	Mercer
Fuller's Point	Coles	Havana	Mason	Kendall	Kendall
Fulton	Whitesides	Havelock	Cook	Kent	Stephenson
Fulton Center	Fulton	Hazel Dell	Cumberland	Kentucky	Vermillion
Galena	Jo Daviess	Hazlett	Rock Island	Kewaunee	Henry
Galesburg	Knox	Hebron	McHenry	Keysport	Clinton
Gallatin	Saline	Hecker	Monroe	Kickapoo	Peoria
Galloway	La Salle	Hemlo	Whitesides	Killbuck	Ogle
Galum	Perry	Henderson	Knox	Kinderhook	Pike
Galva	Henry	Hennepin	Putnam	Kingsbury	Whitesides
Gap Grove	Lee	Henry	Marshall	King's Mills	Kane
Garden Plain	Whitesides	Hermitage	Coles	Kingston	De Kalb
Garden Prairie	Boone	Hermon	Knox	Kingston Mines	Peoria
Gardner	Grundy	Herndon	Montgomery	Kinmundy	Marion
Gard's Point	Wabash	Hersman's	Brown	Kiytyro	Winnebago
Geneva	Kane	Heyworth	McLean	Kishwaukee	"
Genesee	Henry	Hickory	Lake	Knight's Grove	St. Clair
Genesee Grove	Whitesides	Hickory Creek	Fayette	Knot Prairie	Jefferson
Genoa	De Kalb	Hickory Grove	Massac	Knoxville	Knox
Georgetown	Vermillion	Hickory Hill	Marion	Kyte River	Ogle

16 POST OFFICES—ILLINOIS.

Post Office.	County.	Post Office.	County.	Post Office.	County.
La Clair	De Kalb	McLean	McLean	Montezuma	Pike
Lacon	Marshall	McLeansboro'	Hamilton	Montgomery	Kane
Lacey	De Kalb	Macomb	McDonough	Monticello	Piatt
La Clede	Fayette	Madison	Madison	Monument	Pike
Lacuna	Logan	Magnolia	Putnam	Moore's Prairie	Jefferson
Lafayette	Stark	Mahomet	Champaign	Morian's Grove	Wayne
Lafox	Kane	Maine	Cook	Moro	Madison
La Harpe	Hancock	Mainville	"	Morrison	Whitesides
Lake Creek	Williamson	Majority Point	Cumberland	Morris	Grundy
Lake Forrest	Lake	Malden	Bureau	Morristown	Henry
Lake Zurich	"	Malina	De Kalb	Mortansville	Sangamon
Lamb's Point	Madison	Malta	"	Morton	Tazewell
Lamoille	Bureau	Malugin Grove	Lee	Moscow	Masou
Lancaster	Cass	Manchester	Scott	Mossville	Peoria
Lane Depot	Ogle	Maulius	La Salle	Moultonville	Madison
Lane's ½ Roads	Hamilton	Mansfield	Kendall	Mound City	Pulaski
Lanesville	Sangamon	Manteno	Kankakee	Mound Station	Brown
Langdon	Peoria	Maple Grove	Edwards	Mount Auburn	Christian
Laona	Winnebago	Maple's Mill	Fulton	Mount Carmel	Wabash
La Prairie Center	Marshall	Maquon	Knox	Mount Carroll	Carroll
Larkinsburg	Clay	Maradosia	Morgan	Mount Erie	Wayne
La Salle	La Salle	Marceline	Adams	Mount Hawley	Peoria
Lavine	Iroquois	Marcy	Franklin	Mount Meacham	Schuyler
Lawndale	Logan	Marengo	McHeury	Mount Morris	Ogle
Lawn Ridge	Marshall	Margaretta	Clark	Mount Palatine	Putnam
Lawrence	McHenry	Marietta	Fulton	Mount Pleasant	Union
Lawrenceville	Lawrence	Marine	Madison	Mount Prospect	Whitesides
Lebanon	St. Clair	Marion	Williamson	Mount Pulaski	Logan
Lee Center	Lee	Marissa	St. Clair	Mount Sterling	Brown
L'Erable	Iroquois	Markanda	Jackson	Mount Sumner	Jo Daviess
Leesville	Boone	Maroa	Macou	Mount Vernon	Jefferson
Leland	La Salle	Marrowbone	Moultrie	Moweaqua	Shelby
Lemont	Cook	Marseilles	La Salle	Mud Creek	St. Clair
Lena	Stephenson	Martinsburg	Pike	Mulberry Grove	Bond
Lenzburg	St. Clair	Marshall	Clark	Mule Creek	Cumberland
Leroy	McLean	Martinsville	"	Murphysborough	Jackson
Lewistown	Fulton	Marysville	Vermillion	Murrysville	Morgan
Lexington	McLean	Mascoutah	St. Clair	Munson	Henry
Leyden Center	Cook	Mason	Effingham	Myersville	Vermillion
Liberty	Adams	Mason City	Mason	Nachusa	Lee
Libertyville	Lake	Matanzas	"	Nakomis	Montgomery
Lillecash	Will	Mattison	Cook	Naperville	Du Page
Lina	Adams	Mattoon	Coles	Naples	Scott
Limerick	Bureau	Mayestown	Monroe	Nashville	Washington
Limestone	Kankakee	Mazou	Grundy	Nasusay	Kendall
Lincoln	Logan	Mechanicsburg	Sangamon	Nauvoo	Hancock
Lindenwood	Ogle	Melrose	Clark	Neapolis	Shelby
Lisbon	Kendall	Mendon	Adams	Nebo	Pike
Lisle	Du Page	Mendota	La Salle	Neeleyville	Morgan
Litchfield	Montgomery	Mercia	Rock Island	Negro Lick	Greene
Little Detroit	Tazewell	Meriden	La Salle	Nelson	Lee
Little Muddy	Franklin	Metamora	Woodford	Neoga	Cumberland
Little Rock	Kendall	Metropolis City	Massac	Neponset	Bureau
Littleton	Schuyler	Middle Creek	Hancock	New Ark	Kendall
Little York	Warren	Middle Fork	Fulton	New Baltimore	Wayne
Lively	St. Clair	Middle Grove	"	New Bedford	Bureau
Liverpool	Fulton	Middleport	Iroquois	Newbern	Jersey
Livingston	Clark	Middletown	Logan	New Boston	Mercer
Loami	Sangamon	Midway	Fulton	New Bremen	Cook
Lock	La Salle	Mier	Wabash	New Clyde	Whitesides
Lockhart	Macon	Miles' Station	Macoupin	New Columbia	Massac
Lockport	Will	Millford	Iroquois	Newcomb	Champaign
Locust Grove	Williamson	Millburn	Lake	New Erin	Stephenson
Lodi Station	Kane	Milledgeville	Carroll	New Franklin	Wayne
Logan	Edgar	Millersburg	Mercer	New Gennessee	Whitesides
Logansport	Hamilton	Mill Grove	Stephenson	New Hartford	Pike
London City	Fayette	Mills' Prairie	Edwards	New Haven	Gallatin
Lone Tree	Bureau	Millstadt	St. Clair	New Hebron	Crawford
Long Grove	Lake	Millville	Jo Daviess	New Hope	Wabash
Long Point	Livingston	Milo	Bureau	New Jordan	Whitesides
Long Prairie	Wayne	Milroy	Knox	New Lancaster	Warren
Looking Glass	Clinton	Milton	Pike	New Lebanon	De Kalb
Loran	Stephenson	Milton Station	Coles	New Liberty	Pope
Louisville	Clay	Mineral	Bureau	New Market	Gallatin
Lovington	Moultrie	Minersville	Henry	New Massilon	Wayne
Lovilla	Hamilton	Mill Shoals	White	New Maysville	Pike
Lowell	La Salle	Minonk	Woodford	New Michigan	Livingston
Low Point	Woodford	Minooka	Grundy	New Middleton	Marion
Luda	Ogle	Mitchelsville	Saline	New Milford	Winnebago
Lusk	Pope	Mitchie	Monroe	New Philadelphia	McDonough
Lynchburg	Jefferson	Mode	Shelby	New Plato	Kane
Lyndon	Whitesides	Mokena	Will	Newport	Lake
Lynnville	Morgan	Moline	Rock Island	New Providence	Greene
Lyonsville	Cook	Momence	Kankakee	New Rutland	La Salle
Lythesville	McLean	Monce	Will	News	Calhoun
McConnell's Grove	Stephenson	Mounmouth	Warren	New Salem	Pike
McGary	Hancock	Monroe	Mercer	Newton	Jasper
McHenry	McHenry	Monroe Center	Ogle	New Virgil	Kane
Mackinaw	Tazewell	Monroe City	Monron	Ney	De Kalb
		Monterey	Calhoue	Niantic	Macon

POST OFFICES—ILLINOIS.

Post Office.	County.	Post Office.	County.	Post Office.	County.
Night's Prairie	Hamilton	Pekin	Tazewell	Richland Grove	Mercer
Niles	Cook	Pellonia	Massac	Richmond	McHenry
Niles Center	Cook	Pennsylvania	Rock Island	Richview	Washington
Nilwood	Macoupin	Peoria	Peoria	Ridge Farm	Vermillion
Noble	Richland	Perry	Pike	Ridgefield	McHenry
Nora	Jo Daviess	Peru	La Salle	Ridgely	Madison
Northfield	Cook	Peru Station	Champaign	Riley	McHenry
North Fork	Vermillion	Pesotum		Ringgold	Cook
North Hampton	Peoria	Petersburg	Menard	Kingwood	McHenry
North Henderson	Warren	Petty's	Lawrence	Rinosa	Iroquois
North Kingston	De Kalb	Pytons	Adams	Ripley	Brown
North Plato	Kane	Phillipstown	White	Risdon	St. Clair
North Prairie	Knox	Philo	Champaign	Rivola	Mercer
Northville	La Salle	Piasa	Macoupin	Rising Sun	Macoupin
Norway	"	Pickwick	Jasper	Roanoke	Woodford
Noyesville	Cook	Pierce	Will	Robin's Nest	Peoria
Oak	Pope	Pierceville	DeKalb	Robinson	Crawford
Oakland	Coles	Pigeon Creek	Pike	Robinson's Mills	Menard
Oakley	Macon	Pilot	Vermillion	Rochester	Sangamon
Oak Ridge	Menard	Pilot Grove	Hancock	Rochester Mills	Wabash
Oakula	Iroquois	Pinckneyville	Perry	Rock	Pope
Oblong	Crawford	Pingree Grove	Kane	Rockbridge	Greene
Oceola	Stark	Pink Prairie	Henry	Rock Creek	Carroll
Oconee Station	Shelby	Pin Oak	Wayne	Rockford	Winnebago
Ocoya	Livingston	Pioneer	Greene	Rock Grove	Stephenson
Odell	"	Pitman	Adams	Rock Island	Rock Island
Odin	Marion	Pittsfield	Pike	Rockland	Lake
O'Fallon Depo	St. Clair	Plainfield	Will	Rookport	Pike
Ogle Station	Lee	Plain View	Macoupin	Rock Run	Stephenson
Ohio	Bureau	Plano	Kendall	Rockton	Winnebago
Ohio Grove	De Kalb	Plato	Iroquois	Rockville	Kankakee
Okaw	Washington	Plattville	Kendall	Roland	White
Old Farm	Lawrence	Pleasant Grove	Wayne	Rome	Jefferson
Old Ripley	Bond	Pleasant Green	Stark	Rome Farms	Peoria
Olena	Henderson	Pleasant Hill	Pike	Rook's Creek	Livingston
Olive	Lawrence	Pleasant Plains	Sangamon	Roscoe	Winnebago
Olney	Richland	Pleasant Ridge	Rock Island	Rosefield	Peoria
Omega	Marion	Pleasant Vale	Pike	Rose Hill	Jasper
Omph Ghent	Madison	Pleasant Valley	Jo Daviess	Rosemond	Christian
Onargo	Iroquois	Pleasant View	Schuyler	Rosencrans	Lake
Oneco	Stephenson	Plum Hill	Washington	Roseville	Warren
Ono	Adams	Plum River	Jo Daviess	Rosiclare	Hardin
Oneida	Knox	Plymouth	Hancock	Ross Grove	DeKalb
Ontario	"	Pocahontas	Bond	Rossville	Vermillion
Ophir	La Salle	Point Pleasant	Champaign	Rough and Ready	Hancock
Oquawka	Henderson	Polo	Ogle	Round Grove	Whitesides
Orange Prairie	Peoria	Pol's Grove	Carroll	Rozetta	Henderson
Orangeville	Stephenson	Pontiac	Livingston	Ruma	Randolph
Oregon	Ogle	Pontoosac	Hancock	Rural	Rock Island
Oriou	Henry	Pope Creek	Mercer	Rural Retreat	Coles
Orland	Cook	Poplar Grove	Boone	Rush	Jo Daviess
Orleans	Morgan	Port Byron	Rock Island	Rushville	Schuyler
Osage	Franklin	Port Clinton	Lake	Russellville	Lawrence
Osborn	Washington	Portland	Whitesides	Ruthsville	Montgomery
Ostend	McHenry	Prairie	Mason	Rutland	Kane
Oswego	Kendall	Praire Bird	Shelby	Sacton	Clark
Ottawa	La Salle	Prairie City	McDonough	Sagone	Du Pago
Otto	Fulton	Prairie Creek	Logan	St. Albans	Hancock
Otsego	Lake	Prairie Du Rocher	Randolph	St. Anne	Kankakee
Otter Creek	Jersey	Prairiefield	Rock Island	St. Augustine	Fulton
Owaneco	Christian	Prairie Hill	Williamson	St. Charles	Kane
Oxbow	Putnam	Prairie Mound	Fayette	St. Francisville	Lawrence
Oxford	Henry	Prairie Pond	D. Kalb	St. Jacob	Madison
Paddock's Grove	Madison	Pre-emption	Mercer	St. John	Perry
Padua	McLean	Prentice	Morgan	St. Joseph	Champaign
Paine's Point	Ogle	Preston	Randolph	St. Marie	Jasper
Palatine	Cook	Princeton	Bureau	St. Marys	Hancock
Palestine	Crawford	Princeville	Peoria	St. Omer	Coles
Palo Alto	Hamilton	Prophetstown	Whitesides	Salem	Marion
Paloma	Adams	Providence	Bureau	Saline Mines	Gallatin
Palos	Cook	Provise	Cook	Salisbury	Sangamon
Palmyra	Macoupin	Pulaski	Hancock	Salt Creek	Effingham
Pana	Christian	Quincy	Adams	Sandoval	Marion
Panola Station	Woodford	Racoon	Marion	Sandwich	DeKalb
Paradise	Coles	Raleigh	Saline	Sandy Ridge	Grundy
Paris	Edgar	Ramsey	Fayette	Sangamon	Macon
Parker	Clark	Randolph's Grove	McLean	San Jose	"
Parkersburg	Richland	Runtoul Station	Champaign	Santa Anna	De Witt
Park's Corners	Boone	Rapids City	Rock Island	Santa Fe	Alexander
Parrish	Franklin	Raritan	Henderson	Sarahsville	Williamson
Patoka	Marion	Rattlesnake	White	Saratoga	Marshall
Patoku	Marion	Reading	Livingston	Savanna	Carroll
Pavillion	Kendall	Rectorville	Hamilton	Saxon	Henry
Pawnee	Saugamon	Red Bank	Saline	Scales Mound	Jo Daviess
Paw Paw Grove	Lee	Red Bud	Randolph	Scott	La Salle
Parton	Ford	Reed	Sangamon	Scottville	Macoupin
Payson	Adams	Renault	Monroe	Secor	Woodford
Pearl	Pike	Reynoldsburg	Johnson	Selby Station	Bureau
Peatone	· Will	Richfield	Adams	Seluna	McLean
Pocatonica	Winnebago	Richaud	Sangamon	Sonex	"

2

POST OFFICES—ILLINOIS.

Post Office.	County.	Post Office.	County.	Post Office.	County.
Serena	La Salle	Sycamore	De Kalb	Warrensville	Du Page
Seward	Kendall	Sylva	Schuyler	Warrenton	Lake
Shabbona's Grove	DeKalb	Sylvan Dale	Hancock	Warsaw	Hancock
Shalonier	Fayette	Table Grove	Fulton	Washburn	Marshall
Shadsville	White	Tallula	Menard	Washington	Tazewell
Sharon	Henry	Tamaroo	Perry	Wataga	Knox
Shaumburg	Cook	Tamorack	Will	Waterloo	Monroe
Shawneetown	Gallatin	Tamar	Ogle	Watertown	Rock Island
Shaw's Point	Macoupin	Taylor	"	Watson	Sangamon
Sheffield	Bureau	Taylorsville	Christian	Wauconda	Lake
Shelbyville	Shelby	Tennessee	McDonough	Waukegan	"
Sheldon's Grove	Schuyler	Tentopolis	Effingham	Waverly	Morgan
Sherburnville	Kankakee	Terre Haute	Henderson	Wayland	Schuyler
Sherman	Sangamon	Thebes	Alexander	Wayne	Du Page
Shiloh	St. Clair	Thompson's Mills	Jo Daviess	Wayne Center	"
Shiloh Hill	Randolph	Thornton	Cook	Waynesville	De Witt
Shipman	Macoupin	Thornton Station	"	Welch's Prairie	Franklin
Shirland	Winnebago	Timber	Peoria	Webster	Hancock
Shirley	McLean	Time	Pike	Weller	Henry
Shoal Creek Station	Clinton	Tiskilwa	Bureau	Wenona Station	Marshall
Shokokon	Henderson	Tolono	Champaign	Wentworth	Lake
Shop Creek	Montgomery	Toluca	Madison	Wesley City	Tazewell
Shorb	Jasper	Tonica	La Salle	Westfield	Clark
Sidney	Champaign	Toulon	Stark	West Hall	Warren
Siloam	Wabash	Towanda	McLean	West Hebron	McHenry
Sinclair	Morgan	Tower Hill	Shelby	West Jersey	Stark
Slack Water	Stark	Town Mount	Franklin	West Northfield	Cook
Smithton	St. Clair	Tracy	Will	West Point	Hancock
Smallpox	Jo Daviess	Tremont	Tazewell	West Salem	Edwards
Smithville	Peoria	Trenton	Clinton	West Wheeling	Cook
Snackwine	Putnam	Trivoli	Peoria	Wetaug	Pulaski
Sodorus	Champaign	Triumph	La Salle	Wethersfield	Henry
Solon Mills	McHenry	Troy	Madison	Wetweather	Jasper
Somerset	Saline	Troy Grove	La Salle	Wheatland	Will
Somonauk	DeKalb	Troy Mills	Fulton	Wheaton	Du Page
South America	Saline	Trumbull	Macoupin	Wheeling	Cook
Southampton	Peoria	Truro	Knox	Whitefield	Marshall
South Bend	Winnebago	Truxton	Bureau	White Hall	Greene
South Grove	DeKalb	Turner	Du Page	White Oak	Montgomery
South Hampton	Gallatin	Tuscola	Douglas	White Rock	Ogle
South Macon	Macon	Tyler	Winnebago	White Willow	Kendall
South Northfield	Cook	Udina	Kane	Whitley's Point	Moultrie
South Pass	Union	Ulin	Pulaski	Wilkesborough	McLean
South Port	Peoria	Ulm	Adams	Williamsville	Sangamon
Spark's Hill	Hardin	Undulation	Pulaski	Willow	Jo Daviess
Sporland	Marshall	Union	McHenry	Willow Creek	Lee
Sparta	Randolph	Union Grove	Whitesides	Willow Hill	Jasper
Spencer	Will	Union Point	Union	Wilmington	Will
Specie Grove	Kendall	Uniontown	Knox	Wilson	Macon
Spring Bay	Woodford	Unity	Alexander	Wilsonburg	Richland
Springfield	Sangamon	Upper Alton	Madison	Winchester	Scott
Spring Garden	Jefferson	Urbana	Champaign	Windsor	Shelby
Spring Grove	Warren	Ursa	Adams	Winfield	Du Page
Spring Hill	Whitesides	Utah	Warren	Winnebago Depot	Winnebago
Spring Lake	Tazewell	Utica	La Salle	Winnetka	Cook
Spring Valley	Carroll	Valley	Stark	Winslow	Stephenson
Springville	Coles	Valley Forge	Pulaski	Winthrop	Kane
Squaw Grove	DeKalb	Van Buren	De Kalb	Wittemburg	Clinton
Staunton	Macoupin	Vancil's Point	Macoupin	Woburn	Bond
Steam Mill	Schuyler	Vandalia	Fayette	Woodburn	Macoupin
Steele's Mills	Randolph	Vedder	Calhoun	Woodbury	Cumberland
Sterling	Whitesides	Venice	Madison	Woodford	Woodford
Steuben	Marshall	Vergennes	Jackson	Woodhull	Henry
Stiflesville	Crawford	Vermillion	Edgar	Woodside	Sangamon
Stirlup Grove	Macoupin	Vermillionville	La Salle	Woodstock	McHenry
Stockton	Jo Daviess	Vermont	Fulton	Woodville	Adams
Stone Fort	Saline	Versailles	Brown	Wool	Pope
Stone's Prairie	Adams	Victoria	Knox	Woosung	Ogle
Stonington	Christian	Vienna	Johnson	Worthington	Jackson
Strasburg	Cook	Viola	Mercer	Wyant	Bureau
Stout's Grove	McLean	Virden	Macoupin	Wyoming	Stark
Stringtown	Richland	Virgil	Fulton	Wythe	Hancock
Sublette	Lee	Virginia	Cass	Xenia	Clay
Sugar Grove	Kane	Wabash	Wayne	Yale	Jasper
Sullivan	Moultrie	Wakefield	Richland	Yates City	Knox
Sulphur Springs	Williamson	Waltridge	Pulaski	Yellow Creek	Stephenson
Summerfield	St. Clair	Wales	Ogle	Yellow Head Grove	Kankakee
Summer Hill	Pike	Walker	Hancock	York	Clark
Summerville	Peoria	Walker's Grove	Mason	York Center	Du Page
Summit	Cook	Walker's Neck	Brown	Yorktown	Bureau
Summit Hill	Whitesides	Wallingford	Will	Young	McDonough
Summum	Fulton	Walnut	Bureau	Young America	Warren
Sumner	Lawrence	Walnut Grove	Knox	Zabriskie	De Witt
Sunbeam	Mercer	Walnut Hill	Marion	Zanesville	Montgomery
Sunbury	Livingston	Walshville	Montgomery	Zif	Wayne
Sutton's Point	Clay	Wanda	Madison	Zion	Morgan
Swan Creek	Warren	Wapella	De Witt	Zion Hill	Pope
Sweet Water	Menard	Warren	Jo Daviess		

POST OFFICES—INDIANA

Indiana.

Post Office.	County.
Aberdeen	Ohio
Abington	Wayne
Acton	Marion
Adair	"
Adams	Decatur
Akron	Fulton
Alamo	Montgomery
Albany	Delaware
Albion	Noble
Alden	Marshall
Alexandria	Madison
Alfont	"
Alfordsville	Davies
Allensville	Switzerland
Alligator	Owen
Alpha	Scott
Alquina	Fayette
Alto	Howard
Alton	Crawford
Alvarado	Steuben
America	Wabash
Americus	Tippecanoe
Amity	Johnson
Amsterdam	Cass
Anderson	Madison
Andersonville	Franklin
Angola	Steuben
Angnilla	Clay
Annapolis	Parke
Anoka	Cass
Antioch	Huntington
Arba	Randolph
Arcadia	Hamilton
Areana	Grant
Arcola	Allen
Arctic	De Kalb
Argos	Marshall
Armiesburg	Parke
Arney	Owen
Ascension	Sullivan
Ashborough	Clay
Ashley's Mills	Montgomery
Ashland	Henry
Atkinsonville	Owen
Attica	Fountain
Aubbeenaubbee	Fulton
Auburn	De Kalb
Augusta Station	Marion
Aurora	Dearborn
Austin	Scott
Avilla	Noble
Azalia	Bartholomew
Baker's Mills	Jackson
Bainbridge	Putnam
Balaka	Randolph
Ballstown	Ripley
Baltimore	Warren
Barber's Mills	Wells
Barbersville	Jefferson
Barren	Harrison
Bartonia	Randolph
Batcham	Sullivan
Batesville	Ripley
Battle Ground	Tippecanoe
Bayou Mills	Huntington
Bean Blossom	Brown
Bear Branch	Ohio
Bear Creek	Jay
Beaver Dam	Kosciusko
Beck's Mills	Washington
Beckville	Montgomery
Bedford	Lawrence
Beech Grove	Rush
Beechy Mire	Union
Belden	Wabash
Belle Air	Clay
Bellmore	Parke
Bellville	Hendricks
Bonnettsville	Clark
Bennington	Switzerland
Benton	Elkhart
Bentonville	Fayette
Benville	Jennings
Berlin	Clinton
Bethany	Parke
Bethel	Wayne

Post Office.	County.
Bethlehem	Clark
Bigelow's Mills	Laporte
Big Springs	"
Billingzville	Union
Bird's Eye	Dubois
Black Creek	Sullivan
Black Hawk Mills	Posey
Black Oak Ridge	Daviess
Blairsville	Posey
Bloom	Rush
Bloomfield	Greene
Bloomingburg	Fulton
Bloomingdale	Parke
Blooming Grove	Franklin
Bloomingsport	Randolph
Bloomington	Monroe
Blountsville	Henry
Blue Creek	Franklin
Blue Grass	Fulton
Blue Lick	Clark
Blue Ridge	Shelby
Bluff Creek	Johnson
Bluff Point	Jay
Bluffton	Wells
Bock's Mills	Madison
Bono	Lawrence
Boon Grove	Porter
Boonville	Warrick
Boston	Wayne
Boundary	Jay
Bourbon	Marshall
Bourie	Noble
Bovine	Gibson
Bowling Green	Clay
Boxley	Hamilton
Boydston's Mills	Kosciusko
Bradford	Harrison
Branch Creek	Huntington
Braysville	Dearborn
Brazil	Clay
Brenen	Marshall
Brewersville	Jennings
Brick Mill	Sullivan
Bridgeport	Marion
Bridgeton	Parke
Bright	Dearborn
Brighton	La Grange
Bristol	Elkhart
Broad Ripple	Marion
Brook	Newton
Brookfield	Shelby
Brooklyn	Morgan
Brookston	White
Brookville	Franklin
Brownsburg	Hendricks
Brownstown	Jackson
Brown's Valley	Montgomery
Brownsville	Union
Bruce's Lake	Fulton
Braceville	Knox
Brnin's X Roads	Parke
Brunswick	Lake
Brushy Prairie	La Grange
Bryautsburg	Jefferson
Bryantsville	Lawrence
Bryant's Creek	Monroe
Buck Creek	Greene
Buckskin	Gibson
Buffalo	White
Buffaloville	Spencer
Bunker Hill	Miami
Burget's Corners	Clinton
Burlington	Carroll
Burnett's Creek	White
Burnsville	Bartholomew
Busseron	Knox
Butler	DeKalb
Butlerville	Jennings
Byrneville	Harrison
Cadis	Henry
Callao	Laporte
Camargo	Jefferson
Cambridge	Wayne
Camden	Carroll
Campbell	Orange
Campbellsburg	Washington
Camp Morton	Marion
Cana	Jennings
Canaan	Jefferson
Canal	Warwick

Post Office.	County.
Cannelton	Perry
Canoper	Adams
Canton	Washington
Carlisle	Sullivan
Carmel	Hamilton
Carpenter's Creek	Jasper
Carpentersville	Putnam
Carroll	Carroll
Carrsville	Marion
Cartersburg	Hendricks
Carthage	Rush
Cary	Miami
Cassville	Howard
Castleton	Marion
Catalpa Grove	Benton
Cataract	Owen
Cathcart	Jasper
Cave Spring	Decatur
Cedar Grove	Franklin
Cedar Lake	Lake
Celestine	Dubois
Center	Howard
Center Point	Clay
Centerton	Morgan
Center Valley	"
Centerville	Wayne
Cerro Gordo	Randolph
Chalmers	White
Chamberlain	Allen
Chambersburg	Orange
Charlestown	Clark
Charlottesville	Hancock
Chestnut Hill	Washington
Chester	Wayne
Chesterfield	Madison
Chili	Miami
Christy's Prairie	Clay
Churabusco	Whitley
Cicero	Hamilton
Cincinnatus	Hendricks
Clarksburg	Decatur
Clark's Hill	Tippecanoe
Clark's Prairie	Daviess
Clarksville	Hamilton
Clark's Station	Lake
Clay Hill	Bartholomew
Claypool	Kosciusko
Clayton	Hendricks
Claysville	Washington
Clear Spring	Kosciusko
Cleona	Brown
Clermont	Marion
Cleveland	Hancock
Clifford	Bartholomew
Clifton	Union
Clifty	Decatur
Clinton	Vermillion
Clinton Lock	Parke
Cloverdale	Putnam
Cloverland	Clay
Coatesville	Hendricks
Cochran	Dearborn
Coesse	Whitley
Coffee	Clay
Coffee Creek	Porter
Cold Spring	Noble
Cole Creek	Fountain
Cole's Corners	DeKalb
Colfax	Clinton
Collamer	Whitley
Columbia	Fayette
Columbia City	Whitley
Columbus	Bartholomew
Concord	Tippecanoe
Cornersville	Fayette
Conn's Creek	Shelby
Cookerly	Vigo
Cook's Station	Elkhart
Cornucopia	Carroll
Cortland	Jackson
Corunna	DeKalb
Corydon	Harrison
Cottage Grove	Union
Cottage Hill	St. Joseph
Covington	Fountain
Cox's Mill	Wayne
Craig	Switzerland
Crane's Mill	Jackson
Crawfordsville	Montgomery
Crisp's X Roads	Harrison

POST OFFICES—INDIANA.

Post Office.	County.	Post Office.	County.	Post Office.	County.
Crittenden	Cass	Fair View	Randolph	Hagerstown	Wayne
Cromwell	Noble	Fall Creek	Marion	Halbert's Bluff	Martin
Crooked Creek	Steuben	Falmouth	Fayette	Half Way	Jay
Crossing	Laporte	Farabee's Station	Washington	Hall	Morgan
Cross Plains	Ripley	Farm	Clay	Hall's Corners	Allen
Crothersville	Jackson	Farmers	Kosciusko	Hamilton	Steuben
Crown Point	Lake	Farmers' Retreat	Dearborn	Hammond	Marion
Crowville	Warrick	Farmersville	Posey	Hannah Station	Laporte
Cuba	Owen	Farmland	Randolph	Haunegan	Rusk
Culver's Station	Tippecanoe	Fayetteville	Lawrence	Hanover	Jefferson
Cumberland	Marion	Ferdinand	Dubois	Hardinsburg	Washington
Currysville	Sullivan	Fotherbuff's Mills	Carroll	Harian	Allen
Curtis	Madison	Findley's Mills	Jackson	Harmony	Clay
Curtisville	Tipton	Fish Creek	Steuben	Harrisburg	Fayette
Cynthiana	Posey	Fishersburg	Madison	Harrison	Delaware
Dale	Spencer	Fitch	Cass	Harrstown	Washington
Daleville	Delaware	Five Corners	Miami	Harrisville	Randolph
Dalton	Wayne	Flat Rock	Shelby	Harrodsburg	Monroe
Daugola	Gibson	Flint	Steuben	Hartford	Ohio
Danville	Hendricks	Florence	Switzerland	Hartford City	Blackford
Dan Webster	Henry	Flower's Gap	Washington	Hart's Mills	Ripley
Darlington	Montgomery	Flowerville	White	Hartsville	Bartholomew
Davisville	Shelby	Floyd Knobs	Floyd	Harveysburg	Fountain
Dayton	Tippecanoe	Fly Creek	La Grange	Haskell	Laporte
Decatur	Adams	Forest Hill	Decatur	Haubstadt	Gibson
Decker's Station	Knox	Forestville	Madison	Hausertown	Owen
Deem	Owen	Fort Branch	Gibson	Haw Patch	La Grange
Deep River	Lake	Fort Ritner	Lawrence	Hawthorn's Mills	Pike
Deer Creek	Carroll	Fort Wayne	Allen	Haysville	Dubois
Deerfield	Randolph	Foster's Ridge	Perry	Hazleton	Gibson
DeKalb	DeKalb	Fox	Wells	Headley's Mills	Fountain
Delaware	Ripley	Francesville	Pulaski	Hebron	Porter
Delaware Station	"	Francisco	Gibson	Hecla	Noble
Delphi	Carroll	Fraukfort	Clinton	Hector	Jay
Delta	Parke	Frauklin	Johnson	Heffron	Washington
Deming	Hamilton	Frankton	Madison	Heller's Corners	Allen
Derby	Perry	Fredericksburg	Washington	Heltonville	Lawrence
Devon	Henry	Fredonia	Crawford	Hermann	Ripley
Dillsborough	Dearborn	Freelandville	Knox	Hickory Branch	Posey
Dilney Hill	Dubois	Freeport	Shelby	Hickory Point	Lake
Don Juan	Perry	Freetown	Jackson	Highland Station	Greene
Door Village	Laporte	Fremont	Steuben	High Rock	Daviess
Dora	Wabash	French Island	Spencer	Hillsboro'	Fountain
Dover	Boone	French Lick	Orange	Hobart	Lake
Dover Hill	Martin	Fruit Hill	Vigo	Hobbieville	Greene
Down Hill	Crawford	Fulda	Spencer	Holland	Dubois
Drewersburg	Franklin	Fuller's Corners	Whitley	Hollandsburg	Parke
Dublin	Wayne	Fulton	Fulton	Holman	Dearborn
Duck Creek	Madison	Galena	Floyd	Holton	Ripley
Dudleytown	Jackson	Gallandit	Marion	Home	Jefferson
Dundee	Blackford	Galveston	Cass	Homer	Rush
Dunkirk	Jay	Ganson	Pulaski	Hope	Bartholomew
Dunlapsville	Union	Geetingsville	Clinton	Hopewell	Jennings
Dupont	Jefferson	Gentryville	Spencer	Houston	Jackson
Dye	Martin	Georgetown	Floyd	Howard	Parke
Dyer	Lake	Georgia	Lawrence	Howesville	Clay
Eagle Creek	"	Germantown	Marion	Hubbard	Clark
Eagletown	Hamilton	Gibson Station	Lake	Hudson	Laporte
East Germantown	Wayne	Gilead	Miami	Hudsonville	Daviess
East Liberty	Allen	Gillum	Jay	Huntingburg	Dubois
East Orange	Noble	Glenn's Valley	Marion	Huntington	Huntington
Eaton	Delaware	Goldsborough	Bartholomew	Huntsville	Madison
Economy	Wayne	Gold Creek	Brown	Huron	Lawrence
Eden	Hancock	Goshen	Elkhart	Huth	Franklin
Edinburg	Johnson	Gosport	Owen	Hymeria	Sullivan
Edwardsport	Knox	Graham	Jefferson	Iba	De Kalb
Edwardsville	Floyd	Grand View	Spencer	Idaville	White
Elizabeth	Harrison	Grant	Grant	Independence	Warren
Elizabethtown	Bartholomew	Grantsburg	Crawford	Indianapolis	Marion
Elizaville	Boone	Grant's Creek	Switzerland	Indian Field	Monroe
Elkhart	Elkhart	Granville	Delaware	Inwood	Marshall
Elkinsville	Brown	Greenbush	Grant	Ireland	Dubois
Ellittsville	Monroe	Green Castle	Putnam	Island Grove	Greene
Elm	Knox	Greenfield	Hancock	Jack's Creek	"
Elrod	Ripley	Greenfield Mills	La Grange	Jackson	Decatur
Eminence	Morgan	Green Oak	Fulton	Jacksonburg	Wayne
Emmettsville	Randolph	Greensborough	Henry	Jacksonville	Switzerland
English	Crawford	Greensburg	Decatur	Jadden	Grant
English Lake	Stark	Green's Fork	Wayne	Jalapa	"
Enterprise	Spencer	Greentown	Howard	Jamestown	Boone
Epsom	Daviess	Greenville	Floyd	Jarvis	De Kalb
Etna Green	Kosciusko	Greenwood	Johnson	Jasonville	Greene
Eugene	Vermillion	Greysville	Sullivan	Jasper	Dubois
Evansville	Vanderburg	Groomsville	Tipton	Jay	Jay
Everton	Fayette	Groveland	Putnam	Jefferson	Clinton
Ewing	Jackson	Grovertown	Stark	Jeffersonville	Clark
Fairfield	Franklin	Groves	Fayette	Jennings	Franklin
Fairfield Center	DeKalb	Guilford	Dearborn	Jerome	Howard
Fairland	Shelby	Guionsville	"	Jonesborough	Grant
Fairmont	Marshall	Guthrie	Lawrence	Jones' Station	Dearborn

POST OFFICES—INDIANA. 21

Post Office.	County.	Post Office.	County.	Post Office.	County.
Jonesville	Bartholomew	McCutehanville	Vanderburg	Morgantown	Morgan
Jordan	Randolph	McDonald's	Orange	Morgiana	Lawrence
Jordan Village	Owen	McFadden	Posey	Morocco	Newton
Juliet	Lawrence	Madison	Jefferson	Morris	Ripley
Kansas	Bartholomew	Magnolia	Crawford	Morristown	Shelby
Keek's Church	Martin	Mahalasville	Morgan	Morton	Putnam
Kelso	Dearborn	Mahon	Huntington	Moscow	Rush
Kendallville	Noble	Manchester	Dearborn	Mountain Springs	Martin
Kent	Jefferson	Manhattan	Putnam	Mount Auburn	Shelby
Kent Station	Newton	Manilla	Rush	Mount Carmel	Franklin
Kewauna	Fulton	Mansfield	Parke	Mount Comfort	Hancock
Kinder	Hancock	Manville	Jefferson	Mount Etna	Huntington
Kingsbury	Laporte	Maples	Allen	Mount Gilboa	Benton
Kingston	Decatur	Marco	Greene	Mount Hope	De Kalb
Kirkland	Adams	Marcy	La Grange	Mount Jefferson	Carroll
Kirk's X Roads	Clinton	Marengo	Crawford	Mount Liberty	Brown
Knightstown	Henry	Marietta	Shelby	Mount Meridian	Putnam
Knob Creek	Harrison	Marion	Grant	Mount Moriah	Brown
Knox	Matthew	Markle	Huntington	Mount Pleasant	Martin
Kokomo	Howard	Markleville	Madison	Mount Prospect	Crawford
Kossuth	Washington	Marmont	Marshall	Mount Sterling	Switzerland
Laconia	Harrison	Marshfield	Warren	Mount Tabor	Monroe
Ladoga	Montgomery	Mars Hill	Randolph	Mount Vernon	Posey
La Fayette	Tippecanoe	Martinsburg	Washington	Mount Washington	Morgan
La Fontaine	Wabash	Martinsville	Morgan	Muddy Fork	Clark
La Grange	La Grange	Martz	Clay	Mud Lick	Jefferson
La Gro	Wabash	Massillon	Allen	Mulberry	Clinton
Lake City	Stark	Mauckport	Harrison	Muncie	Delaware
Lake Station	Lake	Maxinkuckee	Marshall	Murray	Wells
Laketon	Wabash	Maysville	Huntington	Napoleon	Ripley
Lakeville	St. Joseph	Mechanisburg	Henry	Nash Depot	Vanderburg
Lancaster	Jefferson	Medeline	Parke	Nashville	Brown
Land	Whitley	Medarysville	Pulaski	Natchez	Martin
Lanesville	Harrison	Medora	Jackson	Nebraska	Crawford
Laporte	Laporte	Melrose	Rush	Nebraska	Jennings
Laurel	Franklin	Memphis	Clark	Neff	Randolph
Laurence	Marion	Mercury	Madison	Neil's Station	Wayde
Lawrenceburg	Dearborn	Merom	Sullivan	Nevada	Tipton
Lawrenceville	"	Merrian	Noble	New Albany	Floyd
Leatherwood	Lawrence	Merrillville	Lake	New Alsace	Dearborn
Leavenworth	Crawford	Metamora	Franklin	New Amsterdam	Harrison
Lebanon	Boone	Metun	Cass	New Bellaville	Brown
Lee	Warrick	Mots	Steuben	Newbern	Bartholomew
Leesburg	Kosciusko	Mexico	Miami	Newberry	Greene
Leesville	Lawrence	Miami	"	New Boston	Spencer
Leipsic	Orange	Michigan City	Laporte	New Britton	Hamilton
Leo	Allen	Michigantown	Clinton	Newburg	Warrick
Leopold	Perry	Middlebury	Elkhart	New Burlington	Delaware
Lewis	Vigo	Middle Fork	Clinton	New Carlisle	St. Joseph
Lowis Creek	Shelby	Middletown	Henry	New Castle	Henry
Lewisburg	Cass	Midway	Spencer	New Corner	Delaware
Lewisville	Henry	Mier	Grant	New Corydon	Jay
Lexington	Scott	Mifflin	Crawford	New Durham	Laporte
Liberty	Union	Milan	Ripley	New Elizabeth	Hendricks
Liberty Center	Wells	Milford	Kosciusko	New Farmington	Jackson
Liberty Mills	Wabash	Mill Ark	Fulton	New Garden	Wayne
Ligonier	Noble	Mill Grove	Owen	New Goshen	Vigo
Lilly Dale	Perry	Millersburg	Elkhart	New Harmony	Posey
Lima	La Grange	Millhousen	Decatur	New Haven	Allen
Lumber Lost	Adams	Millport	Jackson	New Holland	Wabash
Lincoln	Cass	Milltown	Crawford	New Lancaster	Tipton
Linden	Montgomery	Millville	Henry	New Lebanon	Sullivan
Linn Grove	Adams	Milo	Brown	New Lisbon	Henry
Linton	Greene	Milroy	Rush	New London	Howard
Lisbon	Noble	Milton	Wayne	New Marion	Ripley
Litte River	Allen	Mishawaka	St. Joseph	New Maysville	Putnam
Little Walnut	Putnam	Mitchell	Lawrence	New Mount Pleasant	Jay
Little York	Washington	Mixersville	Franklin	New Paris	Elkhart
Livonia	"	Mongoquinong	La Grange	New Philadelphia	Washington
Locke	Elkhart	Monmouth	Adams	New Pittsburg	Randolph
Lockport	Carroll	Monon	White	Newport	Vermillion
Lodi	Wabash	Monroe	Jay	New Providence	Clark
Logan	Dearborn	Monrouville	Allen	Now Retreat	Washington
Logansport	Cass	Monrovia	Morgan	New Richmond	Montgomery
London	Shelby	Monterey	Pulaski	New Ross	"
Lone Tree	Greene	Montez	Cass	New Salem	Rush
Longwood	Fayette	Montezuma	Parke	New Salisbury	Harrison
Loogootee	Martin	Montgomery	Jennings	Newton Stewart	Orange
Losantville	Randolph	Montgomery's Station	Daviess	Newtonville	Spencer
Lovely Dale	Knox	Monticello	White	Newtown	Fountain
Lowell Mills	Bartholomew	Montmorency	Tippecanoe	New Trenton	Franklin
Ludlow	Dubois	Montpelier	Blackford	Newville	De Kalb
Luray	Henry	Mooney	Jackson	New Washington	Clark
Lushers	Perry	Moorefield	Switzerland	New Waverly	Cass
Lynn	Randolph	Mooresburg	Pulaski	New Winchester	Hendricks
Lynnville	Warrick	Moore's Hill	Dearborn	Nicholsonville	Putnam
Mace	Montgomery	Mooresville	Morgan	Nieonra	Miami
McCameron	Martin	Moore's Vineyard	"	Nine Mile	Allen
McCordsville	Hancock		Bartholomew	Ninevoh	Johnson
McCoy's Station	Decatur	Morul	Shelby	Noah	Shelby

POST OFFICES—INDIANA.

Post Office.	County.	Post Office.	County.	Post Office.	County.
Noble	Noble	Pittsboro'	Hendricks	Rossville	Clinton
Noblesville	Hamilton	Pittsburg	Carroll	Royal Center	Cass
Normanda	Tipton	Plainfield	Hendricks	Royalton	Boone
North Bend	Stark	Plainville	Daviess	Rushville	Rush
North East	Steuben	Pleasant	Switzerland	Russell's Mills	Parke
Northern Depot	Boone	Pleasant Grove	Jasper	Russellville	Putnam
Northfield	"	Pleasant Hill	Montgomery	Russiaville	Clinton
North Galveston	Kisciusko	Pleasant Lake	Steuben	Rutherford	Switzerland
North Hogan	Ripley	Pleasant Mills	Adams	Saint John	Dearborn
North Judson	Stark	Pleasant Ridge	Greene	Saint Leon	Dearborn
North Liberty	St. Joseph	Plymouth	Marshall	Saint Mary's	Vigo
North Madison	Jefferson	Po	Allen	Saint Omer	Decatur
North Manchester	Wabash	Point Commerce	Greene	Saint Paul	"
Northport	Noble	Point Isabel	Grant	Saint Peter's	Franklin
North Salem	Hendricks	Poland	Clay	Saint Wendel's	Posey
Notre Dame	St. Joseph	Polk Patch	Warrick	Salamonia	Jay
Nottingham	Wells	Polk Run	Clark	Salem	Washingtou
Null's Mills	Fayette	Pond Creek Mills	Knox	Salem Center	Steuben
Nnma	Parke	Poolesville	Warren	Saltilloville	Washington
Oak	Pulaski	Poplar Grove	Howard	Saluda	Jefferson
Oakdale	Jennings	Porter's X Roads	Porter	Saundersville	Vanderburg
Oakdam	Vanderburg	Portersville	Dubois	Sandy Ridge	Steuben
Oakford	Howard	Port Gibson	Gibson	Sandford	Vigo
Oak Forrest	Franklin	Portland	Fountain	San Jacinto	Jennings
Oak Grove	Jasper	Portland Mills	Parke	San Pierce	Stark
Oakland	Spencer	Poseyville	Posey	Santa Claus	Spencer
Oakland City	Gibson	Poston	Ripley	Santa Fe	Miami
Oak Station	Knox	Prailie	Tipton	Sardinia	Decatur
Oak Woods	Grant	Prairie Creek	Vigo	Saturn	Whitley
Oceola	St. Joseph	Prairie Edge	Montgomery	Scipio	Jennings
Ogden	Henry	Prairieton	Vigo	Scotland	Greene
Oldenburg	Franklin	Prescott	Shelby	Scottsville	Floyd
Olean	Ripley	Priam	Blackford	Sellersburg	Clark
Olive Hill	Wayne	Price	Huntington	Selma	Delaware
Oncida	Kosciusko	Princeton	Gibson	Sevastopol	Kosciusko
Ontario	La Grange	Prince William	Carroll	Seymour	Jackson
Onward	Cass	Prosperity	Madison	Shanghai	Howard
Orange	Fayette	Prowsville	Washington	Shannondale	Montgomery
Orangeville	Orange	Puddletown	Laporte	Sharon	Delaware
Orchard Grove	Lake	Pulaski	Pulaski	Sharp's Mills	Harrison
Oregon	Clark	Putnamville	Putnam	Sharpsville	Tipton
Organ Spring	Washington	Queensville	Jennings	Shawnee Mound	Tippecanoe
Orland	Steuben	Quercus Grove	Switzerland	Sheasville	Morgan
Orleans	Orange	Quincy	Owen	Shelville	Hamilton
Osgood	Ripley	Raglesville	Daviess	Shelbyville	Shelby
Ossian	Wells	Rainsville	Warren	Sidney	Fulton
Oswego	Kosciusko	Raleigh	Rush	Silver Lake	Kosciusko
Outlet	Lake	Randall	Allen	Silverville	Lawrence
Ovid	Madison	Raysville	Henry	Simon's Corners	Noble
Owensburg	Greene	Reddington	Jackson	Six Mile	Jennings
Owensville	Gibson	Reelsville	Putnam	Slash	Grant
Oxford	Benton	Reese's Mill	Boone	Slate	Jennings
Padiria	Crawford	Reiffsburg	Wells	Slate Cut	Clark
Palestine	Kosciusko	Rensselaer	Jasper	Sligo	Marshall
Palmyra	Harrison	Reserve	Miami	Smelser's Mills	Rush
Paoli	Orange	Retreat	Jackson	Smithland	Shelby
Paris	Jennings	Reynolds	White	Smithville	Monroe
Parish Grove	Benton	Richardson	St. Joseph	Smyrna	Decatur
Parker	Randolph	Richland	Rush	Snow Hill	Randolph
Parkersburg	Montgomery	Richmond	Wayne	Solsberry	Greene
Parker's Settlement	Posey	Rich Valley	Wabash	Somerset	Wabash
Parkville	Parke	Richwoods	Delaware	Somerville	Gibson
Patoka	Gibson	Ridge Road	Allen	South Bend	St. Joseph
Patricksburg	Owen	Ridgeville	Randolph	South Betheny	Bartholomew
Patriot	Switzerland	Rigdon	Grant	South Boston	Washington
Paw Paw	Miami	Riley	Vigo	South Cleveland	Whitley
Pecksburg	Hendricks	Ringgold	La Grange	South Gate	Franklin
Pekin	Washington	Rising Sun	Ohio	South Martin	Martin
Pendleton	Madison	River Vale	Lawrence	South Milford	La Grange
Pennville	Jay	Roanoke	Huntington	Southport	Marion
Peppertown	Franklin	Rob Roy	Fountain	South West	Elkhart
Perkinsville	Madison	Rochester	Fulton	South Whitley	Whitley
Perry	Allen	Rock Creek	Bartholomew	Spade's Depot	Ripley
Perrysburg	Miami	Rockfield	Carroll	Spauldingville	Knox
Perrysville	Vermillion	Rockford	Jackson	Sparksville	Jackson
Peru	Miami	Rockport	Spencer	Sparta	Dearborn
Petersburg	Pike	Rockville	Parke	Spartanburg	Randolph
Pettit	Tippecanoe	Rogersville	Henry	Spencer	Owen
Philadelphia	Hancock	Rolling Prairie	Laporte	Spencerville	De Kalb
Piattsville	Parke	Rome	Perry	Sticcland	Henry
Pickard's Mills	Clinton	Romney	Tippecanoe	Spring Creek	Cass
Pierceton	Kosciusko	Rono	Perry	Sping Dale	Harrison
Pierceville	Ripley	Root	Allen	Springfield	Franklin
Pigeon Roost	Scott	Roselle	Laporte	Springfield Mills	Noble
Pilot Grove	Newton	Rosedale	Parke	Spring Hill	Decatur
Pilot Knob	Crawford	Rose Hill	Kosciusko	Springtown	Hendricks
Pimento	Vigo	Roseville	Parke	Springville	Lawrence
Pipe City	Morgan	Rosewood	Harrison	Sproatts	Sullivan
Pine Village	Warren	Ross	Lake	Stamper's Creek	Orange
Pinhook	Lawrence	Rossburg	Decatur	Stanford	Monroe

POST OFFICES—IOWA.   23

Post Office.	County.	Post Office.	County.	Post Office.	County.
Star	Rush	Walton	Cass	Zimsburg	Madison
State Line	Warren	Warren	Huntington	Zionsville	Boone
Staunton	Clay	Warrington	Hancock		
Steam Corner	Fountain	Warsaw	Kosciusko		
Steeles	Rush	Washington	Daviess		
Stewartsville	Posey	Washington Center	Whitley	**Iowa.**	
Stilesville	Hendricks	Waterford	La Porte		
Stinesville	Monroe	Waterloo	Fayette	Post Office.	County.
Stip's Hill	Franklin	Waterman	Parke		
Stockdale	Miami	Waveland	Montgomery	Abingdon	Jefferson
Stockton	Owen	Waverly	Morgan	Adair	Adair
Stockwell	Tippecanoe	Wawaka	Noble	Adel	Dallas
Stoney Point	Jefferson	Waw-pe-cong	Miami	Adelphi	Polk
Storm's Creek	Jennings	Way	Ripley	Afton	Union
Strawberry Ridge	Pulaski	Wamansville	Bartholomew	Agency City	Wapello
Strawtown	Hamilton	Waynesburg	Decatur	Agricola	Mahaska
Stringtown	Ripley	Waynetown	Montgomery	Albany	Davis
Sugar Branch	Switzerland	Waynesville	Bartholomew	Albia	Monroe
Sugar Creek	Hancock	Webster	Wayne	Albion	Marshall
Sugar Grove	Tippecanoe	Weisburg	Dearborn	Albright	Des Moines
Sugar River	Montgomery	Wenona	Henry	Alden	Hardin
Sullivan	Sullivan	Wesley	Montgomery	Algona	Kossuth
Sulphur Hill	Shelby	West Buena Vista	Gibson	Algonquin	Butler
Sulphur Springs	Henry	Westchester	Jay	Allemakee	Allemakee
Summit	Whitley	West Creek	Lake	Allen's Grove	Scott
Summitville	Madison	Westfield	Hamilton	Almoral	Delaware
Sumption Prairie	St. Joseph	West Kinderhook	Tipton	Alpine	Wapello
Sunman	Ripley	Westland	Hancock	Alton	Dallas
Swain's Mills	Rush	West Lebanon	Warren	Amador	Wapello
Swan	Noble	West Liberty	Howard	Amboy	Washington
Swanville	Jefferson	West Newton	Marion	Amish	Johnson
Sylvan Grove	Clark	West Point	Tippecanoe	Amity	Scott
Sylvania	Parke	Westport	Decatur	Anamosa	Jones
Syracuse	Kosciusko	Westville	Laporte	Andrew	Jackson
Tampico	Jackson	Wheatland	Knox	Apple Grove	Polk
Taylor's Corners	De Kalb	Wheatonville	Warrick	Aquilla Grove	Winneshiek
Taylorsville	Bartholomew	Wheatville	Miami	Arbor Hill	Adair
Tell City	Perry	Wheeler	Porter	Argo	Lucas
Terre Coupee	St. Joseph	Wheeling	Delaware	Ashland	Wapello
Terro Haute	Vigo	Whitcomb	Franklin	Aspinwall	Dubuque
Tetersburg	Tipton	White Cottage	Harrison	Atalissa	Muscatine
Texas	Washington	White Creek	Jackson	Atlanta	Buchanan
Thorntown	Boone	White Hall	Owen	Attica	Marion
Tippecanoe Town	Marshall	White Lick	Boone	Auburn	Mahaska
Tipton	Tipton	White Oak Grove	Pike	Augusta	Des Moines
Tolleston	Lake	White's Grove	Newton	Aurora	Keokuk
Toronto	Vermillion	Whitestown	Boone	Bach Grove	Wright
Toto	Stark	Whitesville	Montgomery	Bangor	Marshall
Trafalgar	Johnson	White Water	Wayne	Bankston	Dubuque
Transitville	Tippecanoe	Wickliffe	Crawford	Banner Valley	Linn
Trask	Grant	Wild Cat	Carroll	Ballyclough	Dubuque
Trenton	Randolph	Williamsburg	Wayne	Barclay	Black Hawk
Trinity Springs	Martin	Williamsport	Warren	Barryville	Delaware
Tripton	Jennings	Williamstown	Decatur	Bear Creek	Poweshiek
Troy	Perry	Wilmington	Dearborn	Bear Grove	Guthrie
Tunnelton	Lawrence	Winnot	Noble	Beaver City	Chickasaw
Turkey Creek	Steuben	Willow Branch	Hancock	Bedford	Taylor
Tarman's Creek	Sullivan	Willow Valley	Martin	Beetrace	Appanoose
Twelve Mile	Cass	Winchester	Randolph	Belinda	Lucas
Two Mile Prairie	Pulaski	Windfall	Tipton	Belfast	Lee
Tyner City	Marshall	Windsor	Randolph	Belle Air	Johnson
Union	Pike	Winfield	Lake	Belle Fountain	Mahaska
Union City	Randolph	Winnamac	Pulaski	Bellevue	Jackson
Union Mills	Laporte	Winslow	Pike	Belleville	Webster
Unionville	Monroe	Winterrowd	Shelby	Belmond	Wright
Urbana	Wabash	Wintersville	Decatur	Bennington	Marion
Utica	Clark	Wirt	Jefferson	Benton's Port	Van Buren
Valene	Orange	Wollcott's Mills	La Grange	Bertram	Linn
Valonia	Jackson	Wolf Creek	Marshall	Bethel	Fayette
Valparaiso	Porter	Wolf Lake	Noble	Bethlehem	Wayne
Van Buren	Clay	Woodbury	Hamilton	Big Grove	Pottawatomie
Vandalia	Owen	Woodland	St. Joseph	Big Mound	Lee
Vera Cruz	Wells	Wooster	Kosciusko	Big Rock	Scott
Vermont	Howard	Worth	Dubois	Birmingham	Van Buren
Vernon	Jennings	Worthington	Greene	Blakeville	Black Hawk
Versailles	Ripley	Worthsville	Johnson	Bloomfield	Davis
Vevay	Switzerland	Wright	Greene	Bloomington	Polk
Victor	De Kalb	Wright's Mills	Parke	Blue Grass	Scott
Vienna	Scott	Wright's Corners	Dearborn	Bluff Creek	Monroe
Vincennes	Knox	Wyandotte	Tippecanoe	Bluffton	Winnishiek
Vistula	Elkhart	Wyan	Franklin	Bon Accord	Johnson
Volga	Jefferson	Xenia	Miami	Bonaparte	Van Buren
Wabash	Wabash	Yankeetown	Warrick	Boone	Dallas
Wadesville	Posey	Yellow Creek	Kosciusko	Blue Point	Poweshiek
Whitsboro'	Bartholomew	York Center	Steuben	Boonesboro'	Boone
Wakarusa	Elkhart	Yorktown	Delaware	Boon Spring	Clinton
Walkersville	Jasper	Yorkville	Dearborn	Border Plains	Webster
Walkerton	St. Joseph	Yountsville	Montgomery	Botany	Shelby
Wallace	Fountain	Zanesville	Wells	Batavia	Jefferson
Walpole	Hancock	Zenas	Jennings		

POST OFFICES—IOWA.

Post Office.	County.	Post Office.	County.	Post Office.	County.
Boulder	Linn	Clear Lake City	Cerro Gordo	Elk River	Clinton
Bower's Prairie	Jones	Clermont	Fayette	Elm Springs	Butler
Boyer River	Crawford	Cleveland	Allemakee	Elon	Allemakee
Boylin's Grove	Butler	Clifton	Louisa	Elvira	Clinton
Bradford	Chickasaw	Clinton	Clinton	Ely	Marion
Brandon	Buchanan	Clio	Wayne	Emeline	Jackson
Bridgeport	Jackson	Clide	Jasper	Emmet	Emmet
Brighton	Washington	Coal Creek	Keokuk	English Settlement	Marion
Bristol	Worth	Coffin's Grove	Delaware	Enterprise	Black Hawk
Brock	Mahaska	Cold Water	"	Epworth	Dubuque
Brookfield	Clinton	College Spring	Page	Erie	Buchanan
Brookville	Jefferson	Colony	Delaware	Erin	"
Brush Creek	Fayette	Columbia	Marion	Estherville C. H.	Emmet
Brushy	Taylor	Columbus City	Louisa	Eugene	Ringgold
Buckingham	Tama	Communia	Clayton	Eveland Grove	Mahaska
Buena Vista	Clinton	Competine	Wapello	Exira	Audubon
Buffalo	Scott	Confidence	Wayne	Fairbank	Buchanan
Buffalo Grove	Buchanan	Cono	Iowa	Fairfield	Jefferson
Buncombe	Dubuque	Copi	Johnson	Fairport	Muscatine
Burgess	Clinton	Corn Hill	Fayette	Fairview	Jones
Burk	Benton	Cory	Fremont	Fauden	Allamakee
Burlington	Des Moines	Corydon	Wayne	Farley	Dubuque
Burr Oak	Winneshiek	Cottage Hill	Dubuque	Farmersburg	Clayton
Burr Oak Springs	"	Cotton Grove	Henry	Farmer's Creek	Jackson
Business Corner	Van Buren	Cottonville	Jackson	Farmington	Van Buren
Butler	Keokuk	Council Bluffs	Pottawatomie	Festina	Winneshiek
Butler Center	Butler	Council Hill	Clayton	Filmore	Dubuque
Butler Hill	Emmet	Cox Creek	"	Flood Creek	Floyd
Butlerville	Tama	Crawfordsville	Washington	Florence	Benton
Busti	Howard	Crescent City	Pottawatomie	Floris	Davis
Cairo	Louisa	Cresco	Kossuth	Floyd	Floyd
Caledonia	Ringgold	Cross	Ringgold	Fontanelle	Adair
Caldwell	Appanoosa	Croton	Lee	Funtaine	Hardin
Calhoun	Harrison	Crysta	Tama	Forrest City	Winnebago
Calmar	Winneshiek	Cuba	Monroe	Forest Hill	Louisa
Calmus	Clinton	Daggett	Benton	Forest Home	Poweshiek
Caloma	Marion	Dahlonega	Wapello	Foreston	Howard
Camanche	Clinton	Dairy	Washington	Forestville	Delaware
Cambria	Wayne	Dakota	Humbolt	Forfax	Linn
Cambridge	Story	Dallas	Marion	Forks	Tama
Camden	"	Dalmanutha	Guthrie	Fort Atkinson	Winneshiek
Campton	Delaware	Danforth	Johnson	Fort Dodge	Webster
Cana	Buchanan	Danville	Des Moines	Fort Madison	Lee
Canoe	Winneshiek	Davenport	Scott	Fort Plain	Warren
Canton	Jackson	Davis Cree	Washington	Fox	Davis
Capoli	Allemakee	Dayton	Bremer	Frankfort	Montgomery
Cardiff	Mitchell	Decatur	Decatur	Franklin	Decatur
Carl	Adams	Decorah	Winneshiek	Franklin Centre	Lee
Carlisle	Warren	Deep River	Poweshiek	Frank Pierce	Johnson
Carrolton	Carroll	Deerfield	Chickasaw	Frankville	Winneshiek
Carson's Point	Boone	Delanti	Hardin	Frederica	Bremer
Carthage	Johnson	Delaware	Delaware	Fredericksburg	Chickasaw
Cascade	Dubuque	Delhi	"	Fredouia	Louisa
Castalia	Winneshiek	Denison	Crawford	Freedom	Lucas
Castle Grove	Jones	Denmark	Lee	Freeland	"
Cedar Bluff	Cedar	Dennis	Appanoose	Freeport	Winneshiek
Cedar Falls	Black Hawk	Derrinance	Dubuque	Fremont	Mahaska
Cedar Fork	Sac	Des Moines	Polk	French Creek	Allemakee
Cedar Grove	Lucas	De Witt	Clinton	Fryeburg	Wright
Cedar Rapids	Linn	Dixon	Scott	Fuller's Mills	Jones
Cedar Valley	Black Hawk	Dodge	Guthrie	Fulton	Jackson
Cedarville	Washington	Dudgeville	Des Moines	Gainesboro'	Van Buren
Central City	Linn	Duran	Mitchell	Galesburg	Jasper
Centor	Page	Dorchester	Allemakee	Garden Grove	Decatur
Center Point	Linn	Dorrville	Warren	Garnaville	Clayton
Centerville	Appanoose	Douglas	Fayette	Garry Owen	Jackson
Cerro Gordo	Mills	Dover	Lee	Gaston	Fremont
Chandalier	Keokuk	Downey	Cedar	Gem	Clayton
Chapin	Franklin	Drakesville	Davis	Genesee	Cerro Gordo
Chariton C. H.	Lucas	Dry Creek	Linn	Geneva	Franklin
Charleston	Lee	Duane	Jones	Genoa	Wayne
Charlotte	Clinton	Dubuque	Dubuque	Genoa Bluff	Iowa
Charlottsville	Madison	Durango	"	Georgetown	Monroe
Chatham	Buchanan	Durant	Cedar	Germanville	Jefferson
Chattanooga	Dallas	Dutch Creek	Washington	Girard	Clayton
Chelsea	Tama	Dyersville	Dubuque	Gilbert	Scott
Chequist	Davis	Earlville	Delaware	Gilbertville	Black Hawk
Cherokee	Cherokee	East Waterloo	Black Hawk	Glasgow	Jefferson
Cherry	Mahaska	Eatonville	Howard	Glendale	"
Chickasaw	Chickasaw	Eber	Humboldt	Glenn's	Clark
Chilicothe	Wapello	Ebenville	Marshall	Glenwood	Mills
Christiansburg	"	Eddyville	Wapello	Goldfield	Wright
Crystal	Tama	Eden	Fayette	Gomersal	Benton
Churchville	Scott	Edinburg	Jones	Gosport	Marion
Cincinnati	Appanoose	Edna	Cass	Gowando	Marshall
Clauton	Madison	Eldora	Hardin	Grand Meadow	Clayton
Clarinda	Page	El Dorado	Fayette	Grand Mound	Clinton
Clay	Washington	Elgin	"	Grand River	Wayne
Clayton	Clayton	Elkader	Clayton	Grand View	Louisa
Clear Creek	Allemakee	Elkport	"	Grandville	Mahaska

POST OFFICES—IOWA.

Post Office.	County.	Post Office.	County.	Post Office.	County.
Gravity	Taylor	Keosauqua	Van Buren	Masonville	Cerro Gordo
Green Castle	Jasper	Kilbourn	"	Massillon	Cedar
Greenfield	Adair	Kinisaw	Tama	Maysv	Franklin
Green Mountain	Marshall	King	Dubuque	Mechanicsv	Cedar
Greenvale	Dallas	Kingston	Des Moines	Molpine	Muscatine
Greenville	Lucas	Kingston City	Linn	Memphis	Appanoose
Grinnell	Poweshiek	Kirksville	Wapello	Memory	Taylor
Grove Creek	Delaware	Kirkwood	Polk	Mennon	Marion
Grove Hill	Bremer	Knoxville	Marion	Middle River	Madison
Grundy Center	Grundy	Kossuth	Des Moines	Middletown	Des Moines
Guthrie Center	Guthrie	Kossuth Center	Kossuth	Mid Prairie	Louisa
Gutenburg	Clayton	Koszta	Iowa	Milford	Clark
Gwinville	Benton	Lewis	Cass	Mill	Fayette
Halfway Prairie	Monroe	Lowisburg	Wayne	Millrock	Jackson
Hamilton	Marion	Lexington	Taylor	Milleray	Dubuque
Hamlin Grove	Audubon	Liberty	Clark	Millersburg	Iowa
Hammondsburg	Warren	Lima	Fayette	Mill Grove	Poweshiek
Hampton	Franklin	Libertyville	Jefferson	Millville	Clayton
Harbour	Davis	Lacello	Clark	Milton	Van Buren
Hardin	Clayton	Lacona	Warren	Mineral Ridge	Boone
Harian	Shelby	Lacy	Muscatine	Minerva	Jasper
Hartford	Warren	Lafayette	Linn	Mitchell	Mitchell
Hartland	Worth	La Grange	Lucas	Mitchville	Polk
Hartwick	Delaware	Lake	Washington	Modnil	Harrison
Harwell	Cedar	Lake City	Calhoun	Moffitt's Grove	Guthrie
Hawk Eye	Des Moines	Lakin's Grove	Hamilton	Mondieu	Linn
Hawleysville	Page	La Motte	Jackson	Moncek	Winneshiek
Hazle Groen	Delaware	Lancaster	Keokuk	Monmouth	Jackson
Hazelton	Buchanan	Langworthy	Jones	Monona	Clayton
Heath	Tama	Lansing	Allemakee	Monroe	Jasper
Hebron	Adair	Laporte	Clark	Monteroy	Davis
Helena	Tama	Laporte City	Black Hawk	Montezuma	Poweshiek
Hesper	Winneshiek	Laredo	Mahaska	Montizello	Jones
Hesperian	Webster	La Vega	Des Moines	Montrose	Lee
Hibbsville	Appanoose	Lawrenceburg	Warren	Moravia	Appanoose
Hickory	Van Buren	La Yerba	Hardin	Morgan	Winneshiek
Highland	Clayton	Lobanon	Van Buren	Morning Sun	Louisa
Highland Grove	Jones	Le Claire	Scott	Morris	Woodbury
High Point	Decatur	Le Grand	Marshall	Morrisbur	Guthrie
Hillsborough	Henry	Leo	Fayette	Moscow	Muscatine
Holaday's	Adair	Looni	Butler	Mount Algor	Jackson
Holt	Taylor	Leon	Decatur	Mount Ayr	Ringgold
Home	Van Buren	Leroy	Brewer	Mount Calvary	Davis
Homer	Hamilton	Lester	Black Hawk	Mt. Etna	Adams
Homestead	Iowa	Lime Spring	Howard	Mt. Hope	Delaware
Honey Creek	Clayton	Linn	Cerro Gordo	Mt. Joy	Scott
Hopeville	Clark	Linton	Des Moines	Mt. Pleasant	Henry
Hopewell	Mahaska	Linwood	Benton	Mt. Sterling	Van Buren
Hopkinton	Delaware	Lisbon	Linn	Mt. Vernon	Linn
Horton	Bremer	Lithopolis	Hardin	Mullasky's Grove	Black Hawk
Howard	Howard	Littleport	Clayton	Muscatine	Muscatine
Howard Center	"	Little Sioux	Harrison	Nashua	Chickasaw
Howardsville	Floyd	Livingston	Appanoose	National	Clayton
Hudson	Black Hawk	Lockridge	Jefferson	Nautril.	Bremer
Iconium	Appanoose	Locust Lane	Winneshiek	Nocot	Linn
Ida	Ida	Lott's Creek	Kossuth	Nelson	Mitchell
Illinois Grove	Marshall	Lovilia	Monroe	Nevada	Story
Illyria	Fayette	Lowden	Cedar	Nevinville	Adams
Independence C H	Buchanan	Lowell	Henry	Newark	Marion
Indianola C H	Warren	Low Moor	Clinton	Nowbern	"
Indianapolis	Mahaska	Lucerne	Wayne	New Buda	Decatur
Ingart's Grove	Ringgold	Luni	Wright	New Galena	Allemakee
Inland	Cedar	Lura	Cass	New Hampton	Chickasaw
Ioka	Keokuk	Lybrand	Allemakee	New Hartford	Butler
Iola	Marion	Lynn	Warren	New Haven	Washington
Ion	Allemakee	Lyunville	Jasper	New Hope	Union
Iowa Center	Story	Lyons	Clinton	New Jefferson	Greene
Iowa City	Johnson	McGregor	Clayton	New Liberty	Scott
Iowa Falls	Hardin	McKissack's Grove	Fremont	New London	Henry
Iowaville	Van Buren	Macedonia	Pottawattomie	New Market	Van Buren
Iron Hills	Jackson	Maceville	Henry	New Oregon	Howard
Irvington	Kossuth	Madison	Jones	New Philadelphia	Story
Isabell	Jackson	Magnolia	Harrison	Newport	Johnson
Island Grove	Butler	Makee	Allemakee	New Providence	Hardin
Iuka	Tama	Malcom	Poweshiek	New Sharon	Mahaska
Jacksonville	Chickasaw	Malvora	Johnson	New Stand	Clayton
Jamestown	Howard	Manchester	Delaware	Newton	Jasper
Jasper	Carroll	Manti	Fremont	Newport Center	Johnston
Jaynesville	Bremer	Manteno	Shelby	New Town	Pottswatomie
Jeddo City	Harrison	Mapleton	Monona	Now Vienna	Dubuque
Jefferson	Dubuque	Maquoketa	Jackson	New Virginia	Warren
Jeffersonville	Lee	Marble Rock	Floyd	New York	Wayne
Jeromo	Appanoose	Marengo	Iowa	Nezoka	Allemakee
Jessup	Buchanan	Mariotta	Marshall	Niles	Van Buren
Johnson	Jones	Mariner's Hope	Allemakee	Nine Eagles	Decatur
Johnston Grove	Story	Marion	Linn	Nodaway Fork	Page
Johnstown	Appanoose	Marshall	Henry	Nora Springs	Floyd
Jone	Iowa	Marshalltown	Marshall	North Bend	Mitchell
Jollyville	Lee	Martinsburg	Keokuk	North English	Iowa
Keokuk	"	Mason City	Cerro Gordo	Northfield	Des Moines

POST OFFICES—IOWA.

Post Office.	County.	Post Office.	County.	Post Office.	County.
North Liberty	Johnson	Prairie Hill	Boone	Springfield	Keokuk
North Washington	Chickasaw	Prairie Mills	Muscatine	Spring Grove	Linn
Northwood	Worth	Prairie View	Ringgold	Spring Lake	Bremer
Norwalk	Warren	Prairieville	Decatur	Spring Rock	Clinton
Nugent's Grove	Linn	Primrose	Lee	Spring Run	Keokuk
Numa	Appanoose	Princeton	Scott	Spring Valley	Decatur
Oakfield	Audubon	Promise City	Wayne	Springville	Linn
Oak Point	Van Buren	Prospect Hill	Linn	Spruce Mills	Jackson
Oak Spring	Davis	Pulaski	Davis	Staceyville	Mitchell
Occola C. H.	Clark	Quasqueton	Buchanan	Stapleton	Chickasaw
Ogden	Dubuque	Quebec	Hardin	Stelapolis	Iowa
Okoboji	Dickenson	Queen City	Adams	Sterling	Jackson
Ola	Tama	Queen's Point	Madison	Stiles	Davis
Old Mission	Winneshiek	Quincy	Adams	Story City	Story
Ohio	Union	Ramessa	Clinton	Strawberry Hill	Muscatine
Olmstead	Shelby	Rend	Clayton	Strawberry Point	Clayton
Onion Grove	Cedar	Redding	Ringgold	Stringtown	Davis
Ononway	Louisa	Redman	Tama	Sugar Grove	Poweshiek
Onaway City	Monona	Red Oak	Cedar	Sullivan	Jackson
Oran	Fayette	Red Oak Junction	Montgomery	Summerset	Warren
Orange	Clinton	Red Rock	Iowa	Summit	Muscatine
Orlando	Wayne	Reeder's Mills	Harrison	Summitville	Lee
Orleans	Appanoose	Richfield	Fayette	Sumner	Bremer
Osborne	Howard	Richland	Keokuk	Sunny Side	Buchanan
Osage	Mitchell	Richmond	Washington	Swanton	Butler
Oskaloosa	Mahaska	Ridgedale	Polk	Swede Point	Boone
Osprey	Monroe	Ridgeway	Guthrie	Sweetland Center	Muscatine
Ossian	Allemakee	Riley	Clark	Tabor	Fremont
Otho	Webster	Ringgold	Ringgold	Tallahoma	Lucas
Otisville	Franklin	Rippey	Greene	Talleyrand	Keokuk
Otranto	Mitchell	Rising Sun	Polk	Tamaville	Tama
Otsego	Fayette	Rochester	Cedar	Tara	Dubuque
Ottawa	Clark	Rockdale	Dubuque	Turkis	Page
Ottumwa	Wapello	Rockford	Floyd	Taylor	Davis
Ovid	Taylor	Rock Grove City	"	Taylor Hill	Grundy
Owen's Grove	Cerro Gordo	Rockville	Delaware	Taylor's Grove	Benton
Oxford	Johnson	Rolley	Jackson	Taylorsville	Fayette
Ozark	Jackson	Rome	Henry	Timber Creek	Marshall
Pacific City	Mills	Rosetto	Cedar	Time	Lucas
Page City	Page	Ross Grove	Montgomery	Tipton	Cedar
Palestine	Johnson	Rossville	Allemakee	Tivoli	Dubuque
Palmyra	Polk	Round Grove	Scott	Toledo	Tama
Palo	Linn	Sabula	Jackson	Toolsborough	Louisa
Palo Alto	Louisa	Sac City	Sac	Toronto	Clinton
Panther Creek	Clayton	Saint Ansgar	Mitchell	Tower Hill	Delaware
Parkersburg	Butler	Saint Charles	Madison	Trenton	Henry
Parrish	Des Moines	Saint Clair	Monona	Tripoli	Bremer
Parsonville	Jefferson	Saint Charles City	Floyd	Trout Hill	
Peck's	Keokuk	Saint Donatus	Jackson	Troy	Davis
Pedee	Cedar	Saint John	Harrison	Turkey Grove	Cass
Pella	Marion	Saint Paul	Lee	Twelve Mile Grove	Warren
Penora	Guthrie	Salem	Henry	Twin Spring	Winneshiek
Peoria	Mahaska	Salina	Jefferson	Ulster	Floyd
Peoria City	Polk	Sand Spring	Delaware	Union	Hardin
Peosta	Dubuque	Sandysville	Warren	Union City	Union
Perry Valley	Buchanan	Saratoga	Howard	Union Prairie	Allemakee
Peru	Madison	Savannah	Davis	Union Ridge	Franklin
Peterson	Clay	Saylorsville	Polk	Uniontown	Delaware
Philo	Union	Sciola	Montgomery	Unionville	Appanoose
Pickaway	Benton	Scotch Grove	Jones	Unity	Benton
Pierce Point	Dallas	Scott	Mahaska	Upper Grove	Hancock
Pike	Muscatine	Sergeant's Bluff	Woodbury	Upton	Van Buren
Pilot Grove	Lee	Seventy-eight	Johnson	Urbanna	Benton
Pine	Buchanan	Sheffield	Story	Utica	Van Buren
Pin Oak	Dubuque	Sholby	Clark	Valley	Washington
Pittsburg	Van Buren	Shelbyville C. H.	Shelby	Valley Farm	Linn
Plattville	Taylor	Sholl Rock	Butler	Van Buren	Jackson
Pleasant Grove	Des Moines	Shell Rock Falls	Cerro Gordo	Vandalia	Jasper
Pleasant Hill	Cedar	Shelisburg	Benton	Vandyke	Des Moines
Pleasant Plain	Jefferson	Sherrill's Mount	Dubuque	Vega	Henry
Pleasant Prairie	Muscatine	Shuesville	Johnson	Venus	Madison
Pleasant Valley	Scott	Side Hill	Cedar	Vernon	Van Buren
Pleasant View	Jasper	Sidney	Fremont	Vernon Springs	Howard
Pleasantville	Marion	Sigourney	Keokuk	Victor	Poweshiek
Plum Hollow	Fremont	Silver Street	Ringgold	Vienna	Marshall
Plum Spring	Delaware	Simpson	Adams	Village Creek	Allemakee
Plymonth	Cerro Gordo	Sioux City	Woodbury	Vincennes	Lee
Plymouth Rock	Winneshiek	Sisley's Grove	Louisa	Vinton	Benton
Point Isabelle	Wapello	Smithland	Woodbury	Virginia Grove	Louisa
Point Pleasant	Hardin	Snyder	Dallas	Volga City	Clayton
Polk City	Polk	Solon	Johnson	Volney	Allemakee
Polk Precinct	Bremer	South English	Keokuk	Wacousta	Humboldt
Port Allen	Louisa	South Fliut	Des Moines	Wagonersburg	Jackson
Portland	Van Buren	South Fork	Wayne	Wahagbousey	Mills
Port Louisa	Louisa	Spencer	Clay	Walnut	Jefferson
Port Richmoud	Wapello	Spirit Lake	Dickinson	Walnut Fork	Jones
Postville	Allemakee	Spragueville	Jackson	Walnut Grove	Scott
Prairie City	Jasper	Spring Brook	"	Wapello	Louisa
Prairie Creek	Iowa	Spring Creek	Tama	Wapsa	Linn
Prairie Grove	Clark	Spring Dale	Cedar	Warren	Lee

POST OFFICES—KANSAS.

Post Office.	County.	Post Office.	County.	Post Office.	County.
Washington	Washington	Bazaar	Chase	Leavenworth City	Leavenworth
Wassonville	Washington	Beach Valley		Lecompton	Douglas
Waterford	Jackson	Belmont	Woodson	Le Roy	Coffee
Waterloo	Black Hawk	Big Springs	Douglas	Lexington	Johnston
Waterman	O'Brien	Big Turkey		Lincoln	Nemaha
Watertown	Floyd	Black Jack	Douglas	Little Stranger	Leavenworth
Waterville	Allemakee	Blooming Grove	Linn	Lyons	Lykins
Waubeek	Linn	Blue Rapids	Marshall	McKinney	Douglas
Waucoma	Fayette	Brooklyn	Linn	Madison	Madison
Waverly	Bremer	Brushville		Mairestown	Shawnee
Wankou	Allemakee	Burlingame	Shawnee	Manhattan	Riley
Wayne	Henry	Burlington	Coffee	Mantau	Allen
Wayne ⋈ Roads	Wayne	Camp Creek		Mapleton	Bourbon
Webster	Keokuk	Canton	Brown	Marion	Douglas
Webster City	Hamilton	Capioma	Nemaha	Marmaton	Bourbon
Welland	Appanoose	Carlyle	Allen	Maryaville	Marshall
Weiler	Monroe	Carson	Brown	Merrimac	"
Well's Mills	Appanoose	Cato	Bourbon	Miami Village	Lykins
Welton	Clinton	Catholic Mission		Mill Creek	Bourbon
Wentworth	Mitchell	Centerville	Linn	Moneka	Linn
West Branch	Cedar	Central City	Nemaha	Monrovia	Atchison
West Dayton	Webster	Centralia	"	Monticello	Johnston
Western College	Linn	Centropolis	Franklin	Moore's Branch	Marion
Westerville	Decatur	Cherokee City	McGhee	Mound City	Linn
Westfield	Fayette	Chelsea	Butler	Mount Airy	Woodson
West Grove	Davis	Claytonville	Brown	Mount Florence	Jefferson
West Irving	Tama	Clinton	Douglas	Mount Pleasant	Atchison
West Liberty	Muscatine	Columbus	Doniphan	Nashville	Coffee
West Milton	Guthrie	Cottonwood Falls	Chase	Neosho City	"
West Point	Lee	Council Grove	Morris	Neosho Falls	Woodson
West Union	Fayette	Cresco	Brown	Neosho Rapids	Breckinridge
Woxford	Allemakee	Crooked Creek	Jefferson	New Eureka	Jackson
Wheatland	Clinton	Cold Spring	Allen	New Lancaster	Lykins
Wheeling	Marion	Davis	Douglas	Nohart	Richardson
White Cloud	Mills	Dayton	Bourbon	Nottingham	Marshall
White Pigeon	Keokuk	Decora	Breckinridge	Oakwood	Linn
Whitneville	Cass	Delaware City	Leavenworth	Ogden	Riley
Wickliffe	Jackson	Doniphan	Doniphan	Ohio City	Franklin
Williams	Benton	Easton	Leavenworth	Olathe	Johnston
Willow	Pottawatomie	Eden	Atchison	Ole	Jefferson
Williamstown	Chickasaw	El Dorado	Hunter	Osawatomie	Lykins
Willoughby	Butler	Eldon	Pottawatomie	Oskaloosa	Jefferson
Wilson's Ford	Allemakee	Elizabethtown	Brown	Ottawa Creek	"
Willow Junction	Muscatine	Elmendaro	Madison	Ottumwa	Coffee
Wimer's Mills	Keokuk	Elwood	Doniphan	Ozawkie	Jefferson
Winchester	Van Buren	Emporia	Breckenridge	Padoria	Brown
Windham	Johnson	Eudora	Douglas	Palermo	Doniphan
Windsor	Fayette	Eureka	Greenwood	Paola	Lykins
Winfield	Henry	Fairland	Marshall	Pardee	Atchison
Winneshiek	Winneshiek	Forest Hill	Breckinridge	Paris	Linn
Winterset	Madison	Fort Leavenworth		Palmyra	Douglas
Wisonita	Dallas	Fort Riley		Pawnee	Atchison
Wolcot	Scott	Fort Scott	Bourbon	Pawnee Fork	"
Wolf Creek	Tama	Franklin	Douglas	Peoria	Franklin
Woodbine	Harrison	Fremont	Breckinridge	Pleasant Grove	Greenwood
Woodbridge	Cedar	Gardener	Johnston	Pleasant Spring	Nemaha
Woods	Benton	Garnett	Anderson	Plymouth	Breckinridge
Wooster	Jefferson	Geary	Doniphan	Pony Creek	Brown
Worthington	Dubuque	Geneva	Allen	Potosi	Linn
Wyoming	Jones	Grasshopper Falls	Jefferson	Powhattan	Brown
Xenia	Dallas	Greenwood		Prairie City	Douglas
Xniffin	Wayne	Guiltard's Station	Marshall	Quindaro	Leavenworth
Yankee Settlement	Clayton	Hamlin	Brown	Randolph	Riley
Yatton	Washington	Hartford	Madison	Rayville	Bourbon
Yazoo	Harrison	Henryville	Riley	Rides	Brown
York	Delaware	Hiawatha	Brown	Richardson	Shawnee
Yough	Boone	Hibbard	Johnston	Richland	"
Zurich	Jones	Hickory Creek	Franklin	Ridgeway	Osage
Zwingle	Jackson	Highland	Doniphan	Riley City	Davis
		Holton	Jackson	Robinson	Brown
		Humboldt	Allen	Rock Creek	Pottawatomie
Kansas.		Huntsville	Arapahoe	Rockford	Bourbon
		Huron	Atchison	Rodgersville	Washington
Post Office.	County.	Hyatt	Brown	Rosyvale	Brown
		Indianapolis	Lykins	Rovella	Linn
Abilene	Dickinson	Indianola	Shawnee	Sabetha	Nemaha
Agnes City	Breckinridge	Iola	Allen	Saint George	Pottawatomie
Albany	Nemaha	Iowa Point	Doniphan	Saint Mary's Mission	"
Allen	Breckinridge	Irving	Marshall	Saint Nicholas	Atchison
America City	Nemaha	Janesville	Greenville	Scipio	Franklin
Americus	Breckinridge	Junction City	Davis	Seneca	Nemaha
Ashland	Davis	Kanwaka	Douglas	Shawnee	Johnston
Ash Point	Nemaha	Kaw City	Jefferson	Shell Rock Falls	Madison
Atchison	Atchison	Kennekuck	Brown	Shields	Jefferson
Aubrey	Johnston	Kenton	Davis	Six Mile Creek	Morris
Auburn	Shawnee	Kickapoo City	Leavenworth	Solomon's City	Saline
Barnesville	Bourbon	Lafayette	Doniphan	Spencer	Atchison
Barrett	Marshall	Lamb's Point	Dickinson	Spring Dale	Leavenworth
		Lane	Franklin	Spring Hill	Johnston
		Lawrence	Douglas	Squiresville	"

POST OFFICES—KENTUCKY.

Post Office.	County.	Post Office.	County.	Post Office.	County.
Stanton	Lykins	Berry's Lick	Butler	Cave City	Barren
Sumner	Atchison	Berry's Station	Harrison	Cayce's Station	Fulton
Superior	Weller	Bethel	Bath	Caves	Carter
Tecumseh	Shawnee	Bethlehem	Henry	Cedar Creek	Jefferson
Toledo	Breckinridge	Bewleyville	Breckenridge	Cedar Springs	Allen
Tonganoxie	Leavenworth	Big Clifty	Grayson	Center	Metcalfe
Topeka	Shawnee	Big Hill	Madison	Centerfield	Oldham
Towanda	Otoe	Big Ready	Edmonson	Centerpoint	Monroe
Troy	Doniphan	Big Rock	Harlan	Centerville	Bourbon
Turkey Creek	Bourbon	Big Spring	Breckenridge	Ceralvo	Ohio
Twin Mound	Douglas	Birdsville	Livingston	Chapel Hill	Allen
Twin Springs	Linn	Birmingham	Marshall	Chaplin	Nelson
Unadilla	Pottawatomie	Bitter Water	Bullitt	Charleston	Hopkins
Virgil	Madison	Blackford	Hancock	Cherokee	Lawrence
Wakarusa	Douglas	Black Lick	Logan	Cheshire's Store	Anderson
Walker	Brown	Black Walnut	Barren	Chicago	Marion
Walnut Grove	Doniphan	Black Water	Morgan	Christiansburg	Shelby
Walton	Shawnee	Blandville	Ballard	Christy's Fork	Morgan
Waterloo	Breckinridge	Bloomfield	Nelson	Clarksburg	Lewis
Wathena	Doniphan	Bloomington	Maggoffin	Clay	Union
Wabaunsee	Wabaunsee	Blue Lick Springs	Nicholas	Claysville	Harrison
Waushara	Breckinridge	Blue Spring Grove	Barren	Clay's Village	Shelby
Westmoreland	Pottawatomie	Bohan	Mercer	Clear Creek	Knox
White Cloud	Doniphan	Bolton	Lawrence	Clear Fork	Whitley
Whitehead		Boone	Boone	Clear Spring	Graves
Wilmington	Wabaunsee	Boone Furnace	Carter	Cleaveland	Fayette
Winchester	Jefferson	Booneville	Owsley	Clifton's Mills	Breckenridge
Wyandotte	Leavenworth	Bordley	Union	Clifty	Todd
Xenia	Bourbon	Boston	Nelson	Clinton	Hickman
Zeandale	Wabaunsee	Boston Station	Pendleton	Clintonville	Bourbon
		Bowling Green	Warren	Clio	Wayne
		Boyd's Station	Harrison	Cloverport	Breckenridge
		Bradfordsville	Marion	Clyde	Hopkins
		Brandenburg	Mead	Cogar's Landing	Jessamine
Kentucky.		Brasherville	Perry	Cold Spring	Campbell
		Breckenridge	Pike	Cold Water	Callaway
		Breedings	Adair	Colemansville	Harrison
Post Office.	County.	Bremen	Muhlenburg	Columbia	Adair
		Bridgeport	Franklin	Columbus	Hickman
Aaron's Run	Montgomery	Brienalurg	Marshall	Concord	Lewis
Abbottsford	Trimble	Brigg's Mills	Ohio	Connersville	Harrison
Adairsville	Logan	Bristow Station	Warren	Consolation	Shelby
Adams' Mills	Pulaski	Broadwell	Harrison	Constance	Boone
Albany	Clinton	Brook's Station	Bullitt	Cool Spring	Ohio
Alexandria	Campbell	Brookville	Bracken	Coral Hill	Barren
Allendale	Greene	Brownsborough	Oldham	Cordova	Grant
Allenville	Todd	Brownsville	Edmonson	Cornett's Mills	Letcher
Alma	Warren	Bryantville	Garrard	Cornishville	Mercer
Alpha	Clinton	Buckeye		Corydon	Henderson
Amanda	Greenup	Buckhorn	Ohio	Cotton Wood	Christian
Antioch	Washington	Buenna Vista	Harrison	Covington	Kenton
Ashbysburg	Hopkins	Buford	Ohio	Crab Orchard	Lincoln
Ashland	Boyd	Bullittsville	Boone	Creelsburg	Russell
Aspen Grove	Pendleton	Burlington		Crittenden	Grant
Athens	Fayette	Burnsville	Caldwell	Crittenden Springs	Crittenden
Atkinson	Christian	Bush's Store	Laurel	Cromwell	Ohio
Augusta	Bracken	Butlersville	Allen	Cropper's Depot	Shelby
Aurora	Marshall	Buzzard Roost	Nicholas	Cross Plains	Barren
Bacon Creek	Hart	Butler	Pendleton	Crow's Pond	Daviess
Bainbridge	Christian	Cabin Creek	Lewis	Cuba	Graves
Bald Eagle	Bath	Cadiz	Trigg	Cumberland Ford	Knox
Bald Knob	Franklin	Cairo	Henderson	Curdsville	Daviess
Ballardsville	Oldham	Calhoun	McLean	Curry's Run	Harrison
Barboursville	Knox	California	Campbell	Cutshin	Perry
Bark Camp Mills	Whitley	Callahan	Greenup	Cynthiana	Harrison
Bardstown	Nelson	Callaway	Harlan	Cypress	Union
Barksdale	Marshall	Camargo	Montgomery	Dabney	Pulaski
Barrick	Greene	Camdenville	Anderson	Dale	Campbell
Baugh's Station	Logan	Campbellsburg	Henry	Dallman's Creek	Logan
Bear Creek	Owsley	Campbellsville	Taylor	Dallas	Pulaski
Beard's Station	Oldham	Camp Creek	Crittenden	Danville	Boyle
Bear Wallow	Barren	Cane Spring Depot	Bullitt	Daysville	Todd
Beattyville	Owsley	Cane Valley	Adair	Delaware	Daviess
Beaver Dam	Ohio	Caney	Morgan	Demossville	Pendleton
Beaver Lick	Boone	Caneyville	Grayson	Deposit	Jefferson
Bedford	Trimble	Cannonsburg	Greenup	Depot	Graves
Beech Fork	Washington	Canton	Trigg	Devil's Creek	Wolf
Beechland		Carlisle	Nicholas	Dixon	Webster
Bee Lick	Lincoln	Carlow	Hopkins	Donaldson	Trigg
Bee Spring	Edmonson	Carrollton	Carroll	Doughty's Creek	Warren
Bell	Morgan	Carrsville	Livingston	Dover	Mason
Belmont	Bullitt	Carthage	Campbell	Downingsville	Grant
Belle Ombre	Ballard	Casey Creek	Adair	Dry Ridge	Grant
Belle View	Christian	Caseyville	Union	Dublin	Graves
Bell's Mines	Crittenden	Cash's Knob	Montgomery	Ducker's	Woodford
Bell's Trace	Carter	Cassity's Mills	Morgan	Dunaway's	Clark
Bennettsville	Hancock	Catalpa Grove	Greene	Duncan	Mercer
Benson	Franklin	Catawba	Pendleton	Dyousburg	Crittenden
Benton	Marshall	Catlettsburg	Boyd	Eagle Hill	Owen
Berlin	Bracken	Cato	Pulaski	Earle's	Muhlenburg

POST OFFICES—KENTUCKY.

Post Office.	County.	Post Office.	County.	Post Office.	County.
East Fork	Metcalf	Gonge's	Grant	Kansas	Graves
Eddyville	Lyon	Gradyville	Adair	Keene	Jessamine
Edmonton	Metcalf	Gracfenburg	Shelby	Kenton	Kenton
Edmundsville	Barren	Grant's Lick	Campbell	Kentontown	Harrison
Elizabethtown	Hardin	Grassy Creek	Morgan	Keysburg	Logan
Elizaville	Fleming	Gratz	Owen	Kiddville	Clark
Elk Creek	Spencer	Gray Hawk	Jackson	Kingston	Madison
Elk Spring	Warren	Grayson C. H.	Carter	Kinniconick	Lewis
Elkton	Todd	Grayson Springs	Grayson	Kirksville	Madison
Eliston	Madison	Graysville	Todd	Knottsville	Daviess
Ellwood	Muhlenburg	Great Crossings	Scott	Knoxville	Pendleton
Elm	Ballard	Green Castle	Warren	Lacona	Jefferson
Eminence	Henry	Green Grove	Clinton	La Fayette	Christian
Empire Iron Works	Trigg	Green Hall	Owsley	La Fontaine	Harlan
Escipion	Logan	Green River	Hart	La Grange	Oldham
Estel Furnace	Estill	Greensburg	Greene	Lair's Station	Harrison
Exchange	McCracken	Greenup C. H.	Greenup	Lancaster	Garrard
Fair Dealing	Marshall	Greenville	Muhlenburg	Latonia Springs	Kenton
Fairfield	Nelson	Grundy	Pulaski	Laura Furnace	Trigg
Fairview	Todd	Gum Grove	Union	Laurel Bluff	Muhlenburg
Falls of Blain	Lawrence	Hadensville	Todd	Laurel Bridge	Laurel
Falls of Harrod	Jefferson	Hadley	Warren	Laurel Fork	Bath
Falls of Rough	Grayson	Hague	Logan	Lawrenceburg	Anderson
Falmouth	Pendleton	Hall	Hopkins	Lanesville	Floyd
Fancy Farm	Graves	Hamilton	Boone	Lead Hill	Muhlenburg
Farm Dale	Farmer	Hamilton's Store	Pike	Leander	Graves
Farmer's	Rowan	Hammonville	Hart	Lebanon	Marion
Farmersville	Caldwell	Hampton's Mills	Morgan	Leesburg	Harrison
Farmington	Graves	Hanly	Jessamine	Leonard	Harlan
Feliciana	"	Hardensburg	Breckenridge	Levee	Montgomery
Ferguson's Station	Logan	Harlan	Harlan	Lewisport	Hancock
Fern Creek	Jefferson	Hardscrable	Grant	Lexington	Fayette
Fern Leaf	Mason	Harmony	Owen	Liberty	Casey
Felixville	Greene	Harrisonville	Shelby	Licking Station	Morgan
Finchville	Shelby	Harrodsburg	Mercer	Lindsay's Mills	Trigg
Fisherville	Jefferson	Harreldville	Butler	Linn Creek	Pulaski
Flat Creek	Clay	Hartford	Ohio	Litchfield	Grayson
Flagg Spring	Campbell	Haskinsville	Greene	Little Eagle	Scott
Flat Lick	Knox	Havilandsville	Harrison	Little Prairie	Hopkins
Flat Rock	Bourbon	Hawesville	Hancock	Little Sandy	Morgan
Flat Woods	Marshall	Hays' Spring	Jefferson	Livermore	McLean
Flemingsburg	Fleming	Haysville	Marion	Lockport	Henry
Flippin	Monroe	Hazard	Perry	Lockwood	Lawrence
Flint Island	Mead	Hazle Green	Wolfe	Locust Grove	Callaway
Florence	Boone	Hazlewood	Ballard	Locust Mills	Bracken
Flower Creek	Pendleton	Head Qarters	Nicholas	Logan's Mills	Logan
Floydsburg	Oldham	Hebbardsville	Henderson	Logansport	Butler
Ford's Ferry	Crittenden	Hearin's Store	Union	London	Laurel
Fordsville	Ohio	Hebron	Boone	Long Run	Jefferson
Forest Retreat	Nicholas	Helena	Mason	Long View	Christian
Forks of Elkhorn	Franklin	Henderson C. H.	Henderson	Lowville	Pike
Fort Jefferson	Ballard	Henry's X Roads	Todd	Loretto	Marion
Foster	Bracken	Henrysville	Logan	Lost Creek	Breathitt
Fountain Run	Monroe	Hickman	Fulton	Lost Run	Breckenridge
Fowler's Creek	Kenton	Hickory Flat	Simpson	Lot	Whitley
Frankfort	Franklin	Hickory Grove	Graves	Louisa Court House	Lawrence
Franklin	Simpson	Hico	Callaway	Louisville	Jefferson
Franklin X Roads	Hardin	High Grove	Nelson	Lovelaceville	Ballard
Franklinton	Henry	Highland	Bath	Lowell	Garrard
Fredericktown	Washington	Hillsboro'	Fleming	Lone Station	Bourbon
Freedom	Casey	Hilton	Monroe	Lusby's Mills	Owen
Fredonia	Caldwell	Hines' Mills	Ohio	Lynn	Greenup
Friendship	Harlin	Hodgeusville	La Rue	Lynn Camp	Knox
Frozen Creek	Breathitt	Hood's Fork	Johnson	McDanul'sStore	Breckenridge
Fruit Hill	Christian	Hood's Run	Greenup	McKenzie's Mill	Christian
Fulton	Fulton	Hopkinsville	Christian	McAfee	Mercer
Gainesville	Allen	Horse Shoe Bottom	Russell	McGee	Jackson
Galway	Simpson	Horsewell	Barren	McLean's Retreat	Daviess
Gardnersville	Pendleton	Howard's Mills	Montgomery	Macedonia	Grant
Garnettsville	Mead	Horse Cave	Hart	Mackville	Washington
Garrotsburg	Christian	Houston	Bourbon	Madisonville	Hopkins
Garrett	Meade	Howell's Springs	Hardin	Magnolia	La Rue
Garriot's Landing	Trimble	Howe's Valley	"	Mammoth Cave	Edmonson
Geneva	Henderson	Hudsonville	Breckenridge	Manchester	Clay
George's Creek	Lawrence	Hustinville	Lincoln	Mannsville	Taylor
Georgetown	Scott	Hutchison's	Bourbon	Manton	Marion
Germantown	Mason	Independence	Kenton	MarbleCreek	Fayette
Gills' Mills	Bath	Indian Bottom	Letcher	Marino	Lewis
Ghent	Carroll	Indian Spring	Campbell	Marion	Crittenden
Glasgow	Barren	Irvine	Estill	Murrowbone	Cumberland
Glenn Brook	Hart	Irvinsville	Nicholas	Marsh Creek	Whitley
Glen's Fork	Adair	Jackson	Breathitt	Marshall's	Bath
Glencoe	Gallatin	Jamestown	Russell	Martinsburg	Monroe
Glendale	Hardin	Jeffersontown	Jefferson	Masonville	Daviess
Glenville	McLean	Jericho	Henry	Massack	McCracken
Golden Pond	Trigg	Jessamine	Jessamine	Mauldin	Jackson
Goochland	Madison	Jesse's Store	Shelby	Mayfield	Graves
Good's Precinct	Clark	Joe's Lick	Madison	May's Lick	Mason
Gordonville	Logan	Johnson's Forks	Morgan	Maysville	"
Goshen	Oldham	Kane	Campbell	Meadow Creek	Whitley

POST OFFICES—KENTUCKY.

Post Office.	County.	Post Office.	County.	Post Office.	County.
Meadville	Mead	Old Town	Greenup	Robertson's Station	Harrison
Melvin	Ballard	Olive Hill	Carter	Robersonville	Hardin
Menelos	Madison	Olive	Marshall	Robinson's Creek	Pike
Middleburg	Casey	Olympian Springs	Bath	Rochester	Butler
Middle Fork	Jackson	Orangeburg	Mason	Rock Bridge	Monroe
Middletown	Jefferson	Owensboro'	Daviess	Rock Castle	Trigg
Midview	Henry	Owenton	Owen	Rock Dale	Owen
Midway	Woodford	Owingsville	Bath	Rock Haven	Mead
Milburn	Ballard	Oxford	Scott	Rockhold's	Whitley
Milford	Bracken	Pace's	Metcalfe	Rockhouse	Bath
Military Institute	Franklin	Paducah	McCracken	Rockland Mills	Barren
Mills	Christian	Pageville	Barren	Rock Lick	Breckenridge
Milledgeville	Lincoln	Paint Lick	Garrard	Rock Point	Henry
Millersburg	Bourbon	Paintsville	Johnson	Rocky Hill	Barren
Millerstown	Grayson	Palma	Marshall	Rocky Hill Station	Edmonson
Millersville	Russell	Paradise	Muhlenburg	Rogersville	Madison
Mill Grove	Madison	Paris	Bourbon	Rolling Fork	Nelson
Mill Spring	Wayne	Park	Barren	Roscoe	Todd
Milton	Trimble	Parksville	Boyle	Rose Hill	Laurel
Milltown	Adair	Parmleysville	Wayne	Roseville	Barren
Millwood	Mason	Payne's Depot	Scott	Ross' Ferry	Livingston
Minerva	"	Peach Orchard	Lawrence	Rough and Ready	Anderson
Mintonville	Casey	Peeled Oak	Bath	Round Stone	Rock Castle
Mitchellsburg	Boyle	Pekin	Jessamine	Rowena	Russell
Model Mills	Muhlenburg	Pembroke	Christian	Rowlett's Depot	Hart
Monroe	Hart	Perryville	Boyle	Royalton	Russell
Monterey	Owen	Petersburg	Boone	Ruckersville	Clark
Montgomery	Trigg	Pewee Valley	Oldham	Ruddle's Mills	Bourbon
Monticello	Wayne	Piketon	Pike	Rumsey	McLane
Moorefield	Nicholas	Pilot Knob	Todd	Russell's Springs	Russell
Morehead C. H.	Rowan	Pine Bluff	Callaway	Russellville	Logan
Moreland	Bourbon	Pine Grove	Clark	Rutland	Harrison
Morgan	Pendleton	Pitt's Point	Bullitt	Saint Mary's	Marion
Morganfield	Union	Planter's Hall	Breckenridge	Saint Matthew's	Jefferson
Morgantown	Butler	Pleasant Grove	Ohio	Salem	Livingston
Morning View	Kenton	Pleasant Grove Mills	Fleming	Salina	Jefferson
Mortonsville	Woodford	Pleasant Hill	Mercer	Saloma	Taylor
Moscow	Hickman	Pleasant Home	Owen	Salt Lick	La Rue
Motier	Pendleton	Pleasant Point	Daviess	Salvisa	Mercer
Mount Aerial	Allen	Pleasant Ridge	"	Samuel's Depot	Nelson
Mount Carmel	Fleming	Pleasant Vale	Todd	Saudifer's Store	Carroll
Mount Eden	Spencer	Pleasant Valley Mills	Nicholas	Santa Fe	Bracken
Mount Freedom	Jessamine	Pleasant View	Todd	Saratoga	Lyon
Mount Gilead	Mason	Pleasureville	Henry	Sardis	Mason
Mount Ida	Montgomery	Plummer's Mill	Fleming	Savern	Owen
Mount Olivet	Bracken	Point Curve	Graves	Scaffold Cane	Rock Castle
Mount Savage	Carter	Point Pleasant	Ohio	Scottsville	Allen
Mount Sterling	Montgomery	Polkville	Warren	Seventy-six	Clinton
Mount Vernon	Rock	Pollard's Tan Yard	Caldwell	Sexton's Creek	Clay
Mount Washington	Bullitt	Pond River Mills	Muhlenburg	Shady Grove	Crittenden
Mount Zion	Perry	Poole's Mills	Henderson	Sharpsburg	Bath
Mud Lick	Monroe	Poor Fork	Harlan	Shawnun	Bourbon
Munfordville	Hart	Poplar Flat	Lewis	Shelbyville	Shelby
Munday's Landing	Woodford	Poplar Grove	Owen	Shepherdsville	Bullitt
Murray	Callaway	Poplar Hill	Casey	Sherburn Mills	Fleming
Murphysville	Mason	Poplar Neck	Nelson	Shiloh	Callaway
Napoleon	Gallatin	Poplar Plains	Fleming	Short Creek	Grayson
Neatsville	Adair	Portland	Jefferson	Shortsville	Bullitt
Nebo	Hopkins	Port Royal	Henry	Side View	Montgomery
Nelson Furnace	Nelson	Pott's Mills	Jessamine	Simpsonville	Shelby
Nevada	Mercer	Powersville	Bracken	Slack	Mason
Newberry	Wayne	Prestonburg	Floyd	Slaughtersville	Webster
New Castle	Henry	Prestonville	Carroll	Sligo	Henry
New Columbus	Owen	Prewitt's Knob	Barren	Smileytown	Spencer
New Concord	Callaway	Princeton	Caldwell	Smithfield	Henry
New Haven	Nelson	Proctor	Owsley	Smithland	Livingston
New Hope	"	Prosperity	Lawrence	Smith's Grove	Warren
New Liberty	Owen	Providence	Hopkins	Smith's Mills	Henderson
New Market	Marion	Pryorsburg	Graves	Snow Hill	Callaway
Newport	Campbell	Quality Valley	Butler	Social Hill	McLean
New Roe	Allen	Quincy	Lewis	Somerset	Pulaski
Newstead	Christian	Rabbittsville	Logan	Sonora	Hardin
New Woodburn	Warren	Radford	Callaway	South Carrollton	Muhlenburg
New Texas	Hickman	Raleigh	Union	South Fork	Owsley
Newtown	Scott	Randolph	Metcalf	South Union	Logan
Nicholasville	Jessamine	Raven Creek	Harrison	Southville	Shelby
Nobob	Barren	Raywick	Marion	Sparta	Owen
Nolen	Hardin	Readyville	Butler	Speedwell	Madison
Northcutt's Store	Boone	Red Hill	Hardin	Spottsville	Henderson
North Fork	Mason	Red River Iron Works	Estill	Spring Bank	Franklin
North Hill	Wayne	Relief	Morgan	Springfield	Washington
North Middletown	Bourbon	Richland	Butler	Springport	Henry
Oakford	Daviess	Richlieu	Logan	Spring Station	Woodford
Oak Grove	Christian	Richmond	Madison	Spence Grove	Owsley
Oakland Mills	Nicholas	Rich Pond Grove	Warren	Stamperton	Owen
Oakland Station	Warren	Richmond	Boone	Stamping Ground	Scott
Oak Woods	Fleming	Riffe's ⋈ Roads	Lawrence	Stanford	Lincoln
O'Bannon	Jefferson	Rio	Hart	Stanton	Powell
Oddville	Harrison	River View	Jefferson	Stapleton	Mead
Oldhamburg	Oldham	Roaring Spring	Trigg	Star Furnace	Carter

POST OFFICES—LOUISIANA. 31

Post Office.	County.	Post Office.	County.	Post Office.	Parish.
Stateley's Run	Grant	Withesville	Caldwell	Centerville	St. Mary's
State Line	Fulton	Woodbine	Whitley	Charenton	
Stephensburg	Hardin	Woodbary	Butler	Cherry Ridge	Union
Stephensport	Breckenridge	Woodlawn	Morgan	Cheneyville	Rapides
Still Water	Wolf	Woodsonville	Hart	Chicot Pass	St. Martin's
Stoner	Clark	Woodstock	Pulaski	Church	Assumption
Stony Point	Bourbon	Woodville	Ballard	Clinton	East Feliciana
Sugar Creek	Gallatin	Woolridge's Store	Christian	Cloutiersville	Natchitoches
Sugar Grove	Butler	Worthville	Carroll	Cock	Livingston
Sugar Plant	Metcalfe	Wightsville	Pulaski	Collinsburg	Bossier
Sulphur Lick	Monroe	Wyoming	Bath	Columbia	Caldwell
Sulphur Springs	Muhlenburg	Yellow Creek	Knox	Columbus	Sabine
Sulphur Well	Jessamine	Yelvington	Daviess	Convent	St. James
Summerville	Greene	Zion	Henderson	Conshatte Chute	Natchitoches
Suntish	Edmonson			Copenhagen	Caldwell
Swiftsville	Wolf			Cotee Gelee	Lafayette
Symsonia	Graves	**Louisiana.**		Cotile	Rapides
Taylorsville	Spencer			Cotton Valley	Bossier
Temperance Hill	Warren			Covington	St. Tammany
Temperance Mount	Simpson			Crane's Forge	Assumption
Texas	Washington	Post Office.	Parish.	Cypress Point	Point Coupee
Thompsonville	Pulaski			Darlington	East Feliciana
Three Forks	Barren	Abbville	Vermillion	Davidson	Washington
Three Prong	Greenup	Adaies	Natchitoches	Delhi	Carroll
Three Springs	Harp	Adams	Caddo	Dennis' Mills	St. Helena
Tibbatt's × Roads	Campbell	Aimwell	Catahoula	Dillonsville	Sabine
Tilton	Fleming	Albany	Caddo	Donaldsonville	Ascension
Tippecanoe	Ohio	Alexandria	Rapides	Dorcheat	Claiborne
Tolesborough	Lewis	Albemarle	Assumption	Douglass	Jackson
Tompkinsville	Monroe	Algiers	Orleans	Downsville	Union
Tracy	Barren	Alligator	St. Mary's	Dunbarton	St. Landry
Traveler's Rest	Owsley	Allen's Settlement	Claiborne	Edgard	St. John Baptist
Trenton	Todd	Alpha	Caldwell	Enterprise	Catahoula
Troy	Woodford	Amite City	St. Helena	Evergreen	Avoyelles
Truittsville	Greenup	Anacoca	Sabine	Fairview	Concordia
Turkey Foot	Scott	Arcadia	Bienville	Farmersville	Union
Union	Boone	Argus	Claiborne	Fause Point	St. Martin's
Union Star	Breckenridge	Arnandville	St. Landry	Fillmore	Bossier
Uniontown	Union	Ashton	Carroll	Finlay's	Catahoula
Upper Tygart	Carter	Ashwood	Tensas	Flat Lick	Claiborne
Uptonville	La Rue	Assumption	Assumption	Flowery Mound	Concordia
Vanceburg	Lewis	Atchafalaya	St. Landry	Floyd	Carroll
Vandenburg	Hopkins	Athens	Claiborne	Ford's Creek	Catahoula
Van Dyke's Mill	Spencer	Bailey's Mill	Washington	Forest Grove	Claiborne
Verona	Boone	Balize	Plaquemine	Fort Jessup	Sabine
Versailles	Woodford	Ballew's Ferry	St. Landry	Fort Pike	Orleans
Vienna	Clark	Castrop	Morehouse	Franklin	St. Mary's
Vine Grove	Hardin	Paton Rouge	E. Baton Rouge	Franklinton	Washington
Viola Station	Graves	Bayou Barbary	Livingston	French Settlement	Livingston
Visalia	Kenton	Bayou Bocuf	St. Landry	Funny Louis	Catahoula
Volney Station	Logan	Bayou Chicot		Good Water	Winn
Wadesboro'	Marshall	Bayou Chene	St. Martin's	Gordon	Claiborne
Wallonia	Trigg	Bayou La Chute	Caddo	Grand Cane	De Soto
Walnut Flat	Lincoln	Bayou Goula	Iberville	Grand Chenier	Vermillion
Walnut Hill	Fayette	Bayou Tunica	West Feliciana	Grand Coteau	St. Landry
Walnut Valley	Clark	Bear Creek	Rapides	Grand Ecore	Natchitoches
Walton	Boone	Bell River	Assumption	Grand Point	St. James
Warfield	Lawrence	Bellevue	Bossier	Grand Prairie	Plaquemine
Warsaw	Gallatin	Bethany	Caddo	Green's Creek	Catahoula
Washington	Mason	Bienvenue	St. Bernard	Greensburg	St. Helena
Waterford	Spencer	Benton's Ferry	Livingston	Greenwell Springs	East Baton Rouge
Waterloo	Pulaski	Bertrand Prairie	Winn		
Watson's	Marshall	Berwick	St. Mary's	Greenwood	Caddo
Waynesboro'	Lincoln	Big Bend	Avoyelles	Griffin	Claiborne
Weaverton	Wayne	Big Cane	St. Landry	Hamilton	Wachita
Webster	Breckenridge	Big Creek	Rapides	Harrisonburg	Catahoula
Wesley	Hickman	Black Hawk Point	Concordia	Hart's Bluff	De Soto
Weston	Nicholas	Black Jack	De Soto	Haynesville	Claiborne
Westonburg	Crittenden	Black Walnut	St. Helena	Hemp's Creek	Catahoula
West Liberty	Morgan	Bonner	Jackson	Hermitage	West Baton Rouge
West Point	Hardin	Bonnet Carre	St. John Baptist	Hickory Flat	Calcasieu
Westport	Oldham	Bossier Point	Bossier	Hinoston	Rapides
Whippoorwill	Laurel	Bouff Prairie	Franklin	Hog Branch	St. Helena
White Hall	Madison	Brashear	St. Mary's	Holmesville	Avoyelles
White Lilly	Laurel	Breaux's Bridge	St. Martin's	Hollywood	Livingston
White Oak Hill	Fleming	Brookline	Jackson	Homer	Claiborne
Whitesburg	Letcher	Buckeoo	Winn	Houma	Terre Bonne
White Sulphur	Scott	Bruly Landing		Hourna	Terre Bonne
Whitesville	Daviess		West Baton Rouge	Huddleston	Rapides
Whitley C. H.	Whitley	Bush Valley	Bienville	Independence	Livingston
Wickliffe	Nelson	Buck Horn		Indian Village	Wachita
Wild Cat	Whitley	BurrasSettlement	Plaquemine	Iou	Morehouse
Williams	Christian	Burr's Ferry	Sabine	Iverson	Bienville
Williamstown	Grant	Caledonia	Carroll	Jutt	Rapides
Willisburg	Washington	Campti	Natchitoches	Jackson	East Feliciana
Wilson's Creek	Graves	Cane Ridge	Claiborne	Jefferson	Jefferson
Wilsonville	Spencer	Cantrelle	St. James	Jeanerettes	St. Mary's
Winchester	Clark	Carrollton	Jefferson	Jesuits' Bend	Plaquemine
Winona	Trimble	Custo Springs	Catahoula	Joe's Bayou	Carroll
Wise's Mill	Henderson	Castor	Caldwell	Jones' Ferry	Morehouse

POST OFFICES—MAINE.

Post Office.	Parish.	Post Office.	County.	Post Office.	County.
Justice	Sabine	Plankville	Jackson	White Houmas	Ascension
Keatchie	De Soto	Plantersville	Morehouse	White Sulphur Springs	
Kemp's Mills	St. Helena	Plaquemine	Iberville		Catahoula
Kenner	Jefferson	Plaquemine Brulee	St. Landry	Wheeling	Winn
Kingston	De Soto	Pleasant Grove	De Soto	Williamsport	Point Coupee
Kirk's Ferry	Tensas	Pleasant Hill	"	Winfield	Winn
Kisatchee	Natchitoches	Ponchatoula	Livingston	Winsborough	Franklin
Knox Point	Bossier	Point Coupee	Point Coupee	Wiseville	Claiborne
Kyisbe	Winn	Point a la Hache	Plaquemine	Woodland	East Feliciana
Lafayette City	Lafayette	Point Jefferson	Morehouse	Woodville	Jackson
Lake Arthur	Calcasieu	Point Michael	Plaquemine	Yellow Bluff	Franklin
Lake Charles	"	Port Hudson	East Feliciana		
Lake Providence	Carroll	Pompeville	St. Landry		
Lamothe	Rapides	Prairie Mer Rouge	Morehouse		
Lanark	Winn	Provost	Wachita	**Maine.**	
Lawrence	Terre Bonne	Prospect Hill	St. Helena		
La Place	St Martin's	Quay	Claiborne	Post Office.	County.
Laurel Hill	West Feliciana	Quebec	Madison		
Lecompte	Rapides	Raceland	Lafourche	Abbott	Piscataquis
Leouville	St. Landry	Red Bluff	De Soto	Acton	York
Liberty Creek	Rapides	Red Mouth	Franklin	Addison Point	Washington
Lima	St. Tammany	Red River Landing		Albany	Oxford
Lind Grove	Morehouse		Point Coupee	Albion	Kennebec
Line	"	Richmond	Madison	Alexander	Washington
Lisbon	Claiborne	Ringgold	Bienville	Alfred	York
Livonia	Point Coupee	Roberts	Washington	Alton	Penobscot
Live Oak	Ascension	Roberts' Mills	St. Helena	Alton Village	Penobscot
Lobdell's Store	West Baton Rouge	Rocky Mount	Bossier	Alna	Lincoln
		Rosedale	Iberville	Amherst	Hancock
Logansport	De Soto	Rose Hill	Claiborne	Amity	Aroostook
Loggy Bayou	Bienville	St. Charles Court House		Andover	Oxford
Long Street	De Soto		St. Charles	Anson	Somerset
Long Lake	Caldwell	St. Francisville	West Feliciana	Argyle	Penobscot
Louisville	Winn	St. Gabriel	Iberville	Aroostook	Aroostook
Lucky Hit	Rapides	St. Joseph	Tensas	Athens	Somerset
Madisonville	St. Tammany	St. Martinsville	St. Martin's	Atkinson	Piscataquis
McCutcheons' Landing		St. Maurice	Winn	Auburn	Androscoggin
	St. Charles	San Patrice	Sabine	Augusta	Kennebec
Magnolia Springs		Saline	Bienville	Aurora	Hancock
	East Baton Rouge	Salt Spring	"	Avon	Franklin
Manchac	"	Scottsville	Claiborne	Bangor	Penobscot
Mandeville	St. Tammany	Sentell's Store	Bossier	Bancroft	Aroostook
Manny	Sabine	Shady Grove	Washington	Bancroft Mills	Aroostook
Mansfield	De Soto	Shiloh	Union	Baring	Washington
Mansura	Avoyelles	Shongaloo	Claiborne	Bar Mills	York
Marion	Union	Shreveport	Caddo	Bath	Sagadahoc
Marthaville	Natchitoches	Sicily Island	Catahoula	Baileyville	Washington
Marksville	Avoyelles	Simmsport	Avoyelles	Beddington	Washington
Mermenton	St. Landry	South Bend	Concordia	Belfast	Waldo
Midway	Union	Southwest Pass	Plaquemine	Belgrade	Kennebec
Milliken's Bend	Madison	Sparta	Bienville	Belgrade Mills	Kennebec
Mill Creek	Sabine	Spearsville	Union	Belmont	Waldo
Mineral Springs	Union	Spring Creek	Rapides	Benton	Kennebec
Minden	Claiborne	Springfield	Livingston	Bethel	Oxford
Monroe	Wachita	Spring Place	Wachita	Biddeford	York
Montgomery	Winn	Spring Ridge	Caddo	Bingham	Somerset
Monticello	Carroll	Star	Assumption	Blanchard	Piscataquis
Mooringsport	Caddo	Stony Point	East Baton Rouge	Bloomfield	Somerset
Moranville	Avoyelles	Stubbs' Mills	Washington	Blue Hill	Hancock
Morganzia	Point Coupee	Sugar Creek	Claiborne	Blue Hill Falls	Hancock
Mound Bayou	Tensas	Sugartown	Calcasieu	Bolster's Mills	Cumberland
Mount Lebanon	Bienville	Sun	St. Tammany	Bonny Eagle	York
Mount Pleasant	Caldwell	Sunny Side	Caddo	Booth Bay	Lincoln
Mud Branch	Bienville	Tangapaho	St. Helena	Bowdoin	Sagadahoc
Nashborough	Sabine	Taylor	St. Charles	Bowdoin Center	Sagadahoc
Natchitoches	Natchitoches	Tickfaw	Livingston	Bowdoinham	Sagadahoc
Negreet	Sabine	The Village	Point Coupee	Bower Bank	Piscataquis
New Carthage	Madison	Thibodeaux	Lafourche	Bradford	Penobscot
New Iberia	St. Martin's	Tigerville	Terre Bonne	Brewer	Penobscot
New Orleans	Orleans	Tipton	Morehouse	Brewer Village	Penobscot
New River	Ascension	Tone's Bayou	Caddo	Bridgton	Cumberland
Oak Bluffs	Carroll	Tooley's	Concordia	Bridgewater	Aroostook
Oakley	Franklin	Toro	Sabine	Brighton	Somerset
Oakland	East Feliciana	Trenton	Wachita	Bristol	Lincoln
Opelousas	St. Landry	Trinity	Catahoula	Brooklin	Hancock
Old Field	Livingston	Tureand	Ascension	Brooks	Waldo
Omega	Madison	Union ≠ Roads	Union	Brooksville	Hancock
O'Rourke's	St. Tammany	Vacherie Roads	St. James	Brownfield	Oxford
Orchard Grove	Bossier	Vermillionville	Lafayette	Brown's Corner	Kennebec
Ouachita City	Union	Vernon	Jackson	Brownsville	Piscataquis
Paincortville	Assumption	Vienna	"	Brunswick	Cumberland
Palestine	Washington	Villa Platte	St. Landry	Bryant's Pond	Oxford
Parkersville	St. Tammany	Vista Ridge	Carroll	Buckfield	Oxford
Pattersonville	St. Mary's	Wallace Lake	De Soto	Buck's Mills	Hancock
Pecan Grove	Carroll	Walnut Creek	Bienville	Bucksport	Hancock
Perry's Bridge	Vermillion	Warsaw	Franklin	Bucksport Center	Hancock
Pine Ridge	Winn	Washington	St. Landry	Burlington	Penobscot
Pipesville	Union	Waterloo	Point Coupee	Burnham Village	Waldo
Plain'sStore	East Baton Rouge	Water Proof	Tensas	Buxton	York
Plainville	Bossier	West Fork	Calcasieu		

Post Office.	County.	Post Office.	County.	Post Office.	County.
Buxton Center	York	East Lowell	Penobscot	Green Bush	Penobscot
Byron	Oxford	East Machias	Washington	Greene	Androscoggin
Calais	Washington	East Madison	Somerset	Green's Corner	Androscoggin
Cambridge	Somerset	East Monmouth	Kennebec	Greenfield	Penobscot
Camden	Knox	East Montville	Waldo	Green's Landing	Hancock
Canaan	Somerset	East Newport	Penobscot	Greenville	Piscataquis
Canton	Oxford	East New Portland	Somerset	Greenwood	Oxford
Canton Mills	Oxford	East New Sharon	Franklin	Guilford	Piscataquis
Cape Elizabeth Depot	Cumberland	East New Vineyard	Franklin	Hallowell	Kennebec
		East Northport	Waldo	Hampden	Penobscot
Cape Neddick	York	E. N. Yarmouth	Cumberland	Hampden Corner	Penobscot
Carmel	Penobscot	East Orrington	Penobscot	Hancock	Hancock
Carroll	Penobscot	East Otisfield	Cumberland	Hanover	Oxford
Carritunk	Somerset	East Palermo	Waldo	Harmony	Somerset
Carthage	Franklin	East Parsonfield	York	Harrington	Washington
Carver's Harbor	Waldo	East Pittsfield	Somerset	Harrison	Cumberland
Casco	Cumberland	East Pittston	Kennebec	Hartford	Oxford
Castine	Hancock	East Poland	Androscoggin	Hartland	Somerset
Castle Hill	Aroostook	Eastport	Washington	Haynesville	Aroostook
Center Guilford	Piscataquis	East Raymond	Cumberland	Hebron	Oxford
Center Lebanon	York	East Roadfield	Kennebec	Hermon	Penobscot
Center Lincolnville	Waldo	East Rumford	Oxford	Hermon Pond	Penobscot
Center Lovell	Oxford	East Sangerville	Piscataquis	Highland	Somerset
Caribou	Aroostook	East Stetson	Penobscot	Hiram	Oxford
Center Montville	Waldo	East Stoneham	Oxford	Hodgdon	Aroostook
Center Sidney	Kennebec	East Strong	Franklin	Hodgdon's Mills	Lincoln
Charlestown	Penobscot	East Sullivan	Hancock	Holden	Penobscot
Charlotte	Washington	East Sumner	Oxford	Hollis	York
Chester	Penobscot	East Thorndike	Waldo	Hollis' Center	York
Chesterville	Franklin	East Trenton	Hancock	Hope	Knox
China	Kennebec	East Turner	Androscoggin	Houlton	Aroostook
Clinton	Kennebec	East Union	Knox	Howland	Penobscot
Columbia	Washington	East Vassalborough	Kennebec	Hudson	Penobscot
Concord	Somerset	East Wales	Androscoggin	Indian River	Washington
Conway	Aroostook	East Wilton	Franklin	Industry	Franklin
Cooper	Washington	East Windham	Cumberland	Islesborough	Waldo
Cooper Mills	Lincoln	East Winthrop	Kennebec	Isle Au Haut	Hancock
Corinna	Penobscot	Eden	Hancock	Jackson	Waldo
Corinna Center	Penobscot	Edinburgh	Penobscot	Jackson Brook	Washington
Corinth	Penobscot	Eddington	Penobscot	Jay	Franklin
Cornish	York	Edes' Falls	Cumberland	Jefferson	Lincoln
Cornville	Somerset	Edgecomb	Lincoln	Jonesborough	Washington
Cranberry Isles	Hancock	Elliot	York	Katahdin Iron Works	Piscataquis
Crawford	Washington	Elliottsville	Piscataquis		
Cumberland	Cumberland	Elliot Depot	York	Kendall's Mills	Somerset
Cumberland Center	"	Ellingwood's Corner	Waldo	Kenduskeag	Penobscot
Cushing	Lincoln	Ellsworth	Hancock	Kennebunk	York
Cross Hill	Kennebec	Ellsworth Falls	Hancock	Kennebunk Depot	York
Curtis' Corner	Kennebec	Embden	Somerset	Kennebunkport	York
Cutter	Washington	Embden Center	Somerset	Kent's Hill	Kennebec
Damariscotta Mills	Lincoln	Emery's Mills	York	Kezar Falls	York
Danville	Androscoggin	Enfield	Penobscot	Kilmarnock	Piscataquis
Deblois	Washington	Etna	Penobscot	Kingsbury	Piscataquis
Dead River	Somerset	Etna Center	Penobscot	Kingsfield	Franklin
Dedham	Hancock	Exeter	Penobscot	Kittery	York
Deer Isle	Hancock	Exeter Mills	Penobscot	Kittery Depot	York
Denmark	Oxford	Fairfield	Somerset	Kittery Point	York
Dennysville	Washington	Fairfield Corners	Somerset	Knox	Waldo
Detroit	Somerset	Falmouth	Cumberland	La Grange	Penobscot
Dexter	Penobscot	Farmington	Franklin	Lane's Brook	Washington
Dixfield	Oxford	Farmington Falls	Franklin	Larone	Somerset
Dixfield Center	Oxford	Fayette	Kennebec	Lebanon	York
Dixmont	Penobscot	Fayette Ridge	Kennebec	Lee	Penobscot
Dixmont Center	Penobscot	Flagstaff	Somerset	Leeds	Androscoggin
Dover	Piscataquis	Fort Fairfield	Aroostook	Leeds' Junction	Androscoggin
Dover South Mills	Piscataquis	Fort Kent	Aroostook	Levant	Penobscot
Dresden	Lincoln	Foxcroft	Piscataquis	Lewiston	Androscoggin
Dresden Mills	Lincoln	Frankfort Mills	Waldo	Lexington	Somerset
Durham	Androscoggin	Franklin	Hancock	Liberty	Waldo
Dirigo	Kennebec	Freedom	Waldo	Limerick	York
East Auburn	Cumberland	Freeman	Franklin	Limestone	Aroostook
East Baldwin	Cumberland	Fremont	Aroostook	Limington	York
East Benton	Kennebec	Freeport	Cumberland	Lincoln	Penobscot
East Bowdoinham	Sagadahoc	Friendship	Knox	Lincoln Center	Penobscot
East Bradford	Penobscot	Fryeburg	Oxford	Lincolnville	Waldo
East Bucksport	Hancock	Fryeburg Center	Oxford	Linneus	Aroostook
East Corinth	Penobscot	Gardiner	Kennebec	Lisbon	Androscoggin
East Dixfield	Oxford	Garland	Penobscot	Litchfield	Kennebec
East Dixmont	Penobscot	Georgetown	Sagadahoc	Litchfield Corners	Kennebec
East Dover	Piscataquis	Gilead	Oxford	Little River Village	Androscoggin
East Eddington	Penobscot	Glenburn	Penobscot		
East Eden	Hancock	Goodale's Corners	Penobscot	Littleton	Aroostook
East Exeter	Penobscot	Goodwin's Mills	York	Livermore	Androscoggin
East Fryeburg	Oxford	Gorham	Cumberland	Livermore Center	Androscoggin
East Hampden	Penobscot	Gouldsborough	Hancock	Livermore Falls	Androscoggin
East Hebron	Oxford	Grafton	Oxford	Locke's Mills	Oxford
East Holden	Penobscot	Grant Isle	Aroostook	Lovell	Oxford
East Knox	Waldo	Gray	Cumberland	Lowell	Penobscot
East Limington	York	Great Pond	Hancock	Lubec	Washington
East Livermore	Androscoggin	Great Works	Penobscot	Lubec Mills	Washington

POST OFFICES—MAINE.

Post Office.	County.	Post Office.	County.	Post Office.	County.
Lyman Center	York	North Hancock	Hancock	Pittston	Kennebec
Lyndon	Aroostook	North Hermann	Penobscot	Plantation No. 14	Washington
McLain's Mills	Waldo	North Hollis	York	Plymouth	Penobscot
Machias	Washington	North Howland	Penobscot	Poland	Androscoggin
Machiasport	Washington	North Islesborough	Waldo	Porter	Oxford
Madawaska	Aroostook	North Jay	Franklin	Portland	Cumberland
Madison	Somerset	North Kennebunkport	York	Pownal	Cumberland
Madison Center	Somerset	North Lebanon	York	Prentiss	Penobscot
Madrid	Franklin	North Leeds	Androscoggin	Presque Isle	Aroostook
Manchester	Kennebec	North Limington	York	Princeton	Washington
Maple Grove	Aroostook	North Linneus	Aroostook	Prospect Ferry	Waldo
Marion	Washington	North Livermore	Androscoggin	Prospect Harbor	Hancock
Mars Hill	Aroostook	North Lovell	Oxford	Rangeley	Franklin
Masardis	Aroostook	North Mariaville	Hancock	Rawson	Aroostook
Matinicus	Knox	North Monroe	Waldo	Raymond	Cumberland
Mattawamkeag	Penobscot	North Monmouth	Kennebec	Readfield	Kennebec
Maxfield	Penobscot	North Newcastle	Lincoln	Readfield Depot	Kennebec
Mechanic's Falls	Androscoggin	North Newfield	York	Red Beach	Washington
Medford	Piscataquis	North Newport	Penobscot	Richmond	Sagadahoc
Medway	Penobscot	North New Portland	Somerset	Richmond Corner	Sagadahoc
Medybemps	Washington	North Newry	Oxford	Ripley	Somerset
Mercer	Somerset	North Norway	Oxford	Robbinston	Washington
Mexico	Oxford	North Palermo	Waldo	Rockabema	Aroostook
Medford Center	Piscataquis	North Paris	Oxford	Rockland	Knox
Milford	Penobscot	North Parsonfield	York	Rockport	Knox
Millbridge	Washington	North Penobscot	Hancock	Rockville	Knox
Milltown	Washington	North Perry	Washington	Rome	Kennebec
Milo	Piscataquis	North Pittston	Kennebec	Ross Corner	York
Milton Plantation	Oxford	Northport	Waldo	Round Pond	Lincoln
Minot	Androscoggin	North Pownal	Cumberland	Roxbury	Oxford
Monhegan Island	Lincoln	North Prospect	Waldo	Rumford	Oxford
Monmouth	Kennebec	North Raymond	Cumberland	Rumford Center	Oxford
Monson	Piscataquis	North Searsmont	Waldo	Rumford Point	Oxford
Monroe	Waldo	North Searsport	Waldo	Sabatus	Androscoggin
Monroe Center	Waldo	North Sedgwick	Hancock	Saccarappa	Cumberland
Monticello	Aroostook	North Sidney	Kennebec	Saco	York
Montville	Waldo	North Shapleigh	York	St. Albany	Somerset
Moose River	Somerset	North Turner	Androscoggin	St. George	Knox
Moro	Aroostook	North Turner Bridge	"	Salem	Franklin
Morrill	Waldo	North Union	Knox	Salisbury Cove	Hancock
Mount Desert	Hancock	North Vassalborough	Kennebec	Salmon Brook	Aroostook
Mount Vernon	Kennebec	North Vienna	Kennebec	Sandy Beach	Cumberland
Naples	Cumberland	North Waldoborough	Lincoln	Sandy Point	Waldo
Narraguagus	Washington	North Washington	Lincoln	Sanford	York
Newburg	Penobscot	North Waterford	Oxford	Saugerville	Piscataquis
Newburg Center	Penobscot	North Wayne	Kennebec	Scarborough	Cumberland
New Casco	Cumberland	North Whitefield	Lincoln	Seal Cove	Hancock
New Castle	Lincoln	North Wilton	Franklin	Searsmont	Waldo
Newfield	York	North Windham	Cumberland	Searsport	Waldo
New Gloucester	Cumberland	North Winterport	Waldo	Sebago	Cumberland
New Limerick	Aroostook	North Woodstock	Oxford	Sebec	Piscataquis
Newport	Penobscot	North Woodville	Penobscot	Sedgwick	Hancock
New Portland	Somerset	North Yarmouth	Cumberland	Shapleigh	York
Newry	Oxford	Norway	Oxford	Sheepscott Bridge	Lincoln
New Sharon	Franklin	Number Three	Aroostook	Shirley	Piscataquis
New Vineyard	Franklin	Oak Hill	Cumberland	Shirley Mills	Piscataquis
Noblesborough	Lincoln	Oak Hill Station	Cumberland	Sidney	Kennebec
Norridgewock	Somerset	Oceanville	Hancock	Six Mile Falls	Penobscot
North Acton	York	Ogunquit	York	Skowhegan	Somerset
North Albany	Oxford	Olamon	Penobscot	Small Point	Sagadahoc
North Anson	Somerset	Old Town	Penobscot	Smithfield	Somerset
North Appleton	Knox	Orient	Aroostook	Smyrna	Aroostook
North Auburn	Androscoggin	Orland	Hancock	Smyrna Mills	Aroostook
North Baldwin	Cumberland	Oroneville	Piscataquis	Snow Falls	Oxford
North Bangor	Penobscot	Orono	Penobscot	Solon	Somerset
North Belgrade	Kennebec	Orrington	Penobscot	Somerville	Lincoln
North Berwick	York	Otis	Hancock	Somerset Mills	Somerset
North Blue Hill	Hancock	Otisfield	Cumberland	South Acton	York
North Boothbay	Lincoln	Owl's Head	Lincoln	South Albion	Kennebec
North Bradford	Penobscot	Oxford	Oxford	South Andover	Oxford
North Bridgton	Cumberland	Palermo	Waldo	South Atkinson	Piscataquis
North Brooklin	Hancock	Palermo Center	Waldo	South Berwick	York
North Brownsville	Piscataquis	Palmyra	Somerset	South Beddington	Washington
North Buckfield	Oxford	Paris	Oxford	South Berwick Junction	York
North Bucksport	Hancock	Parker's Head	Sagadahoc	South Bridgton	Cumberland
North Carmel	Penobscot	Parkman	Piscataquis	South Bristol	Lincoln
North Castine	Hancock	Parlin Pond	Somerset	South Brooks	Waldo
North Chesterville	Franklin	Parsonfield	York	South Brooksville	Hancock
North Cutler	Washington	Passadumkeag	Penobscot	South Casco	Cumberland
North Dixmont	Penobscot	Parkman Center	Piscataquis	South Charleston	Penobscot
Northeast Dixmont	Penobscot	Patten	Penobscot	South Chesterville	Franklin
North Edgecomb	Lincoln	Pemaquid	Lincoln	South China	Kennebec
North Ellsworth	Hancock	Pembroke	Washington	South Corinth	Penobscot
North Fayette	Kennebec	Penobscot	Hancock	South Deer Isle	Hancock
North Fairfield	Somerset	Perry	Washington	South Dexter	Penobscot
Northfield	Washington	Peru	Oxford	South Dover	Piscataquis
North Frankfort	Waldo	Phillips	Franklin	South Durham	Androscoggin
North Fryeburg	Oxford	Phipsburg	Sagadahoc	South Exeter	Penobscot
North Gray	Cumberland	Pishon's Ferry	Kennebec	South Freedom	Waldo
North Haven	Knox	Pittsfield	Somerset	South Freeport	Cumberland

POST OFFICES—MARYLAND.

Post Office.	County.
South Hartford	Oxford
South Hope	Knox
South Jefferson	Lincoln
South Leeds	Androscoggin
South Levant	Penobscot
South Liberty	Waldo
South Lincoln	Penobscot
South Litchfield	Kennebec
South Livermore	Androscoggin
South Moluncus	Aroostook
South Monmouth	Kennebec
South Montville	Waldo
South Newburg	Penobscot
South Norridgewock	Somerset
South Orrington	Penobscot
South Paris	Oxford
South Parkman	Piscataquis
South Parsonfield	York
South Penobscot	Hancock
Southport	Lincoln
South Princeton	Washington
South Robinson	Washington
South St. George	Knox
South Sanford	York
South Sangerville	Piscataquis
South Sebec	Piscataquis
South Solon	Somerset
South Thomaston	Knox
South Vassalborough	Kennebec
South Waterford	Oxford
South West Harbor	Hancock
South Windham	Cumberland
South Windsor	Kennebec
South Winn	Penobscot
Springfield	Penobscot
Springvale	York
Standish	Cumberland
Stark	Somerset
Steep Falls	Cumberland
Stetson	Penobscot
Steuben	Washington
Stevens' Plains	Cumberland
Stockton	Waldo
Stow	Oxford
Strickland Ferry	Kennebec
Strong	Franklin
Sullivan	Hancock
Sumner	Oxford
Surry	Hancock
Swan's Island	Hancock
Swanville	Waldo
Sweden	Oxford
Temple Mills	Franklin
Tenant's Harbor	Knox
The Forks	Somerset
Thomaston	Knox
Thorndike	Waldo
Tilden	Hancock
Togus Springs	Kennebec
Topsfield	Washington
Topsham	Sagadahoc
Tremont	Hancock
Trenton Point	Hancock
Troy	Waldo
Troy Center	Waldo
Turner	Androscoggin
Union	Knox
Unity	Waldo
Upper Gloucester	Cumberland
Upper Stillwater	Penobscot
Upton	Oxford
Van Buren	Aroostook
Vassalborough	Kennebec
Veazie	Penobscot
Vienna	Kennebec
Waite	Washington
Waldo	Waldo
Waldoborough	Lincoln
Wales	Androscoggin
Waltham	Hancock
Walton Mills	Kennebec
Warren	Knox
Washington	Knox
Waterborough	York
Waterborough Center	York
Waterford	Oxford
Waterville	Kennebec
Wayne	Kennebec
Webb's Mills	Cumberland
Webster	Androscoggin

Post Office.	County.
Weck's Mills	Kennebec
Welchville	Oxford
Weld	Franklin
Wellington	Piscataquis
Wells	York
Wells' Depot	York
Wesley	Washington
West Anson	Somerset
West Auburn	Androscoggin
West Baldwin	Cumberland
West Bethel	Oxford
West Bowdoin	Sagadahoc
West Bridgeton	Cumberland
West Brooksville	Hancock
West Buxton	York
West Camden	Knox
West Charleston	Penobscot
West Corinna	Penobscot
West Cumberland	Cumberland
West Danville	Androscoggin
West Dover	Piscataquis
West Durham	Androscoggin
West Eden	Hancock
West Ellsworth	Hancock
West Enfield	Penobscot
West Falmouth	Cumberland
West Farmingdale	Kennebec
West Freeman	Franklin
West Gardiner	Kennebec
West Garland	Penobscot
West Glenburn	Penobscot
West Gloucester	Cumberland
West Gorham	Cumberland
West Gouldsborough	Hancock
West Great Works	Penobscot
West Hampden	Penobscot
West Jefferson	Lincoln
West Lebanon	York
Wese Levant	Penobscot
West Lubec	Washington
West Minot	Androscoggin
West Moscow	Somerset
West Newfield	York
Weston	Aroostook
West Paris	Oxford
West Parsonfield	York
West Peru	Oxford
West Poland	Androscoggin
West Pownal	Cumberland
Westport	Lincoln
West Ripley	Somerset
West Sedgwick	Hancock
West Sidney	Kennebec
West's Mills	Franklin
West Sumner	Oxford
West Trenton	Hancock
West Troy	Waldo
West Washington	Lincoln
West Waterville	Kennebec
Whitefield	Lincoln
White Rock	Cumberland
Whitneyville	Washington
Whiting	Washington
Williamsburg	Piscataquis
Winnegance	Sagadahoc
Winslow	Kennebec
Wilson's Mills	Oxford
Wilton	Franklin
Windham	Cumberland
Windsor	Kennebec
Winn	Penobscot
Winter Harbor	Hancock
Winthrop	Kennebec
Wiscasset	Lincoln
Woodstock	Oxford
Woodville	Penobscot
Woolwich	Sagadahoc
Winterport	Waldo
Yarmouth	Cumberland
York	York

Maryland.

Post Office.	County.
Abingdon	Hartford
Accident	Alleghany

Post Office.	County.
Adamstown	Frederick
Agricultural College	Prince George's
Airays	Dorchester
Alberton	Howard
Allen's Fresh	Charles
Annapolis	Anne Arundel
Annapolis Junction	"
Aquasco	Prince George's
Bachman's Mills	Carroll
Backlingan	Baltimore
Bakersville	Washington
Baltimore	Baltimore
Bark Hill	Carroll
Barnesville	Montgomery
Barrallville	Alleghany
Barren Creek Spring	Somerset
Barry	Frederick
Barton	Alleghany
Bay Hundred	Talbot
Bay View	Cecil
Beantown	Charles
Beaver Creek	Washington
Bel Air	Harford
Beltsville	Prince George's
Benedict	Charles
Benevola	Washington
Berlin	Worcester
Bethlehem	Carolina
Big Mills	Durchester
Bird Hill	Carroll
Bishop's Head	Dorchester
Bishopsville	Worcester
Black Rock	Baltimore
Bladensburg	Prince George's
Bloomington	Alleghany
Blue Ball	Cecil
Bohemia Mills	Cecil
Bolivar	Frederick
Boonesville	Caroline
Boonsborough	Washington
Brady's Mills	Alleghany
Brandywine	Prince George's
Brick Meeting House	Cecil
Bridgeport	Frederick
Bridgetown	Caroline
Bristol	Anne Arundel
Broad Creek	Queen Anne
Brooklandville	Baltimore
Brookville	Montgomery
Brownsville	Washington
Bruceville	Carroll
Bryantown	Charles
Buchanan	Baltimore
Buckeytown	Frederick
Backlingen	Baltimore
Bucktown	Dorchester
Buena Vista	Prince George's
Burkittsville	Frederick
Burnettsville	Somerset
Burnt Mills	Montgomery
Burrsville	Caroline
Butler	Baltimore
Calverton Mills	"
Cambridge	Dorchester
Carrollton	Carroll
Catonsville	Baltimore
Cavertown	Washington
Cecilton	Cecil
Cedar Creek	Dorchester
Centerville	Queen Anne
Central	Kent
Chapel	Talbot
Chaptico	St. Mary's
Charlestown	Cecil
Charlotte Hall	St. Mary's
Cherry Hill	Cecil
Chesapeake City	"
Chestertown	Kent
Chesterville	"
Chewsville	Washington
Church Creek	Dorchester
Church Hill	Queen Anne
Churchville	Harford
Clarksburg	Montgomery
Clarkaville	Howard
Clayton	Harford
Clear Spring	Washington
Clermont Mills	Harford
Cookeysville	Baltimore

POST OFFICES—MARYLAND.

Post Office.	County.
Colesville	Montgomery
College of St. James	Washington
Collington	Prince George's
Conococheague	Washington
Cooksville	Howard
Cornersville	Dorchester
Cotocton Furnace	Frederick
Cottage	Montgomery
Crampton	Queen Anne
Cragerstown	Frederick
Croom	Prince George's
Crotcher's Ferry	Dorchester
Cumberland	Alleghany
Crownsville	Anne Arundel
Damascus	Montgomery
Darlington	Harford
Daruestown	Montgomery
Davidsonville	Anne Arundel
Deal's Island	Somerset
Delmar	"
Denton	Caroline
Derricksons ⋈ Roads	Worcester
Doncaster	Charles
Dorsey's Store	Howard
Double Pipe Creek	Carroll
Downsville	Washington
Drawbridge	Dorchester
Dublin	Harford
Duffield	Charles
Dulaney's Valley	Baltimore
Dunkirk	Calvert
East New Market	Dorchester
Easton	Talbot
Edesville	Kent
Elk Ridge Landing	Howard
Elkton	Cecil
Ellengowan	Baltimore
Ellicott's Mills	Howard
Emmittsburg	Frederick
Emmorton	Harford
Fair Hill	Cecil
Fair View	Harford
Fallston	"
Farmington	Cecil
Federal Hill	Harford
Federalsburg	Dorchester
Finksburg	Carroll
Fishing Creek	Dorchester
Flintstone	Alleghany
Forest Hill	Harford
Forest Home	Anne Arundel
Forest Oak	Montgomery
Fork Meeting House	Baltimore
Forktown	Somerset
Fort Washington	Prince George's
Four Locks	Washington
Fowling Creek	Caroline
Franklinville	Carroll
Frankville	Alleghany
Frederick	Frederick
Freedom	Carroll
Freeland	Baltimore
Friendship	Anne Arundel
Frizelburg	Carroll
Frostburg	Alleghany
Funkstown	Washington
Galena	Kent
Galestown	Dorchester
Gallant Green	Charles
Glenelg	Howard
Glenville	Harford
Glymont	Charles
Golden Hill	Dorchester
Gorsuck's Mills	Baltimore
Goshen	Montgomery
Govanstown	Baltimore
Governor's Bridge	Anne Arundel
Graceham	Frederick
Grantsville	Alleghany
Grave Run Mills	Baltimore
Great Mills	St. Mary's
Greenfield Mills	Frederick
Greensboro'	Caroline
Green Spring	Baltimore
Green Spring Furnace	Washington
Greenwood	Baltimore
Hagerstown	Washington
Hall's ⋈ Roads	Harford
Hampstead	Carroll
Hancock	Washington
Hanesville	Kent
Harewood	Howard
Harford Furnace	Harford
Harmony	Kent
Harney	Carroll
Harrison	Dorchester
Harrisonville	Baltimore
Haver de Grace	Harford
Head of Sassafras	Kent
Hereford	Baltimore
Hickory Tavern	Harford
Hicksburgh	Dorchester
Hillsboro'	Caroline
Hill's Point	Dorchester
Hood's Mills	Carroll
Hookstown	Baltimore
Hooperville	Dorchester
Hooversville	Anne Arundel
Hope	Somerset
Hopewell ⋈ Roads	Somerset
Horsehead	Prince George's
Honck's Store	Carroll
Huntingtown	Calvert
Hyattstown	Montgomery
Hyattsville	Prince George's
Ijamsville	Frederick
Indian Springs	Washington
Ilchester Mills	Howard
Jarrettsville	Harford
Jefferson	Frederick
Jerusalem Mills	Harford
Johnson's Store	Anne Arundel
Johnstown	Alleghany
Keedysville	Washington
Kemptown	Frederick
Kingston	Somerset
Krigham's	Alleghany
Kroh's Mills	Carroll
Ladiesburg	Frederick
Lakesville	Dorchester
Lapidum	Harford
Lappon's ⋈ Roads	Washington
Lauraville	Baltimore
Laurel Factory	Prince George's
Laytousville	Montgomery
Leitersburg	Washington
Leonardstown	St. Mary's
Lewistown	Frederick
Libertytown	"
Lindsoyville	Worcester
Linganore	Frederick
Lisbon	Howard
Little Gunpowder	Baltimore
Lonaconing	Alleghany
Long Green Academy	Baltimore
Long Marsh	Queen Anne
on Old Fields	Prince George's
Lower Marlboro'	Calvert
Lutherville	Baltimore
McKinstry's Mills	Carroll
Magnolia	Harford
Manchester	Carroll
Marriottsville	Howard
Maryland Line	Baltimore
Massey's ⋈ Roads	Kent
Matthews' Store	Howard
Mechanicstown	Frederick
Melville	Caroline
Michaelsville	Harford
Middlebrook	Montgomery
Middleburg	Carroll
Middletown	Frederick
Milestown	St. Mary's
Milford Mills	Harford
Millersville	Anne Arundel
Mill Green	Harford
Millington	Kent
Millstone Point	Washington
Monkton Mills	Baltimore
Monocacy	Montgomery
Monrovia	Frederick
Mount Airy	Carroll
Mount Olive	St. Mary's
Mount Pleasant	Frederick
Mount Savage	Alleghany
Mount Washington	Baltimore
Myersville	Frederick
Nanjemoy	Charles
Newark	Worcester
Newbury	Charles
New Hope	Caroline
New London	Frederick
New Market	"
Newport	Charles
Newtown	Worcester
New Windsor	Carroll
North Branch	Baltimore
Northeast	Cecil
Nottingham	Prince George's
Oakland	Alleghany
Oak Orchard	Frederick
Oakville	St. Mary's
Oldtown	Alleghany
Olney	Montgomery
Orleans	Alleghany
Owing's Mills	Baltimore
Oxford	Talbot
Paper Mills	Baltimore
Parkton	"
Patuxent	Anne Arundel
Patuxent City	Charles
Perrymansville	Harford
Perryville	Cecil
Petersville	Frederick
Phœnix	Baltimore
Philopolis	"
Pikesville	Baltimore
Piney Creek	Carroll
Piscataway	Prince George's
Pisgah	Charles
Pleasantville	Harford
Point Lookout	St. Mary's
Point of Rocks	Frederick
Pomonkey	Charles
Poolsville	Montgomery
Poplar Springs	Howard
Port Deposit	Cecil
Port Herman	"
Port Republic	Calvert
Port Tobacco	Charles
Potter's Landing	Caroline
Powellsville	Worcester
Powhatan	Baltimore
Preston	Caroline
Prince Fredericktown	Calvert
Princess Anne	Somerset
Principio	Cecil
Principio Furnace	Cecil
Pylesville	Harford
Quantico	Somerset
Queen Anne	Prince George's
Queenstown	Queen Anne
Randallstown	Baltimore
Rawling's Station	Alleghany
Rehoboth	Somerset
Reisterstown	Baltimore
Ridge	St. Mary's
Ringgold	Washington
Rising Sun	Cecil
Riverton	Somerset
Roachville	Somerset
Rock Hall	Kent
Rock Springs	Cecil
Rockville	Montgomery
Roesville	Queen Anne
Roger's Store	Kent
Rohrersville	Washington
Rossville	Baltimore
Rowlandsville	Cecil
Roxbury Mills	Howard
Royal Oak	Talbot
Sabillasville	Frederick
Saint Augustine	Cecil
Saint Dennis	Baltimore
Saint Inegoes	St. Mary's
Saint Leonard's	Calvert
Saint Margaret's	Anne Arundel
Saint Martin's	Worcester
Saint Michael's	Talbot
Salisbury	Somerset
Sam's Creek	Carroll
Sandy Hill	Worcester
Sandy Spring	Montgomery
Savage	Howard
Selbysport	Alleghany
Sharpsburg	Washington
Sharpstown	Somerset

POST OFFICES—MASSACHUSETTS. 37

Post Office.	County.
Shawan	Baltimore
Shawsville	Harford
Shelltown	Somerset
Silver Run	Carroll
Skipton	Talbot
Smithsburg	Washington
Smithville	Caroline
Snow Hill	Worcester
South Milford	Cecil
South River	Anne Arundel
Spencerville	Montgomery
Stablersville	Baltimore
Still Pond	Kent
Sudlersville	Queen Anne
Summitville	Alleghany
Sunderlandville	Calvert
Surratt's	Prince George's
Swanton	Alleghany
Sweet Air	Baltimore
Sykesville	Carroll
Taneytown	"
Taylor	Harford
Taylor's Island	Dorchester
T. B.	Prince George's
Templeville	Queen Anne
Thomas' Run	Harford
Tilghmantown	Washington
Tobacco Stick	Dorchester
Tompkinsville	Charles
Towsontown	Baltimore
Tracy's Landing	Anne Arundel
Trappe	Talbot
Triadelphia	Montgomery
Tyaskin	Somerset
Union Bridge	Carroll
Union Meeting House	Baltimore
Union Mills	Carroll
Uniontown	"
Unionville	Frederick
Unity	Montgomery
Upperco	Baltimore
Upper ½ Roads	Harford
Upper Falls	Baltimore
Upper Marlboro'	Prince George's
Upper Trappe	Somerset
Urbana	Frederick
Urieville	Kent
Utica Mills	Frederick
Vienna	Dorchester
Wakefield	Carroll
Walkersville	Frederick
Warfieldburg	Carroll
Warren	Baltimore
Warwick	Cecil
Watersville	Carroll
Weisesburg	Baltimore
Westernman's Mills	"
Westernport	Alleghany
Westminster	Carroll
West Nottingham	Cecil
West River	Anne Arundel
Wetheredville	Baltimore
Weverton	Frederick
Whaleysville	Worcester
Wheatland	Dorchester
White Hall	Baltimore
White Haven	Somerset
Williamsburg	Dorchester
Williamsport	Washington
Winfield	Carroll
Winston	Alleghany
Wolfsville	Frederick
Woodbury	Baltimore
Woodbine	Carroll
Woodensburg	Baltimore
Wool Lawn	Cecil
Woodsborough	Frederick
Woodstock	Howard
Wye Mills	Queen Anne
Zion	Cecil
Zoucksville	Baltimore

Massachusetts.

Post Office.	County.
Abington	Plymouth
Acton	Middlesex
Adams	Berkshire
Adamsville	Franklin
Agawam	Hampden
Alford	Berkshire
Amesbury	Essex
Amherst	Hampshire
Andover	Essex
Annisquam	Essex
Ashburnham	Worcester
Ashburnham Depot	Worcester
Ashby	Middlesex
Ashfield	Franklin
Ashland	Middlesex
Ashley's Falls	Berkshire
Ashleyville	Hampden
Assabet	Middlesex
Athol	Worcester
Athol Depot	Worcester
Attleborough	Bristol
Auburn	Worcester
Auburn Dale	Middlesex
Baldwinsville	Worcester
Ballard Vale	Essex
Bancroft	Berkshire
Barnstable	Barnstable
Barre	Worcester
Barre Plains	Worcester
Beckett	Berkshire
Bedford	Middlesex
Belchertown	Hampshire
Bellingham	Norfolk
Belmont	Middlesex
Bernardstown	Franklin
Berkley	Bristol
Berkshire	Berkshire
Berlin	Worcester
Beverly	Essex
Beverly Farms	Essex
Billerica	Middlesex
Blackinton	Berkshire
Blackstone	Worcester
Blanford	Hampden
Bolton	Worcester
Bond's Village	Hampden
Boston	Suffolk
Boston Corner	Berkshire
Boxborough	Middlesex
Boxford	Essex
Boylston	Worcester
Boylston Center	Worcester
Bradford	Essex
Braggville	Middlesex
Braintree	Norfolk
Brewster	Barnstable
Bridgewater	Plymouth
Brighton	Middlesex
Brimfield	Hampden
Brookfield	Worcester
Brookline	Norfolk
Buckland	Franklin
Burlington	Middlesex
Burrageville	Worcester
Byfield	Essex
Cambridge	Middlesex
Cambridgeport	Middlesex
Campello	Plymouth
Canton	Norfolk
Carlisle	Middlesex
Carver	Plymouth
Centerville	Barnstable
Charlemont	Franklin
Charles River Village	Norfolk
Charlestown	Middlesex
Charlton	Worcester
Charlton Depot	Worcester
Chatham	Barnstable
Chelmsford	Middlesex
Chelsea	Suffolk
Cherry Valley	Worcester
Cheshire	Berkshire
Chester	Hampden
Chester Factories	Hampden
Chesterfield	Hampshire
Chicopee	Hampden
Chicopee Falls	Hampden

Post Office.	County.
Chilmark	Dukes
Chiltonville	Plymouth
Clappville	Worcester
Cliftondale	Essex
Clinton	Worcester
Cochesett	Plymouth
Cohasset	Norfolk
Cold Brook	Worcester
Cold Spring	Berkshire
Colerain	Franklin
College Hill	Middlesex
Collins' Depot	Hampden
Concord	Middlesex
Conway	Franklin
Cordaville	Worcester
Cotuitport	Barnstable
Cunnington	Hampshire
Cunnington West Village	
	Hampshire
Curtinsville	Berkshire
Dana	Worcester
Dalton	Berkshire
Danvers	Essex
Danvers Center	Essex
Danversport	Essex
Dartmouth	Bristol
Dedham	Norfolk
Deerfield	Franklin
Denn's	Barnstable
Dighton	Bristol
Dorchester	Norfolk
Douglass	Worcester
Dover	Norfolk
Dracut	Middlesex
Dudley	Worcester
Dunstable	Middlesex
Duxbury	Plymouth
East Abington	Plymouth
East Brewster	Barnstable
East Bridgewater	Plymouth
East Brinfield	Hampden
East Brookfield	Worcester
East Cambridge	Middlesex
East Charlemont	Franklin
East Dennis	Barnstable
East Douglass	Worcester
East Falmouth	Barnstable
East Foxborough	Norfolk
East Freetown	Bristol
East Granville	Hampden
East Gloucester	Essex
Eastham	Barnstable
East Hampton	Hampshire
East Harwich	Barnstable
East Haverhill	Essex
East Holliston	Middlesex
East Lee	Berkshire
East Lexington	Middlesex
East Long Meadow	Hampden
East Marshfield	Plymouth
East Medway	Norfolk
East Middleborough	Plymouth
Easton	Bristol
East Orleans	Barnstable
East Pepperell	Middlesex
East Princeton	Worcester
East Randolph	Norfolk
East Salisbury	Essex
East Sandwich	Barnstable
East Sharon	Norfolk
East Sheffield	Berkshire
East Shelburne	Franklin
East Stoughton	Norfolk
East Taunton	Bristol
East Walpole	Norfolk
East Wareham	Plymouth
East Weymouth	Norfolk
East Whately	Franklin
East Windsor	Berkshire
East Woburn	Middlesex
Edgartown	Dukes
Enfield	Hampshire
Erving	Franklin
Essex	Essex
Fairhaven	Bristol
Fairmount	Norfolk
Fall River	Bristol
Falmouth	Barnstable
Farnumsville	Worcester
Feeding Hills	Hampden

38 POST OFFICES—MASSACHUSETTS.

Post Office.	County.	Post Office.	County.	Post Office.	County.
Feltonsville	Middlesex	Long Plain	Bristol	North Easton	Bristol
Fiskedale	Worcester	Lowell	Middlesex	North Eastham	Barnstable
Fitchburg	Worcester	Ludlow	Hampden	North Egremont	Berkshire
Florence	Hampshire	Lunenburg	Worcester	North Fairhaven	Bristol
Florida	Berkshire	Lynn	Essex	North Falmouth	Barnstable
Forge Village	Middlesex	Lynnfield	Essex	Northfield	Franklin
Foxborough	Norfolk	Lynnfield Center	Essex	Northfield Farms	Franklin
Framingham	Middlesex	Malden	Middlesex	North Hadley	Hampshire
Franklin	Norfolk	Manchester	Essex	North Leominster	Worcester
Franklin City	Norfolk	Mansfield	Bristol	North Leverett	Franklin
Freetown	Bristol	Maplewood	Middlesex	North Marshfield	Plymouth
Gardner	Worcester	Marblehead	Essex	N. Middleborough	Plymouth
Georgetown	Essex	Marlborough	Middlesex	North New Salem	Franklin
Gilbertville	Worcester	Marion	Franklin	North Orange	Franklin
Gill	Franklin	Marshfield	Plymouth	North Oxford	Worcester
Glendale	Berkshire	Marston's Mills	Barnstable	North Pembroke	Plymouth
Globe Village	Worcester	Mattapan	Norfolk	North Plymton	Plymouth
Gloucester	Essex	Mattapoisett	Plymouth	North Prescott	Hampshire
Goshen	Hampshire	Medfield	Norfolk	North Reading	Middlesex
Grafton	Worcester	Medford	Middlesex	North Rehoboth	Bristol
Granby	Hampshire	Medway	Norfolk	North Rochester	Plymouth
Graniteville	Middlesex	Melrose	Middlesex	North Sandwich	Barnstable
Grantville	Norfolk	Mendon	Worcester	North Scituate	Plymouth
Granville Corners	Hampden	Methuen	Essex	North Spencer	Worcester
Great Barrington	Berkshire	Middleborough	Plymouth	North Sudbury	Middlesex
Greenfield	Franklin	Middlefield	Hampshire	North Swansea	Bristol
Greenwich	Hampshire	Middlesex Village	Middlesex	North Tewksbury	Middlesex
Greenwich Village	Hampshire	Middleton	Essex	North Truro	Barnstable
Greenwood	Middlesex	Milford	Worcester	North Uxbridge	Worcester
Groton	Middlesex	Millburg	Worcester	North West Bridgewater	Plymouth
Grout's Corners	Franklin	Mill River	Berkshire		Plymouth
Groveland	Essex	Millville	Worcester	North Westport	Bristol
Hadley	Hampshire	Milton	Norfolk	North Weymouth	Norfolk
Halifax	Plymouth	Mirickville	Bristol	North Wilmington	Middlesex
Hamilton	Essex	Mittenague	Hampden	North Woburn	Middlesex
Hancock	Berkshire	Monroe	Franklin	North Wrentham	Norfolk
Hanover	Plymouth	Monson	Hampden	Norton	Bristol
Hanson	Plymouth	Montague	Franklin	Norwich	Hampshire
Hardwick	Worcester	Monterey	Berkshire	Oakdale	Worcester
Harrison Square	Norfolk	Montgomery	Hampden	Oakham	Worcester
Hartsville	Berkshire	Montville	Berkshire	Orange	Franklin
Harvard	Worcester	Monument	Barnstable	Orleans	Barnstable
Harwich	Barnstable	Mount Auburn	Middlesex	Osterville	Barnstable
Harwichport	Barnstable	Nahant	Essex	Otis	Berkshire
Hatchville	Barnstable	Nantucket	Nantucket	Otter River	Worcester
Hatfield	Hampshire	Natick	Middlesex	Oxford	Worcester
Haverhill	Essex	Needham	Norfolk	Palmer	Hampden
Hawley	Franklin	Neponset Village	Norfolk	Paxton	Worcester
Hayden Row	Middlesex	New Ashford	Berkshire	Pelham	Hampshire
Haydenville	Hampshire	New Bedford	Bristol	Pembroke	Plymouth
Heath	Franklin	New Boston	Berkshire	Pepperell	Middlesex
Hingham	Plymouth	New Braintree	Worcester	Peru	Berkshire
Hinsdale	Berkshire	Newburyport	Essex	Petersham	Worcester
Hebronville	Bristol	New England Village	Worcester	Phillipston	Worcester
Hinsdale Depot	Berkshire	New Lenox	Berkshire	Pigeon Cove	Essex
Holden	Worcester	New Marlborough	Berkshire	Pittsfield	Berkshire
Holland	Hampden	New Salem	Franklin	Plainfield	Hampshire
Holliston	Middlesex	Newton	Middlesex	Plainville	Norfolk
Holmes' Hole	Dukes	Newton Center	Middlesex	Plymouth	Plymouth
Holyoke	Hampden	Newton Lower Falls	Middlesex	Plympton Station	Plymouth
Hoosac Tunnel	Berkshire	Newton Upper Falls	Middlesex	Plympton	Plymouth
Hopkinton	Middlesex	Newtonville	Middlesex	Pocasset	Barnstable
Housatonic	Berkshire	North Abington	Plymouth	Prescott	Hampshire
Hubbardston	Worcester	North Adams	Berkshire	Princeton	Worcester
Hull	Plymouth	North Amherst	Hampshire	Provincetown	Barnstable
Huntington	Hampshire	Northampton	Hampshire	Quincy	Norfolk
Hyannis	Barnstable	North Andover	Essex	Quincy Point	Norfolk
Indian Orchard	Hampden	North Andover Depot	Essex	Randolph	Norfolk
Ipswich	Essex	North Attleborough	Bristol	Reading	Middlesex
Ireland	Hampden	North Becket	Berkshire	Rehoboth	Bristol
Jamaica Plains	Norfolk	North Bellingham	Norfolk	Richmond	Berkshire
Kingston	Plymouth	North Beverly	Essex	Ringville	Hampshire
Lancaster	Worcester	North Billerica	Middlesex	Rochester	Plymouth
Lanesborough	Berkshire	North Blanford	Hampden	Rock	Plymouth
Lakeville	Plymouth	North Blackstone	Worcester	Rock Bottom	Middlesex
Lanesville	Essex	Northborough	Worcester	Rockport	Essex
Lawrence	Essex	Northbridge	Worcester	Rockville	Norfolk
Lee	Berkshire	Northbridge Center	Worcester	Rowe	Franklin
Leeds	Hampshire	North Bridgewater	Plymouth	Rowley	Essex
Leicester	Worcester	North Brookfield	Worcester	Roxbury	Norfolk
Lenox	Berkshire	North Cambridge	Middlesex	Royalston	Worcester
Lenox Furnace	Berkshire	North Carver	Plymouth	Russell	Hampden
Leominster	Worcester	North Chatham	Barnstable	Rutland	Worcester
Leverett	Franklin	North Chelmsford	Middlesex	Salem	Essex
Lexington	Middlesex	North Chelsea	Suffolk	Salisbury	Essex
Leyden	Franklin	North Cluster	Hampden	Sandisfield	Berkshire
Lincoln	Middlesex	North Cohasset	Norfolk	Sandwich	Barnstable
Littleton	Middlesex	North Dana	Worcester	Saugus	Essex
Lock's Village	Franklin	North Dartmouth	Bristol	Saugus Center	Essex
Long Meadow	Hampden	North Dighton	Bristol	Saundersville	Worcester

POST OFFICES—MICHIGAN. 39

Post Office.	County.	Post Office.	County.	Post Office.	County.
Savoy	Berkshire	Island	Hampden	Wilkinsonville	Worcester
Saxonville	Middlesex	Topsfield	Essex	Williamsburgh	Hampshire
Scituate	Plymouth	Townsend	Middlesex	Williamstown	Berkshire
Scotland	Plymouth	Townsend Harbor	Middlesex	Willimansett	Hampden
Seekonk	Bristol	Truro	Barnstable	Wilmington	Middlesex
Sharon	Norfolk	Tyngsborough	Middlesex	Winchendom	Worcester
Sheffield	Berkshire	Tyringham	Berkshire	Winchester	Middlesex
Shelburne	Franklin	Upton	Worcester	Windsor	Berkshire
Shelburne Falls	Franklin	Uxbridge	Worcester	Winthrop	Suffolk
Sheldonville	Norfolk	Van Deusenville	Berkshire	Woburn	Middlesex
Sherborn	Middlesex	Wachusett Village	Worcester	Wood's Hole	Barnstable
Shirley	Middlesex	Wales	Hampden	Woodville	Middlesex
Shirley Village	Middlesex	Walpole	Norfolk	Worcester	Worcester
Shrewsbury	Worcester	Ware	Hampshire	Worthington	Hampshire
Sippican	Plymouth	Wareham	Plymouth	Wrentham	Norfolk
Somerset	Bristol	Waltham	Middlesex	Yarmouth	Barnstable
Somerville	Middlesex	Waquoit	Barnstable	Yarmouth Point	Barnstable
South Acton	Middlesex	Warren	Worcester	Zoar	Franklin
South Abington	Plymouth	Warwick	Franklin		
South Amesbury	Essex	Washington	Berkshire		
Southampton	Hampshire	Watertown	Middlesex		
South Attleborough	Bristol	Wayland	Middlesex	## Michigan.	
South Amherst	Hampshire	Webster	Worcester		
South Braintree	Norfolk	Wellfleet	Barnstable		
Southbridge	Worcester	Wendell	Franklin	Post Office.	County.
South Carver	Plymouth	Wendell Depot	Franklin		
South Danvers	Essex	Wenham	Essex	Abscota	Calhoun
Southborough	Worcester	West Acton	Middlesex	Ada	Kent
South Dartmouth	Bristol	West Amesbury	Essex	Adamsville	Cass
South Dedham	Norfolk	West Barnstable	Barnstable	Addison	Lenawee
South Deerfield	Franklin	West Becket	Berkshire	Adrian	"
South Dennis	Barnstable	Westborough	Worcester	Akron	Tuscola
South Easton	Bristol	West Boxford	Essex	Alamo	Kalamazoo
South Egremont	Berkshire	West Boylston	Worcester	Albany	Isabella
Southfield	Berkshire	West Brewster	Barnstable	Albion	Calhoun
South Framingham	Middlesex	West Bridgewater	Plymouth	Algansee	Branch
South Franklin	Norfolk	West Brookfield	Worcester	Algonac	St. Clair
South Gardner	Worcester	West Cambridge	Middlesex	Allison	Lapier
South Groton	Middlesex	West Chatham	Barnstable	Allegan	Allegan
South Groveland	Essex	West Chelmsford	Middlesex	Allendale	Ottawa
South Hadley	Hampshire	West Chesterfield	Hampshire	Alma	Gratiot
South Hadley Falls	Hampshire	West Dedham	Norfolk	Almont	Lapeer
South Hanson	Plymouth	West Dennis	Barnstable	Alpena	Alpena
South Harwich	Barnstable	West Duxbury	Plymouth	Algonquin	Ontonagon
South Hawley	Franklin	West Falmouth	Barnstable	Alto	Kent
South Hingham	Plymouth	Westfield	Hampden	Alton	"
South Lancaster	Worcester	West Fitchburgh	Worcester	Alverton	Ingham
South Lee	Berkshire	Westford	Middlesex	Amboy	Hillsdale
South Malden	Middlesex	West Foxboro'	Norfolk	Ann Arbor	Washtenaw
South Middleboro'	Plymouth	West Gloucester	Essex	Antrim	Shiawassee
South Milford	Worcester	West Grauville	Hampden	Annae	Bay
South Natick	Middlesex	West Groton	Middlesex	Argentine	Genesee
South Orleans	Barnstable	West Hampton	Hampshire	Arland	Jackson
South Plymouth	Plymouth	West Hanover	Hampshire	Arlington	Van Buren
South Randolph	Norfolk	West Harwich	Barnstable	Armada	Macomb
South Reading	Middlesex	West Hawley	Franklin	Ashland	Newago
South Royalston	Worcester	West Mansfield	Bristol	Ashley	Kent
South Sandwich	Barnstable	West Medford	Middlesex	Assyria	Barry
South Scituate	Plymouth	West Medway	Norfolk	Atlas	Genesee
South Seekonk	Bristol	West Millbury	Worcester	Athens	Calhoun
South Walpole	Norfolk	Westminster	Worcester	Attica	Lenawee
South Wellfleet	Barnstable	West Needham	Norfolk	Auburn	Oakland
South Westport	Bristol	West Newbury	Essex	Aurelius	Ingham
South Weymouth	Norfolk	West Newton	Middlesex	Ausable	Iosco
Southwick	Hampden	West Northfield	Franklin	Austerlitz	Kent
South Wilbraham	Hampden	Weston	Middlesex	Austin	Oakland
South Williamstown	Berkshire	West Otis	Berkshire	Avery	Berrien
South Wrentham	Norfolk	West Pittsfield	Berkshire	Avon	Ionia
South Yarmouth	Barnstable	Westport	Bristol	Bainbridge	Berrien
Spencer	Worcester	Westport Point	Bristol	Baldwin's Mills	Jackson
Springfield	Hampden	West Roxbury	Norfolk	Ball Mountain	Oakland
Spring Hill	Barnstable	West Rutland	Worcester	Baltimore	Barry
State Line	Berkshire	West Sandwich	Barnstable	Bangor	Van Buren
Sterling	Worcester	West Scituate	Plymouth	Barnetteville	Huron
Still River	Worcester	West Springfield	Hampden	Barryville	Barry
Stockbridge	Berkshire	West Sterling	Worcester	Base Lake	Washtenaw
Stoneham	Middlesex	West Stockbridge	Berkshire	Batavia	Branch
Stoughton	Norfolk	West Stockbridge Center		Bath	Clinton
Stow	Middlesex		Berkshire	Battle Creek	Calhoun
Sturbridge	Worcester	West Sutton	Worcester	Bay City	Bay
Sudbury	Middlesex	West Tisbury	Dukes	Bear River	Emmet
Sunderland	Franklin	West Townsend	Middlesex	Beaver Creek	Gratiot
Sutton	Worcester	West Wareham	Plymouth	Bedford	Calhoun
Swampscott	Essex	West Worthington	Hampshire	Belle River	St. Clair
Swansea	Bristol	West Wrentham	Norfolk	Belleville	Wayne
Taunton	Bristol	West Yarmouth	Barnstable	Bellevue	Eaton
Templeton	Worcester	Weymouth	Norfolk	Bengal	Clinton
Towksbury	Middlesex	Whately	Franklin	Benningtos	Shiawassee
Thorndike	Hampden	Whitinsville	Worcester	Henona	Oceana
Three Rivers	Hampden	Wilbraham	Hampden	Benton	Washtenaw

POST OFFICES—MICHIGAN.

Post Office.	County.	Post Office.	County.	Post Office.	County.
Benzonia	Leelanau	Clarkston	Oakland	Fairfield	Lenawee
Berlin	Ottawa	Clay Banks	Oceana	Fair Grove	Tuscola
Berrien Center	Berrien	Clayton	Lenawee	Fair Plains	Montcalm
Berrien Spring	"	Clear Lake	Montcalm	Fair View	Mason
Bertrand	"	Clifton	Keweenaw	Fallasburg	Kent
Bethel	Branch	Climax Prairie	Kalamazoo	Farm	Jackson
Big Beaver	Oakland	Clinton	Lenawee	Farmer's	Sanilac
Big Prairie	Newaygo	Clyde Mills	St. Clair	Farmer's Creek	Lapeer
Big Rapids	Mecosta	Cohoctah	Livingston	Farmington	Oakland
Big Spring	Ottawa	Cold Water	Branch	Fawn River	St. Joseph's
Birch Run	Saginaw	Colon	St. Joseph's	Felts	Ingham
Birmingham	Oakland	Coloma	Berrien	Fentonville	Genesee
Blendon	Ottawa	Columbia	Jackson	Ferris	Montcalm
Blissfield	Lenawee	Columbiaville	Lapeer	Ferrysburg	Ottawa
Bloomer Center	Montcalm	Columbus	St. Clair	Fitchburg	Ingham
Bloomingdale	Tuscola	Commerce	Oakland	Flat River	Kent
Blumfield	Saginaw	Comstock	Kalamazoo	Flint	Genesee
Blunt	Isabella	Concord	Jackson	Florence	St. Joseph's
Borodino	Wayne	Conner's Creek	Wayne	Florida	Hillsdale
Bowne	Kent	Convis	Calhoun	Flowerfield	St. Joseph's
Bradley	Allegan	Convis Center	"	Flushing	Genesee
Brady	Kalamazoo	Constantine	St. Joseph's	Ford River	Delta
Branch	Branch	Conway	Livingston	Forest	Genesee
Brandon	Oakland	Cooper	Kalamazoo	Forrester	Sanilac
Breedville	Van Buren	Coopersville	Ottawa	Forest Bay	"
Brest	Monroe	Copper Falls Mine	Keweenaw	Forest City	Ottawa
Brewersville	Van Buren	Copper Harbor	"	Forest Hill	Gratiot
Bridgeport	Saginaw	Cortland Center	Kent	Forestville	Sanilac
Bridgeport Center	"	Corunna	Shiawassee	Four Towers	Oakland
Bridgewater	Washtenaw	Cottrellville	St. Clair	Fowlersville	Livingston
Brighton	Livingston	Crimea	Muskegon	Franciscoville	Jackson
Bristolville	Barry	Crockersville	Genesee	Frankenlust	Saginaw
Brokway	St. Clair	Croton	Newaygo	Frankenmuth	"
Bronson's Prairie	Branch	Crystal	Montcalm	Franklin	Oakland
Brookfield	Eaton	Cuba	Kent	Frankfort	Leelanau
Brooklyn	Jackson	Dalton's Mills	Muskegon	Fredonia	Washtenaw
Brownstown	Wayne	Dallas	Clinton	Fremont	Shiawassee
Brownsville	Cass	Danby	Ionia	Gaines	Genesee
Buchanan	Berrien	Dansville	Ingham	Gaines' Station	"
Brick Creek	Kent	Davisburg	Oakland	Gainesville	Kent
Buel	Sanilac	Davison Center	Genesee	Galesburg	Kalamazoo
Bunker Hill	Ingham	Davisville	Sanilac	Galion	Berrien
Burlington	Calhoun	Day	Muskegon	Ganges	Allegan
Burns	Shiawassee	Dayton	Berrien	Garlick	Ontonagon
Burr Oak	St. Joseph's	Dearbornville	Wayne	Geary	Clinton
Burt	Cheboygan	Decatur	Van Buren	Genesee Village	Genesee
Bushnell Center	Montcalm	Deer Creek	Livingston	Geneva	Lenawee
Butler	Branch	Deerfield	Lenawee	Georgetown	Ottawa
Byron	Shiawassee	Delta	Eaton	Gibraltar	Wayne
Caledonia	Kent	Detroit	Wayne	Gidley's Station	Jackson
California	Branch	De Witt	Clinton	Gilead	Branch
Cambria Mill	Hillsdale	Dexter	Washtenaw	Gilbert	Oakland
Cambridge	Lenawee	Disco	Macomb	Girard	Branch
Camden	Hillsdale	Dover	Lenawee	Glass Creek	Barry
Campbell	Ionia	Dowagiac	Cass	Glen Arbor	Leelanau
Campbellton	St. Clair	Drayton Plains	Oakland	Goodland	Lapeer
Camp Creek	Eaton	Dryden	Lapeer	Goodrich	Genesee
Canton	Wayne	Duncan	Cheboygan	Goss	Clinton
Canandaigua	Lenawee	Dundee	Monroe	Grafton	Monroe
Canonsburg	Kent	Duplain	Clinton	Grahamsville	Kent
Capac	St. Clair	Eagle	Clinton	Grand Blanc	Genesee
Carlisle	Eaton	Eagle Harbor	Keweenaw	Grand Haven	Ottawa
Carlton	Barry	Eagle River	"	Grand Ledge	Eaton
Cascade	Kent	East Dayton	Tuscola	GrandTraverse	GrandTraverse
Casco	St. Clair	East Leroy	Calhoun	Grand Rapids	Kent
Caseville	Huron	Eastmansville	Ottawa	Grandville	"
Casnovia	Muskegon	East Nankin	Wayne	Grass Lake	Jackson
Cass	Hillsdale	East Ogden	Lenawee	Grattan	Kent
Cassapolis	Cass	East Raisinville	Monroe	Gravel Run	Washtenaw
Cato	Montcalm	East Saginaw	Saginaw	Greenbush	Clinton
Catrille	Wayne	East Hetford	Genesee	Greenfield	Wayne
Cayuga	Jackson	East Union	Macomb	Greenland	Ontonagon
Cedar Creek	Barry	Eaton Rapids	Eaton	Green Oak	Livingston
Cedar Lake	Calhoun	Eden	Ingham	Greenville	Montcalm
Cedar Fork	Delta	Edinburg	Hillsdale	Greenwood	Oceana
Cedar Springs	Kent	Edwardsburg	Cass	Groose Isle	Wayne
Centor	Eaton	Elgin	Genesee	Grove	Mecosta
Centerville	St. Joseph's	Elk	"	Groveland	Oakland
Ceresco	Calhoun	Elk Rapids	Antrim	Gun Lake	Barry
Charleston	Kalamazoo	Elm	Wayne	Gun Marsh	Allegan
Charlevoix	Emmett	Elmira	Eaton	Hadley	Lapeer
Charlotte	Eaton	Elm Hall	Gratiot	Hamburg	Livingston
Chelsea	Washtenaw	Elsie	Clinton	Hamburg Village	"
Chesaning	Saginaw	Englishville	Kent	Hamilton	Van Buren
Cheshire	Allegan	Enterprise	Shiawassee	Hancock	Houghton
Chester	Eaton	Erie	Monroe	Hanover	Jackson
China	St. Clair	Erin	Kent	Harrisville	Alcona
Clarence	Calhoun	Esconawba	Delta	Hartford	Van Buren
Clarendon Center	"	Essex	Clinton	Hartland	Livingston
Clark City	Monroe	Exeter	Monroe	Hartwellsville	Shiawassee

POST OFFICES—MICHIGAN. 41

Post Office.	County.	Post Office.	County.	Post Office.	County.
Harvey	Marquette	Mabopae	Oakland	North Star	
Hastings	Barry	Manchester	Washtenaw	North Unity	Leelanau
Havanna	Saginaw	Manistee	Manistee	North Vernon	Shiawassee
Hazleton	Shiawassee	Manlius	Allegan	Northville	Wayne
Henrietta	Jackson	Maple	Ionia	Norvell	Jackson
Hickory Corners	Barry	Mapleton	Grand Traverse	Novi	Oakland
Highland	Oakland	Maple Grove	Barry	Nunica	Ottawa
Hillsdale	Hillsdale	Maple Rapids	Clinton	Oak	Wayne
Hollister	Livingston	Marathon	Lapeer	Oakford	Lenawee
Holland	Ottawa	Marcellus	Cass	Oakfield	Kent
Holly Mills	Oakland	Marengo	Calhoun	Oak Grove	Livingston
Holt	Ingham	Marion	Livingston	Oakland	Oakland
Homer	Calhoun	Marquette	Marquette	Oakville	Monroe
Hopkins	Allegan	Marr	Muskegon	Oakwood	Oakland
Houghton	Houghton	Marshall	Calhoun	Oecola Center	Livingston
Howardsville	St. Joseph's	Martin	Allegan	Olivet	Eaton
Howell	Livingston	Marysville	St. Clair	Omena	Grand Traverse
Hubbardstown	Ionia	Mason	Ingham	Oneida	Clinton
Hudson	Lenawee	Matherton	Ionia	Onondaga	Ingham
Hunter	Van Buren	Mattawan	Van Buren	Ontonagon	Ontonagon
Hunter's Creek	Lapeer	Mattison	Branch	Oporto	St. Joseph's
Ida	Monroe	May	Tuscola	Orange	Ionia
Imlay	Lapeer	Mead's Mills	Wayne	Orangeville Mills	Barry
Indian Creek	Kent	Medina	Lenawee	Orion	Oakland
Ionia	Ionia	Memphis	Macomb	Ortonville	
Irving	Barry	Menden	St. Joseph's	Oshtemo	Kalamazoo
Isabella Center	Isabella	Mere	Macomb	Otisco	Ionia
Ishpeming	Marquette	Merrillsville	St. Clair	Otisville	Genesee
Ithica	Gratiot	Merritt	Barry	Otsego	Allegan
Jackson	Jackson	Metamora	Lapeer	Ottawa Center	Ottawa
Jamestown	Ottawa	Michigan Center	Jackson	Ottawa Lake	Monroe
Jay	Saginaw	Middleburg	Shiawassee	Otter Creek	Jackson
Jefferson	Hillsdale	Middletown	Ingham	Overisel	Allegan
Jersey	Oakland	Middleville	Barry	Ovid	Clinton
Johnstown	Barry	Midland	Midland	Ovid Center	
Jonesville	Hillsdale	Milan	Monroe	Ownsso	Shiawassee
Josco	Livingston	Milo	Barry	Oxford	Oakland
Kalamazoo	Kalamazoo	Milford	Oakland	Paint Creek	Washtenaw
Kalamo	Eaton	Millsburg	Berrien	Palo	Ionia
Kearsley	Genesee	Mill Creek	St. Joseph's	Palmyra	Lenawee
Keelersville	Kent	Millington	Tuscola	Panama	Newaygo
Kenochee	St. Clair	Mill Point	Ottawa	Park	St. Joseph's
Kensington	Oakland	Milton	Macomb	Parkville	
Kewana Bay	Houghton	Minnesota Mine	Ontonagon	Parshallville	Livingston
Keystone	Clinton	Monroe	Monroe	Partello	Calhoun
Kiddville	Ionia	Montcalm	Montcalm	Patterson's Mills	
Kimberhook	Branch	Monterey	Allegan	Pavillion	Kalamazoo
Kossuth	Ionia	Montrose	Genesee	Paw Paw	Van Buren
Lafayette	Gratiot	Morenci	Lenawee	Peal Shanty	Ingham
La Grange	Cass	Morgansville	Hillsdale	Peck	Sanilac
Laingsburgh	Shiawassee	Moscow		Penfield	Calhoun
Lake Mill	Van Buren	Mosherville		Pent Water	Oceana
Lake Port	St. Clair	Mottville	St. Joseph's	Pere Marquette	Mason
Lake Ridge	Lenawee	Moulin Range	Wayne	Perry	Shiawassee
Lakeville	Oakland	Mount Clemens	Macomb	Pewabic	Ontonagon
Lambertsville	Monroe	Mount Morris	Genesee	Pewamo	Ionia
Lamont	Ottawa	Mount Pleasant	Oakland	Phelpstown	Ingham
Lansing	Ingham	Mount Vernon	Macomb	Pickett's Corners	Cass
Laphamsville	Kent	Mud Creek	Eaton	Pierson	Mecosta
Lapeer	Lapeer	Muir	Ionia	Pinckney	Livingston
La Salle	Monroe	Mundy	Genesee	Pine Creek	Calhoun
Lawrence	Van Buren	Muskegon	Muskegon	Pine Grove	Tuscola
Lawton		Nankin	Wayne	Pine Grove Mills	Van Buren
Leland	Leelanau	Napoleon	Jackson	Pine Plain	Allegan
Lenox	Macomb	Negaunee	Marquette	Pine Run	Genesee
Leoni	Jackson	Nelson	Kent	Pipestone	Berrien
Leonidas	St. Joseph's	Nowaygo	Newaygo	Pittsburg	Shiawassee
Le Roy	Ingham	Newman	Sanilac	Plainfield	Livingston
Leslie		New Baltimore	Macomb	Plainwell	Allegan
Lexington	Sanilac	New Buffalo	Berrien	Plunk Road	Wayne
Liberty	Jackson	New Casco	Allegan	Pleasant	Kent
Liberty Church	Cass	New Haven	Macomb	Plumb Brook	Macomb
Lima	Washtenaw	New Hudson	Oakland	Plymouth	Wayne
Lincoln	Mason	Newport	Monroe	Pokagon	Cass
Linden	Genesee	Newton	Calhoun	Pompei	Gratiot
Lisbon	Kent	Niles	Berrien	Pontiac	Oakland
Litchfield	Hillsdale	Noble Center	Branch	Pool	Lapeer
Little Prairie Ronde	Cass	North Adams	Hillsdale	Port Austin	Huron
Livonia Center	Wayne	North Aurelius	Ingham	Portage	Kalamazoo
Lodi	Washtenaw	North Branch	Lapeer	Porter	Van Buren
London	Monroe	North Brighton	Livingston	Port Hope	Huron
Loomisville	Kent	North Brownsville	Kent	Port Huron	St. Clair
Lowell		North Eagle	Clinton	Portland	Ionia
Lyons	Ionia	North Farmington	Oakland	Port Sanilac	Sanilac
Lynn	St. Clair	North Irving	Barry	Portsmouth	Bay
McPhersonville	Macomb	North Oxford	Oakland	Pottersburg	St. Clair
Mackinaw	Michilimackinac	Northport	Leelanau	Prairie Ronde	Kalamazoo
Macomb	Macomb	North Plains	Ionia	Prairieville	Barry
Macon	Lenawee	North Raisinville	Monroe	Proctor	Allegan
Madison	Livingston	North Shade	Gratiot	Prospect Lake	Van Buren

POST OFFICES—MINNESOTA.

Post Office.	County.	Post Office.	County.	Post Office.	County.
Pulaski	Jackson	Summerfield	Monroe	Woodstock	Lenawee
Quincy	Branch	Summersville	Cass	Worth	Tuscola
Ransom	Hillsdale	Summit	Oakland	Wright	Ottawa
Ravenna	Muskegon	Sunfield	Eaton	Wyandott	Wayne
Ransomville	Wayne	Superior	Washtenaw	Yankee Springs	Barry
Ray	Macomb	Swan Creek	St. Clair	York	Washtenaw
Ray Center	"	Swart's Creek	Genesee	Yorkville	Kalamazoo
Reading	Hillsdale	Sylvan	Washtenaw	Ypsilanti	Washtenaw
Red Bridge	Ingham	Sylvanus	Hillsdale	Zilwaukie	Saginaw
Redford	Wayne	Tallmadge	Ottawa	Zealand	Ottawa
Richfield	Genesee	Tarvas City	Josco		
Richland	Kalamazoo	Taymouth	Saginaw		
Richmond	Macomb	Tecumseh	Lenawee		
Richmondville	Sanilac	Tekawsha	Calhoun	## Minnesota.	
Ridgeway	Lenawee	Thetford	Genesee		
Riga	"	Thornton	St. Clair		
Riley	Clinton	Thornville	Lapeer	Post Office.	County.
Rix	Ionia	Three Oaks	Berrien		
Robinson	Ottawa	Three Rivers	St. Joseph's	Acton	Meeker
Rochester	Oakland	Tipton	Lenawee	Afton	Washington
Rollins	Lenawee	Tompkins	Jackson	Alba	Fillmore
Rome	"	Traverse City	Grand Traverse	Albert Lea	Freeborn
Romeo	Macomb	Trenton	Wayne	Albion	Wright
Romulus	Wayne	Troy	Oakland	Alexandria	Douglas
Ronald Center	Ionia	Tyrone	Livingston	Amada	Chisago
Rose	Oakland	Unadilla	"	Anawauk	Le Sueur
Roseville	Macomb	Union	Cass	Anoka	Anoka
Round Lake	Branch	Union City	Branch	Arendahl	Fillmore
Roxana	Eaton	Union House	Clinton	Argo	Winona
Royal Oak	Oakland	Utica	Macomb	Arlington	Sibley
Ruby	St. Clair	Vandalia	Cass	Ashippun	Brown
Saginaw	Saginaw	Vassar	Tuscola	Ashland	Dodge
St. Charles	"	Vergennes	Kent	Austin	Mower
St. Clair	St. Clair	Vermontville	Eaton	Aurora Center	Steele
St. James	Maniton	Vernon	Shiawassee	Bass Lake	Faribault
St. John's	Clinton	Victor	Clinton	Bear Grove	Olmstead
St. Joseph's	Berrien	Vienna	Macomb	Bear Valley	Wabashaw
St. Lewis	Gratiot	Wacousta	Clinton	Beaver	Winona
Salem	Washtenaw	Wahjamaga	Tuscola	Beaver Bay	Superior
Saline	"	Wakeshma	Kalamazoo	Beaver Dam	McLeod
Salt River	Isabella	Waldenburg	Macomb	Bellefontaine	Scott
Sandstone	Jackson	Wales	St. Clair	Belle Creck	Goodhue
Sandford	Ingham	Walled Lake	Oakland	Bell Plain	Scott
Sanilac Mills	Sanilac	Wanicott	Sanilac	Bell Praire	Morrison
Saranac	Ionia	Warren	Macomb	Bellville	Fillmore
Saugatuck	Allegan	Washington	"	Bergen	"
Sault Ste. Marie	Chippewa	Waterford	Oakland	Berlin	Steele
Schoolcraft	Kalamazoo	Waterloo	Jackson	Berne	Dodge
Scio	Washtenaw	Watertown	Tuscola	Bianca	Wright
Sebewa	Ionia	Watervliet	Barrien	Big Bend	"
Secilia	Calhoun	Watrousville	Tuscola	Big Lake	Sherburne
Seneca	Lenawee	Waverly	Van Buren	Big Spring	Filmore
Shave Head	Cass	Wayland	Allegan	Bloomington	Hennepin
Sherwood	Branch	Wayne	Wayne	Blue Earth City	Faribault
Shiawassee Town	Shiawassee	Weaversville	Newaygo	Brantford	Sherburne
Sibewaing	Huron	Webster	Washtenaw	Breckinridge	Toombs
Silver Creek	Allegan	Wesaw	Berrien	Brownsville	Houston
Six Corners	Ottawa	Wellville	Lenawee	Brunswick	Kanabeck
Smithville	Wayne	West Berlin	St. Clair	Buchanan	Saint Louis
Smyrna	Ionia	West Bloomer	Montcalm	Buckeye	Freeborn
Sodus	Berrien	West Bloomfield	Oakland	Buffalo	Wright
Somerset	Hillsdale	West Climax	Kalamazoo	Burlington	Lake
South Boston	Ionia	West Delhi	Ingham	Butternut Valley	Blue Earth
South Cass	"	West Haven	Shiawassee	Caledonia	Houston
Southfield	Oakland	West Leroy	Calhoun	Cambridge	Isante
South Genoa	Livingston	West Novi	Oakland	Canfield	Fillmore
South Haven	Van Buren	West Ogden	Lenawee	Cannon City	Rice
South Henrietta	Jackson	West River	Jackson	Cannon River Falls	Goodhue
South Jackson	"	Westphalia	Clinton	Carimona	Fillmore
South Lyon	Oakland	West Windsor	Eaton	Carver	Carver
South Plymouth	Wayne	Wheatland	Ionia	Caswell	Wright
South Ripley	Clinton	Wheatland Center	Hillsdale	Castle Rock	Dakota
South Sunfield	Eaton	Wheelersville	Shiawassee	Cedar	McLeod
South Wright	Hillsdale	White Lake	Oakland	Cedar Lake	Scott
Sparta	"	White Oak	Ingham	Chain Lake Center	Martin
Sparta Center	Kent	White Pigeon	St. Joseph's	Champlain	Hennepin
Spencer's Mills	"	White River	Muskegon	Chanhassen	Carver
Spring Arbor	Jackson	White Rock	Huron	Chaska	"
Spring Brook	Gratiot	White Water	Grand Traverse	Chatfield	Fillmore
Springfield	Oakland	Whitmore Lake	Washtenaw	Chatham	Wright
Spring Mills	"	Whitneyville	Kent	Chengwatana	Pine
Springport	Jackson	Williamstown	Ingham	Cherry Grove	Fillmore
Springville	Lenawee	Williamsville	Cass	Chester	Rice
Stella	Gratiot	Willow Creek	Huron	Chippewa Lake	Douglas
Stevens' Landing	Sanilac	Windsor	Eaton	Chisago City	Chisago
Stockbridge	Ingham	Wiota	Isabella	Chisago Lake	Chisago
Stony Run	Genesee	Wolf Creek	Lenawee	Christiana	Dakota
Strait's Lake	Oakland	Woodhull	Shiawassee	Claremont	Dodge
Sturgis	St. Joseph's	Woodland	Barry	Clark's Grove	Freeborn
Sugar Island	Chippewa	Wood's Corners	Hillsdale	Clayton	Fairbault

POST OFFICES—MINNESOTA. 43

Post Office.	County.	Post Office.	County.	Post Office.	County.
Clear Lake	Sherburne	Green Lake	Monongalia	Maylardsville	Le Sueur
Clear Water	Wright	Greenville	Wabashaw	Mazeppa	Wabashaw
Cleveland	Le Sueur	Greenwood	Hennepin	Medford	Steele
Clinton	Stearns	Guilford	Freeborn	Medicine Lake	Hennepin
Clinton Falls	Steele	Hackett's Grove	Houston	Melrose	Stearns
Cobb River	Blue Earth	Hader	Goodhue	Mendota	Dakota
Cold Spring City	Stearns	Hallowell	Dodge	Mendin	Steele
Columbus	Anoka	Hampton	Dakota	Miami	Goodhue
Concord	Dodge	Harrisburg	"	Middle Branch	Chisago
Cook's Valley	Wabashaw	Harrison	Meeker	Middlesville	Wright
Cooleysville	Steele	Hartland	Freeborn	Millersburg	Rice
Cordova	Le Sueur	Hastings	Dakota	Mineral Springs	Mower
Cottage Grove	Washington	Haven	Rice	Minneapolis	Hennepin
Crisp's Store	Blue Earth	Hazle Prairie	Fillmore	Minneska	Wabashaw
Crow Wing	Crow Wing	Hazlewood	Rice	Minnesota City	Winona
Cross Roads	Winona	Hebron	Nicolet	Minnesota Lake	Faribault
Crystal Lake	Hennepin	Hoctor	Dodge	Minnetonka	Hennepin
Crystal Spring	Goodhue	Holena	Scott	Minnetrista	"
Dayton	Hennepin	Henderson	Sibly	Money Creek	Houston
Denham	Houston	High Forrest	Olmstead	Monticello	Wright
Deer Creek	Fillmore	Highland	Fillmore	Morristown	Rice
Deerfield	Steele	Hilo	Nicolet	Moscow	Freeborn
Dodge City	"	Hokah	Houston	Mount Pleasant	Wabashaw
Dolphin	Washington	Homer	Winona	Mount Vernon	"
Dresbach City	Winona	Houston	Houston	Mower City	Mower
Dryden	Sibley	Hutchinson	McLeod	Muskootink	Chisago
Duluth	St. Louis	Hyde Park	Wabashaw	Neenah	Stearns
Dundas	Rice	Independence	"	Ness	Meeker
Eagartown	Dakota	Industriana	Hennepin	Nevada	Mower
Eagle Mills	Goodhue	Irving	Monongalia	New Auburn	Sibley
East Prairieville	Rice	Itasca	Benton	New Boston	Winona
Eden Prairie	Hennepin	Jacksonville	Wabashaw	Newburg	Fillmore
Elba	Winona	Jackson	Jackson	New Dublin	Scott
Elgin	Wabashaw	Janesville	Waseka	New Hartford	Winona
Elk Horn	Fillmore	Jessen Land	Sibley	New Haven	Olmstead
Elk River	Sherburne	Juno	Steele	New Munich	Stearns
Ellington	Dodge	Judson	Blue Earth	Newport	Washington
Elliotta	Fillmore	Kandotta	Stearns	New Ulm	Brown
Elwood	Steele	Kasota	Le Sueur	Nicolet	Nicolet
Elysian	Le Sueur	Kelso	Sibley	Nininger	Dakota
Empire City	Dakota	Kennebec	Stearns	Northfield	Rice
Enterprise	Winona	Kenyon	Goodhue	North Warren	Winona
Etna	Fillmore	Kilkenny	Le Sueur	Norway	Goodhue
Ettaville	"	Kingston	Meeker	Nunda	Freeborn
Eureka	Dakota	LaCrescent	Houston	Oakdale	Washington
Excelsior	Hennepin	Lafayette	Nicolet	Oak Glen	Steele
Fairfield	Olmstead	Lake City	Wabashaw	Oak Grove	Ramsey
Fair Haven	Stearns	Lake Land	Washington	Oak Ridge	Winona
Fairmount	Martin	Lake Town	Carver	Odessa	Fillmore
Fair Point	Goodhue	Lakeville	Dakota	Okaman	Waseka
Fair View	Fillmore	Lamoille	Winona	Oneota	Saint Louis
Farmer's Grove	"	Lanesburg	Le Sueur	Oral	Le Sueur
Farmington	Dakota	Langola	Benton	Orlando	Sherburne
Faribault	Rice	Lansing	Mower	Oronoco	Olmstead
Faxon	Sibley	Leavenworth	Brown	Osakis	Todd
Featherston	"	La Villa	Houston	Osseo	Hennepin
Fillmore	Fillmore	Leighton	Hennepin	Otisco	Waseka
Florence	Goodhue	Lemond	Steele	Otsego	Wrigh
Fond du Lac	St. Louis	Lenora	Fillmore	Ottawa	Le Sueur
Forest City	Meeker	Lenz	Hennepin	Otter Tail City	Otter Tail
Forest Mound	Wabashaw	Le Roy	Mower	Owatanna	Steele
Forestville	Fillmore	Le Sueur	Dakota	Papitazec	Brown
Fort Abercrombie (Unknown)		Le Sueur City	Le Sueur	Paynesville	Stearns
Fort Ridgeley	Pierce	Lewiston	Dakota	Pembina	Pembina
Fort Ripley	Todd	Lexington	Le Sueur	Perkinsville	Hennepin
Fort Snelling	Dakota	Liberty	Blue Earth	Pilot Mound	Fillmore
Fowlersville	Rice	Little Canada	Ramsey	Pine Bend	Dakota
Frankfort	Mower	Little Falls	Morrison	Pine Island	Goodhue
Frank Hill	Winona	Long Prairie	Todd	Plainview	Wabashaw
Franklin	Wright	Looking Glass	Fillmore	Plato	McLeod
Freeborn	Freeborn	Looneyville	Houston	Pleasant Grove	Olmstead
Freeborn Springs	"	Lorette	"	Pleasant Prairie	Wabashaw
Freeburg	Houston	Louisville	Scott	Point Douglass	Washington
Free Soil	Fillmore	Lura	Faribault	Poplar Grove	Goodhue
Fremont	McLeod	Madelia	Brown	Portland	Houston
French Lake	Wright	Madison	Mower	Prairie	Mower
Frontenac	Goodhue	Maine Prairie	Stearns	Preston	Fillmore
Garden City	Blue Earth	Manauah	Meeker	Princeton	Benton
Geneva	Freeborn	Mankato	Blue Earth	Putnam	Winona
Glascow	Wabashaw	Manomin	Manomin	Quincy	Olmstead
Glencoe	McLeod	Mantonville	Dodge	Red Stone	Nicolet
Glendale	"	Maple Glen	Scott	Red Wing	Goodhue
Goodhue Center	Goodhue	Maple Lake	Wright	Reed's Landing	Wabashaw
Gopher Prairie	Wabashaw	Maple Plain	Hennepin	Riceford	Houston
Granby	Nicolet	Mapleton	Blue Earth	Rice Lake	Dodge
Grand Meadow	Mower	Marino Mills	Washington	Richfield	Hennepin
Granger	Fillmore	Marlon	Olmstead	Richland	Fillmore
Granite City	Morrison	Marysburg	Le Sueur	Richmond	Winona
Grapeland	Faribault	Marysville	Stearns	Rich Valley	Dakota
Greenfield	Olmstead	Maxson Grove	Waseka	Ridgeway	Winon

POST OFFICES—MISSISSIPPI.

Post Office.	County.	Post Office.	County.	Post Office.	County.
River Point	Steele	Waterford	Dakota	Bolivar	Bolivar
Rochester	Olmstead	Waterloo	Olmstead	Bolton's Depot	Hinds
Rock Dell	"	Watertown	Carver	Bone Yard	Tishemingo
Rockford	Wright	Waterville	Le Sueur	Bovina	Warren
Rocky Run	McLeod	Watonwan	Blue Earth	Booneville	Tishemingo
Rolling Stone	Winona	Wantopa	Wabashaw	Brandon	Rankin
Root River	Mower	Wayland	Winona	Brickley	Jackson
Roscoe	Goodhue	Wentztown	Arroka	Brook Haven	Lawrence
Rosemount	Dakota	West Albany	Wabashaw	Brookville	Noxubee
Roseville	Ramsey	West Union	Todd	Brownsville	Hinds
Rushford	Fillmore	West Saint Paul	Dakota	Bucatunna	Wayne
Rusheby	Chisago	Wheatland	Le Sueur	Buck Creek	Green
St. Anthony's Falls	Hennepin	White Bear Lake	Ramsey	Buck Hill	Yalabusha
St. Augusta	Stearns	White Water Falls	Winona	Buck Horn	Winston
St. Bonnefacius	Hennepin	Wilton	Waseka	Buena Vista	Chickasaw
St Charles	Winona	Winnebago Agency	Blue Earth	Buffalo	Wilkinson
St. Cloud	Stearns	Winnebago City	Faribault	Buckley's	Jasper
St. Francis	Anoka	Winnebago Valley	Houston	Buncomb	Pontotoc
St. Joseph	Pembina	Winona	Winona	Bunker Hill	Smith
St. Lawrence	Scott	Winsted	McLeod	Burkittsville	Attala
St. Mary's	Waseka	Wiscoy	Winona	Burneville	Tishemingo
St. Michael	Wright	Witoka	"	Burtonia	Washington
St. Paul	Ramsey	Woodland	Wabashaw	Burton's	Tishemingo
St. Peter	Nicolet	Worth	Winona	Burtonton	Capino
Salem	Olmstead	Wyattville	"	Buttahatchie	Monroe
Sand Creek	Scott	Wyzata	Hennepin	Byhalia	Marshall
San Jacinto	Houston	Yarmouth	Stearns	Bynum's Creek	Panola
Saratoga	Winona	Young America	Carver	Byram	Hinds
Sauk Center	Stearns	Ypsilanti	Wright	Bywyah	Choctaw
Sauk Rapids	Benton	Yucatan	Houston	Caderata	"
Scandia	Carver	Zumbro	Olmstead	Cairo	Tishemingo
Shakopee	Scott	Zumbrota	Goodhue	Caledonia	Lowndes
Shelbyville	Blue Earth			Calhoun	Pontotoc
Sheldon	Houston			Calvert's Store	Kemper
Shell Rock	Freeborn	## Mississippi.		Camargo	Monroe
Shieldsville	Rice			Camden	Madison
Silver Creek	Wright			Campbellton	Itawamba
Silver Lake	Waseka	Post Office.	Parish.	Canaan	Tippah
Sioux Agency	Brown			Canton	Madison
Sioux Falls City	Big Sioux	Abbeville	Lafayette	Cardiff	Warren
Smithfield	Wabashaw	Aberdeen	Monroe	Carlile's Mills	Perry
South Bend	Blue Earth	Adamsville	Greene	Carolina	Tishemingo
South Troy	Wabashaw	Acona	Holmes	Carolina Landing	Washington
Spencer	Goodhue	Air Mount	Yalabusha	Carollton	Carroll
Spencer Brook	Isanti	Alamucha	Lauderdale	Carson's Landing	Bolivar
Spring Creek	Goodhue	Americus	Jackson	Cartersville	Tishemingo
Spring Grove	Houston	Arcabutta	De Soto	Carthage	Leake
Spring Valley	Fillmore	Armitage	Noxubee	Caseyville	Copiah
Stanton	Goodhue	Artesia	Lowndes	Caswell	Lafayette
Steele Center	Steele	Ascalmore	Tallahatchee	Cato	Rankin
Stewartville	Olmstead	Ash Creek	Oktibbeha	Cayuga	Hinds
Stilwater	Washington	Ashfordsville	Winston	Cedar Bluff	Oktibbeha
Stockton	Winona	Ashland	Monroe	Central Academy	Panola
Sumner	Freeborn	Athens	"	Center	Attala
Snnapee	Goodhue	Attalaville	Attala	Center Hill	De Soto
Sunrise City	Chisago	Augusta	Perry	Centerville	Amite
Swan City	Nicolet	Austin Court House	Tunica	Ceralvo	Carroll
Swan River	Morrison	Australia	Bolivar	Charleston	Tallahatchee
Swavessy	Steele	Bahala	Copiah	Chawata	Pike
Tamarack	Hennepin	Baldwyn	Itawamba	Cherry Creek	Pontotoc
Taylor's Falls	Chisago	Bankston	Choctaw	Cherry Hill	Calhoun
Tepecotah	Wabashaw	Barksdale	Winston	Chesterville	Pontotoc
Tivoli	Blue Earth	Barnes' Store	Tishemingo	Chickasaw Mills	Chickasaw
Torah	Stearns	Barry	Noxubee	China Grove	Pike
Traverse des Sioux	Nicolet	Bartersville	Pontotoc	Chocehama	Tallahatchee
Trenton	Freeborn	Batesville	Panola	Choctaw Agency	Oktibbeha
Troy	Winona	Battlefield	Newton	Choctaw Ridge	Choctaw
Twin Grove	"	Bay Springs	Tishemingo	Chulahoma	Marshall
Twin Lakes	Carlton	Beaver Dam	Clark	Chunkeyville	Lauderdale
Union	Houston	Bellefontaine	Choctaw	Church Hill	Jefferson
Union Lakes	Rice	Bunela	Chickasaw	Claiborne	Jasper
Union Spring	Dodge	Benton	Yazoo	Claysville	Tippah
Utica	Winona	Bethesda	Warren	Clinton	Hinds
Valville	Fillmore	Betlehem	Marshall	Cockrum	De Soto
Vernon	Blue Earth	Beulah	Bolivar	Conadeliah	Neshota
Verona	Faribault	Bigbee Valley	Noxubee	Coffeeville	Yalabusha
Vivian	Waseka	Bigby Fork	Itawamba	Cold Spring	Wilkinson
Wabashaw	Wabashaw	Big Creek	Yalabusha	Cold Water	Marshall
Waconia	Carver	Big Oak	Kemper	College Hill	Lafayette
Wacouta	Goodhue	Biloxie	Harrison	Cole's Creek	Yalabusha
Walcott	Rice	Birmingham	Pontotoc	Columbia	Marion
Walnut Lake	Faribault	Black Hawk	Carroll	Columbus	Lowndes
Wanaminga	Goodhue	Black Land	Tishemingo	Como Depot	Panola
Warren	Winona	Black Water	Kemper	Concord	Calhoun
Warsaw	Rice	Black Wells	Choctaw	Concordia	Bolivar
Wasenta	Toombs	Bluff Spring	Attala	Conehatta	Newton
Washington	Fillmore	Bogue Chitto	Pike	Cunesly's	Pike
Wasioja	Dodge	Bolands	Itawamba	Conway	Leake
Wastedu	Goodhue	Bolingreen	Holmes	Cooksville	Noxubee
Watab	Benton			Coonewar	Pontotoc

POST OFFICES—MISSISSIPPI. 45

Post Office.	County.	Post Office.	County.	Post Office.	County.
Cooper's Well	Hinds	Glencoe	Bolivar	Ludlow	Scott
Coopwood	Winston	Good Hope	Leake	McCall's Creek	Franklin
Cornersville	Marshall	Goodman	Holmes	McLean's Store	Tippah
Corinth	Tishemingo	Goshen Springs	Rankin	McLeod's	Greene
Corona	Pontotoc	Grand Gulf	Claiborne	McNutt	Sun Flower
Cotton Gin Port	Monroe	Graysport	Yalabusha	Mackesville	Clark
Cotton Plant	Tappah	Grenada	"	Macon	Noxubeo
County Line	Newton	Greenleaf	De Soto	Madison Station	Madison
Cow Creek	Kemper	Greensborough	Choctaw	Magnolia	Pike
Crystal Springs	Copiah	Greenville	Washington	Maple Springs	Lafayette
Cuba	Attala	Greenwood	Carroll	Marietta	Itawamba
Cummingsville	Itawamba	Good Hope	Leake	Marion	Lauderdale
Daleville	Lauderdale	Habolochitto	Hancock	Marion Station	"
Dallas	Lafayette	Hamburg	Franklin	Mashulaville	Noxubee
Dalton	Chicasaw	Hamilton	Monroe	Mayhew's Station	Lowndes
Damascus	Scott	Handsboro'	Harrison	Meadville	Franklin
Danville	Tishemingo	Harrisburg	Itawamba	Meadowville	Jackson
Davisville	Jasper	Harrisville	Simpson	Meridian	Lauderdale
Deasonville	Yazoo	Hay's Creek	Carroll	Middleton	Carroll
Decatur	Newton	Hazle Green	Tishemingo	Miles' Landing	Bolivar
Deer Creek	Issaquena	Hazlehurst	Copiah	Milldale	Warren
De Kalb	Kemper	Hazlewood	Tunica	Mississippi City	Harrison
Delay	Lafayette	Herbert	Neshoba	Mitchell's X Roads	"
De Soto	Clark	Hernando	De Soto		Tallahatchie
De Soto Front	De Soto	Hickory	Newton	Molino	Tippah
Dido	Choctaw	Hickory Flat	Tippah	Monroe	Perry
Dixon	Neshoba	Hickory Plains	Tishemingo	Monterey	Rankin
Doolittle Station	Newton	High Hill	Leake	Monto Vista	Choctaw
Dover	Yazoo	Highland	Tishemingo	Monticello	Lawrence
Double Springs	Oktibbeha	Hillsboro'	Scott	Montpelier	Chickasaw
Dry Creek	Covington	Huhenlinden	Chickasaw	Montrose	Jasper
Dry Grove	Hinds	Holly Retreat	Wilkinson	Moody	Marshall
Dry Run	Tishemingo	Holly Springs	Marshall	Moorville	Itawamba
Duck Hill	Carroll	Holmesville	Pike	Mormon Springs	Monroe
Dublin	Choctaw	Holt	Jasper	Morton	Scott
Dumas	Tippah	Homewood	Scott	Mount Carmel	Covington
Dumbarton	Issaquena	Homochitto	Franklin	Mount Hope	Copiah
Durant	Holmes	Hopewell	Chickasaw	Mount Nebo	Yalabusha
Early Grove	Marshall	Hopewell Church	Wilkinson	Mount Olive	Covington
Eastport	Tishemingo	Hopson's	Coahoma	Mount Zion	Simpson
Ebenezer	Holmes	Horn Lake	De Soto	Natchez	Adams
Edgefield	Attala	Houlka	Chickasaw	Neshoba Springs	Neshoba
Edinburg	Leake	Houston	"	New Albany	Pontotoc
Edward's Depot	Hinds	Hope Hill	Pike	New Dublin	Simpson
Eggs Point	Washington	Hudsonville	Marshall	New Ireland	Newton
Egypt	Chickasaw	Huntsville	Choctaw	Newport	Attala
Elder's Ferry	Jackson	Hurricane	Warren	New Prospect	Winston
Ellistown	Pontotoc	Ingraham	"	Newtonia	Wilkinson
Ellisville	Jones	Irene	Tippah	Newton Depot	Newton
Elm Grove	De Soto	Iuka	Tishemingo	Newtonsville	Attala
Emory	Holmes	Jacinto	"	North Mount Pleasant	
Enorgy	Clark	Jackson	Hinds		Marshall
Enow	Perry	Jackson's Point	Adams	Noxapater	Winston
Enterprise	Clark	Jaynesville	Covington	Oak Farm	Itawamba
Eulia	Tallahatchee	Jefferson	Carroll	Oak Grove	Marshall
Erata	Jones	Jonesboro'	Tippah	Oakland	Yalabusha
Erin	Calhoun	Jones' Mills	Yalabusha	Oakland College	Claiborne
Etchoma	Jasper	Keel Boat	Panola	Oakley	Choctaw
Eucutta	Wayne	Kellis' Store	Kemper	Oakohay	Covington
Eudora	De Soto	Kilmichael	Choctaw	Oak Vale	Lawrence
Eulogy	Holmes	Kingston	Adams	Ocean Springs	Jackson
Eureka	Panola	Kirkwood	Madison	Okolona	Chickasaw
Evergreen	Newton	Knoxville	Franklin	Old Hickory	Simpson
Fair River	Lawrence	Kosciusko	Attala	Old Town Creek	Pontotoc
Fairmount	Smith	Kossuth	Tishemingo	Olive Branch	De Soto
Fame	Choctaw	Lacey	Holmes	Orizaba	Tippah
Fannin	Rankin	Lafayette Springs	Lafayette	Osyka	Pike
• Farmington	Tishemingo	Lake	Scott	Owenton	Jones
Fayette Court House	Jefferson	Lake Como	Jasper	Oxford	Lafayette
Fearn's Springs	Winston	Lako Washington	Washington	Ozark	Itawamba
Flewellen's X Roads	De Soto	Lamar	Marshall	Palmetto	Pontotoc
Flint Creek	Harrison	Last Chance	Carroll	Palo Alto	Chickasaw
Flower's Place	Smith	Lauderdale Station	Lauderdale	Panola	Panola
Fordsville	Marion	Laurel Hill	Neshoba	Paris	Lafayette
Fort Adams	Wilkinson	Leakesville	Greene	Parkerville	Noxubee
Fort Stephen's	Kemper	Lebanon	Tippah	Pascagoula	Jackson
Franklin	Holmes	Lexington C. H.	Holmes	Pass Christian	Harrison
Fredonia	Pontotoc	Liberty	Amite	Paulding C. H	Jasper
French Camp	Choctaw	Lightville	Marion	Peach Creek	Panola
Friar's Point	Coahoma	Linden	Copiah	Pearl River	Copiah
Friendship	Franklin	Line Crock	Oktibbeha	Pearl Valley	Neshoba
Fulton	Itawamba	Little Black	Choctaw	Peden	Kemper
Gainsville	Hancock	Lit le Spring	Franklin	Pelahatchee Dep	Rankin
Gallatin	Copiah	Livingston	Madison	Pensacola	Leake
Garlandville	Jasper	Lobutcher	Winston	Percy's Creek	Wilkinson
Garner's Station	Yalabusha	Looxahoma	De Soto	Philadelphia	Neshoba
Gatewood	Yalabusha	Lodi	Choctaw	Phœnix Mills	Attala
Georgetown	Copiah	Long Branch	Oktibbeha	Pickens' Station	Holmes
Gerenton	Carroll	Longtown	Panola	Pierce Springs	Clark
Gholson	Noxubeo	Louisville	Winston	Pigeon Roost	Choctaw

POST OFFICES—MISSOURI.

Post Office.	County.	Post Office.	County.	Post Office.	County.
Pine Bluff	Copiah	Smith's Store	Jones	Zion Hill	Amite
Pine Grove	Tippah	Smithsville	Monroe	Zion Seminary	Covington
Pine Ridge	Copiah	Snow Creek	Marshall		
Pine Valley	Yalabusha	Sookalona	Lauderdale		
Pineville	Smith	Sparta	Chickasaw		
Pinellville	Jones	Splug	Monroe	**Missouri.**	
Pittsborough	Calhoun	Spring Cottage	Marion		
Plattsburg	Winston	Spring Dale	Lafayette		
Plantersville	Itawamba	Springport	Panola	Post Office.	County.
Pleasant Hill	De Soto	Spring Ridge	Hinds		
Pleasant Mount	Panola	Standing Pine	Leake	Acorn Ridge	Stoddard
Pleasant Ridge	Tippah	Starkville	Oktibbeha	Acasto	Clarke
Pleasant Springs	Kemper	State Line Station	Wayne	Akron	Harrison
Pleasanton	Itawamba	Stateland	Choctaw	Alamode	Reynolds
Polkville	Smith	Steam Mill	"	Alba	Jasper
Pontocola	Pontotoc	Steelville	Oktibbeha	Albany	"
Pontotoc	"	Steen's Creek	Rankin	Alanthus Grove	"
Pope's Depot	Panola	Sulphur Springs	Madison	Alemath	Ozark
Poplar Creek	Choctaw	Summit	Pike	Alexander's Mills	Benton
Poplar Spring	Pontotoc	Sunflower Landing	Coahoma	Alexandria	Clarke
Port Gibson	Claiborne	Swan Lake	"	Allen	Randolph
Post Oak	Yalabusha	Tacaluche	Marshall	Allendale	Gentry
Prairie Line	Jasper	Talibenela	Pontotoc	Allenton	St. Louis
Prairie Point	Noxubee	Tallahala	Hinds	Alma	Wright
Prairie Station	Monroe	Tallaloosa	Marshall	Almeda	Newton
Prentiss	Bolivar	Tallulah	Issaquena	Alpha	Grundy
Princeton	Washington	Tampico	Oktibbeha	Altenburg	Perry
Providence	Carroll	Tardyville	Pontotoc	Alton C. H.	Oregon
Queen's Hill	Hinds	Taylor's Depot	Lafayette	Amazonia	Andrew
Quincy	Monroe	Taylorsville	Smith	Appleton	Cape Girardeau
Quitman	Clark	Tchula	Holmes	Arator	Pettis
Raleigh	Smith	Temperance Hill	Monroe	Arbela	Scotland
Randall's Bluff	Winston	Teoc	Carroll	Argo	Crawford
Randolph	Pontotoc	Terry	Hinds	Arno	Taney
Rawsonville	Lauderdale	Thomastown	Leake	Arrow Rock	Saline
Raymond	Hinds	Tibby Station	Lowndes	Ashburn	Pike
Red Bluff	Wayne	Tiro	Marshall	Ash Grove	Greene
Red Bud	Kemper	Toccopola	Pontotoc	Ashland	Boone
Red Land	Pontotoc	Torrance	Yalabusha	Ashley	Pike
Relief	Holmes	Tremont	Itawamba	Ashton	Clarke
Riceville	Hancock	Trenton	Smith	Astoria	Wright
Richland	Holmes	Tripoli	Tishemingo	Athens	Clarke
Richmond	Itawamba	Try Again	Perry	Atlanta	Harrison
Ricazi	Tishemingo	Tunica	Tunica	Auburn	Lincoln
Rio	Kemper	Turkland	Pontotoc	Augusta	St. Charles
Ripley	Tippah	Turnersville	Jasper	Austin	Cass
Robinia	Panola	Tuscahoma	Tallahatchee	Avery	Crawford
Robson's Landing	Coahoma	Twistwood	Jasper	Avilla	Jasper
Rockport	Copiah	Union	Newton	Avoca	Jefferson
Rocky Ford	Pontotoc	Union Church	Jefferson	Avon	St. Genevieve
Rocky Hill	Marion	Union Mills	Tippah	Ayessville	Putnam
Rocky Mount	Kemper	Utica	Hinds	Baden	St. Louis
Rocky Point	Attala	Valley Hill	Carroll	Bailey's Creek	Osage
Rocky Spring	Claiborne	Van Buren	Itawamba	Bairdstown	Sullivan
Rodney	Jefferson	Vaiden	Carroll	Baker's Grove	Barton
Rome	Winston	Vernal	Green	Baruesville	Clinton
Rosalee	Harrison	Vernon	Madison	Barret's Station	St. Louis
Rose Dale	Bolivar	Verona	Itawamba	Barry	Clay
Ruckersville	Tippah	Voto	Franklin	Basin Knob	Johnson
Rushing's Store	Lauderdale	Vicksburg	Warren	Bauff	Taney
Ryan's Well	Itawamba	Vinton	Lowndes	Bay	Gasconade
Salem	Tippah	Wahalack	Kemper	Bear Creek	Cedar
Saltillo	Itawamba	Wahalack Station	"	Bear Creek Station	Marion
Saunder's Creek	Simpson	Wallersville	Pontotoc	Beaufort	Franklin
Sandifer's Mills	Copiah	Wall Hill	Marshall	Beaver Spring	McDonald
Sautee	Covington	Wall's Store	Amite	Bedford	Livingston
Sardis	Panola	Walnut Grove	Leake	Becce	Dunklin
Sarepta	Calhoun	Warrenton	Warren	Bee Hive	Clinton
Satartia	Yazoo	Washington	Adams	Bee Ridge	Knox
Scales	Marshall	Waterford	Marshall	Belew's Creek	Jefferson
Scooba	Kemper	Water Valley	Yalabusha	Bell Air	Cooper
Sebastopol	Scott	Watson	Marshall	Bellemonte	St. Louis
Senatahoba	De Soto	Waynesboro'	Wayne	Bellingsville	Cooper
Sharon	Madison	Webster	Winston	Belle View	Iron
Shelby Creek	Tippah	West Pascagoula	Jackson	Bern	Gasconade
Shell Mound	Sun Flower	West Point	Lowndes	Benton	Scott
Sherman Hill	Scott	West's Station	Holmes	Berger	Franklin
Shieldsboro'	Hancock	Westville	Simpson	Berming	Buchanan
Shoobota	Clark	Whitefield	Oktibbeha	Bessville	Hollinger
Short Branch	Calhoun	White Sand	Lawrence	Bethany C. H.	Harrison
Shufordsville	Coahoma	Wilcox	Choctaw	Bethel	Shelby
Shuqualak	Noxubee	Williamsburg	Covington	Bethpage	McDonald
Sidon	Carroll	Winchester	Wayne	Bible Grove	Scotland
Siloam	Oktibbeha	Winona	Carroll	Big Tavern	Miller
Silver Springs	Tippah	Woodlawn	Itawamba	Big Cedar	Jackson
Singleton	Winston	Woodville	Wilkinson	Big Creek	Johnson
Skipwith's Landing	Isaquena	Wyatt	Lafayette	Big River Mills	St. Francis
Slate Spring	Calhoun	Yazoo City	Yazoo	Big Spring	Montgomery
Smithdale	Amite	Yocony	Itawamba	Billupsville	Scotland
Smith's Mills	Carroll	Zero	Lauderdale	Birch Tree	Oregon

POST OFFICES—MISSOURI. 47

Post Office.	County.	Post Office.	County.	Post Office.	County.
Bird's Point	Mississippi	Casto Valley	Texas	Deerfield	Vernon
Bishop's Store	Benton	Catawissa	Franklin	Deer Ridge	Lewis
Blackwell's Station	St. Francis	Cause Prairie	Cass	DeKalb	Buchanan
Blair's Creek	Shannon	Cave Pump	Camden	Dent C. H.	Dent
Bledsoe	Hickory	Cave Spring	Wright	Dent's Station	St. Francis
Bloomfield	Stoddard	Cedar Bluff	Texas	De Soto	Barton
Bloom Garden	Maries	Cedar Creek	Newton	Des Peres	St. Louis
Blooming Rose	Texas	Cedar Fork	Franklin	De Witt	Carroll
Bloomington	Macon	Central	St. Louis	Diamond Grove	Jasper
Blue Ridge	Harrison	Centralia	Boone	Dido	Livingston
Bluff	Texas	Center	Texas	Dillon	Crawford
Blue Spring	Jackson	Center Grove	Atchison	Dogwood Grove	Morgan
Blytheville	Jasper	Centerville	Reynolds	Doniphan C. H.	Ripley
Bœuf Creek	Franklin	Chalk Level	St. Clair	Douglass	Gentry
Bolivar	Polk	Chambersburg	Clark	Dover	Lafayette
Bolton	Harrison	Chamois	Osage	Dresden	Pettis
Boneta	Clarke	Chaney	Dade	Dry Creek	Crawford
Bonhomme	St. Louis	Chantilly	Lincoln	Dry Fork	Jasper
Bonnot's	Osage	Chapel	Howell	Dry Glaze	Laclede
Boone	Franklin	Chapel Hill	Lafayette	Dry Spring	Ripley
Boone's Lick	Howard	Chariton Mills	Putnam	Dry Wood	Vernon
Booneville	Cooper	Charleston	Mississippi	Dundas	Buchanan
Buttsville	Linn	Cheltenham	St. Louis	Dundee	Franklin
Bourbon	Crawford	Cherry	Camden	Dunkle's Store	Lawrence
Bowdark	Greene	Cherry Box	Shelby	Duuksburg	Pettis
Bower's Mills	Lawrence	Cherry Grove	Scuyler	Duroc	Benton
Bowling Green	Pike	Chesapeake	Lawrence	Durgan's Creek	Lewis
Boydsville	Callaway	Chesnut Ridge	St. Genevieve	Eagle	Harrison
Boyer	Washington	Chilhowee	Johnson	Easton	Buchanan
Boyler's Mill	Benton	Chillicothe	Livingston	Economy	Macon
Brandt's Rock Springs		Clarence	Shelby	Edina	Knox
	Warren	Clarksburg	Moniteau	Edinburg	Grundy
Brannansburg	Butler	Clark's Fork	Cooper	Exe Hill	Reynolds
Brazito	Cole	Clarksville	Pike	Elba	Christian
Breckinridge	Caldwell	Clay Hill	Barry	El Dorado	Clarke
Bridgeport	Cooper	Claysville	Boone	Elk Creek	Texas
Bridgeton	St. Louis	Cleavesville	Gasconade	Elk Fork	Bates
Brighton	Polk	Clifty Dale	Mavies	Elk Grove	Lafayette
Bristol	Webster	Clinton	Henry	Elk Mills	McDonald
Brookfield	Linn	Cloverdale	Benton	Elk Spring	Chariton
Brookville	Marion	Coal Bank	Cooper	Elkton	Hickory
Brown	Cedar	Coal Hill	Boone	Ellisville	St. Louis
Brownsville	Saline	Cogswell's Landing	Jackson	Ellsworth	Texas
Brunot	Wayne	Cold Neck	Cooper	El Paso	Atchison
Brunswick	Chariton	Cold Springs	Moniteau	Elm Grove	Crawford
Brush Creek	Laclede	Cold Water	Wayne	Elm Spring	Newton
Bryan	Saline	Cole Camp	Benton	Elmwood	Saline
Buchanan	Bollinger	College Mound	Macon	Elston Station	Cole
Bucklin	Linn	Colony	Knox	Emerson	Marion
Buck Snort	Christian	Columbia	Boone	Eminence C. H.	Shannon
Buffalo	Dallas	Columbus	Johnson	Empire Prairie	Andrew
Bull Mills	Taney	Commerce	Scott	Enterprise	McDonald
Bunker Hill	Lewis	Competition	Laclede	Erie	"
Burbois	Franklin	Concord	Callaway	Etna	Scotland
Butler C. H.	Bates	Conner's Mills	Cooper	Everett	Cass
Buttsville	Grundy	Cooke's Store	Lafayette	Eureka	St. Louis
Bynumville	Chariton	Coon Creek	Jasper	Fair Grove	Greene
Byron	Mavies	Cooper's Hill	Osage	Fairmont	Clarke
Cadet	Washington	Coplinger's Mills	Cedar	Fair Play	Polk
Cahoka	Clarke	Copper Spring	Douglass	Fair Point	Cooper
Cainesville	Harrison	Cornelia	Johnson	Fair View	Pettis
Cairo	Randolph	Cornersville	Hickory	Falling Spring	Douglass
Caledonia	Washington	Cote Sans Dessien	Callaway	Farley	Platte
Calhoun	Henry	Cuttleville	St. Charles	Farmdale	Moniteau
California	Moniteau	Cottonwood Point	Pemiscot	Farmington	St. Francis
Callao	Macon	Cove Creek	Bates	Farrar's Mill	Madison
Calvy	Franklin	Cow Creek	Saline	Fayette	Howard
Cambridge	Saline	Cow Skin	Douglass	Fayetteville	Johnson
Camden	Ray	Crab Orchard	Ray	Faume Osage	t. Charles
Camden Point	Platte	Crab Tree	Greene	Fenton	St. Louis
Cameron	Clinton	Crawford Seminary	Quawpaw	Fidelity	Jasper
Camphelton	Franklin	Creve Cœur	St. Louis	Fillmore	Andrew
Canaan	Gasconade	Crittenden	Daviess	Finley	Webster
Cane Creek	Butler	Crescent Hill	Bates	Finney's Creek	Saline
Cane Hill	Cedar	Cross Plains	Dallas	Flat Creek	Barry
Canton	Lewis	Cross Roads	St. Francis	Flat Woods	Phelps
Cap Au Gris	Lincoln	Cuba	Crawford	Flint Hill	St. Charles
CapeGirardeau	CapeGirardeau	Cuivro	Lincoln	Florence	Morgan
Capp's Creek	Newton	Curran	Stone	Florida	Monroe
Carbon	Macon	Cypress	Scott	Florisant	St. Louis
Carlisle	Texas	Cross Timbers	Hickory	Floyd's Creek	Adair
Carondelet	St. Louis	Dadesville	Dade	Forest City	Hot
Carpenter's Store	Clinton	Dallas	Greene	Forest Grove	Mississippi
Carrollton	Carroll	Danville	Montgomery	Forest Home	Lawrence
Carthage	Jasper	Darksville	Randolph	Forkner's Hill	Laclede
Caruthersville	Pemiscot	Dawn	Livingston	Forsyth	Taney
Castle Rock	Osage	Dayton	Cass	Fort Henry	Randolph
Cassville	Barry	Debruin	Pulaski	Fourche a Renault	Washington
Castor	Bollinger	Decaturville	Camden	Four Mile	Dunklin
		Deep Water	Henry	Fox Creek	St. Louis

POST OFFICES—MISSOURI.

Post Office.	County.	Post Office.	County.	Post Office.	County.
Frankford	Pike	High Hill	Montgomery	Lamonte	Pettis
Franklin	Howard	High Point	Cole	Lancaster	Schuyler
Fredericksburg	Osage	High Ridge	Jefferson	La Plata	Macon
Fredericktown	Madison	Hilt	Scotland	Lane's Prairie	Osage
Freedom	Lafayette	Hillsborough	Jefferson	Laura	Scotland
French Point	Jasper	Hillsboro' Station	"	Laurel Hill	Perry
French Village	St. Francis	Hill's Landing	Carroll	Layton Mills	Taney
Fulton	Callaway	Hogle's Creek	St. Clair	Load Creek	Montgomery
Gadfly	Barry	Holden	Johnson	Leasburg	Crawford
Gainesville C. H.	Ozark	Holstein	Warren	Lebanon	Laclede
Galena	Stone	Honey Creek	McDonald	Leesville	Henry
Gallatin	Daviess	Hopewell	Mississippi	Lessley	Benton
Gasconade Ferry	Gasconade	Hopewell Furnace	Washington	Lesterville	Reynolds
Gates	McDonald	Houston C. H.	Texas	Lexington	Lafayette
Gatewood	Ripley	Howard Corner	Grundy	Liberty	Clay
Gath	Jefferson	Howard's Mills	St. Clair	Libertyville	St Francis
Gay	Daviess	Howe's Mill	Dent	Lick Creek	Ralls
Gayoso	Pemiscot	Hugginsville	Gentry	Licking	Texas
Gentryville	Gentry	Humansville	Polk	Linden	Atchinson
Georgetown	Pettis	Humboldt	Pulaski	Lindley	Grundy
Glasgow	Howard	Hunnewell	Shelby	Linn	Osage
Glencoe	St. Louis	Huntingdale	Henry	Linn Mills	Jasper
Globe	Johnson	Huntsville	Randolph	Linn Creek	Camden
Golden Grove	Barton	Hutton Valley	Howell	Linneus	Linn
Gooch's Mill	Cooper	Hydesburg	Ralls	Liston	Lafayette
Goodland	Knox	Iatan	Platte	Little Beaver	Taney
Goodwin Mills	Ralls	Iberia	Miller	Little Block	Ripley
Graham	Noddaway	Independence	Jackson	Littleby	Andrian
Granby	Newton	Indian Creek	Monroe	Little Niagara	Camden
Grand Falls	"	Indian Ford	Stoddard	Little Osage	Bates
Grant's Hill	Gentry	Irish Grove	Atchison	Little Piney	Pulaski
Granville	Monroe	Irondale	Washington	Little York	Greene
Grassy Creek	Livingston	Iron Hill	Franklin	Littsville	Noddaway
Gravel Road	Cape Girardeau	Iron Mountain	St. Francis	Livingston	Livingston
Graves' Mills	Morgan	Ironton C. H.	Iron	Locust Hill	Knox
Gray's Summit	Franklin	Isabella	Ozark	Locust Ridge	St. Francis
Greene	Bollinger	Island City	Gentry	Locustville	Putnam
Green Castle	Sullivan	Jackson	Cape Girardeau	Logan's Creek	Reynolds
Green Dale	Camden	Jackson's Corners	Sullivan	Lone Grove	Morgan
Greenfield	Dade	Jacksonville	Randolph	Lone Jack	Jackson
Green Hill	Montgomery	Jake's Creek	Texas	Lone Oak	Bates
Greenland	Boone	Jake's Prairie	Gasconade	Long Branch	Monroe
Green Ridge	Pettis	James's Bayou	Mississippi	Long Hollow	Lawrence
Greensburg	Knox	Jamesport	Daviess	Longwood	Pettis
Greenton	Lafayette	Jamestown	Moniteau	Loomesville	McDonald
Green Top	Schuyler	Japan	Franklin	Loose Creek	Osage
Greenville	Wayne	Jasper	Jasper	Lost Camp	Howell
Greenwood Valley	"	Jefferson Barracks	St. Louis	Lost Branch	Lincoln
Grubville	Franklin	Jefferson City	Cole	Lot's Grove	Gentry
Guilford	Noddaway	Jefferson Mills	Jefferson	Louisiana	Pike
Hager's Grove	Shelby	Jeffriesburg	Franklin	Lonisburg	Dallas
Hainesville	Clinton	Jericho	Laclede	Louisville	Lincoln
Halfway	Polk	Jobe	Oregon	Loutre	Audrian
Hall	Lawrence	John's Branch	Audrain	Loutre Island	Warren
Hailsa's Ferry	Noddaway	Johnstown	Bates	Love	Macon
Hallsville	Boone	Juka	Jasper	Lowell	Holt
Hamburg	St. Charles	Jonesboro'	Saline	Lowndes	Wayne
Hamilton	Caldwell	Jones' Point	Holt	Low Wassie	Oregon
Hampton	Platte	Jones' Tanyard	Callaway	Lucas	Henry
Handy	Barry	Jonesville	Cass	Lutzton	Noddaway
Hannibal	Marion	Kansas	Jackson	McDowell	Barry
Hardin	Bay	Kasliu	Iron	Macon City	Macon
Harmony	Washington	Kelso	Scott	Madison	Monroe
Harrison's Mills	Crawford	Kendall	Clay	Madisonville	Ralls
Harrisonville	Cass	Konnett C. H.	Dunkirk	Mahon's Creek	Shannon
Hartford	Putnam	Kent	Newton	Manchester	St. Louis
Hartville	Wright	Kenton	Christian	Mandeville	Carroll
Hawk Point	Lincoln	Keytesville	Chariton	Manlius	"
Hazel Barrens	Barry	Kidder	Caldwell	Manton	Daviess
Hazel Bottom	"	Kiddville	Sullivan	Maramac	Crawford
Hazel Green	Laclede	Kimmswick	Jefferson	Marble Creek	Iron
Hazel Grove	Saline	King's Point	Dade	Marion	Cole
Hazel Run Mills	St. Francis	Kingston	Caldwell	Marshall	Saline
Hazelwood	Wright	Kingsville	Johnson	Marshfield	Webster
Havana	Gentry	Kirksville	Adair	Marthasville	Warren
Hematite	Jefferson	Kirkwood	St. Louis	Martin	Greene
Henderson	Greene	Knob Noster	Johnson	Martinsburg	Ripley
Houpeck	Shannon	Knob View	Crawford	Martinstown	Putnam
Hermann	Gasconade	Knoxville	Ray	Marvel	Bates
Hermitage	Hickory	Labaddie	Franklin	Maryville	Noddaway
Herron	Camden	La Belle	Lewis	Mattehend	Saline
Hester	Marion	Laclede	Linn	Mattese	St. Louis
Hibernia	Callaway	Laeon	Davies	Maysville C. H.	DeKalb
Hickory Barren	Greene	La Grange	Lewis	Medoc	Jasper
Hickory Creek	Audrain	Lakenan	Shelby	Medora	Osage
Hickory Hill	Cole	Lake Spring	Dent	Melrose	St. Louis
Hickory Port	Grundy	Lakeville	Stoddard	Memphis	Scotland
Hickory Ridge	Cape Girardeau	Lamar	Barton	Menden	Lawrence
Hickory Spring	Texas	Lamar's Station	Noddaway	Mercer	Mercer
High Blue	Cass	La Mine	Cooper	Mexico	Audrain

POST OFFICES—MISSOURI. 49

Post Office.	County.	Post Office.	County.	Post Office.	County.
Miami	Saline	Oakland	Laclede	Pleasant Valley	Wright
Middle Brook	Iron	Oak Point	Moniteau	Pleasant View	Ray
Middlebury	Mercer	Oak Ridge	Cape Girardeau	Plum Creek	Clinton
Middle Fabius	Scotland	Oakwood	St. Charles	Plum Valley	Texas
Middle Grove	Monroe	O'Fallon	"	Pocahontas	Cape Girardeau
Middletown	Montgomery	Ogden	New Madrid	Point Pleasant	New Madrid
Midway	Cooper	Og'e's Mills	Andrew	Poplar Bluff	Butler
Milan	Sullivan	Olio	Macon	Portage Des Sioux	St. Charles
Miles Point	Carroll	Old Alexandria	Lincoln	Port Hudson	Franklin
Mill Creek	Ripley	Old Mines	Washington	Portland	Callaway
Millersburg	Callaway	Omaha	Putnam	Port Perry	Perry
Mill Port	Knox	Oregon	Holt	Port Royal	Jasper
Millville	Ray	Orleans	Polk	Post Oak	Johnson
Millwood	Lincoln	Orr	Webster	Potosi	Washington
Milton	Randolph	Osage	Crawford	Pottersville	Howell
Mine La Motte	Madison	Osage Bluff	Cole	Prairie Bird	Adair
Mineral Point	Washington	Osage City	"	Prairie City	Bates
Minerva	Morgan	Osage Fork	Laclede	Prairie Creek	Osage
Mining	"	Osborn	De Kalb	Prairie Fork	Montgomery
Mint Spring	Wright	Osceola	St. Clair	Prairie Home	Johnson
Mirabile	Caldwell	Otsego	Ray	Prairieville	Pike
Missouri City	Clay	Otter Creek	Wayne	Preston	Jasper
Missouriton	St. Charles	Otterville	Cooper	Price's Branch	Montgomery
Modena	Mercer	Ovid	Cass	Price's Landing	Scott
Monagan	St. Clair	Owasco	Sullivan	Princeton	Mercer
Monroe City	Monroe	Owensville	Gasconade	Prior's Mills	Osage
Moutauk	Texas	Oxford	Worth	Prospect Grove	Scotland
Montevallo	Vernon	Oyster	Lewis	Prospect Hill	Ray
Monticello	Lewis	Ozark	Christian	Providence	Boone
Montgomery City	Montgomery	Pacific	Franklin	Pryor's Store	Taney
Mooresville	Livingston	Pallas	Greene	Punjaub	St. Genevieve
Morgau	Adair	Palmyra	Marion	Quincy	Hickory
Mornington	Webster	Panama	Pulaski	Quitman	Noddaway
Morrison	Gasconade	Paineswick	Davies	Randolph	Randolph
Morse's Mill	Jefferson	Panther Valley	Webster	Ravenna	Mercer
Morristown	Cass	Papinsville	Bates	Readsville	Callaway
Moscow	Greene	Paris	Monroe	Reese Hill	Reynolds
Moss	Lafayette	Parkville	Platte	Reeves' Station	Butler
Mount Helicon	Franklin	Pasco	Dallas	Reform	Callaway
Mount Hope	Lafayette	Paton	Bollinger	Reindeer	Noddaway
Mount Sterling	Gasconade	Patterson	Wayne	Rolfe	Pulaski
Mount Vernon	Lawrence	Pattonsburg	Daviess	Rhineland	Montgomery
Mount View	Benton	Paulville	Adair	Rice's Ferry	Macon
Mule Creek	Cedar	Pay Down	Davies	Rich	Atchison
Munger's Mills	Shannon	Paynesville	Pike	Rich Fountain	Osage
Muscle Mills	Sullivan	Peakesville	Clarke	Richland	Greene
Myers	Howard	Pedee	Schuyler	Richmond	Ray
Napoleon City	Lafayette	Pendleton	Warren	Richmond Hill	Shannon
Narrows	Noddaway	Pennville	Sullivan	Richwoods	Washington
Naylor's Store	St. Charles	Peoples	Cape Girardeau	Ridgely	Platte
Nebo	Pulaski	Peoria	Bates	Ridge Prairie	Saline
Neely's Landing	Cape Girardeau	Perkin's Creek	Bollinger	Right Point	Camden
		Perryville	Perry	King's Point	Adair
Neelyville	Ripley	Petra	Saline	Roanoke	Randolph
Nelsouville	Marion	Pevely	Jefferson	Roaring River	Barry
Neosho	Newton	Phelps	Lawrence	Robertson's Mill	Stone
Nevada	Vernon	Philadelphia	Marion	Rocheport	Boone
Newark	Knox	Philander	Gentry	Rochester	Andrew
New Bloomfield	Callaway	Pierce	Callaway	Rock Bridge	Ozark
New Boston	Macon	Pigeon Creek	Ralls	Rockford	Cass
New Bremen	St. Genevieve	Pike Creek	Ripley	Rock Hill	St. Louis
New Castle	Gentry	Piketon	Stoddard	Rock House Prairie	Buchanan
New Florence	Montgomery	Pilot Grove	Cooper	Rockport	Atchison
New Harmony	Pike	Pilot Knob	Iron	Rock Spring	Washington
New Haven	Franklin	Pinckney	Warren	Rocky Mount	Miller
New Hope	Lincoln	Pine Bluff	Pulaski	Rolla	Phelps
New London	Ralls	Pine Hill	Shannon	Rome	Boone
New Madrid	New Madrid	Pineville	McDonald	Ronda	Polk
New Market	Platte	Pink Hill	Jackson	Roubidoux	Texas
New Melle	St. Charles	Pin Oak	Warren	Round Hill	Cooper
New Offenburg	S.. Genevieve	Pisgah	Cooper	Rowletta	Pettis
New Santa Fe	Jackson	Pitts	Warren	Rucker's Prairie	Franklin
Newtonia	Newton	Pittsburg	Hickory	Rush Ridge	Mississippi
Newtown	Putnam	Pittsville	Johnson	Rushville	Buchanan
New Winchester	Carroll	Plank Road	St. Genevieve	Russell's Hill	Reynolds
Nineveh	Adair	Platin	Jefferson	Russelville	Cole
Noell	Iron	Plato	Texas	Rutledge C. H.	McDonald
Nobleton	Newton	Platte City	Platte	Sacramento	Wright
Norma	Webster	Platte River	Buchanan	Saint Aubert	Callaway
Normandy	St. Louis	Plattsburg	Clinton	St. Catherine	Linn
Norris' Fork	Henry	Pleasant Farm	Miller	St. Charles	St. Charles
Northcutt	Linn	Pleasant Gap	Bates	St. Clair	Franklin
North Point	Holt	Pleasant Green	Cooper	St. Francisville	Clarke
North Salem	Linn	Pleasant Hill	Cass	St. Genevieve C. H.	St. Genevieve
North Star	Atchison	Pleasant Home	Putnam		
Novelty	Knox	Pleasant Hope	Polk	St. James	Phelps
Oakdale	Shelby	Pleasant Mount	Miller	St. John	Putnam
Oakfield	Franklin	Pleasant Park	Carroll	St. Joseph	Buchanan
Oak Grove	Jackson	Pleasant Retreat	Scotland	St. Leger	Ozark
Oak Hill	Gasconade	Pleasant Ridge	Harrison	St. Louis	St. Louis

4

POST OFFICES—NEW HAMPSHIRE.

Post Office.	County.
St. Luke	Webster
St. Mark	"
St. Mary's	St. Genevieve
St. Paul	Webster
St. Peters	St. Charles
St. Thomas	Cole
Salem	Linn
Saline	Mercer
Salt River	Audrian
Sand Hill	Scotland
Sandy Mines	Jefferson
San Francisco	Carroll
Santa Fe	Monroe
Sappington	St. Louis
Sarcoxie	Jasper
Sarvis Spring	Dent
Savannah C. H.	Andrew
Saverton	Ralls
Scotland Ridge	Putnam
Scottville	Sullivan
Sedalia	Pettis
Selden	Douglass
Selma	Jefferson
Sentinel Prairie	Polk
Shady Grove	Dallas
Shamrock	Callaway
Sharpsburg	Marion
Shawnee Mound	Henry
Sheffield	Cape Girardeau
Shelbina	Shelby
Shelbyville	"
Shibley's Point	Adair
Shields	Mavies
Sherwood	Jasper
Shoneytown	Putnam
Short Bend	Crawford
Shotwell	Franklin
Sibley	Jackson
Sidney	Ralls
Sikeston	Scott
Silver Creek	Cedar
Smith City	Pettis
Smithton	Worth
Smithville	Clay
Snell's Mill	Harrison
Snibar	Lafayette
Snow Hill	St. Charles
Solitude	Pemiscot
Somerset	Monroe
Sous Creek	Dade
South Fork	Howell
South Grove	Saline
South Point	Franklin
Spanish Prairie	Phelps
Sparlinville	Newton
Sparta	Buchanan
Spencersburg	Pike
Spring Creek	Pulaski
Springfield	Greene
Spring Fork	Pettis
Spring Garden	"
Spring Grove	Dallas
Spring Hill	Livingston
Spruce	Bates
Stanford	Texas
Stanton Copper Mines	Franklin
Steelsville	Crawford
Stein's Prairie	Mavies
Stewart's	Warren
Stewartsville	De Kalb
Stockland	Montgomery
Stockton	Cedar
Stone House	Morgan
Stono	St. Francis
Stony Point	Jackson
Stringfield's Store	Callaway
Sturgeon	Boone
Sugar Creek	Clarke
Sugar Tree Grove	Clay
Sullivan	Franklin
Sulphur Springs [Landing]	Jefferson
Summit	Macon
Swan	Taney
Sweet Home	Noddaway
Sylvan	Dent
Syracuse	Morgan
Tabo	Lafayette
Tagart's Mill	Carroll

Post Office.	County.
Talladega	Dent
Tallow Hill	Jefferson
Taos	Cole
Ten Mile	Macon
Third Fork	De Kalb
Thomasville	Oregon
Tiger Fork	Shelby
Tinney's Grove	Ray
Tipton	Moniteau
Tiviot	Montgomery
Toledo	Henry
Toronto	Camden
Trail Creek	Harrison
Trenton	Grundy
Troy	Lincoln
Truxton	"
Tuckersville	Camden
Tugne	Warren
Tullvania	Macon
Turkey Creek	Madison
Turnback	Dade
Turnersville	Greene
Tuscumbia	Miller
Tyro	Jefferson
Uman's Ridge	Miller
Union	Franklin
Union Mills	Platte
Unionville	Putnam
Urbana	Dallas
Utica	Livingston
Valparaiso	Sullivan
Van Buren	Carter
Vancill's Landing	Cape Girardeau
Vannoy's Mill	Pike
Vermont	Cooper
Verona	Lawrence
Versailles	Morgan
Vera Cruz	Douglas
Victoria	Davies
Vienna	Mavies
Virginia Mills	Franklin
Wadesburg	Cass
Wagon Knob	Lafayette
Waldo	Webster
Walkersville	Shelby
Wall's Store	Johnson
Walnut Grove	Greene
Walnut Hill	Buchanan
Walnut Shade	Taney
Waltersville	Adair
Wearbleau	St. Clair
Warren	Marion
Warrensburg	Johnson
Warrenton	Warren
Warsaw	Benton
Washburn Prairie	Barry
Washington	Franklin
Waterloo	Clarke
Waverly	Lafayette
Waynesville	Pulaski
Webster	Oregon
Webster Station	St. Louis
Wellington	Lafayette
Wellsburg	St. Charles
Wellsville	Montgomery
Wentzville	St. Charles
Wesley	Schuyler
West Bend	Polk
West Ely	Marion
Westland	Chariton
West Liberty	Putnam
West Locust	Sullivan
Westphalia	Osage
West Plains	Howell
West Point	Bates
Westport	Jackson
West Prairie	Dunklin
West Quincy	Marion
Weston	Platte
West Springfield	Shelby
Wet Glaze	Camden
Wheatland	Morgan
Wheeling	Vernon
Whetstone	Wright
White Cloud	Noddaway
White Hare	Cedar
White Oak	Montgomery
White Oak Grove	Greene
White Rock Prairie	McDonald

Post Office.	County.
Whitesburg	Camden
Whitesville	Andrew
White Water	Bolinger
Willard	Greene
Williamsburg	Callaway
Williamstown	Lewis
Willmathsville	Adair
Wilson	Greene
Wilson Creek	Clarke
Winchester	"
Windsor	Henry
Winslow	Dent
Wintersville	Sullivan
Winthrop	Buchanan
Wolf Creek	Wright
Woodbine	Harrison
Woodbury	Wright
Wood's Fork	"
Woodlawn	Monroe
Woodside	Oregon
Woodville	Macon
Woolam	Gasconade
Wright City	Warren
Wrightsville	Clarke
Wyaconda	Scotland
Xenia	Noddaway
Yancey	Phelps
Yolo	Gentry
Young's Creek	Audrian
Young's Mills	Franklin
Zif	Stoddard
Zion	Henry

New Hampshire

Post Office.	County.
Acworth	Sullivan
Alexandria	Grafton
Allenstown	Merrimack
Alstead	Cheshire
Alton	Belknap
Amherst	Hillsboro'
Amoskeag	Hillsboro'
Andover	Merrimack
Antrim	Hillsboro'
Ashuelot	Cheshire
Atkinson	Rockingham
Atkinson Depot	Rockingham
Auburn	Rockingham
Barnstead	Belknap
Barrington	Strafford
Bartlett	Carroll
Bath	Grafton
Bedford	Hillsboro'
Bennington	Hillsboro'
Benton	Grafton
Berlin	Coos
Berlin Falls	Coos
Bethlehem	Grafton
Boscawen	Merrimack
Bow	Merrimack
Bradford	Merrimack
Brentwood	Rockingham
Bridgewater	Grafton
Bristol	Grafton
Brookfield	Carroll
Brookline	Hillsboro'
Campton	Grafton
Campton Village	Grafton
Canaan	Grafton
Candia	Rockingham
Candia Village	Rockingham
Canterbury	Merrimack
Carroll	Coos
Center Barnstead	Belknap
Center Conway	Carroll
Center Harbor	Belknap
Center Ossipee	Carroll
Center Sandwich	Carroll
Center Strafford	Strafford
Charlestown	Sullivan
Chester	Rockingham
Chesterfield	Cheshire
Chesterfield Factory	Cheshire
Chichester	Merrimack
Claremont	Sullivan

POST OFFICES—NEW HAMPSHIRE. 51

Post Office.	County.	Post Office.	County.	Post Office.	County.
Clarksville	Coös	Hanover	Grafton	Northfield Depot	Merrimack
Colebrook	Coös	Hanover Center	Grafton	North Grantham	Sullivan
Columbia	Coös	Harrisville	Cheshire	North Groton	Grafton
Concord	Merrimack	Haverhill	Grafton	North Hampton	Rockingham
Contoocook Village	Merrimack	Haverhill Center	Grafton	N. Hampton Depot	Rockingham
Conway	Carroll	Hebron	Grafton	North Haverhill	Grafton
Coös	Coös	Henniker	Merrimack	North Lisbon	Grafton
Cornish Flat	Sullivan	Hill	Grafton	North Littleton	Grafton
Crawford's House	Coös	Hillsboro'	Hillsboro'	N. Londonderry	Rockingham
Croyden	Sullivan	Hillsboro' Bridge	Hillsboro'	N. Lyndeborough	Hillsboro'
Croyden Flats	Sullivan	Hillsboro' Center	Hillsboro'	North Monroe	Grafton
Dalton	Coös	Hinsdale	Cheshire	North Richmond	Cheshire
Danbury	Grafton	Holderness	Grafton	North Salem	Rockingham
Danville	Rockingham	Hollis	Hillsboro'	North Sanbornton	Belknap
Deerfield	Rockingham	Hooksett	Merrimack	North Sandwich	Carroll
Deerfield Center	Rockingham	Hopkinton	Merrimack	North Strafford	Strafford
Deering	Hillsboro'	Horn's Mills	Carroll	North Sutton	Merrimack
Derry	Rockingham	Hudson	Hillsboro'	Northumberland	Coös
Derry Depot	Rockingham	Jackson	Coös	North Wakefield	Carroll
Dorchester	Grafton	Jaffrey	Cheshire	North Weare	Hillsboro'
Dover	Strafford	Jefferson	Coös	North Wolfborough	Carroll
Downing's Mills	Strafford	Jefferson Mills	Coös	Nottingham	Rockingham
Drewsville	Cheshire	Keene	Cheshire	Nottingham Turnpike	Rockingham
Dublin	Cheshire	Kensington	Rockingham		
Dunbarton	Merrimack	Kingston	Rockingham	Oil Mill Village	Hillsboro'
Durham	Strafford	Laconia	Belknap	Orford	Grafton
East Andover	Merrimack	Lake Village	Belknap	Orfordville	Grafton
East Canaan	Grafton	Lancaster	Coös	Ossippee	Carroll
East Chester	Rockingham	Landaff	Grafton	Paper Mill Village	Cheshire
East Concord	Merrimack	Langdon	Sullivan	Pelham	Hillsboro'
East Haverhill	Grafton	Lebanon	Grafton	Pembroke	Merrimack
East Jaffrey	Cheshire	Lee	Strafford	Peterborough	Hillsboro'
East Kingston	Rockingham	Leighton's Corners	Carroll	Piermont	Grafton
East Landaff	Grafton	Lempster	Sullivan	Pittsburg	Coös
East Lebanon	Grafton	Lincoln	Grafton	Pittsfield	Merrimack
East Lempster	Sullivan	Lisbon	Grafton	Plainfield	Sullivan
East Madison	Carroll	Littleton	Grafton	Plaistow	Rockingham
East Moultonboro'	Carroll	London	Merrimack	Plymouth	Grafton
East Northwood	Rockingham	London Center	Merrimack	Pottersville	Cheshire
East Plainfield	Sullivan	Londonderry	Rockingham	Portsmouth	Rockingham
East Sanbornton	Belknap	London Ridge	Merrimack	Profile House	Grafton
East Sullivan	Cheshire	Lower Bartlett	Carroll	Randolph	Coös
East Unity	Sullivan	Lower Gilmanton	Belknap	Raymond	Rockingham
East Wakefield	Carroll	Lyman	Grafton	Reed's Ferry	Hillsboro'
East Washington	Sullivan	Lyne	Grafton	Richmond	Cheshire
East Weare	Hillsboro'	Lyndeborough	Hillsboro'	Rindge	Cheshire
East Westmoreland	Cheshire	Mackerel Corners	Carroll	Rochester	Strafford
Eaton Center	Carroll	Madison	Carroll	Rowe's Corner	Merrimack
Effingham	Carroll	Manchester	Hillsboro'	Rumney	Grafton
Effingham Falls	Carroll	Marlborough	Cheshire	Rye	Rockingham
Ellsworth	Grafton	Marlborough Depot	Cheshire	Salem	Rockingham
Enfield	Grafton	Marlow	Cheshire	Salisbury	Merrimack
Enfield Center	Grafton	Mason	Hillsboro'	Salmon Falls	Strafford
Epping	Rockingham	Mason Village	Hillsboro'	Sanbornton	Belknap
Epsom	Merrimack	Mast Yard	Merrimack	Sanbornton Bridge	Belknap
Errol	Coös	Melvin Village	Carroll	Sandown	Rockingham
Exeter	Rockingham	Meredith Center	Belknap	Sandwich	Carroll
Farmington	Strafford	Meredith Village	Belknap	Seabrook	Rockingham
Fernanden Mills	Rockingham	Meriden	Sullivan	Shaker Village	Merrimack
Fishersville	Merrimack	Middleton	Strafford	Shelburn	Coös
Fitzwilliam	Cheshire	Milan	Coös	South Acworth	Sullivan
Flume	Grafton	Milford	Hillsboro'	South Charlestown	Sullivan
Franciestown	Hillsboro'	Mill Village	Sullivan	South Danbury	Grafton
Franconia	Grafton	Milton	Strafford	South Deerfield	Rockingham
Franklin	Merrimack	Milton Mills	Strafford	South Hampton	Rockingham
Freedom	Carroll	Monroe	Grafton	South Kingston	Rockingham
Fremont	Rockingham	Moultonboro'	Carroll	South Lyndeborough	Hillsboro'
George's Mills	Sullivan	Mountain House	Grafton	South Merrimack	Hillsboro'
Gilford Village	Belknap	Mount Vernon	Hillsboro'	South Newbury	Merrimack
Gilmanton	Belknap	Munsonville	Cheshire	S. New Market	Rockingham
Gilmanton Iron Works	Belknap	Nashua	Hillsboro'	South Raymond	Rockingham
Gilsum	Cheshire	Nelson	Cheshire	South Stoddard	Cheshire
Goff town	Hillsboro'	New Alstead	Cheshire	South Tamworth	Carroll
Goffstown Center	Hillsboro'	New Boston	Hillsboro'	South Weare	Hillsboro'
Gonic	Strafford	Newbury	Merrimack	South Wolfborough	Carroll
Gorham	Coös	New Hampton	Belknap	Springfield	Sullivan
Goshen	Sullivan	Newington	Rockingham	Stark	Coös
Grafton	Grafton	New Ipswich	Hillsboro'	Stewartstown	Coös
Grafton Center	Grafton	New London	Merrimack	Stoddard	Cheshire
Grantham	Sullivan	New Market	Rockingham	Strafford	Strafford
Great Falls	Strafford	Newport	Sullivan	Strafford Blue Hill	Strafford
Greenfield	Hillsboro'	Newton	Rockingham	Strafford Corner	Strafford
Greenland	Rockingham	North Barrington	Strafford	Stratford	Coös
Greenland Depot	Rockingham	North Barnstead	Belknap	Stratham	Rockingham
Groton	Grafton	North Branch	Hillsboro'	Sugar Hill	Grafton
Groveton	Coös	North Charleston	Sullivan	Sullivan	Cheshire
Hampstead	Rockingham	North Chichester	Merrimack	Sunapee	Sullivan
Hampton	Rockingham	North Conway	Carroll	Suncook	Merrimack
Hampton Falls	Rockingham	North Dorchester	Grafton	Surry	Cheshire
Hancock	Hillsboro'	North Dunbarton	Merrimack	Sutton	Merrimack

POST OFFICES—NEW JERSEY.

Post Office.	County.
Swanzey	Cheshire
Tamworth	Carroll
Tamworth Iron Works	Carroll
Temple	Hillsboro'
Thornton	Grafton
Thornton's Ferry	Hillsboro'
Troy	Cheshire
Tuftonborough	Carroll
Union	Carroll
Unity	Sullivan
Upper Gilmanton	Belknap
Wadley's Falls	Strafford
Wakefield	Carroll
Walpole	Cheshire
Warner	Merrimack
Warren	Grafton
Washington	Sullivan
Water Village	Carroll
Weare	Hillsboro'
Weir's Bridge	Belknap
Wentworth	Grafton
Wentworth's Location	Coos
West Alton	Belknap
West Andover	Merrimack
West Boscawen	Merrimack
West Campton	Grafton
West Canaan	Grafton
West Claremont	Sullivan
West Concord	Merrimack
West Enfield	Grafton
West Henniker	Merrimack
West Hopkinton	Merrimack
West Lebanon	Grafton
West Littleton	Grafton
West Milan	Coos
West Milton	Strafford
Westmoreland	Cheshire
Westmoreland Depot	Cheshire
West Northwood	Rockingham
West Ossipee	Carroll
West Plymouth	Grafton
Westport	Cheshire
West Rumney	Grafton
West Salisbury	Merrimack
West Springfield	Sullivan
West Stewartson	Coos
West Swanzey	Cheshire
West Thornton	Grafton
West Wilton	Hillsboro'
West Windham	Rockingham
Whitefield	Coos
White Mountain House	Coos
Wilmot	Merrimack
Wilmot Flats	Merrimack
Wilton	Hillsboro'
Winchester	Cheshire
Windham	Rockingham
Wolfborough	Carroll
Woodstock	Grafton
Woodsville	Grafton

New Jersey.

Post Office.	County.
Absecon	Atlantic
Allamuchy	Warren
Allentown	Monmouth
Allowaystown	Salem
Anderson	Warren
Andover	Sussex
Arneytown	Burlington
Asbury	Warren
Atlantic City	Atlantic
Augusta	Sussex
Baker's Basin	Mercer
Baptistown	Hunterdon
Bargaintown	Atlantic
Barnegat	Ocean
Barusborough	Gloucester
Basking Ridge	Somerset
Batsto	Burlington
Beatystown	Warren
Beemerville	Sussex
Beesley's Point	Cape May
Belleville	Essex
Belvidere	Warren
Bennett's Mills	Ocean
Bergen Iron Works	"
Bergen Point	Hudson
Berkshire Valley	Morris
Bethlehem	Hunterdon
Bevan's	Sussex
Beverly	Burlington
Black's Mills	Monmouth
Blackwoodstown	Camden
Blairstown	Warren
Blawanburg	Somerset
Bloomfield	Essex
Bloomingdale	Passaic
Bloomsburg	Hunterdon
Boonton	Morris
Bordentown	Burlington
Boundbrook	Somerset
Brainard's	Warren
Branchville	Sussex
Bridgeboro	Burlington
Bridgeport	Gloucester
Bridgeton	Cumberland
Bridgeville	Warren
Broadway	"
Brotzmanville	"
Brown's Mills	Burlington
Buckshuter	Cumberland
Budd's Lake	Morris
Burlington	Burlington
Caldwell	Essex
Caino	Warren
Camden	Camden
Canton	Salem
Cape Island	Cape May
Cape May	"
Carlstadt	Bergen
Carpenter's Landing	Gloucester
Carpentersville	Warren
Cassville	Ocean
Cedar Creek	"
Cedarville	Cumberland
Centertown	Salem
Centerville	Hunterdon
Changewater	Warren
Chapel Hill	Monmouth
Chatham	Morris
Cherryville	Hunterdon
Chester	Morris
Chetwood	Burlington
Chew's Landing	Camden
Cinnaminson	Burlington
Clarksboro'	Gloucester
Clarksburg	Monmouth
Clarksville	Hunterdon
Clinton	"
Clinton Station	"
Closter	Bergen
Clove	Sussex
Clover Hill	Hunterdon
Cokesburg	"
Cold Spring	Cape May
Colesville	Sussex
Colt's Neck	Monmouth
Columbia	Warren
Columbus	Burlington
Cookstown	"
Copper Hill	Hunterdon
Cranberry	Middlesex
Cranesville	Union
Cresskill	Bergen
Cross Keys	Camden
Cross Wicks	Burlington
Croton	Hunterdon
Crowleyville	Burlington
Danville	Warren
Daretown	Salem
Davisville	Ocean
Deckertown	Sussex
Decosta	Atlantic
Deerfield Street	Cumberland
Delanco	Burlington
Delaware Station	Warren
Dennisville	Cape May
Denville	Morris
Dias Creek	Cape May
Dividing Creek	Cumberland
Dover	Morris
Drakestown	"
Drakesville	"
Dutch Neck	Mercer
East Creek	Cape May
Eatontown	Monmouth
Edinburg	Mercer
Egg Harbor City	Atlantic
Elizabeth	Union
Elizabethport	"
Ellisburg	Camden
Elmer	Salem
Englewood	Bergen
English Creek	Atlantic
English Neighborhood	Bergen
Englishtown	Monmouth
Everittstown	Hunterdon
Ewing's Neck	Cumberland
Ewingsville	Mercer
Fairmount	Hunterdon
Fairton	Cumberland
Farmingdale	Monmouth
Fellowship	Burlington
Fillmore	Monmouth
Fisherville	Gloucester
Fishing Creek	Cape May
Flaggtown	Somerset
Flanders	Morris
Flatbrookville	Sussex
Flemington	Hunterdon
Florence	Burlington
Forest Grove	Cumberland
Forked River	Ocean
Fort Lee	Bergen
Franklin	Essex
Franklin Furnace	Sussex
Franklinville	Gloucester
Freedom	Sussex
Freehold	Monmouth
Frenchtown	Hunterdon
Georgetown	Burlington
German Valley	Morris
Glassboro'	Gloucester
Glendale	Camden
Gloucester City	"
Godwinville	Bergen
Goshen	Cape May
Gratitude	Sussex
Green Bank	Burlington
Green Creek	Cape May
Greensburg	Mercer
Greenwich	Cumberland
Griggstown	Somerset
Groveville	Mercer
Hackensack	Bergen
Hackettstown	Warren
Haddonfield	Camden
Hainesburg	Warren
Hainesville	Sussex
Hamburg	"
Hamilton Square	Mercer
Hammonton	Atlantic
Hancock's Bridge	Salem
Hanover	Morris
Hanover Neck	"
Hardingville	Gloucester
Hardwick	Warren
Harlingen	Somerset
Harmony	Warren
Harrison	Hudson
Harrisonville	Gloucester
Harrisville	Burlington
High Bridge	Hunterdon
Hightstown	Mercer
Hoboken	Hudson
Hohokus	Bergen
Holland	Hunterdon
Holmdel	Monmouth
Hornerstown	Ocean
Hope	Warren
Hopewell	Mercer
Howard	Warren
Hudson	Hudson
Hurffville	Camden
Imlaystown	Monmouth
Irvington	Essex
Jackson	Camden
Jacksonville	Burlington
Jacobstown	"
Jamesburg	Middlesex
Jersey City	Hudson
Jobstown	Burlington
Johnsonburg	Warren

POST OFFICES—NEW JERSEY.

Post Office.	County.
Juliustown	Burlington
Karrsville	Warren
Keyport	Monmouth
Kingston	M'x
Kingwood	Hunterdon
Kinesville	
Knowlton	Warren
Lafayette	Sussex
Lambertville	Hunterdon
Lawrenceville	Mercer
Lebanon	Hunterdon
Lebanon Glass Works	Burlington
Leed's Point	Atlantic
Leedsville	Monmouth
Leesburg	Cumberland
Lesser X Roads	Somerset
Liberty Corners	
Libertyville	Sussex
Little Falls	Passaic
Little York	Hunterdon
Livingston	Essex
Locktown	Hunterdon
Lodi	Bergen
Long-a-coming	Camden
Long Branch	Monmouth
Long Hill	Morris
Lower Bank	Burlington
Lower Squankum	Monmouth
Lumberton	Burlington
Madison	Morris
Malaga	Gloucester
Manahawkin	Ocean
Manalapan	Monmouth
Marksboro'	Warren
Marlboro'	Monmouth
Marlton	Burlington
Martinsville	Somerset
Mauricetown	Cumberland
May's Landing	Atlantic
Mead's Basin	Passaic
Medford	Burlington
Mendham	Morris
Metedeconk	Ocean
Metuchen	Middlesex
Middlebush	Somerset
Middletown	Monmouth
Middletown Point	
Middleville	Sussex
Milford	Hunterdon
Millbrook	Warren
Millburn	Essex
Millington	Morris
Millstone	Somerset
Millville	Cumberland
Milton	Morris
Monroe	Sussex
Montague	Sussex
Moorestown	Burlington
Morristown	Morris
Mountainville	Hunterdon
Mount Bethel	Warren
Mount Ephraim	Camden
Mount Holly	Burlington
Mount Laurel	
Mount Pleasant	Hunterdon
Mount Rose	Mercer
Mount Salem	Sussex
Mullica Hill	Gloucester
Musconetcong	Warren
Neighborsville	Morris
Neshanic	Somerset
Newark	Essex
New Bedford	Monmouth
New Brunswick	Middlesex
New Durham	Hudson
New Egypt	Ocean
Newfoundland	Morris
New Germantown	Hunterdon
New Gretna	Burlington
New Hampton	Hunterdon
New Lisbon	Burlington
New Market	Middlesex
New Monmouth	Monmouth
Newport	Cumberland
New Providence	Union
New Sharon	Monmouth
Newton	Sussex
New Vernon	Morris
New Village	Warren
North Branch	Somerset
Oakdale	Hunterdon
Oak Grove	
Ocean Port	Monmouth
Ogdensburg	Sussex
Old Bridge	Middlesex
Orange	Essex
Oxford Furnace	Warren
Palmyra	Burlington
Parsippany	Morris
Paskack	Bergen
Passaic	Passaic
Passaic Valley	Morris
Pattenburg	Hunterdon
Paterson	Passaic
Paulina	Warren
Paulsboro'	Gloucester
Peapack	Somerset
Podricktown	Salem
Pemberton	Burlington
Pennington	Mercer
Penn's Grove	Salem
Popokating	Sussex
Perrineville	Monmouth
Perryville	Hunterdon
Perth Amboy	Middlesex
Petersburg	Cape May
Philipsburg	Warren
Pine Brook	Morris
Pitt's Grove	Salem
Pittstown	Hunterdon
Plainfield	Union
Plainsborough	Middlesex
Pleasant Run	Hunterdon
Pleasant Valley	Sussex
Pluckemine	Somerset
Point Pleasant	Ocean
Pointville	Burlington
Polkville	Warren
Pompton	Passaic
Pompton Plains	
Port Elizabeth	Cumberland
Port Mercer	Mercer
Port Republic	Atlantic
Potter's Creek	Ocean
Pottersville	Hunterdon
Princeton	Mercer
Progress	Burlington
Prospect Plains	Middlesex
Quakertown	Hunterdon
Railway	Middlesex
Ramsey's	Bergen
Rancocas	Burlington
Raritan	Somerset
Raven's Rock	Hunterdon
Readington	
Reaville	
Recklastown	Burlington
Redbank	Monmouth
Rieeville	
Ringoe's	Hunterdon
Rio Grande	Cape May
Roadstown	Cumberland
Robbinsville	Mercer
Rocksburg	Warren
Rockaway	Morris
Rocky Hill	Somerset
Rowland Mills	Hunterdon
Saddle River	Bergen
Salem	Salem
Satesville	Hudson
Sand Brook	Hunterdon
Schooley's Mountain	Morris
Schraulenburg	Bergen
Scotch Plains	Essex
Scullown	Salem
Seaville	Cape May
Screpta	Warren
Sergeantsville	Hunterdon
Shamong	Burlington
Shark River	Ocean
Sharptown	Salem
Shelltown	Ocean
Shiloh	Cumberland
Shrewsbury	Monmouth
Sidney	Hunterdon
Six Mile Run	Somerset
Smith's Landing	Atlantic
Somer's Point	
Somerville	Somerset
South Amboy	Middlesex
South Branch	Somerset
South Brunswick	Middlesex
South Orange	Essex
South River	Middlesex
Sparta	Sussex
Spotswood	Middlesex
Springfield	Essex
Springtown	Warren
Spring Valley	Bergen
Squam Village	Ocean
Stanhope	Sussex
Stanton	Hunterdon
Stephensburg	Morris
Stewartsville	Warren
Still Valley	
Stillwater	Sussex
Stockholm	Sussex
Stockton	Hunterdon
Suckasunny	Morris
Summit	Essex
Swartswood	Sussex
Sweedsborough	Gloucester
Sykesville	Burlington
Tinton Falls	Monmouth
Titusville	Mercer
Tom's River	Ocean
Townsbury	Warren
Townsend's Inlet	Cape May
Tranquility	Sussex
Trenton	Mercer
Tuckahoe	Cape May
Tuckerton	Burlington
Tumble	Hunterdon
Turkey	Monmouth
Tuttle's Corner	Sussex
Union	Essex
Uniontown	Middlesex
Vanhiseville	Mercer
Vernon	Sussex
Verona	Essex
Vienna	Warren
Vincentown	Burlington
Wading River	
Walnford	Monmouth
Walnut Grove	Morris
Walnut Valley	Warren
Wallpack Center	Sussex
Warrenville	Somerset
Washington	Warren
Waterloo	Sussex
Waterville	Morris
Wawayanda	Sussex
Westville	Hunterdon
West Bloomfield	Essex
West Creek	Ocean
Westfield	Union
West Hoboken	Hudson
West Milford	Passaic
Weston	Somerset
Westville	Gloucester
Weymouth	Atlantic
White Hall	Hunterdon
White House	
Williamstown	Camden
Windsor	Mercer
Winslow	Camden
Wiretown	Ocean
Woodbridge	Middlesex
Woodbury	Gloucester
Woolmansie	Ocean
Woodport	Morris
Woodstown	Salem
Woodville	Mercer
Wrightstown	Burlington
Wykertown	Sussex
Yardville	Mercer

New York.

Post Office.	County.
Academy	Ontario
Accord	Ulster
Acra	Greene
Adams	Jefferson
Adams' Basin	Monroe
Adams' Center	Jefferson
Adamsville	Washington
Addison	Steuben
Adrian	Steuben
Adriance	Dutchess
Afton	Chenango
Akron	Erie
Alabama	Genesee
Albany	Albany
Albion	Orleans
Alden	Erie
Alden Center	Erie
Alder Brook	Franklin
Alder Creek	Oneida
Alexander	Genesee
Alexandria	Jefferson
Alfred	Allegany
Alfred Center	Allegany
Allegany	Cattaraugus
Allen	Allegany
Allen Center	Allegany
Allen's Hill	Ontario
Alma	Allegany
Almond	Allegany
Alpine	Schuyler
Alps	Rensselaer
Altay	Schuyler
Alton	Wayne
Altona	Clinton
Amador	Franklin
Amagansett	Suffolk
Amber	Onondaga
Amboy Center	Oswego
Amenia	Dutchess
Amenia Union	Dutchess
Ames	Montgomery
Amesville	Ulster
Amity	Orange
Amityville	Suffolk
Amsterdam	Montgomery
Ancram	Columbia
Ancram Lead Mine	Columbia
Andes	Delaware
Andover	Allegany
Andrusville	Franklin
Angelica	Allegany
Angola	Erie
Antwerp	Jefferson
Apalachin	Tioga
Apulia	Onondaga
Arcadia	Wayne
Argosville	Schoharie
Argyle	Washington
Arkport	Steuben
Arkwright Summit	Chautauque
Armonk	Westchester
Arthursburg	Dutchess
Ashford	Cattaraugus
Ashland	Greene
Ash Park	Cattaraugus
Astoria	Queens
Athens	Greene
Athol	Warren
Atlanticville	Suffolk
Attica	Wyoming
Attica Center	Wyoming
Attlebury	Dutchess
Auburn	Cayuga
Augusta	Oneida
Aurelius	Cayuga
Auriesville	Montgomery
Aurora	Cayuga
Ausable Forks	Essex
Austerlitz	Columbia
Ava	Oneida
Avoca	Steuben
Avon	Livingston
Ayrshire	Chenango
Babcock Hill	Oneida
Babylon	Suffolk
Bacon Hill	Saratoga

Post Office.	County.
Bainbridge	Chenango
Baiting Hollow	Suffolk
Bald Mountain	Washington
Baldwin	Chemung
Baldwinsville	Onondaga
Ballston	Saratoga
Ballston Center	Saratoga
Bangall	Dutchess
Bangor	Franklin
Barbourville	Delaware
Barcelona	Chautauque
Barkersville	Saratoga
Barnes' Corners	Lewis
Barnerville	Schoharie
Barre Center	Orleans
Barrington	Yates
Barrytown	Dutchess
Barryville	Sullivan
Barton	Tioga
Burton Hill	Schoharie
Batavia	Genesee
Batchellerville	Saratoga
Bath	Steuben
Baitenville	Washington
Bay Ridge	Kings
Bay View	Richmond
Beach Ridge	Niagara
Bearsville	Ulster
Beaver Brook	Sullivan
Beaver Dams	Schuyler
Beaver Kill	Sullivan
Bedford	Westchester
Bedford Station	Westchester
Beech Wood	Sullivan
Beckman	Dutchess
Beckmantown	Clinton
Belcher	Washington
Belfast	Allegany
Belle Isle	Onondaga
Belleville	Jefferson
Bellport	Suffolk
Bellvale	Orange
Belmont	Allegany
Belvidere	Allegany
Bemus Heights	Saratoga
Bennettsburg	Schuyler
Bennet's Corners	Madison
Bennett's Creek	Steuben
Bennettsville	Chenango
Bennington	Wyoming
Benson	Hamilton
Benson Center	Hamilton
Bentley	Richmond
Benton	Yates
Benton Center	Yates
Bergen	Genesee
Bergholtz	Niagara
Berkshire	Tioga
Berlin	Rensselaer
Berne	Albany
Bernhard's Bay	Oswego
Bethany	Genesee
Bethany Mills	Genesee
Bethel	Sullivan
Bethel Corners	Cayuga
Bethlehem Center	Albany
Big Creek	Steuben
Big Flats	Chemung
Big Hollow	Greene
Big Stream Point	Yates
Big Tree Corners	Erie
Binghampton	Broome
Black Brook	Clinton
Big Brook	Oneida
Black Creek	Allegany
Black River	Jefferson
Black Rock	Erie
Blauveltville	Rockland
Bleeker	Fulton
Blockville	Chautauque
Blodget Mills	Cortland
Bloominghurg	Sullivan
Bloomingdale	Essex
Blooming Grove	Orange
Bloomville	Delaware
Blossvale	Oneida
Blue Point	Suffolk
Bluff Point	Yates
Boght	Albany
Bolivar	Allegany

Post Office.	County.
Bolton	Warren
Bombay	Franklin
Bonny Hill	Steuben
Booneville	Oneida
Booth	Herkimer
Borodino	Onondaga
Boscobel	Westchester
Boston	Erie
Bouckville	Madison
Boutonville	Westchester
Bovina	Delaware
Bowen's Corners	Oswego
Bowmansville	Erie
Boylston	Oswego
Bradford	Steuben
Brainard	Rensselaer
Brayman's Corners	Schenectady
Branchport	Yates
Brant	Erie
Brantingham	Lewis
Brasher Falls	St. Lawrence
Brasher Iron Works	St. Lawrence
Breakabeen	Schoharie
Breesport	Chemung
Brewerton	Onondaga
Brewster's Station	Putnam
Bridgehampton	Suffolk
Bridgeport	Madison
Bridgeville	Sullivan
Bridgewater	Oneida
Brier Hill	St. Lawrence
Brigham	Chautauque
Brighton	Monroe
Bristol	Ontario
Bristol Center	Ontario
Broadalbin	Fulton
Brockett's Bridge	Fulton
Brockport	Monroe
Brocton	Chautauque
Bronxville	Westchester
Brookfield	Madison
Brooklyn	Kings
Brook's Grove	Livingston
Broom Center	Schoharie
Brownville	Jefferson
Brushland	Delaware
Brush's Mills	Franklin
Brunswick	Ulster
Buck Tooth	Cattaraugus
Buel	Montgomery
Buena Vista	Steuben
Buffalo	Erie
Buffalo Plains	Erie
Bull's Head	Dutchess
Bullville	Orange
Burdett	Schuyler
Burke	Franklin
Burlingham	Sullivan
Burlington	Otsego
Burlington Flats	Otsego
Burns	Allegany
Burnt Hills	Saratoga
Burtonsville	Montgomery
Bushnell's Basin	Monroe
Bushnellsville	Greene
Bushville	Sullivan
Buskirk's Bridge	Washington
Busti	Chautauque
Butterfly	Oswego
Buttermilk Falls	Orange
Butternuts	Otsego
Byersville	Livingston
Byron	Genesee
Cabin Hill	Delaware
Cadosia Valley	Delaware
Cadyville	Clinton
Cario	Greene
Caldwell	Warren
Caledonia	Livingston
Callanan's Corners	Albany
Callicoon	Sullivan
Callicoon Depot	Sullivan
Cambria	Niagara
Cambridge	Washington
Camden	Oneida
Cameron	Steuben
Cameron Mills	Steuben
Camillus	Onondaga
Campbelltown	Steuben

POST OFFICES—NEW YORK. 55

Post Office.	County.	Post Office.	County.	Post Office.	County.
Campville	Tioga	Chenango Forks	Chenango	Cook's Corners	Franklin
Canaan	Columbia	Cherry Creek	Chautauque	Coomer	Niagara
Canaan Center	Columbia	Cherubusco	Clinton	Cooper's Plains	Steuben
Canaan Four Corners	Columbia	Cheshire	Ontario	Cooperstown	Otsego
Canadice	Ontario	Cheshireville	Chenango	Copake	Columbia
Canajoharie	Montgomery	Cherry Valley	Otsego	Copake Iron Works	Columbia
Canal	Onondaga	Chester	Orange	Copenhagen	Lewis
Canandaigua	Ontario	Chestertown	Warren	Coram	Suffolk
Canarsie	Kings	Chili	Monroe	Corfu	Genesee
Canaseraga	Allegany	China	Wyoming	Corinth	Saratoga
Canastota	Madison	Chittenango	Madison	Corning	Steuben
Candor	Tioga	Chittenango Falls	Madison	Cornwall	Orange
Caneadea	Allegany	Churchtown	Columbia	Cornwallville	Greene
Canisteo	Steuben	Churchville	Monroe	Cortland Village	Cortland
Cannonsville	Delaware	Cicero	Onondaga	Cottage	Cattaraugus
Canoga	Seneca	Cincinnatus	Cortland	County Line	Niagara
Canton	St. Lawrence	Cireleville	Orange	Coventry	Chenango
Cape Vincent	Jefferson	City	Dutchess	Coventryville	Chenango
Cardiff	Onondaga	Clarence	Erie	Covert	Seneca
Carlisle	Schoharie	Clarence Center	Erie	Coveville	Saratoga
Carlton	Orleans	Clarendon	Orleans	Covington	Wyoming
Carmel	Putnam	Clarksburg	Erie	Cowaselon	Madison
Caroline	Tompkins	Clark's Factory	Delaware	Cowlesville	Wyoming
Caroline Center	Tompkins	Clarkson	Monroe	Coxsackie	Greene
Caroline Depot	Tompkins	Clarkson Center	Monroe	Craigsville	Orange
Cartersville	Oswego	Clarkstown	Rockland	Cranberry Creek	Fulton
Carthage	Jefferson	Clarksville	Albany	Cranesville	Montgomery
Carthage Landing	Dutchess	Claryville	Sullivan	Crary's Mills	St. Lawrence
Cassadaga	Chautauque	Claverack	Columbia	Creek Center	Warren
Cassville	Oneida	Clay	Onondaga	Creek Locks	Ulster
Castle	Wyoming	Clayton	Jefferson	Crescent	Saratoga
Castile Creek	Broome	Clayton Center	Jefferson	Cresco	Kings
Castleton	Rensselaer	Clayville	Oneida	Crittenden	Erie
Catatonk	Tioga	Clear Creek	Chautauque	Croghan	Lewis
Catharine	Schuyler	Clermont	Columbia	Cropseyville	Rensselaer
Cato	Cayuga	Cleveland	Oswego	Cross River	Westchester
Caton	Steuben	Clifton	Monroe	Croton	Delaware
Catskill	Greene	Clifton Park	Saratoga	Croton Falls	Westchester
Cattaraugus	Cattaraugus	Clifton Springs	Ontario	Cocoa Landing	Westchester
Caughdenoy	Oswego	Clinton	Oneida	Couse's Store	Dutchess
Cayuga	Cayuga	Clinton Corners	Dutchess	Crown Point	Essex
Cayuta	Chemung	Clintondale	Ulster	Crum Creek	Fulton
Cayutaville	Schuyler	Clinton Hollow	Dutchess	Crum Elbow	Dutchess
Cazenovia	Madison	Clinton Point	Dutchess	Cruso	Seneca
Cedar Hill	Albany	Clintonville	Clinton	Cuba	Allegany
Cedar Lake	Herkimer	Clockville	Madison	Cuddebackville	Orange
Cedar Swamp	Queens	Clove	Dutchess	Cutchogue	Suffolk
Cedarville	Herkimer	Clovesville	Delaware	Cuyler	Cortland
Central Bridge	Schoharie	Clyde	Wayne	Caylerville	Livingston
Central Square	Oswego	Clymer	Chautauque	Dale	Wyoming
Center Almond	Allegany	Cobleskill	Schoharie	Danby	Tompkins
Center Berlin	Rensselaer	Cobleskill Center	Schoharie	Dannemora	Clinton
Center Brunswick	Rensselaer	Cochoc	Sullivan	Danube	Herkimer
Center Cambridge	Washington	Cochecton Center	Sullivan	Dansville	Livingston
Center Canisteo	Steuben	Coeyman's	Albany	Darien	Genesee
Centerfield	Ontario	Coeyman's Hollow	Albany	Dorien Center	Genesee
Center Lisle	Broome	Cohocton	Steuben	Davenport	Delaware
Center Moriches	Suffolk	Cohoes	Albany	Davenport Center	Delaware
Center Point	Orange	Coila	Washington	Davton	Cattaraugus
Centerport	Suffolk	Colchester	Delaware	Dean's Corners	Saratoga
Center Sherman	Chantauque	Cold Brook	Herkimer	Dansville	Oneida
Center Village	Broome	Colden	Erie	De Bruce	Sullivan
Centerville	Allegany	Coldenham	Orange	Decatur	Otsego
Center White Creek		Cold Spring	Putnam	Deerfield	Oneida
	Washington	Cold Spring Harbor	Suffolk	Deer Park	Suffolk
Ceres	Allegany	Colesville	Broome	Deer River	Lewis
Champion	Jefferson	Collaburg	Orange	Defreestville	Rensselaer
Champlain	Clinton	Coll'amer	Onondaga	De Kalb	St. Lawrence
Chapinville	Ontario	College Point	Queens	De Lancey	Madison
Chappaqua	Westchester	Colliersville	Otsego	Delaware Bridge	Sullivan
Charleston	Montgomery	Collins	Erie	Delhi	Delaware
Charleston 4 Corners		Coll'ns Center	Erie	Delphi	Onondaga
Charlotte	Monroe	Collinsville	Lewis	Delta	Oneida
Charlotte Center	Chautauque	Colosse	Oswego	Denmark	Lewis
Charlotteville	Schoharie	Colton	St. Lawrence	Denison	Herkimer
Charlton	Saratoga	Columbia	Herkimer	Denning	Ulster
Chase's Mills	St. Lawrence	Columbus	Chenango	Depauville	Jefferson
Chaseville	Otsego	Comnack	Suffolk	Depeyster	St. Lawrence
Chateaugay	Franklin	Comstock's Landing		Deposit	Broome
Chateauguy Lake	Franklin		Washington	De Ruyter	Madison
Chatham	Columbia	Conesus	Livingston	De Witt	Onondaga
Chatham Center	Columbia	Conesus Center	Livingston	De Wittville	Chantauque
Chatham Four Corners	Columbia	Conesville	Schoharie	Dexter	Jefferson
Chaumont	Jefferson	Conewango	Cattaraugus	Diana	Lewis
Chautauque Valley	Allegany	Conklin Center	Broome	Dickersonville	Niagara
Chazy	Clinton	Conquest	Cayuga	Dickerson	Franklin
Cheektowaga	Erie	Constableville	Lewis	Dickerson Center	Franklin
Chemung	Chemung	Constantia	Oswego	Dix Hills	Suffolk
Chemung Center	Chemung	Constantia Center	Oswego	Dobb's Ferry	Westchester
Chenango	Broome	Cook-burg	Albany	Doraville	Broome

POST OFFICES—NEW YORK.

Post Office.	County.	Post Office.	County.	Post Office.	County.
Dormansville	Albany	East Pierpont	St. Lawrence	Farnham	Erie
Doty's Corner	Steuben	East Pike	Wyoming	Fayette	Seneca
Dover	Dutchess	East Pitcairn	St. Lawrence	Fayetteville	Onondaga
Downsville	Delaware	East Poestenkill	Rensselaer	Federal Store	Dutchess
Dresserville	Cayuga	East Porter	Niagara	Felt's Mills	Jefferson
Dryden	Tompkins	East Randolph	Cattaraugus	Fenner	Madison
Dunne	Franklin	East Rodman	Jefferson	Fentonville	Chautauque
Duanesburg	Schenectady	East Roxbury	Delaware	Ferguson's Corner	Yates
Dugway	Oswego	East Rushford	Allegany	Fillmore	Allegany
Dundee	Yates	East Salem	Washington	Fergusonville	Delaware
Dunkirk	Chautauque	East Schodack	Rensselaer	Findley's Lake	Chautauque
Dunnsville	Albany	East Schuyler	Herkimer	Fine	St. Lawrence
Durham	Greene	East Scott	Cortland	Fire Island	Suffolk
Durhamville	Oneida	East Shelby	Orleans	Fireplace	Suffolk
Dwaar's Kill	Ulster	East Springfield	Otsego	Fisher's	Ontario
Dykeman's	Putnam	East Springwater	Livingston	Fishkill	Dutchess
Eagle	Wyoming	East Troupsburg	Steuben	Fishkill Landing	Dutchess
Eagle Bridge	Rensselaer	East Varick	Seneca	Fishkill Plains	Dutchess
Eagle Harbor	Orleans	East Venice	Cayuga	Five Corners	Cayuga
Eagle Mills	Rensselaer	East Virgil	Cortland	Flackville	St. Lawrence
Eagle's Nest	Hamilton	East Warsaw	Wyoming	Flanders	Suffolk
Eagle Village	Wyoming	East Wilson	Niagara	Flatbrook	Columbia
Earlville	Madison	East Windham	Greene	Flatbush	Kings
East Amherst	Erie	East Worcester	Otsego	Flat Creek	Montgomery
East Ashford	Cattaraugus	Eaton	Madison	Flat Lands	Kings
East Aurora	Erie	Entonsville	Herkimer	Fleming	Cayuga
East Avon	Livingston	Eddystown	Yates	Flemingsville	Tioga
East Beckmantown	Clinton	Eden	Erie	Flint Creek	Ontario
East Berkshire	Tioga	Edenton	St. Lawrence	Florence	Oneida
East Berne	Albany	Edenville	Orange	Florida	Orange
East Bethany	Genesee	Edinburg	Saratoga	Floyd	Oneida
East Bloomfield	Ontario	Edmeston	Otsego	Flushing	Queens
East Boston	Madison	Edwards	St. Lawrence	Fluvanna	Chautauque
East Branch	Delaware	Edwardsville	St. Lawrence	Fly Creek	Otsego
East Candor	Tioga	Eddyville	Cattaraugus	Fly Mountain	Ulster
East Carlton	Orleans	Eggertsville	Erie	Folsomdale	Wyoming
East Chatham	Columbia	Egypt	Monroe	Fonda	Montgomery
East Chester	Westchester	Elba	Genesee	Fordham	Westchester
East China	Wyoming	Elbridge	Onondaga	Forestburg	Sullivan
East Clarkson	Monroe	Elgin	Cattaraugus	Forest City	Tompkins
East Cobleskill	Schoharie	Eden Valley	Erie	Forest Port	Oneida
East Constable	Franklin	Elizabethtown	Essex	Forestville	Chautauque
East Creek	Herkimer	Elizaville	Columbia	Fort Ann	Washington
East DeKalb	St. Lawrence	Ellenburg	Clinton	Fort Covington	Franklin
East Dickinson	Franklin	Ellenburg Center	Clinton	Fort Covington Center	Franklin
East Durham	Greene	Ellenburg Depot	Clinton	Fort Edward	Washington
East Eden	Erie	Ellenville	Ulster	Fort Hamilton	Kings
East Elba	Genesee	Ellery	Chautauque	Fort Hunter	Montgomery
East Evans	Erie	Ellery Center	Chautauque	Fort Miller	Washington
East Fishkill	Dutchess	Ellicott	Erie	Fort Montgomery	Orange
East Florence	Oneida	Ellicottsville	Cattaraugus	Fort Plain	Montgomery
East Gaines	Orleans	Ellington	Chautauque	Fortsville	Saratoga
East Gainesville	Wyoming	Ellisburg	Jefferson	Fosterdale	Sullivan
East Galway	Saratoga	Elma	Erie	Fosterville	Cayuga
East Genoa	Cayuga	Elmira	Chemung	Fowler	St. Lawrence
East German	Chenango	Elm Valley	Allegany	Frankfort	Herkimer
East Glenville	Schenectady	Elton	Cattaraugus	Frankfort Hill	Herkimer
East Grafton	Rensselaer	Eminence	Schoharie	Franklin	Delaware
East Granger	Allegany	Emmonsburg	Herkimer	Franklin Falls	Franklin
East Greenbush	Rensselaer	Enfield	Tompkins	Franklinton	Schoharie
East Greene	Chenango	Enfield Center	Tompkins	Franklinville	Cattaraugus
East Greenwich	Washington	Engellville	Schoharie	Fredonia	Chautauque
East Groveland	Livingston	Ephratah	Fulton	Freedom Plain	Dutchess
East Guilford	Chenango	Erieville	Madison	Freeport	Queens
East Hamburg	Erie	Erin	Chemung	Freetown Corners	Cortland
East Hamilton	Madison	Esopus	Ulster	Fremont	Sullivan
East Hampton	Suffolk	Esperance	Schoharie	Fremont Center	Sullivan
East Hill	Livingston	Essex	Essex	French Creek	Chautauque
East Home	Cortland	Etna	Tompkins	French Mountain	Warren
East Houndsfield	Jefferson	Euclid	Onondaga	Fresh Pond	Suffolk
East Java	Wyoming	Evans	Erie	Frewsburg	Chautauque
East Jewett	Greene	Evans' Mills	Jefferson	Frey's Bush	Montgomery
East Kendall	Orleans	Evansville	Ulster	Friend's Ferry	Cattaraugus
East Lansing	Tompkins	Exeter	Otsego	Friendship	Allegany
East Leon	Cattaraugus	Fabius	Onondaga	Frontier	Clinton
East Line	Saratoga	Factoryville	Tioga	Fullersville Iron Works	St. Lawrence
East McDonough	Chenango	Fair Dale	Oswego	Fulton	Oswego
East Maine	Broome	Fairfield	Herkimer	Fultonham	Schoharie
East Marion	Suffolk	Fair Haven	Cayuga	Fultonville	Montgomery
East Moriches	Suffolk	Fair Mount	Onondaga	Gaines	Orleans
East Nassau	Rensselaer	Fair View	Cattaraugus	Gainesville	Wyoming
East New York	Kings	Fairville	Wayne	Gales	Sullivan
East Norwich	Queens	Falconer	Chautauque	Galesville	Washington
Easton	Washington	Fallsburg	Sullivan	Galesville Mills	Ulster
East Orangeville	Wyoming	Farmer	Seneca	Gallatinville	Columbia
East Otto	Cattaraugus	Farmer's Mills	Putnam	Gallupville	Schoharie
East Painted Post	Steuben	Fairport	Monroe	Galway	Saratoga
East Palmyra	Wayne	Farmersville	Cattaraugus	Gansevoort	Saratoga
East Pembroke	Genesee	Farmingdale	Queens	Gardnersville	Schoharie
East Pharsalia	Chenango	Farmington	Ontario		

POST OFFICES—NEW YORK.

Post Office.	County.	Post Office.	County.	Post Office.	County.
Garoga	Fulton	Hague	Warren	Honeoye Falls	Monroe
Garrattsville	Otsego	Hadeshorough	St. Lawrence	Hooper	Broome
Garrison's	Putnam	Haleottsville	Delaware	Hooper's Val'ey	Tioga
Gasport	Niagara	Hale's Eddy	Delaware	Hoosick	Rensselaer
Gates	Monroe	Half Moon	Saratoga	Hoosick Falls	Rensselaer
Gayhead	Greene	Hall's Corners	Ontario	Hope Center	Hamilton
Geddes	Onondaga	Hallsport	Allegany	Hope Falls	Hamilton
Genegantslet	Chenango	Hallsville	Montgomery	Hopewell	Ontario
Geneseo	Livingston	Halsey Valley	Tioga	Hopewell Center	Ontario
Geneva	Ontario	Hamburg	Erie	Hopkinton	St. Lawrence
Genoa	Cayuga	Hamden	Delaware	Horicon	Warren
Georgetown	Madison	Hamilton	Madison	Hornby	Steuben
German	Chenango	Hamlet	Chautauque	Hornellsville	Steuben
Germantown	Columbia	Hamlin	Monroe	Horseheads	Chemung
Gerry	Chautauque	Hammond	St. Lawrence	Houghton Creek	Allegany
Getzville	Erie	Hammondsport	Steuben	Houseville	Lewis
Ghent	Columbia	Hampton	Washington	Howard	Steuben
Gibson	Steuben	Hancock	Delaware	Howell's Depot	Orange
Gibsonville	Livingston	Hanford's Landing	Monroe	Howlett Hill	Onondaga
Gilbert's Mills	Oswego	Hannibal	Oswego	Hubbardsville	Madison
Gilboa	Schoharie	Hannibal Center	Oswego	Hudson	Columbia
Gilman	Hamilton	Harford	Cortland	Hughsonville	Dutchess
Glasco	Ulster	Harlemville	Columbia	Huguenot	Orange
Glen Aubrey	Broome	Harmony	Chautauque	Hulburton	Orleans
Glen Castle	Broome	Harpersfield	Delaware	Hull's Mills	Dutchess
Glenco Mills	Columbia	Harpersville	Broome	Hume	Allegany
Glen Cove	Queens	Harrisburg	Lewis	Humphrey	Cattarangus
Glenham	Dutchess	Harris' Hill	Erie	Humphreyville	Columbia
Glen Haven	Cortland	Harrison	Westchester	Hunter	Greene
Glenmore	Oneida	Harriscnville	Lewis	Hunter's Home	Franklin
Glenn	Montgomery	Harsenville	New York	Hunter's Land	Schoharie
Glenn's Falls	Warren	Hartfield	Chautauque	Huntington	Suffolk
Glensdale	Lewis	Hartford	Washington	Hunt's Corners	Cortland
Glenville	Schenectady	Hartland	Niagara	Hunt's Hollow	Livingston
Glenwild	Sullivan	Hurt Lot	Onondaga	Hurlbutville	Oneida
Glenwood	Erie	Hurt's Village	Dutchess	Hurley	Ulster
Gloversville	Fulton	Hartwick	Otsego	Huron	Wayne
Goff's Mills	Steuben	Hartwick Seminary	Otsego	Hyde Park	Dutchess
Golden's Bridge	Westchester	Harvard	Delaware	Hyudsville	Schoharie
Good Ground	Suffolk	Hasbrouck	Sullivan	Ilion	Herkimer
Gorham	Ontario	Haskell Flats	Cattarangus	Independence	Allegany
Goshen	Orange	Haskinville	Steuben	Indian Fields	Albany
Gonvernaur	St. Lawrence	Hastings	Oswego	Indian River	Lewis
Gowanda	Cattarangus	Hastings Center	Oswego	Ingraham	Clinton
Grafton	Rensselaer	Hastings-upon-Hudson	Westchester	Inverness	Livingston
Grahamsville	Sullivan			Ira	Cayuga
Granby Center	Oswego	Hauppauge	Suffolk	Ireland Corners	Albany
Grand Island	Erie	Havanna	Schuyler	Irondequoit	Monroe
Granger	Allegany	Haverstraw	Rockland	Irving	Chautauque
Grangerville	Saratoga	Haviland Hollow	Putnam	Irvington	Westchester
Granville	Washington	Hawkinsville	Oneida	Ischua	Cattarangus
Grass River	St. Lawrence	Hawleyton	Broome	Islip	Suffolk
Gravesend	Kings	Hayuerville	Rensselaer	Italy Hill	Yates
Gravesville	Herkimer	Hebron	Washington	Italy Hollow	Yates
Gray	Herkimer	Hecla Works	Oneida	Ithaca	Tompkins
Great Bend	Jefferson	Hector	Schuyler	Jackson	Washington
Great Valley	Cattarangus	Helena	St. Lawrence	Jackson Summit	Fulton
Greece	Monroe	Hemlock Lake	Livingston	Jacksonville	Tompkins
Greenborough	Oswego	Hempstead	Queens	Jack's Reef	Onondaga
Greenbush	Rensselaer	Henderson	Jefferson	Jamaica	Queens
Greene	Chenango	Henrietta	Monroe	Jamesburg	Ulster
Greenfield	Ulster	Hensonville	Greene	Jamesport	Suffolk
Greenfield Center	Saratoga	Herkimer	Herkimer	Jamestown	Chautauque
Green Haven	Dutchess	Hermitage	Wyoming	Janesville	Onondaga
Green Island	Albany	Hermon	St. Lawrence	Jasper	Steuben
Green Point	Kings	Hess Road	Niagara	Java	Wyoming
Greenport	Suffolk	Heuvelton	St. Lawrence	Java Center	Wyoming
Green River	Columbia	Hibernia	Dutchess	Java Village	Wyoming
Greenville	Greene	Hickory Corners	Niagara	Jay	Essex
Greenwich	Washington	Hicksville	Queens	Jeddo	Orleans
Greenwood	Steuben	Higginsville	Oneida	Jefferson	Schoharie
Greenwood Works	Orange	High Falls	Ulster	Jeffersonville	Sullivan
Greig	Lewis	Highland Mills	Orange	Jefferson Valley	Westchester
Greigsville	Livingston	Hillsborough	Oneida	Jenksville	Tioga
Griffin's Corners	Delaware	Hillsdale	Columbia	Jericho	Queens
Griffin's Mills	Erie	Hill Side	Oneida	Jerusalem South	Queens
Griswold's Mills	Washington	Hindsburg	Orleans	Jerusalem Station	Queens
Groom's Corner	Saratoga	Hinmansville	Oswego	Jewett	Greene
Groton	Tompkins	Hinsdale	Cattarangus	Jewett Center	Greene
Groton City	Tompkins	Honx's Corner	Rensselaer	Johnsburg	Warren
Groveland	Livingston	Hobart	Delaware	Johnsonburg	Wyoming
Grovernor's Corners	Schoharie	Hoffman's Ferry	Schenectady	Johnson's Creek	Niagara
Guilderland	Albany	Hogansburg	Franklin	Johnsonville	Rensselaer
Guilderland Center	Albany	Holland	Erie	Johnstown	Fulton
Guilford	Chenango	Holland Patent	Oneida	Johnsville	Dutchess
Guilford Center	Chenango	Holley	Orleans	Jonesville	Saratoga
Gypsum	Ontario	Holtsville	Suffolk	Jordan	Onondaga
Hadley	Saratoga	Homer	Cortland	Jordanville	Herkimer
Haerlem	New York	Homowack	Ulster	Joy	Wayne
Hagaman's Mills	Montgomery	Honeoye	Ontario	Junction	Rensselaer

POST OFFICES—NEW YORK.

Post Office.	County.	Post Office.	County.	Post Office.	County.
Junius	Seneca	Limestone	Cattaraugus	Manorkill	Schoharie
Kanona	Steuben	Linden	Genesee	Manorville	Suffolk
Kasong	Oswego	Lindleytown	Steuben	Mansfield	Dutchess
Katonah	Westchester	Linklean	Chenango	Maple Grove	Otsego
Keck's Center	Fulton	Linlithgo	Columbia	Mahopac	Putnam
Keefer's Corners	Albany	Lion	Onondaga	Mapleton	Niagara
Keene	Essex	Lisbon	St. Lawrence	Marathon	Cortlandt
Keeney's Settlement	Cortland	Lisbon Center	St. Lawrence	Marbletown	Ulster
Keeseville	Essex	Lisha's Kill	Albany	Marcellus	Onondaga
Kelloggsville	Cayuga	Lisle	Broome	Marcellus Falls	Onondaga
Kendall	Orleans	Litchfield	Herkimer	Marcy	Oneida
Kendall Mill's	Orleans	Lithgow	Dutchess	Marengo	Wayne
Kensico	Westchester	Little Britain	Orange	Margaretville	Delaware
Kent	Putnam	Little Falls	Herkimer	Mariaville	Schenectady
Kerhonkson	Ulster	Little Genesee	Allegany	Marietta	Onondaga
Ketcham's Corners	Saratoga	Little Neck	Queens	Marilla	Erie
Ketchumsville	Tioga	Little Rest	Dutchess	Mariners Harbor	Richmond
Kiantone	Chautauque	Little Valley	Cattaraugus	Marion	Wayne
Kidder's Ferry	Seneca	Little York	Cortland	Marlsborough	Ulster
Killbuck	Cattaraugus	Liverpool	Onondaga	Marshall	Oneida
Killawog	Broome	Livingston	Columbia	Marshfield	Erie
Kinderhook	Columbia	Livingstonville	Schoharie	Marshville	Montgomery
Kingsboro'	Fulton	Livonia	Livingston	Martindale Depot	Columbia
King's Bridge	New York	Livonia Station	Livingston	Martinsburg	Lewis
Kingsbury	Washington	Lock Berlin	Wayne	Martinsville	Niagara
King's Ferry	Cayuga	Loch Sheldrake	Sullivan	Martville	Cayuga
King's Settlement	Chenango	Locke	Cayuga	Marvin	Chautauque
Kingston	Ulster	Lockport	Niagara	Maryland	Otsego
Kinney's Four Corners	Oswego	Locust Glen	Dutchess	Masonville	Delaware
Kirkland	Oneida	Locust Valley	Queens	Maspeth	Queens
Kirkville	Onondaga	Lodi	Seneca	Massena	St. Lawrence
Kirkwood	Broome	Lodi Center	Seneca	Massena Center	St. Lawrence
Kiskatom	Greene	Logan	Schuyler	Mattawan	Dutchess
Knowersville	Albany	Long Eddy	Sullivan	Mattituck	Suffolk
Knowlesville	Orleans	Long Island City	Queens	Mayfield	Fulton
Knox	Albany	Long Neck	Richmond	Mayville	Chautauque
Knox Corners	Oneida	Looneyville	Erie	Mead's Creek	Steuben
Kortright	Delaware	Loon Lake	Steuben	Mechanicsville	Saratoga
Kreischerville	Richmond	Lordville	Delaware	Mecklenburg	Schuyler
Kyserike	Ulster	Lorraine	Jefferson	Medina	Orleans
Kysorville	Livingston	Lotville	Fulton	Medusa	Albany
Lackawack	Ulster	Louisville	St. Lawrence	Medway	Greene
Lafargeville	Jefferson	Louisville Landing	St. Lawrence	Mellenville	Columbia
Lafayette	Onondaga			Memphis	Onondaga
Lafayetteville	Dutchess	Lowell	Oneida	Mendon	Monroe
La Grange	Wyoming	Low Hampton	Washington	Mendon Center	Monroe
La Grangeville	Dutchess	Lowville	Lewis	Meredith	Delaware
Lairdsville	Oneida	Loyd	Ulster	Meridian	Cayuga
Lake	Washington	Ludingtonville	Putnam	Merrick	Queens
Lake Hill	Ulster	Ludlowville	Tompkins	Messengerville	Cortland
Lakeland	Suffolk	Lumberland	Sullivan	Mexico	Oswego
Lakeport	Madison	Lumberville	Delaware	Middleburg	Schoharie
Lake Ridge	Tompkins	Lutheranville	Schoharie	Middlefield	Otsego
Lake Road	Niagara	Luzerne	Warren	Middlefield Center	Otsego
Lakeville	Livingston	Lyell	Westchester	Middle Granville	Washington
Lausons	Onondaga	Lyndonville	Orleans	Middle Grove	Saratoga
Lancaster	Erie	Lyons	Wayne	Middle Hope	Orange
Langford	Erie	Lyonsdale	Lewis	Middle Island	Suffolk
Lansingburgh	Rensselaer	Lyon's Falls	Lewis	Middleport	Niagara
Lansingville	Tompkins	Lysander	Onondaga	Middlesex	Yates
Laona	Chautauque	Mabbettsville	Dutchess	Middletown	Orange
Lapeer	Cortland	Macedon	Wayne	Middleville	Herkimer
La Salle	Niagara	Macedon Center	Wayne	Milan	Dutchess
Lassellsville	Fulton	Machias	Cattaraugus	Milford	Otsego
Laurens	Otsego	Macomb	St. Lawrence	Mill Brook	Warren
Lawrenceville	St. Lawrence	McConnellsville	Oneida	Millen's Bay	Jefferson
Lawyersville	Schoharie	McDonough	Chenango	Millerton	Dutchess
Lebanon	Madison	McGrawville	Cortlandt	Millburne	Broome
Ledyard	Cayuga	McLean	Tompkins	Miller's Place	Suffolk
Lee	Oneida	Madison	Madison	Mill Grove	Erie
Lee Center	Oneida	Madrid	St. Lawrence	Mill Port	Chemung
Leeds	Greene	Magnolia	Chautauque	Mills' Corners	Fulton
Leedsville	Dutchess	Maine	Broome	Mills' Mills	Allegany
Leesville	Schoharie	Malden	Ulster	Milltown	Putnam
Leon	Cattaraugus	Malden Bridge	Columbia	Millville	Orleans
Leonardsville	Madison	Malone	Franklin	Milo	Yates
La Raysville	Jefferson	Malta	Saratoga	Milo Center	Yates
LeRoy	Genesee	Maltaville	Saratoga	Milton	Ulster
Levanna	Cayuga	Mamakating	Sullivan	Mina	Chautauque
Levant	Chautauque	Mamaroneck	Westchester	Minaville	Montgomery
Lewis	Essex	Manchester	Ontario	Minden	Montgomery
Lewisborough	Westchester	Manchester Center	Ontario	Mindenville	Montgomery
Lewiston	Niagara	Manhana	Onondaga	Mineola	Queens
Lexington	Greene	Manhasset	Queens	Minerva	Essex
Leyden	Lewis	Manhattanville	New York	Minetto	Oswego
Liberty	Sullivan	Manheim Center	Herkimer	Minisink	Orange
Liberty Falls	Sullivan	Manlius	Onondaga	Mitchellville	Steuben
Libertyville	Ulster	Manlius Center	Onondaga	Modena	Ulster
Lima	Livingston	Manlius Station	Onondaga	Moffett's Store	Columbia
Limerick	Jefferson	Mannsville	Jefferson	Mohawk	Herkimer

POST OFFICES—NEW YORK. 59

Post Office.	County.	Post Office.	County.	Post Office.	County.
Moria	Franklin	New Lebanon Spr'gs	Columbia	North Pembroke	Genesee
Molino	Oswego	New Lisbon	Otsego	North Pharsalia	Chenango
Mongaup	Sullivan	New London	Oneida	North Pitcher	Chenango
Mongaup Valley	Sullivan	New Milford	Orange	Northport	Suffolk
Monroe	Orange	New Ohio	Broome	North Potsdam	St. Lawrence
Monroe Works	Orange	New Oregon	Erie	North Reading	Steuben
Moisey	Rockland	New Paltz	Ulster	North Ridge	Niagara
Montague	Lewis	New Paltz Landing	Ulster	North Ridgeway	Orleans
Montezuma	Cayuga	Newport	Herkimer	North River	Warren
Montgomery	Orange	New Road	Delaware	North Rose	Wayne
Monticello	Sullivan	New Rochelle	Westchester	North Rush	Monroe
Moodna	Orange	New Russia	Essex	North Russel'	St. Lawrence
Moores	Clinton	New Salem	Albany	North Salem	Westchester
Moores' Forks	Clinton	New Scotland	Albany	North Sanford	Broome
Moravia	Cayuga	New Springville	Richmond	North Scriba	Oswego
Morean Station	Saratoga	Newtonville	Albany	North Sheldon	Wyoming
Morehouseville	Hamilton	New Utrecht	Kings	North Shore	Richmond
Moreland	Schuyler	New Village	Suffolk	North Sparta	Livingston
Moresville	Delaware	Newville	Herkimer	North Stephentown	Rensselaer
Morgany I'e	Genesee	New Woodstock	Madison	North Sterling	Cayuga
Moriah	Essex	New York	New York	North Stockholm	St. Lawrence
Moriches	Suffolk	New York Mills	Oneida	Northumberland	Saratoga
Morley	St. Lawrence	Niagara Falls	Niagara	North Urbana	Steuben
Morris	Otsego	Nichols	Tioga	Northville	Fulton
Morrisania	Westchester	Nicholville	St. Lawrence	North Volney	Oswego
Morrisonville	Clinton	Nile	Allegany	North Western	Oneida
Morristown	St. Lawrence	Niles	Cayuga	NorthWhiteCreek	Washington
Morrisville	Madison	Ninevah	Broome	North Wilna	Jefferson
Morseville	Schoharie	Niverville	Columbia	North Winfield	Herkimer
Moreston	Sullivan	Norfolk	St. Lawrence	Norton Hill	Greene
Morton Corners	Erie	Norman's Kill	Albany	Norton's Mills	Ontario
Mortonville	Orange	North Adams	Jefferson	Norway	Herkimer
Moscow	Livingston	North Almond	Allegany	Norwich	Chenango
Mosherville	Saratoga	Northampton	Fulton	Nunda	Livingston
Moslolu	Westchester	North Argyle	Washington	Nunda Station	Livingston
Mott Haven	Westchester	North Bangor	Franklin	Nyack	Rockland
Mott's Corners	Tompkins	North Barton	Tioga	Nyack Turnpike	Rockland
Mottville	Onondaga	North Bay	Oneida	Oakfield	Genesee
Mount Hope	Orange	North Bergen	Genesee	Oak Hill	Greene
Mount Kisko	Westchester	North Bleuheim	Schoharie	Oakland	Livingston
Mount Morris	Livingston	North Bloomfield	Ontario	Oak Orchard	Orleans
Mount Pleasant	Saratoga	North Boston	Erie	Oak Point	St. Lawrence
Mount Reed	Monroe	North Branch	Sullivan	Oak's Corners	Ontario
Mount Sinai	Suffolk	North Bridgewater	Oneida	Oakville	Otsego
Mount Upton	Chenango	North Broadalbin	Fulton	Oblong	Dutchess
Mount Vernon	Westchester	North Brookfield	Madison	Odessa	Schuyler
Mount Vision	Otsego	North Buffalo	Erie	Ogden	Monroe
Mount Washington	Steuben	North Burke	Franklin	Ogdensburgh	St. Lawrence
Munford	Monroe	North Cambridge	Washington	Ohio	Herkimer
Munsville	Madison	North Cameron	Steuben	Ohioville	Ulster
Murray	Orleans	North Castle	Westchester	Olcott	Niagara
Naticoke Springs	Broome	North Chatham	Columbia	Olean	Cattaraugus
Nanuet	Rockland	North Chemung	Chemung	Olive	Ulster
Napanock	Ulster	North Chili	Monroe	Olive Bridge	Ulster
Naples	Ontario	North Clarkson	Monroe	Olmstedville	Essex
Napoli	Cattaraugus	North Cohocton	Steuben	Omar	Jefferson
Narrowsburg	Sullivan	North Colesville	Broome	Oneida	Madison
Nashville	Chautauque	North Copake	Columbia	Oneida Castle	Oneida
Nassau	Rensselaer	North Creek	Warren	Oneida Lake	Madison
Natural Bridge	Jefferson	North East	Dutchess	Oneida Valley	Madison
Naumburg	Lewis	North East Center	Dutchess	Oneonta	Otsego
Navarino	Onondaga	North Easton	Washington	Onondaga	Onondaga
Nelson	Madison	North Elba	Essex	Onondaga Castle	Onondaga
Neperan	Westchester	North Evans	Erie	Onondaga Valley	Onondaga
Neversink	Sullivan	North Franklin	Delaware	Onoville	Cattaraugus
New Albion	Cattaraugus	North Gage	Oneida	Ontario	Wayne
Newark	Wayne	North Galway	Saratoga	Oppenheim	Fulton
Newark Valley	Tioga	North Granville	Washington	Oramel	Allegany
New Baltimore	Greene	North Greece	Monroe	Oran	Onondaga
New Berlin	Chenango	North Greenfield	Saratoga	Orange	Steuben
New Berlin Center	Chenango	North Greenwich	Washington	Orangeburgh	Rockland
New Bremen	Lewis	North Hamden	Delaware	Orangeport	Niagara
New Brighton	Richmond	North Harpersfield	Delaware	Orangeville	Wyoming
Newburg	Orange	North Hartland	Niagara	Oregon	Chautauque
New Castle	Westchester	North Haverstraw	Rockland	Orient	Suffolk
New Centerville	Oswego	North Hebron	Washington	Oriskany	Oneida
New Drop	Richmond	North Hector	Tompkins	Oriskany Falls	Oneida
Newfane	Niagara	North Hempstead	Queens	Orleans	Ontario
Newfield	Tompkins	North Hoosick	Rensselaer	Orleans Four Corners	Jefferson
New Graefenberg	Herkimer	North Hudson	Essex	Orwell	Oswego
New Hackensack	Dutchess	North Huron	Wayne	Osborn's Bridge	Fulton
New Hamburg	Dutchess	North Java	Wyoming	Osborne Hollow	Broome
New Hampton	Orange	North Kortright	Delaware	Osceola	Lewis
New Hartford	Oneida	North Lansing	Tompkins	Ossian	Livingston
New Haven	Oswego	North Lawrence	St. Lawrence	Oswego	Oswego
New Hurley	Ulster	North Linklaen	Chenango	Oswego Falls	Oswego
New Kingston	Delaware	North Maulius	Onondaga	Oswego Village	Dutchess
Newkirk's Mills	Fulton	North Nassau	Rensselaer	Otego	Otsego
New Lebanon	Columbia	North Norwich	Chenango	Otisco	Onondaga
New LebanonCenter	Columbia	North Parma	Monroe	Otisville	Orange

POST OFFICES—NEW YORK.

Post Office.	County.	Post Office.	County.	Post Office.	County.
Otsdawa	Otsego	Pine Woods	Madison	Ramapo Works	Rockland
Otselic	Chenango	Pinckney	Lewis	Randolph	Cattaraugus
Otterville	Orange	Pitcairn	St. Lawrence	Randolph Center	Broome
Otto	Cattaraugus	Pitcher	Chenango	Ransomville	Niagara
Ouaqnaga	Broome	Pitcher Springs	Chenango	Rapids	Erie
Ovid	Seneca	Pittsfield	Otsego	Rathboneville	Steuben
Owasco	Cayuga	Pittsford	Monroe	Ravenswood	Queens
Owasco Lake	Cayuga	Pittstown	Rensselaer	Rawson	Cattaraugus
Owego	Tioga	Plainville	Onondaga	Rawson Hollow	Tompkins
Oxbow	Jefferson	Plank Road	Onondaga	Raymortown	Rensselaer
Oxford	Chenango	Plato	Cattaraugus	Raymondville	St. Lawrence
Oxford Depot	Orange	Plattekill	Ulster	Reading	Steuben
Oyster Bay	Queens	Plattsburg	Clinton	Reading Center	Steuben
Page's Corners	Herkimer	Pleasant Brook	Otsego	Red Creek	Wayne
Paine's Hollow	Herkimer	Pleasant Plains	Dutchess	Red Falls	Greene
Painted Post	Steuben	Pleasant Ridge	Dutchess	Redfield	Oswego
Palatine	Montgomery	Pleasant Valley	Dutchess	Redford	Clinton
Palatine Bridge	Montgomery	Pleasantville	Westchester	Red Hook	Dutchess
Palenville	Greene	Plesis	Jefferson	Red Mills	Putnam
Palermo	Oswego	Plymouth	Chenango	Red Rock	Columbia
Palisades	Rockland	Poestinkill	Rensselaer	Redwood	Jefferson
Palmyra	Wayne	Point Peninsula	Jefferson	Reed's Corners	Ontario
Pamelia Four Corners	Jefferson	Poland	Herkimer	Reidsville	Albany
Panama	Chantauque	Poland Center	Chantauque	Remsen	Oneida
Pantico	Cayuga	Polkville	Onondaga	Rensselaer Falls	St. Lawrence
Paris	Oneida	Pompey	Onondaga	Rensselaerville	Albany
Parish	Oswego	Pompey Center	Onondaga	Reserve	Erie
Parishville	St. Lawrence	Pond Eddy	Sullivan	Rexford Flats	Saratoga
Parksville	Sullivan	Poney Hollow	Tompkins	Rexville	Steuben
Parma	Monroe	Pontiac	Erie	Reynale's Basin	Niagara
Parma Center	Monroe	Poolville	Madison	Reynoldsville	Schuyler
Patchin	Erie	Pope's Mills	Saratoga	Rhinebeck	Dutchess
Patchogue	Suffolk	Popla Ridge	Cayuga	Rhine Cliff	Dutchess
Patten's Mills	Washington	Portageville	Wyoming	Rhinebeck Station	Dutchess
Patterson	Putnam	Port Byron	Cayuga	Richburg	Allegany
Pavilion	Genesee	Port Chester	Westchester	Richfield	Otsego
Pavilion Center	Genesee	Port Crane	Broome	Richfield Springs	Otsego
Pawling	Dutchess	Porter's Corners	Saratoga	Richford	Tioga
Pearl Creek	Wyoming	Port Ewen	Ulster	Richmond	Richmond
Peconia	Suffolk	Port Gibson	Ontario	Richmond Mills	Ontario
Peekskill	Westchester	Port Gilspow	Wayne	Richmondville	Schoharie
Pekin	Niagara	Port Henry	Essex	Richville	St. Lawrence
Pelham	Westchester	Port Jackson	Montgomery	Ridge	Livingston
Pembroke	Genesee	Port Jefferson	Suffolk	Ridgebury	Orange
Penataquit	Suffolk	Port Jervis	Orange	Ridgeway	Orleans
Pendleton	Niagara	Port Kent	Essex	Riga	Monroe
Pendleton Center	Niagara	Portland	Chautauque	Riker's Hollow	Steuben
Penfield	Monroe	Port Leyville	Otsego	Ripley	Chautauque
Penfield Center	Monroe	Port Leyden	Lewis	Risingville	Steuben
Pennellville	Oswego	Port Ontario	Oswego	River Head	Suffolk
Penn Yan	Yates	Port Richmond	Richmond	River Side	Ulster
Peoria	Wyoming	Portville	Cattaraugus	Robert's Corners	Jefferson
Pepacton	Delaware	Port Washington	Queens	Robertsonville	Sullivan
Perch River	Jefferson	Post Creek	Chemung	Rochester	Monroe
Perkinsville	Steuben	Potsdam	St. Lawrence	Rockaway	Queens
Perrine's Bridge	Ulster	Potter	Yates	Rock City	Dutchess
Perry	Wyoming	Potter's Hill	Rensselaer	Rock City Falls	Saratoga
Perry Center	Wyoming	Potter's Hollow	Albany	Rockdale	Chenango
Perry City	Schuyler	Pottersville	Warren	Rockland	Sullivan
Perrysburg	Cattaraugus	Poughkeepsie	Dutchess	Rockland Lake	Rockland
Perry's Mills	Clinton	Poughquag	Dutchess	Rock Rift	Delaware
Perryville	Madison	Pound Ridge	Westchester	Rock Stream	Yates
Perth	Fulton	Prattsburg	Steuben	Rockville	Allegany
Peru	Clinton	Prate's Hollow	Madison	Rockville Center	Queens
Peruville	Tompkins	Prattsville	Greene	Rockwood	Fulton
Peterboro'	Madison	Preble	Cortland	Rodman	Jefferson
Petersburg	Rensselaer	Preston	Chenango	Rome	Oneida
Petersburg Four Corners	Rensselaer	Preston Hollow	Albany	Romulus	Seneca
Pharsalia	Chenango	Prince's Bay	Richmond	Romulus Center	Seneca
Phelps	Ontario	Pricetown	Schenectady	Rondout	Ulster
Philadelphia	Jefferson	Prospect	Oneida	Root	Montgomery
Philipsport	Sullivan	Protection	Erie	Rose	Wayne
Phillip's Creek	Allegany	Providence	Saratoga	Rosebloom	Otsego
Philmont	Columbia	Pulaski	Oswego	Rose Hill	Seneca
Phœnicia	Ulster	Pulver	Reuben	Rosendale	Ulster
Phœnix	Oswego	Pultneyville	Wayne	Roslyn	Queens
Piermont	Rockland	Pulver's Corners	Dutchess	Rossie	St. Lawrence
Pierpont	St. Lawrence	Purdy Creek	Steuben	Rossville	Richmond
Pierrepont Manor	Jefferson	Purdy's Station	Westchester	Rouse's Point	Clinton
Pitard	Livingston	Purvis	Sullivan	Roxbury	Delaware
Pike	Wyoming	Putnam	Washington	Roylton	Niagara
Pike Pond	Sullivan	Quaconkill	Rensselaer	Rural Hill	Jefferson
Pillar Point	Jefferson	Quaker Hill	Dutchess	Rush	Monroe
Pine Bush	Orange	Quaker Springs	Saratoga	Rushford	Allegany
Pine Grove	Steuben	Quaker Street	Schenectady	Rushville	Yates
Pine Hill	Ulster	Quarryville	Ulster	Russell	St. Lawrence
Pine Plains	Dutchess	Queens	Queens	Russia	Herkimer
Pine's Bridge	Westchester	Queensbury	Warren	Rutland	Jefferson
Pine Valley	Chemung	Quogue	Suffolk	Rye	Westchester
		Racket River	St. Lawrence	Sackett's Harbor	Jefferson

POST OFFICES—NEW YORK. 61

Post Office.	County.	Post Office.	County.	Post Office.	County.
Sageville	Hamilton	Sheldrake	Seneca	South Lansing	Tompkins
Sag Harbor	Suffolk	Shelter Island	Suffolk	South Lima	Livingston
Saint Andrews	Orange	Sherburne	Chenango	South Livonia	Livingston
Saint Helena	Wyoming	Sheridan	Chautauque	South New Berlin	Chenango
Saint James	Suffolk	Sherman	Chautauqua	Southold	Suffolk
St. Johnsville	Montgomery	Sherman Hollow	Yates	South Onondaga	Onondaga
St. Johnsburg	Niagara	Sherwoods	Cayuga	South Otselic	Chenango
St. Lawrence	Jefferson	Shin Creek	Sullivan	South Owego	Tioga
St. Regis Lake	Franklin	Shingle Creek	S. Lawrence	South Oxford	Chenango
Salem	Washington	Shirley	Erie	South Oyster Bay	Queens
Salem Center	Westchester	Shokan	Ulster	South Pekin	Niagara
Salina	Onondaga	Shono	Allegany	South Plattsburg	Clinton
Salisbury	Herkimer	Shortsville	Ontario	South Plymouth	Chenango
Salisbury Center	Herkimer	Short Tract	Allegany	Southport	Chemung
Salisbury M'lls	Orleans	Shrub Oak	Westchester	South Pultney	Steuben
Salmon River	Oswego	Siousam	Washington	South Richland	Oswego
Salt Point	Dutchess	Siautte's Corners	Schoharie	South Rutland	Jefferson
Salt Springville	Otsego	Sidney	Delaware	South Salem	Westchester
Sammonsville	Fulton	Sidney Center	Delaware	South Sand Lake	Rensselaer
Samsonville	Ulster	Sidney Plains	Delaware	South Schodack	Rensselaer
Sand Bank	Oswego	Siloam	Madison	South Side	Richmond
Sandburgh	Sullivan	Silver Creek	Chautauque	South Sodus	Wayne
Sand Lake	Rensselaer	Sing Sing	Westchester	South Stephentown	Rensselaer
Sandusky	Cattaraugus	Same Iales	Onondaga	South Stockton	Chautauque
Sandy Creek	Oswego	Siste Hill	Orange	South Thurston	Steuben
Sandy Hill	Washington	Sisterville	Washington	South Trenton	Oneida
Sanford	Broome	Slo aville	Schoharie	South Troupsburg	Steuben
Sanford's Corners	Jefferson	Sodus	Rockland	South Valley	Otsego
Sangerfield	Oneida	Smith's Basin	Washington	Southville	St. Lawrence
Saranac	Clinton	Smith's Mills	Tioga	South Wales	Erie
Saranac Lake	Franklin	Smith's Mills	Chautauque	South Westerlo	Albany
Saratoga Springs	Saratoga	Smithtown	Suffolk	Southwest Oswego	Oswego
Sardinia	Erie	Smithtown Branch	Suffolk	South Wilson	Niagara
Saugerties	Ulster	Sinkin's Valley	Schuyler	South Worcester	Otsego
Sauquoit	Oneida	Smithville	Jefferson	Spafford	Onondaga
Savannah	Wayne	Smithville Flats	Chenango	Spafford Hollow	Onondaga
Saville	Orange	Smoke Hollow	Columbia	Sparrow Bush	Orange
Savona	Steuben	Smyrna	Chenango	Sparta	Livingston
Sayville	Suffolk	Sodus	Wayne	Speedville	Tompkins
Searsdale	Westchester	Sodus Center	Wayne	Spencer	Tioga
Schaghticoke	Rensselaer	Sodus Point	Wayne	Spencerport	Monroe
Schenectady	Schenectady	Sorou	Cortland	Spencertown	Columbia
Schenevus	Otsego	Solsville	Madison	Spooner's Corners	Otsego
Schodack Center	Rensselaer	Somers	Westchester	Spraker's Basin	Montgomery
Schodack Depot	Rensselaer	Somerset	Niagara	Spring Brook	Erie
Schodack Landing	Rensselaer	Somerville	St. Lawrence	Springfield	Otsego
Schoharie	Schoharie	Sodus	Steuben	Spring Mills	Allegany
Schoon Lake	Essex	South Addison	Steuben	Springs	Suffolk
Schroon River	Essex	South Albany	Genesee	Spring Valley	Rockland
Schultsville	Dutchess	South Amboy	Oswego	Springville	Erie
Schuyler's Falls	Clinton	South Amenia	Dutchess	Springwater	Livingston
Schuyler's Lake	Otsego	South Amboy	Suffolk	Sprout Brook	Montgomery
Schuylersville	Saratoga	South Argyle	Washington	Sprout Creek	Dutchess
Scio	Allegany	South Bristol	Livingston	Spuyten Duyvil	Westchester
Sciota	Clinton	South Ballston	Saratoga	Staatsburg	Dutchess
Scipio	Cayuga	South Bare	Orleans	Stafford	Genesee
Scipioville	Cayuga	South Berlin	Rensselaer	Stamford	Delaware
Sconondoa	Oneida	South Leno	Albany	Stanard's Corners	Allegany
Scotch Bush	Montgomery	South Boliver	Allegany	Stanfordville	Dutchess
Scotchtown	Orange	South Bombay	Franklin	Stanley Corners	Ontario
Scotia	Schenectady	South Brenford	Steuben	Stanwix	Oneida
Scott	Cortland	South Bristol	Ontario	Stapleton	Richmond
Scottsburg	Livingston	South Brookfield	Madison	Starkey	Yates
Scottsville	Monroe	South Butler	Wayne	Starkville	Herkimer
Scriba	Oswego	South Byron	Genesee	State Bridge	Oneida
Sculsburg	Tompkins	South Cairo	Greene	State Road	Chemung
Searsville	Orange	South Canunion	Jefferson	Stedman	Chautauque
Seely Creek	Chemung	South Columbia	Herkimer	Stephens' Mills	Steuben
Selden	Suffolk	South Corinth	Saratoga	Stephentown	Rensselaer
Sempronius	Cayuga	South Cortland	Cortland	Sterling	Cayuga
Seneca	Schuyler	South Danby	Tompkins	Sterling Bush	Lewis
Seneca Castle	Ontario	South Dansville	Steuben	Sterlingville	Jefferson
Seneca Falls	Seneca	South Dover	Dutchess	Steuben	Oneida
Seneca River	Cayuga	South Durham	Greene	Stevensville	Sullivan
Sennet	Cayuga	South Easton	Washington	Stittville	Oneida
Setauket	Suffolk	South Edmeston	Otsego	Stillwater	Saratoga
Seward	Schoharie	South Edwards	S. Lawrence	Stillwater Center	Saratoga
Seymour	Allegany	South Galway	Saratoga	Stockbridge	Madison
Shandaken	Ulster	South Gill	Schoharie	Stockholm	St. Lawrence
Sharon	Schoharie	South Glenn's Falls	Saratoga	Stockholm Depot	St. Lawrence
Sharon Center	Schoharie	South Ganby	Oswego	Stockport	Columbia
Sharon Springs	Schoharie	South Granville	Washington	Stockport Station	Delaware
Sharon Station	Dutchess	South Hamilton	Madison	Stockton	Chautauque
Shavetown	Delaware	South Hannibal	Oswego	Stokes	Oneida
Shawangunk	Ulster	South Hartford	Washington	Stone Arabia	Montgomery
Shawnee	Niagara	South Hammick	Oneida	Stone Church	Genesee
Shed's Corners	Madison	South Haven	Suffolk	Stone Mills	Jefferson
Sholdy	Orleans	South Hill	Steuben	Stone Ridge	Ulster
Shelby Basin	Orleans	South Howard	Steuben	Stony Brook	Suffolk
Sheldon	Wyoming	South Kortright	Delaware	Stony Clove	Greene

POST OFFICES—NEW YORK.

Post Office.	County.	Post Office.	County.	Post Office.	County.
Stormville	Dutchess	Union Falls	Clinton	Watkins	Chemung
Stowell's Corners	Jefferson	Union Grove	Delaware	Watson	Lewis
Strait's Corners	Tioga	Union Mills	Fulton	Waverly	Tioga
Stratford	Fulton	Union Settlement	Oswego	Wawarsing	Ulster
Stratton's Falls	Delaware	Union Society	Greene	Wayland Depot	Steuben
Strykersville	Wyoming	Union Springs	Cayuga	Wayne	Steuben
Stuyvesant	Columbia	Union Square	Oswego	Wayne Four Corners	Steuben
Stuyvesant Falls	Columbia	Union Valley	Cortland	Weavertown	Warren
Success	Suffolk	Unionville	Orange	Webb's Mills	Chemung
Sufferns	Rockland	Upper Aquebogue	Suffolk	Webster	Monroe
Suffolk	Suffolk	Upper Jay	Essex	Weedsport	Cayuga
Sugar Hill	Steuben	Upper Lisle	Broome	Wogatchie	St. Lawrence
Sugar Loaf	Orange	Upper Red Hook	Dutchess	Wells	Hamilton
Sullivan	Madison	Utica	Oneida	Wellsburg	Chemung
Sullivanville	Chemung	Vail's Mills	Fulton	Wells' Corner	Orange
Summer Hill	Cayuga	Valatie	Columbia	Wellsville	Allegany
Summit	Schoharie	Valcour	Clinton	Weltonville	Tioga
Suspension Bridge	Niagara	Valhalla	Westchester	West Addison	Steuben
Swainsville	Allegany	Valley Falls	Rensselaer	West Almond	Allegany
Sweden	Monroe	Vallonia Springs	Broome	West Amboy	Oswego
Syosset	Queens	Van Buren	Onondaga	West Bainbridge	Chenango
Syracuse	Onondaga	Van Buren Center	Onondaga	West Bangor	Franklin
Taberg	Oneida	Van Etten	Chemung	West Barre	Orleans
Tachkanick	Columbia	Van Ettenville	Chemung	West Bergen	Genesee
Tallman	Rockland	Van Hornesville	Herkimer	West Bloomfield	Ontario
Tannersville	Greene	Varick	Seneca	West Branch	Oneida
Tappantown	Rockland	Varna	Tompkins	West Brighton	Monroe
Tarrytown	Westchester	Varysburg	Wyoming	West Brook	Delaware
Taylor	Cortland	Venice	Cayuga	West Brookville	Sullivan
Tayloreville	Ontario	Venice Center	Cayuga	West Burlington	Otsego
Texas	Oswego	Verbank	Dutchess	Westbury	Cayuga
Texas Valley	Cortland	Vermillion	Oswego	West Butler	Wayne
The Corner	Ulster	Vermont	Chautauque	West Camden	Oneida
The Glen	Warren	Vernon	Oneida	West Cameron	Steuben
Theresa	Jefferson	Vernon Center	Oneida	West Camp	Ulster
The Square	Cayuga	Verona	Oneida	West Candor	Tioga
Thompson's Station	Suffolk	Verplanck	Westchester	West Carlton	Orleans
Thompsonville	Sullivan	Versailles	Cattaraugus	West Charlton	Saratoga
Thorn Hill	Onondaga	Vesper	Onondaga	West Chary	Clinton
Three Mile Bay	Jefferson	Vestal	Broome	Westchester	Westchester
Three River Point	Onondaga	Vestal Center	Broome	West Clarksville	Allegany
Throopsville	Cayuga	Veteran	Chemung	West Colesville	Broome
Thurman	Warren	Victor	Ontario	West Conesville	Schoharie
Thurston	Steuben	Victory	Cayuga	West Constable	Franklin
Ticonderoga	Essex	Victory Mills	Saratoga	West Danby	Tompkins
Tioga Center	Tioga	Vienna	Oneida	West Davenport	Delaware
Tivoli	Dutchess	Villanova	Chautauque	West Day	Saratoga
Toddsville	Otsego	Virgil	Cortland	West Dresden	Yates
Tomhannock	Rensselaer	Vischer's Ferry	Saratoga	West Dryden	Tompkins
Tompkins' Cove	Rockland	Vista	Westchester	West Eaton	Madison
Tompkinsville	Richmond	Vonk	Yates	West Edmeston	Otsego
Tonawanda	Erie	Volncy	Oswego	Westerlo	Albany
Towlesville	Steuben	Volusia	Chautauque	Westernville	Oneida
Towners	Putnam	Waddington	St. Lawrence	West Exeter	Otsego
Town Line	Erie	Wadham's Mills	Essex	West Falls	Erie
Townsend	Chemung	Wading River	Suffolk	West Farmington	Ontario
Townsendville	Seneca	Walden	Orange	West Farms	Westchester
Tracy Creek	Broome	Waldensville	Schoharie	West Fayette	Seneca
Transit Bridge	Allegany	Wales	Erie	Westfield	Chautauque
Trenton	Oneida	Wales Center	Erie	Westford	Otsego
Trenton Falls	Oneida	Walesville	Oneida	West Fort Ann	Washington
Triangle	Broome	Wallace	Steuben	West Fulton	Schoharie
Tribus Hill	Montgomery	Walmore	Niagara	West Galway	Fulton
Troupsburg	Steuben	Walton	Delaware	West Gilboa	Schoharie
Trout Creek	Delaware	Walworth	Wayne	West Greece	Monroe
Trout River	Franklin	Wampsville	Madison	West Greenfield	Saratoga
Troy	Rensselaer	Wappinger's Falls	Dutchess	West Greenwood	Steuben
Trumansburg	Tompkins	Ward	Allegany	West Groton	Tompkins
Trumansburg Landing	Seneca	Wardborough	Warren	West Hampton	Suffolk
Trumbull Corners	Tompkins	Wardwell	Jefferson	West Hebron	Washington
Truxton	Cortland	Warnerville	Schoharie	West Henrietta	Monroe
Tuckahoe	Westchester	Warren	Herkimer	West Hills	Suffolk
Tully	Onondaga	Warrensburg	Warren	West Hoosick	Rensselaer
Tully Valley	Onondaga	Warren's Corners	Niagara	West Hurley	Ulster
Tuna	Cattaraugus	Warsaw	Wyoming	West Jasper	Steuben
Turin	Lewis	Warwick	Orange	West Junius	Seneca
Turner's	Orange	Washington	Dutchess	West Kendall	Orleans
Tuscarora	Livingston	Washington Heights	New York	West Kill	Greene
Tuthill	Ulster	Washington Hollow	Dutchess	West Kortright	Delaware
Tyre	Seneca	Washington Mills	Oneida	West Laurens	Otsego
Tyrone	Steuben	Wassaic	Dutchess	West Leyden	Lewis
Ulsterville	Ulster	Waterford	Saratoga	West Lowville	Lewis
Unadilla	Otsego	Waterloo	Seneca	West Martinsburg	Lewis
Unadilla Center	Otsego	Waterloo Mills	Orange	West Meredith	Delaware
Unadilla Forks	Otsego	Waterport	Orleans	West Milton	Saratoga
Underwood	Broome	Watertown	Jefferson	West Monroe	Oswego
Union	Broome	Watervale	Onondaga	Westmoreland	Oneida
Union Center	Broome	Water Valley	Erie	West Newark	Tioga
Union Church	Albany	Waterville	Oneida	Weston	Steuben
Union Corners	Livingston	Watervliet Center	Albany	West Oneonta	Otsego

POST OFFICES—NORTH CAROLINA. 63

Post Office.	County.
West Onondaga	Onondaga
West Perth	Fulton
West Plattsburg	Clinton
West Point	Orange
Westport	Essex
West Potsdam	St. Lawrence
West Providence	Saratoga
West Richmondville	Schoharie
West Rush	Monroe
West Sand Lake	Rensselaer
West Schuyler	Herkimer
West Seneca	Erie
West Seneca Center	Erie
West Shandaken	Ulster
West Shelby	Orleans
West Somers	Westchester
West Somerset	Niagara
West Stephentown	Rensselaer
West Stockholm	St. Lawrence
West Taghanick	Columbia
West Town	Orange
West Township	Albany
West Troupsburg	Steuben
West Troy	Albany
West Union	Steuben
West Vienna	Oneida
West View	Livingston
Westville	Otsego
West Walworth	Wayne
West Webster	Monroe
West Windsor	Broome
West Winfield	Herkimer
Westwood	Erie
West Yorkshire	Cattaraugus
Wethersfield	Wyoming
Wethersfield Springs	Wyoming
Whallonsburg	Essex
Wheatville	Genesee
Wheeler	Steuben
White Creek	Washington
Whitehall	Washington
White Lake	Sullivan
White Plains	Westchester
Whitesburg	Fulton
White's Corners	Erie
Whiteside's Corners	Saratoga
White's Store	Chenango
Whitestone	Queens
Whitestown	Oneida
Whitesville	Allegany
Whitney's Crossing	Allegany
Whitney's Point	Broome
Willow	Ulster
Wileysville	Steuben
Willet	Cortland
William's Bridge	Westchester
Williamsburg	Kings
Williamson	Wayne
Williamstown	Oswego
Williamsville	Erie
Willink	Erie
Willsboro	Essex
Willseyville	Tioga
Wilmington	Essex
Wilna	Jefferson
Wilson's	Niagara
Wilson's Creek	Tioga
Wilton	Saratoga
Windham Center	Greene
Windsor	Broome
Winfield	Herkimer
Wing's Station	Dutchess
Winspear	Erie
Wiscoy	Allegany
Wolcott	Wayne
Wolcottsville	Niagara
Woodbourne	Sullivan
Woodbury	Queens
Woodhull	Steuben
Woodland	Ulster
Woodstock	Ulster
Woodville	Jefferson
Woodward's Hollow	Erie
Worcester	Otsego
Worthville	Jefferson
Wright's Corners	Niagara
Wrightvale	Lewis
Wurtsboro	Sullivan
Wynantskill	Rensselaer
Wyoming	Wyoming

Post Office.	County.
Yaphank	Suffolk
Yates	Orleans
Yatesville	Yates
Yonkers	Westchester
York	Livingston
Yorkshire	Cattaraugus
Yorkshire Center	Cattaraugus
Yorktown	Westchester
Yorkville	New York
Young Hickory	Steuben
Youngstown	Niagara
Youngsville	Sullivan

North Carolina.

Post Office.	County.
Abbott's Creek	Davidson
Adam's Creek	Craven
Albemarle	Stanly
Albertson's	Duplin
Alexandriana	Mecklenburg
Alforsville	Robeson
Allemance	Guilford
Allensville	Person
Amau's Store	Onslow
Amity Hill	Iredell
Anderson's Store	Caswell
Angola	New Hanover
Anna Perena	Robeson
Ansonville	Anson
Aquone	Macon
Arcadia	Davidson
Areysville	Sampson
Argyle	Cumberland
Asheborough	Randolph
Asheville	Buncombe
Auburn	Wake
Auman's Hill	Montgomery
Ausburnville	Wilkes
Averysboro'	Harnett
Avery's Creek	Buncombe
Ayersville	Stokes
Bachelor's Creek	Randolph
Bain's Mills	Orange
Baker's X Roads	Franklin
Bakersville	Yancey
Bald Creek	"
Ballard's Bridge	Chowan
Baunerman	New Hanover
Barclaysville	Harnett
Bartonsville	Hertford
Bath	Beaufort
Battleborough	Edgecombe
Battle Hill	Duplin
Bay River	Craven
Bear Branch	Richmond
Bear Swamp	Duplin
Bear Wallow	Henderson
Beattie's Ford	Lincoln
Beatty's Bridge	Bladen
Beaufort	Carteret
Beaumont	Chatham
Beaver Creek	Ashe
Beaver Dam	Union
Bellview	Beaufort
Bellevoir	Chatham
Beman's X Roads	Sampson
Bentonsville	Johnson
Berea	Granville
Bethania	Forsyth
Bethany Church	Iredell
Bethel Hill	Person
Belt's Bridge	Iredell
Belt's Store	Wake
Beulah	Johnson
Big Falls	Orange
Big Laurel	Madison
Big Lick	Stanly
Big Swamp	Columbus
Birchettsville	Cleveland
Black Creek	Wilson
Blackman's Mills	Sampson
Black Mountain	McDowell
Black River Chapel	New Hanover
Black Rock	Brunswick

Post Office.	County.
Blackwell	Caswell
Blakeley	Stokes
Blocker's	Cumberland
Bloomingdale	Mecklenburg
Bloomington	Guilford
Blount's Creek	Beaufort
Blowing Rock	Watauga
Blue Ridge	Henderson
Blue Wing	Granville
Bolston	Henderson
Bowman's Bluff	
Boone	Watauga
Boone Hill	Johnson
Booneville	Yadkin
Bostick's Mills	Richmond
Bost's Mills	Cabarrus
Boyd's Ferry	Pitt
Boyden	Iredell
Branch	Chatham
Branch's Store	Duplin
Brick Church	Guilford
Bridgewater	Burke
Brier Creek	Wilkes
Brindleton	Burke
Bringle's Ferry	Rowan
Brinkleyville	Halifax
Brittain	Rutherford
Broad River	Cleveland
Brooklin	Robeson
Brookville	Granville
Brower's Mills	Randolph
Brownsville	Granville
Brush Creek	Randolph
Bryant's Swamp	Bladen
Buchanan	Granville
Buckhorn	Robeson
Buckland	Gates
Buck Shoals	Caldwell
Bucy's Creek	Harnett
Buena Vista	Duplin
Buffalo	Moore
Buffalo Ford	Randolph
Buggabo	Wilkes
Bug Hill	Columbus
Bunker's Hill	Catawba
Bunn's Level	Harnett
Burnsville	Yancey
Burney's Mills	Randolph
Bushy Fork	Person
Butler	Rutherford
Byrdsville	Brunswick
Cain's Branch	McDowell
Caintuck	New Hanover
Calabash	Davie
Calaubria	Cowan
Caldwell	Orange
Caledonia	Moore
Calhoun	Henderson
Calton	Moore
Camden	Camden
Camp Call	Cleveland
Camp Creek	Chatham
Cane Creek	Chatham
Caraway	Randolph
Carbonton	Chatham
Caroline City	Carteret
Carolina Seminary	Greene
Cary	Wake
Carthage	Moore
Casher's Valley	Macon
Castalia	Nash
Castania Grove	Gaston
Catawba Spring	Lincoln
Catawba Station	Iredell
Catawba View	Caldwell
Catharine Lake	Onslow
Cathey's Creek	Henderson
Cedar Bush	Davidson
Cedar Creek	Rutherford
Cedar Falls	Randolph
Cedar Fork	Wake
Cedar Grove	Orange
Cedar Hill	Anson
Cedar Mountain	Henderson
Center	Guilford
Center Grove	Person
Centerville	Moore
Cerro Gordo	Columbus
Climk Level	Cumberland
Charlotte	Mecklenburg

POST OFFICES—NORTH CAROLINA.

Post Office.	County.	Post Office.	County.	Post Office.	County.
Chapel Hill	Orange	Dunn's Rock	Henderson	Gap Civil	Ashe
Cherry Lane	Ashe	Durham's	Orange	Gap Creek	"
Cherryfield	Henderson	Durham's Creek	Beaufort	Garmon's Mills	Cabarras
Chesnut Hill	Ashe	Dutchville	Granville	Gardner's Ford	Cleveland
Chesnut Oak	Gaston	Dysortville	McDowell	Gerysburg	Northampton
Chesnut Ridge	Yadkin	Eagle Falls	Rockingham	Gaston	Northampton
Childsville	Yancey	Eagle Mills	Iredell	Gatesville	Gates
Chimney Rock	Rutherford	Eagle Rock	Wake	Georgetown	Jackson
China Grove	Rowan	Early Grove	Lincoln	Germanton	Stokes
Chinkapin	Duplin	Earpsborough	Johnson	Gibson's Store	Richmond
Chronicle	Lincoln	East Bend	Yadkin	Gibsonville	Guilford
Clarksberry	Rockingham	East Laporte	Jackson	Gilmer's Store	"
Clark's Creek	Montgomery	Eden	Randolph	Gilopolis	Robeson
Clarksville	Davie	Edenton	Chowan	Glade Creek	Ashe
Clayton	Johnson	Edinboro'	Montgomery	Gladsborough	Randolph
Claytonville	Henderson	Edneyville	Henderson	Glenaloon	Chatham
Clay Valley	Robeson	Efird's Mills	Stanley	Globe	Caldwell
Clear Creek	Mecklenburg	Egypt	Yancey	Golden Place	Onslow
Clemmonsville	Davidson	Elevation	Johnson	Golden Valley	Rutherford
Clinesville	Catawba	Elizabeth City	Pasquotank	Gold Branch	Cherokee
Clinton	Sampson	Elizabethtown	Bladen	Gold Hill	Rowan
Clover Garden	Orange	Elk Creek	Ashe	Gold Region	Moore
Clover Orchard	"	Elk × Roads	"	Goldsboro'	Wayne
Coburn's Store	Union	Elk'n	Surry	Goldston	Chatham
Coddle Creek	Cabarras	Elk Shoals	Alexander	Good Spring	Moore
Corajock	Currituck	Elk Spur	Wilkes	Goose Creek Island	Beaufort
Colerain	Bertie	Elkville	"	Gordonton	Person
Colesville	Stokes	Elm Grove	Rockingham	Governor's Island	Macon
Collettsville	Caldwell	Ellott's Springs	Catawba	Graham	Alamance
Columbia	Tyrrell	Ellisville	Bladen	Granite Hill	Iredell
Columbus	Polk	Enfield	Halifax	Grape Creek	Cherokee
Colvin's Creek	New Hanover	England's Point	Cherokee	Grassy Creek	Yancey
Comfort	Jones	Enola	Iredell	Grassy Knob	Rutherford
Company's Shops	Alamance	Erasmus	Gaston	Gravelly Hill	Bladen
Concord	Cabarras	Erwinsville	Cleveland	Graves	Caswell
Cool Spring	Iredell	Everettsville	Wayne	Gray's Creek	Cumberland
Cooper's Gap	Rutherford	Exchange	Warren	Green Hill	Rutherford
Copenhagen	Caldwell	Fair Bluff	Columbus	Green Level	Wake
Cottage Home	Lincoln	Fairfield	Hyde	Green Plains	Northampton
Cotton Grove	Davidson	Fair Grove	Davidson	Green River	Henderson
County Line	Davie	Fairplay	Robeson	Greensborough	Guilford
Covington	Richmond	Fairport	Granville	Green Swamp	Columbus
Cowan's Ford	Mecklenburg	Fairview	Buncombe	Greenville	Pitt
Cowee	Macon	Faison's Depot	Duplin	Grogansville	Rockingham
Cowper Hill	Robeson	Falkland	Pitt	Grove	Chatham
Cox's Mills	Randolph	Fall Creek	Chatham	Grove Hill	Warren
Coxville	Pitt	Falling Creek	Wayne	Gulf	Chatham
Crab Tree	Haywood	Falls	Yancey	Gum Branch	Onslow
Craghead	Mecklenburg	Fallstown	Iredell	Gun Neck	Tyrrel
Craigsville	Gaston	Fancy Hill	"	Hadley's Mills	Chatham
Crain's Creek	Moore	Farmington	Davie	Hadnot's	Carteret
Cranberry Forge	Watauga	Fayetteville	Cumberland	Halifax	Halifax
Creachville	Johnson	Fentriss	Guilford	Hallsville	Duplin
Cross Rock	Malison	Fine's Creek	Haywood	Hamby's Creek	Davidson
Crooked Creek	Stokes	First Broad	Rutherford	Hamilton	Martin
Crowder's Creek	Gaston	Fish Dam	Wake	Hamptonville	Yadkin
Crowder's Mountain	Gaston	Fisher's	Catawba	Hannersville	Davidson
Cuba	Rutherford	Fisher's Gap	Surry	Happy Home	Burke
Cunningham's Store	Person	Five-Mile Fork	Yadkin	Harrell's Store	New Hanover
Curriesville	Moore	Flag Branch	Union	Harrolsville	Hertford
Currituck C. H.	Currituck	Flat Branches	Forsyth	Harrington	Cumberland
Curcis' Mills	Alamance	Flat Creek	Buncombe	Harris Depot	Cabarras
Cypress Creek	Bladen	Flat River	Orange	Harrison Creek	Cumberland
Dallas	Gaston	Flat Rock	Henderson	Harrisville	Montgomery
Danbury	Stokes	Flat Shoal	Sarry	Hartshorn	Alamance
Dan River	Rockingham	Flint Rock	Catawba	Hatteras	Hyde
Davidson College	Mecklenburg	Floriesville	Robeson	Haw Branch	Onslow
Davidson River	Henderson	Forbush	Yadkin	Hawfields	Orange
Day Book	Yancey	Forestville	Wake	Hawley's Store	Sampson
Deal's Mills	Caldwell	Fort Creek	Randolph	Haw River	Alamance
Deep Creek	Anson	Fork Mountain	Yancey	Hay Meadow	Wilkes
Deep River	Guilford	Forks of Pigeon	Haywood	Hay Stack	Surry
Deep Well	Iredell	Forks of Tenuessee	Macon	Haywood	Chatham
Democrat	Buncombe	Fork Swamp	Beaufort	Hazel Dell	Caldwell
Desrett	Bladen	Fort Defiance	Caldwell	Healing Springs	Davidson
Day's Mills	Currituck	Fort Hembree	Cherokee	Heathville	Halifax
Dick's Creek	Buncombe	Fort Landing	Tyrrell	Helton	Ashe
Dobbinsville	Sampson	Fort Montgomery	Cherokee	Henderson	Granville
Dobson	Surry	Foust's Mills	Randolph	Hendersonville	Henderson
Dickerys' Store	Richmond	Francisco	Stokes	Herringville	Sampson
Dogwood Grove	New Hanover	Franklin	Macon	Hertford	Perquimans
Double Shoals	Cleveland	Franklinburg	Anson	Hester's Store	Person
Downingville	Bladen	Franklinton	Franklin	Hickory Tavern	Catawba
Draughon's Store	Sampson	Franklinville	Randolph	Hicksville	Rutherford
Drowning Creek	Burke	French Broad	Buncombe	High Point	Guilford
Dry Ponds	Lincoln	French Creek Church	Bladen	High Shoals	Rutherford
Dudley	Wayne	Friendship	Guilford	High Top	Jackson
Dunning Creek	Richmond	Fullwood Store	Mecklenburg	Hightown	Caswell
Duncan's Creek	Cleveland	Fulton	Davie	Hilliardston	Nash
Dundarrack	Robeson	Gaddeysville	Robeson	Hillsboro'	Orange

POST OFFICES—NORTH CAROLINA.

Post Office.	County.	Post Office.	County.	Post Office.	County.
Hillsdale	Guilford	Leesville	Robeson	Montrose	Cumberland
Hill's Store	Randolph	Leicester	Buncombe	Mooresborough	Cleveland
Hintonsville	Pasquotank	Lewisville	Forsyth	Moore's Creek	New Hanover
Hitchcock	Macon	Lenoir	Caldwell	Mooshannee	Moore
Hogan's Creek	Rockingham	Lenox Castle	Rockingham	Moretz Mill	Watauga
Holly Springs	Wake	Lee	Stanley	Morehead City	Carteret
Holtsburg	Davidson	Lewis' Fork	Wilkes	Morgan's Mills	Union
Holt's Store	Alamance	Letho	Richmond	Morgantown	Burke
Holly Grove	Madison	Lexington	Davidson	Morringsville	Chatham
Hookerstown	Greene	Liberty Hill	Iredell	Morrison's Tan Yard	
Hopewell	Mecklenburg	Lilesville	Anson		Mecklenburg
Hornet's Nest		Lillington	New Hanover	Morrisville	Wake
Hommony Creek	Buncombe	Lincolnton	Lincoln	Morton's Store	Alamance
Horse Creek	Ashe	Lindley's Store	Alamance	Morren	Anson
Horse Cove	Jackson	Linville River	Burke	Moseley Hall	Lenoir
Hotel	Bertie	Linton	Richmond	Mountain Creek	Catawba
Houstonville	Iredell	Little Mills		Mountain Island	Gaston
Howellsville	Robeson	Little Rock Fish	Cumberland	Mount Airy	Surry
Hoover Hill	Randolph	Little River	Caldwell	Mount Gilead	Montgomery
Hunsucker's Store	Montgomery	Littleton	Halifax	Mount Mourne	Iredell
Hunter's Bridge	Beaufort	Little Yadkin	Stokes	Mount Nebo	Yadkin
Hunting Creek	Wilkes	Locust Hill	Caswell	Mount Olive	Wayne
Huntsville	Yadkin	Logan's Store	Rutherford	Mount Piggah	Alexander
Hardle's Mills	Person	Long's Mills	Randolph	Mount Pleasant	Cabarras
Independence	Caswell	Long Ridge	Washington	Mount Tabor	Forsyth
Indesville	Surry	Long Street	Moore	Mount Tirza	Person
Indiantown	Currituck	Long Town	Catawba	Mount Ulla	Rowan
Inverness	Cumberland	Louisburg	Franklin	Mount Verd	Union
Island Creek	Duplin	Lowrance's Mills	Lincoln	Mount Vernon	Rowan
Island Ford	Rutherford	Lovelace	Wilkes	Mount Willing	Orange
Ivy	Yancey	Lovelady	Caldwell	Moyock	Currituck
Ivy Bend	Madison	Love's Level	Union	Mud Creek	Henderson
Ivy Gap		Lowell	Johnson	Muddy Fork	Cleveland
Ivy Hill	Haywood	Lumber Bridge	Robeson	Mud Lick	Chatham
Jackson	Northampton	Lumberton		Mulberry	Wilkes
Jackson's Creek	Randolph	McCray's Store	Orange	Mull Grove	Lincoln
Jackson's Hill	Davidson	McDaniel	Alamance	Murfreesboro'	Hertford
Jackson Spring	Moore	McLeansville	Guilford	Murphey	Cherokee
Jacob's Fork	Catawba	Macedonia	Montgomery	Nahonta	Wayne
Jamestown	Guilford	Mackey's Ferry	Washington	Nail Factory	Gaston
Jamesville	Martin	Macon Depot	Warren	Nantihala	Macon
Jefferson	Ashe	Madison	Rockingham	Nashville	Nash
Jonkin's Store	Union	Magnolia	Duplin	Nathan's Creek	Ashe
Jericho	Wayne	Manchester	Cumberland	Neatman	Stokes
Jerusalem	Davie	Mangum	Richmond	Negro Head Depot	Union
Jewell Hill	Madison	Minson	Warren	Nettle Knob	Ashe
Job's Cabin	Wilkes	Maple Springs	Wilkes	Newbern	Craven
Johnson's Mills	Pitt	Margaretsville	Northampton	Newby's Bridge	Perquimans
Johnsonville	Cumberland	Marion	McDowell	Now Castle	Wilkes
Jonathan's Creek	Haywood	Marlboro'	Pitt	New Garden	Guilford
Jones' Creek	Anson	Marley's Mills	Randolph	New Gilead	Moore
Jones' Mine	Randolph	Marshall	Madison	New Hill	Wake
Jonesville	Yadkin	Mars Hill College		New Hope	Iredell
Joyner's Depot	Edgecomb	Martha's Vineyard	Chatham	New Hope Academy	Randolph
Kenansville	Duplin	Martindale	Mecklenburg	New Light	Wake
Kendall's Store	Stanley	Martin's Limekiln	Stokes	New Market	Randolph
Kernersville	Forsyth	Maxwell	Brunswick	New Salem	
Killian's Mills	Lincoln	Mayfield	Rockingham	New Sterling	Iredell
Kimbolton	Chatham	Mayo		Newton	Catawba
King's Creek	Caldwell	Maysville	Greene	Newton Grove	Sampson
King's Mountain	Gaston	Meadow Creek	Orange	Newtonville	Caswell
Kinnie's Creek	Cumberland	Mebanesville	Alamance	Nicholsonville	Cleveland
Kinston	Lenoir	Melrose	Robeson	North Cove	McDowell
Kirkland	Cabarras	Meat Camp	Watauga	North Fork	Ashe
Kittrell	Granville	Melville	Alamance	Northington	Cumberland
Klutts' Tan Yard	Cabarras	Melvinsville	Bladen	Norval	Harnett
Knap of Reeds	Granville	Merry Hill	Bertie	Norwood	Stanly
Knob Creek	Cleveland	Merry Mount	Warren	Nottla	Cherokee
Knott's Island	Currituck	Middle Creek	Wake	Nuthush	Warren
Kyle's Landing	Cumberland	Middletown	Hyde	Oak Forest	Iredell
La Grange	Randolph	Midway	Davidson	Oak Grove	Union
Lake Comfort	Hyde	Millbank	Granville	Oak Hill	Granville
Lake Landing		Milbernie	Wake	Oakland	Chatham
Lanesborough	Anson	Milledgeville	Montgomery	Oaklawn	Cabarras
Lano's Creek	Union	Mill Creek	Randolph	Oak Level	Yadkin
Lantz Grove	Lincoln	Mill Hill	Cabarras	Oakley	New Hanover
Lapland	Madison	Mill River	Henderson	Oak Ridge	Guilford
Lassiter's Mills	Randolph	Mill Landing	Bertie	Oaks	Orange
Laurenburg	Richmond	Milton	Caswell	Oak Spring	Rutherford
Laurel	Franklin	Mineraville	McDowell	Oakville	Union
Laurel Branch	Rowan	Mint Hill	Mecklenburg	Ocona Lufty	Haywood
Laurel Spring	Ashe	Mintonsville	Gates	Ooracoko	Hyde
Laurel Valley	Cherokee	Miranda	Rowan	Old Fort	McDowell
Lawhorn's Hill	Moore	Mocksville	Davie	Old Furnace	Gaston
Lawsonville	Rockingham	Moffit's Mills	Randolph	Old Richmond	Forsyth
Leochburg	Johnson	Munk's Store	Sampson	Old Shop	Wake
Leaksville	Rockingham	Monroe	Union	Old Town	Forsyth
Leasburg	Caswell	Monrooton	Rockingham	Olin	Iredell
Ledger	Yancey	Monticello	Guilford	Olive Branch	Union
Lecohville	Beaufort	Montpelier	Richmond	Olive Hill	Person

5

POST OFFICES—NORTH CAROLINA.

Post Office.	County.	Post Office.	County.	Post Office.	County.
Onslow C. H.	Onslow	Rosaca	Duplin	Smithfield	Johnson
Orange Factory	Orange	Reynoldson	Gates	Smith Grove	Davie
Oregon	Rockingham	Rialto	Chatham	Smith's Store	Alamance
Orrville	Mecklenburg	Richardson's Creek	Union	Smith's Valley	Stokes
Otter Creek	Rutherford	Rich Fork	Davidson	Smithville	Brunswick
Outlaws' Bridge	Duplin	Richlands	Onslow	Smyrna	Carteret
Owensville	Sampson	Richland Creek	Randolph	Snead's Ferry	Onslow
Oxford	Granville	Richland Valley	Haywood	Snipe's Store	Chatham
Pacific	Franklin	Richmond Hill	Yadkin	Snow Camp	Alamance
Pactolus	Pitt	Rich Square	Northampton	Snow Creek	Iredell
Paint Gap	Yancey	Ridge Spring	Pitt	Snow Hill	Greene
Palmyra	Halifax	Ridgeway	Warren	Soapstone Mount	Randolph
Palo Alto	Onslow	Riggsher's Store	Chatham	Solemn Grove	Moore
Pantegal	Beaufort	Ringwood	Halifax	South Creek	Beaufort
Panther Creek	Surry	Roanoke	Martin	South Fork	Ashe
Parks' Store	Cabarrus	Roaring Gap	Wilkes	South Lowell	Orange
Patterson	Caldwell	Robeson	Brunswick	South Mills	Camden
Patterson's Store	Alamance	Rock Creek	Alamance	South Point	Gaston
Patten's Home	Rutherford	Rock Cut	Iredell	South River	Rowan
Peach Tree	Cherokee	Rock Fish	Duplin	Spaightesville	Craven
Peach Tree Grove	Nash	Rockford	Surry	Sparta	Edgecombe
Peacock's Store	Columbus	Rockingham	Richmond	Speight's Bridge	Greene
Pedlar's Hill	Chatham	Rock Mills	Lincoln	Spencer	Davidson
Peodee	Anson	Rock Spring	Orange	Spring Creek	Madison
Pekin	Montgomery	Rockville	Rowan	Springfield	Richmond
Perkinsville	Burke	Rocky Mount	Edgecombe	Spring Hill Forge	Lincoln
Persimmon Creek	Cherokee	Rocky Point	New Hanover	Spring Hope	Nash
Petersburg	Cleveland	Rodger's Store	Wake	Spruce Pine	Yancey
Peru	Haywood	Rolesville	"	Staceyville	Rockingham
Peter's Creek	Stokes	Rollins' Store	Moore	Stagville	Orange
Pharr's Mills	Moore	Rose Hill	Pitt	Stanhope	Nash
Philadelphus	Robeson	Roseman's Store	Rowan	Stanley's Creek	Gaston
Pierceville	Cleveland	Rosova e	Mecklenburg	Stantonsburgh	Edgecombe
Pigeon River	Haywood	Rotherwood	Watauga	State Road	Surry
Pikeville	Wayne	Round Hill	Orange	Satosville	Iredell
Pilot Mountain	Stokes	Rowan's Mills	Rowan	Steele Creek	Mecklenburg
Pine Grove	Montgomery	Roxborough	Person	Stevens' Mills	Union
Pine Hall	Stokes	Roxobel	Bertie	Stice's Shoal	Cleveland
Pine Level	Johnson	Rudy Branch	Moore	Stikoih	Cherokee
Pineville	Mecklenburg	Rum's Creek	Buncombe	Stocksville	Buncombe
Piney Creek	Alleghany	Rural Hall	Forsyth	Stone Mountain	McDowell
Piney Green	Onslow	Rush's Mills	Montgomery	Stone Lick	Randolph
Piney Grove	Sampson	Rusk	Surry	Stone's Bay	Onslow
Pink Hill	Lenoir	Rutherfordton	Rutherford	Stony Fork	Watauga
Pioneer Mills	Cabarrus	Saint Charles	Johnson	Stony Point	Alexander
Pitch Landing	Hertford	Saint John	Hertford	Stony Ridge	Surry
Pittsboro'	Chatham	Saint Lawrence	Chatham	Stowesville	Gaston
Pleasant Exchange	Bladen	Saint Pauls	Robeson	Strabane	Lenoir
Pleasant Grove	Alamance	Salem	Forsyth	Straits	Carteret
Pleasant Hill	Northampton	Salem Church	Randolph	Suck Creek	Rutherford
Pleasant Retreat	Duwell	Salem Chapel	Forsyth	Sugar Grove	Watauga
Pleasant Ridge	Gaston	Salisbury	Rowan	Sugar Hill	McDowell
Pleasantville	Rockingham	Sanders' Hill	Montgomery	Sulphur Springs	Buncombe
Plymouth	Washington	Sandy Creek	Randolph	Summerfield	Guilford
Pocket	Moore	Sandy Foundation	Lenoir	Summerville	Harnett
Polkville	Cleveland	Sandy Grove	Chatham	Summit	Northampton
Pollocksville	Jones	Sandy Level	Johnson	Sunbury	Gates
Poplar Branch	Currituck	Sandy Mush	Buncombe	Sunny South	Nash
Poplar Hill	Union	Sandy Plains	Rutherford	Supply	Brunswick
Portsmouth	Carteret	Saratoga	Wilson	Swangstown	Cleveland
Potecasi	Northampton	Sassafras Fork	Granville	Swannano	Buncombe
Powellton	Richmond	Saxapahaw	Alamance	Swan Pond	Wilkes
Prescott	Duplin	Sawyersville	Randolph	Swan Quarter	Hyde
Prospect Hall	Bladen	Science Hill	"	Swansboro'	Onslow
Prospect Hill	Caswell	Scotland Neck	Halifax	Sweet Home	Iredell
Prosperity	Moore	Scottsville	Ashe	Sweet Water	Watauga
Providence	Mecklenburg	Scott's Hill	New Hanover	Swift Creek Bridge	Craven
Purlear's Creek	Wilkes	Scuppernong	Washington	Swift Island	Montgomery
Purley	Caswell	Seaboard	Northampton	Sycamore Alley	Halifax
Quallatown	Haywood	Sedges Garden	Forsyth	Tabb's Creek	Granville
Queensdale	Robeson	Siegel's Store	Lincoln	Tally Ho	Granville
Query's	Mecklenburg	Shady Grove	Davidson	Tarborough	Edgecombe
Raft Swamp	Robeson	Shallotte	Brunswick	Taylor's Bridge	Sampson
Raleigh	Wake	Shallow Ford	Alamance	Taylorsville	Alexander
Ramseytown	Yancey	Sharon	Mecklenburg	Teachey's	Duplin
Ranaleburg	Mecklenburg	Shaw's Mills	Guilford	Tennessee River	Macon
Randallsville	Robeson	Shelby	Cleveland	Terebinthe	Cumberland
Ransom's Bridge	Nash	Shephardsville	Carteret	Thomasville	Davidson
Rawlingsburg	Rockingham	Sherrill's Ford	Lincoln	Thompsonville	Rockingham
Raysville	Madison	Shiloah	Camden	Tom's Creek	Surry
Raywood	Union	Shocco Springs	Warren	Topsail Sound	New Hanover
Reddie's River	Wilkes	Shuffordville	Buncombe	Townesville	Granville
Red Hill	Yancey	Sill's Creek	New Hanover	Tranquility	"
Red Mountain	Orange	Siloam	Surry	Trapp Hill	Wilkes
Red Plains	Yadkin	Silver Hill	Davidson	Trenton	Jones
Red Shoals	Stokes	Six Runs	Sampson	Trinity College	Randolph
Red Springs	Robeson	Skeench	Macon	Troublesome	Rockingham
Reed Creek	Randolph	Sladesville	Hyde	Troy	Montgomery
Reidsville	Rockingham	Sleepy Creek	Wayne	Troy's Store	Randolph
Republic	Yadkin	Smith's Bridge	Robeson	Tyron	Polk

POST OFFICES—OHIO.

Post Office.	County.
Snekasaga	Mecklenburg
Tulin	Iredell
Turkey Cove	McDowell
Turnersburg	Iredell
Turnpike	Buncombe
Turtle Town	Cherokee
Tusquittee	"
Uchella	Macon
Union Grove	Iredell
Union Mills	Jones
Union Ridge	Alamance
Unionville	Robeson
University Station	Orange
Valle Crusis	Watauga
Valley Town	Cherokee
Van Hook's Store	Person
Vestal's Ford	Gaston
Vesuvius Furnace	Lincoln
Vienna	Forsyth
Wadesboro'	Anson
Wakefield	Wake
Waknlla	Robeson
Walkerstown	Forsyth
Walkersville	Union
Wallers	Granville
Walnut Cove	Stokes
Walnut Creek	Buncombe
Walnut Grove	Orange
Walnut Hill	Ashe
Walnut Lane	Yadkin
Walnut Shade	Gaston
Warm Springs	Buncombe
Warren Plains	Warren
Warrensville	Sampson
Warrenton	Warren
Warrior Creek	Wilkes
Warsaw	Duplin
Washington	Beaufort
Watauga Falls	Watauga
Waterloo	Granville
Watson's Bridge	Moore
Waughtown	Forsyth
Waynesville	Haywood
Weaver's Mills	Forsyth
Weaver's Ford	Ashe
Webb's Ford	Rutherford
Webster	Jackson
Weldon	Halifax
Wentworth	Rockingham
West Brook	Bladen
Western Prong	"
Westfield	Stokes
Westland	Halifax
Westminster	Guilford
West Point	Orange
Wheelersville	Northampton
White Creek	Bladen
White Cross	Orange
White Hall	Mecklenburg
White Hill	Union
White House	Randolph
White Oak	Bladen
White Pine	Gaston
White Plains	Cleveland
White Road	Forsyth
White Rock	Madison
White's Creek	Bladen
White's Store	Anson
Whiteville	Columbus
Why Not	Randolph
Wilkesborough	Wilkes
Wilbar	"
Williamsboro'	Granville
Williamsburg	Iredell
Williams' Mills	Chatham
Williamston	Martin
Wilmington	New Hanover
Wilson	Edgecombe
Wilson's Store	Stokes
Wilton	Granville
Winchester	Union
Wind Hill	Montgomery
Windsor	Bertie
Winslow	Harnett
Winston	Forsyth
Winton	Hertford
Wittenburg	Alexander
Wolf Creek	Cherokee
Wolf Pitt	Onslow
Wolf Pond	Union
Wolfsville	Union
Woodland	Northampton
Woodlawn	Gaston
Woodleaf	Rowan
Woodsdale	Person
Woodville	Perquimans
Woodworth	Granville
Yadkin Institute	Davidson
Yadkinville	Yadkin
Yanceyville	Caswell
Yellow Mountain	Yancey
York College Institute	
	Alexander
Young's X Roads	Granville
Zimmerman	Wilkes
Zion	Yadkin

Ohio.

Post Office.	County.
Abbeyville	Medina
Aberdeen	Brown
Achor	Columbiana
Acadia	Allen
Ada	Hardin
Adams	Seneca
Adams' Mills	Muskingum
Adamsville	"
Adairo	Richland
Addison	Gallia
Adelphi	Ross
Adena	Jefferson
Adrian	Seneca
Ai	Fulton
Aid	Lawrence
Agatha	Jackson
Akron	Summit
Alba	Hancock
Albany	Tuscarawas
Albion	Ashland
Alert	Butler
Alexandersville	Montgomery
Alexandria	Licking
Alfred	Meigs
Algonquin	Carroll
Allens	Miami
Allensburg	Highland
Allentown	Allen
Allensville	Vinton
Alliance	Stark
Alpha	Greene
Alton	Franklin
Alum Creek	Delaware
Amanda	Fairfield
Amboy	Ashtabula
Amelia	Clermont
Amesville	Athens
Amherst	Lorain
Amsterdam	Jefferson
Andover	Ashtabula
Angola	Clermont
Andrews	Morrow
Anna	Shelby
Annapolis	Jefferson
Anselm	Gallia
Ansenia	Darke
Antioch	Monroe
Antrim	Guernsey
Antwerp	Paulding
Apple Creek	Wayne
Apple Grove	Meigs
Appleton	Licking
Arabia	Lawrence
Arcadia	Hancock
Arcanum	Darke
Archbold	Fulton
Archer	Harrison
Arlington	Hancock
Armstrong's Mills	Belmont
Arnheim	Brown
Arrowsmith's	Defiance
Ashury	Perry
Ash Cave	Hocking
Ashland	Ashland
Ashley	Delaware
Ash Ridge	Brown
Ashtabula	Ashtabula
Ashville	Pickaway
Athalia	Lawrence
Athens	Athens
Atlas	Belmont
Attica	Seneca
Atwater	Portage
Auburn	Geauga
Auglaize	Van Wert
Augusta	Carroll
Aurora	Portage
Austin	Ross
Austinburg	Ashtabula
Ava	Noble
Avon	Lorain
Avon Lake	"
Ayersville	Defiance
Bacon	Coshocton
Bailey's Mills	Belmont
Bainbridge	Ross
Baker's	Champaign
Bakersville	Coshocton
Baltimore	Fairfield
Bantam	Clermont
Barlow	Washington
Barnes'	Richland
Barnesville	Belmont
Barry	Cuyahoga
Barryville	Stark
Bartramville	Lawrence
Bartlett	Washington
Bascom	Seneca
Basil	Fairfield
Bashan	Meigs
Batavia	Clermont
Batesville	Guernsey
Bath	Summit
Baughman	Wayne
Bayard	Columbiana
Bazetta	Trumbull
Beallsville	Monroe
Beamsville	Darke
Beasley's Fork	Adams
Beaver	Pike
Beaver Dam	Allen
Beckett's Store	Pickaway
Bedford	Cuyahoga
Beech	Licking
Belfast	Clermont
Bell	Highland
Bell Air	Belmont
Bell Brook	Greene
Bell Center	Logan
Bellefontaine	"
Belmont	Belmont
Belle Vernon	Wyandott
Belleville	Richland
Bellevue	Huron
Belle Point	Delaware
Belmore	Putnam
Belpre	Washington
Bennington	Morrow
Benton	Holmes
Bentonville	Adams
Benton Ridge	Hancock
Belea	Cuyahoga
Berkshire	Delaware
Berlin	Holmes
Berlin Center	Mahoning
Berlin X Roads	Jackson
Berlin Hights	Erie
Berlin Station	"
Berlinville	"
Berne	Noble
Berrysville	Highland
Berwick	Seneca
Beta	Henry
Bethany	Butler
Bethel	Clermont
Bethesda	Belmont
Bettsville	Seneca
Bevis Tavern	Hamilton
Beverly	Washington
Big Island	Marion
Big Lick	Hancock
Big Plain	Madison
Big Prairie	Wayne
Big Run	Washington
Big Sand Furnace	Vinton
Bird's Run	Guernsey

POST OFFICES—OHIO.

Post Office.	County.	Post Office.	County.	Post Office.	County.
Bishopville	Morgan	Burnett Wood	Hamilton	Chickasaw	Mercer
Birmingham	Erie	Butler	Richland	Chili	Coshocton
Bissell's	Geauga	Butlerville	Warren	Chilicothe	Ross
Black Creek	Holmes	Byhalia	Union	Chilo	Clermont
Black Jack	Hocking	Byington	Pike	Chippewa	Wayne
Black Lick	Franklin	Byron	Greene	Christiansburg	Champaign
Blacklysville	Wayne	Caballo	Carroll	Church Hill	Trumbull
Black River	Lorain	Cadiz	Harrison	Cincinnati	Hamilton
Black Swamp	Sandusky	Cadwallader	Tuscarawas	Circleville	Pickaway
Bladensburg	Knox	Caldwell	Noble	Claridon	Geauga
Blanc	Fulton	Cairo	Stark	Clarington	Monroe
Blanchard Bridge	Hancock	Calais	Monroe	Clark's	Coshocton
Blanchester	Clinton	Calcutta	Columbiana	Clarksburg	Ross
Blendon	Franklin	Caledonia	Marion	Clark's Corners	Ashtabula
Bloody Eagle	Hancock	California	Clermont	Clarksfield	Huron
Bloom	Wood	Calvary	Athens	Clarkson	Columbiana
Bloom Center	Logan	Camba	Jackson	Clarksville	Clinton
Bloomfield	Morrow	Cambridge	Guernsey	Clay	Jackson
Bloomingburg	Fayette	Camden	Preble	Clay Lick	Licking
Bloomingdale	Jefferson	Camden Station	Lorain	Clayton	Montgomery
Bloomington	Clinton	Cameron	Monroe	Claytona	Noble
Bloomingville	Erie	Campbell	Lawrence	Claysville	Guernsey
Bloom Rose	Brown	Campbelltown	Preble	Clear Port	Fairfield
Bloomville	Seneca	Camp Charlotte	Pickaway	Clear Creek	..
Blue Ball	Butler	Camp Run	Crawford	Clement	Hancock
Blue Creek	Adams	Canaan	Wayne	Cleveland	Cuyahoga
Blue Lick	Allen	Canaanville	Athens	Cleves	Hamilton
Blue Rock	Muskingum	Canal Dover	Tuscarawas	Clifton	Greene
Boardman	Mahoning	Canal Fulton	Stark	Clinton	Summit
Boetia	Mercer	Canal Lewisville	Coshocton	Clinton Valley	Clinton
Boke's Creek	Union	Canal Winchester	Franklin	Clintonville	Franklin
Bolivar	Tuscarawas	Canfield	Mahoning	Clio	Greene
Bonn	Washington	Canonsburg	Hancock	Clover	Clermont
Boston	Summit	Cannon's Mill	Columbiana	Clyde	Sandusky
Boswell	Mahoning	Canton	Stark	Coal Dale	Muskingum
Bourneville	Ross	Captina	Belmont	Coal Grove	Lawrence
Bowerston	Harrison	Cardington	Morrow	Coal Run	Washington
Bowersville	Greene	Carey	Wyandott	Cochran's Landing	Monroe
Bowling Green	Wood	Carlisle Station	Warren	Cochranton	Marion
Bowshersville	Wyandott	Carmel	Highland	Coe Ridge	Cuyahoga
Boyd's Mills	Coshocton	Carroll	Fairfield	Coitsville	Mahoning
Braceville	Trumbull	Carrollton	Carroll	Cold Spring	Harrison
Brady	Tuscarawas	Carson	Huron	Cold Water	Mercer
Bradyville	Adams	Carthagena	Mercer	Colerain	Belmont
Brandt	Miami	Carthage	Hamilton	Cullomer	Cuyahoga
Brandon	Knox	Carysville	Champaign	College Corner	Butler
Bremen	Fairfield	Cass	Hancock	College Hill	Hamilton
Bricksville	Cuyahoga	Casstown	Miami	Collinsville	Butler
Bridge Creek	Geauga	Cassville	Harrison	Colton	Henry
Bridgeport	Belmont	Castalia	Erie	Columbia	Hamilton
Bridgeville	Muskingum	Castine	Darke	Columbia Center	Licking
Bridgewater	Williams	Catawba	Clark	Columbiana	Columbiana
Briar Hill	Mahoning	Cedar Valley	Wayne	Columbia Station	Lorain
Brighton	Lorain	Cedarville	Greene	Columbus	Franklin
Brimfield	Portage	Cedar Hill	Fairfield	Concord	Lake
Brinley's Station	Preble	Cedron	Clermont	Concordia	Darke
Brinton	Champaign	Celina	Mercer	Condit	Delaware
Bristol	Morgan	Central College	Franklin	Congress	Wayne
Bristolville	Trumbull	Centor	Montgomery	Conneaut	Ashtabula
Brock	Darke	Center Belpre	Washington	Conotton	Harrison
Broken Sword	Crawford	Center Bend	Morgan	Conover	Miami
Bronson	Huron	Centerburg	Knox	Constantia	Delaware
Brookfield	Trumbull	Centerfield	Highland	Constitution	Washington
Brooklyn	Cuyahoga	Centerton	Huron	Contreras	Butler
Brookville	Montgomery	Center View	Monroe	Convenience	Fayette
Brown's Corners	Wood	Center Village	Delaware	Coolville	Athens
Brownhelm	Lorain	Centerville	Montgomery	Copley	Summit
Brown's Mills	Washington	Chagrin Falls	Cuyahoga	Copopa	Lorain
Brownsville	Licking	Chalfant	Champaign	Cork	Ashtabula
Browuson Station	Franklin	Chambersburg	Montgomery	Cornersburg	Mahoning
Brunersburg	Defiance	Chandlersville	Muskingum	Corsica	Morrow
Brunswick	Medina	Chanticleer	Knox	Coshocton	Coshocton
Bryan	Williams	Chapel Hill	Perry	Cottage Hill	Muskingum
Brushy Fork	Licking	Chardon	Geauga	Covington	Miami
Buchanan	Perry	Charlestown	Portage	Cove	Jackson
Buck's	Columbiana	Charloe	Paulding	Cox	Licking
Buckeye	Putnam	Chatfield	Crawford	Cranberry	Allen
Buckeye Cottage	Perry	Chatham	Licking	Cranberry Prairie	Mercer
Buckeye Furnace	Jackson	Chatham Center	Medina	Cranesville	Paulding
Bucyrus	Crawford	Chauncey	Athens	Crandall	Lorain
Buena Vista	Tuscarawas	Cherry Fork	Adams	Creighton	Guernsey
Buffalo	Guernsey	Cherry Grove	Hamilton	Crestline	Crawford
Buford	Highland	Cherry Valley	Ashtabula	Cridersville	Auglaize
Bundysburg	Geauga	Cheshire	Gallia	Croghan	Allen
Bunker Hill	Butler	Chester	Meigs	Crooked Tree	Noble
Burbank	Wayne	Chester ½ Roads	Geauga	Cross Creek	Jefferson
Burlingham	Meigs	Chesterfield	Fulton	Cross Roads	Madison
Burlington	Lawrence	Chester Hill	Morgan	Croton	Licking
Burgh Hill	Trumbull	Chesterville	Morrow	Croxton	Jefferson
Burton	Geauga	Cheviot	Hamilton	Cuba	Clinton

POST OFFICES—OHIO.

Post Office.	County.	Post Office.	County.	Post Office.	County.
Cumberland	Guernsey	East Orange	Delaware	Frankfort	Ross
Cumminsville	Hamilton	East Palestine	Columbiana	Franklin	Warren
Cuyahoga Falls	Summit	East Plymouth	Ashtabula	Franklin Furnace	Scioto
Cutler	Washington	East Richland	Belmont	Franklin Mills	Portage
Cynthiana	Pike	East Ringgold	Pickaway	Franklin Square	Columbiana
Dallas	Highland	East Rochester	Columbiana	Franklin Station	Coshocton
Dallasburg	Warren	East Rockport	Cuyahoga	Frazeysburg	Muskingum
Dalton	Wayne	East Rush Creek	Perry	Frease's Store	Stark
Damascus	Henry	East Springfield	Jefferson	Frederick	Mahoning
Damascoville	Columbiana	East Sycamore	Hamilton	Fredericksburg	Wayne
Danville	Knox	East Toledo	Lucas	Fredericktown	Knox
Darby	Franklin	East Townsend	Huron	Freeburg	Stark
Darby Creek	Madison	East Trumbull	Trumbull	Fredonia	Licking
Darby Plains	Union	East Union	Wayne	Freedom	Portage
Darbyville	Pickaway	Eaton	Preble	Freeport	Harrison
Darke	Darke	Eckmansville	Adams	Fremont	dusky
Darrtown	Butler	Economy	Highland	Friendship	Scioto
Dawn	Darke	Edenton	Clermont	Fryburg	Auglaize
Dawkin's Mills	Jackson	Edgerton	Williams	Fulton	Hamilton
Dayton	Montgomery	Edinburg	Portage	Fultonham	uskingum
Davis	Carroll	Edwardsville	Warren	Gahannah	Franklin
Deardorff's Mills	Tuscarawas	Egypt	Wood	Galena	Delaware
		El Dorado	Preble	Galion	Crawford
Denvertown	Morgan	Elida	Allen	Gallia Furnace	Gallia
Decatur	Brown	Elizabethtown	Hamilton	Gallipolis	"
Decaturville	Washington	Elk	Vinton	Galigher	Guernsey
Deer Creek	Pickaway	Elkton	Columbiana	Gambier	Knox
Deep Cut	Mercer	Elliott's ½ Roads	Morgan	Ganges	Richland
Deerfield	Portage	Elliottsville	Jefferson	Garden	Athens
Deerfield Village	Warren	Ellsworth	Mahoning	Gardner	Noble
Deer Lick	Williams	Elm Grove	Hancock	Garrettsville	Portage
Deersville	Harrison	Elmore	Ottawa	Gates' Mills	Cuyahoga
Defiance	Defiance	Elmira	Fulton	Gavers	Columbiana
De Graff	Logan	Elyria	Lorain	Geneva	Ashtabula
De La Palma	Brown	Emery	Fulton	Genoa	Ottawa
Delaware	Delaware	Emerald	Adams	Genoa ½ Roads	Delaware
Delhi	Hamilton	Emmett	Paulding	Georgesville	Franklin
De Lisle	Darke	Enoch	Monroe	Georgetown	Brown
Delphos	Van Wert	Enon	Clark	German	Darke
Delta	Fulton	Enterprise	Preble	Germano	Harrison
Demas	Belmont	Etna	Licking	Germantown	Montgomery
Democracy	Knox	Euclid	Cuyahoga	Gettysburg	Darke
Denmark	Ashtabula	Euphemia	Preble	Ghent	Summit
Dent	Hamilton	Evansburg	Coshocton	Gibsonville	Hocking
Dewitt Ridge	Holmes	Evansport	Defiance	Gibson	Pike
Dexter	Meigs	Ewing	Hocking	Gibson's Station	Guernsey
Dille's Bottom	Belmont	Ewington	Gallia	Gilboa	Putnam
Dinsmore	Shelby	Exeter	Sandusky	Gilead	Wood
Dodson	Montgomery	Fairfax	Highland	Gillespieville	Ross
Dodsonville	Highland	Fairfield	Greene	Gilmore	Tuscarawas
Dog Creek	Putnam	Fair Haven	Preble	Girard	Trumbull
Domestic	Williams	Fair Play	Jefferson	Glasgow	Columbiana
Donnel's	Allen	Fairview	Guernsey	Glencoe	Belmont
Donnelsville	Clark	Fallsburg	Licking	Gendale	Hamilton
Dorset	Ashtabula	Farmer	Defiance	Gnadenhutten	Tuscarawas
Dover	Cuyahoga	Farmer's Station	Clinton	Golden Corner	Wayne
Downington	Meigs	Farmersville	Montgomery	Gomber	Guernsey
Dresden	Muskingum	Farmington	Trumbull	Good Hope	Fayette
Dry Ridge	Hamilton	Fayetteville	Brown	Gomer	Allen
Dublin	Franklin	Fearing	Washington	Gordon	Darke
Duck Creek	Trumbull	Federalton	Athens	Gore	Hocking
Dudley	Hardin	Feesburg	Brown	Gorham	Fulton
Damontville	Fairfield	Felicity	Clermont	Goshen	Clermont
Dunbar	Washington	Fidelity	Miami	Grafton	Lorain
Dunbarton	Adams	Fife	Harrison	Grand View	Washington
Duncan's Falls	Muskingum	Fillmore	Washington	Granger	Medina
Dundas	Vinton	Fincastle	Brown	Granville	Licking
Dundee	Tuscarawas	Finley	Hancock	Grape Grove	Greene
Dunham	Washington	Fitchville	Huron	Gratiot	Licking
Dunkinsville	Adams	Five Mile	Brown	Gratis	Preble
Dunkirk	Hardin	Five Points	Pickaway	Gray's Corners	Morrow
Dungannon	Columbiana	Flat	Pike	Graysville	Monroe
Dunlap	Hamilton	Flat Rock	Seneca	Graytown	Ottawa
Dunlevy	Warren	Fletcher	Miami	Greasy Ridge	Lawrence
Durand	Henry	Flint's Mills	Washington	Great Bend	Meigs
Durbin's Corners	Williams	Florence	Erie	Green	Licking
Dyson's	Guernsey	Florida	Henry	Greenbush	Preble
Eagle	Hancock	Flushing	Belmont	Green Camp	Marion
Eagle Mills	Vinton	Ford	Geauga	Green Castle	Fairfield
Eagleville	Ashtabula	Forest	Hardin	Greenfield	Highland
East Claridon	Geauga	Fort Ancient	Warren	Greenford	Mahoning
East Clarksfield	Huron	Fort Jefferson	Darke	Green Hill	Columbiana
East Cleveland	Cuyahoga	Fort Jennings	Putnam	Greenland	Ross
East Fairfield	Columbiana	Fort Recovery	Mercer	Greensburg	Trumbull
East Greenville	Stark	Fort Seneca	Seneca	Greensburg ½ Roads	Sandusky
East Lewistown	Mahoning	Foster's Crossings	Warren	Green Spring	Seneca
East Liberty	Logan	Fostoria	Seneca	Greentown	Stark
East Liverpool	Columbiana	Four Corners	Huron	Greenville	Darke
East Monroe	Highland	Fowler	Trumbull	Greenwick Station	Huron
Easton	Wayne	Franconia	Putnam	Greersville	Knox

POST OFFICES—OHIO.

Post Office.	County.	Post Office.	County.	Post Office.	County.
Groesbeck	Hamilton	Houston	Shelby	Lake	Stark
Grove City	Franklin	Howland	Trumbull	Lake Fork	Ashland
Grove Port	"	Hubbard	"	Lamartine	Carroll
Guilford	Medina	Hudson	Summit	Lamira	Belmont
Gustavus	Trumbull	Hudsonville	Hardin	Lampsville	"
Gustin	Adams	Hull's	Athens	Lancaster	Fairfield
Guysville	Athens	Humphrey's Villa	Holmes	Langsville	Meigs
Hale	Harden	Hunter	Belmont	La Porte	Lorain
Hale's Creek	Scioto	Huntersville	Hardin	Larue	Marion
Hall's Valley	Morgan	Huntington	Lorain	Latham	Pike
Hallsville	Ross	Huntsburg	Geauga	Lattas	Ross
Hamburg	Fairfield	Huntsville	Logan	Laura	Miami
Hamer	Paulding	Huron	Erie	Laurel	Clermont
Hamilton	Butler	Hyattsville	Miami	Lavona	Fulton
Hamersville	Brown	Iberia	Morrow	Lawrence	Washington
Hammondsville	Jefferson	Islesboro'	Hocking	Layman	"
Hampden	Geauga	Independence	Cuyahoga	Leatherwood	Guernsey
Handy	Fulton	Indian Camp	Guernsey	Leavitt	Carroll
Hanging Rock	Lawrence	Indian Hill	Hamilton	Lebanon	Warren
Hanna's Mills	Mahoning	Indigo	Monroe	Lecompton	Monroe
Hannibal	Monroe	Inland	Summit	Ledlies	Meigs
Hanover	Licking	Inverness	Columbiana	Lee	Athens
Hanoverton	Columbiana	Ione	Erie	Leesburg	Highland
Hardin	Shelby	Iron Furnace	Scioto	Lee's Creek	Clinton
Harlem	Delaware	Ironton	Lawrence	Leesville	Carroll
Harlem Spring	Carroll	Iron Valley	Jackson	Leesville X Roads	Crawford
Harmar	Washington	Irwin	Union	Leipsic	Putnam
Harmony	Clark	Island Creek	Jefferson	Lena	Fulton
Harper	Logan	Ithaca	Drke	Lenox	Ashtabula
Harpersfield	Ashtabula	Jackson Furnace	Jackson	Leon	"
Harrietsville	Noble	Jacksontown	Licking	Leonardsburg	Delaware
Harris	Gallia	Jacobsburg	Belmont	Le Roy	Medina
Harrison	Hamilton	Jamestown	Greene	Leslie	Van Wert
Harrisburg	Franklin	Jasper	Pike	Le Sourdsville	Butler
Harrisonville	Meigs	Jasper Mills	Fayette	Letart Falls	Meigs
Harrisville	Harrison	Java	Lucas	Letimberville	Marion
Harshmansville	Montgomery	Jaysville	Darke	Level	Warren
Hartford	Trumbull	Jackson Center	Shelby	Levering	Knox
Hartland	Huron	Jackson C. H.	Jackson	Levi	Jackson
Hartleyville	Athens	Jacksonborough	Butler	Lewis	Brown
Hart's Grove	Ashtabula	Jeddo	Jefferson	Lewisburg	Preble
Hartville	Stark	Jefferson C. H.	Ashtabula	Lewis Center	Delaware
Harveysburg	Warren	Jeffersonville	Fayette	Lewistown	Logan
Hassan	Hancock	Jelloway	Knox	Lewisville	Monroe
Hastings	Richland	Jerome	Union	Lexington	Richland
Havana	Huron	Jeromesville	Ashland	Liberty	Montgomery
Haverhill	Scioto	Jersey	Licking	Liberty Center	Henry
Hawk Eye	Licking	Jewett	Harrison	Liberty Corner	Crawford
Hays	Jackson	Johnsonville	Trumbull	Liberty Hill	Washington
Haysville	Ashland	Johnson's Corners	Summit	Lick Run	Hamilton
Hebbardsville	Athens	Johnstown	Licking	Licking Valley	Muskingum
Hebron	Licking	Johnsville	Montgomery	Likens	Crawford
Hedge's Store	Pickaway	Jolly	Monroe	Lilly	Scioto
Hemlock Grove	Meigs	Jones' Station	Butler	Lima	Allen
Henly	Montgomery	Jones' Corner	Coshocton	Limaville	Stark
Hendrysburg	Belmont	Junction	Paulding	Lincoln	Monroe
Henning's Mills	Clermont	Kalida	Putnam	Lindonville	Ashtabula
Henrietta	Lorain	Keene	Coshocton	Limeville	Licking
Herring	Allen	Kansas	Seneca	Linton	Jefferson
Hibbetts	Carroll	Keiths	Noble	Linton Mills	Coshocton
Hickory	Lucas	Kelley's Island	Erie	Linwood	Hamilton
Hicksville	Defiance	Kelley's Mills	Lawrence	Litchfield	Medina
Higginsport	Brown	Kelloggsville	Ashtabula	Lithopolis	Fairfield
High Hill	Muskingum	Kennedy's X Roads	Lawrence	Little Beaver Bridge	
Highland	Highland	Kenon	Belmont		Columbiana
Hill Grove	Darke	Kennonsburg	Noble	Little Bull's Skin	Delaware
Hillhouse	Lake	Kenton	Hardin	Little Sandusky	Wyandot
Hilliard's	Franklin	Keystone	Jackson	LittleHockhocking	Washington
Hillsboro'	Highland	Killbourne	Delaware	Little York	Montgomery
Hill's Fork	Adams	Killbuck	Holmes	Liverpool	Medina
Hinckley	Medina	Kilgore	Carroll	Lock	Knox
Hiram	Portage	Kinholton	Guernsey	Lockbourne	Franklin
Hiramsburg	Noble	Kinderhook	Pickaway	Lockington	Shelby
Hockingport	Athens	Kingston	Ross	Lockport	Williams
Hog Creek	Allen	Kingston Center	Delaware	Lockville	Fairfield
Holland	Lucas	Kingsville	Ashtabula	Lockland	Hamilton
Holmes Mill	Jefferson	Kinsmans	Trumbull	Lockland Station	"
Holmesville	Holmes	Kirby	Wyandott	Locust Corner	Clermont
Holt	Wood	Kirkersville	Licking	Locust Grove	Adams
Home	Highland	Kirkland	Lake	Locust Point	Ottawa
Homer	Licking	Kneisley	Greene	Locust Ridge	Brown
Homerville	Medina	Knox	Knox	Lodi	Medina
Hoopoole	Ross	Knoxville	Jefferson	Logan	Hocking
Hope	Franklin	Koch's	Wayne	Loganville	Logan
Hopedale	Harrison	Kossuth	Auglaize	Log Cabin	Morgan
Hope Ridge	Monroe	Kyger	Gallia	Loudon	Madison
Hopewell	Muskingum	Laceyville	Harrison	Londonderry	Guernsey
Hopkinsville	Noble	La Fayette	Madison	Long Bottom	Meigs
Hopkinsville	Warren	La Grange	Lorain	Long Run	Licking
Horatio	Darke	Laing's	Monroe	Loramie's	Shelby

POST OFFICES—OHIO.

Post Office.	County.	Post Office.	County.	Post Office.	County.
Lordstown	Trumbull	Means	Harrison	Moscow	Clermont
Lottridge	Athens	Mecca	Trumbull	Moscow Mills	Morgan
Londonville	Ashland	Mechanicsburg	Champaign	Moss Run	Washington
Louisville	Stark	Mechanicstown	Carroll	Moultrie	Columbiana
Loveland	Clermont	Medary	Putnam	Moulton	Auglaize
Lovett's	Adams	Medill	Athens	Mount Airy	Hamilton
Lovett's Grove	Wood	Medina	Medina	Mount Blanchard	Hancock
Lowell	Washington	Medoc	Hamilton	Mount Blanco	Meigs
Lowellville	Mahoning	Medway	Clark	Mount Carmel	Clermont
Lower Lawrence	Washington	Meigs' Creek	Morgan	Mount Carrick	Monroe
Lower Newport	"	Meigsville	"	Mount Eaton	Wayne
Lower Salem	"	Melmore	Seneca	Mount Ephraim	Noble
Loydsville	Belmont	Mendon	Mercer	Mount Gilead	Morrow
Lucas	Richland	Mentor	Lake	Mount Healthy	Hamilton
Lucasville	Scioto	Mercer	Mercer	Mount Heron	Darke
Lucerne	Knox	Mercerville	Gallia	Mount Holly	Warren
Ludlow	Miami	Mesopotamia	Trumbull	Mount Hope	Holmes
Luke's Corners	Williams	Metamora	Fulton	Mount Liberty	Knox
Lumberton	Clinton	Mexico	Wyandott	Mount Olive	Clermont
Lynchburg	Highland	Miami	Hamilton	Mount Orab	Brown
Lyndon Station	Ross	Miami City	Montgomery	Mount Perry	Perry
Lyons	Fulton	Miamiburg	"	Mount Pisgah	Clermont
Lyra	Scioto	Miamiville	Clermont	Mount Pleasant	Jefferson
McArthur	Vinton	Middle Branch	Stark	Mount Sterling	Madison
McCluney	Perry	Middlebourne	Guernsey	Mount Union	Stark
McCleary	Noble	Middleburg	Cuyahoga	Mount Vernon	Knox
McCanley's	Defiance	Middlebury	Summit	Mount Victory	Hardin
McComb	Hancock	Middle Creek	Noble	Mount Washington	Hamilton
McConnellsville	Morgan	Middle Fork	Hocking	Mowrystown	Highland
McCutchenville	Wyandott	Middle Field	Geauga	Muchinippe	Logan
McDaniels	Gallia	Middle Point	Van Wert	Mulberry	Clermont
McDonald	Hardin	Middleport	Meigs	Mulberry Corners	Geauga
McDonaldsville	Stark	Middletown	Butler	Munnsville	Coshocton
McKwen's X Roads	Morrow	Mifflin	Ashland	Munson	Geauga
McGill	Paulding	Milan	Erie	Mutual	Champaign
Motionigle's Station	Butler	Milford	Clermont	Murat	Paulding
McKay	Ashland	Milford Center	Union	Muse	Muskingum
Mabee's	Jackson	Milfordton	Knox	Nairo	Scioto
Macedon	Mercer	Millbury	Wood	Nankin	Ashland
Macedonia Depot	Summit	Mill Creek	Fulton	Napoleon	Henry
Macon	Lake	Milldale	Defiance	Nashport	Muskingum
Madison	Morrow	Mill Grove	Morgan	Nashville	Holmes
Madisonburg	Wayne	Millers	Lawrence	Navarre	Stark
Madisonville	Hamilton	Millersburg	Holmes	Nebo	Jefferson
Magnolia	Stark	Millersport	Fairfield	Neelysville	Morgan
Mainville	Warren	Millerstown	Champaign	Nelson	Portage
Malaga	Monroe	Millfield	Athens	Nelsonville	Athens
Mallet Creek	Medina	Milligan	Tuscarawas	Neptune	Mercer
Malta	Morgan	Millwood	Knox	Nettle Lake	Williams
Malvern	Carroll	Milnersville	Guernsey	Nevada	Wyandott
Manchester	Adams	Milo	Defiance	Neville	Clermont
Mansfield	Richland	Millville	Butler	Nevin	Highland
Mantua	Portage	Milton	Mahoning	New Albany	Mahoning
Manton Station	"	Miltonsburg	Monroe	New Alexander	Columbiana
Maple	Brown	Milton Station	Wood	New Alexandria	Jefferson
Mapleton	Stark	Miltonville	"	New Antioch	Clinton
Marathon	Clermont	Mineral	Athens	Newark	Licking
Marble Furnace	Adams	Mineral Point	Tuscarawas	New Athens	Harrison
Marblehead	Ottawa	Minersville	Meigs	New Baltimore	Stark
Marcellus	Mercer	Mingo	Vinton	New Bavaria	Henry
Maroy	Fairfield	Minerva	Stark	New Bedford	Coshocton
Marengo	Morrow	Minster	Auglaize	New Berlin	Stark
Maria Stein	Mercer	Mississinawa	Darke	New Bloomington	Marion
Marietta	Washington	Mitchell'sSaltWorks	Jefferson	New Bremen	Auglaize
Marion	Marion	Mogadore	Summit	Newburg	Cuyahoga
Marlts	Morrow	Mohawk Village	Coshocton	New Burlington	Clinton
Mark	Logan	Mohican	Ashland	Newbury	Geauga
Marlborough	Stark	Monclova	Lucas	New California	Union
Marseilles	Wyandott	Monroe	Butler	New Carlisle	Clark
Marshall	Highland	Monroe Center	Ashtabula	New Castle	Coshocton
Marshallville	Wayne	Monroe Mills	Knox	NewChambersburg	Columbiana
Martin	Ottawa	Monroeville	Huron	New Comerstown	Tuscarawas
Martinsburg	Knox	Montauk	Hamilton	New Concord	Muskingum
Martin's Ferry	Belmont	Monterey	Clermont	New Corwin	Highland
Martinsville	Clinton	Montezuma	Mercer	New Cumberland	Tuscarawas
Marshfield	Athens	Montgomery	Hamilton	New Dover	Union
Marysville	Union	Montpelier	Williams	New England	Athens
Mason	Warren	Montra	Shelby	New Franklin	Stark
Massillon	Stark	Montrose	Summit	New Garden	Columbiana
Masterton	Monroe	Montville	Geauga	New Guilford	Coshocton
Matchett	Darke	Moons	Fayette	New Hagerstown	Carroll
Maumee City	Lucas	Moore's Salt Works	Jefferson	New Hampshire	Auglaize
Maximo	Stark	Mooreland	Wayne	New Harmony	Brown
Maxville	Perry	Moorefield	Harrison	New Harrisburg	Carroll
Maxwell	Delaware	Morgan	Ashtabula	New Haven	Huron
Mayfield	Cuyahoga	Morgan's Fork	Pike	New Holland	Pickaway
May Hill	Adams	Morning Sun	Preble	New Hope	Brown
Maysville	Columbiana	Morristown	Belmont	New Jasper	Greene
Meadow Farm	Muskingum	Morrisville	Clinton	New Knoxville	Montgomery
Meadow Branch	Jackson	Morrow	Warren	New Lebanon	Montgomery

72   POST OFFICES—OHIO.

Post Office.	County.	Post Office.	County.	Post Office.	County.
New Lexington	Perry	Olena	Huron	Plank Road	Belmont
New Lisbon	Columbiana	Olive	Noble	Plato	Lorain
New London	Huron	Olive Branch	Clermont	Plattsville	Shelby
New Lyme	Ashtabula	Olive Center	Meigs	Pleasant	Putnam
New Madison	Darke	Olive Furnace	Lawrence	Pleasant Corners	Franklin
New Market	Highland	Olive Green	Noble	Pleasant Hill	Miami
New Martinsburg	Fayette	Olivesburg	Richland	Pleasant Plain	Warren
New Matamoras	Washington	Olmsted	Cuyahoga	Pleasant Ridge	Hamilton
New Middletown	Mahoning	Omega	Pike	Pleasant Run	Hamilton
New Milford	Portage	Oneida Mills	Carroll	Pleasanton	Athens
New Moscow	Coshocton	Ontario	Richland	Pleasant Valley	Morgan
New Palestine	Clermont	Orange	Mahoning	Pleasantville	Fairfield
New Paris	Preble	Orange Station	Delaware	Plimpton	Holmes
New Petersburg	Highland	Orangeville	Trumbull	Plymouth	Richland
New Philadelphia	Tuscarawas	Oregon	Warren	Poast Town	Butler
New Pittsburg	Wayne	Orrville	Wayne	Poe	Medina
New Plymouth	Vinton	Orwell	Ashtabula	Point Isabel	Clermont
Newport	Washington	Oshorn	Greene	Point Pleasant	"
New Portage	Summit	Osman's	Adams	Poland	Mahoning
New Prospect	Wayne	Osnaburg	Stark	Polk	Ashland
New Richland	Logan	Ostend	Washington	Polktown	Clermont
New Richmond	Clermont	Ostrander	Delaware	Pomeroy	Meigs
New Rochester	Wood	Otsego	Muskingum	Pond	Geauga
New Rumley	Harrison	Ottawa	Ottawa	Pond Run	Scioto
New Salem	Fairfield	Ottokee C. H.	Fulton	Pontiac	Huron
New Somerset	Jefferson	Otways	Scioto	Poplar	Crawford
New Springfield	Mahoning	Outville	Licking	Poplar Ridge	Darke
Newton Falls	Trumbull	Overpeck's Station	Butler	Portage	Wood
Newtonville	Clermont	Ovid	Franklin	Portage Center	Hancock
Newville	Richland	Owensville	Clermont	Port Clinton	Ottawa
Newtown	Hamilton	Oxford	Butler	Porter	Delaware
New Vienna	Clinton	Ozark	Monroe	Portersville	Perry
New Washington	Crawford	Paddy's Run	Butler	Port Homer	Jefferson
New Waterford	Columbiana	Painesville	Lake	Portland	Meigs
New Way	Licking	Paint	Highland	Portsmouth	Scioto
New Westfield	Wood	Painter Creek	Darke	Port Union	Butler
New Westville	Preble	Paintersville	Greene	Port Washington	Tuscarawas
Ney	Defiance	Palestine	Pickaway	Port William	Clinton
Nicholsville	Clermont	Pallow	Stark	Potsdam	Miami
Niles	Trumbull	Palmyra	Portage	Powell	Delaware
Nimisila	Summit	Palo Alto	Seneca	Powellsville	Scioto
Nonpareil	Knox	Panama	Defiance	Powhatan Point	Belmont
North Benton	Mahoning	Pancoastburg	Fayette	Prairie Depot	Wood
North Berne	Fairfield	Paris	Stark	Prairieville	Erie
North Bloomfield	Trumbull	Parisville	Portage	Pratt	Shelby
North Camden	Lorain	Parkman	Geauga	Pruttsville	Vinton
North Clayton	Miami	Park's Mills	Franklin	Preston	Hamilton
North Columbus	Franklin	Parma	Cuyahoga	Pricetown	Highland
North Dover	Cuyahoga	Pataskala	Licking	Primrose	Williams
North Eaton	Lorain	Patmos	Mahoning	Princeton	Butler
North Fairfield	Huron	Patriot	Gallia	Propstville	Pickaway
Northfield	Summit	Patterson	Delaware	Prospect	Marion
North Georgetown	Columbiana	Paulding	Paulding	Providence	Lucas
North Hampton	Clark	Payne	"	Puebla	Brown
North Industry	Stark	Pemberton	Shelby	Pugh	Belmont
North Jackson	Mahoning	Pendleton	Putnam	Pulaski	Williams
North Lawrence	Stark	Penfield	Lorain	Pulaskiville	Morrow
North Lewisburg	Champaign	Peninsula	Summit	Put-in Bay	Ottawa
North Liberty	Knox	Pennsville	Morgan	Putnam	Muskingum
North Lima	Mahoning	Peoli	Tuscarawas	Pyrmont	Montgomery
North Madison	Lake	Perin's Mills	Clermont	Quaker Bottom	Lawrence
North Newbury	Geauga	Perote	Ashland	Quincy	Logan
North Ridge	Hancock	Perry	Lake	Racine	Meigs
North Ridgeville	Lorain	Perrysburg	Wood	Raccoon Island	Gallia
North Royalton	Cuyahoga	Perryton	Licking	Radnor	Delaware
North Salem	Guernsey	Perryville	Ashland	Rainsboro'	Highland
North Sheffield	Ashtabula	Peru	Huron	Randolph	Portage
North Solon	Cuyahoga	Petersburg	Mahoning	Rapids	"
North Springfield	Summit	Pettisville	Fulton	Rarden	Scioto
North Star	Darke	Pharisburg	Union	Ravenna	Portage
North Uniontown	Highland	Phelps	Ashtabula	Rawsonville	Lorain
North Washington	Hardin	Philanthropy	Butler	Raymonds	Union
Northwest	Williams	Philipsburg	Jefferson	Rays	Jackson
Norton	Delaware	Philo	Muskingum	Reading	Hamilton
Norton Center	Summit	Pickerington	Fairfield	Red Lion	Warren
Norwalk	Huron	Pickereltown	Logan	Reid's	Paulding
Norwich	Muskingum	Pierce	Stark	Reed's Mills	Vinton
Nottingham	Harrison	Pierpont	Ashtabula	Reedsburg	Wayne
Nova	Ashland	Pike	Perry	Reedtown	Seneca
Oakfield	Perry	Piketon	Pike	Reesville	Clinton
Oak Hill	Jackson	Pilcher	Belmont	Regneir's Mills	Washington
Oakland	Clinton	Pine Grove	Gallia	Reboloth	Perry
Oak Ridge	Hancock	Pioneer	Williams	Reiley	Butler
Oberlin	Lorain	Piqua	Miami	Reinersville	Morgan
Oceola	Crawford	Pisgah	Butler	Remson's Corners	Medina
Odessa	Henry	Pittsburg	Darke	Renrock	Noble
Ohl's Town	Trumbull	Pittsfield	Lorain	Republic	Seneca
Oil Diggings	"	Plain	Wayne	Republican	Darke
Okeana	Butler	Plainfield	Coshocton	Reservoir	Mercer
Old Hickory	Wayne	Plainville	Hamilton	Reynoldsburg	Franklin

POST OFFICES—OHIO.

Post Office.	County.	Post Office.	County.	Post Office.	County.
Richfield	Summit	Sciotoville	Scioto	Stony Ridge	Wood
Richland	Richland	Scotch Ridge	Wood	Storrs	Hamilton
Richmond	Jefferson	Scott	Adams	Stouts	Adams
Richmond Center	Ashtabula	Scroggsfield	Carroll	Stoutsville	Fairfield
Richmond Dale	Ross	Seal	Wyandott	Stovertown	Muskingum
Richwood	Union	Sego	Perry	Strasburg	Tuscarawas
Ridgeland	Henry	Selma	Clark	Strait Creek	Brown
Ridgeville	Warren	Seneeaville	Guernsey	Straitsville	Perry
Ridgeville Corners	Henry	Seven Mile	Butler	Streetsborough	Portage
Riga	Lucas	Seven Mile Prairie	Darke	Strongsville	Cuyahoga
Rinehart	Auglaize	Sewellsville	Belmont	Stryker	Williams
Ringgold	Morgan	Shade	Athens	Suffield	Portage
Rio Grande	Gallia	Shadeville	Franklin	Sugar Grove	Fairfield
Ripley	Brown	Shalersville	Portage	Sugar Ridge	Putnam
River Styx	Medina	Shaler's Mills	Knox	Sugar Tree Ridge	Highland
Rives	Richland	Shanandoah	Richland	Sugar Valley	Preble
Rix's Mills	Muskingum	Shane's Crossing	Mercer	Sullivan	Ashland
Rochester Depot	Lorain	Shanesville	Tuscarawas	Sulphur Spring	Crawford
Rocksford	Tuscarawas	Shannon	Muskingum	Summerbeld	Noble
Rock Camp	Lawrence	Sharon	Noble	Summerford	Madison
Rock House	Hocking	Sharon Center	Medina	Summit	Summit
Rockport	Cuyahoga	Sharonville	Hamilton	Summitville	Columbiana
Rockville	Adams	Shaucks	Morrow	Sunbury	Delaware
Rocky Fork	Licking	Shefield	Lorain	Swan	Vinton
Rocky Hill	Jackson	Sheffield Lake	"	Swan Creek	Gallia
Rock Oak	Athens	Shelby	Richland	Swauton	Lucas
Rodney	Gallia	Shepherdstown	Belmont	Sweet Wine	Hamilton
Rogersville	Tuscarawas	Sherman	Huron	Sycamore	Wyandott
Rokeby	Morgan	Sherodsville	Carroll	Sylvania	Lucas
Rollersville	Sandusky	Short Creek	Harrison	Sylvia	Hardin
Rome	Ashtabula	Shreve	Wayne	Symmes' Corner	Butler
Rootstown	Portage	Shunk	Henry	Symmes' Run	Lawrence
Roscoe	Coshocton	Sicily	Highland	Syracuse	Meigs
Rose	Carroll	Sidney	Shelby	Tallmadge	Summit
Rosedale	Madison	Silver Run	Meigs	Tampico	Darke
Roseville	Muskingum	Sinking Spring	Highland	Tank Town	Delaware
Ross	Butler	Six Corners	Richland	Tappan	Harrison
Rosseau	Morgan	Sixteen Mile Stand	Hamilton	Tariton	Pickaway
Round Bottom	Monroe	Skeel's ½ Roads	Mercer	Tawawa	Shelby
Round Head	Hardin	Slate Mills	Ross	Taylor's Center	Union
Rows	Ashland	Sligo	Clinton	Taylor's Creek	Hamilton
Rowville	Licking	Smithfield	Jefferson	Taylorsville	Montgomery
Roxabell	Ross	Smithfield Station	Mahoning	Teegardin	Pickaway
Roxbury	Morgan	Smithville	Wayne	Tedrow	Fulton
Royalton	Fairfield	Smyrna	Harrison	Temperanceville	Belmont
Ruggles	Ashland	Snow Hill	Clinton	Terre Haute	Champaign
Rural	Clermont	Solon	Cuyahoga	Texas	Henry
Rural Dale	Muskingum	Somerset	Perry	Thivener	Gallia
Rush Creek	Union	Somerton	Belmont	Thompson	Geauga
Rush	Tuscarawas	Somerville	Butler	Thornville	Perry
Rush Run	Jefferson	Sonora	Muskingum	Three Locusts	Marion
Rushville	Fairfield	South Arlington	Montgomery	Thurman	Gallia
Rushsylvania	Logan	South Bloomfield	Pickaway	Tiffin	Seneca
Russell	Geauga	South Bloomingville	Hocking	Tippecanoe	Harrison
Russell's Place	Lawrence	South Charleston	Clark	Tiro	Crawford
Russellville	Brown	Southington	Trumbull	Tiverton	Coshocton
Russell's Station	Highland	South Kirkland	Lake	Toboseo	Licking
Russia	Shelby	South New Castle	Gallia	Todd's	Morgan
Rutland	Meigs	South Olive	Noble	Toledo	Lucas
Sabina	Clinton	South Perry	Hocking	Tompkins	Hamilton
Saint Charles	Butler	South Plymouth	Fayette	Tontogany	Wood
Saint Clair	Columbiana	South Point	Lawrence	Torch	Athens
Saint Clairsville	Belmont	South Ridge	Ashtabula	Townsend	Sandusky
Saint Henry's	Mercer	South Salem	Ross	Tradersville	Madison
Saint John's	Auglaize	South Solon	Madison	Tranquility	Adams
Saint Joseph	Williams	South Warsaw	Allen	Transit	Hamilton
Saint Joseph College	Perry	Sparta	Morrow	Tremont	Clark
Saint Louisville	Licking	Spencer	Medina	Trenton	Butler
Saint Mary's	Auglaize	Spencer Station	Guernsey	Trindelphia	Morgan
Saint Paris	Champaign	Springborough	Warren	Trimble	Athens
Sago	Muskingum	Spring Dale	Hamilton	Troy	Miami
Salesville	Guernsey	Springfield	Clark	Trumbull	Ashtabula
Salem	Columbiana	Spring Hills	Champaign	Tully	Van Wert
Salem Center	Meigs	Spring Lake	Williams	Tunnell	Washington
Salineville	Columbiana	Spring Mountain	Coshocton	Tupper's Plains	Meigs
Salt Creek	Holmes	Spring Valley	Greene	Turner	"
Saltillo	"	Springville	Wayne	Tuscarawas	Tuscarawas
Samanth	Highland	Stafford	Monroe	Twenty Mile Stand	Warren
Samsonville	Jackson	Stanley	Putnam	Twinsburg	Summit
Sandusky	Erie	Starr	Hocking	Tymochtee	Wyandott
Sandy	Columbiana	Station Fifteen	Harrison	Tyrone	Coshocton
Sandyville	Tuscarawas	Staunton	Fayette	Uhricksville	Tuscarawas
Sarahsville	Noble	Stamburg	Ashtabula	Underwood's	Marion
Sardinia	Brown	Stelvideo	Darke	Union	Montgomery
Sardis	Monroe	Steuben	Huron	Union Plain	Brown
Savannah	Ashland	Steubenville	Jefferson	Union Port	Jefferson
Saybrook	Ashtabula	Stillwater	Tuscarawas	Union Town	Belmont
Schooley's Station	Ross	Stockport	Morgan	Unionville	Lake
Scio	Harrison	Stone Creek	Tuscarawas	Unionville Center	Union
Scioto	Scioto	Stone Lick	Clermont	Uniopolis	Auglaize

POST OFFICES—OREGON.

Post Office.	County.	Post Office.	County.	Post Office.	County.
Unison	Delaware	West Independence	Hancock	Young Hickory	Muskingum
Unity	Columbiana	West Jefferson	Madison	Young's Mills	Monroe
Updegraff's	Jefferson	West Lafayette	Coshocton	Youngstown	Mahoning
Upper Sandusky	Wyandott	West Lancaster	Fayette	Youngsville	Adams
Upsbur	Preble	West Lebanon	Wayne	Zaleski	Vinton
Urbana	Champaign	West Liberty	Logan	Zanesfield	Logan
Utica	Licking	West Lodi	Seneca	Zanesville	Muskingum
Vail's X Roads	Morrow	West Manchester	Preble	Zimmerman	Greene
Valley Ford	Meigs	West Middleburg	Logan	Zoar	Tuscarawas
Vanatta	Licking	West Mill Grove	Wood	Zoar Station	''
Van Buren	Hancock	West Milton	Miami		
Vandalia	Montgomery	Westminster	Allen		
Vanlue	Hancock	Weston	Wood		
Van's Valley	Delaware	West Newton	Allen	**Oregon.**	
Van Wert	Van Wert	West Point	Columbiana		
Vaughsville	Putnam	West Rushville	Fairfield		
Venice	Erie	West Sonora	Preble	Post Office.	County.
Vermillion	''	West Salem	Wayne		
Vernon	Trumbull	West Union	Adams	Albany	Linn
Vito	Washington	West Unity	Williams	Amity	Yam Hill
Versailles	Darke	West View	Cuyahoga	Applegate	Jackson
Vienna	Trumbull	Westville	Champaign	Ashland Mills	''
Vienna X Roads	Clarke	West Williamsfield	Ashtabula	Astoria	Clatsop
Vigo	Ross	West Windsor	Richland	Aurora Mills	Marion
Vincent	Washington	West Woodville	Clermont	Belpassi	''
Vineyard Hill	Adams	West Zanesville	Muskingum	Bloomington	Polk
Vinton	Gallia	Weymouth	Medina	Bridgeport	Polk
Vinton Station	Vinton	Wheatland Mills	Belmont	Brownsville	Linn
Wadsworth	Medina	Wheat Ridge	Adams	Butenville	Marion
Waggoner's Ripple	Adams	Wheelersburg	Scioto	Champoeg	Marion
Wahoo	Madison	Whetstone	Morrow	Chetco	Curry
Wakatonika	Coshocton	Whigville	Noble	Cole's Valley	Douglas
Wakeman	Huron	Whipstown	Perry	Coose River	Coose
Waldo	Marion	White Cottage	Muskingum	Corvallis	Benton
Wales	Gallia	White Eye's Plains	Coshocton	Cottage Grove	Lane
Walhonding	Coshocton	White House	Lucas	Dallas	Polk
Waller	Ross	White Oak	Fayette	Dayton	Yam Hill
Walnut	Fairfield	White Oak Valley	Brown	Diamond Hill	Linn
Walnut Creek	Holmes	White Sulphur Springs		Elkton	Umpqua
Walnut Hill	Hamilton		Delaware	Ellenberg	Curry
Walnut Ridge	Gallia	Whittlesey	Medina	Empire City	Coos
Wapakoneta	Anglaize	Wickliffe	Lake	Eola	Polk
Warnock	Belmont	Wilkesville	Vinton	Etna	Polk
Warren	Trumbull	Wilkins	Union	Eugene City	Lane
Warrensville	Cuyahoga	Wilkin's Run	Licking	Fairfield	Marion
Warrenton	Jefferson	Willetville	Highland	Forest Grove	Washington
Warsaw	Coshocton	Williamsburg	Clermont	Franklin	Lane
Washington	Guernsey	Williams' Center	Williams	Freedom	''
Washington C. H.	Fayette	Williamsfield	Ashtabula	Galeville	Douglas
Washingtonville	Columbiana	Williamsport	Pickaway	Glad Tidings	Clackamas
Waterford	Washington	Williamsville	Delaware	Grand Ronde	Polk
Waterloo	Gallia	Willoughby	Lake	Harrisburg	Linn
Watson's X Roads	Seneca	Whartonsburg	Wyandott	Hillsboro'	Washington
Watson's Station	''	Willow Dale	Trumbull	Hood River	Wascopum
Watertown	Washington	Will's Creek	Coshocton	Independence	Polk
Waterville	Lucas	Wilshire	Van Wert	Jacksonville	Jackson
Watkins	Union	Wilmington	Clinton	Kellogg's	Umpqua
Wattsville	Carroll	Wilson's Station	''	Kirby	Josephine
Wauseon	Fulton	Winameg	Fulton	King's Valley	Benton
Waverly	Pike	Winchester	Guernsey	Lackamute	Polk
Waynesburg	Stark	Windham	Portage	Lafayette	Yam Hill
Waynesfield	Anglaize	Windham Station	''	Lawn Arbor	Polk
Waynesville	Warren	Windsor	Ashtabula	Lebanon	Linn
Webster	Darke	Winesburg	Holmes	Leland	Josephine
Wegee	Belmont	Windfield	Tuscarawas	Liberty	Benton
Weilersville	Crawford	Winter's Station	Sandusky	Locust Grove	Umpqua
Wellington	Lorain	Wintersville	Jefferson	Long Tom	Lane
Wellsville	Columbiana	Withamsville	Clermont	McMinnville	Yam Hill
Welshfield	Geauga	Wittens	Monroe	Milwaukie	Clackamas
Wesley	Washington	Wolf Creek	Morgan	Monmouth	Polk
West Alexandria	Preble	Woodbury	Wood	Mount Hood	Yam Hill
West Andover	Ashtabula	Woodington	Darke	Myrtle Creek	Douglas
West Baltimore	Montgomery	Wood Grove	Morgan	Needy	Clackamas
West Barre	Fulton	Woodsfield	Monroe	North Canyonville	Douglas
West Beaver	Columbiana	Woodstock	Champaign	North Yam Hill	Yam Hill
West Bedford	Coshocton	Woodview	Morrow	Oakland	Douglas
Westboro'	Clinton	Woodville	Sandusky	Oregon City	Clackamas
West Brookfield	Stark	Woodland	Darke	Oswego	''
West Buffalo	Williams	Wood Yard	Athens	Parkersville	Marion
West Cairo	Allen	Wooster	Wayne	Peoria	Linn
West Canaan	Madison	Worth	Perry	Phenix	Jackson
West Carlisle	Coshocton	Worthington	Franklin	Pine	Linn
West Charleston	Miami	Wynant	Shelby	Pleasant Hill	Lane
West Chester	Butler	Wyandott	Wyandott	Plum Valley	Polk
West Elkton	Preble	Xenia	Greene	Portland	Multnomah
Western Star	Summit	Yankee Ridge	Coshocton	Port Orford	Curry
Westerville	Franklin	Yankeetown	Darke	Randolph	Coos
Westfield	Morrow	Yellow Pond	Ross	Rockpoint	Jackson
West Florence	Preble	Yellow Springs	Greene	Roseburg	Douglas
West Fremont	Sandusky	York	Union	Round Prairie	''

POST OFFICES—PENNSYLVANIA. 75

Post Office.	County.	Post Office.	County.	Post Office.	County.
St. Clair	Marion	Asylum	Bradford	Bethesda	Lancaster
St. Helen	Columbia	Athens	"	Big Bend	Venango
Salem	Marion	Atkinson's Mills	Mifflin	Bigler	Adams
Salt Creek	Polk	Attleborough	Bucks	Big Run	Jefferson
Sandy	Clackamas	Auburn	Schuylkill	Big Spring	Cumberland
Santiam City	Marion	Auburn Center	Susquehannah	Bingham	Potter
Scio	Linn	Auburn Four Corners	"	Binkley's Bridge	Lancaster
Scottsburg	Umpqua	Aughwick Mills	Huntingdon	Birchardsville	Susquehannah
Siuslaw	Lane	Augusta	Northumberland	Birdsboro'	Berks
Silverton	Marion	Avon	Lebanon	Birmingham	Huntingdon
Slate Creek	Josephine	Avondale	Chester	Black Ash	Crawford
Sunvies Island	Washington	Ayers	Indiana	Black Creek	Luzerne
Springville	Multnomah	Ayer's Hill	Potter	Black Fox	Clarion
Starr's Point	Benton	Baden	Beaver	Black Hawk	Beaver
Sublimity	Marion	Bailey Creek	Tioga	Black Horse	Chester
The Dalles	Wasco	Bailey Hollow	Luzerne	Black Lick Mills	Indiana
Umpqua City	Umpqua	Bainbridge	Lancaster	Blain	Perry
Valfontis	Polk	Baker Bank	Beaver	Blairsville	Indiana
Wascopum	Wascopum	Bakerstown	Alleghany	Blakely	Luzerne
Wapatoo	Washington	Bakersville	Somerset	Blanket Hill	Armstrong
Waldo	Josephine	Bald Eagle	York	Blockley	Philadelphia
Williamsburg	"	Bald Hill	Clearfield	Bloody Run	Bedford
Williamette Forks	Lane	Bald Mount	Luzerne	Bloomfield	Crawford
Willamina	Yam Hill	Baldwin	Butler	Blooming Valley	"
Winchester	Douglas	Balm	Mercer	Bloomsburg	Columbia
Yoncalla	Umpqua	Harbour's Mills	Lycoming	Bloomville	Clearfield
		Bareville	Lancaster	Blossburg	Tioga
		Barnesville	Schuylkill	Bloserville	Cumberland
		Barnhart's Mills	Butler	Blue Ball	Lancaster
Pennsylvania.		Barro Forge	Huntingdon	Blue Bell	Montgomery
		Barron Hill	Montgomery	Blue Mountain	Northampton
Post Office.	County.	Barry	Schuylkill	Blue Rock	Chester
		Bart	Lancaster	Boalsburg	Center
Aaronsburg	Center	Bartonsville	Monroe	Bodinesville	Lycoming
Abbottstown	Adams	Bartville	Lancaster	Boiling Spring	Cumberland
Abington	Montgomery	Bastross	Lycoming	Bolivar	Westmoreland
Academia	Juniata	Bath	Northampton	Booth Corner	Delaware
Achey's Corner	Lehanon	Bavington	Washington	Boquette	Westmoreland
Adams	Armstrong	Baumstown	Berks	Bossardsville	Monroe
Adamsburg	Westmoreland	Beach Grove	Luzerne	Boston	Northampton
Adamstown	Lancaster	Beach Haven	"	Bovard's Store	Butler
Adamsville	Crawford	Beach Pond	Wayne	Bower	Clearfield
Addison	Somerset	Beallsville	Washington	Bower Hill	Washington
Agnew's Mills	Venango	Bear Creek	Luzerne	Bower's Station	Berks
Airy Dale	Huntingdon	Bear Gap	Northumberland	Bowman's Creek	Wyoming
Akersville	Fulton	Bearmont	Schuylkill	Bowmansville	Lancaster
Alba	Bradford	Beartown	Lancaster	Boyerstown	Berks
Albany	Berks	Beaver Center	Crawford	Brackney	Susquehannah
Alberts	Luzerne	Beaver C. H.	Beaver	Braddock's Field	Alleghany
Albion	Erie	Beaver Meadows	Carbon	Bradenville	Westmoreland
Albrightsville	Carbon	Beaver Springs	Snyder	Bradford	McKean
Aldenville	Wayne	Beavertown	"	Brady	Indiana
Alexandria	Huntingdon	Beaver Valley	Columbia	Brady's Bend	Armstrong
Alleghany	Alleghany	Bechtelsville	Berks	Braintrem	Wyoming
Alleghany Bridge	McKean	Buck's Mills	Washington	Branch Dale	Schuylkill
Allen	Cumberland	Beekersville	Berks	Branch Junction	Westmoreland
Allentown	Lehigh	Bedford	Bedford	Brandywine Manor	Chester
Allensville	Mifflin	Bedminster	Bucks	Breakneck	Butler
Alsace	Berks	Beech Bottom	Elk	Breinigsville	Lehigh
Altoona	Blair	Beech Creek	Clinton	Brickerville	Lancaster
Alum Bank	Bedford	Belfast	Northampton	Bridesburg	Philadelphia
Alvan	Jefferson	Belknap	Armstrong	Bridgeport	Montgomery
Alvira	Lycoming	Bella Sylva	Wyoming	Bridge Valley	Bucks
Amberson's Valley	Franklin	Bellefonte	Center	Bridgewater	"
Amity	Washington	Bellemonte	Lancaster	Brinkerton	Clarion
Analomink	Monroe	Belle Valley	Erie	Bristol	Bucks
Anandale	Butler	Belle Vernon	Fayette	Broad Axe	Montgomery
Andalusia	Bucks	Belleview	Lebanon	Broad Mountain	Schuylkill
Andersonburg	Perry	Bellsville	Mifflin	Broad Top	Huntingdon
Anderson's Mills	Butler	Bendersville	Adams	Brockwayville	Jefferson
Andesville	Perry	Beuvenue	Dauphin	Broadhead	Alleghany
Andora	Philadelphia	Benezette	Elk	Brodbeck's	York
Annin Creek	McKean	Benford's Store	Somerset	Brodheadville	Monroe
Annville	Lebanon	Benner	Center	Brookdale	Susquehannah
Ansonville	Clearfield	Bentley Creek	Bradford	Brookfield	Tioga
Antes	Center	Bentleyville	Washington	Brookland	Potter
Antestown	Blair	Benton	Columbia	Brooklyn	Susquehannah
Apollo	Armstrong	Benzinger	Elk	Brookville	Jefferson
Applebacksville	Bucks	Berkley's	Somerset	Brower	Berks
Apple Grove	York	Berlin	"	Brownington	Butler
Ararat	Susquehannah	Berlin Center	Wayne	Brownsburg	Berks
Archbald	Luzerne	Berlinsville	Northampton	Brown's Mills	Jefferson
Arch Spring	Blair	Bermudian	Adams	Browntown	Bradford
Arendtsville	Adams	Bernville	Berks	Brownsville	Fayette
Ariel	Wayne	Berrysburg	Dauphin	Bruin	Butler
Armaugh	Indiana	Berwick	Columbia	Brumfieldville	Berks
Arroyo	Elk	Bethany	Wayne	Brush Creek	Beaver
Arsenal	Alleghany	Bethel	Berks	Brush Run	Washington
Ashland	Schuylkill	Bethel Station	Cambria	Brush Valley	Indiana
		Bethlehem	Northampton	Bryansville	York

POST OFFICES—PENNSYLVANIA.

Post Office.	County.	Post Office.	County.	Post Office.	County.
Buchanan	Alleghany	Chapman	Snyder	Cookstown	Fayette
Buck	Lancaster	Charleston	Tioga	Coolbaughs	Monroe
Buck Horn	Columbia	Charlesville	Bedford	Cool Spring	Jefferson
Buckingham	Bucks	Chartier	Alleghany	Coon Island	Washington
Buckstown	Somerset	Chatham	Chester	Coopersburg	Lehigh
Bucksville	Bucks	Chatham Run	Clinton	Cooperstown	Venango
Buck Valley	Fulton	Chatham Valley	Tioga	Cornplanter	
Buena Vista	Alleghany	Chelsea	Delaware	Cornwall	Lebanon
Buffalo	Washington	Cheltenham	Montgomery	Corsica	Jefferson
Buffalo Mills	Bedford	Chenango	Lawrence	Corsons	Lycoming
Buffalo Cross Roads	Union	Cherry Flats	Tioga	Corydon	Warren
Buffalo Run	Center	Cherry Hill	Erie	Cosgrave Hall	Union
Bunker Hill	Bucks	Cherry Ridge	Wayne	Cottage	Huntingdon
Burgettstown	Washington	Cherry Tree	Venango	Coultersville	Butler
Burlington	Bradford	Cherry Valley	Washington	Covesville	Monroe
Burns	Crawford	Cherryville	Northampton	Covington	Tioga
Burnside	Clearfield	Chesnut Grove	Lycoming	Cowansville	Armstrong
Burnt Cabins	Fulton	Chesnut Hill	Philadelphia	Cowdersport	Potter
Burrell	Westmoreland	Chesnut Level	Lancaster	Coxtown	Berks
Bursonville	Bucks	Chess Springs	Cambria	Coyleville	Butler
Burtville	McKean	Chest	Clearfield	Crab Tree	Westmoreland
Bushkill	Pike	Chester	Delaware	Cranberry	Venango
Bush Kiln Center	Northampton	Chester Springs	Chester	Cresson	Cambria
Bustleton	Philadelphia	Chester Valley	"	Cressona	Schuylkill
Butler	Butler	Chesterville	"	Crooked Creek	Tioga
Butztown	Northampton	Cheyney	Delaware	Crooked Hill	Montgomery
Byberry	Philadelphia	Chillisquaque	Northumberland	Cronover's Mills	Huntingdon
Cabinet	Montgomery	Choconut	Susquehannah	Cross-Creek Village	Washington
Caernarvon	Berks	Christiana	Lancaster	Cross Cut	Lawrence
Cains	Lancaster	Chulasky	Northumberland	Cross Forks	Clinton
Caledonia	Elk	Church Hill	Luzerne	Crossingville	Crawford
Callensburg	Clarion	Churchtown	Lancaster	Cross Kill Mills	Berks
Cain	Chester	Clara	Potter	Cross Roads	York
Calvin	Huntingdon	Clarington	Forest	Crow's Mills	Greene
Camargo	Lancaster	Clarion	Clarion	Culley	Sullivan
Cambra	Luzerne	Clark	Mercer	Culmerville	Alleghany
Cambridge	Lancaster	Clarksburg	Indiana	Cumberland Valley	Bedford
Cameron	Clinton	Clark's Green	Luzerne	Cumminsville	Huntingdon
Campbellstown	Lebanon	Clarksville	Greene	Cumra	Berks
Campbellville	Sullivan	Clanssville	Lehigh	Carlsville	Clarion
Camptown	Bradford	Claysville	Washington	Cartin	Dauphin
Canaan	Wayne	Clayton	Berks	Cirwinsville	Clearfield
Canal	Venango	Clearfield	Clearfield	Cush	"
Candor	Washington	Clearfield Bridge	"	Cussawago	Crawford
Canoe Creek	Blair	Clear Spring	York	Custards	"
Cannonsburg	Washington	Clearville	Bedford	Daggett's Mills	Tioga
Canton	Bradford	Clermontville	McKean	Dale	Berks
Carbon	Carbon	Clifford	Susquehannah	Daleville	Luzerne
Carbondale	Luzerne	Clifton	Luzerne	Dallas	"
Carlisle	Cumberland	Clinton	Alleghany	Dallastown	York
Carlisle Springs	"	Clinton Corner	Wyoming	Dalmatia	Northumberland
Carmichael's	Greene	Clintonville	Venango	Damacus	Wayne
Carrick	Alleghany	Clokey	Washington	Danborongh	Bucks
Carrick Furnace	Franklin	Clonmell	Lancaster	Danielsville	Northampton
Carroll	Clinton	Coalmont	Huntingdon	Danville	Montour
Carrolltown	Cambria	Coal Port	Indiana	Darby	Delaware
Carter Camp	Potter	Coals Bluff	Washington	Darlington	Beaver
Carter Hill	Erie	Coal Valley	Alleghany	Dauphin	Dauphin
Carversville	Bucks	Coatesville	Chester	Davidsburg	York
Carverton	Luzerne	Cocalico	Lancaster	Davidson	Sullivan
Cascade	Wayne	Cochran's Mills	Armstrong	Davidson's Ferry	Fayette
Cashtown	Adams	Cochransville	Chester	Davidsville	Somerset
Cass	Venango	Cochranton	Crawford	Davis	Armstrong
Cassville	Huntingdon	Codurus	York	Davistown	Greene
Castle Fin	York	Coffee Run	Huntingdon	Davieville	Bucks
Catasauqua	Lehigh	Cogan Honse	Lycoming	Dawson	Fayette
Catawissa	Columbia	Cogan Station	"	Dayton	Armstrong
Catfish Furnace	Clarion	Cold Spring	Wayne	Day's Store	Greene
Cavettsville	Westmoreland	Colebrook	Lebanon	Decatur	Mifflin
Cedar Run	Lycoming	Colebrookdale	Berks	Decker's Point	Indiana
Cedar Springs	Clinton	Colemansville	Lancaster	Defranceville	Clinton
Central	Columbia	Colerain	"	Delaware	Pike
Center	Perry	Colerain Forge	Huntingdon	Delaware Grove	Mercer
Center Bridge	Bucks	Colesburg	Potter	Delaware Water Gap	Monroe
Center Hall	Center	Colo's Creek	Columbia	Delhi	Indiana
Center Hill	"	Collamer	Chester	Dempseytown	Venango
Center Line	"	Columbia	Lancaster	Dent	Greene
Center Moreland	Wyoming	Columbia X Roads	Bradford	Derry Church	Dauphin
Center Route Station	Crawford	Columbus	Warren	Dewart	Northumberland
Center Square	Montgomery	Commettsburg	Washington	Dickinson	Cumberland
Centertown	Mercer	Concord	Franklin	Dillingersville	Lehigh
Center Valley	Lehigh	Concordville	Delaware	Dillsburg	York
Centerville	Crawford	Conestoga	Lancaster	Dill's Ferry	Northampton
Chadd's Ford	Delaware	Conneautville	Crawford	Dilworthtown	Chester
Chambersburg	Franklin	Connellsville	Fayette	Dimock	Susquehannah
Chambersville	Indiana	Conshohocken	Montgomery	Dingman's Ferry	Pike
Chanceford	York	Conyngham	Luzerne	Diximont	Alleghany
Chaudlerville	Chester	Cook	Erie	Doe Run	Chester
Chaneyville	Bedford	Cooksport	Indiana	Dolington	Bucks
Chapinville	Crawford	Cook's Run	Clinton	Donaldson	Schuylkill

POST OFFICES—PENNSYLVANIA.

Post Office.	County.	Post Office.	County.	Post Office.	County.
Donation	Huntingdon	Eleven Mile	Potter	Florence	Washington
Donegal	Westmoreland	Elinsport	Lycoming	Fogelsville	Lehigh
Donnally's Mills	Perry	Elizabeth	Alleghany	Forest	Clearfield
Dorrance	Luzerne	Elizabethtown	Lancaster	Forest Hill	Union
Dorseyville	Alleghany	Elizabethville	Dauphin	Forest Lake	Susquehannah
Double Sale	Butler	Elk Creek	Erie	Forks	Columbia
Douglass	Montgomery	Elk Dale	Chester	Forkston	Wyoming
Douglassville	Berks	Elkland	Tioga	Forksville	Sullivan
Dover	York	Elk Lick	Somerset	Fort Littleton	Fulton
Downington	Chester	Elk Run	Tioga	Forty Fort	Luzerne
Doylesburg	Franklin	Ellisburg	Potter	Forwardstown	Somerset
Doylestown	Bucks	Elliottsburg	Perry	Fostoria	Blair
Drakestown	Somerset	Elm	Fayette	Foundryville	Columbia
Drum's	Luzerne	Elwell	Bradford	Fountain Dale	Adams
Drury's Run	Chester	Elwood	Schuylkill	Fountain Green	Chester
Dry Ridge	Bedford	Elysburg	Northumberland	Fowlersville	Columbia
Dry Run	Chester	Emans	Lehigh	Foxburg	Forest
Dryville	Berks	Embreeville	Chester	Fox Chase	Philadelphia
Dublin	Bucks	Emigsville	York	Frampton	Clarion
Dublin Mills	Fulton	Emilie	Bucks	Franconia	Montgomery
Dunbar	Fayette	Emlenton	Venango	Frankford	Philadelphia
Duncannon	Perry	Enders	Dauphin	Frankfort Springs	Beaver
Duncansville	Blair	English Center	Lycoming	Franklin	Venango
Dundaff	Susquehannah	Ennisville	Huntingdon	Franklin Corner	Erie
Dunkard	Greene	Enon Valley	Lawrence	Franklindale	Bradford
Dunmore	Luzerne	Enterline	Dauphin	Franklintown	York
Dunnings	"	Enterprise	Lancaster	Frankstown	Blair
Dunningsville	Washington	Ephrata	"	Frazer	Chester
Dunnsburg	Clinton	Equinunk	Wayne	Frederick	Montgomery
Duquesne	Alleghany	Kroildown	Chester	Fredericksburg	Lebanon
Durell	Bradford	Erie	Erie	Fredericksville	Berks
Durham	Bucks	Erwinna	Bucks	Fredericktown	Washington
Durlack	Lancaster	Espy	Columbia	Freeburg	Snyder
Dushore	Sullivan	Espyville	Crawford	Freedom	Beaver
Dyberry	Wayne	Etna	Alleghany	Freehold	Warren
Eagle	Warren	Ettors	York	Freemansburg	Northampton
Eagle Foundry	Huntingdon	Eulalie	Potter	Freeport	Armstrong
Eaglesmere	Sullivan	Evansburg	Crawford	French Creek	Mercer
Eagleville	Montgomery	Evan's Falls	Wyoming	French Mills	Bradford
Eakin	Alleghany	Evansville	Columbia	Frenchtown	"
Earlville	Berks	Evendale	Juniata	Frenchville	Clearfield
East Barro	Huntingdon	Ewing's Mills	Alleghany	Friedensville	Lehigh
East Berlin	Adams	Exchange	Montour	Friendsville	Susquehannah
East Bethlehem	Washington	Exeter	Luzerne	Frostburg	Jefferson
Eastbrook	Lawrence	Experiment Mills	Monroe	Fryburg	Clarion
East Charleston	Tioga	Factoryville	Wyoming	Fulmerville	Pike
East Finley	Washington	Fagleysville	Montgomery	Fulton	Westmoreland
East Freedom	Blair	Fairdale	Susquehannah	Fulton House	Lancaster
East Green	Erie	Fairfield	Adams	Furman Hill	Wyoming
East Hanover	Lebanon	Fairmont Springs	Luzerne	Furnace	Berks
East Hempfield	Lancaster	Fairview	Erie	Gaines	Tioga
East Homer	Potter	Fairview Village	Montgomery	Gallilee	Wayne
East Liberty	Fayette	Fairville	Chester	Gallitzin	Cambria
East Nantmeal	Chester	Fallen Timber	Cambria	Gamble's	Alleghany
East Penn	Carbon	Falls	Wyoming	Gap	Lancaster
East Pine Grove	Warren	Fullsington	Bucks	Garland	Warren
East Salem	Juniata	Falls of Schuylkill	Philad'a	Gardenville	Bucks
East Sandy	Venango	Fallston	Beaver	Gebharts	Somerset
East Sharon	Potter	Falmouth	Lancaster	Geiger's Mills	Berks
East Smithfield	Bradford	Fanuettsburg	Franklin	General Wayne	Montgomery
East Springhill	"	Farmers	York	Genesee Forks	Potter
East Sterling	Wayne	Farmers' Valley	McKean	Georgetown	Beaver
East Troy	Bradford	Farmersville	Lancaster	Germania	Potter
Easton	Northampton	Farmington	Fayette	Germansville	Lehigh
East Waterford	Juniata	Farmington Center	Tioga	Germantown	Philadelphia
Eaton	Wyoming	Farm School	Center	Germany	Warren
Ebenezer	Indiana	Farrandsville	Clinton	Gery's	Buck's
Ebensburg	Cambia	Fawn Grove	York	Gettysburg	Adams
Eberly's Mill	Cumberland	Fayette	Alleghany	Gibson	Susquehannah
Echo	Armstrong	Fayette Springs	Fayette	Gilbertsville	Montgomery
Eckley	Luzerne	Fayetteville	Franklin	Gill Hall	Alleghany
Economy	Beaver	Feltonville	Philadelphia	Ginger Hill	Washington
Eddington	Bucks	Feuersville	Monroe	Girard	Erie
Eddyville	Armstrong	Fertiga	Venango	Glade Mills	Butler
Eden	McKean	Fertility	Lancaster	Glatfelters	York
Edenville	Erie	Fetherolffsville	Berks	Glen Hope	Clearfield
Edgemont	Delaware	Finleyville	Washington	Glen Mills	Delaware
Edgewood	Bucks	First Fork	Cameron	Glenn	McKean
Edenborough	Erie	Fisher	Clarion	Glen Riddle	Delaware
Edinburg	Lawrence	Fisher's Ferry	Northumberland	Glen Rock	York
Edsailville	Bradford			Glen Roy	Chester
Edort	Monroe	Fishersville	Dauphin	Glenshaw	Alleghany
Egypt Mills	Pike	Fishing Creek	Columbia	Glenwood	Susquehannah
Elbinsville	Bedford	Fitz Henry	Westmoreland	Golden Hill	Wyoming
Elder's Mills	Beaver	Fitzwatertown	Montgomery	Good Hope	Cumberland
Elder's Ridge	Indiana	Flatwoods	Fayette	Good Intent	Washington
Eldersville	Washington	Fleetville	Luzerne	Goodville	Lancaster
Elderton	Armstrong	Fleming	Center	Gordon	Schuylkill
Eldred	Wayne	Flemington	Clinton	Gordonsville	Lancaster
Eldredsville	Sullivan	Flicksville	Northampton	Goshen	"

78 POST OFFICES—PENNSYLVANIA.

Post Office.	County.	Post Office.	County.	Post Office.	County.
Goshenville	Chester	Heidlersburg	Adams	Ickesburg	Perry
Gouglersville	Berks	Heilman's Dale	Lebanon	Idaville	Adams
Gouldsborough	Luzerne	Heistersburg	Fayette	Independence	Washington
Grafensburg	Adams	Hellam	York	Indiana	Indiana
Grahamton	Clearfield	Hellen	Elk	Indian Run	Mercer
Grahamville	York	Hellen Furnace	Clarion	Indian Orchard	Wayne
Grampian Hills	Clearfield	Hellertown	Northampton	Industry	Beaver
Granite Hill	Adams	Hemlock	Cambria	Intercourse	Lancaster
Granville	Bradford	Hempfield	Lancaster	Irish Ripple	Lawrence
Granville Summit	"	Henderson	Mercer	Irishtown	Mercer
Gratz	Dauphin	Hendler	Schuylkill	Iron Hill	Northampton
Gray's Valley	Tioga	Hendricksburg	Luzerne	Irvine	Warren
Graysville	Huntingdon	Henrysville	Monroe	Irwin's Station	Westmoreland
Great Bend	Susquehannah	Hensingersville	Lehigh	Ivy Mills	Delaware
Greene	Lancaster	Hepler	Schuylkill	Jackson	Susquehannah
Green Bank	Lancaster	Hereford	Berks	Jackson Hal	Franklin
Greenbrier	Northumberland	Herndon	Northumberland	Jackson Station	Erie
Green Castle	Franklin	Hermitage	Mercer	Jackson Valley	Susquehannah
Greenfield	Erie	Herrick	Bradford	Jacksonville	Lehigh
Green Garden	Beaver	Herrick Center	Susquehannah	Jacksville	Butler
Green Grove	Luzerne	Herrickville	Bradford	James' Creek	Huntingdon
Greenland	Lancaster	Herriottsville	Alleghany	Jamestown	Mercer
Green Mount	Adams	Hetricks	York	Jeansville	Luzerne
Greene Ridge	"	Hickory	Washington	Jefferson	Greene
Greensboro'	Greene	Hickory Corners	"	Jefferson Furnace	Clarion
Greensburg	Westmoreland		Northumberland	Jefferson Line	Clearfield
Green Tree	Alleghany	Hickory Hill	Chester	Jefferson Station	York
Green Village	Franklin	Hickory Run	Carbon	Jeffersonville	Montgomery
Greenwood	Columbia	Hickorytown	Montgomery	Jeffries	Clearfield
Greenwood Furnace		Hick's Run	Elk	Jenkintown	Montgomery
	Huntingdon	High House	Fayette	Jenner's X Roads	Somerset
Greshville	Berks	High Lake	Wayne	Jennersville	Chester
Grimville	"	Highland	Bradford	Jenningsville	Wyoming
Grinnel's	Crawford	High Spire	Dauphin	Jericho	Wayne
Groff's Store	Lancaster	Highville	Lancaster	Jersey Mills	Lycoming
Gulf Mills	Montgomery	Hill	Mercer	Jersey Shore	"
Gum Tree	Chester	Hillegass	Montgomery	Jerseytown	Columbia
Guthrieville	"	Hillsboro'	Washington	Joanna Furnace	Berks
Guy's Mills	Crawford	Hillsdale	Indiana	Johnstown	Cambria
Gwynned	Montgomery	Hill's Grove	Sullivan	Jollytown	Greene
Hagersville	Bucks	Hillside	Westmoreland	Jones' Mills	Westmoreland
Half Moon	Center	Hill's View	"	Jonestown	Lebanon
Halifax	Dauphin	Hillsville	Lawrence	Juniata	Perry
Hall	York	Hilltown	Bucks	Kahle's	Clarion
Hamburg	Berks	Hiner's Run	Clinton	Kantz	Snyder
Hamilton	Jefferson	Hinkletown	Lancaster	Karthous	Clearfield
Hamlinton	Wayne	Hobbie	Luzerne	Keating	Clinton
Hammersley's Fork	Clinton	Hockersville	Dauphin	Keeper's Store	Franklin
Hammond's Creek	Tioga	Hogestown	Cumberland	Keelersburg	Wyoming
Hamorton	Chester	Holland	Venango	Keeneyville	Tioga
Hampton	Adams	Hollidaysburg	Blair	Keiserville	Wyoming
Hancyville	Lycoming	Hollisterville	Wayne	Kellersville	Monroe
Hannah Center	Center	Holmesburg	Philadelphia	Kelleysville	Delaware
Hanover	York	Home	Indiana	Kemblesville	Chester
Hanover Junction	"	Homer	Potter	Kendall	Beaver
Harbor Creek	Erie	Honesdale	Wayne	Kendall Creek	McKean
Harford	Susquehannah	Honey Brook	Chester	Kennett's Square	Chester
Hardensburg	Lawrence	Honey Grove	Juniata	Kensington	Philadelphia
Harleysville	Montgomery	Hookstown	Beaver	Kent	Indiana
Harmarville	Alleghany	Hop Bottom	Susquehannah	Kepnersville	Schuylkill
Harmansburg	Crawford	Hope Church	Alleghany	Kerr's Station	Washington
Harmony	Butler	Hopewell	Bedford	Kerr's Store	Clarion
Harnedsville	Somerset	Hopewell Center	York	Kerrsville	Cumberland
Harrisburg	Dauphin	HopewellCottonWorks	Chester	Kersey's	Elk
Harrison City	Westmoreland	Hoppenville	Montgomery	Kessler's	Northampton
Harrison Valley	Potter	Hornbrook	Bradford	Kettle Creek	Potter
Harrisonville	Fulton	Horsham	Montgomery	Kilgore	Venango
Harrisville	Butler	Horton's	Indiana	Kimberton	Chester
Harshaville	Beaver	Hosensack	Lehigh	King of Prussia	Montgomery
Harthugig	Mercer	Host	Berks	Kingsleys	Crawford
Hartleton	Union	Houston	Alleghany	Kingsessing	Philadelphia
Hartstown	Crawford	Howard	Center	Kingston	Luzerne
Hartsville	Bucks	Howe	Venango	Kingsville	Clarion
Harvey's	Greene	Howellville	Delaware	Kingwood	Somerset
Harvey's Five Points		Hublersburg	Center	Kintnersville	Bucks
	Westmoreland	Hughes	Schuylkill	Kinzers	Lancaster
Harveysville	Luzerne	Hughesville	Lycoming	Kinzua	Warren
Hatboro'	Montgomery	Hulmesville	Bucks	Kirby	Greene
Havensville	Bradford	Hulton	Alleghany	Kirbyville	Berks
Haverford	Delaware	Hummelstown	Dauphin	Kirk's Mills	Lancaster
Hawley	Wayne	Humphreysville	Luzerne	Kirkwood	"
Hayfield	Crawford	Hunlock Creek	"	Kishacoquillas	Mifflin
Hayesville	Chester	Hunter's Cave	Greene	Kiskiminitas	Armstrong
Hazleton	Luzerne	Hunterstown	Adams	Kittaning	"
Hebron	Potter	Huntersville	Lycoming	Kleckuersville	Northampton
Heckshirville	Schuylkill	Huntingdon	Huntingdon	Kline'sGrove	Northumberland
Hecla	"	Huntingdon Valley		Klinesville	Berks
Hector	Potter		Montgomery	Klingerstown	Schuylkill
Hecktown	Northampton	Huntsville	Luzerne	Knauer's	Berks
Hegins	Schuylkill	Hyde Park	"	Knox	Clarion

POST OFFICES—PENNSYLVANIA. 79

Post Office.	County.	Post Office.	County.	Post Office.	County.
Knox Dale	Jefferson	Light Street	Columbia	McKee's Half Falls	Snyder
Knoxville	Tioga	Ligonier	Westmoreland	McKeesport	Alleghany
Knuckle	Luzerne	Lima	Delaware	McLaughlin's Store	
Kossuth	Clarion	Lime Hill	Bradford		Westmoreland
Kratzerville	Snyder	Lime Ridge	Columbia	McSherrytown	Adams
Kreamer	"	Limerick	Montgomery	McVeytown	Mifflin
Kreidersville	Northampton	Limerick Bridge	"	McWilliamstown	Chester
Kresgeville	Monroe	Limestone	Washington	Macedonia	Bradford
Kulpsville	Montgomery	Limestoneville	Montour	Macungie	Lehigh
Kunkletown	Monroe	Linden	Lycoming	Maddenville	Huntingdon
Kutztown	Berks	Lindly's Mills	Washington	Madera	Clearfield
Kutzville	"	Line Lexington	Montgomery	Madison	Westmoreland
Kylerstown	Clearfield	Line Mills	Crawford	Madisonburg	Center
Laceyville	Wyoming	Line Mountain		Mahanoy	Northumberland
Lackawanna	Luzerne		Northumberland	Mahoning	Indiana
Lackawaxen	Pike	Lineville	Clarion	Maiden Creek	Berks
Laddsburg	Bradford	Linglestown	Dauphin	Mainesburg	Tioga
Lafayette	McKean	Linwood Station	Delaware	Maineville	Columbia
La Grange	Wyoming	Lionville	Chester	Manada Hill	Dauphin
Lahaska	Bucks	Lisburn	Cumberland	Manatawny	Berks
Lairdsville	Lycoming	Litchfield	Bradford	Manayunk	Philadelphia
Lake	Luzerne	Litiz	Lancaster	Manchester	York
Lamar	Clinton	Little Britain	Lancaster	Manheim	Lancaster
Lamartine	Clarion	Little Cooley	Crawford	Mann's Choice	Bedford
Lampeter	Lancaster	Little Gap	Carbon	Manor	Lancaster
Lancaster	"	Little Marsh	Tioga	Manor Dale	Westmoreland
Landingsville	Schuylkill	Little Meadows	Susquehannah	Manor Hill	Huntingdon
Landisburg	Perry	Littlestown	Adams	Manor Station	Westmoreland
Landis' Store	Berks	Livermore	Westmoreland	Mansfield	Tioga
Landis Valley	Lancaster	Liverpool	Perry	Maple Furnace	Butler
Lanesboro'	Susquehannah	Llewellyn	Schuylkill	Maple Grove	Venango
Landisville	Lancaster	Long	Chester	Maple Ridge	Tioga
Landsdale	Montgomery	Lobachsville	Berks	Mapleton Depot	Huntingdon
Laporte	Sullivan	Lockhaven	Clinton	Mapletown	Greene
Larraer's Station		Locko's Mills	Mifflin	Marchand	Indiana
	Westmoreland	Lockport Station		Margaretta Furnace	York
Larry's Creek	Lycoming		Westmoreland	Marietta	Lancaster
Lathrop	Susquehannah	Locust Hill	Washington	Marion	Franklin
Lathrop's Lake	"	Locust Valley	Lehigh	Marionville	Forest
Latrobe	Westmoreland	Logan Mills	Clinton	Markelaville	Perry
Laubach	Northampton	Loganville	York	Marlboro'	Chester
Laughlintown	Westmoreland	London	Mercer	Marple	Delaware
Laurelton	Union	Londonderry	Chester	Marr	Lawrence
Laurelville	Westmoreland	Loudon Grove	"	Marron	Clearfield
Lavansville	Somerset	Long Run	Armstrong	Marsh	Chester
Lawrenceburg	Armstrong	Long Swamp	Berks	Marshfield	Tioga
Lawrenceville	Tioga	Long Valley	Monroe	Marshall's Corners	Crawford
Larry's Station	Lehigh	Lord's Valley	Pike	Marshall's Creek	Monroe
Lawsonham	Clarion	Loretto	Cambria	Marshallton	Chester
Lawsville Center		Lottsville	Warren	Martickville	Lancaster
	Susquehannah	Loudon	Franklin	Martinsburg	Blair
Lazaretto Station	Delaware	Lovelton	Wyoming	Martin's Creek	Northampton
Leacock	Lancaster	Lower Bern	Berks	Martinsville	Lancaster
Leaman Place	"	Lower Chanceford	York	Marvin	Lawrence
Leasureville	Butler	Lower Mahatango	Schuylkill	Masontown	Fayette
Leatherwood	Clarion	Lower Merion	Montgomery	Masseysburg	Huntingdon
Lebanon	Lebanon	Lower Saucon	Northampton	Masthope	Pike
Lebœuf	Erie	Lowhill	Lehigh	Mastersonville	Lancaster
Leconte's Mills	Clearfield	Loyalsock	Lycoming	Matamoras	Pike
Lederachsville	Montgomery	Lucesco	Westmoreland	Matildaville	Clarion
Ledge Dale	Wayne	Lucinda Furnace	Clarion	Mauch Chunk	Carbon
Leechburg	Armstrong	Lumber City	Clearfield	Maxatawney	Berks
Leesburg	Mercer	Lumberville	Bucks	May	Lancaster
Lee's ½ Roads	Cumberland	Lundy's Lane	Erie	Maysville	Mercer
Leesport	Berks	Luthersburg	Clearfield	Maytown	Lancaster
Lehigh Gap	Carbon	Lykens	Dauphin	Meadow Gap	Huntingdon
Leighton	"	Lyles	Lancaster	Mead Corners	Crawford
Lehigh Valley	Lehigh	Lymansville	Potter	Meadville	"
Lehman	Luzerne	Lynn	Susquehannah	Mechanicsburg	Cumberland
Leidy	Clinton	Lynnville	Lehigh	Mechanics' Grove	Lancaster
Leinbach	Berks	Lyon Valley	"	Mechaniesville	Bucks
Leipersville	Delaware	Lyon's Station	Berks	Media	Delaware
Leithsville	Northampton	McAllisterville	Juniata	Mehoopany	Wyoming
Lemon	Wyoming	McAlevy's Ford	Huntingdon	Menallen	Adams
Lenartsville	Berks	McCall's Ferry	York	Mendon	Westmoreland
Lenni Mills	Delaware	McCalmont	Venango	Menno	Mifflin
Lenox	Susquehannah	McCandless	Butler	Mercer	Mercer
Lenoxville	"	McClancy	Beaver	Mercersburg	Franklin
Leonard Hollow	Bradford	McClellandtown	Fayette	Merritstown	Fayette
Le Raysville	"	McConnellsburg	Fulton	Merryall	Bradford
Le Roy	"	McConnellstown	Huntingdon	Mertztown	Berks
Leverington	Philadelphia	McCoysville	Juniata	Merwinsburg	Monroe
Lewisberry	York	McCulloch's Mills	Juniata	Meshannon	Center
Lewisburg	Union	McDowel's	Crawford	Meshoppin	Wyoming
Lewistown	Mifflin	McElhattan	Clinton	Mexico	Juniata
Lewisville	Chester	McEwensville	Northumberland	Meyer's Mills	Somerset
Liberty	Tioga	McKean	Erie	Middaghs	Northampton
Liberty Corners	Bradford	McKeansburg	Schuylkill	Middleburg	Snyder
Liberty Square	Lancaster	McKean's Old Stand		Middleburg Center	Tioga
Library	Alleghany		Westmoreland	Middle Creek	Union

POST OFFICES—PENNSYLVANIA.

Post Office.	County.	Post Office.	County.	Post Office.	County.
Middle Lancaster	Butler	Mount Pleasant	Westmoreland	New Salem	Fayette
Middleport	Schuylkill	Mount Pleasant Mills	Snyder	New Scottsville	Beaver
Middle Spring	Cumberland	Mount Rock	Cumberland	New Sheffield	
Middletown	Dauphin	Mount Union	Huntingdon	New Springfield	Clarion
Middletown Center		Mount Vernon	Chester	New Stanton	Westmoreland
	Susquehannah	Mountville	Lancaster	New Texas	Alleghany
Middle Valley	Wayne	Mount Zion	Lebanon	Newton Hamilton	Mifflin
Mifflinburg	Union	Muddy Creek	Lancaster	Newtown	Bucks
Mifflintown	Juniata	Muhlenburg	Luzerne	Newtown Square	Delaware
Mifflinville	Columbia	Mummasburg	Adams	New Tripoli	Lehigh
Milan	Bradford	Muncy	Lycoming	New Vernon	Mercer
Milanville	Wayne	Muncy Bottom	Sullivan	Newville	Cumberland
Milesburg	Center	Muncy Station	Lycoming	New Washington	Clearfield
Miles Grove	Erie	Munntown	Washington	New Wilmington	Lawrence
Milestown	Philadelphia	Munster	Cambria	Nicholson	Wyoming
Milford	Pike	Murdocksville	Washington	Nine Points	Lancaster
Milford Square	Bucks	Murrinsville	Butler	Nippenose	Lycoming
Mill Creek	Huntingdon	Murrysville	Westmoreland	Nittany	Center
Milledgeville	Mercer	Myersburg	Bradford	Niven	Susquehannah
Milligan's Mills	Westmoreland	Myerstown	Lebanon	Nohlestown	Alleghany
Mellersburg	Dauphin	Naglesville	Monroe	Nora	Berks
Miller's Eddy	Armstrong	Nauticoke	Luzerne	Norristown	Montgomery
Millerstown	Perry	Narrows	Pike	Norritonville	"
Millersville	Lancaster	Nawood	Tioga	North East	Erie
Mill Hall	Clinton	Nazareth	Northampton	North Hope	Butler
Millheim	Center	Nebraska	Venango	North Jackson	Susquehannah
Millport	Potter	Neffs	Lehigh	North Liberty	Mercer
Milltown	Chester	Neffsville	Lancaster	North Oakland	Butler
Millview	Sullivan	Nelson	Tioga	North Orwell	Bradford
Millville	Columbia	Nelsonport	Potter	North Penn	Schuylkill
Millwood	Westmoreland	Nescopeck	Luzerne	North Pine Grove	Clarion
Millsboro'	Washington	Neshannock Falls	Lawrence	North Rome	Bradford
Milroy	Mifflin	Nesquehoning	Carbon	North's Mills	Mercer
Milton	Northumberland	New Albany	Bradford	North Sewickly	Beaver
Milwaukie	Luzerne	New Alexandria	Westmoreland	North Shenango	Crawford
Mineral Point	Cambria	New Bedford	Lawrence	North Smithfield	Bradford
Minersville	Schuylkill	New Berlin	Union	North Star	Washington
Missemer's Mills	Lebanon	Newberry	Lycoming	North Towanda	Bradford
Mitchell's Creek	Tioga	Newberrytown	York	Northumberland	
Mitchell's Mills	Indiana	New Bethlehem	Clarion		Northumberland
Mixtown	Tioga	New Bloomfield	Perry	Northville	Erie
Mohontougo	Juniata	New Bridgeville	York	North Washington	
Mohn's Store	Berks	New Bridgeport	Bedford		Westmoreland
Mohrsville	"	New Brighton	Beaver	North Whartou	Potter
Molltown	"	New Britain	Bucks	North Whitehall	Lehigh
Monongahela City	Washington	New Buffalo	Perry	Norwich	McKean
Monroe Furnace	Huntingdon	Newburg	Cumberland	Nottingham	Chester
Monroetown	Bradford	New Castle	Lawrence	Nyce's	Pike
Monroeville	Alleghany	New Centerville	Chester	Oakdale	Delaware
Monterey	Berks	New Chester	Adams	Oakford	Bucks
Mont Alto	Franklin	New Columbia	Union	Oak Forest	Greene
Montgomery's Ferry	Perry	New Columbus	Luzerne	Oak Grove	Erie
Montgomery Station	Lycoming	New Cumberland	Cumberland	Oak Grove Furnace	
Montgomeryville	Montgomery	New Derry	Westmoreland		Westmoreland
Monturesville	Lycoming	New Era	Bradford	Oak Hill	Lancaster
Montrose	Susquehannah	New Florence	Westmoreland	Oakland	Armstrong
Montrose Depot	Susquehannah	Newfoundland	Wayne	Oakland X Roads	
Moon	Alleghany	New Freedom	York		Westmoreland
Mooresburg	Montour	New Freeport	Greene	Oakland Mills	Juniata
Moorestown	Northampton	New Galilee	Beaver	Oakley	Susquehannah
Moorheadville	Erie	New Garden	Chester	Oak Shade	Lancaster
Moosic	Luzerne	New Geneva	Fayette	Oakville	Cumberland
Mordansville	Columbia	New Germantown	Perry	Ocoola	Tioga
Moredocks	Greene	New Grenada	Fulton	Octoraro	Lancaster
Moreland	Lycoming	New Guilford	Franklin	Ogdensburg	Tioga
Morgantown	Berks	New Hamburg	Mercer	Ogle	Butler
Morleytown	Perry	New Hanover	Montgomery	Ohioville	Beaver
Morris	Tioga	New Harbor	"	Oil Creek	Crawford
Morris Cross Roads	Fayette	Newhart's	Northampton	Old Forge	Luzerne
Morrisdale	Clearfield	New Highland	Elk	Old Hickory	Bradford
Morrison	Luzerne	New Holland	Lancaster	Old Line	Lancaster
Morrisville	Bucks	New Hope	Bucks	Oley	Berks
Mortonville	Chester	New Jerusalem	Berks	Olivet	Armstrong
Moscow	Luzerne	New Kingston	Cumberland	Olivia	Blair
Moselem	Berks	New Lebanon	Mercer	Ono	Lebanon
Mount Ætna	"	New Lexington	Somerset	Orange	Luzerne
Mount Airy	Philadelphia	New London	Chester	Orangeville	Columbia
Mountain Eagle	Center	New Mahoning	Carbon	Orbisonia	Huntingdon
Mount Bethel	Northampton	Newman's Mills	Indiana	Orcutt Creek	Bradford
Mount Campbell	York	New Milford	Susquehannah	Orofield	Lehigh
Mount Carmel	Northumberland	New Millport	Clearfield	Oregon	Lancaster
Mount Creek Forks	York	New Milltown	Lancaster	Orrstown	Franklin
Mount Hope	Lancaster	New Mount Pleasant	Monroe	Orrsville	Armstrong
Mount Jackson	Lawrence	New Oxford	Adams	Orwell	Bradford
Mount Holly Springs		Newport	Perry	Orwigsburg	Schuylkill
	Cumberland	Newportville	Bucks	Ostend	Clearfield
Mount Joy	Lancaster	New Providence	Lancaster	Oswayo	Potter
Mount Lebanon	Alleghany	New Richmond	Crawford	Ottsville	Bucks
Mount Morris	Greene	New Ringgold	Schuylkill	Oval	Lycoming
Mount Nebo	Lancaster	Newry	Blair	Overton	Bradford

POST OFFICES—PENNSYLVANIA.

Post Office.	County.	Post Office.	County.	Post Office.	County.
Oxford	Chester	Pleasant View	Juniata	Rich Valley	Alleghany
Oxford Church	Philadelphia	Pleasantville	Montgomery	Riddle's ⋈ Roads	Butler
Oxford Valley	Bucks	Plum	Venango	Ridgebury	Bradford
Packer	Jefferson	Plumer	Venango	Ridgeway	Elk
Palmyra	Lebanon	Plumsteadville	Bucks	Ridleyville	Delaware
Paoli	Chester	Plumville	Indiana	Rileysville	Wayne
Palo Alto	Bedford	Plymouth	Luzerne	Rimersburg	Clarion
Paradise	Lancaster	Plymouth Meeting	Montgomery	Ringgold	Jefferson
Paradise Furnace	Huntingdon	Pocahontas	Somerset	Ringtown	Schuylkill
Paradise Valley	Monroe	Point Pleasant	Bucks	Rising Sun	Philadelphia
Paris	Washington	Polk	Venango	Rittersville	Lehigh
Parksburg	Chester	Polkville	Columbia	Roaring Creek	Montour
Parkersville	"	Port Alleghany	McKean	Robeson	Berks
Parnassus	Westmoreland	Port Blanchard	Luzerne	Robisonville	Bedford
Parrysville	Carbon	Port Carbon	Schuylkill	Rochester	Beaver
Patterson	Juniata	Port Clinton	"	Rockdale	Crawford
Patterson's Mills	Washington	Porter	Jefferson	Rock Lake	Wayne
Pattonville	Bedford	Porterfield	Venango	Rockland	Venango
Paupac	Pike	Porter's Seidling	York	Rockport	Carbon
Paxinos	Northumberland	Porterville	Butler	Rock Spring	Center
Peach Bottom	York	Port Kennedy	Montgomery	Rockton	Clearfield
Peckville	Luzerne	Port Matilda	Center	Rockville	Chester
Pencador	"	Port Perry	Alleghany	Rogersville	Greene
Penfield	Clearfield	Port Providence	Montgomery	Rohrsburg	Columbia
Penn	Lancaster	Port Richmond	Philadelphia	Rome	Bradford
Penn Hall	Center	Port Royal	Juniata	Roseburg	Perry
Penn Haven	Carbon	Port Treverton	Snyder	Roseland	Cambria
Penn Line	Crawford	Potter	Beaver	Rose Point	Lawrence
Penningtonville	Chester	Potter's Mills	Center	Rose Tree	Delaware
Penn Run	Indiana	Potterville	Bradford	Rossland	Monroe
Pennsburg	Montgomery	Pott's Grove	Northumberland	Rosston	Armstrong
Penn's Creek	Snyder	Pottstown	Montgomery	Rossville	York
Penn's Station	Westmoreland	Pottsville	Schuylkill	Rostraver	Westmoreland
Penn's Square	Montgomery	Powelton	Huntingdon	Rothsville	Lancaster
Pennsville	Fayette	Powl's Valley	Dauphin	Rough and Ready	Schuylkill
Pequea	Lancaster	Prentiss Vale	McKean	Roulette	Potter
Perkiomen Bridge	Montgomery	President Furnace	Venango	Round Hill	Adams
Perkiomenville	"	Preston	Wayne	Roxbury	Franklin
Perrino	Mercer	Priceburg	Monroe	Royalton	Crawford
Perry	Venango	Pricetown	Berks	Roger's Ford	Montgomery
Perryopolis	Fayette	Priceville	Wayne	Rucksville	Lehigh
Perrysville	Alleghany	Princeton	Lawrence	Ruff Creek	Greene
Perrytown	Westmoreland	Prompton	Wayne	Rummersfield Creek	Bradford
Pershing	Cambria	Prospect	Butler	Rundell's	Crawford
Peru Mills	Juniata	Prospectville	Montgomery	Rupert	Columbia
Petersburg	Butler	Prosperity	Washington	Ruppaville	Lehigh
Peter's Creek	Lancaster	Providence	Luzerne	Rural Ridge	Alleghany
Petersville	Northampton	Pughtown	Chester	Rural Valley	Armstrong
Phelp's Mills	Clinton	Pulaski	Lawrence	Rush	Susquehannah
Philadelphia	Philadelphia	Punxutawny	Jefferson	Rushtown	Northumberland
Philipsburg	Center	Puseyville	Lancaster	Rushville	Susquehannah
Philip's Mills	Indiana	Putneyville	Armstrong	Russellsburg	Warren
Phœnixville	Chester	Quakertown	Bucks	Russell Hill	Wyoming
Phœnix	Armstrong	Quarryville	Lancaster	Russellville	Chester
Pickering	Chester	Quincy	Franklin	Rutland	Tioga
Pierce	Armstrong	Radnor	Delaware	Ryerson's Station	Greene
Pierceville	Wyoming	Railroad	York	Sabbath Rest	Blair
Pike	Bradford	Rainsburg	Bedford	Sabinsville	Tioga
Pike Mills	Potter	Ralston	Lycoming	Sacramento	Schuylkill
Pike Run	Washington	Ranch's Gap	Clinton	Sadsburyville	Chester
Pike Township	Berks	Randolph	Crawford	Saegerstown	Crawford
Pike Valley	Potter	Ransom	Luzerne	Safe Harbor	Lancaster
Pillow	Dauphin	Rawlinsville	Lancaster	Saint Augustine's	Cambria
Pine Creek	Tioga	Raymonds	Potter	Saint Clair	Schuylkill
Pine Glen	Center	Ray's Hill	Bedford	Saint Clairsville	Bedford
Pine Grove	Schuylkill	Reading	Berks	Saint Johns	Bradford
Pine Grove Mills	Center	Reamstown	Lancaster	Saint Joseph's	Susquehannah
Pine Hill	York	Rebersburg	Center	Saint Mary's	Chester
Pine Street	Elk	Rebucks	Northumberland	Saint Peter's	"
Pine Township	Armstrong	Red Bank Furnace	Armstrong	Saint Thomas	Franklin
Pine Valley	Warren	Red Hill	Montgomery	Saint Vincent's	Westmoreland
Pineville	Bucks	Rod Rock	Luzerne	Salem	Mercer
Perry	Clarion	Red Stone	Fayette	Salem ⋈ Roads	Westmoreland
Pipersville	Bucks	Reedsville	Mifflin	Salfordville	Montgomery
Pitman	Schuylkill	Rehrersburg	Berks	Salisbury	Lancaster
Pittsburg	Alleghany	Reidsburg	Clarion	Salladaysburg	Lycoming
Pittsfield	Warren	Reiglesville	Bucks	Salona	Clinton
Pittston	Luzerne	Reinholdsville	Lancaster	Salt Lick	Clearfield
Plainfield	Cumberland	Remington	Alleghany	Saltsburg	Indiana
Plane Grove	Lawrence	Reppert's ⋈ Roads	Fayette	Salunga	Lancaster
Plainsville	Luzerne	Reynoldsville	Jefferson	Sand Patch Tunnel	Somerset
Plateu	Erie	Rhoadestown	Columbia	Sandy Creek	Crawford
Plattville	Cambria	Rice's Landing	Greene	Sandy Hill	Perry
Pleasant Gap	Center	Riceville	Crawford	Sandy Lake	Mercer
Pleasant Grove	Lancaster	Richardsville	Jefferson	Sarah	Blair
Pleasant Hall	Franklin	Richborough	Bucks	Sardis	Westmoreland
Pleasant Mount	Wayne	Richfield	Juniata	Sarversville	Butler
Pleasant Run	Montgomery	Richland Station	Lebanon	Sartwell	McKean
Pleasant Unity	Westmoreland	Richlandtown	Bucks	Satterfield	Mercer
Pleasant Valley	Bucks	Richmond	Northampton	Saucon Valley	Lehigh

6

POST OFFICES—PENNSYLVANIA.

Post Office.	County.	Post Office.	County.	Post Office.	County.
Saxenburg	Butler	Slate Hill	York	Stewart's Run	Venango
Saylorsburg	Monroe	Slate Lick	Armstrong	Stewartstown	York
Scalp Level	Cambria	Slat Ridge	York	Stewartsville	Westmoreland
Schellsburg	Bedford	Slatington	Lehigh	Stillwater	Columbia
Schnecksville	Lehigh	Slippery Rock	Butler	Stockertown	Northampton
Schœneck	Lancaster	Sloyersville	Luzerne	Stockton	Luzerne
Schœffner's Corners	Jefferson	Smicksburg	Indiana	Stoddartsville	
Schuylkill	Chester	Smiley	Susquehannah	Stone Church	Northampton
Schuylkill Haven	Schuylkill	Smithfield	Fayette	Stonerstown	Bedford
Schwenck's Store	Montgomery	Smithfield Summit	Bradford	Stonersville	Berks
Scotch Hill	Clarion	Smithport	McKean	Stony Creek	Somerset
Scotland	Franklin	Smith's Ferry	Beaver	Stony Fork	Tioga
Scottsville	Wyoming	Smith's Mills	Clearfield	Stoinville	Monroe
Scranton	Luzerne	Smith's Station	York	Stouchburg	Berks
Scrub Grass	Armstrong	Smithville	Lancaster	Stoughstown	Cumberland
Searights	F.yette	Smitten	Indiana	Stouts	Northampton
Second Fork	Elk	Smyrna	Lancaster	Stoyestown	Somerset
Seiberlingsville	Lehigh	Snapp's Station	Crawford	Strabane	Washington
Seidersville	Northampton	Snow Shoe	Centre	Strasburg	Lancaster
Seigfried's Bridge	"	Snydertown	Northumberland	Strattonville	Clarion
Seisholtzville	Berks	Snydersville	Monroe	Straustown	York
Selin's Grove	Union	Somerfield	Somerset	Strawbridge	Berks
Seller's Tavern	Bucks	Somerset	Somerset	Street Road	Chester
Seneca	Venango	Somerton	Philadelphia	Street's Run	Allegheny
Sereno	Columbia	Sonestown	Sullivan	Strickersville	Chester
Sergeant	McKean	Sonman	Cambria	Strinestown	York
Service	Beaver	Sorrel Horse	Montgomery	Stode's Mills	Mifflin
Setzler's Store	Chester	Sondersburg	Lancaster	Strongstown	Indiana
Seventy-Six	Beaver	Southampton	Somerset	Strondsburg	Monroe
Seven Valleys	York	South Auburn	Susquehannah	Sugar Grove	Warren
Sewickleyville	Allegheny	S uth Bend	Armstrong	Sugar Lake	Crawford
Shade Furnace	Somerset	South Creek	Bradford	Sugar Run	Bradford
Shade Gap	Huntingdon	South Easton	Northampton	Sugartown	Chester
Shady Grove	Franklin	South Eaton	Wyoming	Sugar Valley	Clinton
Shaefferstown	Lebanon	South Evansville	Berks	Sullivan	Tioga
Shamokin	Northumberland	South Gibson	Susquehannah	Summer Hill	Cambria
Shamokin Dam	Snyder	South Hermitage	Lancaster	Summersville	Jefferson
Shanesville	Berks	South Hill	Bradford	Summit	Cambria
Shanksville	Somerset	South Shenango	Crawford	Summit Hill	Carbon
Shannondale	Clarion	South Sterling	Wayne	Summit Mills	Somerset
Shannonsville	Montgomery	South Warren	Bradford	Summit Station	Schuylkill
Sharon	Mercer	South West	Warren	Sumneytown	Montgomery
Sharon Center	Potter	South Whitehall	Lehigh	Sunbury	Northumberland
Sharpsburg	Allegheny	Spang's Mills	Blair	Suuville	Venango
Shartlesville	Berks	Spangsville	Berks	Surgeon's Hall	Allegheny
Shaver's Creek	Huntingdon	Sparta	Washington	Susquehannah	Dauphin
Shearer's X Roads	Westmoreland	Spartansburg	Crawford	Susquehannah Depot	Susquehannah
Shawnee	Monroe	Spiersville	Fulton	Sutersville	Westmoreland
Shawsville	Clearfield	Spinnerstown	Bucks	Sutton's Corners	Crawford
Shrakleysville	Mercer	Sporting Hill	Lancaster	Swan Station	Erie
Sheffield	Warren	Spraggs	Greene	Swan's Mills	Lancaster
Shohola	Pike	Sprankle's Mills	Jefferson	Swartzville	"
Shelocta	Indiana	Spread Eagle	Chester	Swatara	Schuylkill
Shepherdstown	Cumberland	Spring	Crawford	Swatara Station	Dauphin
Sherman's Dale	Perry	Spring Church	Armstrong	Sweden	Potter
Shisheguin	Bradford	Spring Creek	Warren	Sweet Valley	Luzerne
Shickshinny	Luzerne	Spring Dale	Allegheny	Sybertsville	"
Shimerville	Lehigh	Springfield	Bradford	Sylvan	Franklin
Shingle House	Potter	Springfield X Roads	Erie	Sylvania	Bradford
Shippen	Cameron	Springfield Furnace	Blair	Table Rock	Adams
Shippensburg	Cumberland	Spring Forge	York	Tacony	Philadelphia
Shippensville	Clarion	Spring Hill	Bradford	Tafton	Pikes
Shiremantown	Cumberland	Spring Hill Furnace	Fayette	Tallotville	Chester
Shirland	Allegheny	Spring Mills	Centre	Talley Covey	Allegheny
Shirleysburg	Huntingdon	Spring House	Montgomery	Tallmansville	Wayne
Shoemakers	Monroe	Spring Run	Franklin	Tamaqua	Schuylkill
Shoemakerstown	Montgomery	Springtown	Bucks	Tamarac	Crawford
Shoem kervill	Berks	Springville	Susquehannah	Tanner's Falls	Wayne
Shoenersville	Lehigh	Spruce Creek	Huntingdon	Tannersville	Monroe
Short Mountain	Dauphin	Spruce Hill	Juniata	Tannery	Indiana
Shoustown	Allegheny	Square Corner	Adams	Tarentum	Allegheny
Shrewsbury	York	Stahlstown	Westmoreland	Taylorstown	Washington
Shunk	Sullivan	Standing Stone	Bradford	Taylorsville	Bucks
Sidousburg	York	Stants' Store	Clarion	Teepleville	Crawford
Silver Creek	Schuylkill	Star	Warren	Temperanceville	Allegheny
Silver Lake	Susquehannah	Starucca	Wayne	Temple	Berks
Silver Spring	Lancaster	State ine	Franklin	Ten Mile	Washington
Simpson's Store	Washington	Steamburg	Crawford	Ten Mile Bottom	Venango
Sinking Spring	Berks	Steam Mill	Warren	Terre Hill	Lancaster
Sinking Valley	Blair	Steeleville	Chester	Texas	Lycoming
Sinnamahoning	Cameron	Steinsburg	Bucks	Thompson	Susquehannah
Sipe's Mills	Fulton	Steinsville	Lehigh	Thompsontown	Juniata
Sipesville	Somerset	Stembersville	Cambria	Thompsonville	Washington
Siverlings	Crawford	Sterling	Wayne	Thorndale Iron Works	Chester
Six Mile Run	Bedford	Sterretania	Erie	Thornbury	"
Skinner's Eddy	Wyoming	Sterrett's Gap	Perry	Three Springs	Huntingdon
Skippack	Montgomery	Stevenson's Mills	Wayne	Three Tuns	Montgomery
Slack Water	Lancaster	Steuben	Crawford	Thurlow	Delaware
Slute Ford	Northampton	Stevensville	Bradford	Tidionte	Warren
		Stewart	Erie		

POST OFFICES—PENNSYLVANIA. 83

Post Office.	County.	Post Office.	County.	Post Office.	County.
Tinker Run	Westmoreland	Walker's Mills	Alleghany	West Springfield	Erie
Tioga	Tioga	Wallace	Chester	West Vincent	Chester
Tioga Valley	Bradford	Wallaceville	Venango	West Warren	Bradford
Tionesta	Venango	Wallaville	Luzerne	West Whiteland	Chester
Tippecanoe	Fayette	Walnut	Juniata	West Windham	Bradford
Tipton	Blair	Walnut Bottom	Cumberland	Wexford	Alleghany
Titusville	Crawford	Walts' Mills	Westmoreland	Wharton	Potter
Tivoli	Lycoming	Wapwallopen	Luzerne	Wheatland Mills	Lancaster
Todd	Huntingdon	Warfordsburg	Fulton	White Ash	Alleghany
Tomb's Run	Lycoming	Warminster	Bucks	White Cottage	Greene
Towanda	Bradford	Warm Springs	Perry	White's Corners	Potter
Town Hill	Luzerne	Warren C. H.	Warren	White Deer	Lycoming
Town Line	"	Warren Center	Bradford	White Deer Mills	"
Trappe	Montgomery	Warrenham	"	White Hall	Montour
Trexbleville	Monroe	Warrensville	Lycoming	White Hall Station	Lehigh
Tremont	Schuylkill	Warren Tavern	Chester	Whitehallville	Bucks
Truskow	Carbon	Warrington	Bucks	White Haven	Luzerne
Troverton	Northumberland	Warrior's Mark	Huntingdon	White House	Cumberland
Trexlertown	Lehigh	Warsaw	Jefferson	Whiteley	Greene
Trout Run	Lycoming	Washington	Washington	White Marsh	Montgomery
Troutville	Clearfield	Washingtonville	Montour	White Mills	Wayne
Troxelville	Snyder	Water Cure	Beaver	White Oaks	Lancaster
Troy	Bradford	Waterford	Erie	White Pine	Lycoming
Troy Center	Crawford	Waterloo	Juniata	White Springs	Union
Trucksville	Luzerne	Waterloo Mills	Chester	White's Tannery	Monroe
Trumbaursville	Bucks	Water Street	Huntingdon	Whitestown	Butler
Tuckerton	Berks	Waterville	Lycoming	Wiconisca	Dauphin
Tullytown	Bucks	Watsontown	Northumberland	Wilcox	Elk
Tulpehocean	Berks	Watterson's Ferry	Clarion	Wilkesbarre	Luzerne
Tunkhannock	Wyoming	Wattsburg	Erie	Wilkins	Alleghany
Turbotville	Northumberland	Waverly	Luzerne	Wilkinsburg	"
Turkey Foot	Somerset	Waymart	Wayne	Willet	Indiana
Turner Creek	Potter	Wayne	Erie	Williamsburg	Blair
Turnersville	Crawford	Waynesboro'	Franklin	Williams' Grove	Clearfield
Turtle Creek	Alleghany	Waynesburg	Greene	Williamsport	Lycoming
Tuscarora	Schuylkill	Weaver's Mill	Lancaster	Williamsville	Elk
Two Taverns	Adams	Weaversville	Northampton	Williston	Potter
Tylers	Clearfield	Weatherly	Carbon	Willistown Inn	Chester
Tylersburg	Clarion	Webster	Westmoreland	Willow Grove	Montgomery
Tylersport	Montgomery	Weaver's Old Stand	"	Willow Street	Lancaster
Tylersville	Clinton	Webster's Mills	Fulton	Willow Tree	Greene
Tyrone	Blair	Woisenburg	Lehigh	Willmore	Cambria
Tyrone Mills	Fayette	Weisport	Carbon	Wilsonia	Huntingdon
Tyrrel	Venango	Welsh Run	Franklin	Wilson's Mills	Venango
Uhlersville	Northampton	Wellersburg	Somerset	Wind Gap	Northampton
Ulster	Bradford	Welliversville	Columbia	Windham	Bradford
Ulysses	Potter	Wellsboro'	Tioga	Wind Ridge	Greene
Ulysses Center	"	Wells' Corners	Erie	Windsor	York
Umstead's	Berks	Wells' Tannery	Fulton	Windsor Castle	Berks
Union	York	Wellsville	York	Winfield	Union
Union Corner	Northumberland	Wernersville	Berks	Wittenburg	Somerset
Union Dale	Susquehannah	Weteosville	Lehigh	Wintersville	Bucks
Union Deposit	Dauphin	Wesley	Venango	Wolf Creek	Mercer
Union Forge	Lebanon	Wesleyville	Erie	Wolf Run	Lycoming
Union Mills	Erie	West Alexander	Washington	Wolf's Store	Center
Union Square	Montgomery	West Auburn	Susquehannah	Womelsdorf	Berks
Uniontown	Fayette	West Barre	Huntingdon	Woodbury	Bedford
Unionville	Chester	West Brownsville	Washington	Woodcock	Crawford
Unity	Crawford	West Burlington	Bradford	Woodland	Clearfield
Unityville	Lycoming	Westchester	Westchester	Woodrow	Washington
Upper Black Eddy	Bucks	West Dublin	Fulton	Woodside	Schuylkill
Upper Darby	Delaware	West Earl	Lancaster	Woodville	Alleghany
Upper Dublin	Montgomery	West Elizabeth	Alleghany	Woodward	Center
Upper Mahantango	Schuylkill	West Earl	Bedford	Worcester	Montgomery
Upper Middleton	Fayette	West Fairfield	Westmoreland	Worth	Mercer
Upper St. Clair	Alleghany	West Fairview	Cumberland	Worthington	Armstrong
Upper Strasburg	Franklin	Westfall	Pike	Wrightstown	Bucks
Upsonville	Susquehannah	Westfield	Tioga	Wrightsville	York
Upton	Franklin	West Finley	Washington	Wurtemburg	Lawrence
Urohland	Chester	West Franklin	Bradford	Wyalusing	Bradford
Utah	Indiana	West Freedom	Clarion	Wyoming	Luzerne
Utena	Butler	West Greenville	Mercer	Wysox	Bradford
Utica	Venango	West Greenwood	Crawford	Xenia	"
Valley Forge	Chester	West Grove	Chester	Yardleyville	Bucks
Van Buren	Washington	West Hanover	Dauphin	Yellow Creek	Bedford
Van Camp	Columbia	West Haverford	Delaware	Yellow Spring	Blair
Venango	Crawford	West Lebanon	Indiana	Yocumtown	York
Vera Cruz	Lehigh	West Manchester	Alleghany	Yohogany	Westmoreland
Vernon	Wyoming	West Manheim	York	Young Womanstown	Clinton
Verona	Westmoreland	West Middlesex	Mercer	York	York
Village Green	Delaware	West Middletown	Washington	York Furnace	"
Vincent	Chester	West Nanticoke	Luzerne	York Sulphur Springs	Adams
Vineyard Mills	Huntingdon	West Newton	Westmoreland	Youngstown	Westmoreland
Virginsville	Berks	West Penn	Schuylkill	Youngsville	Warren
Vazausville	Lancaster	West Pike	Potter	Zelionople	Butler
Volant	Lawrence	Westport	Clinton	Zion	Center
Wagontown	Chester	West Salem	Mercer	Zigglersville	Montgomery
Wakefield	Lancaster	West Shoffield	Warren	Zollersville	Washington
Walkor	Center	West Spring Creek	"		

84 POST OFFICES—RHODE ISLAND—SOUTH CAROLINA.

Rhode Island.

Post Office.	County.
Adamsville	Newport
Albion	Providence
Allenton	Washington
Arcadia	Washington
Ashaway	Washington
Barrington	Bristol
Bliss Four Corners	Newport
Bristol	Bristol
Burrillville	Providence
Carolina Mills	Washington
Centerdale	Providence
Centerville	Kent
Charlestown	Washington
Chepachet	Providence
Coventry	Kent
Cumberland Hill	Providence
Davisville	Washington
Diamond Hill	Providence
Dorrville	Washington
East Greenwich	Kent
Escoheag	Kent
Exeter	Washington
Fiskeville	Providence
Foster	Providence
Foster Center	Providence
Georgiaville	Providence
Green?	Kent
Greenville	Providence
Harmony	Providence
Hopkinton	Washington
Jamestown	Newport
Kingston	Washington
Knightsville	Providence
Lafayette	Washington
Lime Rock	Providence
Little Compton	Newport
Lonsdale	Providence
Manton	Providence
Manville	Providence
Mapleville	Providence
Mount Vernon	Providence
Mohegan	Providence
Narragansett	Washington
Natick	Kent
Nayatt Point	Bristol
Newport	Newport
New Shoreman	Newport
Nooseneck Hill	Kent
North Scituate	Providence
Oneyville	Providence
Pascoag	Providence
Pawtucket	Providence
Pawtuxet	Kent
Pearce Dale	Washington
Perryville	Washington
Phenix	Kent
Pine Hill	Washington
Portsmouth	Newport
Porter's Hill	Washington
Providence	Providence
Quonochontaug	Washington
Quidnick	Kent
Rice City	Kent
Rockland	Providence
Rockville	Washington
Rocky Brook	Washington
Shamrock Mills	Washington
Slatersville	Providence
Slocumville	Washington
South Foster	Providence
South Portsmouth	Newport
South Scituate	Providence
Summit	Kent
Tiverton	Newport
Tiverton Four Corners	Newport
Tower Hill	Washington
Usquepaugh	Washington
Valley Falls	Providence
Wakefield	Washington
Warren	Bristol
Warwick	Kent
Warwick Neck	Kent
Westerly	Washington
West Gloucester	Providence
West Greenwich Center	Kent
Wickford	Washington
Woodville	Washington
Woonsocket Falls	Providence
Wyoming	Washington

South Carolina.

Post Office.	County.
Abbeville C. H.	Abbeville
Adam's Run	Colleton
Aiken	Barnwell
Algood	Spartanburg
Allen Bridge	Marion
Allison Creek	York
Alpha	Abbeville
Alston	Fairfield
Anderson C. H.	Anderson
Anderson's Mills	Pickens
Andersonville	Anderson
Antioch	York
Arnold's Mills	Pickens
Arrowwood	Spartanburg
Ashapoo Ferry	Colleton
Ashmore's Store	Greenville
Bachelor's Retreat	Pickens
Bamberg	Barnwell
Barleywood	Spartanburg
Barnwell C. H.	Barnwell
Batesville	Spartanburg
Beach Branch	Beaufort
Beaufort C. H.	Beaufort
Beaver Pond	Lexington
Beckamsville	Chester
Beech Island	Edgefield
Bee Tree	Kershaw
Belair	Lancaster
Bell's Store	Fairfield
Blount	Newberry
Belton	Anderson
Bennettsville	Marlborough
Beth Eden	Newberry
Bethlehem	Sumter
Big Creek	Edgefield
Bishopville	Sumter
Bivingsville	Spartanburg
Black Oak	Charleston
Black River	Sumter
Blackville	Barnwell
Blairsville	York
Blanton's X Roads	Horry
Blue House	Colleton
Bluff Rabun	Laurens
Bluffton	Beaufort
Boiling Spring	Spartanburg
Bordeaux	Abbeville
Bounty Land	Pickens
Bowlingsville	Union
Boydton	York
Bradford Springs	Sumter
Branch Island	Pickens
Branchville	Orangeburg
Brewerton	Laurens
Brighton	York
Brightsville	Marlborough
Britton's Neck	Marion
Brown's	Fairfield
Broxton's Bridge	Colleton
Brushy Creek	Anderson
Buchanan	Anderson
Buck Creek	Spartanburg
Buckhead	Fairfield
Buckhead Causey	Colleton
Buck Swamp	Marion
Bucksville	Horry
Buena Vista	Greenville
Bunford's Bridge	Barnwell
Bug Swamp	Horry
Bullock Creek	York
Bull Swamp	Orangeburg
Burnt Factory	Spartanburg
Butler	Lancaster
Butlersville	Anderson
Cain Creek	Pickens
Cairo	Edgefield
Calhoun	Anderson
Calhoun's Mills	Abbeville
Calk's Ferry	Lexington
Camden	Kershaw
Cameronville	Spartanburg
Camp Ground	Pickens
Campobello	Spartanburg
Camp Ridge	Williamsburg
Cannon's Store	Spartanburg
Carmel Hill	Chester
Cartersville	Darlington
Cashville	Spartanburg
Catarrh	Chesterfield
Catfish	Marion
Cavin's Old Fields	Spartanburg
Cedar Bluff	Union
Cedar Falls	Greenville
Cedar Hill	Spartanburg
Cedar Shoal	Chester
Cedar Springs	Spartanburg
Centreville	Laurens
Chappell's Bridge	Newberry
Charleston	Charleston
Cheohee	Pickens
Cheraw	Chesterfield
Cherokee Heights	Abbeville
Cherokee Iron Works	York
Chester C. H.	Chester
Chesterfield C. H.	Chesterfield
Chick's Springs	Greenville
Claremont	Pickens
Clark's Fork	York
Clark's Mills	Lexington
Clay Hill	York
Clayton's Mills	Pickens
Clear Spring	Greenville
Clinton	Laurens
Clio	Marlborough
Cokesbury	Abbeville
Cold Spring	Edgefield
Cold Water	Laurens
Cold Well	Union
Coleman's X Roads	Edgefield
Collier's	
Colonel's Fork	Pickens
Columbia	Richland
Conway's Borough	Horry
Cornwall's Turnout	Chester
Cottswood	Newberry
Countsville	Lexington
Cowpen Branch	Barnwell
Cowpens	Spartanburg
Craigsville	Lancaster
Crawfordsville	Spartanburg
Cripple Creek	Greenville
Croshyville	Chester
Cross Anchor	Spartanburg
Cross Hill	Laurens
Cross Keys	Union
Crowsville	Spartanburg
Cureton's Store	Lancaster
Dacusville	Pickens
Damascus	Spartanburg
Danner's X Roads	Charleston
Danielton	Beaufort
Darlington C. H.	Darlington
Diamond Hall	Abbeville
Dogwood Neck	Horry
Doko	Richland
Donaldsville	Abbeville
Dorn's Gold Mines	
Dorn's Mills	Edgefield
Double Branches	Anderson
Douthet	
Draft's Mills	Lexington
Draytonsville	Union
Dry Creek	Lancaster
Dublin	Greenville
Dudley	Lancaster
Duck Branch	Barnwell
Due West Corner	Abbeville
Dunbarton	Barnwell
Danklin	Greenville
Dyson's Mills	Edgefield
Earlesville	Spartanburg
Eastaloe	Pickens
Ebenezerville	York
Echaw	Charleston
Eden	Laurens
Edisto Island	Colleton
Edisto Mills	Edgefield
Effingham Station	Marion
Eighteen Miles	Pickens
Eda's Grove	Marion

POST OFFICES—SOUTH CAROLINA. 85

Post Office.	County.	Post Office.	County.	Post Office.	County.
Elmville	Colleton	Horse Creek	Greenville	Merritt's Bridge	Barnwell
Elton	Edgefield	Horse Gall	Beaufort	Merrittsville	Greenville
Enoree	Spartanburg	Horse Shoe	Pickens	Midway	Barnwell
Equality	Anderson	Huntersville	Greenville	Milford	Greenville
Erwington	Barnwell	Huntington	Laurens	Milburg	
Fair Forest	Union	Hurricane	Spartanburg	Millersville	Barnwell
Fair Play	Pickens	Indian Creek	Newberry	Millville	Spartanburg
Fairview	Greenville	Indian Town	Williamsburg	Milton	Laurens
Feasterville	Fairfield	Ivy Island	Edgefield	Mims	Barnwell
Fingersville	Spartanburg	Jacksonboro' Depot	Colleton	Mine Creek	Edgefield
Five Forks	Anderson	Jackson Creek	Fairfield	Moffettsville	Anderson
Five Mile	Pickens	Jacksonham	Lancaster	Monterey	Abbeville
Flat Rock	Kershaw	Jackson Hill	Spartanburg	Monticello	Fairfield
Flat Shoals	Pickens	Jalappa	Newberry	Moultrie	Spartanburg
Flint Ridge	Lancaster	Jamison	Orangeburg	Mountain Creek	Anderson
Florence	Darlington	Jefferson	Chesterfield	Mountain Ridge	Spartanburg
Floydsville	Marion	Jeffrey's Creek	Marion	Mountain Shoals	"
Forestville	"	Johnson	Barnwell	Mountain View	Abbeville
Fort Mill	York	Johnsonville	Williamsburg	Mount Bethel	Newberry
Fort Mottee	Orangeburg	Jolly Street	Newberry	Mount Carmel	Abbeville
Fort Prince	Spartanburg	Jonesville	Union	Mount Croghan	Chesterfield
Fountain Inn	Greenville	Jordan's Mills	Orangeburg	Mount Gallaher	Laurens
Four Mile Branch	Barnwell	Kaolin	Edgefield	Mount Joy	Union
Fowler's Creek	Pickens	Kelton	Union	Mount Lebanon	Spartanburg
Frazierville	Abbeville	Kinnard's Turnout	Newberry	Mount Pleasant	Laurens
Friendfield	Marion	King Creek	Barnwell	Mount Tabor	Union
Friendship	Clarendon	Kingstree	Williamsburg	Mountville	Laurens
Fruit Hill	Edgefield	Kirksey's X Roads	Edgefield	Mount Willing	Edgefield
Fulton	Clarendon	Kitching's Mills	Orangeburg	Mullin's Depot	Marion
Gadsden	Richland	Lancaster C. H.	Lancaster	Murray's Ferry	Williamsburg
Gantsville	Abbeville	Landsford	Chester	Mush Creek	Greenville
George's Creek	Pickens	Laurens C. H.	Laurens	Natural Grove	Williamsburg
Georgetown	Georgetown	Lawtonville	Beaufort	Newberry C. H.	Newberry
Germanville	Edgefield	Leavenworth	Darlington	New Center	York
Gilchrist's Bridge	Marion	Leesville	Lexington	Newell	Anderson
Gilder	Greenville	Leunde's Ferry	Williamsburg	New House	York
Gillisonville	Beaufort	Level Land	Abbeville	New Market	Spartanburg
Gladden's Grove	Fairfield	Lowisville	Chester	New Prospect	"
Glassy Mountain	Pickens	Lexington C. H.	Lexington	New Zion	Clarendon
Glenn's Springs	Spartanburg	Liberty Hall	Newberry	Nine Times	Pickens
Glympville	Newberry	Liberty Hill	Kershaw	Ninety Six	Abbeville
Golden Grove	Greenville	Lickville	Greenville	North Creek	Laurens
Golden Springs	Anderson	Lightwood Creek	Lexington	North Santee	Charleston
Goshen Hill	Union	Lima	Greenville	Oak Grove	Union
Gowansville	Greenville	LimestoneSprings	Spartanburg	Oakland	Edgefield
Gowdeyville	Union	Lime Creek	Laurens	Oak Lawn	Greenville
Graham's Turnout	Barnwell	Lisbon	Darlington	Oakton	Marion
Grahamville	Beaufort	Little Mountain	Newberry	Oakville	Lexington
Graniteville	Edgefield	Little River	Horry	Oak Way	Pickens
Grassy Pond	Spartanburg	Little Rock	Marion	Oconee Station	"
Great Cypress	Barnwell	Locust Hill	Anderson	Oil Camp	Greenville
Greenfield	Beaufort	Long Branch	Beaufort	Old Store	Chesterfield
Greenland	Barnwell	Long Cane	Abbeville	Orangeburg C. H.	Orangeburg
Green Pond	Colleton	Long Creek	Pickens	Orrville	Anderson
Greenville C. H.	Greenville	Long Hollow	Lexington	Pacolett Depot	Spartanburg
Grove Hill	Edgefield	Longmire's Store	Edgefield	Pacolett Mills	Union
Grove Station	Greenville	Long Pond	Newberry	Pacolett Springs	Spartanburg
Gully	Darlington	Long Run	Fairfield	Packsville	Sumter
Gum Swamp	Marion	Longstreet	Lancaster	Parks	Edgefield
Gunter's Store	Lexington	Lotts	Edgefield	Park's Creek	Abbeville
Guthriesville	York	Lower Three Runs	Barnwell	Parnassus	Marlborough
Haddrell's	Charleston	Lowrysville	Chester	Peedee	Marion
Halsellville	Chester	Lowndesville	Abbeville	Pendleton	Anderson
Hamburg	Edgefield	Lylesford	Fairfield	Perry's X Roads	Edgefield
Hammond	Barnwell	Lydia	Darlington	Philadelphia	Darlington
Hanging Rock	Kershaw	Lynchburg	Sumter	Phoenix	Edgefield
Hardeeville	Beaufort	Lynch's Creek	Marion	Pickens C. H.	Pickens
Harmony	York	Lynch's Lake	Williamsburg	Pickensville	Pickens
Harmony College	Sumter	Lynchwood	Kershaw	Piercetown	Anderson
Harper's Ferry	Abbeville	McConnellville	York	Pine Tree	Chesterfield
Harrisburg	Abbeville	McInnis Bridge	Marion	Pineville	Charleston
Hartsville	Darlington	McQueen	"	Plain	Greenville
Hazlewood	Chester	Manchester	Sumter	Plantersville	Williamsburg
Hebron	Spartanburg	Manning	Clarendon	Pleasant Grove	Greenville
Hickory Grove	York	Mapleton	Abbyville	Pleasant Hill	Lancaster
Hickory Head	Lancaster	Marengo	Laurens	Pleasant Lane	Edgefield
Highland Grove	Greenville	Marietta	Greenville	Pleasant Mound	Laurens
Highland Home	Laurens	Marion C. H.	Marion	Pleasant Spring	Lexington
Highway	Greenville	Mars Bluff	"	Pleasant Valley	Lancaster
Hobbysville	Spartanburg	Martin's Creek	Pickens	Pliny	Greenville
Hodges	Abbeville	Martin's Depot	Laurens	Plowden's Mills	Sumter
Hokerville	Greenville	Martinsville	Spartanburg	Pocotaligo	Beaufort
Holland's Store	Anderson	Maxwell's Mills	Pickens	Ponaria	Newberry
Hollow Creek	Lexington	Maybinton	Newberry	Poolsville	Spartanburg
Holly Springs	Pickens	Maysville	Sumter	Poverty Hill	Edgefield
Honey Path	Anderson	Meansville	Union	Powell's Store	Marlborough
Hope Station	Lexington	Mechaniesville	Sumter	Power's Shop	Laurens
Popewell	"	Meck's Hill	York	Privateer	Sumter
Hopkins' Turnout	Richland	Meeting Street	Edgefield	Prosperity	Newberry
Hornsborough	Chesterfield	Melville	Anderson	Providence	Sumter

POST OFFICES—TENNESSEE.

Post Office.	County.	Post Office.	County.	Post Office.	County.
Queensborough	Anderson	Tincker's Creek	Barnwell	Ashwood	Maury
Red Hill	Kershaw	Tirza	York	Aspen Hill	Giles
Reedy Creek	Marion	Tomsville	Chester	Athens	McMinn
Rehoboth	Edgefield	Torbit's Store	"	Auburn	Cannon
Reidsville	Spartanburg	Townsville	Anderson	Austin	Wilson
Reynosa	Laurens	Toxaway	Pickens	Bagdad	Smith
Richardsonville	Edgefield	Tucker's Pond	Edgefield	Baker's Gap	Johnson
Rich Hill ⋈ Roads	Chester	Tumbling Shoals	Laurens	Ball Camp	Knox
Ridge	Edgefield	Tunnell Hill	Pickens	Ball Play	Monroe
Ridgeville	Colleton	Twelve-Mile	Pickens	Barnardsville	Roane
Ridgeway	Fairfield	Twenty-Six	Anderson	Barren	Williamson
Rish's Store	Lexington	Tylersville	Laurens	Barren Plain	Robertson
Roadville	Charleston	Unionville	Union	Barton's Creek	Dickson
Roberteville	Beaufort	Valley Falls	Spartanburg	Basin Spring	Williamson
Rock Hill	York	Vance's Ferry	Orangeburg	Bean's Station	Grainger
Rock Mills	Anderson	Varennes	Anderson	Bear Creek	Putnam
Rockville	Lexington	Vernonsville	Orangeburg	Beardstown	Perry
Rocky Mount	Fairfield	Walhalla	Pickens	Beaver Creek	Sullivan
Rocky Ridge	Anderson	Walker's	Colleton	Beaver Ridge	Knox
Rocky Well	Lexington	Wallace	Chester	Beech	Sumner
Rogers' Bridge	Spartanburg	Walterborough	Colleton	Beech Grove	Coffee
Rossville	Chester	Walton	Newberry	Bee Creek	Bledsoe
Rumph Bridge	Colleton	Warrenton	Abbeville	Belleville	Roane
Russell's Place	Kershaw	Warsaw	Pickens	Belfast	Marshall
Saddler's Creek	Anderson	Waterloo	Laurens	Bell Buckle	Bedford
St. George's	Colleton	Wateree	Richland	Bellsburg	Dickson
St. Matthew's	Orangeburg	Webster's Store	Spartanburg	Bell's Depot	Haywood
Salem	Sumter	Well Ridge	Chester	Belltown	Monroe
Saltketcher Bridge	Colleton	West Creek	Edgefield	Bellville	Roane
Salubrity	Pickens	West's Spring	Union	Bennett's Ferry	Jackson
Saluda Mills	Newberry	Whetstone	Pickens	Benton	Polk
Sandersville	Chester	Whippy Swamp	Beaufort	Benton Hill	Benton
Sandover	Abbeville	White Cane	Orangeburg	Berlin	Marshall
Sand Hill	Beaufort	White Hill	Pickens	Bersheba Springs	Grundy
Sandy Flat	Greenville	White Horse	Greenville	Bethel	Giles
Sandy Grove	Williamsburg	White Plains	Chesterfield	Bethesda	Williamson
Sandy Run	Lexington	White Pond	Barnwell	Bethlehem	Robertson
Sautuck	Union	White Sand	Greenville	Big Barren Forge	Claiborne
Sawyer's Mills	Lexington	Whitmires	Newberry	Big Bottom	Humphreys
Scuffletown	Laurens	Wideman's	Abbeville	Bigbyville	Maury
Selkirk	Marion	Wild Cat	Lancaster	Big Creek	Shelby
Seneca	Anderson	Williamson's Mills	Lexington	Big Hill	McNairy
Shallowford	"	Williamston	Anderson	Big Rock	Stewart
Sharon Valley	York	Willington	Abbeville	Big Spring	Wilson
Shelton	Fairfield	Williston	Barnwell	Birch Wood	Hamilton
Shiloh	Sumter	Willow Creek	Marion	Black Jack	Robertson
Shop Spring	Newberry	Willow Swamp	Orangeburg	Black Oak	Weakley
Silver Glade	Anderson	Wilson's Creek	Abbeville	Blain's ⋈ Roads	Grainger
Silver Hill	Beaufort	Windsor	Barnwell	Blanton's Store	Bedford
Silverton	Barnwell	Winnsboro'	Fairfield	Bloomington	Tipton
Simpson's Mills	Laurens	Woodlawn	Edgefield	Blountsville	Stewart
Simsville	Union	Woodruff's	Spartanburg	Bluff Point	Hickman
Singletarysville	Williamsburg	Wood Shop	Darlington	Bluff Springs	Gibson
Sister Springs	Edgefield	Woodward	Barnwell	Boatland	Fentress
Skull Shoals	Union	Wright's Bluff	Clarendon	Bodenham	Giles
Slabtown	Anderson	Yancy	Anderson	Bolivar	Hardeman
Smith's Ford	York	Yanhanna	Georgetown	Bon Eau	Hardin
Smith's Store	Spartanburg	Yonguesville	Fairfield	Boon's Creek	Washington
Smith's Turnout	York	Yorkville	York	Boon's Hill	Lincoln
Smithville	Abbeville	Young's Store	Laurens	Booth's Point	Dyer
Snow Creek	Pickens	Zeno	York	Boston	Williamson
Society Hill	Darlington			Bowling Green	Stewart
Sparta	Spartanburg			Boyd's Creek	Sevier
Spartanburg	"			Boydsville	Weakley
Speedwell	Barnwell	**Tennessee.**		Bradshaw	Giles
Spring Grove	Laurens			Bradyville	Cannon
Springtown	Barnwell	Post Office.	County.	Brentwood	Williamson
Stateburg	Sumter			Brick Mill	Blount
Steedman's	Lexington	Adams' Station	Robertson	Britt's Landing	Perry
Steele's	Anderson	Adamsville	McNairy	Brodie's Landing	Decatur
Steep Bottom	Beaufort	Afton	Shelby	Brook's Tan Yard	Macon
Sterling Grove	Greenville	Alanthus Hill	Hancock	Brownsville	Haywood
Stognersville	Lancaster	Albany	Henry	Broylesville	Washington
Stoke's Bridge	Darlington	Alexandria	DeKalb	Brush Creek	Polk
Stony Point	Anderson	Altamont	Grundy	Buck Point	Jackson
Strother	Fairfield	Alto	Franklin	Buchman	Henry
Summerville	Charleston	Alton Hill	Macon	Buena Vista	Carroll
Sumter	Sumter	Amity Hill	Hardeman	Buffalo	Humphreys
Sunny Dale	Pickens	Anderson	Franklin	Buffalo Ridge	Washington
Swanson's Ferry	Abbeville	Anderson's Store	McNairy	Bull Run	Knox
Table Mountain	Pickens	Andrew Chapel	Madison	Bull's Gap	Hawkins
Taylor's	Sumter	Antioch	Gibson	Bunker's Hill	Giles
Taylor's Creek	York	Appleton	Lawrence	Butler	Carter
Temperance Hill	Marion	Arcadia	Sullivan	Butler's Landing	Jackson
Temple of Health	Abbeville	Arrington	Williamson	Byrne	Putnam
Thomas' ⋈ Roads	Darlington	Arizonia	Shelby	Cable's Valley	Johnson
Thomason's Creek	Spartanburg	Ashland City	Cheatham	Cade's Cove	Blount
Tiller's Ferry	Kershaw	Ashland	Wayne	Cageville	Haywood
Timber Ridge	Union	Ashport	Lauderdale	Cainsville	Wilson
Timmonsville	Darlington			Caleb's Valley	Stewart

POST OFFICES—TENNESSEE. 87

Post Office.	County.	Post Office.	County.	Post Office.	County.
Caledonia	Henry	Cotton Grove	Madison	Falls Branch	Washington
Calhoun	McMinn	Cotton Port	Meigs	Fall River	Lawrence
Camargo	Lincoln	County Line	Lincoln	Falling Water	Putnam
Camden	Benton	Couchville	Davidson	Farmington	Marshall
Campbell's Rest	Sullivan	Covington	Tipton	Farmville	Henderson
Campbell's Station	Knox	Cowan	Franklin	Fayette Corners	Fayette
Campbellsville	Giles	Coxburn	Benton	Fayettville	Lincoln
Camp Creek	Greene	Cox's Store	Washington	Fillmore	Bledsoe
Canasauga	Polk	Coytee	Monroe	Fincastle	Campbell
Cane Bottom	Lauderdale	Crab Orchard	Cumberland	Fisherville	Shelby
Cane Creek	Lincoln	Crab Orchard	Bledsoe	Flag Pond	Washington
Caney Branch	Greene	Craighead	Lincoln	Flat Creek	Bedford
Caney Spring	Marshall	Crainsville	Hardeman	Flintville	Lincoln
Cannon's Store	Sevier	Craven's Mills	Wayne	Flynn's Lick	Jackson
Centrall's X Roads	McMinn	Crocket's Station	Obion	Fordtown	Sullivan
Carlockville	Rutherford	Crooked Fork	Morgan	Forrest Hill	Dyer
Carolina	Haywood	Cross Bridges	Maury	Forest Mills	Coffee
Carter's Creek	Maury	Cross Plains	Robertson	Forked Deer	Haywood
Carter's Depot	Carter	Cross Rock	Wilson	Fort Blount	
Cartersville	Maury	Crossville	Cumberland	Forts Station	Robertson
Carthage	Smith	Crown Point	Marion	Foster's X Roads	Hickson
Cass	Lawrence	Cuba	Shelby	Fosterville	Rutherford
Castalian Springs	Sumner	Cullooka	Maury	Fountain Creek	Maury
Cave	White	Cumberland Gap	Claiborne	Fountain Head	Sumner
Cave Spring	Carter	Cumberland Institute	White	Fountain Hill	McMinn
Cedar Creek	Greene	Cumberland Iron Works		Four Mile Branch	Monroe
Cedar Ford	Union		Stewart	Fowler's Landing	Humphreys
Cedar Grove Furnace	Perry	Cynthiana	Jefferson	Fox Spring	Overton
Celina	Jackson	Creaston	Lincoln	Franklin	Williamson
Centre Mound	Haywood	Daneyville	Haywood	Franklin College	Davidson
Center Point	Henderson	Danielsville	Dickson	Frank's Branch	Jackson
Centerville	Hickman	Danville	Benton	Frank's Ferry	White
Chapel Hill	Marshall	Dandridge	Jefferson	Fredonia	Montgomery
Charity	Lincoln	Decatur	Meigs	Freedom	Washington
Charleston	Bradley	Decaturville	Decatur	Fremont	Obion
Charlotte	Dickson	Deshard	Franklin	Friendship	Dyer
Chaseville	Benton	Dedham	Weakley	Friendsville	Blount
Chattanooga	Hamilton	Delta	Shelby	Fallon's	Greene
Chawalla	McNairy	Denmark	Madison	Fulton	Lauderdale
Cheap Valley	Henry	Dixon's Springs	Smith	Galdson	Madison
Cheekville	Marion	De River Cove	Carter	Gainesborough	Jackson
Cherry Grove	Washington	Dunelson	Davidson	Gallcher's	Knox
Cherry Mount	Robertson	Doable Branch	Hamilton	Gallatin	Sumner
Cherry Valley	Wilson	Double Bridges	Lauderdale	Galway	Fayette
Chestnut Bluffs	Dyer	Double Springs	Jackson	Gamble's Store	Blount
Chestnut Grove	Cheatham	Douglass Springs	Decatur	Gap Creek	Knox
Chestnut Hill	Jefferson	Dover	Stewart	Gas Factory	Lincoln
Chestnut Mound	Smith	Dresden	Weakley	Gatlinburg	Sevier
Chestnut Ridge	Lincoln	Dry Hill	Lauderdale	George's Store	Lincoln
Chestnut Valley	White	Dry Valley	Putnam	Germantown	Shelby
Chickamauga	Hamilton	Duck River	Hickman	Gibbs X Roads	Smith
Chilhowee	Blount	Ducktown	Polk	Gibson's Store	Campbell
Christiana	Williamson	Digger's Ferry	Carter	Gibson's Wells	Gibson
Christinasville	Carroll	Dukedom	Weakley	Gibsonville	Giles
Church Grove	Knox	Dumplin	Jefferson	Gillis' Mills	Hardin
Clarksburg	Carroll	Dannington	Hickman	Glades	Morgan
Clarktown	White	Dunlap	Marion	Gladeville	Wilson
Clarksville	Montgomery	Darhamville	Lauderdale	Glenlock	Lawrence
Clear Branch	Washington	Dyer's Station	Gibson	Globe Creek	Marshall
Clear Creek	Greene	Dyersburg	Dyer	Godfield	Meigs
Clearmont	Warren	Eagle Furnace		Goodletsville	Davidson
Clear Spring	Grainger	Eagleville	Williamson	Goose Creek	Macon
Cleaveland	Bradley	East Fork	Anderson	Gordonsville	Smith
Clements	Montgomery	Eaton	Gibson	Gourley's Bridge	Greene
Clementsville	Jackson	Echo	Macon	Goshen	Lincoln
Clifton	Wayne	Eclipse	Macon	Gott's X Roads	Sullivan
Clinton	Anderson	Eden's Ridge	Sullivan	Grand Junction	Hardeman
Clover Bottom	Sullivan	Edgeworth	"	Greasbrough	Campbell
Clover Hill	Blount	Egypt	Fayette	Granville	Jackson
Cloyd's Creek	"	Elba	"	Grassy Cove	Cumberland
Coal Creek	Campbell	Elizabethton	Carter	Graysburg	Greene
Cobb's Creek	Johnson	Elkmont Spring	Giles	Gray's Hill	Roane
Coffee Landing	Hardin	Elk River	Franklin	Gravel Hill	McNairy
Cog Hill	McMinn	Elkton	Giles	Green Bottom	Shelby
Coker Creek	Monroe	Ellejoy	Blount	Green Hill	Wilson
Collierville	Shelby	Elm Grove	Carter	Green Tree	White
College Grove	Williamson	Elm Tree	Weakley	Greeneville	Greene
Columbia	Maury	Eron College	Sumner	Greenwood	Shelby
Commerce	Wilson	Entreprise	Gibson	Grobns Green	Sumner
Cona	Henry	Equality	Jackson	Grove Mount	Dyer
Concord	Knox	Erie	Roane	Gum Grove	Shelby
Convenient	Smith	Estill's Springs	Franklin	Gustavus	Greene
Conyerville	Henry	Eureka	McMinn	Huckberry	Roane
Cookville	Putnam	Eulia	Macon	Haglesville	Henry
Coshalla	Bradley	Eve Mills	Monroe	Hale's Mill	Fentress
Cooptown	Robertson	Facility	McMinn	Hall's Creek	Humphreys
Coopersville	Fentress	Factor's Fork	Wayne	Hall's Hill	Rutherford
Cornersville	Giles	Fairfield	Bedford	Hamburg	Hardin
Cosby	Cocke	Fair Garden	Sevier	Hamilton Landing	Jackson
Cottage Grove	Henry	Fairmount	Montgomery	Hammond's Store	Giles

POST OFFICES—TENNESSEE.

Post Office.	County.	Post Office.	County.	Post Office.	County.
Hampshire	Maury	Lagnardo	Wilson	Mill's Branch	Van Buren
Hanna's	Sumner	Lagrange	Fayette	Miller's Chapel	Dyer
Happy Valley	Carter	Lake	Rhea	Millersville	Robertson
Hardison's Mills	Maury	Lancaster	Smith	Mill Point	Sullivan
Harrisburg	Sevier	Lanefield	Haywood	Millville	Lincoln
Harrison	Hamilton	Laurel Gap	Greene	Mill Wood	Washington
Harrison's Store	Shelby	Laurel Hill	DeKalb	Milton	Rutherford
Hartsville	Sumner	Lawrenceburg	Lawrence	Mint Springs	Stewart
Hartwood	Bedford	La Vergne	Rutherford	Mitchellsville Station	Sumner
Hatchie	McNairy	Luvinia	Carroll	Molino	Lincoln
Haw's X Roads	Washington	Lead Vale	Jefferson	Monroe	Overton
Hay's Store	Wilson	Lebanon	Wilson	Monterey	McNairy
Hazel Flat	Shelby	Leesburg	Washington	Montezuma	"
Haynes	Grainger	Lee Valley	Hawkins	Monticello	Hardin
Head of Barren	Claiborne	Lenoir's	Roane	Montrose	Smith
Hecla	Carroll	Lenora Springs	Hamilton	Montvale Spring	Blount
Henderson's Mill	Greene	Lewisburg	Marshall	Moore's X Roads	Meigs
Henderson's Spring	Sevier	Lexington	Henderson	Moore's Rest	Anderson
Hendersonville	Sumner	Liberty	DeKalb	Mooresville	Marshall
Henrietta	Cheatham	Lick Creek	Hickman	Morell's Mill	Sullivan
Henry's Station	Henry	Limestone	Hamilton	Morgan	Morgan
Henry's X Roads	Sevier	Limestone Cove	Carter	Morgan's Creek	Benton
Henryville	Lawrence	Limestone Springs	Greene	Morgantown	Blount
Herbertsville	Hardin	Linden	Perry	Morning Sun	Shelby
Hermitage	Decatur	Lineport	Stewart	Morrison	Warren
Hickory Hill	Bedford	Linwood	Wilson	Morristown	Jefferson
Hickory Creek	Coffee	Little Chucky	Greene	Moscow	Fayette
Hickory Valley	Hardeman	Little Doe	Johnson	Mossy Creek	Jefferson
Hickory Withe	Fayette	Live Well	Anderson	Mountain	Tipton
Hico	Carroll	Livingston	Overton	Mountain Creek	Warren
Higdon's Store	Polk	Lobelville	Perry	Mount Airy	Bledsoe
Highland	Jackson	Lockport	Wilson	Mount Carmel	Wilson
Hilham	Overton	Locust Grove	Weakley	Mount Comfort	Fayette
Hillsboro'	Coffee	Locust Mount	Washington	Mount Harmony	McMinn
Hilton's	Sullivan	Locust Shade	Overton	Mount Holyoke	Henry
Holly Leaf	Gibson	Loddy	Hamilton	Mount Pelia	Weakley
Holston Valley	Sullivan	Lodi	Jackson	Mount Pinson	Madison
Holt's Corners	Marshall	London	Roane	Mount Pisgah	Overton
Hope	Stewart	Longmire	Washington	Mount Pleasant	Maury
Hope's Creek	Roane	Long Savannah	Hamilton	Mount Vernon	Monroe
Hope Hill	Gibson	Looney's Creek	Marion	Mount Vista	Henry
Hopewell	Maury	Lost Creek	Union	Mount Zion	Tipton
Horner's Store	Grainger	Louisville	Blount	Mouth of Hiwassee	Meigs
Horse Creek	Greene	Lowryville	Hardin	Mouth of Sandy	Henry
Howard's Quarter	Claiborne	Loy's X Roads	Anderson	Mouth of Wolf	Overton
Howesville	Decatur	Lynchburg	Lincoln	Mud Creek	McNairy
Humbolt	Gibson	Lynnville	Giles	Mulberry	Lincoln
Huntington	Carroll	Lyons' Store	Hawkins	Mulberry Gap	Hancock
Hunt's Station	Franklin	McAllister's X Roads		Murfreesborough	Rutherford
Huntsville	Scott		Montgomery	Nashville	Davidson
Hurricane	Franklin	McDonald	Bradley	Nebraska	Jefferson
Hurt's X Roads	Maury	McLemoresville	Carroll	Nelson Hill	Wilson
Increase	Warren	McMillan	Knox	Netherland	Overton
Independence	Dickson	McMinnville	Warren	Nettle Carrier	"
Independent Hill	Rutherford	Macedonia	Carroll	Newark	White
Indian Creek	Washington	Macon	Fayette	Newbern	Dyer
Indian Mound	Stewart	Madison	Davidson	New Boston	Henry
Ingleside	Hardin	Madisonville	Monroe	Newburg	Lewis
Iron Mountain	Stewart	Magnolia	Stewart	New Centon	Hawkins
Irvine's Store	Weakley	Manchester	Coffee	New Castle	Hardeman
Irving College	Warren	Maulyville	Henry	New Hope	Marshall
Isom's Store	Maury	Munsfield	"	Newmanville	Greene
Jacksborough	Campbell	Maple Spring	Cumberland	New Market	Jefferson
Jack's Creek	Henderson	Marble Hall	Hawkins	New Middleton	Smith
Jackson	Madison	Marble Hill	Franklin	Newport	Cocke
Jacksonville	Obion	Marlborough	Carroll	New Providence	Montgomery
Jalappa	Monroe	Murrowbone	Davidson	New York	"
Jamestown	Fentress	Marshall's Ferry	Grainger	Nicojack	Marion
Jasper	Marion	Marysville	Blount	Nine Mile	Bledsoe
Jefferson	Rutherford	Mason's Grove	Madison	Nolensville	Williamson
Jennings' Fork	Smith	Mason Hall	Obion	Normandy	Bedford
Jenkins' Depot	Hardeman	Mayfield	Jackson	Norris Creek	Lincoln
Jessamine	Shelby	Maynardsville	Union	North Fork	Henry
Johnston's Mill	Monroe	Mechanicsville	Cannon	North Springs	Jackson
Johnson's Depot	Washington	Mecklenburg	Knox	Oak Flat	Giles
Jonesborough	"	Medium	Marshall	Oak Forest	Henderson
Junesville	Cocke	Medon	Madison	Oak Grove	Jefferson
Jordan's Store	Williamson	Meesville	Bradley	Oak Hill	Overton
Jordan's Springs	Montgomery	Meigsville	Jackson	Oak Hill Seminary	Coffee
Jordan's Valley	Rutherford	Memphis	Shelby	Oakland	Fayette
Juno	Henderson	Midbridge	Giles	Oakley	Overton
Kansas	Jefferson	Middleburg	Hardeman	Oak Retreat	Wilson
Kelso	Lincoln	Middle Creek	McMinn	Oakwood	Montgomery
Kenton	Obion	Middle Cypress	Wayne	Occola	Cheatham
Kinsey's Store	Polk	Middle Fork	Henderson	Ocoa	Polk
Kincannon's Ferry	Meigs	Middleton	Rutherford	Okolono	Carter
Kingsport	Sullivan	Midway	Greene	Old Hickory	Weakley
Kingston	Roane	Mifflin	Henderson	Old Town	Claiborne
Knoxville	Knox	Milan Depot	Gibson	Oliver's	Anderson
Lafayette	Macon	Mill Bend	Hawkins	Olympus	Overton

POST OFFICES—TENNESSEE.

Post Office.	County.	Post Office.	County.	Post Office.	County.
Onecho	Cheatham	Ripley	Lauderdale	Stantonville	McNairy
Ones	Greene	River Bend Forge	Sullivan	Statesville	Wilson
Oregon	Lincoln	River Hill	White	Steam Mills	Giles
Orme's Store	Bledsoe	Roan Mountain	Carter	Stephen's Chapel	Bledsoe
Ottewah	Hamilton	Robertsville	Anderson	Stewart's Ferry	Davidson
Owl Hill	Morgan	Rob Camp	Claiborne	Stockton's Valley	Roane
Oxford	McWinn	Roberson's X Roads	Bledsoe	Stony Point	Bradley
Palestine	Lewis	Robinson's Store	Lincoln	Straight Fork	Campbell
Pall Mall	Fentress	Rockford	Blount	Strawberry Plains	Jefferson
Palmetto	Bedford	Rock Island	White	Sulphur Springs	Rhea
Palmyra	Montgomery	Rockport	Benton	Sulphur Well	Shelby
Palo Alto	Lawrence	Rocky Mount	Jackson	Sugar Wood	Humphreys
Pandora	Johnson	Rocky River	Warren	Summittville	Coffee
Panther Springs	Jefferson	Rocky Spring	Grainger	Swallow Bluff	Hardin
Paperville	Sullivan	Rogersville Junction	Hawkins	Sweet Gum Plains	Overton
Paradise	Humphreys	Rogersville	"	Sweet Water	Monroe
Paris	Henry	Rome	Smith	Swingleville	Washington
Parker's X Roads	Henderson	Romeo	Greene	Sycamore	Claiborne
Parksville	Polk	Roseberry	Knox	Sycamore Mills	Cheatham
Parottsville	Cocke	Rose Creek	McNairy	Tabor	Roane
Patriot	Wayne	Ross	Anderson	Talbott's Mills	Jefferson
Paw Paw Ford	Roane	Rossville	Fayette	Tampico	Grainger
Peacher's Mills	Montgomery	Rough and Ready	Warren	Tank	Davidson
Pea Ridge	"	Round Top	Wilson	Taylorsville	Johnson
Pekin	Jackson	Rover	Bedford	Taylorsburg	Cocke
Pelham	Grundy	Rowesville	"	Tazewell	Claiborne
Perryville	Decatur	Running Water	Marion	Tellico Plains	Monroe
Peyton's Creek	Lincoln	Rural Hill	Wilson	Temperance Hall	De Kalb
Petersburg	Smith	Russellville	Jefferson	Ten Mile Stand	Meigs
Peytonsville	Williamson	Rutherford's Depot	Gibson	Terry	Carroll
Philadelphia	Monroe	Rutledge	Grainger	Thomasville	Robertson
Pigeon Forge	Sevier	Sadlersville	Robertson	Thompson's Station	Williamson
Pikeville	Bledsoe	Sagefield	Morgan	Thorn Grove	Knox
Pillowville	Weakley	Sail Creek	Hamilton	Thorn Hill	Grainger
Pilot Knob	Greene	Sailor's Rest	Montgomery	Three Forks	Wilson
Pine Bluff	Warren	Saint Clair	Hawkins	Timber Ridge	Greene
Pine Land	Meigs	Salem	Franklin	Tobasco	Henderson
Pine Ridge	McMinn	Salisbury	Hardeman	Tobacco Port	Stewart
Pine Springs	Fentress	Saltillo	Hardin	Toone's Station	Hardeman
Pine Top	Morgan	Sandy Bridge	Carroll	Towee Falls	Monroe
Pine Wood	Hickman	Sandy Hill	Henry	Totty's Bend	Hickman
Piney Flats	Sullivan	Sandy Mills	Cumberland	Trace Creek	Jackson
Piscah	Giles	Santa Fe	Maury	Tracy City	Madison
Pitts X Roads	Bledsoe	Saundersville	Sumner	Trade	Johnson
Pleasant	Claiborne	Savannah	Hardin	Trammel	Sumner
Pleasant Exchange	Henderson	Scott's Hill	Henderson	Travisville	Fentress
Pleasant Hill	Cumberland	Sevierville	Sevier	Trenton	Gibson
Pleasant Mound	Montgomery	Sewee	Meigs	Trezevant	Carroll
Pleasant Plains	Lincoln	Shady	Johnson	Trion	Jefferson
Pleasant Shade	Smith	Shady Hill	Henderson	Triune	Williamson
Pleasantville	Hickman	Sharon	Tipton	Troy	Obion
Pocahontas	Hardeman	Shelbyville	Bedford	Trundle's X Roads	Sevier
Point Mason	Benton	Shiloh	Gibson	Tucahoe	Jefferson
Poland Springs	Weakley	Shop Spring	Wilson	Tucker's X Roads	Wilson
Pomona	Cumberland	Shown's X Roads	Johnson	Tuckaleechee Cove	Blount
Ponville	Wilson	Silesia	Humphreys	Tullahoma	Coffee
Poor Hill	Sullivan	Silver Creek	Marshall	Tannell Hill	Knox
Poplar Spring	Henderson	Silver Spring	Wilson	Turnbull	Dickson
Portersville	Tipton	Silver Top	Obion	Turnersville	Robertson
Port Royal	Montgomery	Sluydensville	Robertson	Twinville	Knox
Post Oak Springs	Roane	Sligo	De Kalb	Tynersville	Hamilton
Potter's Branch	Bradley	Smith's X Roads	Rhea	Tyree Springs	Sumner
Pouch Creek	Scott	Smith's Fork	Hardin	Tyrone	Marshall
Powder Spring Gap	Grainger	Smithville	De Kalb	Union	Maury
Prestonville	Rhea	Smyrna	Rutherford	Union City	Obion
Prospect Depot	Giles	Sneedville	Hancock	Union Depot	Sullivan
Pulaski	Giles	Snoddyville	Jefferson	Unionville	Bedford
Puncheon Camp	Macon	Snow Hill	Hamilton	Unitia	Blount
Purdy	McNairy	Solon	White	University Place	Franklin
Quarryville	Hawkins	Solsborg	Wilson	Vale Mills	Giles
Quincy	Gibson	Somerville	Fayette	Vandergriff's	Knox
Racoon Valley	Knox	Sorby	Wayne	Van Hill	Hawkins
Raleigh	Shelby	South Carroll	Carroll	Vernon	Hickman
Randolph	Tipton	South Gibson	Gibson	Versailles	Rutherford
Readyville	Rutherford	South Rock Island	Van Buren	Vervilla	Warren
Red Boiling Springs	Macon	Spain's	Henderson	Vine Dale	Knox
Red Bridge	Hawkins	Sparta	White	Viola	Warren
Red Hill	Grainger	Speedwell	Claiborne	Viney Grove	Lincoln
Red Mound	Henderson	Spencer	Van Buren	Walden's Creek	Sevier
Red River	Robertson	Spring Creek	Madison	Walden's Ridge	Marion
Reynolds Depot	Giles	Springfield	Robertson	Wallace's X Roads	Anderson
Rheatown	Greene	Spring Grove	Maury	Walnut Grove	Overton
Riceville	McMinn	Spring Hill	"	Walnut Post	Lauderdale
Richardson's	Montgomery	Spring Hill Academy	Henry	Walnut Valley	Marion
Richland Station	Sumner	Spring House	Grainger	Walter Hill	Rutherford
Richmond	Bedford	Spring Place	Marshall	Wansville	Bradley
Ridge Post	Davidson	Springtown	Polk	War Creek	Hancock
Ridgeville	Franklin	Spring Vale	Jefferson	War Gap	Hawkins
Rigg's X Roads	Williamson	Standing Rock	Stewart	Ward's Forge	Johnson
Linggold	Montgomery	Stanton Depot	Haywood	Warrensburg	Greene

POST OFFICES—TEXAS.

Post Office.	County.	Post Office.	County.	Post Office.	County.
Wartrace Depot	Bedford	Austin	Travis	Cat Spring	Austin
Washington	Rhea	Bagdad	Williamson	Cedar	Fayette
Washington College	Wash'gton	Balch	Parker	Cedar Bayou	Chambers
Wataga Bend	Washington	Bandera	Bandera	Cedar Creek	Bastrop
Watertown	Wilson	Banqueto	Nueces	Cedar Fork	Kaufman
Waverly	Humphreys	Barrowdale	Guadaloupe	Cedar Grove	"
Wayland's Springs	Lawrence	Barton	Anderson	Cedar Hill	Dallas
Waynesborough	Wayne	Basin Springs	Grayson	Centreville	Leon
Wear's Cove	Sevier	Bastrop	Bastrop	Chamber's Creek	Ellis
Weaw	Humphreys	Baytown	Harris	Chamberain	Liberty
Webster	Roane	Bear Creek	Sabine	Chance Prairie	Burleson
Welcker's Mill	Roane	Bearden	Lavacca	Chapel Hill	Washington
Well Spring	Campbell	Bear Grass	Limestone	Charco	Goliad
Wellwood	Haywood	Beaumont	Jefferson	Charleston	Hopkins
West Fork	Overton	Beaver	Anderson	Chaseland	Angelina
West Point	Lawrence	Beckville	Panola	Cherokee	Llano
West's Store	Washington	Bedi	Grimes	Cherry Springs	Gillespie
Whitaker's Blu	Wayne	Beeville	Bee	Cherino	Nacogdoches
White Bluffs	Dickson	Belgrade	Newton	Circleville	Williamson
White Oak	Humphreys	Belleview	Rusk	Cistern	Fayette
White Plains	Jackson	Bellville	Austin	Clapp's Creek	Leon
White Bend	Davidson	Belmont	Gonzales	Clarksville	Red River
Whitesburg	Jefferson	Belton	Bell	Clay's Mound	Shelby
Whitsville	Hardeman	Ben Franklin	Lamar	Clayton	Grayson
Whitleyville	Jackson	Berlin	Washington	Clear Fork	Parker
Whitfield	Hickman	Bethel	Anderson	Clifton	Bosque
Williamsport	Maury	Bevilport	Jasper	Clinton	De Witt
Williamsville	Dickson	Big Creek	Fort Bend	Coffeeville	Upshur
Will's Point	Benton	Big Hill	Gonzales	Cold Springs	Polk
Willis' Station	Fayette	Big Rock	Vanzant	Colita	"
Wilson's	Anderson	Billum's Creek	Tyler	College Mound	Kaufman
Wilsonville	Cocke	Birdsville	Tarrant	Colthorp	Houston
Wilton Springs	"	Black Jack Grove	Hopkins	Columbia	Brazoria
Winchester	Franklin	Black Oaks	"	Columbus	Colorado
Winfield	Scott	Blanco	Blanco	Comanche	Comanche
Winston	Weakley	Blossom Prairie	Lamar	Comfort	Kerr
Wixsville	Jefferson	Blue Branch	Burleson	Concord	Jefferson
Wolf Creek	Cooke	Bluff Springs	Travis	Concrete	De Witt
Wolf River	Fayette	Boerne	Comal	Cook's Ferry	Austin
Woodbourne	Union	Bois d'Arc Mills	Fannin	Copano	Refugio
Woodbury	Cannon	Bold Spring	McLennan	Copper Hill	Parker
Woodford	Montgomery	Bonham	Fannin	Cora	Comanche
Wood Lawn	"	Bonito	Guadaloupe	Corn Hill	Williamson
Woods	Perry	Booneville	Brazos	Corpus Christi	Nueces
Wood's Hill	Roane	Bosqueville	McLennan	Corsicanna	Navarro
Wootton's X Roads	Claiborne	Boston	Bowie	Cottage Hill	Bexar
Woreville	Haywood	Bovine	Lavacca	Coryell	Coryell
Wrightsville	Roane	Bowling	Leon	Cotton Gin	Freestone
Yandell	Gibson	Box Creek	Cherokee	Cotton Plant	Risk
Yellow Creek	Cumberland	Brazoria	Brazoria	Courtland	Cass
Yellow Crk Furnace	Montgmry	Brazos Bottom	Burleson	Courtney	Grimes
Yellow Springs	Claiborne	Brazos Santiago	Cameron	Covington	Hill
Yellow Store	Hawkins	Breckinridge	Dallas	Coxville	"
Yellow Sulpher	Blount	Brenham	Washington	Crain's Mills	Comal
Yorkville	Gibson	Bright Star	Hopkins	Crescent Village	Refugio
Zion Hill	Hamilton	Brockville	Ellis	Crima	Hill
		Brownsborough	Henderson	Crockett	Houston
		Brownsville	Cameron	Crockett's Bluff	Smith

Texas.

Post Office.	County.	Post Office.	County.	Post Office.	County.
		Brownstown	Brown	Cross Roads	Williamson
		Bryant's Station	Milam	Cuba	Colorado
		Buchanan	Johnson	Cuero	De Witt
		Buena Vista	Shelby	Cummingsville	Goliad
		Buffalo	Henderson	Cummin's Creek	Ellis
Aberdeen	Henderson	Bunn's Bluff	Orange	Cunningham's	Bastrop
Air Hall	Bell	Burkeville	Newton	Cassetta	Cass
Alabama	Houston	Burnett C. H.	Burnett	Cypress	Upshur
Albade	Caldwell	Butler	Freestone	Cypress Top	Harris
Algana	San Patricio	Caddo Villa	Hunt	Cyral	Bosque
Alley's Mills	Cass	Cairo	Jasper	Daidgerfield	Titus
Allayton	Colorado	Caldwell	Burleson	Dalby's Springs	Bowie
Alma	Rusk	Caldwell's Hill	Gillespie	Dallas	Dallas
Alta Springs	Falls	Caledonia	Rusk	Danville	Montgomery
Alto	Cherokee	Calloway	Upshur	Day	Washington
Alum Creek	Bastrop	Cameron	Milam	Dayton	Polk
Alvarado	Johnson	Camanche Peak	Johnson	Decatur	Wise
Anacostia	Panola	Camanche Springs	Gillespie	De Harris	Medina
Anaqua	Victoria	Camp Hudson	Kinney	De Kalb	Bowie
Anderson	Grimes	Camp Stockton	Bexar	Dimming's Bridge	Matagorda
Angelina	Angelina	Camp Verde	Kerr	Denton	Denton
Antelope	Jack	Caney	Matagorda	Double Horn	Burnett
Antioch	Lavacca	Canton	Vanzant	Douglass	Nacogdoches
Aquilla	Hill	Capt's Mills	Hays	Douglassville	Cass
Aransas	Refugio	Carrizo	Webb	Dresden	Navarro
Arcade	Cooke	Carolina	Falls	Drew's Corners	Polk
Ashland	Tarrant	Carrollton	Upshur	Dripping Springs	Hays
Ash Spring	Harrison	Carter	Denton	Duck Creek	Dallas
Atchison's Point	Tarrant	Carthage C. H.	Panola	Duffau	Erath
Athens	Henderson	Casa Blanca	Nueces	Duncan's Woods	Orange
Augusta	Houston	Castroville	Medina	Eagle Ford	Dallas
		Catlett's Creek	Wise	Eagle Lake	Colorado

POST OFFICES—TEXAS. 91

Post Office.	County.	Post Office.	County.	Post Office.	County.
Eagle Pass	Maverick	Hancock	Houston	Lewisville	Denton
Eagle Valley	Leon	Hardeman	Matagorda	Lexington	Burleson
Earpville	Upshur	Hardin	Hardin	Liberty	Liberty
Echo	Live Oak	Harmony Hill	Rusk	Liberty Hill	Williamson
Ecleto	Wilson	Harrisburg	Harris	Linden	Cass
Edom	Vanzandt	Hartville	Austin	Lineville	Panola
Egypt	Wharton	Havana	Cass	Linn Flat	Nacogdoches
Eliza	Houston	Haw Grove		Linwood	Cherokee
Elkhart		Hawkinsville	Tarrant	Little Elm	Denton
Ella	Titus	Head of Elm	Montague	Live Oak	DeWitt
Elm Creek	Bell	Hedwig's Hill	Mason	Liverpool	Brazoria
El Paso	El Paso	Helena	Karnes	Livingstone	Polk
Elwood	Madison	Hemphill C. H.	Sabine	Llano	Llano
Elysian Fields	Harrison	Hempstead	Austin	Lockhart	Caldwell
Elysium	Angelina	Henderson	Rusk	Locust Grove	Navarro
Erin	Jasper	Hendersonville	Anderson	Lodi	Wilson
Estill's Station	Tarrant	Henson Creek	Coryell	London	Rusk
Eutaw	Limestone	Herrington	Anderson	Lone Star	Titus
Evergreen	Washington	Hersfield	Mason	Lone Tree	Collin
Fairfield	Freestone	Hickory Hill	Cass	Long Branch	Panola
Fairmount	Sabine	Hico	Hamilton	Long Point	Washington
Fairplay	Panola	High Hill	Fayette	Long Prairie	Fayette
Farmer's Branch	Dallas	Highland	Collin	Lookout	Leon
Farmersville	Collin	Hilliard's	Shelby	Lynchburg	Harris
Fayetteville	Fayette	Hillsboro'	Hills	Lyons	Fayette
Fincastle	Henderson	Hockley	Harris	McKinney	Collin
Fish Creek	Cooke	Hodge's Bend	Fort Bend	McMillan's	Panola
Flag Pond	Bosque	Hodge's Mill	Blanco	Macomb	Grayson
Flintham's Tan Yard		Hollandale	Grimes	Madisonville	Madison
	Red River	Holley Springs	Wood	Magnolia	Anderson
Flora	Smith	Home Valley	Karnes	Magnolia Spring	Jasper
Florence	Williamson	Homer	Angelina	Mahomet	Burnett
Flowerdale	Freestone	Honey Grove	Fannin	Malakoff	Henderson
Forest Home	Cass	Hooker	Hunt	Manchac	Hays
Fork Point	Panola	Hope	Lavacca	Mansfield	Tarrant
Fort Belknap	Young	Hopkinsville	Gonzales	Mantua	Collin
Fort Chadbourne	Runnels	Horn Hill	Limestone	Maple Springs	Red River
Fort Clark	Kinney	Hornsby	Travis	Marienne	Polk
Fort Davis	Bexar	Houston	Harris	Mariou	Angelina
Fort Graham	Hill	Howard	Bell	Marlin	Falls
Fort Quitman	El Paso	Huntsville	Walker	Marshall	Harrison
Fort Turan	Angelina	Independence	Washington	Mason	Mason
Fort Worth	Tarrant	Indianola	Calhoun	Matagorda	Matagorda
Four Milo Prairie	Vanzandt	Industry	Austin	Melrose	Nacogdoches
Frankville	Leon	Ingleside	Nueces	Meridian	Bosque
Fredericksburg	Gillespie	Ioni	Anderson	Merrilltown	Travis
Freedom	Harrison	Iron Mountains	Rusk	Meyersville	DeWitt
Frelsburg	Colorado	Isleta	El Paso	Midway	Madison
Friendship	Harrison	Jacksborough	Jack	Milan	Sabine
Gabriel Mills	Williamson	Jacksonburg		Milford	Ellis
Gainesville	Cooke	Jacksonville	Cherokee	Mill Creek	Red River
Galatsa	Harrison	Jamestown	Smith	Millheim	Austin
Galveston	Galveston	Jasper	Jasper	Millican	Brazos
Gamma	Parker	Jefferson	Cass	Millville	Rusk
Garden Valley	Smith	Jena	Falls	Millwood	Collin
Garnett's Bluffs	Fannin	Johnson's Station	Tarrant	Minden	Rusk
Gatesville	Coryell	Jonesville	Harrison	Mission Valley	Victoria
Gay Hill	Washington	Jordan's Saline C. H.		Mitts	Anderson
Gaytown	Bosque		Vanzandt	Monroe	Rusk
Georgetown	Williamson	Kaufman	Kaufman	Montague	Montague
Georgiaville	Lamar	Keechii	Freestone	Montgomery	Montgomery
Gertrude	Wise	Kemp	Kaufman	Monticello	Titus
Gillelan Creek	Travis	Kemper City	Victoria	Moody's X Roads	Leon
Gilmer C. H.	Upshur	Kenner	Matagorda	Moore's	Bowie
Glade Spring	Harrison	Kentuckytown	Grayson	Morales De Lavacca	Jackson
Goliad	Goliad	Kerrsville	Kerr	Morgansville	Polk
Golinda	Falls	Kickapoo	Anderson	Murman's Mills	Burnett
Gonzales	Gonzales	Kidd's Mills	Leon	Moscow	Polk
Goshen	Walker	Kimball	Bosque	Moss Hill	Moss Hill
Gouldsboro'	Titus	Kiomatia	Red River	Mosquito Prairie	Burleson
Graham's Mills	Shelby	Knoxville	Cherokee	Moulton	Gonzales
Grand Bluff	Panola	Ladonia	Fannin	Mountain City	Hays
Grand Cane	Liberty	Lafayette	Upshur	Mount Calm	Limestone
Grand View	Johnson	La Grange	Fayette	Mount Carmel	Smith
Grape Creek	Gillespie	Lake	Trinity	Mount Enterprise	Rusk
Grape Vine	Tarrant	Lake	Wood	Mount Pleasant	Titus
Gray Rock	Titus	Lamar	Refugio	Mount Sylvan	Smith
Green's Point	Hunt	Lampasas	Lampasas	Marral	Rusk
Greenville		Lancaster	Dallas	Muskete	Navarro
Greenwade's Mills	Hill	Lane	Bowie	Mustang	Vanzant
Greenwood	Nacogdoches	Laredo	Webb	Natches	Houston
Griffin	Cherokee	Larissa	Cherokee	Nacogdoches	Nacogdoches
Griggsby's Bluff	Jefferson	Lattington	Bee	Nashville	Milam
Gulf Prairie	Brazoria	Laverna	Wilson	Navarro	Leon
Gussettsville	Live Oak	Leal	Bexar	Navasota	Grimes
Hazanport	Titus	Lebanon	Collin	New Braunfels	Comal
Hallettsville	Lavacca	Leona	Leon	Newburg	Parker
Hamburg	Vanzant	Leon Springs	Bexar	New Danville	Risk
Hamilton	Shelby	Leonville	Coryell	New Fountain	Medina
Hampton	Hamilton	Lewis' Ferry	Jasper	New Loren	Dallas

POST OFFICES—TEXAS.

Post Office.	County.	Post Office.	County.	Post Office.	County.
Newport	Walker	Refugio	Refugio	Springfield	Limestone
New Salem	Rusk	Resley's Creek	Camanche	Spring Hill	Navarro
Newton	Newton	Retina	Hopkins	Springville	Wood
New Ulm	Austin	Retreat	Grimes	Squaw Creek	Erath
Nockenut	Gaudaloupe	Reunion	Dallas	Stafford's Point	Fort Bend
Nogallis Prairie	Trinity	Richland Crossing	Navarro	Stark Grove	McLennan
Nolaud's River	Johnson	Richmond	Fort Bend	Starkesville	Lamar
Nopal	McMullin	Ridge	Colorado	Starrville	Smith
Norman Hill	Bosque	Ringgold	Leon	Station Creek	Coryell
Norton's Grove	Tarrant	Rio Grande City	Starr	Steele's Creek	Limestone
Nueces	Nueces	Roadville	Anderson	Stephensville	Erath
Oak Hill	Fannin	Robbinsville	Red River	Stover's ⋈ Roads	Kaufman
Oakland	Lavacca	Robinson's Mills	Tarrant	Stewart's Creek	Denton
Oakville	Live Oak	Rock Creek	Johnson	Stricklinge	Burnett
Oat Meal	Burnett	Rock Hill	Collin	Sugar Hill	Panola
Odessa	Wise	Rockwall	Kaufman	Sugar Land	Fort Bend
Ogburn	Smith	Roma	Starr	Sulphur Bluff	Hopkins
Omega	Upshur	Rogersville	Parker	Sulphur Springs	Cherokee
Orange	Orange	Rose Hill	Harris	Sumpter C. H.	Trinity
Orangeville	Fannin	Round Lake	Gonzales	Sutherland Springs	Wilson
Orizaba	Fayette	Round Mountain	Hays	Swartout	Liberty
Oso	"	Round Rock	Williamson	Sweeten	Panola
Owensville	Robertson	Round Top	Fayette	Sweet Home	Lavacca
Palace Hill	Dallas	Rural Shade	Navarro	Taos	Navarro
Palestine	Anderson	Rush Creek	"	Tarkington Prairie	Liberty
Palo Alto	Gonzales	Rusk	Cherokee	Tarrant	Hopkins
Palo Pinto	Palo Pinto	Russell's Store	Palo Pinto	Telico	Ellis
Pamplin's Creek	Tyler	Rutersville	Fayette	Ten Mile	Henderson
Pana Maria	Karnes	Sabinal	Bexar	Tennessee Colony	Anderson
Papalota	Bee	Sabine Lake	Hunt	Tewockony Springs	Limestone
Paris	Lamar	Sabine Pass	Jefferson	Texanna	Jackson
Parker's Mills	Houston	Sabine Town	Sabine	Tiswell's Creek	Hunt
Parkersville	Anderson	Saint Mary's	Refugio	Timber Creek	"
Parryville	Wood	Salado	Bell	Town Bluff	Tyler
Pattouville	Lamar	Salem	Newton	Travis	Austin
Peach Tree Village	Tyler	Saltillo	Hopkins	Trinidad	Kaufman
Pennington	Houston	Salt Hill	Jack	Trinity Mills	Dallas
Peoria	Hill	Saluria	Calhoun	Troupe	Smith
Perdinalus	Travis	San Anders	Milam	Troy	Freestone
Perry	McLennan	San Antonio	Bexar	Truit's Store	Shelby
Personville	Limestone	San Augustine	San Augustine	Turner's Point	Kaufman
Petersburg	Lavacca	San Barnard	Colorado	Tuscaloosa	Walker
Piedmont Springs	Grimes	San Cosme	Rusk	Twin Sisters	Blanco
Pierpont Place	De Witt	San Domingo	Bee	Tyler	Smith
Pilot Grove	Grayson	Sand Fly	Burleson	Union	Washington
Pilot Point	Denton	Sand Spring	Wood	Union Bridge	Titus
Pine Hill	Rusk	Sandy Fork	Gonzales	Unionville	Cass
Pine Island	Jefferson	Sandy Mountain	Llano	Uvalde	Uvalde
Pinetown	Cherokee	Sandy Point	Brazoria	Valetta Rancho	Denton
Pine Tree	Upshur	San Elizaria	El Paso	Valley	Guadaloupe
Pin Oak	Fayette	San Felipe	Austin	Veal's Station	Parker
Pittsburg	Upshur	San Gabriel	Milam	Velasco	Brazoria
Plano	Collin	San Jacinto	Harris	Victoria	Victoria
Plantersville	Grimes	San Marcos	Travis	Village Creek	Jefferson
Pleasant Hill	Hopkins	San Patricio	San Patricio	Vine Grove	Washington
Pleasauton	Atascosa	San Pedro	Houston	Waco Village	McLennan
Pleasant Valley	Palo Pinto	San Saba	San Saba	Wakefield	Freestone
Plentitude	Anderson	Santa Gertrude	Nueces	Wallor's Store	Austin
Plum Creek	Caldwell	Santa Rosa	Cameron	Wallings' Ferry	Rusk
Plum Grove	Fayette	Sardis	McLennan	Wallisville	Chambers
Point Isabel	Cameron	Sattler's	Comal	Walnut Hill	Panola
Point Monterey	Cass	Savannah	Red River	Warren	Fannin
Point Pleasant	Upshur	Scyene	Dallas	Washington	Washington
Pond Spring	Williamson	Science Hill	Henderson	Waterville	Wharton
Ponton	"	Searsville	McLennan	Waverly	Walker
Port Caddo	Harrison	Sebastopol	Trinity	Waxahatchie	Ellis
Port La Vacca	Calhoun	Seguin	Gandaloupe	Weathersford	Parker
Port Sullivan	Milam	Selma	Bexar	Webster	Wood
Port Oak Island	Williamson	Sempronius	Austin	Webberville	Travis
Powellton	Harrison	Serlin	Bastrop	Wesatch	Goliad
Prairie	Houston	Seven Leagues	Smith	Westbrook	Hays
Prairie Home	Montgomery	Sexton	Sabine	West Fork	Wise
Prairie Lea	Caldwell	Shady Grove	Houston	West Liberty	Liberty
Prairie Mount	Lamar	Shelby	Austin	West Mountain	Upshur
Prairie Plains	Grimes	Shelbyville	Shelby	Weston	Collin
Prairie Point	Wise	Sherman	Grayson	Wharton	Wharton
Prairieville	Kaufman	Shiloh	Hunt	Wheelock	Robertson
Prewitt's Tan Yard	Anderson	Shockley's Prairie	Lamar	Wherry's	Rusk
Price's Creek	De Witt	Shook's Bluff	Cherokee	White Cottage	Shelby
Price's Store	Lamar	Simpsonville	Upshur	White Oak	Hopkins
Prospect	Burleson	Sisterdale	Marion	White Rock	Hill
Providence Hill	Tyler	Smithland	Cass	Whitesboro'	Grayson
Pulaski	Panola	Smithson's Valley	Comal	Wiess' Bluff	Jasper
Quitman	Wood	Snow Hill	Titus	Wigfall	Houston
Rainey's Creek	Coryell	Sour Spring	Caldwell	Willow Creek	Robertson
Rancho	Gonzales	Suwell's Bluff	Fannin	Willow Hole	Madison
Randolph	Houston	South Sulphur	Hunt	Willow Springs	Milam
Reagan	Rusk	Spear's Mill	Denton	Wilton	Ellis
Red Oak	Ellis	Spencer	Red River	Winnsboro'	Wood
Reed's Settlement	Panola	Spring Branch	Comal	Woodland	Hopkins

POST OFFICES—VERMONT. 93

Post Office.	County.	Post Office.	County.	Post Office.	County.
Woodsboro'	Grayson	Dover	Windham	Jamaica	Windham
Woods	Panola	Dummerstown	Windham	Jay	Orleans
Woodville C. H.	Tyler	East Barre	Washington	Jeffersonville	Lamoille
Ye Gua	Washington	East Barnard	Windsor	Jericho	Chittenden
Yorktown	De Witt	East Berkshire	Franklin	Jericho Center	Chittenden
Young's Settlement	Bastrop	East Bethel	Windsor	Johnson	Lamoille
Zanzenburg	Kerr	East Brookfield	Orange	Jonesville	Chittenden
		East Burke	Caledonia	Land Grove	Bennington
		East Calais	Washington	Larrabee's Point	Addison

Vermont.

Post Office.	County.	Post Office.	County.	Post Office.	County.
Addison	Addison	East Charleston	Orleans	Leicester	Addison
Albany	Orleans	East Clarendon	Rutland	Lemington	Essex
Alburg	Grand Isle	East Corinth	Orange	Lincoln	Addison
Alburg Springs	Grand Isle	East Craftsbury	Orleans	Londonderry	Windham
Andover	Windsor	East Dorset	Bennington	Lowell	Orleans
Arlington	Bennington	East Fairfield	Franklin	Lower Waterford	Caledonia
Athens	Windham	East Franklin	Franklin	Ludlow	Windsor
Ascutneyville	Windsor	East Georgia	Franklin	Lunenburg	Essex
Baker's Field	Franklin	East Greensborough	Orleans	Lyndon	Caledonia
Barnard	Windsor	East Hardwick	Caledonia	Lyndon Center	Caledonia
Barnet	Caledonia	East Haven	Essex	McIndoe's Falls	Caledonia
Barre	Washington	East Highgate	Franklin	Manchester	Bennington
Barton	Orleans	East Hubbardtown	Rutland	Marlborough	Windham
B rton's Landing	Orleans	East Middlebury	Addison	Marshfield	Washington
Bartonsville	Windham	East Montpelier	Washington	Mechanicsville	Rutland
Bellows Falls	Windham	East Orange	Orange	Mendon	Rutland
Belvidere	Lamoille	East Poultney	Rutland	Middlebury	Addison
Bennington	Bennington	East Putney	Windham	Middlesex	Washington
Bennington Center	Bennington	East Randolph	Orange	Middletown	Rutland
Benson	Rutland	East Richford	Franklin	Milton	Chittenden
Benson's Landing	Rutland	East Roxbury	Washington	Monkton	Addison
Berkshire	Franklin	East Rupert	Bennington	Montgomery	Franklin
Berlin	Washington	East Sheldon	Franklin	Montgomery Center	Franklin
Bethel	Windsor	East Thetford	Orange	Montpelier	Washington
Bloomfield	Essex	East Wallingford	Rutland	Moretown	Washington
Bolton	Chittenden	East Warren	Washington	Morgan	Orleans
Bondville	Bennington	Eden	Lamoille	Morristown	Lamoille
Bradford	Orange	Eden Mills	Lamoille	Morrisville	Lamoille
Bradford Center	Orange	Elmore	Lamoille	Mount Holly	Rutland
Braintree	Orange	Enosburg	Franklin	Newark	Caledonia
Brandon	Rutland	Enosburg Falls	Franklin	Newbury	Orange
Brattleborough	Windham	Essex	Chittenden	New Haven	Addison
Bridgewater	Windsor	Factory Point	Bennington	New Haven Mills	Addison
Bridport	Addison	Fairfax	Franklin	Newport	Orleans
Bristol	Addison	Fairfield	Franklin	North Bennington	Bennington
Brookfield	Orange	Fairhaven	Rutland	North Cambridge	Lamoille
Brookline	Windham	Fairlee	Orange	North Chester	Windsor
Brooksville	Addison	Fayetteville	Windham	North Clarendon	Rutland
Brownington	Orleans	Felchville	Windsor	North Craftsbury	Orleans
Brownsville	Windsor	Ferrisburg	Addison	North Danville	Caledonia
Brunswick	Essex	Fletcher	Franklin	North Dorset	Bennington
Buck Hollow	Franklin	Forrest Dale	Rutland	North Duxbury	Washington
Burke	Caledonia	Franklin	Franklin	North Enosburg	Franklin
Burlington	Chittenden	Gazett's Station	Windsor	North Fairfax	Franklin
Cabot	Washington	Gaysville	Windsor	North Ferrisburg	Addison
Cady's Falls	Lamoille	Georgia	Franklin	Northfield	Washington
Calais	Washington	Georgia Plain	Franklin	North Greensboro'	Orleans
Cambridge	Lamoille	Glover	Orleans	North Hartland	Windsor
Cambridgeport	Windham	Grafton	Windham	North Hero	Grand Isle
Canaan	Essex	Granby	Essex	North Hyde Park	Lamoille
Castleton	Rutland	Grand Isle	Grand Isle	North Montpelier	Washington
Cavendish	Windsor	Grauville	Addison	North Pownal	Bennington
Center Rutland	Rutland	Green River	Windham	North Randolph	Orange
Charlotte	Chittenden	Greensborough	Orleans	North Sheldon	Franklin
Chelsea	Orange	Groton	Caledonia	North Sherburne	Rutland
Chester	Windsor	Guildhall	Essex	North Springfield	Windsor
Chimney Point	Addison	Guilford	Windham	North Thetford	Orange
Chipman's Point	Addison	Guilford Center	Windham	North Troy	Orleans
Chittenden	Rutland	Halifax	Windham	North Tunbridge	Orange
Clarendon	Rutland	Hancock	Addison	North Wolcott	Lamoille
Clarendon Springs	Rutland	Hardwick	Caledonia	Norwich	Windsor
Colchester	Chittenden	Hartford	Windsor	Orange	Orange
Concord	Essex	Hartland	Windsor	Orwell	Addison
Copperas Hill	Orange	Hartland's Four Corners		Painesville	Chittenden
Corinth	Orange		Windsor	Panton	Addison
Cornwall	Addison	Hartwellville	Bennington	Passumsick	Caledonia
Coventry	Orleans	Healdville	Rutland	Pawlet	Rutland
Craftsbury	Orleans	Highgate	Franklin	Peacham	Caledonia
Cuttingsville	Rutland	Hinesburg	Chittenden	Perkinsville	Windsor
Danby	Rutland	Holland	Orleans	Peru	Bennington
Danby Four Corners	Rutland	Hortonville	Rutland	Pittsfield	Rutland
Danville	Caledonia	Houghtonville	Windham	Pittsford	Rutland
Derby	Orleans	Hubbardton	Rutland	Plainfield	Washington
Derby Line	Orleans	Huntington	Chittenden	Pleasant Valley	Chittenden
Dorset	Bennington	Hyde Park	Lamoille	Plymouth	Windsor
		Hydeville	Rutland	Pomfret	Windsor
		Ira	Rutland	Pompanoosuc	Windsor
		Irasburg	Orleans	Post Mill Village	Orange
		Isle La Mott	Grand Isle	Poultney	Rutland
		Island Pond	Essex	Pownal	Bennington
		Jacksonville	Windham	Pownal Center	Bennington

POST OFFICES—VIRGINIA.

Post Office.	County.	Post Office.	County.	Post Office.	County.
Proctorsville	Windsor	Walden	Caledonia	Acorn Hill	Frederick
Putney	Windham	Wallingford	Rutland	Acquinton	King William
Queechy	Windsor	Wardsboro'	Windham	Adaline	Marshall
Randolph	Orange	Warren	Washington	Adamsville	Harrison
Reading	Windsor	Washington	Orange	Adkinsville	Wayne
Readsborough	Bennington	Waterbury	Washington	Afton	Nelson
Richford	Franklin	Waterbury Center	Washington	Aldie	Loudoun
Richmond	Chittenden	Waterford	Caledonia	Alexandria	Alexandria
Ripton	Addison	Waterville	Lamoille	Alkire's Mills	Lewis
Rochester	Windsor	Weathersfield	Windsor	Albright	Preston
Rockingham	Windham	Weathersfield Center	Windsor	Alleghany Springs	Montgomery
Roxbury	Washington	Wells	Rutland	Allen's Creek	Amherst
Royalton	Windsor	Wells River	Orange	Alma	Page
Rupert	Bennington	West Addison	Addison	Alone	Rockbridge
Rutland	Rutland	West Albany	Orleans	Alpine Depot	Morgan
Ryegate	Caledonia	West Alburg	Grand Isle	Alta Vista	Russell
Saint Albans	Franklin	West Arlington	Bennington	Alto	Louisa
Saint Albans Bay	Franklin	West Barnet	Caledonia	Allum Springs	Rockbridge
Saint George	Chittenden	West Berkshire	Franklin	Alvon	Greenbrier
Saint Johnsbury	Caledonia	West Bolton	Chittenden	Amacetta	Wayne
Saint Johnsbury Center	Caledonia	West Braintree	Orange	Ambler's Mills	Louisa
St. Johnsbury East	Caledonia	West Brattleborough	Windham	Amelia C H	Amelia
Salisbury	Addison	West Burke	Caledonia	Amherst C H	Amherst
Sandgate	Bennington	West Castleton	Rutland	Amissville	Rappahannock
Saudasky	Addison	West Charleston	Orleans	Amsterdam	Botetourt
Saxe's Mills	Franklin	West Concord	Essex	Anandale	Fairfax
Saxton's River	Windham	West Cornwall	Addison	Andrews	Spotsylvania
Searsburg	Bennington	West Corinth	Orange	Angerona	Jackson
Shaftsbury	Bennington	West Danville	Caledonia	Anna	Fairfax
Sharon	Windsor	West Derby	Orleans	Apperson's	Charles City
Sheffield	Caledonia	West Dover	Windham	Appomattox C H	Appomattox
Shelburn	Chittenden	West Dummerston	Windham	Ararat	Patrick
Sheldon	Franklin	West Enosburg	Franklin	Arbor Hill	Augusta
Sherburne	Rutland	West Fairlee	Orange	Arbuckle	Mason
Shoreham	Addison	Westfield	Orleans	Arcola	Loudoun
Shrewsbury	Rutland	Westford	Chittenden	Arden	Berkeley
Simonsville	Windsor	West Georgia	Franklin	Arnettsville	Monongalia
Snow's Store	Windsor	West Halifax	Windham	Arnoldsburg	Calhoun
South Barre	Washington	West Hartford	Windsor	Arnoldton	Campbell
South Dorset	Bennington	West Haven	Rutland	Arrington	Nelson
South Halifax	Windham	West Marlborough	Windham	Ashland	Hanover
South Hardwick	Caledonia	West Milton	Chittenden	Aspen Grove	Pittsylvania
South Hero	Grand Isle	Westminster	Windham	Aspen Wall	Charlotte
South Londonderry	Windham	Westminster West	Windham	Assamosick	Southampton
South Newberry	Orange	West Newport	Orleans	Auburn	Fauquier
South Pomfret	Windsor	Weston	Windsor	Auburn Mills	Hanover
South Reading	Windsor	West Pawlet	Rutland	Austinville	Wythe
South Royalton	Windsor	West Randolph	Orange	Australia	Nansemond
South Ryegate	Caledonia	West Rochester	Windsor	Avon	Nelson
South Shaftsbury	Bennington	West Rupert	Bennington	Axton	Pittsylvania
South Starksboro'	Addison	West Rutland	Rutland	Aylett's	King William
South Strafford	Orange	West Salisbury	Addison	Ayr Hill	Fairfax
South Walden	Caledonia	West Topsham	Orange	Bachelor's Hall	Pittsylvania
South Wallingford	Rutland	West Townshend	Windham	Buck Creek Valley	Frederick
South Wardsboro'	Windham	West Wardsboro'	Windham	Bacon's Castle	Surry
South Windham	Windham	West Waterford	Caledonia	Baileysburg	
South Woodstock	Windsor	Weybride Lower Falls	Addison	Baker's Run	Hardy
Springfield	Windsor	Wheelock	Caledonia	Balcony Falls	Rockbridge
Stamford	Bennington	White River Junction	Windsor	Bald Knob	Boone
Starksboro'	Addison	Whiting	Addison	Ballardsville	
Stockbridge	Windsor	Whittingham	Windham	Ballsville	Powhatan
Stowe	Lamoille	Williamstown	Orange	Baptist Valley	Tazewell
Strafford	Orange	Williamsville	Windham	Barboursville	Orange
Stratton	Windham	Williston	Chittenden	Barhamsville	New Kent
Sudbury	Rutland	Willoughby Lake	Orleans	Barkesdale	Halifax
Sunderland	Bennington	Wilmington	Windham	Barracksville	Marion
Sutherland Falls	Rutland	Windham	Windham	Barren Springs	Wythe
Sutton	Caledonia	Windmill Point	Grand Isle	Barter Brook	Augusta
Swanton	Franklin	Windsor	Windsor	Basnettsville	Marion
Swanton Center	Franklin	Winooski Falls	Chittenden	Batesville	Albemarle
Taftsville	Windsor	Winhall	Bennington	Bath Alum	Bath
Taetford	Orange	Wolcott	Lamoille	Bath Court House	Northampton
Taetford Center	Orange	Woodbury	Washington	Bay View	Northampton
Tinmouth	Rutland	Woodford	Bennington	Bealeton	Fauquier
Topsham	Orange	Woodstock	Windsor	Beaty's Mills	Marion
Townshend	Windham	Worcester	Washington	Beaver Dam Depot	Hanover
Troy	Orleans			Beaver Mills	Nicholas
Tonbridge	Orange			Beech Bottom	Webster
Tyson Furnace	Windsor			Beech Springs	Lee
Underhill	Chittenden	**Virginia.**		Beeler's Station	Marshall
Underhill Center	Chittenden			Belfast Mill's	Russell
Union Village	Orange	Post Office.	County.	Belington	Barbour
Upper Falls	Windsor			Bellfair Mills	Stafford
Vergennes	Addison	Abb's Valley	Tazewell	Belleville	Wood
Vernon	Windham	Abingdon	Washington	Bolle Haven	Accomack
Vershire	Orange	Academy	Pocahontas	Belle Point	Giles
Victory	Essex	Accomack C H	Accomack	Bell's Cross Roads	Louisa
Waitsfield	Washington	Accokeek	Stafford	Bolton	Marshall
Wait's River	Orange	Acotink	Fairfax	Belmont	Loudoun
				Belmede Mills	Powhatan

POST OFFICES—VIRGINIA. 95

Post Office.	County.	Post Office.	County.	Post Office.	County.
Bennett's Mills	Lewis	Broadway Depot	Rockingham	Center	Monongalia
Bent Creek	Appomattox	Brockenburg	Spottsylvania	Center Cross	Essex
Bentivoglio	Albemarle	Brooklyn	Halifax	Centerville	Fairfax
Bent Mountain	Roanoke	Brook Neal	Campbell	Ceredo	Wayne
Benton	Brunswick	Browne Hill	Wythe	Chalk Level	Pittsylvania
Benton's Ferry	Marion	Brownsburg	Rockbridge	Chamblissburg	Bedford
Bentonville	Warren	Brown's Cove	Albemarle	Chancellorsville	Spottsylvania
Benwood	Marshall	Brown's Creek	Harrison	Chantilly	Fairfax
Berger's Store	Pittsylvania	Brown's Mills	"	Chapel Hill	Fluvanna
Berkeley Springs	Morgan	Braceton Mills	Preston	Chapmansville	Logan
Berlin	Southampton	Brucetown	Frederick	Charlemont	Bedford
Berry's Ferry	Clark	Bruington	King and Queen	Charles City C H	Charles City
Berryville	"	Brushy Run	Pendleton	Charlestown	Jefferson
Bestland	Essex	Buckhannon	Upshur	Charlotte C H	Charlotte
Bethany	Brooke	Buckingham C H	Buckingham	Charlottesville	Albemarle
Bethel	Mercer	Buckingham Mine	"	Chatham Hill	Smyth
Beverly	Randolph	Buckland	Prince William	Cherry Camp	Harrison
Bickley's Mills	Russell	Buckton	Warren	Cherry Grove	Rockingham
Big Bend	Calhoun	Buena Vista Furnace	Rockbridge	Cherry Hill	Brooke
Big Clear Creek	Greenbrier	Buffalo	Putnam	Cherry Run Depot	Morgan
Big Island	Bedford	Buffalo Fork	Braxton	Chesnut Fork	Bedford
Bigler's Mills	York	Buffalo Pond	Washington	Chesnut Hill	Kanawha
Big Lick	Roanoke	Buffalora	Logan	Chester	Chesterfield
Big Meadow	Grayson	Buffalo Springs	Amherst	Chickahominy	Hanover
Big Rock	Tazewell	Buford's	Bedford	Childress's Store	Montgomery
Big Spring	Pocahontas	Bula	Goochland	Chilesburg	Caroline
Big Spring Depot	Montgomery	Bull Creek	Wood	Chincoteague	Accomack
Big Stone Gap	Wise	Bulltown	Braxton	Christiansburg	Montgomery
Big Skin Creek	Lewis	Bunger's Mills	Greenbrier	Christiansville	Mecklenburg
Big Sycamore	Clay	Bunker Hill	Bedford	Chuckatuck	Nansemond
Bingamon	Marion	Burgess' Store	Northumberland	Chula Depot	Amelia
Birch Grove	Morgan	Bumpass	Louisa	Churchland	Norfolk
Birch River	Nicholas	Burke's Garden	Tazewell	Church View	Middlesex
Birchtown	Braxton	Burke's Mills	Augusta	Churchville	Augusta
Black Fork	Tucker	Burke's Station	Fairfax	Circleville	Loudoun
Black Heth	Chesterfield	Burkesville	Nottoway	City Point	Prince George
Blacks and Whites	Nottoway	Burnersville	Harbour	Claremont Wharf	Surry
Blacksburg	Montgomery	Burning Spring	Wirt	Clarksburg	Harrison
Blacksville	Monongalia	Burnt Ordinary	James City	Clark's Creek	Patrick
Black Walnut	Halifax	Burntville	Brunswick	Clarksville	Mecklenburg
Blackwater	Sussex	Burton	Wetzel	Clay C H	Clay
Bloomery	Hampshire	Burwell's Bay	Isle of Wight	Clayville	Hampshire
Bloomfield	Loudoun	Bush's Mills	Lewis	Clear Branch	Washington
Bloomingdale	Cabell	Burr Hill	Orange	Clear Fork	Tazewell
Bloomsburg	Halifax	Cabbage Farm	Mecklenburg	Cleek's Mills	Bath
Blossom Hill	Princess Anne	Cabell C H	Cabell	Clendenin	Kanawha
Blue Creek	Kanawha	Cabin Point	Surry	Clift Mills	Fauquier
Blue Ridge	Botetourt	Caenpon Depot	Morgan	Clifton	King George
Blue Spring	Smyth	Cady's Tunnell	Bath	Clifton Forge	Alleghany
Blue Stone	Tazewell	Ca Ira	Cumberland	Clifty	Fayette
Blue Sulphur	Greenbrier	Cairo	Ritchie	Clinton	Ohio
Bluff Bridge	Washington	Calfee's Ferry	Pulaski	Clinton Furnace	Monongalia
Hunt's Depot	Southampton	Calhoun	Harbour	Clintonville	Greenbrier
Body Camp	Bedford	Callaghan's	Alleghany	Clover Creek	Highland
Boggsville	Jackson	Callands	Pittsylvania	Cloverdale	Botetourt
Bolington	Loudoun	Cameron	Marshall	Clover Depot	Halifax
Bombrook	Franklin	Campbell C H	Campbell	Clover Green	Spottsylvania
Bone Creek	Ritchie	Canuelton	Kanawha	Clover Valley	Mason
Bonnineld's Mills	Tucker	Canicello	Rockbridge	Coal Hill	Goochland
Bonsack's	Roanoke	Cuney Hollow	Lee	Coal River Marshes	Raleigh
Boone's Mills	Franklin	Capeville	Northampton	Coalsmonth	Kanawha
Boothsville	Marion	Capon Bridge	Hampshire	Cobb's Creek	Matthews
Bothwick	Dinwiddie	Capon Iron Works	Hardy	Cobham	Albemarle
Boston	Culpeper	Capon Springs	Hampshire	Cold Spring	Carroll
Botetourt	Roanoke	Cappahosic	Gloucester	Cold Stream	Hampshire
Bowers	Southampton	Capper's Spring	Frederick	Cole's Ferry	Charlotte
Bowling Green	Caroline	Carbonvale	Kanawha	Collerstown	Rockbridge
Bowman's Mills	Rockingham	Carlton's Store	King and Queen	Collinsville	Frederick
Boyd's Tavern	Albemarle	Carron Furnace	Franklin	Cologne	Mason
Boydton	Mecklenburg	Carrsville	Isle of Wight	Columbia	Fluvanna
Boykin's Depot	Southampton	Carsonville	Grayson	Columbia Furnace	Shenandoah
Branchville	"	Carter's Bridge	Albemarle	Columbia Grove	Lunenburg
Brandon Church	Prince George	Cartersville	Cumberland	Coman's Well	Sussex
Brandonville	Preston	Cascade	Pittsylvania	Comer's Rock	Grayson
Brandy Station	Culpeper	Cassville	Monongalia	Comorn	King George
Brandywine	Fauquier	Castle Craig	Campbell	Concord Depot	Campbell
Braxton C H	Braxton	Castleman's Ferry	Clark	Confluence	Warren
Breckinridge	Henry	Castleton	Culpeper	Conrad's Store	Rockingham
Bremo Bluff	Fluvanna	Catlett	Fauquier	Contrary	Buchanan
Brentsville	Prince William	Cave Spring	Roanoke	Cool Well	Amherst
Brickland	Lunenburg	Cedar Bluff	Tazewell	Coon's Mills	Boone
Bridgeport	Harrison	Cedar Creek	Frederick	Coopers	Franklin
Bridgewater	Rockingham	Cedar Fork	Caroline	Cootes' Store	Rockingham
Bridle Creek	Grayson	Cedar Grove Mills	Rockbridge	Copper Hill	Floyd
Briscoe Run	Wood	Cedar Point	Page	Copper Valley	"
Bristersburg	Fauquier	Cedar Springs	Wythe	Cornwallis	Ritchie
Bristoe Station	Prince William	Centenary	Buckingham	Cottageville	Jackson
Bradford	Smyth	Central Plains	Fluvanna	Cotton Hill	Fayette
Broad Run	Loudoun	Central Point	Caroline	County Line X Roads	Charlotte
Broad Run Station	Fauquier	Central Station	Doddridge	County Line Mills	Henry

POST OFFICES—VIRGINIA.

Post Office.	County.	Post Office.	County.	Post Office.	County.
Cove Creek	Tazewell	Elamsville	Patrick	Franklin	Pendleton
Covesville	Albemarle	Eldorado	Culpeper	Franklin Depot	Isle of Wight
Coveton	Barbour	Elk	Pocahontas	Franktown	Northampton
Covington	Alleghany	Elk Creek	Grayson	Frazier Bottom	Putnam
Cowpasture Bridge		Elk Fork	Jackson	Fredericksburg	Spottsylvania
Cox's Mills	Gilmer	Elk Run	Fauquier	Frederickshall	Louisa
Crab Orchard	Wythe	Ellenborough	Ritchie	Freeman's Landing	Hancock
Craig's Creek	Craig	Elliaville	Louisa	Freeport	Wirt
Craigsville	Augusta	Elm Grove	Ohio	Freeshade	Middlesex
Cranberry Plains	Carroll	Emans	Bedford	Free Union	Albemarle
Craney	Wyoming	Emory	Washington	French Creek	Upshur
Craussville	Preston	Enfield	King William	French Hay	Hanover
Crichton's Store	Brunswick	Erin Shades	Henrico	Frenchton	Upshur
Criglersville	Madison	Estillville	Scott	Frenchville	Mercer
Crimea	Dinwiddie	Etna	Hanover	Friendship	Fairfax
Croftsville	Tazewell	Evansport	Prince William	Front Royal	Warren
Cross Keys	Rockingham	Evansville	Preston	Frost	Pocahontas
Crow's	Alleghany	Evergreen	Appomattox	Frozen Camp	Jackson
Cuckooville	Louisa	Faber's Mills	Nelson	Fulkerson	Scott
Culpeper C. H.	Culpeper	Fabius	Hardy	Gainesboro'	Frederick
Cumberland C. H.	Cumberland	Fairfax Court House	Fairfax	Gains X Roads	Rappahannock
Curdsville	Buckingham	Fairfax Station	Fairfax	Gainesville	Prince William
Cypress Island	Alleghany	Fairfield	Rockbridge	Galt's Mills	Amherst
Dagger's Springs	Botetourt	Fair Hill	Marshall	Gap Mills	Monroe
Dallas	Marshall	Fairmount	Marion	Garland's	Albemarle
Danielsville	Spottsylvania	Fairview	Hancock	Garrisonville	Stafford
Danville	Pittsylvania	Falling Spring	Greenbrier	Gary's Store	Buckingham
Darkesville	Berkeley	Falling Waters	Berkeley	Garysville	Prince George
Darlington Hights	Prince Edward	Falls Church	Fairfax	Gauley Bridge	Fayette
Davenport	Wetzel	Falls of Tug	Wayne	Genito	Powhatan
Davis' Mills	Bedford	Falls of Twelve Pole		Gerardstown	Berkeley
Davis' Store		Falmouth	Stafford	Germanna	Orange
Davisville	Wood	Fancy Gap	Carroll	German Settlement	Preston
Dawsonville	Greene	Fancy Grove	Bedford	Gholsonville	Brunswick
Dayton	Rockingham	Fancy Hill	Rockbridge	Gibsonville	Russell
Deatonsville	Amelia	Fanlight	Wetzel	Gilboa	Louisa
Decapolis	Madison	Farmer's Grove	Southampton	Gilead Spring	McDowell
Deep Creek	Norfolk	Farmington	Marion	Gilmore's Mills	Rockbridge
Deep Lick	Mercer	Farmville	Prince Edward	Gill's Creek	Franklin
Deerfield	Augusta	Farmwell	Loudoun	Gishe's Mills	Roanoke
Deer Lick	Mason	Farnham	Richmond	Glade Farms	Preston
Deer Walk	Wood	Fayetteville	Fayette	Glade Hill	Franklin
De Kalb	Gilmer	Federal Hill	Ritchie	Gladesboro'	Carroll
Diamond Grove	Brunswick	Fellowsville	Preston	GladeSpringDepot	Washington
Diana Mills	Buckingham	Fetterman	Taylor	Gladesville	Preston
Dickenson's	Franklin	Fifes	Goochland	Glady Fork	Pittsylvania
Dickensonville	Russell	Fillmore	Randolph	Glebe Cottage	Alexandria
Dick's Creek	Tazewell	Fincastle	Botetourt	Glen Easton	Marshall
Dillon's Run	Hampshire	Fine Creek Mills	Powhatan	Glengary	Berkeley
Dinwiddie C. H.	Dinwiddie	Fink's Creek	Lewis	Glenmore	Buckingham
Disputanta	Prince George	Finney's Mills	Amelia	Glenn's	Gloucester
Doe Hill	Highland	Fisher's Point	Jackson	Gleaville	Gilmer
Double Bridge	Lunenburg	Fishersville	Augusta	Glenwood	Rockbridge
Dover Mills	Goochland	Five Oaks	Tazewell	Gloucester C. H.	Gloucester
Dovesville	Rockingham	Flat Creek	Boone	Glover's Gap	Marion
Drake's Branch	Charlotte	Flat Fork	Roane	Gogginsville	Franklin
Dranesville	Fairfax	Flat Head	Floyd	Gold Hill	Buckingham
Draper's Valley	Pulaski	Flat Top	Mercer	Goochland C. H.	Goochland
Drapersville	Mecklenberg	Flat Woods	Braxton	Goodson	Washington
Drewryville	Southampton	Fleetwood Academy	King and Queen	Good View	Bedford
Dry Fork	Randolph	Flemington	Taylor	Goodwynsville	Dinwiddie
Dry Run	Pendleton	Flint Hill	Rappahannock	Goose Creek	Ritchie
Dry Valley	Montgomery	Flippo's	Caroline	Gordonsville	Orange
Dublin	Pulaski	Floyd C H	Floyd	Goresville	Loudoun
Duck Creek	Braxton	Fluke's	Botetourt	Goshen Bridge	Rockbridge
Duffield's	Jefferson	Ford's Depot	Dinwiddie	Grafton	Taylor
Dug Spur	Carroll	Forest Depot	Bedford	Graham's Forge	Wythe
Dumfries	Prince William	Forest Hill	Monroe	Granville	Monongalia
Duncan's Mills	Scott	Forestville	Shenandoah	Grape Island	Tyler
Dunmore	Pocahontas	Forkland	Nottoway	Grass Lick Fork	Jackson
Dunnsville	Essex	Fork Lick	Webster	Grassland	Harrison
Dufree's Old Store	Charlotte	Forks	Washington	Grassy Meadows	Greenbrier
Durrettsville	Richmond	Forksburg	Marion	Gravel Hill	Buckingham
Dyer's Store	Henry	Forks of Buffalo	Amherst	Gravel Spring	Frederick
Dye's Mill	Fairfax	Forks of Potomac	Hampshire	Grave's Mill	Madison
Eagle Mills	Doddridge	Forks of Twelve Pole	Wayne	Gray's Flat	Marion
Earleysville	Albemarle	Forksville	Mecklenburg	Grayson C. H.	Grayson
East Liberty	Page	Fork Union	Fluvanna	Grayson Sulphur Springs	Carroll
Easton	Monongalia	Fort Blackimore		Greasy Creek	Floyd
East River	Mercer	Fort Furnace	Shenandoah	Great Bridge	Norfolk
Eastville	Northampton	Fort Martin	Monongalia	Green Bank	Pocahontas
Edenburg	Shenandoah	Fountain Spring	Wood	Green Bay	Prince Edward
Edge Hill	King George	Fowler's	Brooke	Greenbrier Run	Doddridge
Edmunds	Brunswick	Fowler's Knob	Nicholas	Greenfield	Nelson
Edna Mills	Charles City	Foxville	Fauquier	Green Hill	Campbell
Edom	Rockingham	Frametown	Braxton	Greenland	Hardy
Edray	Pocahontas	Francisco's Mills	Craig	Green Level	Southampton
Eggleston Springs	Giles	Frankford	Greenbrier	Green Mount	Rockingham
Egypt	Monroe	Frankfort	Hampshire	Green Plain	Southampton

POST OFFICES—VIRGINIA.

Post Office.	County.	Post Office.	County.	Post Office.	County.
Greensburg	Preston	Hillsville	Carroll	Keswick's Depot	Albemarle
Green Shoal	Logan	Hockett's Bottom	Amherst	Ketteman's	Hardy
Green Spring Run	Hampshire	Holcombe's Rock	Bedford	Keysville	Charlotte
Green Sulphur Springs	Greenbrier	Holliday's Cove	Hancock	Kidwell	Tyler
Green Valley	Bath	Holly Meadows	Tucker	Kilmarnock	Lancaster
Greenville	Augusta	Holly River	Braxton	Kimberlin	Giles
Greenwood	Doddridge	Holston	Washington	Kincheloe	Harrison
Greenwood Depot	Albemarle	Holston Bridge	Scott	King and Queen C. H.	
Griffinsburg	Culpeper	Holston Springs			King and Queen
Grotto Dell	Roane	Holy Neck	Nansemond	Kingsville	Nansemond
Grove Hill	Page	Homeland	Culpeper	King William C. H.	
Groveton	Prince William	Hoodsville	Marion		King William
Grundy	Buchanan	Hookersville	Nicholas	Kingwood	Preston
Guest's Station	Russell	Hooke's Mills	Hampshire	Kinsale	Westmoreland
Guilford	Accomack	Hope Mills	Page	Kirkwood	Caroline
Guilford Station	Loudoun	Horeb	Bedford	Knob	Tazewell
Gniney's	Caroline	Horntown	Accomack	Knob Fork	Wetzel
Gum Springs	Louisa	Horse Pasture	Henry	Kossuth	Marshall
Gunville	Henry	Horse Shoe Run	Preston	Lacy Spring	Rockingham
Guseman's Store	Preston	Hot Springs	Bath	La Fayette	Montgomery
Guyandotte	Cabell	Howard's Lick	Hardy	La Fayette Hill	Fluvanna
Hacker's Creek	Lewis	Howardsville	Albemarle	Lake Drummond	Norfolk
Hacker's Valley	Webster	Hoysville	Loudoun	Lancaster C. H.	Lancaster
Hackersville	Barbour	Huffville	Floyd	Land of Promise	Princess Anne
Hadensville	Goochland	Hughesville	Loudoun	Lanesville	King William
Hadlock	Northampton	Hunter's Mill	Fairfax	Langley	Fairfax
Hague	Westmoreland	Huntersville	Pocahontas	Landsdown	Prince William
Hainesville	Berkeley	Hurricane Bridge	Putnam	Lantz's Mills	Shenandoah
Hale's Ford	Franklin	Huttonsville	Randolph	Laurel	Washington
Haleysburg	Lunenburg	Hyco	Halifax	Laurel Fork	Carroll
Half-Way House	York	Hyco Falls	"	Laurel Grove	Pittsylvania
Halifax C. H.	Halifax	Hydraulic Mills	Albemarle	Laurel Hill	Lunenburg
Hallsborough	Chesterfield	Ice's Ferry	Monongalia	Laurel Mills	Rappahannock
Halltown	Jefferson	Independence	Grayson	Laurel Point	Monongalia
Hambaugh's	Warren	Independent Hill		Laurelton	Hardy
Hamburg	Shenandoah		Prince William	Lawrenceville	Brunswick
Hamilton	Loudoun	Indian Creek	Monroe	Lead Mine	Tucker
Hamlin	Cabell	Indian Valley	Floyd	Leadsville	Randolph
Hampden Sidney College		Inkermann	Hardy	Leakesville	Page
	Prince Edward	Ireland	Lewis	Leatherwood's Store	Henry
Hampstead	King George	Irishburg	Henry	Lebanon	Russell
Hampton	Elizabeth	Ironvillo	Tazewell	Lebanon Church	Shenandoah
Hanging Rock	Hampshire	Isle of Wight	Isle of Wight	Lebanon White Sulphur	
Hannahsville	Tucker	Issequeane	Goochland	[Springs	Augusta
Hanover C. H.	Hanover	Ivor	Southampton	Lecompton	Wise
Hansonville	Russell	Ivy Depot	Albemarle	Leesburg	Loudoun
Happy Creek Station	Warren	Ive's Store	Princess Anne	Lee's Mills	Wirt
Hardwicksville	Nelson	Jackson	Louisa	Leesville	Campbell
Hargrove's Tavern	Nansemond	Jackson C. H.	Jackson	Leetown	Jefferson
Harmony	Halifax	Jackson's Ferry	Wythe	Leon	Madison
Harmony Village	Middlesex	Jacksonville	Lewis	Leroy	Jackson
Harper's Ferry	Jefferson	Jacob's Church	Shenandoah	Letcher	Bath
Harper's Mills	Pendleton	Jakes' Run	Monongalia	Letter Gap	Gilmer
Harris	Louisa	Jamaica	Middlesex	Level Green	Craig
Harrisonburg	Rockingham	Janelew	Lewis	Lewisburg	Greenbrier
Hartford City	Mason	Jarratt's	Sussex	Lewis's Store	Spottsylvania
Hartmonsville	Hampshire	Jarrett's Ford	Kanawha	Lewisville	Brunswick
Hartwood	Stafford	Jarrold's Valley	Raleigh	Lexington	Rockbridge
Harvey's Store	Charlotte	Jefferson	Powhatan	Liberty	Bedford
Hat Creek	Campbell	Jeffersonton	Culpeper	Liberty Furnace	Shenandoah
Hawk's Nest	Fayette	Jeffress' Store	Nottoway	Liberty Hall	Washington
Haye's Store	Gloucester	Jenkins' Bridge	Accomack	Limestone Hill	Wood
Hay Market	Prince William	Jennings' Gap	Augusta	Linden	Warren
Haymond's Store	Braxton	Jennings' Ordinary	Nottoway	Linside	Monroe
Head Waters	Highland	Jerusalem	Southampton	Lisbon	Bedford
Healing Springs	Bath	Jeter ville	Amelia	Little Georgetown	Berkeley
Henthsville	Northampton	Jobe	Monongalia	Little Ottar	Braxton
Hebron	Pleasants	Johnson's ⋈ Roads	Monroe	LittlePlymouth	King&Queen
Hedgesville	Berkeley	Johnson's Spring	Goochland	Little River	Floyd
Hemlock	Jackson	Johnsontown	Northampton	Little Shin Creek	Lewis
Hendrick's Mills	Russell	Johnstonville	Hardy	Littleton	Sussex
Hendrick's Store	Bedford	Jonesborough	Brunswick	Litwalton	Lancaster
Henry	Sussex	Jones' Springs	Berkeley	Lloyds	Essex
Henry's Mills	Halifax	Jonesville	Lee	Lockleven	Lunenburg
Hereford's	Mason	Joyceville	Mecklenburg	Loch Lomond	Goochland
Hermitage	Augusta	Jumping Branch	Mercer	Locust Bottom	Botetourt
Herndon	Fairfax	Junction	Hanover	Locust Creek	Louisa
Hesaville	Harrison	Junction Store	Botetourt	Locust Dale	Madison
Hickory Flats	Lee	Kabletown	Jefferson	Locust Grove	Orange
Hickory Fork	Gloucester	Kanawha	Wood	Locust Hill	Middlesex
Hickory Ground	Norfolk	Kanawha C. H.	Kanawha	Locust Level	Louisa
Hicksford	Greenville	Kanawha Saline	"	Locust Mount	Accomack
Hicksville	Tazewell	Kasey's	Bedford	Locustvillo	"
Higginsville	Hampshire	Koczletown	Rockingham	Lodi	Washington
Highland	Ritchie	Kellysville	Culpeper	Lodoro	Amelia
Hightown	Highland	Kempsville	Princess Anne	Logan C H	Logan
High View	Frederick	Kennedy's	Brunswick	Lombardy Grove	Mecklenburg
Hill Grove	Pittsylvania	Kerneysville	Jefferson	London Bridge	Princess Anne
Hillsborough	Loudoun	Korr's Creek	Rockbridge	Lone Pine	Bedford
		Keeler's ⋈ Lanes	Nicholas	Lone Tree	Tyler

7

POST OFFICES—VIRGINIA.

Post Office.	County.	Post Office.	County.	Post Office.	County.
Long Branch	Franklin	Metompkin	Accomack	Mount Solon	"
Long Creek	Louisa	Meyerhoeffer's Store		Mount Storm	Hardy
Long Glade	Augusta		Rockingham	Mount Vernon	Monroe
Long Run Station	Doddridge	Middlebourne	Tyler	Mount Vernon Tannery	
Longwood	Rockbridge	Middlebrook	Augusta		Frederick
Lorentz's Store	Upshur	Middleburg	Loudoun	Mountville	Loudoun
Lorenzoville Foundry		Middle Ferry	Brooke	Mount Vinco	Buckingham
	Shenandoah	Middle Fork	Upshur	Mount Zion	Campbell
Loretto	Essex	Middle Mountain	Craig	Mouth of Buffalo	Logan
Lost River	Hardy	Middleport	Webster	Mouth of Indian	Monroe
Lottsburg	Northumberland	Middletown	Frederick	Mouth of Pigeon	Logan
Louisa C H	Louisa	Middleway	Jefferson	Mouth of Pocu	Kanawha
Lovells Creek	Carroll	Midlothian	Chesterfield	Mouth of Seneca	Pendleton
Lovely Mount	Montgomery	Midway	Craig	Mouth of Wilson	Grayson
Love's Mills	Washington	Milford	Caroline	Muddy Creek	Preston
Lovettsville	Loudoun	Milboro' Springs	Bath	Mud River	Boone
Loving Creek	Bedford	Millbrook	Greenbrier	Mulberry Inn	Dinwiddie
Livingston	Nelson	Mill Creek	Berkeley	Murphy's Mill	Wood
Lowry	Bedford	Milldale	Warren	Murraysville	Jackson
Lowry's Mills	Greenbrier	Miller's Tavern	Essex	Murrill's Shop	Nelson
Lowsville	Nelson	Mill Falls	Marion	Muse's Bottom	Jackson
Luleck	Wood	Mill Gap	Highland	Muscville	Pittsylvania
Lumberport	Harrison	Millington	Albemarle	Muster Ground	Scott
Lunenburg C H	Lunenburg	Mill Point	Pocahontas	Naff's	Franklin
Luncy's Creek	Hardy	Millview	Fauquier	Natural Bridge	Rockbridge
Luray	Page	Millville	Westmoreland	Natural Tunnel	Scott
Lyell's Store	Richmond	Millwood	Clark	Nealsco Mills	Prince William
Lynchburg	Campbell	Milo	Wetzel	Nebraska	Appomattox
Lynn Camp	Marshall	Mingo Flat	Randolph	Necrsville	Loudoun
Lynnuville Mills	Franklin	Minnora	Calhoun	Negro Foot	Hanover
McDonald's Mills	Montgomery	Mint Spring	Augusta	Nelson's Station	Nelson
McDowell	Highland	Miracle Run	Monongalia	Nestorville	Barbour
McFarland's	Lunenburg	Mitchell's Station	Culpeper	Newark	Wirt
McGaheysville	Rockingham	Mock's Mills	Washington	New Baltimore	Fauquier
McMullin's Mill	Greene	Modest Town	Accomack	Newburn	Pulaski
Mack's Meadow	Wythe	Moffatt's Creek	Augusta	New Brighton	Fauquier
Macon	Powhatan	Molchill	Ritchie	Newburg	Preston
Madison C H	Madison	Monaskon	Lancaster	New Canton	Buckingham
Madison Mills	"	Monclova	Morgan	New Castle	Craig
Madison Run Station	Orange	Monmouth	Rockbridge	New Church	Accomack
Maiden Spring	Tazewell	Montague	Essex	New Creek Station	Hampshire
Maidsville	Monongalia	Monterey	Highland	New Cumberland	Hancock
Mallory's Ford	Orange	Montgomery Springs		New Dale	Wetzel
Mallows	Pendleton		Montgomery	New England	Wood
Malouesville	Dinwiddie	Montpelier	Hanover	New Garden	Russell
Manchester	Chesterfield	Montross	Westmoreland	New Geneva	Jackson
Mangohick	King William	Moorefield	Hardy	New Glasgow	Amherst
Mannington	Marion	Mooresville	Monongalia	New Hampden	Highland
Mannborough	Amelia	Moore's	Tyler	New Hope	Augusta
Mansfield	Louisa	Moore's Ordinary		New Interest	Randolph
Marengo	Mecklenburg		Prince Edward	New Kent C H	New Kent
Marion	Smyth	Moore's Store	Shenandoah	New London	Campbell
Markham Station	Fauquier	Moreman's River	Albemarle	New Marks	Shenandoah
Marksville	Page	Morgantown	Monongalia	New Martinsville	Wetzel
Marlin Bottom	Pocahontas	Morgan Valley	Wyoming	New Milton	Doddridge
Marple's Store	Upshur	Morris	Hanover	New Plymouth	Lunenburg
Marshallsville	Greenbrier	Morris Hill	Alleghany	Newport	Giles
Martinsburg	Berkeley	Morrisonville	Loudoun	New Salem	Harrison
Martin's Mills	Nelson	Morris Church	Campbell	News Ferry	Halifax
Martinsville	Henry	Morrisville	Fauquier	Newsom's Depot	Southampton
Marysville	Campbell	Morven	Amelia	New Store	Buckingham
Mason	Mason	Mossingford	Charlotte	Newton	Kanawha
Mason's Depot	Amherst	Mossy Creek	Augusta	Newtown	King and Queen
Masontown	Preston	Moundsville	Marshall	Newtown Stephensburg	
Massanutton	Page	Mountain Cove	Fayette		Frederick
Massie's Mills	Nelson	Mountain Falls	Frederick	New Upton	Gloucester
Matamoras	Montgomery	Mountain Grove	Bath	Newville	Sussex
Matissary	Spottsylvania	Mountain Home	Hardy	Nicholas C H	Nicholas
Matoax	Amelia	Mountain House	Alleghany	Nickell's Mills	Monroe
Matthew's Court House		Mountain Lake	Giles	Nickelsville	Scott
	Matthews	Mountain View	Craig	Nineveh	Warren
Mayo	Halifax	Mount Athos	Campbell	Nominy Grove	Westmoreland
Mayo Forge	Patrick	Mount Carmel	Halifax	Non-Intervention	Lunenburg
Maysville	Greenbrier	Mount Clifton	Shenandoah	Norfolk	Norfolk
Meadow Bluff		Mount Clinton	Rockingham	Normantown	Gilmer
Meadow Creek	Grayson	Mount Crawford	"	North Bend Mills	Tyler
Meadow Dale	Highland	Mount Freedom	Pendleton	North End	Matthews
Meadows of Dan	Patrick	Mount Gilead	Loudoun	North Fork	Washington
Meadowville	Barbour	Mount Hebron	Hardy	North Garden	Albemarle
Meadville	Halifax	Mount Hope	Mecklenburg	North Mayo	Henry
Mechanicsburg	Giles	Mount Horeb	Nelson	North Mountain	Berkeley
Mechanicsville	Louisa	Mount Jackson	Shenandoah	North River Meeting House	
Mechum's River	Albemarle	Mount Landing	Essex		Hampshire
Melon	Barbour	Mount Laurel	Halifax	North River Mills	"
Melrose	Rockingham	Mount Meridian	Augusta	North View	Giles
Mendota	Washington	Mount Murphy	Pocahontas	North West River Bridge	
Mercer Salt Works	Mercer	Mount Olive	Shenandoah		Norfolk
Mercer's Bottom	Mason	Mount Pierce	Fairfax	Nottoway Chapel	Southampton
Meredith's Tavern	Marion	Mount Pleasant	Spottsylvania	Nottoway C H	Nottoway
Messongo	Accomack	Mount Sidney	Augusta	No 12 Water Station	Morgan

POST OFFICES—VIRGINIA. 99

Post Office.	County.	Post Office.	County.	Post Office.	County.
Nuzum	Marion	Phillippa	Barbour	Reed Creek	Henry
Oakdale	Rockbridge	Philomont	Loudoun	Reedy	Jackson
Oak Flat	Pendleton	Piedmont	Hampshire	Reedy Ripple	Wirt
Oak Forest	Cumberland	Piedmont Station	Fauquier	Reedy Springs	Appomattox
Oak Grove	Westmoreland	Piercevillle	Bedford	Reedyville	Roane
Oak Hill	Fayette	Pigeon Run	Campbell	Rehoboth	Lunenburg
Oakland	Morgan	Pigeon Trace	Logan	Reidsville	Preston
Oak Level	Henry	Pine Creek	Calhoun	Republican Grove	Halifax
Oakley	Mecklenburg	Pine Grove	Wetzel	Republican Mills	Fairfax
Oak Park	Madison	Pine Spring	Russell	Retreat	Franklin
Oak Shade	Culpeper	Pine View	Fauquier	Rice Depot	Prince Edward
Oakville	Appomattox	Piper's Gap	Carroll	Rice's Store	Westmoreland
Oak Woods	Orange	Pipe Stem	Mercer	Riceville	Pittsylvania
Oatlands	Loudoun	Pittsylvania C H	Pittsylvania	Richardsville	Culpeper
Occoquan	Prince William	Plain View	King and Queen	Rich Creek	Tazewell
Oceana	Wyoming	Plantersville	Lunenburg	Richland	Tazewell
Okonoko	Hampshire	Pleasant Creek	Taylor	Richmond	Henrico
Old Church	Hanover	Pleasantdale	Hampshire	Richman Falls	Raleigh
Oldham's ½ Roads	Westmoreland	Pleasant Flats	Wirt	Rich Patch	Alleghany
Old Hickory	Botetourt	Pleasant Gap	Pittsylvania	Ridgeville	Hampshire
Old Point Comfort	Elizabeth	Pleasant Grove	Lunenburg	Ridgeway	Henry
Olympia	Smyth	Pleasant Hill	Fayette	Ringgold	Pittsylvania
Omega	Halifax	Pleasant Oaks	Brunswick	Ripley's	Tyler
Onancock	Accomack	Pleasant Ridge	Princess Anne	Rippon	Jefferson
Orange C H	Orange	Pleasant Run	Tucker	Ritchie Court House	Ritchie
Orange Springs	"	Pleasant Shade	Greenville	Rivesville	Marion
Orkney Springs	Shenandoah	Pleasant Valley	Fairfax	Roanoke Red Sulphur	
Orlena	Fauquier	Pleasant View	Jackson	[Springs	Roanoke
Oronoco	Amherst	Pocotaligo	Kanawha	Roaring Creek	Randolph
Osborn's Ford	Scott	Poindexter's Store	Louisa	Roaring Run	Botetourt
Osborne's Mills	Kanawha	Point Hope	Grayson	Robert's Mills	Nelson
Otter Bridge	Bedford	Point of RockMills	Cumberland	Rochelle	Madison
Otter Hill	Mecklenburg	Point Pleasant	Mason	Rockbridge Baths	Rockbridge
Ottobine	Rockingham	Point Truth	Russell	Rock Castle	Patrick
Overalls	Warren	Pomona	Loudoun	Rock Cave	Upshur
Overhill	Upshur	Pond Creek	Wood	Rock Farm	Russell
Owl Run	Fauquier	Pond Gap	Augusta	Rock Fish	Nelson
Oxford	Doddridge	Pond's Shop	Southampton	Rock Fish Depot	"
Pack's Ferry	Monroe	Poplar Hill	Pulaski	Rockland Mills	Augusta
Paddy's Mills	Shenandoah	Poplar Mount	Greenville	Rock Lick	Marshall
Painesville	Amelia	Port Conway	King George	Rock Mills	Rappahannock
Paint Creek	Kanawha	Porter's Falls	Wetzel	Rock Spring	Patrick
Paint Lick	Tazewell	Portland	Preston	Rock Valley	Marshall
Palatine	Marion	Port Republic	Rockingham	Rockview	Wyoming
Palestine	Greenbrier	Port Royal	Caroline	Rockville	Hampshire
Palmer'sSprings	Mecklenburg	Portsmouth	Norfolk	Rocky Gap	Tazewell
Palmetto	Wayne	Potomac Furnace	Loudoun	Rocky Hill	Fayette
Palmyra	Fluvanna	Pound	Russell	Rocky Mount	Franklin
Palo Alto	Highland	Powellton	Brunswick	Rocky Point	Scott
Pamplin's Depot	Prince Edward	Powhattan C H	Powhatan	Rocky Point Mills	Botetourt
Parham's Store	Sussex	Price's Factory	Washington	Rocky Station	Lee
Paris	Fauquier	Pride's Church	Amelia	Rolling Hill	Charlotte
Parkersburg	Wood	Prillman's	Franklin	Rollingsburg	Monroe
Parnassus	Augusta	Prince Edward C H	Prince Edward	Romine's Mills	Harrison
Partlow's	Spottsylvania	Prince George C H	Prince George	Romney	Hampshire
Patrick C H	Patrick	Princess Anne C H	Princess Anne	Rosby's Rock	Marshall
Patrick Springs	"			Rosedale	Russell
Patterson's Depot	Hampshire	Princeton	Mercer	Rose Hill	Lee
Pattonsburg	Botetourt	Proctor	Wetzel	Roseland	Nelson
Pattonsville	Scott	Proctor's Creek	Chesterfield	Rose Mills	Amherst
Paw Paw	Morgan	Prospect	Prince Edward	Rough and Ready Mills	Henry
Paw Paw Bottom	Cabell	Prospect Hill	Fairfax	Rough Creek	Charlotte
Peach Bottom	Grayson	Prospect Valley	Harrison	Round Bottom	Wayne
Peach Grove	Fairfax	Providence	Halifax	Round Glade	Raleigh
Peaksville	Bedford	Pranty's	Henry	Round Hill	Loudoun
Pearisburg	Giles	Pruntytown	Taylor	Round Meadows	Patrick
Peck's Run	Upshur	Pryor's Yule	Amherst	Rowlesburg	Preston
Pedlar's Mills	Amherst	Pungoteague	Accomack	Roxalana	Roane
Peel Tree	Barbour	Purcellville	Loudoun	Royal Oaks	Cumberland
Pemberton	Goochland	Purgittsville	Hampshire	Ruckersville	Greene
Pembroke	Giles	Purinton	Preston	Rural Dale	Upshur
Pembroke Springs	Frederick	Quiet Dell	Harrison	Rural Retreat	Wythe
Penhook	Franklin	Quillinsville	Scott	Rusk	Ritchie
Pennsborough	Ritchie	Raccoon Ford	Culpeper	Russell's Mills	Tyler
Penn's Store	Patrick	Raleigh C H	Raleigh	Russellville	Scott
Penola	Caroline	Randolph Macon College		Ruther Glen	Caroline
Pentress	Monongalia		Mecklenburg	Rye Cove	Scott
Peola Mills	Madison	Rapid Ann Station	Culpeper	Rye Valley	Smyth
Perkins' Mills	Braxton	Rapp's Mills	Rockbridge	Ryland's Depot	Greenville
Perkinsville	Goochland	Ravou's Nest	Washington	Sago	Upshur
Peru	Hardy	Ravenswood	Jackson	Saint Clara Colony	Doddridge
Petersburgh	Dinwiddie	Rectortown Station	Fauquier	Saint George	Tucker
Peter's Creek	Patrick	Red Bank	Halifax	Saint Mary's	Pleasants
Peterstown	Monroe	Red Creek	Randolph	Saint Stephen's	Fauquier
Petroleum	Ritchie	Red House	Charlotte	Saint Stephen's Church	
Peytona	Boone	Red House Shoals	Putnam		King and Queen
Peytonsburg	Pittsylvania	Red Oak Grove	Charlotte	Saint Tammany	Mecklenburg
Phenixville	Morgan	Red Sulphur Springs	Monroe	Salem	Roanoke
				Salem Fauquier	Fauquier
				Salina	Randolph

POST OFFICES—VIRGINIA.

Post Office.	County.	Post Office.	County.	Post Office.	County.
Salt Creek	Amherst	Speedwell	Wythe	Thaxton's	Bedford
Salt Lick Bridge	Braxton	Spencer	Roane	Theological Seminary	Fairfax
Salt Peter Cave	Botetourt	Sperryville	Rappahannock	The Plains	Fauquier
Salt Sulphur Springs	Monroe	Spottsylvania C. H.		The Rock	Mercer
Saltville	Washington		Spottsylvania	Thompson's X Roads	Louisa
Saluda	Middlesex	Spout Spring	Appomattox	Thompson's Valley	Tazewell
Sanders' Store	Rockbridge	Spring Hill	Mecklenburg	Thorndike	Cabell
Sandidge's	Amherst	Spring Creek	Wirt	Thorn Hill	Orange
Sand Run	Webster	Springdale	Preston	Thornburg	Spottsylvania
Sandy	Jackson	Springfield	Hampshire	Thornton's Depot	Fairfax
Sandy Bottom	Middlesex	Spring Garden	Pittsylvania	Thorny Creek	Pocahontas
Sandy Hook	Rappahannock	Spring Grove	Surry	Thoroughfare	Prince William
Sandy Level	Pittsylvania	Spring Level	Hanover	Three Forks	Taylor
Sandy Plains	Patrick	Spring Vale	Fairfax	Three Springs	Washington
Sandy River	Pittsylvania	Spring Valley	Grayson	Timber Ridge	Rockbridge
Sangerville	Augusta	Springville	Tazewell	Timberville	Rockingham
Sangster's Station	Fairfax	Spruce Hill	Highland	Tinker Knob	Botetourt
San Marino	Dinwiddie	Stafford C. H.	Stafford	Todd's	Spottsylvania
Sardis	Harrison	Stafford's Store	"	Tolersville	Louisa
Saumsville	Shenandoah	Staffordsville	Giles	Tomahawk Springs	Berkeley
Savage Grant	Wayne	Stanardsville	Greene	Tom's Brook	Shenandoah
Savageville	Accomack	Starry Creek	Franklin	Tower Hill	Appomattox
Sayer's Mills	Doddridge	Staunton	Augusta	Townsend's Mills	Gilmer
Scottsburg	Halifax	Staunton's Precinct		Traveler's Repose	Pocahontas
Scottsville	Albemarle		Buckingham	Traylorsville	Henry
Sea View	Northampton	Stoele's Tavern	Augusta	Trevillian's Depot	Louisa
Second Creek	Greenbrier	Steer Creek	Gilmer	Triadelphia	Ohio
Selma	Alleghany	Stephenson's Depot	Frederick	Tudor Hall	Prince William
Seven Fountains	Shenandoah	Stevensburg	Culpeper	Tuggle's Gap	Patrick
Seven Islands	Fluvanna	Stevensville	King and Queen	Tug River	McDowell
Seville	Madison	Stewartstown	Monongalia	Tumbling Creek	Tazewell
Seven Mile Ford	Smyth	Stewartsville	Bedford	Tunnelton	Preston
Sewall's Mountain	Fayette	Stickleysville	Lee	Turkey Cove	Lee
Shadwell	Albemarle	Stillwell	Wood	Tussekiah	Lunenburg
Shady Grove	Franklin	Stock Creek	Scott	Twelve Pole	Wayne
Shady Springs	Raleigh	Stone Mountain	Carroll	Two Lick Run	Braxton
Shackelford's	King and Queen	Stone Wall Mills	Appomattox	Two Mile Branch	Smyth
Shanghai	Berkeley	Stony Creek Warehouse	Sussex	Twyman'sStore	Spottsylvania
Shannon Hill	Goochland	Stony Cross	Mecklenburg	Tye River Warehouse	Nelson
Sharon	Wythe	Stony Fork	Amherst	Tyler Mountain	Kanawha
Shawsville	Montgomery	Stony Hill	Richmond	Turnstalls	New Kent
Sheetz Mill	Hampshire	Stony Man	Page	Tye River Depot	Nelson
Shellville	Montgomery	Stony Point	Albemarle	Uffington	Monongalia
Shenandoah Iron Works	Page	Stony Point Mills	Cumberland	Unger's Store	Morgan
Shepard's Grove	Culpeper	Stout's Mills	Gilmer	Union	Monroe
Shepardstown	Jefferson	Strait Creek	Highland	Union Furnace	Patrick
Sherando	Augusta	Strasburg	Shenandoah	Union Halt	Franklin
Sherrard	Marshall	Stribling Springs	Augusta	Union Level	Mecklenburg
Shiloh	King George	Stuart's Draft		Union Mills	Fluvanna
Shinnston	Harrison	Sturgeonville	Brunswick	Union Village	Northumberland
Shirley	Tyler	Sublett's Tavern	Powhatan	Unionville	Orange
Short Creek	Brooke	Suffolk	Nansemond	Unison	Loudoun
Shrewsbury	Kanawha	Sugar Grove	Pendleton	University of Virginia	
Silver Hill	Wetzel	Summerdean	Augusta		Albemarle
Simmonsville	Craig	Summer's	Rockbridge	Upland	Mason
Simpson's	Floyd	Summit Point	Jefferson	Upper Cheat	Randolph
Simpson's Creek	Taylor	Sun Hill	Wyoming	Upper Falls of Coal	Kanawha
Sinclair's Bottom	Smyth	Sunny Side	Cumberland	Upper Flats	Mason
Singer's Glen	Rockingham	Sunrise	Bath	Upper Tract	Pendleton
Sinking Creek	Craig	Sunset	Pocahontas	Upperville	Fauquier
Sinks' Grove	Monroe	Surry C. H.	Surry	Urbanna	Middlesex
Sir John's Run	Morgan	Sussex C. H.	Sussex	Valley	Tazewell
Sissonville	Kanawha	Sutherland	Pittsylvania	Valleyburg	Page
Sistersville	Tyler	Swansonville	"	Valley Falls	Marion
Skinquarter	Chesterfield	Sweedlin Hill	Pendleton	Valley Grove	Ohio
Stanesville	Hampshire	Sweet Chalybeate	Alleghany	Valley Head	Randolph
Slate Mills	Rappahannock	Sweet Springs	Monroe	Valley Mills	Morgan
Slatersville	New Kent	Swift Run	Greene	Valley Point	Preston
Sleepy Creek Bridge	Morgan	Swoope's Depot	Augusta	Van Buren Furnace	
Smithfield	Isle of Wight	Sycamore Dale	Harrison		Shenandoah
Smith's Creek	Washington	Sycamore Grove	Putnam	Van Camp	Wetzel
Smith's Gap	Hampshire	Sydnorsville	Franklin	Van Clevesville	Berkeley
Smithton	Doddridge	Table Rock	Raleigh	Variety Mills	Nelson
Smoky Ordinary	Brunswick	Tackett's Mill	Stafford	Verdierville	Orange
Sneadsville	Washington	Talcott	Charlotte	Verdon	Hanover
Snickersville	Loudoun	Tanner's Store	Mecklenburg	Vernon Hill	Halifax
Snow Creek	Franklin	Tannery	Preston	Vicksville	Southampton
Snowhill	Nicholas	Tappahannock C. H.	Essex	Villa	Franklin
Snowville	Pulaski	Taylor Oil Mines	Taylor	Villa Green	Hanover
Somerset	Orange	Taylor's Store	Franklin	Wade's	Bedford
Somerton	Nansemond	Taylorsville	Hanover	Wadestown	Monongalia
Somerville	Fauquier	Tazewell C. H.	Tazewell	Wadesville	Clark
Sontag	Franklin	Teaze's Valley	Putnam	Wagram	Accomack
South Anna	Louisa	Temperance	Amherst	Wakefield Station	Sussex
South Boston Depot	Halifax	Temperanceville	Accomack	Walker	Wood
South Hill	Mecklenburg	Templeton	Prince George	Walker's Church	Appomattox
South Quay	Nansemond	Ten Mile	Cabell	Walkerton	King and Queen
Spanishburg	Mercer	Tenth Legion	Rockingham	Walnut Grove	Putnam
Spanish Oaks	Appomattox	Torrill's Store	Louisa	Walnut Hill	Lee
Sparta	Caroline	Texas	Tucker	Walton	Roane

POST OFFICES—WISCONSIN. 101

Post Office.	County.
Walton Mills	Cumberland
Wardensville	Hardy
Wardville	Hampshire
Ware's ⋈ Roads	Louisa
Warren	Albemarle
Warrenton	Fauquier
Warrenton Springs	"
Warsaw	Richmond
Warwick Court House	Warwick
Washington	Rappahannock
Waskey's Mills	Botetourt
Waterford	Loudoun
Water Lick	Warren
Waterloo	Fauquier
Wattsborough	Lunenburg
Waverlie	Rockingham
Waverly Station	Sussex
Wayland	Scott
Waylandsburg	Culpeper
Wayne Court House	Wayne
Waynesborough	Augusta
Wayside	Mecklenburg
Webb's Mills	Ritchie
Webster	Taylor
Welch Glade	Webster
Wellsburg	Brooke
Wellville	Nottoway
Well Water	Buckingham
West Columbia	Mason
Westham Locks	Henrico
West Liberty	Ohio
West Milford	Harrison
Weston	Lewis
West Point	King William
West Union	Doddridge
West View	Augusta
Wheatland	Loudoun
Wheatley	Fauquier
Wheeling	Ohio
Whissen's Mills	Rockingham
White Chimney	Caroline
White Day	Monongalia
White Flint	Craig
White Gate	Giles
White Hall	Frederick
White House	Mecklenburg
White Oak	Ritchie
White Oak Springs	Lee
White Plains	Brunswick
White Post	Clark
White Rock	Bedford
Whitesburg	Lee
White's Mills	Logan
White Stone	Lancaster
White Sulphur Springs	Greenbrier
Whitesville	Halifax
Whitlock	Halifax
Whitwell	Pittsylvania
Whittle's Mills	Mecklenburg
Wick	Tyler
Wicomico Church	Northumberland
Wilcox's Wharf	Charles
Wilderness	Spottsylvania
Williamsburg	James City
Williamsport	Hardy
Williamstown	Wood
Williamsville	Bath
Willow Bank	Nelson
Willow Island	Pleasants
Willow Springs	Russell
Willis's Ridge	Floyd
Wilmington	Fluvanna
Wilsonburg	Harrison
Wilson's Depot	Dinwiddie
Wilsonville	Highland
Winchester	Frederick
Windsor Station	Isle of Wight
Windfield	Putnam
Winterham	Amelia
Winterpock	Chesterfield
Wirt C. H.	Wirt
Wise	Jackson
Wise C. H.	Wise
Wiseville	Accomack
Wolf Creek	Monroe
Wolf Glade	Carroll
Wolf Summit	Harrison

Post Office.	County.
Wolftown	Madison
Wolf Trap	Halifax
Woodland's	Marshall
Wood's ⋈ Roads	Gloucester
Woodside	Preston
Woodstock	Shenandoah
Woodville	Rappahannock
Woolfolk	Orange
Worthington	Marion
Wylliesburg	Charlotte
Wytheville	Wythe
Wood Lawn	Carroll
Yancey's Mills	Albemarle
Yatesville	Lunenburg
Yellow Branch	Campbell
Yellow Spring	Hampshire
Yellow Sulphur Springs	Montgomery
Yokum Station	Lee
Yorktown	York
Young's Store	Franklin
Zackville	Wirt
Zion's Mills	Lee
Zuni Station	Isle of Wight

Wisconsin.

Post Office.	County.
Adams	Walworth
Adamsville	Iowa
Adell	Sheboygan
Addison	Washington
Afton	Rock
Ahnepee	Kewaunee
Aken	Richland
Albany	Greene
Albion	Dane
Alcove	Fond du Lac
Alden's Corners	Dane
Alderly	Dodge
Allen's Grove	Walworth
Alma	Buffalo
Almand	Portage
Alvaretta	Rock
Amherst	Portage
Amick	Burnett
Angelk	Monroe
Appleton	Outagamie
Arcadia	Trempealeau
Arena	Iowa
Argylo	Lafayette
Arlington	Columbia
Armenia	Juneau
Ashipum	Jefferson
Ashford	Fond du Lac
Ashland	Ashland
Ashton	Dane
Attica	Greene
Atwater	Dodge
Auburn	Fond du Lac
Augusta	Eau Claire
Aurora	Washington
Auroraville	Waushara
Avoca	Iowa
Avalance	Vernon
Aztalan	Jefferson
Bad Axe	B dA
Badger	Portage
Bailey's Harbor	Door
Bangor	La Crosse
Baraboo	Sauk
Bark River	Jefferson
Barton	Washington
Bay City	Pierce
Batavia	Crawford
Bayfield	La Pointe
Beaver Dam	Dodge
Bear Creek	Waupaca
Bear Valley	Sauk
Beechwood	Sheboygan
Beetown	Grant
Boldenville	Pierce
Belgium	Ozaukee
Bell Center	Crawford
Bellefoutaine	Columbia
Bellville	Dane

Post Office.	County.
Beloit	Rock
Bem	Greene
Benicia	Trempeleau
Benton	Lafayette
Berdo	Polk
Bergen	Bad Axe
Berlin	Green Lake
Berry	Dane
Big Bend	Waukesha
Big Foot Prairie	Walworth
Big Spring	Adams
Big Valley	Monroe
Black Earth	Dane
Black River Falls	Jackson
Blanchardsville	Lafayette
Bloomer Prairie	Chippewa
Bloomfield	Walworth
Bloomingdale	Bad Axe
Blue Mound	Dane
Bluff	Sauk
Boaz	Richland
Boltonville	Washington
Bonches	St. Croix
Bothelle	Fond du Lac
Boscobel	Grant
Branch	Manitowoc
Brandon	Fond du Lac
Brant	Calumet
Breckinridge	Bad Axe
Bridgeport	Crawford
Briggsville	Marquette
Brighton	Kenosha
Brillion	Manitowoc
Bristol	Kenosha
British Hollow	Grant
Brodhead	Greene
Brookfield Center	Waukesha
Brookville	St. Croix
Brothertown	Calumet
Buena Vista	Portage
Buffalo	Buffalo
Bunker's Hill	Grant
Burke	Dane
Burr Oak	La Crosse
Burlington	Racine
Burnett	Dodge
Burns	La Crosse
Burnett's Station	Dodge
Butler	Milwaukie
Butte de Morts	Winnebago
Byron	Fond du Lac
Cadiz	Greene
Calamine	Lafayette
Caldwell's Prairie	Racine
Caledonia	"
Caledonia Center	"
Calumet Village	Fond du Lac
Cambria	Columbia
Cambridge	Dane
Campbell	Winnebago
Carlton	Kewaunee
Casco	Kewaunee
Cascade	Sheboygan
Cassell Prairie	Sauk
Cassville	Grant
Castle Rock	"
Cataract	Monroe
Cazenovia	Richland
Cedarsburg	Washington
Cedar Creek	"
Cedar Grove	Sheboygan
Cedar Lake	Waushara
Cedar Valley	Polk
Centralia	Wood
Center	Rock
Charlestown	Calumet
Charlotte	Grant
Chester Station	Dodge
Chickatock	Door
Chilton	Calumet
Chippewa	Pepin
Chippewa City	Chippewa
Chippewa Falls	"
Christiana	Dane
Clairville	Winnebago
Clark's Mills	Manitowoc
Clifton Mills	Pierce
Clifton	Monroe
Clinton	Sheboygan
Clintonville	Waupaca

POST OFFICES—WISCONSIN.

Post Office.	County.	Post Office.	County.	Post Office.	County.
Clyde	Iowa	Fairplay	Grant	Hellenville	Jefferson
Clyman	Dodge	Fairwater	Fond du Lac	Hemlock	Wood
Cold Spring	Jefferson	Fall City	Dunn	Henrietta	Richland
Cole Brook	Waushara	Fall River	Columbia	Herman	Dodge
Coloma	"	Falls of St. Croix	Polk	Herseyville	Monroe
Columbus	Columbia	Fancy Creek	Richland	High Cliff	Calumet
Concord	Jefferson	Farmer's Grove	Greene	Highland	Iowa
Cooksville	Rock	Farmer's Valley	Monroe	Hika	Manitowoc
Coon Prairie	Bad Axe	Farmersville	Dodge	Hillsborough	Bad Axe
Cooperstown	Manitowoc	Farmington	Jefferson	Hinesburg	Fond du Lac
Corfu	Waushara	Fayette	Lafayette	Hingham	Sheboygan
Coryville	Kewaunee	Fennimore	Grant	Hixton	Jackson
Cottage Grove	Dane	Ferryville	Crawford	Hockley	Bad Axe
Cottage Inn	Lafayette	Fife	Monroe	Hoffman's Corners	Monroe
Crandall's Corners	Polk	Fillmore	Washington	Holland	Brown
Cross Plains	Dane	Fish Creek	Door	Homer	Grant
Crossville	Calumet	Fisk's Corners	Winnebago	Honey Creek	Walworth
Crystal Lake	Waupacca	Fitchburg	Dane	Hoosick	Greene
Cypress	Kenosha	Fond du Lac	Fond du Lac	Hoosier	Richland
Dakota	Waushara	Fordham	Adams	Horris Corners	Ozaukee
Dane	Dane	Forest	Richland	Horicon	Dodge
Danville	Dodge	Footville	Rock	Hortonville	Outogamie
Darien	Walworth	Fort Atkinson	Jefferson	Houghton	Ashland
Darlington	Lafayette	Fort Howard	Brown	Howard's Grove	Sheboygan
Dartford	Marquette	Fort Winnebago	Columbia	Howe's Corners	Waushara
Davis' Corners	Adams	Foster	Fond du Lac	Hubbleton	Jefferson
Dayton	Greene	Fountain	Adams	Hudson	St. Croix
Deansville	Dane	Fountain City	Buffalo	Humboldt	Sauk
Debello	Bad Axe	Fowler's Prairie	Juneau	Huntingdon	St. Croix
Deerfield	Dane	Fox Lake	Dodge	Hurricane Grove	Grant
De Korra	Columbia	Francis Creek	Manitowoc	Hustisford	Dodge
Delafield	Waukesha	Frankfort	Dunn	Iola	Waupaca
Delavan	Walworth	Frankville	Clark	Iron Ridge	Dodge
Delhi	Winnebago	Fredonia	Ozaukee	Ironton	Sauk
Dellona	Sauk	Freedom	Outagamie	Ithica	Richland
Dell Prairie	Adams	Fremont	Waupaca	Ives' Grove	Racine
Dalton	Sauk	Frenchtown	Wood	Ixonia	Jefferson
Denmark	Brown	Freistadt	Washington	Ixonia Center	"
Densmore Mills	Walworth	Friendship	Adams	Jamestown	Grant
Depere	Brown	Fulton	Rock	Janesville	Rock
De Soto	Bad Axe	Galesville	Trempleau	Jenny	Marathon
Dexterville	Wood	Garden Valley	Jackson	Jennicton	Iowa
Diamond Bluff	Pierce	Geneva	Walworth	Jeddo	Marquette
Dickeysville	Grant	Geneva Bay	"	Jefferson	Jefferson
Dodge Corners	Waukesha	Genesco	Waukesha	Johnson's Creek	"
Dodgeville	Iowa	Genesee Depot	"	Johnstown	Rock
Door Creek	Dane	Georgetown	Lafayette	Johnstown Center	"
Dorsett	Monroe	Germantown	Juneau	Jordan	Greene
Dousman	Waukesha	Germany	La Crosse	Juda	"
Dotyville	Fond du Lac	Gibbsville	Sheboygan	Juneau	Dodge
Dundas	Calumet	Gill's Landing	Waupaca	Junins	Fond du Lac
Dunkirk	Dane	Gilmanton	Buffalo	Josephine	Greene
Dunville	Dunn	Glenbeulah	Sheboygan	Kaukauna	Outagamie
Duplainville	Waukesha	Glencoe	Buffalo	Kansasville	Racine
Durand	Pepin	Glendale	Monroe	Kokkoktagon	Marathon
Durham Hill	Waukesha	Glen Haven	Grant	Kekoskoo	Dodge
Dyckesville	Kewaunee	Glenmont	St. Croix	Kenosha	Kenosha
Eagle	Waukesha	Golden Lake	Jefferson	Keshena	Shawano
Eastman	Crawford	Good Hope	Milwaukie	Kewaskum	Washington
East Oasis	Waushara	Goole	Bad Axe	Kewannee	Kewannee
East Randolph	Columbia	Grafton	Ozaukee	Kickapoo	Bad Axe
East Troy	Walworth	Grand Marsh	Adams	Kilbourn City	Columbia
Eaton	Manitowoc	Grand Prairie	Marquette	Kildare	Juneau
Eau Claire	Eau Claire	Grand Rapids	Wood	Kingston	Marquette
Eau Galle	Dunn	Granville	Milwaukie	Kinnick Kinnick	St. Croix
Eau Pleine	Portage	Gratiot	Lafayette	Kirchain	Washington
Edna	Adams	Green Bay	Brown	Koro	Winnebago
Edgerton	Rock	Green Bush	Sheboygan	Koskonong	Jefferson
Edwards	Sheboygan	Greenfield	Milwaukie	La Crosse	La Crosse
Eight Mile	Polk	Green Lake	Marquette	Lacote St. Marie	Marquette
El Dorado	Fond du Lac	Greenville	Brown	Ladoga	Fond du Lac
Elk Grove	Lafayette	Grove	Wallworth	Lafayette	Chippewa
Elk Horn	Walworth	Groveland	Winnebago	La Grange	Walworth
Ellenboro'	Grant	Grovesville	Calumet	Lake Five	Waukesha
Elma	Waushara	Hale's Corners	Milwaukie	Lake Maria	Marquette
Elm Grove	Waukesha	Half Moon	Eau Claire	Lake Mills	Jefferson
El Paso	Pierce	Half Way Creek	La Crosse	Lake View	Dane
Embarrass	Waupaca	Hammond	St. Croix	Lamartine	Fond du Lac
Emerald Grove	Rock	Hampton	Columbia	Lamberton	Milwaukie
Emmett	Dodge	Hanchettsville	Dane	Lancaster	Grant
Empire	Fond du Lac	Hancock	Waushara	Lannon Springs	Waukesha
Empire Junction	Columbia	Hanover	Rock	Lansing	Outagamie
Eolia	Dane	Harrisburg	Milwaukie	La Pointe	La Pointe
Etna	Layfayette	Harrisville	Marquette	Larahee	Manitowoc
Eureka	Winnebago	Harmony	Bad Axe	Lavalle	Sauk
Evansville	Rock	Hartford	Washington	Leeds	Columbia
Evanswood	Waupaca	Hartland	Waukesha	Leeds Center	"
Excelsior	Richland	Hazel Green	Grant	Leicester	Dane
Exeter	Greene	Heart Prairie	Walworth	Lemonweir	Juneau
Fairfield	Rock	Helena	Iowa	Lenape	Waushara

POST OFFICES—WISCONSIN.

Post Office.	County.	Post Office.	County.	Post Office.	County.
Leon	Monroe	Monterey	Waukesha	Omro	Winnebago
Leroy	Dodge	Montfort	Grant	Onalaska	La Crosse
Leyden	Rock	Monticello	Greene	Oneida	Brown
Liberty	Kenosha	Montreal Falls	La Pointe	Onion River	Sheboygan
Lima Center	Rock	Morrison	Brown	Ontario	Bad Axe
Lincoln	Kewaunee	Moria	Fond du Lac	Orange	Juneau
Lind	Waupaca	Moscow	Iowa	Ora Oak	Grant
Linden	Iowa	Mosinee	Marathon	Ordino	Marquette
Line Ridge	Sauk	Moundville	Marquette	Oregon	Dane
Linwood	Portage	Mountain	Monroe	Orfordville	Rock
Lisbon	Waukesha	Mount Hope	Grant	Orion	Richland
Little Chute	Outagamie	Mount Ida	"	Osborne	Rock
Little Grant	Grant	Mount Morris	Waushara	Oshkuta	Columbia
Little Lake	Adams	Mount Pisgah	Monroe	Oshkosh	Winnebago
Little Prairie	Walworth	Mount Pleasant	Racine	Otsego	Columbia
Little Sturgeon	Door	Mount Sterling	Crawford	Ottawa	Waukesha
Little Suamico	Oconto	Mount Tabor	Bad Axe	Otter Creek	Eau Claire
Little Wolf	Waupaca	Mount Vernon	Dane	Our Town	Sheboygan
Lodi	Columbia	Mount Zion	Juneau	Oxford	Marquette
Loganville	Sauk	Mukwanago	Waukesha	Ozaukee	Ozaukee
Lomira	Dodge	Murone	Fond du Lac	Pacific	Columbus
Lone Pine	Portage	Muscoda	Grant	Pakwaukee	Marquette
Lone Rock	Richland	Muskego Center	Waukesha	Palmyra	Jefferson
Long Lake	Marquette	Myra	Washington	Pan Yan	Racine
Lowell	Dodge	Mound Spring	Jackson	Paoli	Dane
Lower Lynxville	Crawford	Nanaupa	Fond du Lac	Paquette	Manitowoc
Lowville	Columbia	Nasewaupee	Door	Pardeeville	Columbia
Loyd	Richland	Nasonville	Wood	Paris	Racine
Luna	Pepin	Navary	Jackson	Patch Grove	Grant
Lyons	Walworth	Necedah	Juneau	Peatville	Dane
McFarland	Dane	Neillsville	Clark	Pedee	Greene
Madely	Portage	Nelson	Buffalo	Pensaukio	Oconto
Madison	Dane	Neenah	Winnebago	Pepin	Dunn
Magnolia	Rock	Nekama	"	Perry	Dane
Maiden Rock	Pierce	Nenno	Washington	Perrytown	Pierce
Malden	Polk	Neosho	Dodge	Peshtigo	Oconto
Manchester	Green Lake	Nepeuskun	Winnebago	Pewaukee	Waukesha
Manitowoc	Manitowoc	Neptune	Richland	Pheasant Branch	Dane
Manitowoc Rapids	"	Neshonoc	La Crosse	Pigeon Grove	Columbia
Maple Grove	"	Neshoto	Manitowoc	Pilot Knob	Adams
Mapleton	Waukesha	Neshkoro	Marquette	Pine Bluff	Dane
Maple Works	Clark	New Amsterdam	La Crosse	Pine Hill	Jackson
Marcellon	Columbia	New Berlin	Milwaukee	Pine Lake	Waukesha
Marble Ridge	Sauk	Newburg	Washington	Pine River	Waushara
Marcus	Door	New California	Grant	Pinery	Juneau
Marcy	Waukesha	New Centerville	St. Croix	Pineville	Clark
Marietta	Crawford	New Chester	Adams	Plain	Sauk
Markesan	Marquette	New Diggins	Lafayette	Plainville	Adams
Marinetta	Oconto	Newfare	Fond du Lac	Plainfield	Waushara
Marquette	Marquette	New Franken	Brown	Platteville	Grant
Martell	Pierce	New Glarus	Greene	Pleasant Ridge	Clark
Martinville	Grant	New Holstein	Calumet	Plover	Portage
Maxville	Buffalo	New Koeln	Milwaukee	Plymouth	Sheboygan
Maytown	Fond du Lac	Newkirk	Greene	Point Bluff	Adams
Mayfield	Washington	New London	Waupaca	Pole Grove	Jackson
Mayville	Dodge	Newport	Sauk	Portage City	Columbia
Mazo Manie	Dane	New Richmond	St. Croix	Port Andrew	Richland
Meanston	Juneau	New Rome	Adams	Port Hope	Columbia
Mecker	Washington	Newtonburg	Manitowoc	Portland	Dodge
Mecker's Grove	Lafayette	Newville	Bad Axe	Potosi	Grant
Medina	Outagamie	Niles	Manitowoc	Poygan	Winnebago
Meeme	Manitowoc	North Bend	Jackson	Poynett	Columbia
Melrose	Jackson	North Cape	Racine	Poysippi	Waushara
Menasha	Winnebago	North Elk Grove	Lafayette	Prairie	Racine
Menominee	Dunn	North Lake	Waukesha	Prairie du Chien	Crawford
Menominee Falls	Waukesha	North Lamartine	Fond du Lac	Prairie du Sac	Sauk
Menokano	Oconto	North Leeds	Columbia	Prescott	Pierce
Mequon River	Ozaukee	Northport	Waupaca	Primrose	Dane
Meridian	Monroe	North Prairie Station	"	Princeton	Marquette
Merrimac	Sauk	"	Waukesha	Prospect Hill	Waukesha
Merton	Waukesha	North Royalton	Waupaca	Quincy	Adams
Metomen	Fond du Lac	Norway	Racine	Racine	Racine
Middleton	Dane	Oaks	Sauk	Randall	Portage
Midland	Marquette	Oak Creek	Milwaukee	Randolph Center	Columbia
Mifflin	Iowa	Oakfield	Fond du Lac	Rantoul	Calumet
Millard	Walworth	Oakfield Center	"	Rathbun	Sheboygan
Mill Creek	Richland	Oak Grove	Dodge	Raymond	Racine
Milford	Jefferson	Oak Hill	Jefferson	Readstown	Bad Axe
Mill Haven	Juneau	Oakland	"	Reedsburg	Sauk
Millville	Grant	Oakley	Greene	Readfield	Waupaca
Milton	Rock	Oasis	Waushara	Reeseville	Dodge
Milwaukie	Milwaukie	Oconto	Oconto	Retreat	Bad Axe
Mineral Point	Iowa	Oceola	Fond du Lac	Rheinberg	Richland
Minodro	La Crosse	Oceola Mills	"	Rhine	Sheboygan
Minnesota Junction	Dodge	Oconomowoc	Waukesha	Richland Center	Richland
Mischicot	Manitowoc	Odanah	La Pointe	Richland City	"
Monches	Waukesha	Ogden	Rock	Richfield	Washington
Mondovia	Buffalo	Ogdensburg	Waupaca	Richford	Waushara
Monroe	Greene	Okee	Columbia	Richmond	Walworth
Montello	Marquette	Oliver's Mills	Grant	Richwood	Jefferson

POST OFFICES—WISCONSIN.

Post Office.	County.	Post Office.	County.	Post Office.	County.
Ridgeville	Monroe	Spring Dale	Dane	Walnut Springs	Greene
Ridgeway	Iowa	Springfield	Walworth	Walworth	Walworth
Rio	Columbia	Spring Green	Sauk	Wanoka	Dunn
Ripon	Fond du Lac	Spring Grove	Greene	Warner's Landing	Bad Axe
Rising Sun	Crawford	Spring Lake	Waukesha	Washburn	Grant
River Falls	Pierce	Spring Prairie	Walworth	Washington Harbor	Door
Roaring Creek	Jackson	Springville	Bad Axe	Waterford	Racine
Robinson	Brown	Spring Valley	Rock	Waterloo	Jefferson
Rookbridge	Richland	Spring Water	Waushara	Watertown	
Rochester	Racine	Star	Bad Axe	Waterville	Waukesha
Roche-a-Cri	Adams	Stantsville	Washington	Waubeck	Pepin
Rock Falls	Dunn	State Line	Walworth	Wauconsta	Fond du Lac
Rock Prairie	Rock	Station	Washington	Waukau	Winnebago
Rockville	Dunn	Stephensville	Outagamie	Waukesha	Waukesha
Rocky Run	Columbia	Stevenstown	La Crosse	Waumandee	Buffalo
Rolling Ground	Crawford	Stevens' Point	Portage	Waupaca	Waupaca
Rolling Prairie	Dodge	Stiles	Oconto	Waupun	Fond du Lac
Romance	Bad Axe	Stockbridge	Calumet	Wausau	Marathon
Rome	Jefferson	Stockholm	Pepin	Wautoma	Waushara
Root Creek	Milwaukie	Stockton	Portage	Wauwatsa	Milwaukie
Rosendale	Fond du Lac	Stone Bank	Waukesha	Wauzeka	Crawford
Roslin	Marquette	Stone Hill	Marquette	Weister	Bad Axe
Rousseau	Brown	Stoner's Prairie	Dane	Weelnunee	Winnebago
Roxbury	Dane	Stonghton	"	Wellington	Monroe
Rubicon	Dodge	Strang's Prairie	Adams	Welch Prairie	Columbia
Rural	Waupaca	Sturgeon Bay	Door	Wequinock	Brown
Rush Lake	Fond du Lac	Suamico	Brown	Weruer	Juneau
Rush River	Pierce	Sugar Bush	Outagamie	West Bend	Washington
Russell	Sheboygan	Sugar Creek	Walworth	West Branch	Richland
Russell's Corners	Sauk	Sullivan	Jefferson	West Blue Mound	Iowa
Rutland	Dane	Summit	Waukesha	Westfield	Marquette
Sacramento	Green Lake	Sumner	Trempeleau	West Granville	Milwaukie
Saint Mary's	Monroe	Sun Prairie	Dane	West Green Lake	Marquette
Saint Rose	Grant	Superior	Douglas	West Lima	Richland
Salem	Kenosha	Sussex	Waukesha	West Middleton	Dane
Sandusky	Sauk	Sweet Home	Dane	West Milton	Rock
Saratoga	Wood	Sylvania	Racine	West Point	Columbia
Sauk City	Sauk	Sylvester	Greene	West Port	Dane
Saukville	Ozaukee	Sylvan	Richland	West Rosendale	Fond du Lac
Saxeville	Waushara	Tafton	Grant	Weston	Marathon
Scandinavia	Waupaca	Tavcheeda	Fond du Lac	West Salem	La Crosse
Schlessingerville	Washington	Teller's Corners	Crawford	Westville	Walworth
Schlswig	Manitowoc	Ten Mile House	Milwaukie	Weyauwega	Waupaca
Scotia	Trempeleau	Theresa	Dodge	Wheatland	Kenosha
Scott	Sheboygan	Tiffany	Rock	Wheat Valley	Sheboygan
Schiller	Brown	Tirade	Walworth	White Oak Springs	Lafayette
Seneca	Crawford	Toland's Prairie	Washington	White Creek	Juneau
Sentinel	Juneau	Tomah	Monroe	White Mound	Sauk
Sextonville	Richland	Towerville	Crawford	Whitesville	Racine
Sharon	Walworth	Transit	Jefferson	White Water	Walworth
Shaw-wu-no	Outagamie	Trempeleau	Trempeleau	Willett	Greene
Sheboygan	Sheboygan	Trenton	Pierce	Wilmot	Kenosha
Sheboygan Falls	"	Trim Belle	"	Wilson's Creek	Sauk
Sheldon	Monroe	Troy	Walworth	Wilton	Monroe
Sherwood	Calumet	Troy Center	"	Winchester	Winnebago
Shiocton	Outagamie	Troy Lakes	"	Windsor	Dane
Shopiere	Rock	Tunnel City	Monroe	Winneconne	Winnebago
Shuey's Mills	Greene	Twin Valley	Adams	Winooska	Sheboygan
Shullsburg	Warren	Two Rivers	Manitowoc	Wiota	Lafayette
Sierra	Bad Axe	Ulao	Ozaukee	Wishua	Columbia
Silver Lake	Waushara	Union	Rock	Wonewoc	Juneau
Sinsinawa Mound	Grant	Union Center	Juneau	Woodland	Dodge
Skinner	Greene	Union Church	Racine	Woodman	Grant
Sladesburg	Crawford	Union Grove	Racine	Woodstock	Richland
Smeltzer's Grove	Grant	Utica	Dane	Wright's Ferry	Crawford
Snidersville	Outagamie	Vernon	Waukesha	Wrightstown	Brown
Solon	Monroe	Verona	Dane	Wyocena	Columbia
Somerset	St. Croix	Victory	Bad Axe	Wyoming	Iowa
Somerville	Crawford	Vienna	Walworth	Wyalusing	Grant
South Bend	Trempeleau	Vinland	Winnebago	Yankee Town	Crawford
South Bristol	Racine	Viola	Richland	Yellow Stone	Lafayette
South Genesee	Waukesha	Viroqua	Bad Axe	York	Dane
South Grove	Walworth	Waitesville	Jefferson	Yorkville	Racine
Sparta	Monroe	Wakefield	Outagamie	Young Hickory	Washington
Spafford	Lafayette	Walhain	Kewaunee	Yuba	Richland
Spring Bluff	Adams				

TERRITORIES.

Colorado.

Post Office.	County.
American Ranche	Weld
Boulder City	Boulder
Breckinridge	Summit
Canon City	Fremont
Colorado City	El Paso
Delaware Flats	Summit
Denver City	Arapahoe
Empire City	Clear Creek
Fleming's Ranche	Weld
Fort Lupton	Weld
Fort Wise	
Golden City	Jefferson
Gold Dirt	"
Golden Gate	"
Huntsville	Douglas
Michigan House	Jefferson
Missouri City	Gilpin
Mountain City	"
Mount Vernon	Jefferson
Nevada	Gilpin
Oro City	Lake
Parkeville	Summit
Pueblo	Pueblo
Ralstons	Jefferson
Saint Vrain	Weld
Spanish Bar	Clear Creek
Tarryall	

Dacota.

Elk Point	
Fort Abercrombie	
Fort Randall	
James River	
Vermillion	
Yancton	

Idaho.

Durkeeville	
Mount Idahoe	

Nebraska.

Post Office.	County.
Activity	Dixon
Albavillo	Hall
Archer	Richardson
Aspinwall	Nemaha
Athens	Richardson
Austin	Clay
Avoca	Cass
Beatrice	Gage
Belle Creek	Washington
Bellevue	Sarpy
Blue Springs	Gage
Bonhomme City	L'Eau Qui Court
Brownsville	Nemaha
Buchanan	Platte
Center Valley	Cass
Colona	
Columbus	Platte
Conotia	
Cottonwood Falls	Shorter
Cottonwood Springs	Shorter
Covington	Dakota
Cumming City	Washington
Dakota	
Daniel's Branch	Jones
Decatur	Burt
Deer Creek	
Dennison	Gage
De Soto	Washington
De Witt	Cumming
Dixon	Dixon
El Dorado	Platte
Elk Horn City	Douglas
Fair View	Pawnee
Falls City	Richardson
Florence	Douglas
Fontanelle	Washington
Fort Calhoun	"
Fort Kearney	Clackamas
Fort Laramie	(Unknown)
Fort Randall	
Frankfort	L'Eau Qui Court
Franklin	Dodge
Fremont	"
Genoa	Platte
Glendale	Cass
Glen Rock	Nebama
Grand Island City	Hall
Greenwood	
Hazleton	Sarpy
Helena	Johnston
Hendricks	Otoe
Humboldt	Richardson
Ionia	Dixon
Jacobaville	Lander
Jalapa	Dodge
Julesburg	
Kanoshe	Cass
Kingston	Johnston
Lewisburg	Dodge
Middleburg	Richardson
Monroo	Platte
Mount Pleasant	Cass
Mount Vernon	Nemaha
Monterey	Richardson
Nebraska Center	Buffalo
Nebraska City	Otoe
Nemaha City	Nemaha
Niobrara	L'Eau Qui Court
Nursery Hill	Otoe
O'Fallon's Bluff	
O'Gorman	Dakota
Omadi	Dakota
Omaha City	Douglas
Oreapolis	Cass
Otoe City	Otoe
Pawnee City	Pawnee
Platt Valley	Sarpy
Platte's Mouth	Cass
Plattford	Sarpy
Pleasant Valley	Pawnee
Poncah	Dixon
Ponca's Agency	
Rock Bluffs	Cass
Rulo	Richardson
Saint Helena	Cedar
Saint James	"
Saint Stephen	Richardson
Salem	"
Salt Creek	Cass
Shylock	L'Eau Qui Court
South Pass City	
Stewart's	Johnston
Susquehanna	Butler
Table Rock	Pawnee
Tecumseh	Johnston
Tekamah	Burt
Three Grove	Cass
Turkey Creek	Johnston
Vesta	"
Wacaponna	Cedar
Wallace	Dodge
Weeping Water	Cass
West Point	Cuming
Wood River	Buffalo
Worrallton	Nemaha
Wyoming	Otoe

Nevada.

Fort Churchill	
Silver City	
Virginia City	
Washoe	

New Mexico.

Post Office.	County.
Albuquerque	Bernalillo
Arizona	Dona Ana
Casa Blanca	"
Fernandez de Taos	Taos
Fort Buchanan	Dona Ana
Fort Craig	"
Fort Defiance	Bernalillo
Fort Stanton	Dona Ana
Fort Union	Taos
Las Cruzces	"
Las Vegas	San Miguel
Los Luceros	Rio Arriba
Mesilla	Dona Ana
Pimo Village	Dona Ana
Pino Forest	"
Santa Fe	Santa Fe
Socorro	Socorro
Tecolote	San Miguel
Tucson	"

Washington.

Post Office.	County.
Arkada	Sawamish
Baker's	Thurston
Beaver	
Boistfort	Lewis
Bracoport	Chehalis
Cascades	Clark
Castle Rock	Cowelitz
Cathlemet	Wankiakum
Cedarville	Chehalis
Chehalis Point	
Chenook	Pacific
Claquato	Lewis
Coal Bank	Thurston
Cosmopolis	Chehalis
Coveland	Island
Cowlitz	Lewis
Fisher's Landing	Clark
Fort Colville	Walla-Walla
Fort Willopa	Chehalis
Franklin	Pierce
Grand Mound	Thurston
Highland	Lewis

POST OFFICES—TERRITORIES.

Post Office.	County.
Lake River	Clark
Montesano	Chehalis
Monticello	Cowelitz
Nesqually	Pierce
Newaucum	Lewis
New Dungeness	Clallam
Oakland	Sawamish
Oak Point	Thurston
Olympia	
Oysterville	Pacific
Port Ludlow	
Port Madison	Kitsap
Port Towuseud	Jefferson
Rockland	Clicatat
Saunders' Prairie	Lewis
eatter Creek	Thurston
Seabeck	Kitsap
Seattle	King
Skookumchuck	Thurston
Skokomish	Sawamish
Spauaway	Pierce
Steilacoom City	
Teakalet	Kitsap
Union	Chehalis
Vancouver	Clark
Warlepta	Walla-Walla
Washongal	Clark
Whatcom	Whatcom
Yelm	Thurston

Utah.

Post Office.	County.
Alpine City	Utah
American Fork	
Beaver	Beaver
Brigham City	Box Elder
Camp Floyd	Cedar
Carey's Mills	Carson
Carson City	
Carson Valley	
Cedar City	Iron
Cedar Valley	Utah
Centerville	Davis
Draper	Salt Lake
Ephraim	San Pete
Farmington	Davis
Fillmore City	Millard
Fort Bridger	Green River
Fountain Green	San Pete
Gardner's Mills	Salt Lake
Harmony	Washington
Hyrum	Cache
Kaysville	Davis
Lehigh City	Utah
Logan	Cache
Manti	San Pete
Mendon	Cache
Mill Creek	Salt Lake

Post Office.	County.
Millville	Cache
Moneville	Joab
Mormon	Salt Lake
Muroni	San Pete
North Ogden	Weber
Ogden City	
Paronau	Iron
Payson	Utah
Pine Valley	Iron
Pleasant Grove	Utah
Provo City	Provo
Providence	Cache
Salt Creek	Joab
Salt Lake City	Salt Lake
Santa Clara	Washington
Santaquin	Utah
South Weber	Davis
Spanish Fork	Utah
Springville	
Stoker	Davis
Summit	Iron
Susanville	Joab
Tokersville	Washington
Union	Salt Lake
Virgen City	Washington
Washington	
Wellsville	Cache
Willard	Box Elder

INDEX

— TO —

UNITED STATES POST OFFICE DIRECTORY.

Alabama	1
Arkansas	4
California	6
Connecticut	8
Delaware	9
District of Columbia	9
Florida	9
Georgia	10
Illinois	13
Indiana	19
Iowa	23
Kansas	27
Kentucky	28
Louisiana	31
Maine	32
Maryland	35
Massachusetts	37
Michigan	39
Minnesota	42
Mississippi	44
Missouri	46

New Hampshire	50
New Jersey	52
New York	54
North Carolina	63
Ohio	67
Oregon	74
Pennsylvania	75
Rhode Island	84
South Carolina	84
Tennessee	86
Texas	90
Vermont	93
Virginia	94
Wisconsin	101
Colorado	105
Dacotah	105
Nebraska Territory	105
New Mexico	105
Nevada	105
Utah	106
Washington	105

www.ingramcontent.com/pod-product-compliance
Lightning Source LLC
Chambersburg PA
CBHW022111230426
43672CB00008B/1348